FRONTIERS OF QUANTITATIVE ECONOMICS

CONTRIBUTIONS
TO
ECONOMIC ANALYSIS

Volume 71

Honorary Editor

J. TINBERGEN

Editors

J. JOHNSTON

D. W. JORGENSON

J. WAELBROECK

1971

NORTH-HOLLAND PUBLISHING COMPANY · AMSTERDAM · LONDON

FRONTIERS
OF
QUANTITATIVE ECONOMICS

Papers Invited for Presentation at the
Econometric Society Winter Meetings, New York, 1969

Edited by

MICHAEL D. INTRILIGATOR
University of California, Los Angeles

1971

NORTH-HOLLAND PUBLISHING COMPANY · AMSTERDAM · LONDON

Library of Congress Catalog Card Number: 70-134645
ISBN North-Holland: 0 7204 3171 9

PUBLISHERS:

NORTH-HOLLAND PUBLISHING COMPANY – AMSTERDAM
NORTH-HOLLAND PUBLISHING COMPANY, LTD. – LONDON

PRINTED IN BELGIUM

INTRODUCTION TO THE SERIES

This series consists of a number of hitherto unpublished studies, which are introduced by the editors in the belief that they represent fresh contributions to economic science.

The term *economic analysis* as used in the title of the series has been adopted because it covers both the activities of the theoretical economist and the research worker.

Although the analytical methods used by the various contributors are not the same, they are nevertheless conditioned by the common origin of their studies, namely theoretical problems encountered in practical research. Since for this reason, business cycle research and national accounting, research work on behalf of economic policy, and problems of planning are the main sources of the subjects dealt with, they necessarily determine the manner of approach adopted by the authors. Their methods tend to be "practical" in the sense of not being too far remote from application to actual economic conditions. In addition they are quantitative rather than qualitative.

It is the hope of the editors that the publication of these studies will help to stimulate the exchange of scientific information and to reinforce international cooperation in the field of economics.

THE EDITORS

INTRODUCTION

MICHAEL D. INTRILIGATOR

University of California, Los Angeles

The papers in this volume were invited for presentation at the Winter Meetings of the Econometric Society held in New York in December, 1969. The ten subjects covered in the papers were chosen to represent areas of active current interest to economists, and the authors were invited to summarize and evaluate previous work and to indicate possible future developments in the field. While the subjects covered are being actively studied by economists, certain of them will also be of interest to people in other fields, especially business, political science, and statistics.

The papers are grouped into three parts. The first part consists of three papers on economic methodology and theory. Chapter 1, by Kenneth J. Arrow, discusses the impact of transaction costs, market failure, public goods, and externalities on economic theory — especially on the problem of economic efficiency. One area touched upon by Arrow, information, its value and cost, is discussed in detail in Chapter 2, by Jacob Marschak, on the economics of information systems. Another area touched upon by Arrow, collective action, is discussed in detail in Chapter 3, by Charles R. Plott, on the theory of voting and public choice.

The second part of the book is concerned with econometric techniques. Lawrence R. Klein, in Chapter 4, surveys large-scale econometric models, discussing both the techniques of working with such models and their application to forecasting and policy evaluation. Chapter 5 consists of two papers, one by Arnold Zellner and one by Thomas J. Rothenberg, giving two views of the Bayesian approach and alternatives in econometrics. Chapter 6 also consists of two papers, one by Thomas H. Naylor and one by A. N. Halter, M. L. Hayenga, and T. J. Manetsch on macro-simulation models. The paper by Naylor discusses simulation techniques and their application to macro-econometric models, including the large-scale models discussed by Klein. The paper by Halter et al. discusses a specific macro-simulation model used to study the Nigerian agricultural economy.

The third part of the book is concerned with quantitative approaches to traditional topics in economics. The first traditional topic is monetary theory, and, in Chapter 7, Harry G. Johnson and Robert W. Clower present their views on a question of current interest in monetary theory — 'Is there an Optimal Money Supply?' The second traditional topic is the theory of capital markets, and, in Chapter 8, Eugene F. Fama reviews the theoretical and empirical literature on efficient capital markets. The third traditional topic is industrial organization, and, in Chapter 9, Leonard Weiss reviews the modern quantitative approaches to this subject. The fourth and last traditional topic is economic history, and, in Chapter 10, Gavin Wright reviews recent econometric studies of history.

This book is the product of efforts by many people — the authors and discussants whose papers and comments appear here; the members of the Program Committee for the 1969 Winter Meetings of the Econometric Society, who advised in the selection of topics and speakers; and the editors of the Contributions to Economic Analysis Series, who encouraged its publication.

CONTENTS

Part 1

ECONOMIC METHODOLOGY AND THEORY

Frontiers of Quantitative Economics, ed. M.D. Intriligator. © *North-Holland Publishing Company.*

CHAPTER 1

POLITICAL AND ECONOMIC EVALUATION OF
SOCIAL EFFECTS AND EXTERNALITIES

KENNETH J. ARROW
Harvard University

0. Introduction

The concept of public goods has been developed through a process of successive refinement over a long period of time. Yet surprisingly enough there does not seem to exist anywhere in the literature a clear general definition of this concept or the more general one of "externality". The accounts given are usually either very general and discursive, difficult of interpretation in specific contexts, or else they are rigorous accounts of very special situations. What exactly is the relation between externalities and such concepts as "appropriability" or "exclusion"?

Also, there is considerable ambiguity in the purpose of the analysis of externalities. The best developed part of the theory relates to only a single question: the statement of a set of conditions, as weak as possible, which insure that a competitive equilibrium exists and is Pareto-efficient. Then the denial of any of these hypotheses is presumably a sufficient condition for considering resort to non-market channels of resource allocation — usually thought of as government expenditures, taxes, and subsidies.

At a second level the analysis of externalities should lead to criteria for non-market allocation. We are tempted to set forth these criteria in terms analogous to the profit-and-loss statements of private business; in this form, we are led to benefit-cost analysis. There are, moreover, two possible aims for benefit-cost analysis; one, more ambitious but theoretically simpler, is specification of the non-market actions which will restore Pareto efficiency;

the second involves the recognition that the instruments available to the government or other non-market forces are scarce resources for one reason or another, so that all that can be achieved is a "second-best".

Other concepts that seem to cluster closely to the concept of public goods are those of "increasing returns" and "market failure". These are related to Pareto inefficiency on the one hand and to the existence and optimality of competitive equilibrium on the other; sometimes the discussions in the literature do not adequately distinguish these two aspects. I contend that market failure is a more general category than externality; and both differ from increasing returns in a basic sense, since market failures in general and externalities in particular are relative to the mode of economic organization, while increasing returns are essentially a technological phenomenon.

Current writing has helped bring out the point that market failure is not absolute; it is better to consider a broader category, that of transaction costs, which in general impede and in particular cases completely block the formation of markets. It is usually though not always emphasized that transaction costs are costs of running the economic system. An incentive for vertical integration is replacement of the costs of buying and selling on the market by the costs of intra-firm transfers; the existence of vertical integration may suggest that the costs of operating competitive markets are not zero, as is usually assumed in our theoretical analysis.

Monetary theory, unlike value theory, is heavily dependent on the assumption of positive transaction costs; the recurrent complaint about the difficulty of integrating these two branches of theory is certainly governed by the contradictory assumptions made about transaction costs. The creation of money is in many respects an example of a public good.

The identification of transaction costs in different contexts and under different systems of resource allocation should be a major item on the research agenda of the theory of public goods and indeed of the theory of resource allocation in general. Only the most rudimentary suggestions are made here. The "exclusion principle" is a limiting case of one kind of transaction cost, but another type, the costliness of the information needed to enter and participate in any market, has been little remarked. Information is closely related on the one hand to communication and on the other to uncertainty.

Given the existence of Pareto inefficiency in a free market equilibrium, there is a pressure in the system to overcome it by some sort of departure from the free market, i.e., some form of collective action. This need not be undertaken by the government. I suggest that in fact there is a wide variety of social institutions, in particular generally accepted social norms of behavior, which serve in some means as compensation for failure or limitation of the market, though each in turn involves transaction costs of its own. The question also arises how the behavior of individual economic agents in a social institution (especially in voting) is related to their behavior on the market. A good deal of theoretical literature has arisen in recent years which seeks to describe political behavior as analogous to economic, and we may hope for a general theory of socio-economic equilibrium. But it must always be kept in mind that the contexts of choice are radically different, particularly when the hypotheses of perfectly costless action and information are relaxed. It is not accidental that economic analysis has been successful only in certain limited areas.

1. Competitive equilibrium and Pareto efficiency

A quick review of the familiar theorems on the role of perfectly competitive equilibrium in the efficient allocation of resources will be useful. Perfectly competitive equilibrium has its usual meaning: households, possessed of initial resources, including possibly claims to the profits of firms, choose consumption bundles to maximize utility at a given set of prices; firms choose production bundles so as to maximize profits at the same set of prices; the chosen production and consumption bundles must be consistent with each other in the sense that aggregate production plus initial resources must equal aggregate consumption.[1] The key points in the definition are the parametric role of the prices for each individual and the identity of prices for all individuals. Implicit are the assumptions that all prices can be known by all individuals and that the act of charging prices is not itself a consumer of resources.

A number of additional assumptions are made at different points in the theory of equilibrium, but most are clearly factually valid in the usual contexts and need not be mentioned. The two hypotheses frequently not

---

[1] Sometimes this is stated to permit an excess of supply over demand, with a zero price for such free goods; but this can be included in the above formulation by postulating the existence of production processes (disposal processes), which have such surpluses as inputs and no outputs.

valid are (C), the convexity of household indifference maps and firm production possibility sets, and (M), the universality of markets. While the exact meaning of the last assumption will be explored later at some length, for the present purposes we mean that the consumption bundle which determines the utility of an individual is the same as that which he purchases at given prices subject to his budget constraint and that the set of production bundles among which a firm chooses is independent of decisions made by other agents in the economy.

The relations between Pareto efficiency and competitive equilibrium are set forth in the following two theorems:

(1) *If (M) holds, a competitive equilibrium is Pareto-efficient.* This theorem is true even if (C) does not hold.
(2) *If (C) and (M) hold, then any Pareto-efficient allocation can be achieved as a competitive equilibrium by a suitable reallocation of initial resources.*

When the assumptions of Proposition (2) are valid, then the case for the competitive price system is strongest. Any complaints about its operation can be reduced to complaints about the distribution of income, which should then be rectified by lump-sum transfers. Of course, as Pareto already emphasized, the proposition provides no basis for accepting the results of the market in the absence of accepted levels of income equality.

The central role of competitive equilibrium both as a normative guide and as at least partially descriptive of the real world raises an analytically difficult question: does a competitive equilibrium necessarily exist?

(3) *If (C) holds, then there exists a competitive equilibrium.* This theorem is true even if (M) does not hold.

If both (C) and (M) hold, we have a fairly complete and simple picture of the achievement of desirable goals, subject always to the major qualification of the achievement of a desirable income distribution. The price system itself determines the income distribution only in the sense of preserving the status quo. Even if costless lump-sum transfers are possible, there is needed a collective mechanism reallocating income if the status quo is not regarded as satisfactory.

Of course (C) is not a necessary condition for the existence of a competitive equilibrium, only a sufficient one. From Proposition (1), it is possible to have an equilibrium and therefore efficient allocation without convexity (when (M) holds). However, in view of the central role of (C) in these theorems, the implications of relaxing this hypothesis have been examined intensively in recent years by Farrell (1959), Rothenberg (1960), Aumann (1966), and Starr (1969). Their conclusions may be summarized as follows: Let (C') be the weakened convexity assumption that there are no indivisibilities large relative to the economy.

(4) *Propositions (2) and (3) remain approximately true if (C) is replaced by (C').*

Thus, the only non-convexities that are important for the present purposes are increasing returns over a range large relative to the economy. In those circumstances, a competitive equilibrium cannot exist.

The price system, for all its virtues, is only one conceivable form of arranging trade, even in a system of private property. Bargaining can assume extremely general forms. Under the assumptions (C') and (M), we are assured that not everyone can be made better off by a bargain not derived from the price system; but the question arises whether some members of the economy will not find it in their interest and within their power to depart from the perfectly competitive price system. For example, both Knight (1921, pp. 190-194) and Samuelson (1967, p. 120) have noted that it would pay all the firms in a given industry to form a monopoly. But in fact it can be argued that unrestricted bargaining can only settle down to a resource allocation which could also be achieved as a perfectly competitive equilibrium, at least if the bargaining itself is costless and each agent is small compared to the entire economy. This line of argument originated with Edgeworth (1881, pp. 20-43) and has been developed recently by Shubik (1959), Debreu and Scarf (1963), and Aumann (1964).

More precisely, it is easy to show:

(5) *If (M) holds and a competitive equilibrium prevails, then no set of economic agents will find any resource allocation which they can accomplish by themselves (without trade with the other agents) which they will all prefer to that prevailing under the equilibrium.*

Proposition (5) holds for any number of agents. A deeper proposition is the following converse:

(6) *If (C') and (M) hold, and if the resources of any economic agent are small compared with the total of the economy, then, given any allocation not approximately achievable as a competitive equilibrium, there will be some set of agents and some resource allocation they can achieve without any trade with others which each one will prefer to the given allocation.*

These two propositions, taken together, strongly suggest that when all the relevant hypotheses hold, (a) a competitive equilibrium, if achieved, will not be upset by bargaining even if permitted, and (b) for any bargain not achievable by a competitive equilibrium there is a set of agents who would benefit by change to another bargain which they have the full power to enforce.

The argument that a set of firms can form a monopoly overlooks the possibility that the consumers can also form a coalition, threaten not to buy, and seek mutually advantageous deals with a subset of the firms; such deals are possible since the monopoly allocation violates some marginal equivalences.

In real life, monopolizing cartels are possible for a reason not so far introduced into the analysis: bargaining costs between producers and consumers are high, those among producers low — a point made most emphatically by Adam Smith (1937, p. 128): "People of the same trade seldom meet together, even for merriment or diversion, but the conversation ends in a conspiracy against the public, or in some contrivance to raise prices". *It is not the presence of bargaining costs per se but their bias that is relevant.* If all bargaining costs are high, but competitive pricing and the markets are cheap, then we expect the perfectly competitive equilibrium to obtain, yielding an allocation identical with that under costless bargaining. But if bargaining costs are biased, then some bargains other than the competitive equilibrium can be arrived at which will not be upset by still other bargains if the latter but not the former are costly.

Finally, in this review of the elements of competitive equilibrium theory, let me repeat the obvious and well-known fact that in a world where time is relevant, the commodities which enter into the equilibrium system include those with future dates. In fact, the bulk of meaningful future transactions cannot be carried out on any existing present market, so that assumption (M), the universality of markets, is not valid.

2. Imperfectly competitive equilibrium

There is no accepted and well-worked out theory corresponding to the title of this section. From the previous section it is clear that such a theory is forcibly needed in the presence of increasing returns on a scale large relative to the economy (hereafter, the phrase "increasing returns" will always be understood to include the prepositional phrase just employed), and is superfluous in its absence.

There are two approaches to a theory of general equilibrium in an imperfectly competitive environment; most writers who touch on public policy questions implicitly accept one or the other of these proto-theories without always recognizing that they have made a choice. One assumes all transactions are made according to the price system, i.e., the same price is charged for all units of the same commodity; this is the *monopolistic competition* approach. The alternative approach assumes unrestricted bargaining; this is the *game theory* approach. The first might be deemed appropriate if the costs of bargaining are high relative to the costs of ordinary pricing, while the second assumes costless bargaining.[2]

It cannot be too strongly emphasized that neither approach is, at the present stage, a fully developed theory, and it is misleading to state any implications about the working of these systems. Chamberlain's (1933) purpose was certainly the incorporation of monopoly into a general equilibrium system, together with a view that the commodity space should be viewed as infinite-dimensional, with the possibility of arbitrarily close substitutes in consumption; Triffin (1941) emphasized this aspect, but the only completely worked-out model of general monopolistic equilibrium is that of Negishi (1960-61), and he made the problem manageable by regarding the demand functions facing the monopolists as those perceived by them, with only loose relations to reality. Such a theory would have little in the way of deducible implications (unless there were a supplementary psychological theory to explain the perceptions of demand functions) and certainly no clear welfare implications.

Of course, whatever a monopolistic competitive equilibrium means, it must imply inefficiency in the Pareto sense if there are substantial increasing returns. For a firm can always make zero profits by not existing; hence, if it operates, price must at least equal average cost which is greater than marginal cost. Kaldor (1935) and Demsetz (1964), however, have argued that in the "large numbers" case, the welfare loss may be supposed very small. I would

---

[2] Within the framework of each proto-theory attempts have been made to modify it in the direction of the other. Thus, price discrimination is a modification of the price system in the pure theory of monopoly, though I am aware of no attempt to study price discrimination in a competitive or otherwise general equilibrium context. Some game theorists (Luce 1954, 1955a, b; Aumann and Maschler 1964) have attempted to introduce bargaining costs in some way by simply limiting the range of possible coalitions capable of making bargains.

conjecture that this conclusion is true, but it is not rigorously established, and indeed the model has never been formulated in adequate detail to discuss it properly.[3]

With unrestricted bargaining it is usual to conclude that the equilibrium, whatever it may be, must be Pareto-efficient for, by definition, it is in the interest of all economic agents to switch from a Pareto-inefficient allocation to a suitably chosen Pareto-efficient one. This argument seems plausible, but is not easy to evaluate in the absence of a generally accepted concept of solution for game theory. Edgeworth (1881) held the outcome of bargaining to be indeterminate within limits, and Von Neumann and Morgenstern (1944) have generalized this conclusion. But when there is indeterminacy, there is no natural or compelling point on the Pareto frontier at which to arrive. It is certainly a matter of common observation, perhaps most especially in the field of international relations, that mutually advantageous agreements are not arrived at because each party is seeking to engross as much as possible of the common gain for itself. In economic affairs a frequently cited illustration is the assembly of land parcels for large industrial or residential enterprises whose value (net of complementary costs) exceeds the total value of the land in its present uses. Then each owner of a small parcel whose acquisition is essential to the execution of the enterprise can demand the entire net benefit. An agreement may never be reached or may be long delayed; at positive discount rates even the latter outcome is not Pareto-efficient. It is to avoid such losses that the coercive powers of the state are invoked by condemnation proceedings.

There is, however, another tradition within game theory which argues for the determinacy of the outcome of bargaining. Zeuthen (1930, Chapter IV) had early propounded one such solution. After Von Neumann and Morgenstern, Nash (1950, 1953) offered a solution, which Harsanyi (1956) later showed to be identical with that of Zeuthen. Nash's analysis of bargaining has been extended by Harsanyi (1959, 1963, 1966); variant but related approaches have been studied by Shapley (1953) and Selten (1964). The analysis has proceeded at a very general level, and its specific application to resource allocation has yet to be spelled out. In the simplest situation,

---

[3] Suppose that the degree of increasing returns is sufficient to prevent there being more than one producer of a given commodity narrowly defined, but not to prevent production of a close substitute. Is this degree of returns sufficiently substantial to upset the achievement of an approximately perfect competitive equilibrium, as discussed in the last section?

bargaining between two individuals who can cooperate but cannot injure each other except by withholding cooperation and who can freely transfer benefits between them, the conclusion of the theories is the achievement of a joint optimum followed by equal splitting of the benefits of cooperation net of the amounts each bargainer could obtain without cooperation. Thus, in a land assembly, if the participation of all parcels is essential, each owner receives the value of his parcel in its present (or best alternative) use plus an equal share of the net benefits of the project. Without further analytic and empirical work it is not easy to judge the acceptability of this conclusion.

An elementary example may bring out the ambiguities of allocation with unrestricted bargaining. Since the perfectly competitive equilibrium theory is satisfactory (in the absence of marketing failures and costs) when increasing returns on a substantial scale are absent, the problem of imperfectly competitive equilibrium arises only when substantial increasing returns are present. In effect, then, there are small numbers of effective participants. Suppose there are only three agents. Production is assumed to take place in coalitions; the output of each coalition depends only on the number of members in it. If the average output of the members of a coalition does not increase with the number of members, then the equilibrium outcome is the perfectly competitive one, where each agent produces by himself and consumes his own product. If the average output of a coalition increases with the number of members, then clearly production will take place in the three-member coalition; but the allocation is not determined by the threats of individuals to leave the coalition and go on their own, nor by threats of pairs to form coalitions (for any one member can claim more than one-third of the total output and still leave the other two more than they could produce without him). But perhaps the most interesting case is that where the average output is higher for two individuals than for either one or three, i.e., increasing returns followed by diminishing returns. For definiteness, suppose that one agent can produce one unit, two agents can produce four units, and all three agents together can produce five units. Clearly, Pareto efficiency requires the joint productive activity of all three. Since each pair can receive four units by leaving the third agent out, it would appear that each pair must receive at least four units. But this implies that the total allocated to keep the three-man coalition together must be at least six, more than is available for distribution.[4]

---

[4] The general principle illustrated by this example has been briefly alluded to by Shapley and Shubik (1967, footnote 5, p. 98).

(Theories of the Nash-Harsanyi type arrive at solutions in cases like this by assuming that the economic agents foresee these possible instabilities and recognize that any attempt by any pair to break away from the total coalition can itself be overturned. If each is rational and assumes the others are equally rational, then they recognize, in the completely symmetric situation of the example, that only a symmetric allocation is possible.)

The point of this lengthy discussion of possible game theory concepts of equilibrium is to suggest caution in accepting the proposition that bargaining costs alone prevent the achievement of Pareto efficiency in the presence of increasing returns, as Buchanan and Tullock (1962, p. 88) and Demsetz (1968, p. 61) assert.

3. Risk and information

The possible types of equilibria discussed in the previous two sections are not, in principle, altered in nature by the presence of risk. If an economic agent is uncertain as to which of several different states of the world will obtain, he can make contracts contingent on the occurrence of possible states. The real-world counterparts of these theoretical contingent contracts include insurance policies and common stocks. With these markets for contingent contracts, a competitive equilibrium will arise under the same general hypotheses as in the absence of uncertainty. It is not even necessary that the economic agents agree on the probability distribution for the unknown state of the world; each may have his own subjective probabilities. Further, the resulting allocation is Pareto-efficient if the utility of each individual is identified as his expected utility according to his own subjective probability distribution.

But, as Radner (1968) has pointed out, there is more to the story. Whenever we have uncertainty we have the possibility of information and, of course, also the possibility of its absence. No contingent contract can be made if, at the time of execution, either of the contracting parties does not know whether the specified contingency has occurred or not. This principle eliminates a much larger number of opportunities for mutually favorable exchanges than might perhaps be supposed at first glance. A simple case is that known in insurance literature as "adverse selection". Suppose, e.g., there are two types of individuals, A and B, with different life expectancies, but the insurance company has no way to distinguish the two;

it cannot in fact identify the present state of the world in all its relevant aspects. The optimal allocation of resources under uncertainty would require separate insurance policies for the two types, but these are clearly impossible. Suppose further that each individual knows which type he belongs to. The company might charge a rate based on the probability of death in the two types together, but the insurance buyers in the two types will respond differently; those in the type with the more favorable experience, say A, will buy less insurance than those in type B, other things (income and risk-aversion) being equal. The insurance company's experience will be less favorable than it intended, and it will have to raise its rates. An equilibrium rate will be reached which is, in general, between those corresponding to types A and B separately but closer to the latter. Such an insurance arrangement is, of course, not Pareto-efficient. It is not *a priori* obvious in general that this free market arrangement is superior to compulsory insurance even though the latter is also not Pareto-efficient because it typically disregards individual differences in risk-aversion.

As the above example shows, the critical impact of information on the optimal allocation of risk-bearing is not merely its presence or absence but its inequality among economic agents. If neither side knew which type the insured belonged to, then the final allocation would be Pareto-efficient if it were considered that the two types were indistinguishable; but in the above example the market allocation is Pareto-efficient neither with the types regarded as indistinguishable nor with them regarded as distinguishable.

There is one particular case of the effect of differential information on the workings of the market economy (or indeed any complex economy) which is so important as to deserve special comment: one agent can observe the joint effects of the unknown state of the world and of decisions by another economic agent, but not the state or the decision separately. This case is known in the insurance literature as "moral hasard", but because the insurance examples are only a small fraction of all the illustrations of this case and because, as Pauly (1968) has argued, the adjective "moral" is not always appropriate, the case will be referred to here as the "confounding of risks and decisions". An insurance company may easily observe that a fire has occurred but cannot, without special investigation, know whether the fire was due to causes exogenous to the insured or to decisions of his (arson, or at least carelessness). In general, any system which, in effect, insures against adverse final outcomes automatically reduces the incentives to good decision-making.

In these circumstances there are two extreme possibilities (with all intermediate possibilities being present): full protection against uncertainty of final outcome (e.g., cost-plus contracts for production or reseach) or absence of protection against uncertainty of final outcome (the one-person firm; the Admiral shot for cowardice "pour encourager les autres"). Both policies produce inefficiency, though for different reasons. In the first, the incentive to good decision-making is dulled for obvious reasons; in the second, the functions of control and risk-bearing must be united, whereas specialization in these functions may be more efficient for the workings of the system.

The relations between principals and agents (e.g., patients and physicians, owners and managers) further illustrate the confounding of risks and decisions. In the professions in particular they also illustrate the point to be emphasized later: that ethical standards may to a certain extent overcome the Pareto inefficiencies.

So far we have taken the information structure as given. But the fact that particular information structures give rise to Pareto inefficiency means that there is an economic value in transmitting information from one agent to another, as well as in the creation of new information. Marschak (1968), Hirshleifer (unpublished), and others have begun the study of the economics of information, but the whole subject is in its infancy. Only a few remarks relevant to our present purpose will be made here.

(1) As both communications engineering and psychology suggest, the transmission of information is not costless. Any professor who has tried to transmit some will be painfully aware of the resources he has expended and, perhaps more poignantly, of the difficulties students have in understanding. The physical costs of transmission may be low, though probably not negligible, as any book buyer knows; but the "coding" of the information for transmission and the limited channel capacity of the recipients are major costs.

(2) The costs of transmitting information vary with both the type of information transmitted and the recipient and sender. The first point implies a preference for inexpensive information, a point stressed in oligopolistic contexts by Kaysen (1949, pp. 294-5) and in other bargaining contexts by Schelling (1957). The second point is relevant to the value of education and to difficulties of transmission across cultural boundaries (so that production functions can differ so much across countries).

(3) Because the costs of transmission are non-negligible, even situations which are basically certain become uncertain for the individual; the typical economic agent simply cannot acquire in a meaningful sense the knowledge of all possible prices, even where they are each somewhere available. Markets are thus costly to use, and therefore the multiplication of markets, as for contingent claims as suggested above, becomes inhibited.

4. Externalities illustrated

After this long excursus into the present state of the theory of equilibrium and optimality it is time to discuss some of the standard concepts of externality, market failure, and public goods generally. The clarification of these concepts is a long historical process, not yet concluded, in which the classic contributions of Knight (1924), Young (1913, pp. 676-684), and Robertson (1924) have in more recent times been enriched by those of Meade (1952), Scitovsky (1954), Coase (1960), Buchanan and Stubblebine (1962), and Demsetz (1966). The concept of externality and the extent to which it causes non-optimal market behavior will be discussed here in terms of a simple model.

Consider a pure exchange economy. Let x_{ik} be the amount of the kth commodity consumed by the ith individual ($i = 1, \ldots, n$; $k = 1, \ldots, m$) and $\bar{x}_k$ be the amount of the kth commodity available. Suppose in general that the utility of the ith individual is a function of the consumption of all individuals (not all types of consumption for all individuals need actually enter into any given individual's utility function); the utility of the ith individual is $U_i(x_{11}, \ldots, x_{nm})$. We have the obvious constraints:

$$\sum_i x_{ik} \leqq \bar{x}_k. \tag{1}$$

Introduce the following definitions:

$$x_{jik} = x_{ik}. \tag{2}$$

With this notation a Pareto-efficient allocation is a vector maximum of the utility functions $U_j(x_{j11}, \ldots, x_{jmn})$, subject to the constraints (1) and (2). Because of the notation used, the variables appearing in the utility function relating to the jth individual are proper to him alone and appear in no one else's utility function. If we understand now that there are $n^2 m$ commodities, indexed by the triple subscript *jik*, then the Pareto efficiency problem has a thoroughly classical form. There are $n^2 m$ prices, p_{jik}, attached to the constraints (2), plus m prices, q_k, corresponding to constraints (1). Following the maximization procedure formally, we see, much as in Samuelson (1954), that Pareto efficiency is characterized by the conditions:

$$\lambda_j(\partial U_j/\partial x_{ik}) = p_{jik},\qquad(3)$$

and

$$\sum_j p_{jik} = q_k,\qquad(4)$$

where λ_j is the reciprocal of the marginal utility of income for individual j. (These statements ignore corner conditions, which can easily be supplied.)

Condition (4) can be given the following economic interpretation: Imagine each individual i to be a producer with m production processes, indexed by the pair (i,k). Process (i,k) has one input, namely commodity k, and n outputs, indexed by the triple (j,i,k). In other words, what we ordinarily call individual i's consumption is regarded as the production of joint outputs, one for each individual whose utility is affected by individual i's consumption.

The point of this exercise is to show that by suitable and indeed not unnatural reinterpretation of the commodity space, externalities can be regarded as ordinary commodities, and all the formal theory of competitive equilibrium is valid, including its optimality.

It is not the mere fact that one man's consumption enters into another man's utility that causes the failure of the market to achieve efficiency. There are two relevant factors which cannot be discovered by inspection of the utility structures of the individual. One, much explored in the literature, is the appropriability of the commodities which represent the external repercussions; the other, less stressed, is the fact that markets for externalities usually involve small numbers of buyers and sellers.

The first point, Musgrave's "exclusion principle" (1959, p. 86) is so well known as to need little elaboration. Pricing demands the possibility of excluding non-buyers from the use of the product, and this exclusion may be technically impossible or may require the use of considerable resources. Pollution is the key example; the supply of clean air or water to each individual would have to be treated as a separate commodity, and it would have to be possible in principle to supply to one and not the other (though the final equilibrium would involve equal supply to all). But this is technically impossible.

The second point comes out clearly in our case. Each commodity (j, i, k) has precisely one buyer and one seller. Even if a competitive equilibrium could be defined, there would be no force driving the system to it; we are in the realm of imperfectly competitive equilibrium.

In my view, the standard lighthouse example is best analyzed as a problem of small numbers rather than of the difficulty of exclusion, though both elements are present. To simplify matters, I will abstract from uncertainty so that the lighthouse keeper knows exactly when each ship will need its services, and also abstract from indivisibility (since the light is either on or off). Assume further that only one ship will be within range of the lighthouse at any moment. Then exclusion is perfectly possible; the lighthouse need only shut off its light when a non-paying ship is coming into range. But there would be only one buyer and one seller and no competitive forces to drive the two into a competitive equilibrium. If in addition the costs of bargaining are high, then it may be most efficient to offer the service free.

If, as is typical, markets for the externalities do not exist, then the allocation from the point of view of the "buyer" is determined by a rationing process. We can determine a shadow price for the buyer; this will differ from the price, zero, received by the seller. Hence, formally, the failure of markets for externalities to exist can also be described as a difference of prices between buyer and seller.

In the example analyzed, the externalities related to particular named individuals; individual i's utility function depended on what a particular individual, j, possessed. The case where it is only the total amount of some commodity (e.g., handsome houses) in other people's hands that matters is a special case, which yields rather simpler results. In this case, $\partial U_j / \partial x_{ik}$ is independent of i for $i \neq j$, and hence, by (3), p_{jik} is independent of i for $i \neq j$. Let,

$$p_{iik} = p_{ik}, \ p_{jik} = \bar{p}_{jk} \ \text{for} \ i \neq j.$$

Then (4) becomes,

$$p_{ik} + \sum_{j \neq i} \bar{p}_{jk} = q_k,$$

or,

$$(p_{ik} - \bar{p}_{ik}) + \sum_{j} \bar{p}_{jk} = q_k,$$

from which it follows that the difference, $p_{ik} - \bar{p}_{ik}$, is independent of i. There are two kinds of shadow prices, a price $\bar{p}_{ik}$, the price that individual i is willing to pay for an increase in the stock of commodity k in any other individual's hands, and the premium, $p_{ik} - \bar{p}_{ik}$, he is willing to pay to have the commodity in his possession rather than someone else's. At the optimum, this premium for private possession must be the same for all individuals.

Other types of externalities are associated with several commodities simultaneously and do not involve named individuals, as in the case of neighborhood effects, where an individual's utility depends both on others' behavior (e.g., aesthetic, criminal) and on their location.

There is one deep problem in the interpretation of externalities which can only be signalled here. What aspects of others' behavior do we consider as affecting a utility function? If we take a hard-boiled revealed preference attitude, then if an individual expends resources in supporting legislation regulating another's behavior, it must be assumed that that behavior affects his utility. Yet in the cases that students of criminal law call "crimes without victims", such as homosexuality or drug-taking, there is no direct relation between the parties. Do we have to extend the concept of externality to all matters that an individual cares about? Or, in the spirit of John Stuart Mill, is there a second-order value judgement which excludes some of these preferences from the formation of social policy as being illegitimate infringements of individual freedom?

5. Market failure

The problem of externalities is thus a special case of a more general phenomenon, the failure of markets to exist. Not all examples of market failure can fruitfully be described as externalities. Two very important examples have already been alluded to: markets for many forms of risk-bearing and for most future transactions do not exist and their absence is surely suggestive of inefficiency.

Previous discussion has suggested two possible causes for market failure: (1) inability to exclude; (2) lack of the necessary information to permit market transactions to be concluded.

The failure of futures markets cannot be directly explained in these terms. Exclusion is no more a problem in the future than in the present. Any contract to be executed in the future is necessarily contingent on some events (e.g., that the two agents are still both in business), but there must be many cases where no informational difficulty is presented. The absence of futures markets may be ascribed to a third possibility: (3) supply and demand are equated at zero; the highest price at which anyone would buy is below the lowest price at which anyone would sell.

This third case of market failure, unlike the first two, is by itself in no way presumptive of inefficiency. However, it may usually be assumed that its occurrence is the result of failures of the first two types on complementary markets. Specifically, the demand for future steel may be low because of uncertainties of all types: sales and technological uncertainty for the buyer's firm, prices and existence of competing goods, and the quality specification of the steel. If, however, adequate markets for risk-bearing existed, the uncertainties could be removed, and the demand for future steel would rise.

6. Transaction costs

Market failure has been presented as absolute, but in fact the situation is more complex than this. A more general formulation is that of transaction costs, which are attached to any market and indeed to any mode of resource allocation. Market failure is the particular case where transaction costs are so high that the existence of the market is no longer worth while. The distinction between transaction costs and production costs is that the former can be varied by a change in the mode of resource allocation, while the latter depend only on the technology and tastes, and would be the same in all economic systems.

The discussions in the preceding sections suggest two sources of transaction costs: (1) exclusion costs; (2) costs of communication and information, including both the supplying and the learning of the terms on which transactions can be carried out. An additional source is (3) the costs of disequilibrium; in any complex system, the market or authoratitive allocation, even under perfect information, it takes time to compute the optimal allocation, and either transactions take place which are inconsistent with the final equilibrium or they are delayed until the computations are completed (see Marschak 1959).

These costs vary from system to system; thus, one of the advantages of a price system over either bargaining or some form of authoritative allocation is usually stated to be the economy in costs of information and communication. But the costs of transmitting and especially of receiving a large number of price signals may be high; thus, there is a tendency not to differentiate prices as much as would be desirable from the efficiency viewpoint; e.g., the same price is charged for peak and off-peak usage of transportation or electricity.

In a price system, transaction costs drive a wedge between buyer's and seller's prices and thereby give rise to welfare losses as in the usual analysis. Removal of these welfare losses by changing to another system (e.g., governmental allocation on benefit-cost criteria) must be weighed against any possible increase in transaction costs (e.g., the need for elaborate and perhaps impossible studies to determine demand functions without the benefit of observing a market).

The welfare implications of transaction costs would exist even if they were proportional to the size of the transaction, but in fact they typically exhibit increasing returns. The cost of acquiring a piece of information, e.g., a price, is independent of the scale of use to which it will be put.

7. Collective action: the political process

The state may frequently have a special role to play in resource allocation because, by its nature, it has a monopoly of coercive power, and coercive power can be used to economize on transaction costs. The most important use of coercion in the economic context is the collection of taxes; others are regulatory legislation and eminent domain proceedings.

The state is not an entity but rather a system of individual agents, a widely extensive system in the case of a democracy. It is appealing and fruitful to analyze its behavior in resource allocation in a manner analogous to that of the price system. Since the same agents appear in the two systems, it becomes equally natural to assume they have the same motives. Hotelling (1929, pp. 54-55) and Schumpeter (1942, Chapter XXII) had sketched such politico-economic models, and Von Neumann and Morgenstern's monumental work is certainly based on the idea that all social phenomena are governed by essentially the same motives as economics. The elaboration of more or less complete models of the political process along the lines of economic theory is more recent, the most prominent contributors being Black (1958), Downs (1957), Buchanan and Tullock (1962), and Rothenberg (1965).

I confine myself here to a few critical remarks on the possibilities of such theories. These are not intended to be negative but to suggest problems that have to be faced and are raised by some points in the preceding discussion.

(1) If we take the allocative process to be governed by majority voting, then, as we well know, there are considerable possibilities of paradox. The possible intransitivity of majority voting was already pointed out by Condorcet (1785). If, instead of assuming that each individual votes according to his preferences it is assumed that they bargain freely before voting (vote-selling), the paradox appears in another form, a variant of the bargaining problems already noted in section 2. If a majority could do what it wanted, then it would be optimal to win with a bare majority and take everything; but any such bargain can always be broken up by another proposed majority.

Tullock (1967, Chapter III) has recently argued convincingly that if the distribution of opinions on social issues is fairly uniform and if the dimensionality of the space of social issues is much less than the number of individuals, then majority voting on a sincere basis will be transitive. The argument is not, however, applicable to income distribution, for such a policy has as many dimensions as there are individuals, so that the dimensionality of the issue space is equal to the number of individuals.

This last observation raises an interesting question. Why, in fact, in democratic systems has there been so little demand for income redistribution? The current discussion of a negative income tax is the first serious attempt at a purely redistributive policy. Hagström (1938) presented a mathematical model predicting on the basis of a self-interest model for voters that democracy would inevitably lead to radical egalitarianism.

(2) Political policy is not made by voters, not even in the sense that they choose the vector of political actions which best suits them. It is in fact made by representatives in one form or another. Political representation is an outstanding example of the principal-agent relation. This means that the link between individual utility functions and social action is tenuous, though by no means completely absent. Representatives are no more a random sample of their constituents than physicians are of their patients.

Indeed, the question can be raised: to what extent is the voter, when acting in that capacity, a principal or an agent? To some extent, certainly, the voter is cast in a role in which he feels some obligation to consider the social good, not just his own. It is in fact somewhat hard to explain otherwise

why an individual votes at all in a large election, since the probability that
his vote will be decisive is so negligible.

8. Collective action: social norms

It is a mistake to limit collective action to state action; many other departures
from the anonymous atomism of the price system are observed regularly.
Indeed, firms of any complexity are illustrations of collective action, the
internal allocation of their resources being directed by authoritative and
hierarchical controls.

I want, however, to conclude by calling attention to a less visible form
of social action: norms of social behavior, including ethical and moral codes.
I suggest as one possible interpretation that they are reactions of society
to compensate for market failures. It is useful for individuals to have some
trust in each other's word. In the absence of trust, it would become very
costly to arrange for alternative sanctions and guarantees, and many
opportunities for mutually beneficial cooperation would have to be foregone.
Banfield (1958) has argued that lack of trust is indeed one of the causes of
economic underdevelopment.

It is difficult to conceive of buying trust in any direct way (though it can
happen indirectly, e.g., a trusted employee will be paid more as being more
valuable); indeed, there seems to be some inconsistency in the very concept.
Non-market action might take the form of a mutual agreement. But the
arrangement of these agreements and especially their continued extension to
new individuals entering the social fabric can be costly. As an alternative,
society may proceed by internalization of these norms to the achievement
of the desired agreement on an unconscious level.

There is a whole set of customs and norms which might be similarly
interpreted as agreements to improve the efficiency of the economic system
(in the broad sense of satisfaction of individual values) by providing
commodities to which the price system is inapplicable.

The social conventions may be adaptive in their origins, but they can
become retrogressive. An agreement is costly to reach and therefore costly
to modify; and the costs of modification may be especially large for
unconscious agreements. Thus, codes of professional ethics, which arise out
of the principal-agent relation and afford protection to the principals, can
serve also as a cloak for monopoly by the agents.

References

Aumann, R.J., 1964, Markets with a continuum of traders. *Econometrica* 32, 39-50.

Aumann, R.J., 1966, The existence of competitive equilibria in markets with a continuum of traders. *Econometrica* 34, 1-17.

Aumann, R.J. and M. Maschler, 1964, The bargaining set for cooperative games. In: *Advances in Game Theory*, edited by M. Dresher, L.S. Shapley and A.W. Tucker. *Annals of Mathematics Study*, Princeton, N.J., Princeton University Press, 52, 443-476.

Banfield, E.C., 1958, *The moral basis of a backward society*. Glencoe, Ill., The Free Press.

Black, D., 1958, *The theory of committees and elections*. Cambridge, Cambridge University Press.

Buchanan, J. and W.C. Stubblebine, 1962, Externality. *Economica* 29, 371-384.

Buchanan, J. and G. Tullock, 1962, *The calculus of consent*, Ann Arbor, Mich., University of Michigan Press.

Chamberlain, E.H., 1933, *The theory of monopolistic competition*. Cambridge, Mass. Eighth edition: 1965.

Coase, R.H., 1960, The problem of social cost. *Journal of Law and Economics* 3, 1-44.

Condorcet, Marquis de, 1785, *Essai sur l'application de l'analyse à la probabilité des décisions rendues à la pluralité des voix*. Paris.

Debreu, G. and H. Scarf, 1963, A limit theorem on the core of an economy. *International Economic Review* 4, 235-246.

Demsetz, H., 1964, The welfare and empirical implications of monopolistic competition. *Economic Journal* 74, 623-641.

Demsetz, H., 1966, Some aspects of property rights. *Journal of Law and Economics* 9, 61-70.

Demsetz, H., 1968, Why regulate utilities. *Journal of Law and Economics* 11, 55-66.

Downs, A., 1957, *An economic theory of democracy*. New York, Harper.

Edgeworth, F.Y., 1881, *Mathematical psychics: an essay on the application of mathematics to the moral sciences*. London, C. Kegan Paul & Co.

Farrell, M.J., 1959, The convexity assumption in the theory of competitive markets. *Journal of Political Economy* 67, 377-391.

Hagström, K.G., 1938, A mathematical note on democracy. *Econometrica* 6,381-383.

Harsanyi, J.C., 1956, Approaches to the bargaining problem before and after the theory of games: A critical discussion of Zeuthen's, Hicks', and Nash's Theories. *Econometrica* 24, 144-157.

Harsanyi, J.C., 1959, A bargaining model for the cooperative n-person game. In: *Contributions to the Theory of Games IV*, edited by A.W. Tucker and R.D. Luce. *Annals of Mathematics Study*, Princeton, N.J., Princeton University Press, 40, 325-255.

Harsanyi, J.C., 1963, A simplified bargaining model for the n-person cooperative game. *International Economic Review* 4, 194-220.

Harsanyi, J.C., 1966, A general theory of rational behavior in game situations. *Econometrica* 34, 613-634.

Hotelling, H., 1929, Stability in competition. *Economic Journal* 39, 41-57.

Kaldor, N., 1935, Market imperfection and excess capacity. *Economica, N.S.* 2, 35-50.

Kaysen, Carl, 1949, Basing point pricing and public policy. *Quarterly Journal of Economics* 63, 289-314.

Knight, F.H., 1921, *Risk, Uncertainty, and profit*. Boston and New York, Houghton-Mifflin. Reprinted by London School of Economics and Political Science, 1948.

Knight, F.H., 1924, Some fallacies in the interpretation of social cost. *Quarterly Journal of Economics* 38, 582-606.

Luce, R.D., 1954, A definition of stability for n-person games. *Annals of Mathematics* 59, 357-366.

Luce, R.D., 1955a, ψ-stability: a new equilibrium concept for n-person game theory. In: *Mathematical Models of Human Behavior*. Stamford, Conn., Dunlap and Associates, pp. 32-44.

Luce, R.D., 1955b, k-stability of symmetric and quota games. *Annals of Mathematics* 62, 517-555.

Marschak, J., 1968, Economics of inquiring, communicating, deciding. *American Economic Review Papers and Proceedings* 58, 1-18.

Marschak, T., 1959, Centralization and decentralization in economic organizations. *Econometrica* 27, 399-430.

Meade, J.E., 1952, External economies and diseconomies in a competitive situation. *Economic Journal* 62, 54-67.

Musgrave, R.A., 1959, *The theory of public finance: a study in public economy*. New York, McGraw-Hill Book Company.

Nash, J.F. jr., 1950, The bargaining problem. *Econometrica* 18, 155-162.

Nash, J.F. jr., 1953, Two person cooperative games. *Econometrica* 21, 128-140.

Negishi, T., 1960-61, Monopolistic competition and general equilibrium. *Review of Economic Studies* 28, 196-201.

Pauly, M.V., 1968, The economics of moral hazard: comment. *American Economic Review* 58, 531-537.

Radner, R., 1968, Competitive equilibrium under uncertainty. *Econometrica* 36, 31-58.

Robertson, D.H., 1924, Those empty boxes. *Economic Journal* 34, 16-30.

Rothenberg, J., 1960, Non-convexity, aggregation, and Pareto optimality. *Journal of Political Economy* 68, 435-468.

Rothenberg, J., 1965, A model of economic and political decision-making. In: *The public economy of urban communities*, edited by J. Margolis. Washington, D.C., Resources for the Future.

Samuelson, P.A., 1954, The pure theory of public expenditures. *Review of Economic Statistics* 36, 387-389.

Samuelson, P.A., 1967, The monopolistic competition revolution. In: *Monopolistic competition theory: studies in impact*, edited by R.E. Kuenne. New York, London and Sydney, Wiley, 105-138.

Schelling, T., 1957, Bargaining, communication, and limited war. *Journal of Conflict Resolution* 1, 19-36.

Schumpeter, J., 1942, *Capitalism, socialism, and democracy*. New York, Harper. Third Edition: 1950.

Scitovsky, T., 1954, Two concepts of external economies. *Journal of Political Economy* 62, 143-151.

Selten, R., 1964, Valuation of n-person games. In: *Advances in Game Theory*, edited by M. Dresher, L.S. Shapley and A.W. Tucker. Princeton, N.J., Princeton University Press, 52, 577-626.

Shapley, L.S., 1953, A value for n-person games. In: *Contribution to the Theory of Games II*, edited by H.W. Kuhn and A.W. Tucker. *Annals of Mathematics Study*, Princeton, N.J., Princeton University Press, 28, 307-317.

Shapley, L.S. and M. Shubik, 1967, Ownership and the production function. *Quarterly Journal of Economics* 81, 88-111.

Shubik, M., 1959, Edgeworth market games. In: *Contribution to the Theory of Games IV*, edited by A. W. Tucker and R. D. Luce. *Annals of Mathematics Study*, Princeton, N.J., Princeton University Press, 40, 267-278.

Smith, A., 1937, *An enquiry concerning the causes of the wealth of nations.* New York, Modern Library.

Starr, R., 1969, Quasi-equilibria in markets with nonconvex preferences. *Econometrica* 37, 25-38.

Triffin, R., 1941, *Monopolistic competition and general equilibrium theory.* Cambridge, Mass., Harvard University Press.

Tullock, G., 1967, *Toward a mathematics of politics.* Ann Arbor, Mich., University of Michigan Press.

Von Neumann, J. and O. Morgenstern, 1944, *Theory of games and economic behavior.* Princeton, N.J., Princeton University Press. Second edition: 1947.

Young, A. A., 1913, Pigou's wealth and welfare. *Quarterly Journal of Economics* 27, 672-686.

Zeuthen, F., 1930, *Problems of monopoly and economic warfare.* London, George Routledge & Sons Ltd.

COMMENTS BY OTTO A. DAVIS

Carnegie-Mellon University

Let me begin by saying that it is both a pleasure and an honor to have the opportunity to comment on a paper by Professor Kenneth Arrow. As everyone doubtlessly already knows, Professor Arrow is one of the most distinguished economists of this century and, indeed, probably of the entire history of our discipline. Accordingly, it is with extreme trepidation that a mere mortal might make bold enough to advance critical comments.

At the risk of appearing trite, it may be advisable to review the major contributions of Professor Arrow's paper. First, it is a masterpiece of exposition. This fact in itself merits special notice because it is extremely rare for someone with a truly exceptional gift for abstract theorizing to be at the same time a master at exposition. But Arrow has both talents.

The second contribution stems from the fact that the paper ties together a literature that is not only varied but also disparate. The extensive literature concerned with the existence and optimality of competitive equilibria, which is still not very widely known due to its abstractness, is briefly and eloquently summarized into six beautifully clear propositions. The nature of an imperfectly competitive equilibrium is illustrated through the modern developments of game theoretic notions of solutions. The problems of risk and information, as these affect the functioning of market systems, are given an insightful treatment. Difficulties associated with externalities and public goods, which are claimed to be less general than market failure, are considered along with issues associated with transaction costs. Arrow also reviews some of the modern work on collective decision making, and with characteristic modesty he fails to mention or reference any of his own substantial contributions to this or any of the other areas. Finally, he concludes with some remarks on the role of social norms within our society. Who could help but admire such an intellectual *tour de force?*

Despite the above, and at least if one judges by listed references and citations within the text, Arrow might regard the section on externalities as the most original part of the paper. With brilliant insight and simplicity, he demonstrates that if the commodity space is suitably redefined, then externalities can be regarded as ordinary commodities so that all the formal theory of competitive equilibrium is still valid and applicable, including its optimality. This result amounts to saying that in principle, if they could be made to exist and function properly, markets could take care of all of our externality problems so that our system should automatically attain Pareto optimality. While some may view this result as most remarkable and fundamental, one can argue that it is at best irrelevant and at worst misleading. What use is there in knowing that in principle markets can take care of our problems when, as Arrow himself emphasizes, they cannot be made to exist or work properly in the presence of externalities? How does such a result help us solve the very real externality problems which abound in our society? The result appears to leave us without a clue as to what should be done.

A second point concerns the originality of the suggested redefinition of the commodity space. Although Arrow appears to be unaware of the fact, some 10 years ago Andrew Whinston in his doctoral dissertation and subsequent publications made that exact point. Unlike Arrow, Whinston used the suggested redefinition as a point of departure for the examination of market-like devices which might be used within decentralized firms or economic systems to accommodate existing externalities. Professor Arrow, on the other hand, appears content to point out that although markets can "in principle" handle such problems, they cannot do so "in reality" because of problems associated with appropriability and small numbers of participants.

Perhaps a more fundamental criticism of the paper, and the entire literature to which it refers, concerns the narrowness of the meaning of optimality and the failure of those who write within this tradition to make explicit comparisons between alternative allocative devices. Although one would not wish to accuse Professor Arrow of holding such a view, the message appears to be implied quite strongly in much of the literature, and in the paper under consideration, that whenever the system does not achieve Pareto optimality, because of externalities or other reasons, then market allocations should be abandoned or altered in some way by collective action. Such a view overlooks the possibility that replacing the market with alternative allocative devices, or even modifying it, might result in situations which are even less desirable than those which are not now Pareto optimal.

The basic point here is that this entire body of literature is incapable of providing what is needed. It is seldom, and perhaps never, that one is asked to choose between allocative devices when one device can achieve optimality and the other cannot. Instead, the usual situation involves making a choice between alternative devices when none of them are capable of leading the system to optimality. What is needed is a theory that helps one choose between imperfect alternatives.

In the paper under consideration here, as well as in much of the literature to which it refers, there appears to be a clear bias in perspective. One may point, e.g., to Professor Arrow's remark that the nonexistence of futures markets for many classes of possible transactions is suggestive of inefficiency. No one could deny that there are no futures markets for many kinds of commodities. But what are the alternatives? Arrow mentions none. Is one to conclude that collective action is required? If so, what action? Are we to argue that the nonexistence of some futures markets means that shortsighted consumers should turn to collective action when we know, e.g., that in the American political system there are evident pressures for the time perspective to be somewhat less than a maximum of 8 years?

One of the basic points at issue here is our clear lack of understanding of the manner in which nonmarket allocative devices might operate. While Arrow does review some of the contributions to the emerging theory of collective decision making, not including the author's own, the discussion reveals the relatively undeveloped nature of that subdiscipline. Not only is there little in that literature, including Arrow's own contributions, which might serve as a basis for making explicit comparisons between market and collective allocations; but the manner in which he covers the models of collective choice serves to illustrate what may well be a little noticed dual set of standards which economic theorists tend to apply to their own and the collective theory. While Arrow emphasizes in this particular section the fact that the allowance for redistribution of income might cause special problems for the collective theory, he barely mentions (and not at all in this section) the problem of information. Yet, informational difficulties are emphasized in his analysis of market allocations, although he does admit that the subject is in its infancy. On the basis of a superficial examination, however, it would appear that informational problems are orders of magnitude larger in political, as opposed to market, systems. Consumers making choices in a market, e.g., surely have a self-interest directed motivation to inform themselves about the characteristics of products under consideration. While one would not want to minimize the consumer's informational problem, it is worthy of note that he does have the aid of certain Federal and local statutes and agencies. On the other hand, the voter, as Gordon Tullock is fond of pointing out, has only minuscule direct self-interest based motivation to inform himself about political issues and the system must rely upon such secondary sources as social norms and individual desires to appear informed in private conversations to provide informational motivation. Further, it is not clear that the natural competitiveness of political campaigns, which are not conducted under the watchful eye of some agency seeking to enforce truth-in-advertising legislation, provides candidates with strong motivations to clearly and truthfully inform the voters about the various issues. Indeed, there may be political advantage, at least in some situations, for candidates to provide incorrect information to the electorate as certainly must have happened, e.g., when one of our late Presidents claimed in his campaign that there was a "missile gap" when in fact the gap was in the opposite direction. The main point here is that some of the very problems which cause markets to operate inefficiently also plague the functioning of the political system. Hence, comparisons of alternative allocative devices inherently involves choices between imperfect alternatives, and at the present time our theories are not structured to aid such choices.

If we really wish to examine the issues upon which choices between market and nonmarket allocations should be based, then it is clear that greatly increased attention must be turned to nonmarket mechanisms. On the other hand, being serious about such a choice also raises the question of whether one would be content with the existing analyses of market allocations which, as Professor Arrow so correctly indicates, concentrate solely upon the criterion of efficiency. In short, it may be that analyses which rely solely upon notions of Pareto optimality and social welfare functions are simply inadequate for such a choice. Surely, if one goes back to, say, the American Founding Fathers, one finds many values other than mere efficiency reflected in their writings. It would be strange, indeed, if such issues as the distribution of power or such problems as the protection of minorities were found to be irrelevant in a choice between market and nonmarket allocations.

It is obvious, of course, that Professor Arrow is not responsible for the inadequacies of economic theory. Yet, his essay does clearly indicate that there is much work to be done before we can even hope to achieve anything even approaching an adequate basis for the design of an economic and political system.

COMMENTS BY PETER A. DIAMOND

Massachusetts Institute of Technology

Professor Arrow has given us a lucid and insightful introduction to the problems of economic analysis for the choice of market vs. nonmarket allocation. I want to follow his basic line adding some elements, giving somewhat different emphasis to others, and combining some of his ideas from different parts of the paper.

The potential difference in transaction costs between market and nonmarket allocation receives considerable attention from Professor Arrow. It seems odd to find no mention of possible differences in production costs depending on whether bureaucrats or entrepreneurs are managing a particular enterprise. Perhaps the theoretical proposition that government can in principle accomplish anything that private industry can has dulled interest in the question of relative efficiencies in practice. There are also differences arising from management when there is discrimination in hiring or other market imperfections arising from individual decision making rather than the form of production possibilities. Further, when the government is using a rationing device like the draft, there are income distribution implications that are different from those arising with the use of a market by the government.

In discussing competitive equilibrium we are told that any allocation not approximately achievable as a competitive equilibrium can be blocked by a coalition acting in isolation. In the discussion of social norms we are told that some ethical and moral codes may serve to compensate for market failure. Combining these two elements we can see that some social norms may help a part of society to enforce an allocation different from a competitive equilibrium by preventing certain types of coalitions from forming. Particularly when the social norm has a class or race element limiting interracial or interclass coalitions this possibility seems very real indeed.

The first part of Arrow's discussion is really a normative analysis of government action. Toward the end he considers problems of having a positive theory of public action. In a world of at least partially decentralized government decision making, unless all parts of the government are acting optimally with respect to the same social welfare function, it is necessary, in general, to have a positive theory of the rest of government to do applicable normative analysis of any part of government decision making. For example, one cannot develop criteria for public investment without a theory of the response of tax rates and debt policy to the level of public investment. This inseparability of different government decisions becomes particularly important in the context of income distribution problems. As Arrow is careful to point out, lump sum transfers are essential to his discussion of the merits of competitive equilibrium. In the absence of optimal redistribution whenever the situation changes unexpectedly, nothing, in general, can be said about the allocation of resources to maximize a social welfare function without explicitly considering income distribution. More specifically, Pareto optimality loses its interest as a theoretical tool when we can only improve income distribution by introducing distortions (e.g., taxes) which prevent Pareto optimality. Thus we have a guide to the problems of resource allocation. Without considering income distribution we do not have a guide to solving them. In practice, political discussion of income distribution takes the form of altering some of the small number of parameters which determine the shape of the income tax or of considering some welfare programs which again usually are described in terms of a small number of parameters. Such a discussion in terms of a few parameters does not give the options of income redistribution necessary to appeal directly to the theorems on competitive equilibrium nor does it present a discussion which has nearly as many dimensions as the number of voters, so Arrow's criticism of Tullock on this point does not seem appropriate.

In the section on collective action I was struck by Arrow's reference to the State's monopoly of coercive power. In both the political and economic realms there are many individuals who take to the streets or slip through second story windows and cause political decisions or the distribution of income to be different from what it would have been. It is standard in economic models to think of individuals as playing a game with fixed rules which they obey. They do not buy more than they know they can pay for, they do not embezzle funds, they do not rob banks. Similarly, political models have individuals vote and perhaps contribute time or money to political campaigning. They do not bribe officials, burn down buildings, or plan revolution. Neither economic nor political reality are games played with fixed rules. They are not even games with vague rules interpreted by an umpire (like court cases). Rather they are games where the rules are made up as the game proceeds and are always subject to revision, in other words, games without rules. I presume it is not necessary to cite specific instances of government violation of the Bill of Rights to make this point. This may alter the nature of political model building more than economic model building but seems relevant for both as soon as one considers models with uncertainty.

Frontiers of Quantitative Economics, ed. **M.D.** *Intriligator.* © *North-Holland Publishing Company.*

CHAPTER 2

ECONOMICS OF INFORMATION SYSTEMS*

JACOB MARSCHAK

University of California, Los Angeles

0. Introduction

0.0. *The economist's general information problem*

Out of several pushbuttons, each of a different color, you select one. A slight push, and massive amounts of energy are released, and are transformed in the manner you have prescribed. The button colors which you have perceived and from which you have selected, exemplify signs, symbols. Your "manipulation of symbols", equally vaguely called "handling of information" (or somewhat more precisely, "sorting") has involved little energy but has discharged and directed a large amount. You have done "brain work". No economist will deny that a large part of our national product is contributed by symbol manipulation — telephoning orders, discussing in conferences, shuffling papers, or just performing some of the humble tasks required of the inspector, or even an ordinary worker, on the assembly line.[1]

---

* Expanded version of paper presented at a session of Econometric Society, December 1969. — Supported partially by the Office of Naval Research and the National Science Foundation. Much is owed to discussions with Carlo Brumat, James MacQueen, Michel Pham-Huu-Tri, and other members of the Western Management Science Institute.

[1] See Marschak (1968a), a paper addressed to a wider audience and, in essence, revised here in a somewhat more precise fashion. For some earlier results see Marschak (1964).

The economist asks, first: what determines the demand and supply of the goods and services used to manipulate symbols. This may help him, second, to understand how social welfare is affected by the manner in which resources are allocated to those goods and services.

A pre-requisite is, to define concepts and study their interrelations in a way that would prove useful for the answering of these questions. The economist begins by assuming that those who demand and use, and those who produce and supply, the goods and services considered, make choices that are "economical" (= "rational") in some usefully defined way, and are made under well-defined constraints. The constraints may include limitations on the choosers' memories and other mental abilities. The economic theorist leaves the door open to psychologists, sociologists, historians, and to his own "institutionalist" colleagues in the hope they will help to determine the values of underlying parameters — provided (another hope!) they do not establish that the assumption of "economical" choice fails to yield usefully close approximations to begin with. I take this back: even then, he will offer his results as recommendations to users and producers of "information-handling", or "informational", goods and services.[2]

0.1. *The user's problem, viewed by non-economists*

Besides its interest to economists, the manipulation of symbols, or information processing, has been the domain of philosophers and linguists; of computer scientists, control theorists and communication engineers; and of statisticians. The latter, following the path of J. Neyman and A. Wald, have become more and more concerned with the economical manner of obtaining "information", and have discovered much that is useful to the economist. Engineers have proposed a "measure of information" based on probability relations between classes of arbitrary signs. This arose out of practical, "economic" needs of the communication industry. My task will be, in part, to see how those results fit into the general economics of symbol-manipulating goods and services — including, e.g., the services of statisticians, and of men who design or handle computers and control mechanisms. (The task of the last-named men is indeed to apply economics to to-day's most varied and complete combinations of informational goods and

---

[2] See Marschak (1968b).

services!). Finally, attempts have been made on the part of linguists and philosophers to apply the engineers' measure of information to the probabilities of sequences of signs in a natural language (Miller and Chomsky 1963); or else to define a measure of "semantic information", a "content measure" — essentially by substituting for an arbitrary class of sign sequences its partition into equivalence classes consisting of sequences with identical "meaning" (Carnap and Bar-Hillel 1952).

In recent years, the approach *via* economic rationality — (bluntly: via the expected utility to the decision maker) — has begun to penetrate the work of both engineers and philosophers. An important, though still not sufficiently well known step was made by pioneer Shannon himself (1960) when he removed his earlier tacit assignment[3] of equal penalty for all communication errors. He introduced, instead, a "fidelity criterion" that does correspond to a component (we call it "benefit") of the utility itself — albeit confined, as we shall see, to the context of communication only and therefore defined on a very special class of actions and events. Howard (1966) writes, in a broader context:

> ... The early developers stressed that the information measure was dependent only on the probabilistic structure of the communication process. For example, if losing all your assets in the stock market and having whale steak for dinner have the same probability, then the information associated with the occurence of either event is the same. ... No theory that involves just the probabilities of outcomes without considering their consequences could possibly be adequate in describing the importance of uncertainty to the decision maker.

He concludes his analysis of a neat model with a challenge to his profession (and perhaps to mine as well):

> If information value and associated decision theoretic structures do not in the future occupy a large part of the education of engineers, then the engineering profession will find that its traditional role of managing scientific and economic resources for the benefit of man has been forfeited to another profession.

And philosopher R. Carnap, whom we have mentioned as one of the early proponents of a "semantic" information measure ("content measure"), wrote in a more recent (1966) paper:

> When I consider the application of the concept of probability in science then I usually have in mind in the first place the probability of predictions and only secondarily the probability of laws or theories. Once we see clearly which features of prediction are desirable, then we may say that a given theory is preferable to another one if the

---

[3] For the case of a "discrete source", see section 7.0 below.

predictions yielded by the first theory possess on the average more of the desirable features than the prediction yielded by the other theory...

He then proceeds to show that if "a practically acting man"

bases his choice either on content measure alone or on probability alone, he will sometimes be led to choices that are clearly wrong. ... We should choose that action for which the expectation value of the utility of outcome is a maximum (pp. 252, 253-4, 257).[4]

0.2. *Individual demand for information services*

Thus encouraged by the spread of understanding of the economic approach to information use, I shall proceed with my task, a more special one than the general economic information problem outlined at the beginning. I shall study the rational choice-making of an individual from among available information systems, or available components of such systems. The availability constraint specifies, in particular, the costs and the delays associated with given components (or with chains or networks of components) of information systems. As is familiar to students of the market, the available set depends on the choices made by suppliers, and joint choices by demanders and suppliers would determine which information systems are in fact produced and used under given external conditions. These conditions include the technological knowledge of those concerned.

I shall not be able to make more than casual remarks on the supply. The first of the two general questions to be asked by the economist, the joint determination of demand and supply, will therefore receive only a partial answer. The second question, that of socially optimal allocation of resources to informational goods and services, is pushed away still farther. This is not to say that the allocation question cannot be studied until the demand and supply of informational goods and services is fully understood. Significant work of Hurwicz (1960), Stigler (1961, 1962), Hirshleifer (1967), Radner (1967, 1968) testifies to the contrary.

---

[4] In the quoted paper, he refers to an earlier paper (Carnap 1962) (strongly influenced by Ramsey's, De Finetti's, and Savage's logic of expected utility) that "gives an exposition of my view on the nature of inductive logic which is clearer and from my present point of view more adequate than that which I gave in my book", viz. in Carnap (1950).

1. Processing

1.0. Processing P

Processing P is defined as:

$$P = \langle X, Y, \eta, \varkappa, \tau \rangle,$$

where $X =$ set of inputs x, $Y =$ set of outputs y, $\eta =$ transformation from X to Y, including the case of stochastic transformation (see below), $\varkappa =$ transformation from X to non-negative reals, measuring cost (in cost units), and $\tau =$ transformation from X to non-negative reals, measuring delay (in time units).

X, Y are, generally, random sets. As to η, in the special *deterministic* (or *noiseless*) case η is an ordinary function; i.e., it associates every x in X with a unique $y = \eta(x)$ in Y. However, we must consider the more general *stochastic* (or *noisy*) case in which η associates every x in X with some (conditional) probability distribution on Y. For simplicity of presentation we shall usually (except for some economically interesting examples) assume X and Y finite:

$$X = (1, \ldots, m), \quad Y = (1, \ldots, n),$$

so that $\eta_{ij} = \text{Prob}(y = j \,|\, x = i)$. Hence $\eta = [\eta_{xy}]$ is a $m \times n$ Markov matrix i.e., all $\eta_{xy} \geq 0$ and $\sum_y \eta_{xy} = 1$ for all x.[5] Clearly, the deterministic case occurs if one element in each row of the matrix $[\eta_{xy}]$ equals unity, in which case[6]:

$$\eta_{xy} = \begin{Bmatrix} 1 \\ 0 \end{Bmatrix} \quad \text{if} \quad y \begin{Bmatrix} = \\ \neq \end{Bmatrix} \eta(x). \tag{1}$$

As to $\varkappa$, we shall assume $\varkappa(x)$, the *cost of processing* a given input x, to be constant. We thus forego the discussion of a more general, stochastic case, in which $\varkappa(x)$ is a probability distribution of costs, given x. Similarly, we assume that the time $\tau(x)$ required to process a given input x is constant.

---

[5] See Blackwell (1953) for an extension of the concept of stochastic transformation to infinite sets.

[6] Example: let $m = 3$, $n = 2$ and

$$\eta = \begin{Bmatrix} 1 & 0 \\ 0 & 1 \\ 0 & 1 \end{Bmatrix}; \text{ then } \eta(1) = 1; \, \eta(2) = \eta(3) = 2.$$

1.1. *Cost-relevant inputs*

In important cases, exemplified by processings called *storage* and *transportation*, two otherwise different inputs, $x = i$ and $x = i'$, say, are such that $\varkappa(i) = \varkappa(i')$. (It costs about the same to transport, over 100 miles, a gallon of whiskey or of gasoline; but see section 7.0.) It is then convenient to replace the original set X by a *reduced set* $X/\varkappa$ consisting of equivalence classes $x/\varkappa$, such that all elements of the same class are associated with the same cost.

1.2. *Available (feasible) processings*

For given X, Y, not all triples $(\eta, \varkappa, \tau)$ are available. For example, to implement a given transformation η at lowered delays $\tau(x)$ for all x may require raised costs $\varkappa(x)$. The set of *available processings* will be denoted by $\mathscr{P}$.

1.3. *Purposive processing*

Consider a case in which the y in Y [now to be rewritten as a in $A = (1, \ldots, n)$] can be interpreted as the *actions (decisions)* of a person who obeys certain axioms of decision logic[7], and the inputs x in X [now to be rewritten as $Z = (1, \ldots, m)$] are *events* beyond his control. Then there exists a probability distribution $\pi = $ vector $[\pi_z]$ and a bounded real-valued *utility function* $\omega(a, z, \varkappa(z), \tau(z))$, such that, given two available processings:

$$P' = \langle Z', A', \eta', \varkappa', \tau' \rangle; \quad P'' = \langle Z'', A'', \eta'', \varkappa'', \tau'' \rangle,$$

the chooser of a processing will choose P' only if:

$$U_{\pi\omega}(P') \geq U_{\pi\omega}(P''),$$

---

[7] I refer to the work of F.P. Ramsey, B. De Finetti, L.J. Savage, accepted in recent years by professional logicians R. Carnap and R.C. Jeffrey. For a survey see Marschak (1968b). Also, regarding Carnap and the relation of probability to frequency see Marschak (1970). That certain observed behavior is not really inconsistent with the expected utility rule if cost or feasibility of storing or other processing is accounted for, was brilliantly shown by Winter (1966). Among the many merits of Raiffa's delightful introduction to the field (1968) is his forceful emphasis on the need for and the possibility of training people for consistency.

where, for any processing P, its (expected) utility is:

$$U_{\pi\omega}(P) = \Sigma_{za}\pi_z\eta_{za}\omega(a, z, \varkappa(z), \tau(z)). \tag{2}$$

It follows that, given the characteristics of the chooser (viz., π, ω, listed in the subscript under U for convenience) and given the available set $\mathscr{P}$, processing P^* will be chosen only if[8]:

$$P^* \in \mathscr{P}, \ U_{\pi\omega}(P^*) \geq U_{\pi\omega}(P), \quad \text{all } P \text{ in } \mathscr{P}.$$

1.4. *Timing*

Utility depends on action. Accordingly, we consider that the utility is "earned", and the action a is taken, at the same time. But the cost $\varkappa(z)$ is incurred $\tau(z)$ time units earlier.

1.5. *Continued purposive processing*

It is often necessary to reinterpret the output a and input z as time-sequences, with a *horizon* equal to T, possibly infinite:

$$a = \{a_t\}, \ z = \{z_t\}, \ t = 1, ..., T. \tag{3}$$

An element η_{za} of the transformation η is then the conditional probability of a particular sequence of T actions, given a sequence of T events. Using the results of Koopmans (1960), implied by some plausible axioms he has suggested, the utility $\omega(a, z, \varkappa(z), \tau(z))$ entering the definition (2) of the utility of processing can be decomposed thus:

$$\omega(a, z, \varkappa(z), \tau(z)) = \sum_{t=1}^{T} \upsilon(\bar{a}_t, \bar{z}_t, \varkappa(z_t))d^{\sum_{s=1}^{t}\tau(z_s)}, \tag{4}$$

where the *discount constant* d $(0 < d \leq 1)$ and the function υ are independent of time and $\bar{a}_t, \bar{z}_t$ are, respectively, the *histories* up to t:

$$\bar{a}_t = (a_1, ..., a_t), \ \bar{z}_t = (z_1, ..., z_t). \tag{5}$$

---

[8] Note that the word "chooser" was used, rather than "decision-maker"; see also section 2.1, where the chooser of P will be called "meta-decider".

1.6. *Additive costs and discounted benefits*

A convenient though rather special assumption is often tacitly made in practice. It is assumed that, given any distribution π, the utility of processing, $U_{\pi\omega}(P)$ increases in "expected discounted benefit", B, and decreases in "expected cost", K. Before defining B and K precisely, let us state the assumption in two other, obviously equivalent, forms: for any given π, (1) "of all processings with the same K, the one with highest B has highest utility"; and (2) "the efficient subset of $\mathscr{P}$ consists of all those available processings for which the pair $(-K, B)$ is not dominated by any other such available pair".

If, on the other hand, the assumption does not hold, then a processing may exceed in utility, and hence be preferable to, another processing, even though the latter has lower expected cost and higher expected discounted benefit. It will be shown that the stated tacit assumption implies that the utility function ω is decomposable in a certain sense.

More precisely, we define:

$$K \equiv K_\pi(\varkappa) \equiv \Sigma_z \pi_z \varkappa(z), \tag{6}$$

$$B \equiv B_{\pi\beta d}(\eta, \tau) \equiv \Sigma_{zy} \beta(a, z) d^{\tau(z)} \pi_z \eta_{zy}, \tag{7}$$

where β is the *benefit function* from $Z \times A$ to the reals, and d is the discount constant, and, as in (2), subscripts under K, B convey the relevant characteristics of the decision maker. Note that d occurs in (7) but not in (6) because of the assumption on timing in section 1.4. This difference will be removed when we study processing chains, as in section 1.8.

It follows from the general theorem on multi-criterion decisions (see Appendix 1) that $U_{\pi\omega}$ is monotone increasing in B and in $-K$ if and only if there exists a function β and constants d and c such that:

$$\omega(a, z, \varkappa(z), \tau(z)) = -c\varkappa(z) + \beta(a, z) d^{\tau(z)}, \tag{8}$$

where c is a positive conversion factor, fixing the choice of units. It then follows by (2) that the utility of processing is monotone in $-K$ and B (for all π) if and only if it is a linear combination[9]:

$$U = -cK + B, \quad c > 0. \tag{9}$$

---

[9] Elsewhere, B was called *expected gross payoff*. See Marschak end Radner (1971).

1.7. *Benefit-relevant events and actions*

It is convenient to define Z and A in such a manner that:

$\beta(a, z) = \beta(a, z')$, all $a \in A$, only if $z = z'$,

$\beta(a, z) = \beta(a', z)$, all $z \in Z$, only if $a = a'$.

Thus if Z and A are finite, so that β can be represented as a *benefit matrix*,

$\beta = [\beta_{az}]$,

then no two columns and no two rows are identical.[10] No generality is lost if all the dominated rows are deleted.

1.8. *Processing chains*

Define a sequence:

$P^1, \ldots, P^N$,

where:

$$P^k = \langle X^k, X^{k+1}, \eta^k, \varkappa^k, \tau^k \rangle, \quad k = 1, \ldots, N \tag{10}$$

as a *processing chain*.

Let X^k have n_k elements, so that η^k is of order $n_k \times n_{k+1}$. Such a sequence is equivalent to a processing:

$$P = \langle X^1, X^{N+1}, \eta, \ldots \rangle, \tag{11}$$

where:

$$\eta_{x^1 x^{N+1}} = \sum_{x^2 \ldots x^N} \eta_{x^1 x^2} \eta_{x^2 x^3} \ldots \eta_{x^N x^{N+1}}, \text{ so that}$$

$$\eta = \prod_{k=1}^{N} \eta^k. \tag{12}$$

With P in (11) equivalent to the sequence (10), the utilities achieved by P and by that sequence should be, in a purposive case, equal. This makes it impossible, in general, to fill the places indicated by dots in (11) by single real-valued functions. Rather, the utility of P (if P is purposive) would

---

[10] Note that z and z' may be equivalent with respect to costs but not equivalent with respect to benefits. See section 1.1.

depend on the sequences $\{\varkappa^k\}$, $\{\tau^k\}$, $k = 1, \ldots, N$. This is easily seen by applying the decomposition of utility over time as in (4) to the case (8) of additive costs and benefits.

1.9. *Networks*

More general than a chain is a *network*, in which each transformation may have several input and output variables, some possibly shared with other transformations. We shall not pursue this here. See Marschak and Radner (1971), Chapter 8.

2. Symbols as outputs and inputs

2.0. *A purposive processing chain*

Consider a chain (10) consisting of N successive processing links, with:

$X^{N+1} = $ set A of actions a,

$X^1 \quad = $ set Z of events z,

where a and z are typical arguments of the benefit function $\beta(a, z)$. Each may be a time-sequence as in (3). Some physical processes cause an action and event to jointly yield some physical consequence (again possibly a time-sequence: e.g., a sequence of annual monetary profits), to which a benefit number is attached. But we shall not be concerned with these physical processes and the chains (or networks) that they form.

The intermediate inputs and outputs, that is $X^2, \ldots, X^N$ do not enter the benefit function. As in section 1.1, two elements x_1^k, x_2^k of the set X^k, $k = 2, \ldots, N$, can be considered equivalent if their processing costs are equal:

$$\varkappa^k(x_1^k) = \varkappa^k(x_2^k).$$

It will be convenient to reserve the term "symbols" for the "benefit-neutral" but "cost-relevant" inputs and outputs. Thus the links $P^2, \ldots, P^N$ will be said to process symbols onto symbols. Typical examples are: translation (e.g., encoding, decoding) of messages; transmission of messages over distances; and their storage over time. On the other hand, an event or an action (even that of a painter or composer) will not be called a symbol;

but processing link P^1 will be said to transform event into a symbol; and P^N will be said to transform a symbol into action.

2.1. *Choosing the chain: a meta-decision*

The action, or decision, $a \equiv x^{N+1}$, the output of the last link in the purposive chain must be distinguished from the decision to choose one rather than another chain. The difference between expected benefit and cost is maximized by the chooser of the chain. The chooser may hire men or machines to perform the successive processings, including the ultimate one, viz., the choice of action, or decision. If this ultimate processing link is called "deciding", the choice of it and of other links of the chain may be called *meta-deciding*.

2.2. *Some information systems*

A purposive processing chain is often called an *information system*, the word "information" presumably bearing some relation to transformations from and into symbol sets. Information about a physical fact is not the fact itself but some "symbols" (e.g., words) associated with it. Historically, two kinds of "shortened" chains have been considered by specialists: statisticians on the one hand, and communication engineers on the other. They are.

(a) a two-link chain, with

$$X^1 = Z = \text{events} \qquad\qquad P^1 = \text{experiment, inquiry}$$
$$X^2 = Y = \text{data, observations} \qquad P^2 = \text{strategy.}$$
$$X^3 = A = \text{actions decisions.}$$

(b) a four-link chain, with

$$X^1 = Z = \text{messages to be sent} \qquad P^1 = \text{storing}$$
$$X^2 = \text{long stored sequences of messages} \quad P^2 = \text{encoding}$$
$$X^3 = \text{encoded messages} \qquad\qquad P^3 = \text{transmission}$$
$$X^4 = \text{received messages} \qquad\qquad P^4 = \text{decoding.}$$
$$X^5 = A = \text{decoded messages.}$$

The chains (a) and (b) are linked together on fig. 1.

To suit special applications, some special assumptions are usually made, different in (a) and in (b), regarding the sets of inputs and outputs, the sets of available processings, the cost and delay functions $\varkappa$ and τ, and the

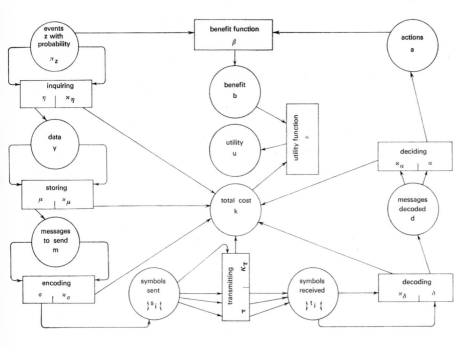

Greek letters η , μ , σ , τ , δ , a , β, v, for processors;
corresponding Latin letters y , m , s , t , d , a , b, u, for their outputs.
The cost functions are $\varkappa_\eta$, $\varkappa_\mu$, $\varkappa_\sigma$, $\varkappa_\tau$, $\varkappa_\delta$, $\varkappa_a$, with k as joint output.

Fig. 1. Inquiring, communicating, deciding.

benefit function β. We shall indicate some of those assumptions and the implications of removing them in due course.

Both (a) and (b) can be considered as special cases of some longer chain. It seems that such longer chains are necessary to describe, in their full richness, the operations of a computer (including problem-solving, simulation, pattern recognition, etc.). The popular description of these operations as *informa ion processing* would then appear a felicitous one. This would include, e.g., programmed navigation. See Chernoff (1968).

In the following three sections, 3, 4, and 5, we deal with the two-links chain (a), and study the consequences of some simplifying assumptions used, in effect, in the literature on statistical decision theory. These results are, in fact, applicable also to information systems consisting of any number of links, with actions based not directly on observations (outputs of the "inquiring" link) but on the outputs of subsequent processings (e.g., encoding, transmitting) of observations. By (12), the system's transformation matrix η is the product of the successive transformation matrices, n^k, of its links; only the last one needs to be specified if the assumptions listed in section 3 are made. Accordingly, in the next four sections, η will be called, interchangeably, the inquiry matrix or simply inquiry; or, to be more general, the transformation matrix of an information system or, briefly, information matrix.

Of the assumptions to be listed in section 3 that of additive cost is perhaps least offensive. It also leads to important results since it permits concentrating on the properties of the information matrix η. On the other hand, the question of successive delays (operation speeds and capacities at successive links), mostly neglected in the two-link theory and introduced in our section 4 in general terms only, will become a serious one when the processing chain is lengthened by inserting links that implement the communication between the observer and the decision-maker.

3. Inquiring and deciding in statistical theory

3.0. *The two-link chain*

Link P^1 in the two-link chain (a) of section 2.2 has been variously called *experiment*, *taking observations*, also *making a diagnosis*. Link P^2, *strategy*, has been also called *decision rule*. Reflecting certain though surely not all aspects of statistical practice, the usual analysis of the two-link chain makes tacitly some restrictions which do not appear necessary or justifiable in the broader context of economic comparison of purposive processings. In particular, the delays $\tau^1(z)$, $\tau^2(y)$ are neglected as are often the constraints on strategies and their cost, $\varkappa^2(y)$.

On the other hand, in most statistical writings, our environmental variable z is generalized, as follows. The event (or, in the case of continued processing, a time-sequence of events) is replaced by a probability distribution called *hypothesis*, so that our π becomes a distribution on the space of probability distributions of some variable v. However, this complicated description of the problem is equivalent, and can be reduced, to the original problem, with v playing the role of the event z. We shall, therefore, not pursue this further.

3.1. *Neglecting delays*

While, as will be shown, the speed of processing is attached great importance in the existing work of communication engineers who study the several-links chain (b) described in section 2.2, processing speed is completely neglected in the statistical theory of the two-links chain (a). No explicit attention is paid to whether it takes an hour or a month to collect a sample, or to apply a given decision rule. Accordingly, the question of "overloaded capacity" of an observation equipment or decision-making equipment is not, to my knowledge, treated explicitly in statistical literature. It is assumed in effect that for all processing chains considered, $\tau^1(z)$ is the same constant, and $\tau^2(y)$ is the same constant so that, when comparing the values of two processings, one can assume for both, without loss of generality:

$$\tau^1(z) = \tau^2(y) = 0. \tag{13}$$

No doubt this assumption is not made in actual statistical practice. If the expected benefit can be strongly diminished when decisions are based on obsolete data (see section 5), the chooser of the experiment and the strategy will give preference to accelerated ones, costs permitting. Moreover, it is not economical to accelerate the experiment if this results in piling up unused data because decisions are taken too slowly. Such considerations surely arise in industrial quality control, in marketing research, in the preparation of economic indices for public policy, and, very likely also in much of scientific laboratory and clinical work. See, e.g., Anderson (1969).

3.2.

With delays out of the way, the *Statistical Decision Problem* takes the following form. Changing notations somewhat, write:

$$\eta_{zy}^1 = p(y\,|\,z) = \eta_{zy}; \; \varkappa^1(z) = \varkappa_z; \; P^1 = \langle \eta, \varkappa \rangle$$

$$\eta_{ya}^2 = p(a\,|\,y) = \alpha_{ya}; \; \kappa^2(y) = \delta_y; \; P^2 = \langle \alpha, \delta \rangle. \tag{14}$$

In this context, $\eta = [\eta_{zy}]$ is often called the *matrix of likelihoods*, and $\alpha = [\alpha_{ya}]$ is called a *(randomized, mixed) strategy*. The sets Z and A are regarded as fixed. This assumption and the fact that Y is the range of η and the domain of α justifies the above abbreviated definition of the links P^1, P^2. Then the processing chain (P^1, P^2), if available, can be written as:

$$P \equiv (\eta, \alpha, \varkappa, \delta) \in \mathscr{P}, \tag{15}$$

where $\mathscr{P}$ is the feasible set. We assume additive cost as in section 1.6 but postpone till later (section 5) the consideration of continued processing introduced in section 1.5. The chooser then maximizes, subject to the constraint (15), the expected utility U which is the difference between expected benefit B (no discounting for delay need be considered) and expected cost K, where[11]:

$$B = B_{\pi\theta}(P) = \Sigma_{zya}\beta(a, z)\pi_z\eta_{zy}\alpha_{ya}, \tag{16}$$

$$K = K_\pi(P) = \Sigma_z\pi_z\varkappa_z + \Sigma_{zy}\pi_z\eta_{zy}\delta_y, \tag{17}$$

$$U = U_{\pi\beta}(P) = B_{\pi\beta}(P) - K_\pi(P). \tag{18}$$

As in section 1.6, the subscripts under B, K, U characterize the chooser. Together with the feasible set $\mathscr{P}$, they form the givens of the chooser's problem. Hence the optimal chain P^* is a function of π, β, $\mathscr{P}$. So is the efficient set, which consists of all elements of $\mathscr{P}$ for which the pair $(-K, B)$ is not dominated by any other such feasible pair.

3.3. *Action as a subset of events*

In general, there is no need to assume any formal, logical relation between Z and A. For example, Z may be the set (cancer, no cancer), and A may be the set (surgery, radiotherapy, no treatment). The benefit function β would then assign a value to each of the $2 \times 3 = 6$ pairs (a, z). In statistical literature, an action that can be considered relevant to the benefit of the statistician's "employer" can be identified with the choice of one of disjoint subsets ("alternative hypotheses") of the set of benefit-relevant events. Such actions cannot be more numerous than events.

True, the action of the statistician is, in other cases, said to consist in choosing from a set of overlapping subsets of events: e.g., in naming an interval.[12] He is then supposed to use choice criteria relevant, I think, to his own, not his employer's, benefit.

For purposes of economics of information, it is more useful to say that the statistician's task is to derive, from observations y, the likelihoods η_{zy} for all events z relevant to his employer's benefit. Given the prior probabilities π_z,

---

[11] In statistical literature the negative of β is called the *loss function*, and the negative of B is called *risk*. As M. Loève remarked to this writer, "we statisticians minimize losses, you economists maximize profits" — which is clearly the same thing.

[12] Contrast Examples 1-3 with Example 4 in Lehmann (1959), section 1.2. See also Pratt (1961). I am indebted to M. DeGroot and W. Kruskal for discussions of this question.

one can then determine the joint probabilities $\pi_z \eta_{zy}$ or, for that matter, the posterior probabilities $(\pi_z \eta_{zy}/\sum_t \pi_t \eta_{ty})$. The employer or his operations research man (possibly identical with the statistician) will combine these probabilities with the benefits yielded to the employer by *his* actions, given the events, and choose the action that maximizes expected benefit.

Accordingly, we shall permit the employer's (user's) actions to be more numerous than events. This will lead to interesting results in the economics of comparing information systems (see section 6.4).

To be sure, a problem of communication arises. It is, in fact, the problem of optimal encoding, in the sense of section 7, below. It may be costly or even non-feasible to communicate in all detail the posterior or the joint probability distributions involved, to the employer, or to his operations research man, or to a low-echelon decision-making man or machine. With this in mind, a condensed message may be used: e.g., the posterior probability that z lies in a particular interval. The choice of the interval will then depend, not on the statistician's "tastes", but on the "meta-decider's" judgment as to the contributions of alternative codes to *his* benefit and cost.

3.4. *Neglecting the constraints and costs of deciding*

In important parts of statistical literature decision-making is, in effect, assumed costless and unconstrained. This strong assumption has led to a fruitful discussion of "comparative informativeness" of the matrices $\eta = [\eta_{zy}]$. We shall pursue it in some detail in sections 4 and 5.

The assumption of costless and unconstrained deciding is too strong to have been actually accepted in practice. For example, in the case where observations y and decisions $a = \alpha(y)$ are both real-valued, attention was paid, quite early, to a special class of decision rules, viz., to the class of *linear* α, presumably because linear functions require less computational effort. (The theorem that, among unbiased *linear* estimators the least-squares estimator is best, goes back to Gauss.) The search for good "robust" statistics is motivated by the low prior probabilities of narrowly specified models. But it is also due to considerations of computational economy, I suppose; as is, of course, the rounding-off of digits in the computational process.

3.5. *Value of information*

With decision undelayed, costless and unconstrained, and inquiry undelayed, the problem of the chooser of a two-link chain P is simplified. Denote by $\{\alpha\}$ the set of *all* stochastic transformations from Y to A (remember that any such transformation was assumed feasible) and let $\{\eta, \varkappa\}$ be the set of feasible pairs of inquiry transformations η and inquiry cost functions $\varkappa$. Then the constraint (15) is relaxed into:

$$P \equiv (\eta, \alpha, \varkappa) \in \{\alpha\} \times \{\varkappa, \eta\}, \tag{19}$$

since $\delta = 0$. Further, equation (16) is unaffected, but in (17) the term involving δ vanishes. Therefore, (18) can be rewritten as:

$$U = U_{\pi\beta}(\eta, \alpha, \varkappa) = B_{\pi\beta}(\eta, \alpha) - K_{\pi}(\varkappa) \tag{20}$$

where:

$$B_{\pi\beta}(\eta, \alpha) = \Sigma_{zya} \beta(a, z) \pi_z \eta_{zy} \alpha_{ya} \tag{21}$$

$$K_{\pi}(\varkappa) = \Sigma_z \pi_z \varkappa_z. \tag{22}$$

Define the *information value* of η as:

$$V_{\pi\beta}(\eta) \equiv \max_{\alpha \in \{\alpha\}} B_{\pi\beta}(\eta, \alpha) \equiv B_{\pi\beta}(\eta, \alpha^*), \text{ say.} \tag{23}$$

Then, maximizing expected utility U with respect to $\eta, \alpha, \varkappa$ over their feasible set, given π, β, is equivalent to:

$$\max_{\eta} V_{\pi\beta}(\eta) - \min_{\varkappa} K_{\pi}(\varkappa), \tag{24}$$

subject to the cost constraint:

$$(\varkappa, \eta) \in \{(\varkappa, \eta)\}. \tag{25}$$

With the meta-decider's problem reduced to (24) and (25) it is useful to consider the expected cost $K_{\pi}(\varkappa)$ as fixed and to compare various information matrices $\eta, \eta', \ldots$ according to their values $V_{\pi\beta}(\eta), V_{\pi\beta}(\eta'), \ldots$.

3.6. *Appropriate action, a_y; value of observation, V_y*

The optimal decision rule α^* defined in (23) depends only on η and π, β. Now, for each η, given π and β, there will exist a deterministic optimal decision rule; for it is well-known that in a one-person game there exists a pure optimal strategy (the average of several quantities cannot exceed everyone of them). Thus, no generality is lost if we define $\{\alpha\}$ as the set of all mappings from Y to A. The assumption of costless and non-restricted decisions excludes the case when the hired (and presumably cheap) decision-making man or machine uses a non-optimal deterministic rule and also the case when he (it) makes "random errors", unless they happen to constitute an optimal random strategy.

With $\{\alpha\}$ reduced to the set of all *pure* strategies, i.e., all functions α from Y to A we can write $a = \alpha(y)$ so that [similar to (1)]:

$$\alpha_{ya} = \begin{Bmatrix} 1 \\ 0 \end{Bmatrix} \quad \text{if} \quad a \begin{Bmatrix} = \\ \neq \end{Bmatrix} \alpha(y). \tag{26}$$

Denote the action that is "appropriate" (i.e., optimal) in response to y by:

$$a_y = \alpha^*(y);$$

that is, for a given y:

$$\max_{a \in A} \sum_z \beta(a, z)\pi_z \eta_{zy} \equiv \sum_z \beta(a_y, z)\pi_z \eta_{zy} \equiv V_y(\eta), \text{ say.} \tag{27}$$

$V_y(\eta)$ may be called "value of the observation y". Later, it will prove convenient to define:

$$\gamma_z(a) \equiv \pi_z \beta(a, z), \tag{28}$$

the benefit of action a at event z, *weighted* by that event's probability. Then (27) becomes:

$$V_y(\eta) \equiv \max_a \Sigma_z \gamma_z(a)\eta_{zy} = \Sigma_z \gamma_z(a_y)\eta_{zy}. \tag{29}$$

By (21), (26) and (23), the value of an inquiry is:

$$V(\eta) = \sum_y V_y(\eta). \tag{30}$$

Note that $\Sigma_z \gamma_z(a)$ is the "prior expectation of benefit" of action a.

3.7. *Labelling of observations*

It is clear from (21) and (23) that $V(\eta)$ is invariant under interchange of columns in η. Therefore, if η is of order $m \times n$ and P a permutation matrix of order n, we shall agree that:

$$\eta \text{ and } \eta P \text{ are equivalent.} \tag{31}$$

Thus if (with $m = n = 2$), $z = 1$ means "stock price will rise" and $z = 2$ means "stock price will not rise", then the datum "my broker says stock price will rise" can be labelled, indifferently, as $y = 1$ or as $y = 2$. There is no loss of generality in choosing any one particular labelling.

Also, no generality is lost if we agree to eliminate any column of η that consists of zeros only and thus designates (with Y finite, as we recall!) an observation that never occurs.

It is seen from (29) that two observations $y = j, k$, whose conditional probabilities, given any event z, are pairwise equal, yield the same appropriate action $a_j = a_k$ and the same value $V_j = V_k$. It is convenient therefore, and involves no loss of generality, to redefine every such inquiry by adding any two identical columns, and thus to make every inquiry matrix η to consist of non-identical columns only.

3.8.

Null-information is said to be provided by any matrix η^0 whose rows are identical, so that we can write:

$$\eta_{zy}^0 = \lambda_y, \text{ all } z; \quad \sum_{y=1}^{n} \lambda_y = 1.$$

Then by (29), (30):

$$V_y(\eta^0) = \lambda_y \max_a \Sigma_z \gamma_z(a)$$

$$V(\eta^0) = \max_a \Sigma_z \gamma_z(a) = \Sigma_z \gamma_z(a^0), \text{ say.} \tag{32}$$

Thus action a^0 is optimal, independently of observations; and all null-inquiries have the same value.[13] As their canonical form we can conveniently

---

[13] A terminological note: in some earlier writings (Marschak 1954; Marschak and Radner 1971) information value of an inquiry η was defined as the difference:

$$V(\eta) - V(1),$$

which, by (37), is never negative. Thus the value of null-information was chosen as the origin to measure information values. The present terminology is simpler.

choose the $(m \times 1)$ matrix with all elements $\eta_{z1} = 1$, $z = 1, \ldots, m$. That is, the same unique observation is obtained, with certainty, whatever the event. Then η^0 is the column vector of order m, with all elements equal to unity: a "sum vector", sometimes denoted by $\eta^0 = \mathbf{1}$. It will be shown in section 4.2 that no inquiry can have a value smaller than that of a null-inquiry. This justifies writing:

$$V(\eta^0)\,V(\mathbf{1}) = V^{\min}. \tag{33}$$

3.9. *Essential set of inquiry matrices*

Let H_m be the set of all Markov matrices with m rows and with all columns non-zero and not pairwise identical. Summarizing the conventions made in 3.7, the essential set of inquiries about m events is defined as the partition H_m/e into equivalence classes; where η and η' in H_m are equivalent, $\eta = [\eta_{zy}]e$ $\eta' = [\eta'_{zy}]$, if $\eta' = \eta P$ for some permutation matrix P or if every η_{zy}, η'_{zy} is independent of z.[14] Accordingly, when η and η' are both noiseless, then $\eta \, e \, \eta'$ means that the sets Y and Y' are permutations of each other.

3.10.

Perfect information will be said to be provided by a matrix η of order $m \times m$ such that the correspondence between Z and Y is 1-1. That is, one element in each row of η equals unity [and hence the other elements in the row equal zero and η is noiseless, as in (1)]; and, moreover, in each column one element equals unity and other elements equal zero. Thus η is a permutation matrix, $\eta = Q$, say. Its transpose Q^T is clearly a permutation matrix, too, $Q^T = P$, say; and it is well known that:

$$I = QP,$$

where I is the identity matrix. Then by (31), I and Q will be considered equivalent: without loss of generality, perfect information will be represented by the identity matrix I as its canonical form.

---

[14] On fig. 2, the unit square represents the set $H_{2 \times 2}$ of all inquiry matrices of order 2×2. The corresponding essential set $H_{2 \times 2}/e$ is, then, in $1-1$ correspondence with the set consisting of all points above the main diagonal and an arbitrary point on that diagonal.

3.11. *Useless inquiries*

Given π, β (and, thus, given γ) an inquiry η is called *useless* if an optimal action, the same for all observations, exists; that is, for all y, $a_y = a^*$, say. Clearly all null-inquiries are useless. But the converse is not, in general, true, as will be seen in sections 6.3 and 6.4. Furthermore we have the following:

Theorem: $V(\eta) = V^{\min}$ *if and only if η is useless.*

To prove sufficiency, let a^* be optimal for a useless inquiry η^*. That is, $a_y = a^*$ for all y:

$$V_y(\eta^*) = \Sigma_z \gamma_z(a^*) \eta_{zy}^* \geq \Sigma_z \gamma_z(a) \eta_{zy}^*, \quad \text{all } a, \quad \text{all } y;$$

summing over y we have, by (30) and, since $\Sigma_y \eta_{zy}^* = 1$:

$$V(\eta^*) = \Sigma_z \gamma_z(a^*) \geq \Sigma_z \gamma_z(a), \quad \text{all } a;$$

$$V(\eta^*) = \max_a \Sigma_z \gamma_z(a) = V^{\min}.$$

To prove necessity, suppose

$$V(\eta) = V^{\min};$$

that is,

$$V(\eta) = \max_a \Sigma_z \gamma_z(a)$$

$$= \Sigma_z \gamma_z(a^*),$$

say. Then a (not necessarily unique) optimal strategy is

$$a_y = a^*, \quad \text{all } y; \tag{34}$$

that is, η is useless.

3.12. *Convexity of the information value function $V_{\pi\beta}(\eta)$*

It follows by (23) and a well-known theorem (see e.g., Karlin 1959, Appendix B.4), that the information value:

$$V_{\pi\beta}(\eta) = \max_\alpha B_{\pi\beta}(\eta, \alpha)$$

is a convex function of η; it is represented by the upper envelope of a family of hyperplanes.[15] The same is true of V_y in (27). Figs. 3, 4, and 5 will give examples.

4. Comparative informativeness

The assumptions of statistical theory set out in the preceding section will be maintained in the present and the two subsequent sections. In particular, deciding is assumed unconstrained so that, for given sets Y, A, the feasible set of strategies consists of all functions from Y to A; and the cost of deciding is zero (or, more generally, constant).

4.0. *More informative than*

We say, following Blackwell[16], that η is *more informative than* η', and write $\eta > \eta'$, if and only if[17]:

$$V_{\pi\beta}(\eta) \geq V_{\pi\beta}(\eta') \quad \text{for all } \pi, \beta,$$

where π, β are defined on fixed sets Z and $A \times Z$, respectively. By fixing these sets rich enough we can apply the definition of "more informative than" to an arbitrarily large set of meta-deciders concerned with the choice among information matrices.

Clearly " $>$ " is a transitive and reflexive relation, and thus induces an ordering on the set of information matrices. It is a partial ordering on this set; for it is easy to construct cases when, depending on π, β, the information matrix η has a larger or a smaller value than η'. Clearly the relation " $>$ " induces also a partial ordering on the essential set H_m/e defined in section 3.9.

[15] See also DeGroot (1970), section 8.4. Chapters 6-7 of Savage (1954) are also relevant.

[16] Several papers by Blackwell and also some earlier work by Bohnenblust, Shapley and Sherman are summarized, as far as "informativeness" is concerned, in Chapter 12 of Blackwell and Girshick (1954). See also Marschak and Miyasawa (1968).

[17] The "more" (rather than "not less") and the sign " $>$ " (rather than " $\geq$ ") should not confuse. Blackwell's notation has the advantage of reserving the sign " $=$ " (usually equivalent to " $\geq$ and $\leq$ ") for the case of identity. The same would be achieved by symbols " $\gtrsim$ " and " $\sim$ " used in the economics of preference.

In particular, when $\eta\, e\, \eta'$ then obviously both $\eta > \eta'$ and $\eta' < \eta$. But the converse is not true: see footnote 20.

4.1. *Garbling*

Consider an information matrix $\eta = [\eta_{zy}]$ and suppose that, whenever the observation $y(= 1, \ldots, n)$ is made, the decision-maker does not learn it. Instead, a random device is used such that, given the observation y, he will receive, with probability $g_{yy'}$, a signal $y' = 1, \ldots, n'$. Clearly $g_{yy'} \geq 0$, $\sum_{y'} g_{yy'} = 1$. The random device is thus characterized by a Markov matrix $G = [g_{yy'}]$, of order $n \times n'$. It follows that, given the event $z = 1, \ldots, m$, the decision-maker receives signal y' with probability:

$$\Sigma_y \eta_{zy} g_{yy'} = \eta'_{zy'}, \text{ say,} \tag{35}$$

where $\eta'_{zy'} \geq 0$, $\sum_{y'} \eta'_{zy'} = 1$. In effect, he has used an information matrix $\eta' = [\eta'_{zy'}]$ of order $m \times n'$ such that:

$$\eta' = \eta G. \tag{36}$$

It seems to agree with common usage to say that η' is obtained from η by *garbling*.[18] And it is intuitively clear that a garbled information matrix cannot exceed in value the original one: for the decision-maker receiving a "garbled" signal will, at best, choose an action appropriate to that signal, not to the original observation. Formally, we have:

Theorem: If η, η', G are Markov matrices with $\eta' = \eta G$, then: $\eta' > \eta$.

---

[18] In Marschak and Miyasawa (1968), "garbling" was defined by a stronger condition, viz., the statistical dependence of y' on y only; that is, by the requirement that, for all z, y, y':

$$p(y'|y, z) = p(y'|y),$$

where $p(s|t)$ denotes the conditional probability of s given t. Since the left side is identical with $p(y, y'|z)/p(y|z)$, the requirement is equivalent to:

$$p(y, y'|z) = p(y'|y) \cdot p(y|z);$$

and this implies, by summing over y, a weaker condition:

$$\eta' = \eta \Gamma,$$

where $\Gamma = [\gamma_{yy'}]$, $\gamma_{yy'} = p(y'|y)$. The present "garbling" condition (36) is still weaker as it does not involue z.

Proof: By (29), (30), and (35):

$$V(\eta') = \Sigma_{y'z}\gamma_z(a_{y'})\eta_{zy'} = \Sigma_{y'z}\gamma_z(a_{y'})\Sigma_y\eta_{zy}g_{yy'}$$

$$= \Sigma_{y'}g_{yy'}\Sigma_{yz}\gamma_z(a_{y'})\eta_{zy}$$

$$= 1\,\Sigma_{yz}\gamma_z(a_{y'})\eta_{zy} \leqslant \Sigma_{yz}\gamma_z(a_y)\eta_{zy} = V(\eta),$$

by (29), (30).

4.2. *Maximal and minimal information matrices*

Theorem:

$$I_m > \eta$$

$$\eta > \mathbf{1}_m, \tag{37}$$

where η has m rows and I_m and $\mathbf{1}_m$ (identity matrix and sum vector of order m) correspond to perfect and to null-information (sections 3.10, 3.8).

Proof: Verify that:

$$\eta = I_m\eta, \ \mathbf{1}_m = \eta\mathbf{1}_n,$$

for any η of order $m \times n$; then, noting that η and $\mathbf{1}_n$ are Markov matrices, apply the theorem of section 4.1 on "garbling".

Thus the canonical forms of the perfect information and the null-information matrices constitute, respectively, the maximal and minimal elements of the lattice in which the essential set of information matrices is partially ordered by the relation "more informative than".

4.3. *Comparative coarseness*

Suppose the garbling matrix G in (36) is noiseless, i.e., analogous to (1):

$$g_{yy'} = \begin{Bmatrix} 1 \\ 0 \end{Bmatrix} \quad \text{if} \quad y' \begin{Bmatrix} = \\ \neq \end{Bmatrix} g(y), \tag{38}$$

for all y, y'. That is, G is reduced to a many-to-one mapping, g, from $Y = (1, \ldots, n)$ to $Y' = (1, \ldots, n')$ and clearly $n' \leq n$. Then it seems to agree with common usage to say that Y' is *coarser* than Y (or, equivalently,

Y is *finer* than Y'). For example, two elements y_1 and y_2 may be real numbers (or vectors), identical except for the last digit (or the last component), and this digit (or component) is omitted in the element $y_1' = g(y_1) = g(y_2)$ of Y'. "Some details are suppressed"; or more generally (to include the limiting case $G = I_n$, $n' = n$), "no details are added". Applying (38) to (35):

$$\eta'_{zy'} = \sum_{y \in S_{y'}} \eta_{zy}, \quad \text{where} \quad S_{y'} = \{y \mid g(y) = y'\}:$$

an intuitively obvious result.[19] It follows from the theorem of section 4.1 that:

$$\text{if } \eta \text{ is coarser than } \eta' \text{ then } \eta > \eta'. \tag{39}$$

This confirms the intuitive assertion that adding detail (at no cost!) cannot do damage, since the detail can be ignored.

4.4. Blackwell's theorem

We give this name to the proposition that:

$$\eta > \eta' \text{ if and only if } \eta' = \eta G \text{ for some Markov matrix } G.$$

The sufficiency part was proved in section 4.1. For proof of necessity, see Blackwell (1954) or Marschak and Miyasawa (1968).

4.5. The case of noiseless information

Theorem: If η and η' are noiseless then $\eta > \eta'$ if and only if η' is coarser than η.

Proof: Sufficiency follows from (39). Necessity follows from Blackwell's theorem, noting that if $\eta' = \eta G$ and η, η' are noiseless then by (35) every entry in G is either 1 or 0, i.e., G is noiseless. (For a possibly more instructive, direct proof see Marschak and Radner 1971.)

It follows that *two noiseless inquiries η and η' have equal information value for any given π, β if, and only if, they are identical up to a permutation of columns.* The sufficiency part of this proposition is obvious. The necessity

---

[19] Example:

$$\eta = \begin{pmatrix} 0.6 & 0.3 & 0.1 \\ 0.2 & 0.1 & 0.7 \end{pmatrix}; \; G = \begin{pmatrix} 1 & 0 \\ 1 & 0 \\ 0 & 1 \end{pmatrix}; \; \eta' = \begin{pmatrix} 0.9 & 0.1 \\ 0.3 & 0.7 \end{pmatrix}.$$

part follows from the previous theorem: for if $\eta > \eta'$ and $\eta' > \eta$, and hence each of the two inquiries is coarser than the other, then to each y in Y corresponds a unique y' in Y', and conversely. Hence the correspondence between Y and Y' is 1-1.

Thus the partial ordering induced by the relation "more informative than" is a strong one over the noiseless subset of the essential set H_m/e of inquiries defined in section 3.9.[20]

5. Informativeness of systems over time

5.0. *Environment, action, and observation as time-sequences*

One or both of the arguments a, z of the benefit function β can be interpreted as time-sequences, as in (3), assuming additive costs, as in section 1.6. With z a time-sequence, it will be convenient (changing our terminology somewhat) to call z the *environment* and to reserve the term *successive events* for the components of the sequence $z = \{z_t\}$, $t = t_1, \ldots, t_T$; to give unit-length to each of the intervals (t_i, t_{i+1}), $i = 1, \ldots, T-1$; and sometimes to make $t_1 = 1$, so that $t = 1, \ldots, T$. Each component a_t of a will be called *successive action*. If the benefit can be represented as a sum of discounted *successive benefits*:

$$\beta(a, z) = \sum_{t=1}^{T} d^t \beta^*(a_t, z_t), \text{ say,} \tag{40}$$

[as would be implied by the assumption (4) combined with (8)], then it is important to agree that a_t and z_t need not "physically" occur simultaneously: e.g., a_t may be "sell stock short to-day" and z_t may be "stock price a month from to-day".

A successive action a_t is taken, using the decision rule α_t, in response to $\bar{y}_t$ (note the bar!) where $\bar{y}_t$ is the *remembered past history of successive observations*:

$$\bar{y}_t = (y_{t-\mu}, \ldots, y_{t-1}, y_t); \tag{41}$$

---

[20] It can be also shown that this ordering is strong over the subset of H_m/e that consists of square non-singular matrices. For the general case, however, David Rosenblatt (in a personal communication for which I am greatly indebted) has constructed η, η' (each square and singular) such that

$\eta > \eta', \eta' > \eta$; and not: $\eta \, e \, \eta'$.

the time-length μ measures the *length of memory*. Again, the subscript t in $\bar{y}_t$ means only that the action taken at time t is based on $\bar{y}_t$; it does not necessarily mean that y_t, the last component of $\bar{y}_t$, was "physically" observed at time t.

In this interpretation, π becomes a distribution on the set Z of sequences z. The information matrix η transforms (stochastically, in general) the environment z into a sequence of remembered histories:

$$y = (\bar{y}_{t-\mu}, ..., \bar{y}_T) \in Y ; \tag{42}$$

that is, η_{zy} is the probability of the sequence y of remembered histories, given a particular environment (i.e., a particular sequence of successive events), $z = (z_1, ..., z_T)$. A *strategy* α is a sequence of functions $\alpha_1, ..., \alpha_T$, where $a_t = \alpha_t(\bar{y}_t)$, thus α is a function from Y to the set A of action-sequences. With these generalizing interpretations, the results of section 4 apply.

5.1. *Effect of memory length on informativeness*

Let $\mu' < \mu$, and let inquiry η' yield remembered history:

$$\bar{y}'_t = (y_{t-\mu'}, ..., y_t) \tag{43}$$

whenever inquiry η yields remembered history:

$$\bar{y}_t = (y_{t-\mu}, ..., y_{t-\mu'}, ..., y_t) . \tag{44}$$

Clearly η' is coarser than η; hence by (39) η is more informative than η'.

5.2. *Prompt vs. delayed perfect information*

Prompt perfect information and *delayed perfect information* are defined, respectively, by:

$$y_t = z_t, \quad t = 1, ..., T ; \qquad y_t \in Y ;$$

$$y'_t = z_{t-\theta}, \ t = \theta+1, ..., T ; \quad y'_t \in Y',$$

where θ is the *delay*, an integer with $0 < \theta < T$. Now, there is a 1-1 correspondence between the set Z of environments z (sequences of successive events) on the one hand, and, on the other, the set $\bar{Z}$ (say) of sequences $\bar{z} = (\bar{z}_1, ..., \bar{z}_T)$ of past histories, $\bar{z}_t = (z_1, ..., z_t)$, of successive events:

for $\bar{z}_{t+1} = (\bar{z}_t, z_{t+1})$. Replace Z by $\bar{Z}$ and redefine β and π accordingly. Then *prompt perfect inquiry*, a mapping η from $\bar{Z}$ to Y, is represented by the identity matrix I; but *delayed perfect inquiry*, a mapping η' from $\bar{Z}$ to Y', is not. Hence $\eta > \eta'$, by (37). A delay cannot improve perfect information. However, if prompt information is not perfect, its value can be exceeded by that of delayed (perfect or imperfect) information. Thus, detailed survey data, even when 2 years old, may be more valuable (because less "coarse": see section 4.3) than those of a less detailed survey made at the time the action is taken.

5.3. *Perfect information with long vs. short delay when the environment is Markovian*

Given the distribution π on the set of environments (sequences of successive events) we can derive the conditional probability of the event z_t given the preceding past history[21]:

$$\bar{p}_t \equiv p(z_t \mid \bar{z}_{t-1}),$$

and also the conditional probability of z_t given z_{t-1}:

$$p_t \equiv p(z_t \mid z_{t-1}).$$

The environment z is said to be Markovian if:

$$\bar{p}_t = p_t. \tag{45}$$

Theorem: If z is Markovian then a perfect inquiry with shorter delay is more informative than a perfect inquiry with longer delay.

Outline of proof: We omit the proof of the following

Lemma: If z is Markovian and $t_1 < t_2 < t_3$ then $p(z_{t_3} \mid z_{t_2}, z_{t_1}) = p(z_{t_3} \mid z_{t_2})$.

Now let two perfect inquiries, η_θ and $\eta_{\theta'}$, be characterized, respectively, by:

$$y_t = z_{t-\theta}, \quad y'_t = z_{t-\theta'}, \tag{46}$$

where $\theta < \theta'$. If z is Markovian then, by the Lemma:

$$p(z_t \mid y_t, y'_t) = p(z_t \mid y_t), \tag{47}$$

---

[21] We use the same functional symbol p for various conditional and joint probabilities, $p(\cdot \mid \cdot)$, $p(\cdot, \cdot)$; no ambiguity arises if one pays attention to the arguments within the parentheses. For what follows in the text see also footnote 18.

or, temporarily omitting the subscript t for brevity:

$$p(z|y, y') = p(z|y),$$

that is:

$$p(z, y, y')/p(y, y') = p(z, y)/p(y);$$

hence:

$$p(z, y, y') \cdot p(y) = p(y, y') \cdot p(z, y).$$

The left side equals $p(y, y'|z) \cdot p(z) \cdot p(y)$; and the right side equals $p(y'|y) \cdot p(y) \cdot p(y|z) \cdot p(z)$. Hence

$$p(y, y'|z) = p(y|z) \cdot p(y'|y), \text{ as in footnote 18.}$$

Summing over y and restoring the subscript t:

$$p(y'_t | z_t) = \sum_{y_t} p(y_t | z_t) \cdot p(y'_t | y_t).$$

Thus inquiry $\eta_{\theta'}$ can be obtained from η_θ by garbling, as in (35). Hence, by the theorem of section 4.1, η_θ is more informative than $\eta_{\theta'}$.

As in the case $\theta = 0$ discussed in section 5.2 for all (not necessarily Markovian) environments, the condition $\theta' > \theta$ does not imply greater informativeness of η_θ compared with $\eta_{\theta'}$, if $\eta_{\theta'}$, η_θ, are not perfect inquiries in the sense of (46); for then, even if z is Markovian, (47) would not follow. So that, again, a shorter delay can be profitably traded off against greater precision.

Furthermore, shorter delay is not necessarily advantageous if the environment is not Markovian but is, e.g., periodic. Restaurant menus do not vary much as between Sundays, and also, in Catholic countries, as between Fridays. And both differ from each other and from the menus of other days of the week. In a Catholic country, before deciding on a Thursday where to eat next Sunday, it is best to know next Sunday's menu ($\theta = 0$, as in section 5.2); but the next best is to learn the menu, not of next Friday ($\theta = 2$ days) but of the previous Sunday ($\theta = 7$ days)!

5.4. *Obsolescence and impatience*

The discount constant d, as used in sections 1.5 and 1.6, reflects a feature of the utility function, sometimes called *impatience*. It is one reason why delays diminish the value of an inquiry (and, more generally, of information systems; see end of section 2.2). We see now another reason, which, when it is applicable, may be more powerful: the obsolescence of the inputs to the decision-making.[22]

5.5. *Sequential inquiries and adaptive programming*

The concept a_t of a successive action (decision) can be usefully extended to include decisions about the observations to be taken at the next point of time. Thus:

$$a_t = (a_t', \eta_{t+1}), \tag{48}$$

where a_t' may be called, *successive action* in the ordinary sense (it enters the benefit function) and η_{t+1} is *inquiry at time* $t+1$. Both are chosen simultaneously, on the basis of remembered history, $\bar{y}_t$. Sequential sampling in statistics is a special case, in which a_t' includes among its values the null-action: "do nothing that would directly influence the benefit", and η_{t+1} includes among its values the null-inquiry **1**; a_t is null (i.e., ordinary action is postponed) and η_{t+1} is non-null (i.e. further observations are taken), till some point τ such that $\eta_{\tau+1}$ is null (observations cease) and a_τ' is non-null ("terminal action"). The more general case is "earn while you learn".

Inquiring and deciding over time, including the general, sequential case just discussed is sometimes called *adaptive programming*. This is sometimes described as a sequence of step-wise revisions of the probability distribution of the environment, starting with the prior distribution π and replacing it with posterior distributions, given past histories, $p(z|\bar{y}_t)$, $t = 1, \ldots$. This description can lead to misapplications, if the researcher estimates each of these successive distributions by some conventional parameters (e.g., means, variances). The parameter actually needed is the optimal action a_t^* (say) itself! Also, a misleading distinction is sometimes made between "stochastic programming" in which the distribution of z is known, and "adaptive programming" in which it is gradually learned. But actually, once the knowledge of the prior distribution π is admitted the mathematical processes needed to compute the optimal sequence of actions [including inquiries as in (48)] are equivalent.[23]

---

[22] Further analysis, using some special classes of environment distributions π and benefit functions β is given in Chapter 7 of Marschak and Radner (1971).

[23] See Bellman (1961), Marschak (1963), Miyasawa (1968).

6. Optimal inquiries[24]

6.0. *Binary inquiries as an example*

The "likelihood matrix" $\eta = [\eta_{zy}]$ is called *binary* if it is of order 2×2, so that $Z = (1, 2)$, $Y = (1, 2)$ and we can denote the likelihoods by:

$$\eta_{11} = 1 - \eta_{12} = p_1$$

$$\eta_{22} = 1 - \eta_{21} = p_2. \tag{49}$$

(This notation makes the subscripts of the p_i conveniently symmetrical.) To avoid triviality, we assume the probabilities π_z of the two events to be both positive:

$$0 < \pi_2 = 1 - \pi_1 < 1. \tag{50}$$

Binary inquiries are widely used in statistics. In testing against a null-hypothesis, the "error probabilities of first and second kind" are related to η_{11}, η_{22} or their complements. Binary "channel matrices" are much used in the theory of communication. We shall look to both fields for examples when, in sections 6.9-6.10, we search for the *optimal inquiry*, i.e., one that maximizes the difference between expected benefit and expected cost, using sampling costs as well as the cost of a transmission channel.

One rather obvious result of section 6.3 will be that, by appropriately permuting the columns of the binary inquiry matrix η we can make its diagonal elements $\eta_{11}(= p_1)$ and $\eta_{22}(= p_2)$ play the role of economic "goods" in the following sense: for any user of information (i.e., for any π, β) its value $V_{\pi\beta}(\eta)$ is monotonically non-decreasing in p_1, p_2. On the other hand, it was seen in section 3.12 that quite generally $V_{\pi\beta}(\eta)$ is a convex function of η. In the case of η binary, writing $V_{\pi\beta}(\eta) = V(p_1, p_2) = V$ for brevity, it follows that V can be represented, over the region of the 2-space where p_1, p_2 qualify as "goods", either by a linear surface (a plane rising with p_1, p_2 except in the trivial case of V constant), or by a non-linear, though possibly piece-wise linear convex surface. And it will be shown that, while a linear V-surface over that region obtains in trivial cases, it will be, in general, a *non-linear convex*, and possibly a *strictly convex* surface.

---

[24] As stipulated in section 2.2 we continue to speak, for brevity, of "inquiries" instead of "information matrices" even when we may be, in fact, concerned with the stochastic transformation η characterizing the whole information processing chain except its last link.

The convexity of the V-surface over the region of the "goods" p_1, p_2 makes it different from the surface representing the utility function of a consumer who maximizes utility subject to a convex constraint (the constraint being linear when the goods have constant prices). To explain why the consumer's choice is an "interior solution", i.e., does not allocate extreme amounts to either good, the utility function is assumed to be *quasi-concave*.[25] Therefore the consumer's indifference sets (loci of equal utility) are *convex* "indifference lines". On the contrary, if a set such as

$$\{\eta : V(\eta) = \text{const.}\},$$

consisting of inquiries with equal information value, is a line, it turns out to be a (possibly *strictly*) *concave line*. In addition, one set (viz., the "useless" set):

$$\{\eta : V(\eta) = V^{\min}\}$$

may turn out to be a part of the (p_1, p_2)-plane, rather than a line.

Accordingly, no "interior solution" could, in general, obtain if the "prices" of the two likelihoods, to be paid by the user of information, were constant. In other words the set of binary inquiries all of whom have the same expected cost to the user:

$$\{\eta : K(\eta) = \text{const.}\}$$

must *not* be a straight line. A few examples will touch on the properties of the cost function $K(\cdot)$ that are required for the existence of an interior solution: $K(\cdot)$ must be, in a sense, "sufficiently convex" relative to $V(\cdot)$.

The analysis carried out in this section will exploit the simple properties of a binary inquiry or its even simpler, symmetric sub-case $(p_1 = p_2)$. Perhaps the insight gained can be later used to handle non-binary inquiries; some beginnings will be attempted in section 6.6.

6.1. *Informativeness of binary inquiries*

Given the inquiry matrix:

$$\eta = [\eta_{zy}] = \begin{pmatrix} p_1 & 1-p_1 \\ 1-p_2 & p_2 \end{pmatrix}, \quad 0 \le p_i \le 1, \quad i = 1, 2, \tag{51}$$

---

[25] See Arrow and Enthoven (1961).

there is no loss of generality in permuting the columns so as to make the determinant $|\eta|$ non-negative:

$$|\eta| = p_1 + p_2 - 1 \geq 0. \tag{52}$$

The reader will easily see that $|\eta| = 0$ is the case of null-information: see section 3.8. Define the two *likelihood ratios*:

$$\lambda_1 = p_1/(1-p_2); \quad \lambda_2 = p_2/(1-p_1). \tag{53}$$

Then under the convention (52):

$$\lambda_1 \geq 1, \quad \lambda_2 \geq 1. \tag{54}$$

Denote by p_i', $\lambda_i'(i = 1, 2)$, respectively, the two likelihoods and two likelihood ratios characterizing another inquiry, η'. Write for brevity:

$\lambda > \lambda'$ when $\lambda_1 \geq \lambda_1'$ and $\lambda_2 \geq \lambda_2'$,

$p > p'$ when $p_1 \geq p_1'$ and $p_2 \geq p_2'$.

The relation denoted by " $>$ " induces a partial ordering on the set of pairs $\lambda = (\lambda_1, \lambda_2)$ and on the set of pairs $p = (p_1, p_2)$ as it does on the set of inquiries η. When neither $\eta > \eta'$ nor $\eta' > \eta$ we write $\eta \| \eta'$; and a similar meaning attaches to $\lambda \| \lambda'$ and $p \| p'$ (as when, e.g., $p_1 > p_1'$ and $p_2' > p_2$).

Theorem: (1) *If $\lambda > \lambda'$ then $\eta > \eta'$ and conversely.*

(2) *If $p > p'$ then $\eta > \eta'$ but the converse is not true.*

Proof of (1): By definition of λ_1, η, η':

$$\lambda_1 - \lambda_1' \equiv (\eta_{11}\eta_{21}' - \eta_{11}'\eta_{21})/\eta_{21}\eta_{21}' \geq 0 \tag{55}$$

if the numerator ≥ 0. Now suppose $\eta > \eta'$. Then by Blackwell's theorem (section 4.4 above):

$$\eta_{ij}' = \eta_{i1}g_{1j} + \eta_{i2}g_{2j} \quad (i = 1, 2; \, j = 1, 2),$$

where g_{kj} is an element of a 2×2 Markov matrix. The numerator in (55) becomes, in the notation of (51):

$$g_{21}(p_1 + p_2 - 1) \geq 0 ;$$

hence, by (52), $\lambda_1 \geq \lambda_1'$; and, by symmetry of subscripts, $\lambda_2 \geq \lambda_2'$. This proves the "converse" part of (1):

if $\eta > \eta'$ then $\lambda > \lambda'$.

Hence, interchanging η and η':

if $\eta' > \eta$ then $\lambda' > \lambda$.

The same symmetry implies that if $\eta \| \eta'$ then neither $\lambda > \lambda'$ nor $\lambda < \lambda'$, and therefore:

if $\eta \| \eta$ then $\lambda \| \lambda'$.

Since these three possibilities are exhaustive, it follows that:

$$\text{if } \lambda > \lambda' \text{ then } \eta > \eta', \tag{56}$$

completing the proof of part (1) of the theorem. On fig. 2, the region:

$$R_\eta^+ = \{\eta' : \eta' > \eta\} = \{\eta' : \lambda' > \lambda\}$$

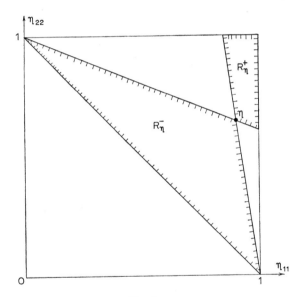

Fig. 2.

is bounded from below by two straight lines:

$$\{\eta' : \lambda_1' = \lambda_1\} \text{ and } \{\eta' : \lambda_2' = \lambda_2\},$$

which go through the point $\eta = (\eta_{11}, \eta_{22})$ and $(0, 1)$ or $(1, 0)$, respectively. [The content of section 4.2 is readily illustrated, with perfect information represented by the point $(1, 1)$, and null-information by any point on the main diagonal.]

As to part (2) of the theorem, it follows from (55), (51), and (56) that $p > p'$ implies $\lambda > \lambda'$ and hence also $\eta > \eta'$. But the converse is not true; for let:

$$p_1 - p_1' > p_1 p_2' - p_2 p_1' > p_2' - p_2 > 0;$$

then $\lambda > \lambda'$ but $p \| p'$. On fig. 2, the sets:

$$\{\eta' : p' > p\} \quad \text{and} \quad \{\eta' : p > p'\}$$

would be represented, respectively, by the upper-right and lower-left rectangles (not shown on the figure) bounded by lines through η, parallel to the axes. Clearly, these rectangles are *proper* sub-regions of R_η^+ and R_η^-, respectively (except trivially at the vertices of the unit square). This illustrates (2): it is possible to increase informativeness by increasing the error probability of one kind, provided the error probability of the other kind is sufficiently decreased. Here the error probabilities are interpreted as in (85) below.

6.2. Symmetric binary information matrices

This is a special case of (51), with:

$$p_1 = p_2 = p, \text{ say.}$$

Thus p will denote here a scalar, not a pair. The convention (52) becomes:

$$p \geq \tfrac{1}{2},$$

and it follows from the theorem of the preceding section that informativeness increases as p increases; an intuitively obvious result. On fig. 2, the symmetric matrices would be represented by the line (not drawn) connecting $(\tfrac{1}{2}, \tfrac{1}{2})$ and $(1, 1)$.

6.3. Value of binary inquiry: the case of two actions

As stated in section 1.7, no two rows and no two columns of the benefit matrix $\beta = [\beta_{az}]$ are identical; and any action represented by a dominated row is eliminated. Suppose that after such elimination there remain two rows, i.e. $A = (1, 2)$. Then there is no loss of generality in writing:

$$\beta = [\beta_{az}] = \begin{pmatrix} b_1 & b_2 - r_2 \\ b_1 - r_1 & b_2 \end{pmatrix}, \quad r_z > 0, \quad z = 1, 2; \tag{57}$$

the r_z are often called *regrets* (about not having used the action $a = z$, optimal under certainty). This benefit matrix is, in effect, used in statistics when the two actions are: "reject the hypothesis" and "accept it". The r_z are then penalties for committing an error of first or second kind.

The value of information is, by (30):

$$V(\eta) = V_1(\eta) + V_2(\eta); \tag{58}$$

and by (29), writing $\pi_z \beta_{az} = \gamma_z(a) = \gamma_{az}$ *(weighted benefits)*:

$$V_1(\eta) = \max(\gamma_{11}\eta_{11} + \gamma_{12}\eta_{21}, \gamma_{21}\eta_{11} + \gamma_{22}\eta_{21})$$

$$V_2(\eta) = \max(\gamma_{11}\eta_{12} + \gamma_{12}\eta_{22}, \gamma_{21}\eta_{12} + \gamma_{22}\eta_{22}). \tag{59}$$

Write $s_z \equiv \pi_z r_z$ *(weighted regrets)*. Then, by (57), (50):

$$[\gamma_{az}] = \begin{pmatrix} \pi_1 b_1 & \pi_2 b_2 - s_2 \\ \pi_1 b_1 - s_1 & \pi_2 b_2 \end{pmatrix}, \quad s_z > 0, \quad z = 1, 2. \tag{60}$$

Since it is always true that:

$$\max(g_1, h_1) + \max(g_2, h_2) =$$

$$\max(g_1 + g_2, h_1 + h_2, g_1 + h_2, h_1 + g_2);$$

we obtain from (58)-(60):

$$V(\eta) = \pi_1 b_1 + \pi_2 b_2 - \min(s_1, s_1 \eta_{12} + s_2 \eta_{21}, s_1 \eta_{11} + s_2 \eta_{22}, s_2). \tag{61}$$

When information is perfect, $\eta_{12} = \eta_{21} = 0$; and, since both $s_z > 0$;

$$V^{\max} = \pi_1 b_1 + \pi_2 b_2.^{26} \tag{62}$$

Since the labelling of events z is arbitrary, let, without loss of generality and using (60):

$$s_2 \geq s_1 > 0, \tag{63}$$

Then with the observations y labelled to yield (52), $\eta_{11} + \eta_{22} \geq 1$:

$$s_1 \eta_{11} + s_2 \eta_{22} \geq s_1.$$

---

[26] If we considered inquiry costs fixed, the comparison between expected utilities (net benefits) of inquiries would not be affected by putting $b_1 = b_2 = V^{\max} = 0$. This is usually done in statistics.

The loss due to the imperfection of η becomes then, by (61) and (62):

$$L(\eta) = V^{\max} - V(\eta) = \min (s_1, s_1\eta_{12} + s_2\eta_{21}). \tag{64}$$

By (37), maximum loss, $L^{\max}$ obtains at null-information, i.e., when the rows of η are identical. Then:

$$\eta_{12} + \eta_{21} = 1, \tag{65}$$

and hence $s_1\eta_{12} + s_2\eta_{21}$ is a weighted average of s_1, s_2 so that by (63):

$$s_1\eta_{12} + s_2\eta_{21} \geq s_1. \tag{66}$$

Therefore, by (64):

$$L^{\max} = s_1.$$

Clearly (65), while sufficient, is not necessary for (66). All inquiries satisfying (66) have the same information value:

$$V^{\min} = V^{\max} - L^{\max}$$

$$= \pi_1 b_1 + \pi_2 b_2 - s_1,$$

equal to the value of null-information. They constitute the *useless indifference set*, H^0:

$$H^0 = \{\eta : s_1\eta_{12} + s_2\eta_{21} \geq s_1\};$$

hence:

$$H^0 = \{\eta : s_1\eta_{11} + s_2\eta_{22} \leq s_2\}. \tag{67}$$

If η is not in H^0 then by (64):

$$L(\eta) = s_1\eta_{12} + s_2\eta_{21} = s_1 + s_2 - (s_1\eta_{11} + s_2\eta_{22}).$$

In general, then [but with the z and y labelled as stated above and using the notations of (51) and (60)]:

$$V(p_1, p_2) = \pi_1 b_1 + \pi_2 b_2 - \left\{\begin{matrix} s_1 \\ s_1(1-p_1) + s_2(1-p_2) \end{matrix}\right\}$$

$$\text{as } p_1/(1-p_2) \left\{\begin{matrix} \geq \\ \leq \end{matrix}\right\} s_2/s_1. \tag{68}$$

Fig. 3 is drawn in the (p_1, p_2)-plane assuming $s_1 = 4$, $s_2 = 5$. The useless set H_0 consists of the points in and on the triangle bounded by the main diagonal, the p_2-axis and the straight line

$$s_1 p_1 + s_2 p_2 = s_2. \tag{69}$$

All other indifference sets are straight lines parallel to (69). If the convention (52) (but not (63)) were dropped, the indifference sets below the main diagonal would replicate those of fig. 3 in an obvious way, preserving the slope $-s_1/s_2$.

Note that all users with the same ratio s_1/s_2 of weighted regrets have the same system of indifference sets of binary inquiries (in the case of two actions).

If η is symmetrical (as in section 6.2), $\eta_{11} = \eta_{22} = p = 1 - q \geq \frac{1}{2}$, (68) becomes:

$$V(\eta) = \pi_1 b_1 + \pi_2 b_2 - \begin{Bmatrix} s_1 \\ (s_1 + s_2)q \end{Bmatrix} \text{ as } p/q \begin{Bmatrix} \leq \\ \geq \end{Bmatrix} s_2/s_1.$$

Thus the information value of a symmetric binary information (in the case of two actions), if plotted against the probability $p \geq \frac{1}{2}$ consists of a "useless" horizontal segment till p reaches a certain bound; and is a positively sloped straight line for larger p. On fig. 3s the information value is plotted, assuming $b_1 = b_2 = 0$ and, as before, $s_1 = 4$, $s_2 = 5$.

6.4. *Binary inquiries with more than two actions*[27]

If the number of non-dominated, benefit-relevant actions exceeds two, the convex function $V_{\pi\beta}(\eta)$, where η is a binary inquiry, may, but need not, retain the shape just derived for the case of two actions. In particular, $V_{\pi\beta}$ may become a strictly convex function of η.

We shall write:

$$\beta(a, z) = \beta_z(a); \quad \pi_z \beta_z(a) = \gamma_z(a); \quad z = 1, 2; \ a \in A.$$

Let a and a' be two distinct elements of A. Then:

$$\beta_1(a) > \beta_1(a') \text{ implies } \beta_2(a) < \beta_2(a') \tag{70}$$

---

[27] These are *multiple decisions*, treated by Ferguson (1967, Chapter 6) with somewhat different purposes.

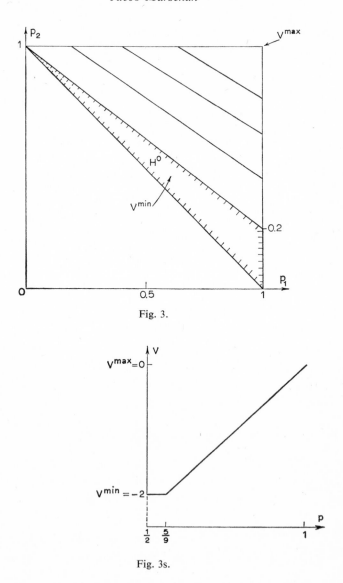

Fig. 3.

Fig. 3s.

lest a' be dominated by a. The case $\beta_1(a) = \beta_1(a')$, $\beta_2(a) = \beta_2(a')$ is also eliminated since A was defined as benefit-relevant (section 1.7). We can therefore order all actions completely and strongly according to $\beta_1(a)$. Moreover, we shall consider A to be closed. If A is finite we can index its N elements a^i so that:

$$\beta_1(a^{i+1}) > \beta_1(a^i); \quad \beta_2(a^{i+1}) < \beta_2(a^i), \quad i = 1, ..., N-1. \tag{71}$$

When A is infinite we shall represent it by the closed interval $A = (0, 1]$, with $\beta_1(a)$ strictly increasing and $\beta_2(a)$ strictly decreasing in a. If, in particular, these two functions are differentiable, it follows that:

$$\beta_1'(a) > 0, \quad \beta_2'(a) < 0, \tag{72}$$

and we say that the *marginal benefits* are, respectively, positive or negative, given z.

We shall consider the case of increasing or constant marginal benefits as well as the economically more plausible case of decreasing marginal benefits. If $\beta_z(a)$ is smooth (twice differentiable) the two cases are, respectively:

$$(\text{I}) \ \beta_z''(a) \geq 0; \quad (\text{II}) \ \beta_z''(a) < 0; \tag{73}$$
$$z = 1, 2.$$

More broadly, the two cases can be interpreted for any continuous function $\beta_z(a)$ by requiring it to be convex or strictly concave, respectively. Stretching the definitions still further, we may let A be finite, arrange and label its elements as in (71) and be concerned with the signs of second differences instead of second derivatives. That is, writing:

$$\Delta_{zi}^2 = [\beta_z(a^{i+1}) - \beta_z(a^i)] - [\beta_z(a_i^i) - \beta_z(a^{i-1})],$$

the two cases in (73) are replaced, respectively, by:

$$(\text{I}) \ \Delta_{zi}^2 \geq 0; \quad (\text{II}) \ \Delta_{zi}^2 < 0; \tag{74}$$
$$z = 1, 2$$
$$i = 2, ..., N-1.$$

(Moreover, it can be shown that we can put $\beta_1(a^1) = 0 = \beta_2(a^N)$ without loss of generality.) An example is that of section 3.3, with cancer absent or present and with three treatments available: see pp. 76-77 below.

Here is, on the other hand, an example of a smooth benefit function, which we shall use later. A farmer wishes to maximize the amount harvested, and he must decide on how to allocate his total acreage $(= 1)$ between two crops, the "wet" crop being favored by wet weather (denoted by $z = 1$), and the "dry" crop by dry weather $(z = 2)$. The action a is the acreage allotted to the *wet* crop. Denote the harvest from x acres of the wet crop when the weather is or is not favorable to it by, respectively, $f_w(x)$ and $g_w(x)$, $0 \le x < 1$. Correspondingly $f_d(x)$ and $g_d(x)$ are the dry crop harvests. Thus:

$$f_w(x) > g_w(x), \quad f_d(x) > g_d(x),$$

and these four functions have positive first derivatives. The combined harvest of the two crops is:

$$\beta_1(a) = f_w(a) + g_d(1-a) \text{ in wet weather}$$

$$\beta_2(a) = g_w(a) + f_d(1-a) \text{ in dry weather.} \tag{75}$$

If no action is dominated, we have by (72):

$$\beta'_1(a) = f'_w(a) - g'_d(1-a) > 0,$$

$$\beta'_2(a) = g'_w(a) - f'_d(1-a) < 0. \tag{75'}$$

Now, if the farming of each crop obeys the "law of decreasing marginal returns to land" the second derivatives of all the four functions f_w, g_w, f_d, g_d are negative and therefore:

$$\beta''_1(a) = f''_w(a) + g''_d(1-a) < 0,$$

$$\beta''_2(a) = g''_w(a) + f''_d(1-a) < 0. \tag{75''}$$

(The inequality signs are reversed if the marginal returns to land are increasing.)

To express the value of inquiry, V, in the general case, denote by $B_y(a)$ the expected benefit of an observation y when action a is taken:

$$B_y(a) = \gamma_1(a)\eta_{1y} + \gamma_2(a)\eta_{2y}, \quad y = 1, 2. \tag{76}$$

By (29) the *value of observation y* is:

$$V_y(\eta) = \gamma_1(a_y)\eta_{1y} + \gamma_2(a_y)\eta_{2y} \ge \gamma_1(a)\eta_{1y} + \gamma_2(a)\eta_{2y}, \quad a \in A; \tag{77}$$

and the *value of inquiry* is:

$$V(\eta) = V_1(\eta) + V_2(\eta).$$

If the functions $\beta_z(a)$ are both *convex*, then so are the functions $\gamma_z(a)$, and consequently their increasing linear combination $B_y(a)$ is convex. Hence $B_y(a)$ will be maximized by one of the extreme values of a; that is, by (71):

$$a_y = a^1 \text{ or } a^N, \quad y = 1, 2.$$

The case of convex benefit functions is thus reduced to that of two actions (section 6.3), so that the function $V(p_1, p_2)$ is again as represented on figs. 3 and 3s. The same applies to the case of A finite and appropriately ordered, with first differences increasing or constant as in (74, I).

We shall show, on the other hand, that if the two benefit functions $\beta_z(a)$ are smooth and strictly concave then V is strictly convex in p_1, p_2. Note that, if $\beta_z''(a) < 0$ then $\gamma_z''(a) < 0$ since $\pi_z > 0$. Define

$$V_y' \equiv \frac{dB_y(a)}{da}\Bigg]_{a=a_y} ; \quad V_y'' \equiv \frac{d^2 B_y(a)}{da^2}\Bigg]_{a=a_y} ; \quad y = 1, 2.$$

Then by (77) we have, for $y = 1, 2$:

$$V_y' = \gamma_1'(a_y)\eta_{1y} + \gamma_2'(a_y)\eta_{2y} = 0 \tag{77'}$$

since, with $\gamma_z''(a) < 0$:

$$V_y'' = \gamma_1''(a_y)\eta_{1y} + \gamma_2''(a_y)\eta_{2y} < 0. \tag{77''}$$

Note that under these conditions all useless inquiries are null-inquiries. For let η be useless as defined in section 3.11. Then $a_1 = a_2 = a^*$, say; and by (77'):

$$\gamma_1'(a^*)\eta_{11} + \gamma_2'(a^*)\eta_{21} = 0 \text{ [repeated in the equation}$$

$$\gamma_1'(a^*)\eta_{12} + \gamma_2'(a^*)\eta_{22} = 0]; \text{ hence}$$

$$\eta_{11}/\eta_{21} = -\gamma_2'(a^*)/\gamma_1'(a^*) = \eta_{12}/\eta_{22},$$

$$\eta_{11}/(1-\eta_{22}) = \eta_{22}/(1-\eta_{11}),$$

$$\eta_{11} + \eta_{22} = 1. \tag{78}$$

The set of useless inquiries, $\{\eta : V(\eta) = V^{\min}\}$ is therefore represented by the main diagonal of the unit square, provided both benefit functions are strictly concave and smooth.

Strict convexity of V in p_1, p_2 when the $\gamma_z(a)$ are strictly concave and smooth, can be proved without solving equation (77') explicitly. It suffices to show — as is done in Appendix 2 — that

$$w_{11} > 0, \quad \begin{vmatrix} w_{11} & w_{12} \\ w_{21} & w_{22} \end{vmatrix} > 0, \tag{79}$$

where:

$$w_{ij} \equiv \partial^2 V/\partial p_i \partial p_j. \tag{80}$$

However, for the sake of illustration and to construct fig. 4, we shall derive an explicit solution by assuming the benefit function quadratic and concave. Specifically[28], let:

$$\gamma_1(a) = (1+4a-2a^2)/4; \quad \gamma_1(a) = (3-2a^2)/4. \tag{81}$$

Differentiating with respect to a, substituting onto (77') and solving, we obtain:

$$a_1 = p_1/(p_1+q_2), \quad a_2 = q_1/(q_1+p_2),$$

where $p_i = 1-q_i = \eta_{ii}$. Then, by (77) and (81), the value of inquiry is:

$$V = V_1 + V_2 = 1 + \tfrac{1}{2} \cdot \frac{p_1 p_2 + q_1 q_2}{(p_1+q_2)(p_2+q_1)}, \tag{82}$$

symmetric and strictly convex in p_1, p_2. The contour lines over the unit square are portions of ellipses, $V = \text{const.}$, whose major axis is the main diagonal (the line $p_1 + p_2 = 1$) and whose minor axes range in length from zero to $\sqrt{2}$. The former extreme corresponds to the set of useless inquiries, which is represented by the main diagonal and thus coincides with the set of null-inquiries, agreeing with the result just stated for all strictly concave smooth benefit functions. At the other extreme, the indifference set is reduced to two points, $(1, 1)$ and $(0, 0)$: perfect information. If, applying the convention (52) (i.e., eliminating the half-square below the main diagonal), we qualify the likelihoods p_1, p_2 as "goods", then the indifference sets (except at the extremes) are represented by strictly concave curves; see fig. 4. When the binary inquiry is symmetric, write $p_1 = p_2 = p$, and (82) becomes:

$$V = \tfrac{3}{2} - p + p^2, \tag{83}$$

a convex parabola with a minimum at $p = \tfrac{1}{2}$, the only useless inquiry. If p is a "good", $p \geq \tfrac{1}{2}$, V is rising and strictly convex in p. See fig. 4s.

---

[28] By (75), the specified functions $\gamma_z(a)$ are consistent with our example of the farmer optimizing the proportion of wet to dry acreage, provided:

$$\pi_1 = \pi_2 = \tfrac{1}{2}$$
$$g_w(x) = g_d(x) = x(3-x)/4 ; f_w(x) = f_d(x) = 3x(3-x)/4 ;$$

implying, for each crop and each weather condition, "decreasing marginal returns to land".

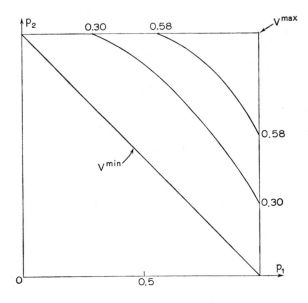

Fig. 4.

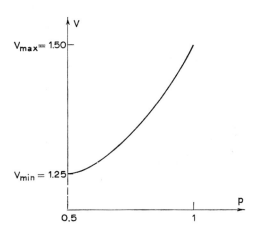

Fig. 4s.

We return now briefly to the case of *A finite*. Condition (77) applies, so that again the information value is:

$$V(\eta) = V_1 + V_2$$

$$= \max_a (\gamma_{a1}\eta_{11} + \gamma_{a2}\eta_{21}) + \max_a (\gamma_{a2}\eta_{21} + \gamma_{a2}\eta_{22}), \text{ where } \gamma_{a2} = \gamma_2^{(a)}.$$
$$(84)$$

Corresponding to the case of *strictly concave* smooth benefit functions, (73, II) that we have just studied, is now condition (74, II) on the second differences. The surface $V(\eta)$ is then again convex and non-linear, but piece-wise linear. The contour lines for $V > V^{\min}$ are piece-wise linear; and they are again concave over the region $p_1 + p_2 > 1$. But, in contrast to the case of smooth benefit functions, the set of useless inquiries ($V = V^{\min}$) is now not confined to the main diagonal (i.e., to null inquiries), but is represented by a flat region. As an example fig. 5 is drawn for the case of 3 actions, $A = (1, 2, 3)$, with the matrix of weighted benefits:

$$[\gamma_{az}] = \begin{pmatrix} 5 & 0 \\ 4 & 2 \\ 0 & 3 \end{pmatrix}.$$

Applying (84) in the region $p_1 + p_2 \geq 1$, we have:

$V_1 = \max (5p_1, 4p_1 + 2q_2)$, corresponding to the appropriate actions
$a_1 = \qquad 1, \qquad 2 \qquad$. Similarly,

$V_2 = \max (5q_1, 4q_1 + 2p_2, 3p_2)$, corresponding to
$a_2 = \qquad 1, \qquad 2 \qquad, 3 \quad$. Hence, omitting dominated values,

$V = \max (p_1 + 2p_2 + 4, 5p_1 + 3p_2, 6, 4p_1 + p_2 + 2)$, corresponding to the
optimal strategies $\alpha^* = (a_1, a_2)$:
$\alpha^* = (1, 2), (1, 3), (2, 2), (2, 3)$.

Perfect information ($p_1 = p_2 = 1$) yields $V^{\max} = \max (6, 8, 6, 7) = 8$. Information is useless when $a_1 = a_2 = 2$, hence $V^{\min} = 6$. The useless region is bounded, on fig. 5, by the shaded piecewise linear concave curve, and its optimal strategy (2, 2) is indicated. The regions corresponding to the other three optimal strategies are indicated similarly; and the broken line — also piecewise linear and concave — is the contour line for $V = 6\frac{1}{4}$.

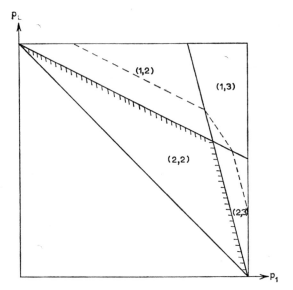

Fig. 5.

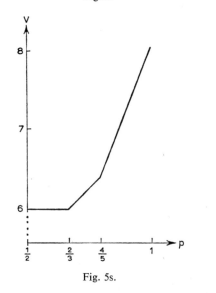

Fig. 5s.

When only symmetric inquiries are considered, $p_1 = p_2 = p \geq \frac{1}{2}$, and

$$V = \max (6, 3p+4, 8p),$$

as plotted on fig. 5s: V is piecewise linear and convex in p.

6.5. *On indifference sets of binary inquiries*

In the case of two actions, the results of sec. 6.3 and fig. 3 are consistent with the indifference lines drawn by Savage (1962) in the space of the "error probabilities of two kinds". In the spirit presented here, he defines an error probability as that of "*doing the wrong thing*" if one of the two possible events, hypotheses, obtains; rather than by the usual, non-operational phrase, "probability of *rejecting*" a true hypothesis. He also points out that these two probabilities depend on the experiment (characterized, in our notation, by the matrix η) *and* on the decision rule used. Note that, if this rule is optimal, the error probability takes, in our notation, the form

$$1 - \Pr(a = a_y | z) = 1 - p(y | z) = 1 - \eta_{zy}, \qquad (85)$$

provided that for each datum y there is a distinct appropriate action, a_y. The space of error probabilities is then essentially identical with the space of likelihoods as on our figs. 3, 4, 5. Savage states, correctly but without proof, that (consistently with our fig. 3 for the case of two actions) the slope of the parallel straight indifference lines is the negative of the "personal odds... when the two errors are equally expensive". (The "useless" region H^0 is not mentioned.)

However, he avoided such concepts when providing "an imperfect and special demonstration" for a (perhaps "non-Bayesian") audience. This demonstration leads to parallel straight indifference lines *regardless of the number of actions*. This contradicts our sect. 6.4 and figs. 4 and 5.

The demonstration considers, in effect, three inquiry matrices η, η', η'' where

$$\eta = k\eta' + (1 - k)\eta'', \ 0 < k < 1, \qquad (86)$$

so that the points representing the three inquiries are collinear. Now denote by

$$g \equiv (\eta', \eta''; k) \qquad (87)$$

a gamble which yields the inquiries η' and η'' with respective probabilities k and $1 - k$. Clearly an inquirer indifferent between η' and η'' is also indifferent between them and g. Therefore, if g and η were *identical objects* it would indeed follow that the straight line containing η, η', η'' is an indifference line. Moreover, for any η^*, our inquirer must be indifferent between the gambles

$$g' \equiv (\eta', \eta^*; k) \quad \text{and} \quad g'' \equiv (\eta'', \eta^*; k);$$

and again: should these two gambles be, respectively, *identical* with the inquiries whose matrices are the convex combinations

$$k\eta' + (1-k)\eta^* \quad \text{and} \quad k\eta'' + (1-k)\eta^*,$$

then it would further follow that the indifference lines must be parallel, regardless of the number of available actions.

This conflict with the results of our sect. 6.5 is explained if we realize that gamble g is in general *not identical* with inquiry η (and similarly, the other two gambles are not identical with the associated convex combinations of inquiries). For action a_y, appropriate to the outcome y of experiment η, may be quite different from the actions a'_y and a''_y (say) that are appropriate to the same outcome y of experiments η' and η'' which are yielded by gamble g. This makes the demonstration inapplicable whenever more than two actions are available.*

6.6. *A remark on non-binary inquiries*

With non-binary inquiries obvious difficulties arise. For example, with $m > 2$, the elimination of dominated actions fails to yield an ordering of actions as in (71), with its simple implications for the case of convex benefit functions. Methods of mathematical programming are called for, especially when the benefit functions are non-smooth.

It is interesting to note some properties of the sets of useless and of null-inquiries. In the case of strictly concave smooth benefit functions, the two sets coincide when $m = n = 2$. But in general the useless set may have higher dimensionality than the set of null-inquiries. To see this, note that, since:

$$\sum_{y=1}^{n} \eta_{zy} = 1, \quad z = 1, ..., m,$$

the set of all inquiries can be represented by a unit-cube of $m(n-1)$ dimensions. The set of all null-inquiries obeys in addition the $(m-1)(n-1)$ equations:

$$\eta_{1y} = ... = \eta_{my}, \quad y = 1, ..., n-1, \tag{88}$$

and is therefore a hyperplane of

$$m(n-1) - (m-1)(n-1) = n-1 \text{ dimensions.}$$

---

* I am grateful to M. DeGroot and T. Ferguson for discussing this matter with me.

It goes through a diagonal of the unit cube. On the other hand, the set of useless inquiries is defined by the $(n-1)$ equations:

$$a_1 = \ldots = a_n. \tag{89}$$

The dimensionality of that set is therefore $(m-1)(n-1) > n-1$ if $m > 2$. If the $\gamma_z(a)$ are smooth and strictly concave, the $n-1$ equations (89) defining the useless set can be rewritten as:

$$\Sigma_z \gamma_z'(a^*) \eta_{zy} = 0, \quad y = 1, \ldots, n-1. \tag{90}$$

Therefore, if the $\gamma_z(a)$ are concave and quadratic, so that the $\gamma_z'(a)$ are linear, then fig. 4 is generalized as follows: the indifference surfaces are portions of hyper-ellipsoids, and the set of useless inquiries is a hyper-plane (90), of higher order than (88). The latter represents the set of null-inquiries.

6.7. *Cost and feasibility conditions*

So far, we have explored, at least for the case of binary information matrices, the behavior of the information value function $V(\eta)$ which associates each η with the maximum expected benefit. If utility can be represented as the difference between benefit and information cost, an optimal matrix η maximizes the difference between $V(\eta)$ and the expected information cost, subject to a constraint on feasible pairs $(\eta, \varkappa)$ of inquiries and cost functions discussed in section 3.5:

$$(\eta, \varkappa) \in \{(\eta, \varkappa)\}.$$

A simple assumption is to associate each η with just one cost function $\varkappa_z(\eta)$. In addition we shall make $\varkappa_z(\eta)$ independent of z:

$$\varkappa_z(\eta) = \varkappa(\eta), \text{ say.}$$

Thus, if η is obtained by a sampling survey of families, the cost $\varkappa(\eta)$ will depend on the size of the sample needed to obtain η (i.e., to attain some preassigned error probabilities) but not on the properties of the families — disregarding, e.g., the fact that households of certain types may require second visits.

Under these assumptions, expected utility is simply:

$$U(\eta) = V(\eta) - \varkappa(\eta).$$

Often cost is considered to be bounded from above so that the feasible set of inquiries has the form:

$$\{\eta : \varkappa(\eta) \leq \text{const.}\}. \tag{91}$$

Still confining ourselves to binary information matrices, we shall give examples illustrating the possible behavior of the cost functions $\varkappa(\eta)$. An important question is: under what conditions does the expected utility, as a function of η, and thus of p_1, p_2:

$$U(p_1, p_2) = V(p_1, p_2) - \varkappa(p_1, p_2) \tag{92}$$

behave in such a way that the optimal information matrix is an "interior solution", in the sense stated in section 6.0. If it does not, optimal information may be null-information; or we may have $p_1 = 1$, $p_2 = 1$, a case of "large scale economies".

6.8. *Cost increasing in channel capacity*

The *capacity* $C = C(p_1, p_2)$ of a channel transmitting one digit per time unit (see below, section 7.3) is given by[29]:

$$2^C = 2^{L_1} + 2^{L_2}; \text{ where:} \tag{93}$$

$$L_1 = (q_1 H_2 - p_2 H_1)/|\eta|; \quad L_2 = (q_2 H_1 - p_1 H_2)/|\eta|,$$

$$|\eta| = p_1 + p_2 - 1, \quad q_i = 1 - p_i,$$

$$H_i = -(p_i \log_2 p_i + q_i \log_2 q_i), \quad i = 1, 2.$$

C is quasi-convex in (p_1, p_2). The contour lines of equal capacity are strictly concave for $p_1 + p_2 > 1$; all points on the straight line $p_1 + p_2 = 1$ have equal capacity $C = 0$; and maximum capacity is $C(1, 1) = 1$. See fig. 6.
Suppose that the contour lines of equal information value are strictly concave as in the "farmer's case" of section 6.4 and fig. 4. Suppose further that the "observations" $y = 1, 2$ are messages ("wet", "dry") received through a channel whose inputs are the "true" events (viz. actual future

---

[29] See, e.g., Ash (1965), Theorem 3.3.3 (p. 56) and problem 3.7 (p. 304).

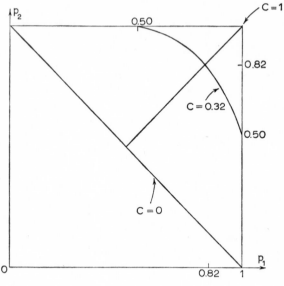

Fig. 6.

weather), $z = 1, 2$. Suppose information cost strictly increases with channel capacity. If, as in (91), the maximum cost is fixed, then so is the capacity $C = C_0$, say. An optimal information system (consisting in this case of the channel and nothing else) is an "interior" optimum if the contour line of equal information value tangent to the contour line of capacity C_0 has, at the point of tangency, a lesser curvature. This happens to be so in the case of our farmer[30], but need not happen if a different benefit function is given.[31]

---

[30] Since both V and C are symmetric functions of p_1, p_2 we must have $p_1 = p_2$ at the point of tangency. Using (102) (for $C = 0.32$) and (82) we have approximately

$$C(0.82, 0.82) = C(0.50, 1.00) = C(1.00, 0.50), \text{ but}$$
$$V(0.82, 0.82) = V(0.58, 1.00) = V(1.00, 0.58);$$

thus a C-curve is less flat than the V-curve touching it. See also figs. 4 and 6.

[31] In general, an interior optimum would exist if the determinant

$$\begin{vmatrix} 0 & c_1 & c_2 \\ c_1 & w_{11} & w_{12} \\ c_2 & w_{21} & w_{22} \end{vmatrix}$$

is positive, where $c_i = \partial C/\partial p_i$, $w_{ij} = \partial^2 V/\partial p_i \partial p_j$. See, e.g., Samuelson (1948, p. 378).

If the information cost is not fixed then, under our assumption and by (92):

$$U(p_1, p_2) = V(p_1, p_2) - f[C(p_1, p_2)],$$

where f is a strictly increasing function. An interior solution will exist if U is quasi-concave; and this will depend on f. In the symmetric case, $p_1 = p_2 = p \geq \frac{1}{2}$:

$$C = 1 + p \log_2 p + (1-p) \log_2 (1-p),$$

increasing and strictly convex in p (since $C''(p) > 0$). Using the strictly convex information value (83) of our farmer's case, it is easily seen that $U = V - f(C)$ is maximized at $p = \frac{1}{2}$ or 1 (no interior solution exists) if f is linear; but f strictly convex may yield an interior solution.

6.9. *Cost of inferring sign of mean of finite population from sign of mean of sample*

Suppose n random variables $u_i (i = 1, \ldots, n)$ are jointly normal, with:

$$E(u_i) = 0, \quad E(u_i u_j) = \begin{Bmatrix} 1 \\ 0 \end{Bmatrix} \quad \text{if} \quad j \begin{Bmatrix} = \\ \neq \end{Bmatrix} i.$$

Define the events z and the "observations" (usually called "statistics") y by:

$$z = \begin{Bmatrix} 1 \\ 2 \end{Bmatrix} \quad \text{if} \quad \sum_1^n u_i \begin{Bmatrix} > \\ \leq \end{Bmatrix} 0; \quad y = \begin{Bmatrix} 1 \\ 2 \end{Bmatrix} \quad \text{if} \quad \sum_1^m u_i \begin{Bmatrix} > \\ \leq \end{Bmatrix} 0$$

$$1 \leq m \leq n.$$

Thus m is the size of the sample, and n is the size of the population. Then (see Cramer 1946, p. 290) the joint distribution of z and y is given by:

$$Pr(z = 1, y = 1) = Pr(z = 2, y = 2) = \frac{1}{4} + (\text{arc sin } \rho)/2\pi$$

$$Pr(z = 1, y = 2) = Pr(z = 2, y = 1) = \frac{1}{4} - (\text{arc sin } \rho)/2\pi,$$

where $\rho = \sqrt{m/n}$.[32] Hence η is binary symmetric, with:

$$\eta_{11} = Pr(y = 1 \mid z = 1) = \tfrac{1}{2} + \text{arc sin } \sqrt{m/n}/\pi = \eta_{22} = p > \tfrac{1}{2};$$

$$m = n \sin^2 \pi(p - \tfrac{1}{2})$$

$$dm/dp = \pi n \sin \pi(2p - 1)$$

$$d^2 m/dp^2 = 2\pi^2 n \cos \pi(2p - 1) \begin{Bmatrix} > \\ < \end{Bmatrix} 0 \quad \text{if} \quad p \begin{Bmatrix} < \\ > \end{Bmatrix} 3/4.$$

The sample size m is thus an increasing function of p, convex for small (and hence less informative; see section 6.2) values of p, and concave for larger ones. So is the cost of information (sampling cost) if we assume it to increase linearly with m.

7. Economics of communication

7.0. *The fidelity criterion as benefit*

In the preceeding three sections, the benefit $\beta(a, z)$ depends on the "action" a in A and the "event" (or hypothesis[33]) z in Z. A probability function π is defined on Z. Event z is transformed into "observation" y by a processing η; and y is transformed into a by a subsequent processing called "strategy" (these processings are possibly stochastic).

Now let us interpret, instead, z in Z as a "message sent", occurring with probability π_z. Interpret processing η as "communication" (to be specified later as a chain: storing, encoding, transmitting), transforming message z into y, the latter to be interpreted as some signals received by the decision-maker. An important restriction is that *the set A of actions a is identical with the set Z of messages sent*. The strategy α consists then in a rule of "decoding" the received signals y, i.e., in prescribing which element a of Z (or which conditional distribution of a) should be associated with a given y. The information system of our fig. 1 is reduced to its "communication" segment.

---

[32] See Marschak (1964), equation (55). The example given in that paper has n stocks in a portfolio and a sample of m of them. With population infinite the sample size would be convex in p (instead of exhibiting an inflexion), so that the example would not add much to that of the preceding section.

[33] See second paragraph of section 3.0.

The early writings on communication theory — most importantly the pioneering work of Shannon (1948) — impose, in effect a further restriction, by assuming equal penalty for all communication errors, so that "a miss is as bad as a mile". That is, the benefit function is taken to be simply:

$$\beta(a, z) = \begin{Bmatrix} 0 \\ -1 \end{Bmatrix} \quad \text{if} \quad a \begin{Bmatrix} = \\ \neq \end{Bmatrix} z. \tag{94}$$

Then the expected benefit is, by (21):

$$B_{\pi\beta}(\eta, \alpha) = \Sigma_{zya}\beta(a, z)\pi_z\eta_{zy}\alpha_{ya}$$

$$= -\sum_{z \neq a}\sum_{y}\pi_z\eta_{zy}\alpha_{ya} = -p_e, \tag{95}$$

where p_e denotes the *probability of error*. For a given set Z (characterized by π), p_e depends then only on the properties of the communication processing η and the decoding strategy α.

To be sure, the special assumption (94) was abandoned in the last chapter of Shannon's (1948) early work for the case when, in our notation, Z is the real line. In this case exact communication ($p_e = 0$) is practically impossible and, in fact, not needed. This property of "continuous sources" moved Shannon to suggest various measures of a (possibly non-metric) "distance" between the message sent and message received. "It measures how undesirable it is ... to receive" (p. 76) *a* when *z* is sent. Thus Shannon's "distance" would correspond to our "penalty", the negative of our "benefit": a function that can take more than just two values. Later, Shannon (1960) extended the idea to "discrete" sources, presumably recognizing its general importance. He defined the *fidelity criterion* (and its negative, the *distortion*), as a general real-valued function of the message sent and the message decoded. This function is identical with our general benefit function that maps $Z \times A$ into reals; except for the restriction (mentioned above) that replaces $Z \times A$ by $Z \times Z$. A fidelity criterion does, then, assign different penalties (negative benefits) to different errors of communication and decoding. To use Shannon's example: it is more dangerous to mistake the emergency signal for "all's well" than conversely.[34]

---

[34] These ideas have not yet penetrated the bulk of literature, certainly not the textbooks, on communication theory. See, however, Jellinek (1968) and Pham-Huu-Tri (1968).

There is an important analogy between communicating information, on the one hand, and, on the other, the storing and transporting of physical commodities. By and large (as indicated in section 1.1), the costs and delays involved in storage and transportation of commodities are independent of the cost of producing and of the use to be made of them. Similarly, the costs and delays in retaining and transmitting knowledge are, by and large, independent of the cost of producing and the value of using it. Pursuing the analogy further, the "amount" (as distinct from cost and value) of information would correspond to the physical volume or weight of goods in warehouses and in transit. Essentially it should measure the *number of symbols* needed to store and transmit a message; for, the larger the collection of symbols — a spoken or written English or coded sentence, a picture — the more time or effort or equipment is required to handle it. Under assumption (94) the number of required symbols is independent of the benefit function of the ultimate user — the "meta-decider" (section 2.1) as distinct from the decoder.

However, to return to our analogy, the storage and transportation costs of a commodity are not completely independent of its value in use. The more valuable a commodity the greater will be the diminishment of profit due to breakage or leakage, per pound or gallon. Similarly, some distortions of messages are more dangerous, diminish the benefit more, than others. They require a larger number (e.g., a repetition) of symbols to mitigate the resulting damage. Shannon's fidelity criterion, replacing the simple assumption (94) takes account of the benefit function. The number of symbols needed is recomputed, still considering the information system of our fig. 1 as consisting of its communication segment only.

7.1. *Capacity of noiseless channel*

We mentioned in section 3.1 that statistical decision theory neglects delays in processing. Communication theory does not neglect them. Concepts like the speed of a processing (thruput per time unit), and the maximum of this speed, achievable with a given processing instrument arise naturally. As a simple case, imagine a noiseless transmission channel. Its inputs are sequences of symbols such as dots and dashes or numerical digits. Let us call them "digits". They are the outputs of the preceding processing link, the encoding, to be discussed next, in section 7.2. The digits are transmitted through the channel one by one and received at the other end with no distortion. If the channel is a cable consisting of several wires several symbols can be transmitted simultaneously. We can diminish delays by increasing the number of wires, and the measure of the channel capacity, analogous to the capacity of a pipeline, is the maximum number of digits that can be transmitted per unit of time.

Channel capacity — already in the noiseless case — is economically significant for two reasons. First, if the inflow of input digits per time unit exceeds the channel capacity, untransmitted, and therefore useless, inputs will pile up indefinitely, with an obvious detriment to the expected benefit. Second, any further increase of capacity, in excess of the inflow of inputs, will diminish the delay between input and output of the channel.

Why delays can diminish expected benefit is due to *impatience* (preference for early results of actions) as well as to the obsolescence of data (in our case, of the channel outputs) on which the choice of action is based. (See sections 1 and 5.)

While increased channel capacity thus increases expected benefit, it will, in general, also require an increase in cost.

Expected benefit is diminished by delay. But benefit is not necessarily a linear function of delay. Hence expected utility (difference between expected benefit and expected cost) need not be monotone in expected delay. Therefore, it is *not* correct to present the economics of communication — even in the simplest case of a noiseless channel — as that of minimizing expected cost for a given expected delay, or a given expected speed of transmission. Yet, just this approach seems to be taken, in this or similar contexts, in much of the literature, where, essentially, the problem is presented as that of determining an efficient set in the space of expectations of various "criteria", as discussed in our Appendix 1.[35]

7.2. *Minimum expected length of code word, as the "uncertainty at source"*

If only two possible messages z ($= 1$ or 0, say) can be sent, each can be encoded as a single binary digit, to be transmitted through the (noiseless) channel. However, if a time sequence of T such two-valued messages is to be communicated, less than T digits (and hence less than one digit per

---

[35] The clearest formulation of such an efficient set is given by Wolfowitz (1961), in the context of optimal coding for a noisy channel. See below, section 7.7. It seems that the assumption of utility linear in its criteria is implicit in the discussion of optimal design in many fields of engineering. See e.g., English (1968).

message) will be needed on the average if one uses "code words" (that is, binary sequences) with few digits for the more probable and with more digits for the less probable sequences of messages. For example, if one uses this principle and if the odds for z taking its two values are $9:1$, then, even if the sequences of messages occur independently ("have no pattern"), it is possible to devise codes which will use, on the average, approximately only 0.64 or 0.53 digits per message when $T = 2$ or $T = 3$, respectively. In general, as established in the "Fundamental Theorem for a Noiseless Channel" by Shannon (1948), the minimum expected length of the code word decreases as T increases, and it converges towards the (never negative) quantity:

$$- \sum_{z \in Z} \pi_z \log_2 \pi_z \equiv H(\pi), \text{ also written as } H(Z), \tag{96}$$

and called the (negative of) *entropy*. This limit is valid not only for the case of two-valued messages (as in our example, with $H(\pi) = 0.47$) but for a set Z of any size m. Since $H(\pi)$ increases with m, and, furthermore, since $H(\pi)$ is largest when all the m elements of Z are equiprobable [so that every $\pi_z = 1/m$, and $H(\pi) = m$], the name "amount of uncertainty" (about z) occasionally given to $H(\pi)$ does agree with English usage. Alternatively, one says that $H(\pi)$ units of information are gained if this uncertainty is removed (by learning the actual value of z). Indeed $H(\pi)$ has been proposed as a *measure of uncertainty* (or *of information*) because it is additive (as any measure ought to be), in the following sense. Let π', π'' characterize two statistically independent sets Z' and Z''; that is, the joint occurrence $z = (z'$ and $z'')$ of given messages from the two sets occurs with probability:

$$\pi_z = \pi'_{z'} \cdot \pi''_{z''}.$$

Then, by the definition (96) of the distribution parameter H:

$$H(\pi) = H(\pi') + H(\pi''). \tag{97}$$

Similar additivity properties can be derived for certain related distribution parameters (such as "uncertainty removed by transmission", of which more later). Since $H(\pi)$ measures, at least in the limit, the average length of a sequence of *binary digits*, the measurement unit of "uncertainty" (or its negative, "information") is called, briefly, a *bit*, following a suggestion of J.W. Tukey.

It is not clear, however, for what economic purpose one should use this measure of uncertainty or information. Because of the additive property (97) of the distribution parameter H, specialists in various fields (mathematics, statistics, psychology) have expressed enthusiasm: the subtle, intangible concept of information has now become measurable "in a way similar to that as money is used in everyday life" (Rényi 1966). Indeed a paper currency bill can be measured by the number of dollars it represents and thus by the amount of some useful commodity at a given price. But it can be also measured in square inches of its area, and if I use it for papering my walls, the latter, not the former, measurement is appropriate!

Somewhat anticipating the subsequent more detailed discussion, note that a distribution parameter such as $H(\pi)$ cannot alone determine the information value of a system. For $H(\pi)$ depends only on the distribution π, not on the benefit function β. To be sure, the special assumption (94) of equal penalty for all communication errors does remove variations of the benefit function. This fact may have been the source of misunderstandings about the economic significance of the number of bits gained or lost, regardless of the use the decision-maker can make of them. If a general fidelity criterion (presumably reflecting the decision-maker's needs) is introduced, $H(\pi)$ fails to determine the information value of the system.

What *is* economically important about $H(\pi)$ is its meaning as the greatest lower bound of the expected length of a code word, given the distribution π. For, the shorter a code word the less is, presumably, the time needed to transmit it, digit by digit; and therefore, for reasons just stated in section 7.1, the larger the expected benefit.[36]

On the other hand, note that, to bring the expected length of code words down close to its lower limit, $H(\pi)$, one may have to wait until a very long sequence of messages (T large) is piled up. The resulting delay may offset the acceleration due to the shortening of code words. In addition, there are storage costs. Like other entropy formulas, to be dealt with later in this section, $H(\pi)$ loses economic significance unless messages flow in at a fast rate (see section 7.6).

---

[36] Wolfowitz (1961) writes that the function H should "for convenience and brevity have a name. However, we shall draw no implicit conclusions from its name, and shall use only such properties of H as we shall explicitly prove. In particular, we shall not erect any philosophical systems on H as a foundation. One reason for this is that we shall not erect any philosophical systems at all, and shall confine ourselves to the proof of mathematical theorems [namely, theorems on optimal coding]." The present writer, though guided by economic rather than mathematical interest, tends to agree.

We can now refer to the "four-link" chain (b) of section 2.1. Messages to be sent are stored, encoded, received, and decoded. The benefit will depend on the messages to be sent and on the decoded messages and the expected benefit will depend on the probability distribution π characterizing the source (i.e., the messages to be sent) and on the Markov matrices characterizing consecutive processings. Costs and delays arise at each processing link, and their distribution (and hence expectation) depends, too, on π and the Markov matrices. However, the four-link chain is merely a part of the total information system. Benefit depends on events and actions. Events are transformed, by inquiry, into observations ("data"). These are the messages to be sent, the initial inputs of the communication system; and its final output, the decoded messages, are transformed into actions by applying strategies. We have thus added two links, one at each end of the communication chain. It remains true that the probability distribution (and hence the expectation) of benefits, costs, and delays depends on the initial distribution π (now attached to events, not to messages received) and on the successive Markov matrices.

Alternatively, we can regard a communication system as a special case of the general information system; viz., one in which the processing of events into data and the processing of decoded messages into action are characterized by identity transformations and by zero-costs and zero-delays.

7.3. *Noisy channel: transmission rate and capacity*

To concentrate on the properties of a channel, it will be convenient to reinterpret our notational symbols again. Let us now designate channel inputs by z in Z, and its outputs by y in Y, analogous to the "events" and "observations" of sections 3-5. Channel inputs z, the digits of the encoded message, occur with probabilities π_z. Channel outputs, y, the digits received at the channel's end, occur, for a given z, with conditional probabilities $p(y|z) = \eta_{zy}$, elements of the Markov matrix η, called the *channel matrix*. The channel is noiseless if η is the identity matrix. The joint probability of z and y and the marginal probability of y are, respectively (see footnote 21 on notations):

$$p(z, y) = \pi_z \eta_{zy}$$

$$p(y) = \sum_{z \in Z} \pi_z \eta_{zy}.$$

It will be convenient to give a special symbol, δ_{yz} (an element of the Markov matrix $\delta = [\delta_{yz}]$) to the posterior probability of z, given y. Clearly δ depends on π and η:

$$\delta_{yz} = p(z|y) = p(z, y)/p(y)$$

$$\delta_{yz} = \pi_z \eta_{zy} / \sum_{u \in Z} \pi_u \eta_{uy}.$$

We may call "uncertainty about z, retained after digit y was received through the channel", the expression:

$$H(Z|y) = -\sum_z \delta_{yz} \log \delta_{yz},$$

and to call its expectation:

$$-\sum_y p(y) H(Z|y) = H(Z|Y), \tag{98}$$

the *uncertainty retained*, in Breiman's (1970) suggestive language. It is clear from its definition that $H(Z|Y)$ depends only on the probability distributions π and η, and we want to emphasize this by writing occasionally:

$$H(Z|Y) \equiv G(\pi, \eta).$$

The quantity (never negative):

$$H(Z) - H(Z|Y) \equiv I(Z, Y) \equiv I(Y, Z) \tag{99}$$

has been called *uncertainty removed* or *amount of information transmitted*. Because of the symmetry with respect to Z, Y, which is easily shown (but is not relevant for our purposes), $I(Y, Z)$ has also been called *mutual information*.[37] Clearly it depends on π and η only. This will be brought out clearly if we rewrite (99) thus:

$$H(\pi) - G(\pi, \eta) = J(\pi, \eta). \tag{100}$$

Shannon's "generalized first theorem" states that $J(\pi, \eta)$ is the greatest

---

[37] Theil (1967), uses the difference $H(Z) - H(Z|Y)$ to measure, e.g., the discrepancy between the predicted and the actual composition of a balance sheet, the national income, or some other total. Of course, this measure can be used outside of economics as well; and it is related to information mainly because the same formula has been used in the theory of communication as developed by Shannon and others. This explains the difference in content between Theil's studies and those presented here, in spite of the similarity of titles.

lower bound of the expected number of binary digits needed to identify (by appropriately decoding the digit sequence received) each digit put through the channel. Thus $J(\pi, \eta)$ is measured in bits per digit.

In section 7.1, the speed of a channel, v digits per time unit (say) was introduced. If we multiply it by $J(\pi, \eta)$ bits per digit, we obtain:

$$v(\text{digits/time}) \times J(\pi, \eta) \,(\text{bits/digit}) = v \cdot J(\pi, \eta) \,(\text{bits/time}), \qquad (101)$$

a quantity called *transmission rate*. Some confusion is present in textbooks, though certainly not in engineering practice, by choosing the time unit so as to make $v = 1$ for convenience and not stating this very explicitly. Yet the distinction between "uncertainty removed" and "uncertainty removed per time unit" is of economic importance.

If matrix η undergoes garbling, in the formal sense of our section 4.1, the number $J(\pi, \eta)$ of bits per digit decreases.[38] Thus variations of "uncertainty removed" affect expected benefit in the case of possible garbling. But another factor affecting expected benefit is the delay in transmission, due to decreasing the factor v, not $J(\pi, \eta)$. An accurate but slow transmission may have the same value to the user as an inaccurate but fast one.

By (101) the transmission rate depends on v, π, and η. If v and η are kept constant but π varies over the set of all probability vectors of order m, the transmission rate will vary, and its maximum is called the *capacity of the channel*. It depends on v and η (and thus also on m, the number of rows in η). However, in theoretical discussion v is often equated to unity, making the capacity, denoted by C, depend on η only. In our notation we have, for any v:

$$\max_{\pi} J(\pi, \eta)v = C(\eta) \cdot v \text{ bits per time unit.}$$

7.4. *Capacity and cost*

It can be presumed that the cost of channel increases with v. It is also usually assumed, I think, that channel cost increases with $C(\eta)$. This assumption was used in section 6.6, where a formula for $C(\eta)$ was given for η binary and $v = 1$. However, it is not too clear why two channels with two different

---

[38] It is easily seen that when the channel is noiseless (i.e., η is an identity matrix) then $G(\pi, \eta) = 0$, $J(\pi, \eta) = H(\pi)$. That is, for given π, uncertainty retained is at its minimum and uncertainty removed reaches its maximum when the channel is noiseless. See also section 7.5.

matrices η, η' should require equal costs (of construction, maintenance and operation) whenever $C(\eta) = C(\eta')$. For example, formula (93) yields approximately (see fig. 6):

$$C \begin{pmatrix} 0.82 & 0.18 \\ 0.18 & 0.82 \end{pmatrix} = 0.32 = C \begin{pmatrix} 0.5 & 0.5 \\ 1.0 & 0 \end{pmatrix}. \tag{102}$$

The matrix on the right is exemplified by a channel which transmits every "no" without fault, but transforms a "yes" into a "no" half of the time: "You will send me a word (through a rather unreliable messenger) only if you decide to come." It is not clear why the use of such a channel should equal in cost the use of a somewhat more reliable messenger who mistakes a "yes" for a "no", or conversely, about one time out of six, as in the matrix on the left and should be more costly than a messenger who makes the mistake one time out of five. I suppose data on such cost questions are at the disposal of the communication industry. As far as I can see, theoretical literature does, in effect, regard all channels with equal capacity as equivalent with respect to cost. It answers, e.g., the question: "What is the best code for a channel with a given capacity?" Yet, the user's economic question should be: "What is the best code for a channel with a given cost?" The answers are the same only when messages are transmitted in sequences of very great length.

7.5. *Does informativeness always increase with "information transmitted?"*

The answer is "no". Let φ be any convex function of a non-negative variable. One such function is:

$$\varphi_0(x) = x \ln x, \quad 0 \le x \le 1, \tag{103}$$

since $\varphi_0''(x) = 1/x > 0$. The following has been proved[39]:

Theorem: If $\eta^{(1)} = [\eta_{zy^{(1)}}^{(1)}]$ and $\eta^{(2)} = [\eta_{zy^{(2)}}^{(2)}]$ are two information matrices then $\eta^{(1)} > \eta^{(2)}$ if and only if, for any convex function φ:

$$\sum_{y^{(1)}} p(y^{(1)}) \sum_z \varphi(\delta_{y^{(1)}z}) \ge \sum_{y^{(2)}} p(y^{(2)}) \sum_z \varphi(\delta_{y^{(2)}z}), \tag{104}$$

where, as in section 7.3, $p(y^{(k)})$ and $\delta_{y^{(k)}z}$ are, respectively, the marginal

---

[39] See Blackwell and Girshick (1954), part 4 of Theorem 12.2.2; and DeGroot (1962).

probability of $y^{(k)}$ and the posterior probability of z, given $y^{(k)}$, both dependent on the distribution π and $\eta^{(k)}$. Consider now the particular convex function φ_0 defined in (103). By the definitions of section 7.3:

$$-\sum_y p(y) \sum_z \varphi_0(\delta_{yz}) = G(\pi, \eta) / \ln 2,$$

where $\eta = [\eta_{zy}]$. It follows from the above theorem that:

$$G(\pi, \eta^{(1)}) \leqslant G(\pi, \eta^{(2)}) \quad \text{if} \quad \eta^{(1)} > \eta^{(2)};$$

it also follows that the converse is not true since the theorem requires condition (104) to hold for all convex functions and not just for φ_0. It further follows, by (100), that the condition:

$$J(\pi, \eta^{(1)}) \geq J(\pi, \eta^{(2)})$$

is necessary but not sufficient for $\eta^{(1)}$ to be more informative than $\eta^{(2)}$. This means that there exist distributions π and benefit functions (fidelity criteria) β such that an increase in J, the information transmitted, can be consistent with a decrease in the expected benefit.

7.6. *Efficient coding, given a fidelity (benefit) function*

Let us continue with the notations of section 7.3. A channel is characterized by speed v, and by a Markov matrix η, which transforms channel inputs z in Z (occurring with probabilities π_z) into channel outputs y in Y. Now, the channel is a processing link intermediary between two others. On the one hand, at its exit, outputs must be decoded; and, as before, we identify, in the context of communication theory, the results of decoding (decoded messages) with benefit-relevant actions a in A (where the sets A and Z are identical), and, hence, identify the decoding transformation with the strategy α. On the other hand, the benefit-relevant events are not the channel inputs but the messages to be sent. These are transformed into channel inputs by a processing called encoding, possibly preceded by storing, as indicated in section 7.2. Neglect storing for a moment (i.e., assume it to be characterized by identity transformation, zero costs and zero delays) and denote the messages to be sent by s in S, and their probability distribution by σ. Denote by w the speed of inflow of these messages. An encoding Markov matrix ε (possibly noiseless) transforms S into Z; and clearly σ and ε completely determine the distribution π on Z. To be feasible, an encoding matrix ε is conditioned on some costs and delays, as is the decoding matrix α. These costs and delays are presumably increasing with the length of code words, and also with the number of code words (size of "dictionary"). The pair (ε, α) is called *code*.

Given σ and the benefit (fidelity) function β on $A \times S$, we can express the expected benefit thus, analogous to (21):

$$B_{\sigma\beta}(\eta, \varepsilon, \alpha) = \sum_{s,z,y,a} \beta(a, s)\sigma_s \varepsilon_{sz} \eta_{zy} \alpha_{ya}. \tag{105}$$

It is in these terms[40] consonant with the general economics of information that I shall try to express the main results of Shannon (1960), more general and appropriate, for the reasons stated, than those of his original paper (1948). Let B^* be some expected benefit, disregarding any losses due to communication delays. Of course, B^* cannot exceed the expected benefit obtained under perfect information (i.e., with a noiseless channel with a speed not less than that of the inflow of messages. Nor can B^* be less than the expected benefit under null-information. Define:

$Q = Q_\beta(B^*, \sigma, \varepsilon, \alpha)$ (bits per digit)

$\quad = \min_{\eta'} J(\sigma, \eta')$ subject to

$\quad B_{\sigma\beta}(\eta', \alpha, \varepsilon) \geq B^*,$

and provided η' has as many rows (columns) as there are elements in $Z(Y)$.

That is, given the benefit function β and the probabilities σ of the messages sent, Q is the least amount of information that needs to be transmitted in order to achieve an expected benefit not less than B^*, using code (ε, α) and a varying channel matrix η'. Now let an available channel have matrix η and speed v and let the messages flow in at a speed w (digits per time unit). It was proved by Shannon that, if

$\quad v \cdot C(\eta) \geq w \cdot Q_\beta(B^*, \sigma, \varepsilon, \alpha),$

then for each positive k and every σ, η there exists a code (ε, α) such that:

$$B^* - B_{\sigma\beta}(\eta, \varepsilon, \alpha) \leq k. \tag{106}$$

Thus, the number of bits per time unit, encoded, transmitted and decoded

---

[40] To translate into Shannon's notation, substitute i for s; j for a; d_{ij} ("distortion measure") for $-\beta(a, s)$; D (= "average distortion") for $-B$ (= "minus expected benefit"); and $R(D^*)$ for $Q(B^*)$. The formulation is due to H. M. Pham-Huu-Tri.

to achieve B^* can be brought down arbitrarily close to that number of bits per time unit which can be transmitted through the available channel — provided an appropriate code is used.[41]

More precisely, for each positive k there exists a number $N(k)$, and a sequence of codes $(\varepsilon_1, \alpha_1), \ldots, (\varepsilon_n, \alpha_n)$ such that for $n > N(k)$, (106) holds. For k small the code $(\varepsilon_n, \alpha_n)$ will, in general, require long words, making it necessary to wait for long sequences of messages before encoding and sending them. As discussed earlier (sections 7.1 and 7.2), long code words cause delays. Long sequences of messages presuppose storing. Therefore, to realize a good code for a small k, it is not possible to neglect (as we have done at the beginning of this section) the storage of messages that must precede their encoding, introducing additional delays, and resulting in diminished benefits (section 5). *Unless messages come in very fast, the entropy amounts H, G, J lose economic relevance.*

7.7. *Demand for communication links*

The cost of each processing link (storing, encoding, transmitting, decoding) will depend on the characteristics of its transformation matrix but it may also, in general, vary with its inputs, as in section 1.0. Thus the expected cost of encoding and expected cost of delays will depend on probabilities σ_s of the various messages to be encoded; the expected cost of transmitting will depend depend on the $\sigma_s \varepsilon_{sz}$; and that of decoding, on the $\sigma_s \varepsilon_{sz} \eta_{zy}$. The problem is simplified if, as in section 6.7, the cost and delay of each processing depends on the transformation characterizing it $(\varepsilon, \eta, \alpha)$ but not on the input. The sum of costs of the links is then subtracted from the expected benefit; and the latter is affected by the delays in the several links, especially because of the diminution of expected benefit, caused by the obsolescence of actions (here: decodings), as in section 5.

However, most of the existing literature lets each link be associated, not with its costs and delays, but with characteristics such as channel capacity, length of the code word, and size of the code dictionary. A question such as the following is asked:

---

[41] When the benefit function and expected benefit are the simple ones of (94) and (95) (i.e., all errors are equally undesirable), $B_{\sigma\beta} = -p_e$, J is minimized at $\eta' = 1$ (null-information: section 3.8), $Q = H(\sigma)$ and the result is reduced to the "Fundamental Theorem for Discrete Channel with Noise" in Shannon's original paper (1948): an appropriate code can make the error probability arbitrarily small, provided $v \cdot C(\eta) \geq w \cdot H(\sigma)$.

Given the channel capacity, the (expected) word length, and the code size, how large an expected fidelity can be achieved? [42]

Answering such a question would not really provide the set of communication systems efficient from the point of view of a given user characterized by a fidelity function and a probability distribution of messages to be sent. We remarked in section 7.4 that two channels with equal capacity (and speed) need not have equal cost. The length (or more generally, the expected length) of code words causes delays and these delays influence expected utility to the user, not by being added to costs but through a complicated effect on expected benefit, especially by making decisions obsolete, as we have just remarked. Expected utility cannot be decomposed additively into expected benefit, channel capacity and (expected) word length; that is, utility is not linear in these quantities. (Similar considerations would apply to the size of code.) Yet without such additivity, answers to a question like that above would not provide the set that is efficient from a given user's point of view: see Appendix 1.

In a sense, the set of non-dominated quadruples (expected fidelity, channel capacity, expected word length, code size) is the result of a crude "averaging" over all users. Delays, being undesirable for all users, are replaced by what amounts to an additive cost, as a make-do. This gives a rough guidance to the supplier of the communication links in estimating the demand for them. The demand of the individual user (if he is "rational") is rather different, and hence that crude average cannot represent the aggregate demand.

8. Market for information

8.0. *Demand for systems and sub-systems*

Return now to the general outline of purposive processing chains (and networks, for that matter) that we gave in sections 1 and 2, with especial regard to information systems. The individual user (meta-decider) can

---

[42] This is the formulation given by Wolfowitz (1961), but generalized in two respects: by introducing a general fidelity criterion instead of an equal penalty for all errors and by permitting the code words to vary in length, thus presumably increasing coding efficiency. I must acknowledge a great debt to Wolfowitz's clear presentation of the economic problem.

achieve a given sequence of transformations only at certain costs and with certain delays (or, more generally, a certain probability distribution of costs and delays). Subject to these constraints, he should maximize the expected benefit simultaneously with respect to all of the transformations. Just like an ideal plant designer decides simultaneously about the size and composition of the personnel as well as of the machine park, the warehouses and the transportation facilities! This is, of course, hardly ever achieved in reality.[43] The humbler meta-decider makes his choices separately for each of several sub-systems; this is what the term "sub-optimization" is often intended to mean, I believe. Hopefully, he partitions the total system in such a way that the complementarity between sub-systems (with regard to expected benefit) is small.

The failure to maximize over all system components simultaneously is just one of many allowances for "lack of rationality" that must be made before we claim a modicum of descriptive validity to the result of aggregating the demands of individual users into the total demand for system components of various kinds, given the constraints.

8.1. *The supply side*

The "demand side" of the market, the relation associating the set of constraints with the set of demands, depends on the benefit functions β and the probability distributions π characterizing individual users. The "supply side" is the relation between those constraints and the supplies, and depends on the "production conditions" ("technology") characterizing each supplier. As usual, the economist is almost completely ignorant of technology.

Let me conclude just with three, rather casual, remarks on these production conditions. It is superfluous to remind the economist that the market is supposed to equalize demand and supply.

8.2. *Standardization*

In many cases, it does not pay to produce "on order". Mass production may be cheaper. This may explain why our Sunday newspaper is so bulky (it gives all things to all subscribers), and why our telephones have such a

---

[43] For an attempt to deal more formally with the limitations of the meta-decider ("organizer") see Marschak and Radner (1971), Chapter 9.

high fidelity. The individual user is "forced" to purchase information services which, for him, would be wasteful if they were not so cheap.

8.3. *Packaging*

In our scheme, inquiry was presented as a component separate from storing the data, encoding as separate from transmission, etc. The producer of automata and control mechanisms may find it cheaper to produce them jointly, in fixed "packages". This, again, imposes constraints on the user, similar to those of standardization.[44]

8.4. *Man vs. machine*

The competition between machines and human nerves (not muscles) is much discussed today. Some symbol-manipulating services consist in many-to-one mapping, variously called "sorting" and "pattern-recognition". Encoding and decoding are of this nature, but not the (generally noisy) transmission. To be sure, we have, in section 7, characterized encoding and decoding by Markov matrices, thus allowing for "randomized codes". Such codes have been used for the convenience of mathematical proofs. But, as in any one-person game, there exists an optimal non-randomized choice. Except to allow for (non-rational) error-making encoders and decoders, we may as well consider these activities as many-to-one mappings. We can imagine the encoder to partition a set of visible or audible stimuli, including verbal sentences, into equivalence classes, variously called "patterns" and "meanings". These are translated, in turn, into the language of channel inputs and outputs, and then decoded back into "patterns" or "meanings". Even when we are little concerned with transmission noise — newspaper misprints or slips of the tongue — the problem of the best code remains: what is the best way to make the receiver (e.g., a listener or reader) to "understand" the sender (a lecturer or writer)? The sender must encode into a well-chosen set of patterns (e.g., an "effective style" of speech, or writing), such that the receiver would be able to recognize them, and respond to them by benefit-maximizing actions.

We are told by psycholinguists — e.g., Miller (1967) — that man's

---

[44] Standardization and packaging are, of course, not peculiar to the production of information services and are present in other markets.

effectiveness as a channel (and also as a storage facility) is poor compared with inanimate equipment such as telephones (and record tapes). But his coding ability seems superb in many cases. It is variously called "insight", "judgment", "ability to recognize a Gestalt (pattern)" ...

Appendix 1: Requirement of commensurable criteria

In the text, utility was defined on each pair "event, action". It is sometimes useful to introduce an additional concept — the *result*, *r* (also called consequence) of the given pair "event, action", and to define utility as a function of the result. The result need not be numerical. For example, the result's values can be "getting cured; dying; continuing in ill health". When the result is a numerical vector, and utility is monotone increasing in each of its components, we call each component a (desirable) criterion* or in another, now customary, terminology, an "attribute".

Thus

action $= a$;   event $= z$;

result $r = (r_1, ..., r_n)$, with every r_i numerical;

$r_i = \rho_i(a, z)$ (ith "result function");

utility $u = v(r_1, ..., r_n)$;

$$v(r_1, ..., r_n) > v(r'_1, ..., r'_n) \text{ if}$$

$$r_i > r'_i \text{ for some } i, r_i \geq r'_i \text{ for all } i.$$

Consider a case when $n = 1$: suppose, e.g., the decision-maker maximizes the expected utility of money profit. The unique component of the criterion vector is then a dollar amount. It is well known that, in this case, expected utility is not necessarily monotone in expected money profit (independently of some other parameters of the distribution of money profit such as variance) unless utility is linear in money.

Before we generalize to the case of *n* components, note, as an example, that the pair "*minus* cost, numerical benefit" constitutes a vector consisting of two criteria.

---

* In fact, a suggestion has been made to replace the commodity space of usual economic theory by a space of criteria that may "explain" the consumers' preferences: e.g., a car becomes a bundle of criteria such as speed, mileage per gallon of fuel, etc. See Lancaster (1966).

In section 7.8 the following criteria, used in communication theory, are listed: fidelity criterion; length of code word; size of code; capacity of channel (provided of course that the last three numbers be replaced by their negatives).

Given the distribution π of events z, the action a will result in some joint distribution of $r_1, \ldots, r_n$, to be denoted by

$$\pi^a(r_1, \ldots, r_n).$$

Consequently, action a will yield expected utility

$$E_a(u) \equiv \sum_{r_1 \ldots r_n} v(r_1, \ldots, r_n)\, \pi^a(r_1, \ldots, r_n). \tag{A.1.1}$$

Given the action a, and thus the joint distribution π^a, the marginal probability distribution of a particular criterion, for example of r_1, will be denoted by

$$\pi^a(r_1) \equiv \sum_{r_2 \ldots r_n} \pi^a(r_1, \ldots, r_n);$$

no ambiguity results from using the same symbol — here π^a — for two different functions, made distinguishable by their different arguments, in parentheses.

Then the expected value of r_i, given action a, is

$$E_a(r_i) \equiv \Sigma_{r_i} r_i \pi^a(r_i). \tag{A.1.2}$$

The vector of expected criterion values will be denoted by

$$[E_a] = [E_a(r_1), \ldots, E_a(r_n)].$$

Given two actions a and b, we say, as usual, that $[E_a]$ dominates $[E_b]$, and write $[E_a]$ *dom* $[E_b]$, if

$$E_a(r_i) \geq E_b(r_i), \quad \text{all } i$$

$$E_a(r_i) > E_b(r_i), \quad \text{some } i.$$

We shall then also say that action a dominates b with *respect to criterion expectations*.

Suppose that

$$E_a(u) > E_b(u) \text{ whenever}$$

$$[E_a]\ dom\ [E_b]. \tag{A.1.3}$$

Clearly this is equivalent to saying that expected utility $E_a(u)$ is a monotone increasing function of the expected criterion values $E_a(r_1), \ldots, E_a(r_n)$. If this is the case then, and only then, the feasible action a^* (say) that maximizes each of the $E_a(r_i)$ will also maximize $E_a(u)$.

Suppose the utility function v is not known; but the monotonicity of $E_a(u)$ with respect to the criterion expectations $E_a(r_1), \ldots, E_a(r_n)$ is known to hold. Then, while it is not possible to determine an optimal action one can at least eliminate all actions that are dominated by some feasible action. The remaining subset of feasible actions is then the *efficient set*.

Consider now the case

$$u = v(r) = r_1 + r_2 + \ldots + r_n;$$

then by (A.1.1)

$$E_a(u) = \sum_{r_1 \ldots r_n} r_1 \pi^a(r_1, \ldots, r_n) + \ldots + \sum_{r_1 \ldots r_n} r_n \pi^a(r_1, \ldots, r_n);$$

then by (A.1.2)

$$E_a(u) = \sum_{r_1} r_1 \pi^a(r_1) + \ldots + \sum_{r_n} r_n \pi^a(r_n)$$

$$= E_a(r_1) + \ldots + E_a(r_n),$$

an obvious result ("Expectation of sum = sum of expectations"). We shall now prove the following.

Theorem: Expected utility is monotone in expected criterion values if and only if utility is linear in the criteria. Clearly, the conclusion of this theorem ("the expected utility is monotone in expected criterion values") is equivalent to the following propositions:

(i)   "If action a dominates action b with respect to expected criterion values then a is preferred to b";

(ii) "The efficient set consists of all those feasible actions which are not dominated, with respect to expected criterion values, by any feasible action."

(iii) "An action that maximizes, over the set of feasible actions, the expected value of each criterion, is optimal."

By substituting any of these three sentences for the conclusion of the Theorem, we obtain three theorems equivalent to it.

The "if" part of Theorem is obvious since a sum is a monotone increasing function of its components. It is unfortunate that the "only if" part is also true. For it follows that unless it is known that utility is additive the computation of expected criterion values loses much of its usefulness: an action b dominated by some other action a with respect to the expected criteria may still be preferable to a, and may indeed be optimal, unless of course some further conditions are known to exist [e.g., if the distributions $\pi^a(r)$, $\pi^b(r)$, ... yielded by all feasible actions are known to belong to some special class-Gaussian, for example].

I shall now give a proof (suggested orally by Roy Radner) of the "only if" part of the above Theorem. Consider three vectors

$$r'' = (r_1^o, ..., r_n^o); \quad r' = (r_1^o, ..., r_n^o); \quad \bar{r} = (\bar{r}_1, ..., \bar{r}_n),$$

where $\bar{r}_i = \alpha r_i^o + (1-\alpha)r_i'$ (all i), and $0 < \alpha < 1$. That is, $\bar{r}$ is a convex combination of r^o and r' (geometrically, $\bar{r}$ is represented by a point on a straight line between r^o and r'). Let two actions, a and b, result, respectively, in the following two joint distributions on the n-vector space:

$$\pi^a : \quad \pi^a(r_1^o, ..., r_n^o) = \alpha, \quad \pi^a(r_1', ..., r_n') = 1-\alpha;$$

$$\pi^b : \quad \pi^b(\bar{r}_1, ..., \bar{r}_n) = 1.$$

Then for every $i = 1, ..., n$,

$$E_a(r_i) = \alpha r_i^o + (1-\alpha)r_i',$$

$$E_b(r_i) = 1 \cdot \bar{r}_i = \alpha r_i^o + (1-\alpha)r_i'.$$

Hence

$$E_b(r_i) = E_a(r_i), \quad \text{all } i.$$

On the other hand,

$$E_a(u) = \alpha v(r^o) + (1-\alpha) v(r')$$

$$E_b(u) = v(\alpha r^o + (1-\alpha)r').$$

Suppose expected utility of any action is monotone in the expected criterion values (resulting from that action). Then, since $E_b(r_i) = E_a(r_i)$ for all i, we must have

$$E_a(u) = E_b(u),$$

$$\alpha v(r^\circ) + (1-\alpha)\, v(r') = v(\alpha r^\circ + (1-\alpha)\, r').$$

This is possible only if the function v on the space of vectors r is linear, i.e., if there exist $w_i (i = 0, 1, \ldots, n)$ such that

$$v(r_1, \ldots, r_n) = w_0 + \sum_{i}^{n} w_i r_i.$$

It is then often said that the criteria are "commensurable" (among each other and with utility itself). In the most common case they are converted into dollars, under the (sometimes tacit) assumption that utility is linear in dollars.

Appendix 2 (to section 6.4)

To prove (79), write $\partial a_j/\partial p_i \equiv a_{ji}$. Differentiate V_y in (77) with respect to $p_i (= \eta_{ii})$, using 77'):

$$\partial V_i/\partial p_i = V_i'(a_i) a_{ii} + \gamma_i(a_i) = 0 + \gamma_i(a_i)$$

$$\partial V_j/\partial p_i = V_j'(a_j) a_{ji} - \gamma_i(a_j) = 0 - \gamma_i(a_j); \quad i \neq j;$$

and since $V = V_1 + V_2$:

$$\partial V/\partial p_1 = \gamma_1(a_1) - \gamma_2(a_2); \quad \partial V/\partial p_2 = -\gamma_2(a_1) + \gamma_2(a_2).$$

Then, by (80), writing $\gamma_i'(a_j) = \gamma_{ij}$:

$$w_{11} = \gamma_{11} a_{11} - \gamma_{12} a_{21} \qquad w_{12} = \gamma_{11} a_{12} - \gamma_{12} a_{22}$$

$$w_{21} = -\gamma_{21} a_{11} + \gamma_{22} a_{21} \qquad w_{22} = -\gamma_{21} a_{12} + \gamma_{22} a_{22}$$

(it will be confirmed presently that $w_{12} = w_{21}$). To evaluate the a_{ji}, differentiate with respect to p_i the equations (77') which are identities in the a_j:

$$\partial V_1'/\partial p_1 = 0 = V_1'' \cdot a_{11} + \gamma_{11} \quad \partial V_1'/\partial p_2 = 0 = V_1'' a_{12} - \gamma_{21}$$

$$\partial V_2'/\partial p_1 = 0 = V_2'' \cdot a_{21} - \gamma_{12} \quad \partial V_2'/\partial p_2 = 0 = V_2'' a_{22} - \gamma_{22};$$

solve for the a_{ji}, writing for brevity:

$$V_j'' \equiv 1/k_j < 0, \ j = 1, 2 \ [\text{by } (77'')];$$

then:

$$a_{jj} = -k_j \gamma_{jj} ; \quad a_{ji} = k_j \gamma_{ij}, \quad i \neq j ;$$

$$w_{11} = -\gamma_{11}^2 k_1 - \gamma_{12}^2 k_1 \quad w_{22} = -\gamma_{21}^2 k_1 - \gamma_{22}^2 k_2 > 0$$

$$w_{12} = \gamma_{11} \gamma_{21} k_1 + \gamma_{12} \gamma_{22} k_2 = w_{21}$$

$$w_{11} w_{22} - w_{12}^2 = k_1 k_2 (\gamma_{11} \gamma_{22} - \gamma_{12} \gamma_{21})^2 > 0,$$

thus establishing condition (79), and completing the proof.

References

Anderson, N.G., 1969, Computer interfaced fast analyzers. *Science* 166, 317-324.

Arrow, K.J. and A.C. Enthoven, 1961, Quasi-concave programming. *Econometrica*, 779-800.

Ash, R., 1965, *Information theory*. New York, Wiley.

Bellman, R., 1961, *Adaptive control processes: a guided tour*. Princeton, N.J., Princeton University Press.

Blackwell, D., 1953, Equivalent comparisons of experiments. *Annals of Mathematical Statistics* 24, 265-272.

Blackwell, D. and A. Girshick, 1954, *Theory of games and statistical decisions*. New York, Wiley.

Breiman, L., 1970, Discrete signaling and coding systems. In: *Conceptual bases of communication*, edited by E. Beckenbach. New York, Wiley.

Carnap, R., 1950, *Logical foundations of probability*. Chicago, University of Chicago Press.

Carnap, R., 1962, The aim of inductive logic. In: *Logic, Methodology, and Philosophy of science*, edited by P. Suppes and A. Tarski. Stanford, Calif., Stanford University Press.

Carnap, R., 1966, Probability and content measure. In: *Mind, matter and method· essays in philosophy and science in honor of M. Feigl*, edited by P. Feyerabend and G. Maxwell. Minneapolis, Minn., University of Minnesota Press.

Carnap, R. and Y. Bar-Hillel, 1952, An outline of a theory of semantic information. Res. Lab. Electronics, Cambridge, Mass., M.I.T. Techn. Rept. 247, 1952. Reprinted in Y. Bar-Hillel, *Language and information*. New York, Addison-Wesley, 1964.

Chernoff, H., 1968, Optimal stochastic control. In: *Mathematics of the decision sciences, Part 2*, edited by G. Dantzig and A.F. Veinott. American Mathematical Society, 149-172.

Cramér, H., 1946, *Mathematical methods of statistics*. Princeton, N.J., Princeton University Press.

DeGroot, M.H., 1962, Uncertainty, information and sequential experiments. *Annals of Mathematical Statistics* 602-605.

DeGroot, M.H., 1970, *Optimal statistical decisions*. New York, McGraw-Hill.

English, J.M. (editor), 1968, *Cost effectiveness: economic evaluation of engineering systems*. New York, Wiley.

Ferguson, Th.S., 1967, *Mathematical statistics. A decision theoretic approach*. New York, Academic Press.

Good, I.J., 1950, *Probability and the weighing of evidence*. New York, Hafner.

Good, I.J., 1960, Weight of evidence, corroboration, explanatory power, information, and the utility of experiments. *Journal of the Royal Statistical Society*, Series B, 319-331.

Good, I.J. and G.H. Toulmin, 1968, Coding theorems and weight of evidence, *J. Inst. Math. Applics*. 94-105.

Hirshleifer, J., 1967, Notes on the private and social value of information. Working Paper No. 114, Western Management Science Institute, University of California, Los Angeles, Calif.

Howard, R.A., 1966, Information value theory. *IEEE Transactions in Systems Science and Cybernetics*. SSC-2, No. 1. 22-33.

Hurwicz, L., 1960, Optimalty and information efficiency in resource allocation processes. In: *Mathematical methods in the social sciences*, edited by K. Arrow et al. Stanford, Calif., Stanford University Press, 27-46.

Jellinek, F., 1968, *Probabilistic information theory*. New York, McGraw-Hill.

Karlin, S., 1959, *Mathematical methods and theory in games, programming, and economics*. New York, Addison-Wesley.

Koopmans, T.C., 1960, Stationary ordinal utility and impatience. *Econometrica* 287-309.

Lancaster, J., 1966, Change and innovation in the technology of consumption. *American Economic Review*.

LaValle, J., 1968, On cash equivalents and information evaluation in decisions under uncertainty. *Journal of American Statistical Association*.

Lehmann, E., 1959, *Testing statistical hypotheses*. New York, Wiley.

Marschak, J., 1954, Towards an economic theory of information and organization. In: *Decision Processes*, edited by R.M. Thrall et al. New York, Wiley, 187-220.

Marschak, J., 1960, Remarks on the economics of information. *Contributions to Scientific Management*. Wesretn Data Processing Center, University of California, Los Angeles, Calif., 79-98.

Marschak, J., 1963, Adaptive programming. *Management Science* 517-526.

Marschak, J., 1964, Problems in information economics. In: *Management Controls: New Directions in Basic Research*, edited by C.P. Bonini et al. New York, McGraw-Hill, 38-74.

Marschak, J., 1968a, Economics of inquiring, communicating, deciding. *American Economic Review* 58, No. 2, 1-18.

Marschak, J., 1968b, Decision-making: Economic aspects. In: *Induction, Growth and Trade*, ed. M. Scott and W. Ellis, *International Encyclopedia of Social Sciences*, Vol. 4, 42-55.

Marschak, J., 1970, The economic man's inductive logic. In: *Volume in Honor of Sir Roy Harrod*, Clarendon Press, Oxford.

Marschak, J. and K. Miyasawa, 1968, Economic comparability of information systems. *International Economic Review* 137-174.

Marschak, J. and R. Radner, 1971, *Economic theory of teams*. Cowles Foundation Monograph 22. New Haven, Conn., Yale University Press.

Miller, G.A., 1967, *The psychology of communication*. New York, Basic Books.

Miller, G.A. and N. Chomsky, 1963, Finitary models of language users. In: *Handbook of Mathematical Psychology*, Vol. II. New York, Wiley, 419-492.

Miyasawa, K., 1968, Information structures in stochastic programming problems. *Management Science* 275-291.

Pham-Huu-Tri, H.M., 1968, Processing and transmitting information, given a payoff function. Working Paper No. 143, Western Management Science Institute, University of California, Los Angeles, Calif. (Ph.D. dissertation).

Radner, R., 1967, Equilibre des marchés à terme et au comptant en cas d'incertitude. *Cahiers d'Econometrie* 9, 30-47.

Radner, R., 1968, Competitive equilibrium under uncertainty. *Econometrica* 36, No 1, 31-58.

Raiffa, H., 1968, *Decision analysis*. New York, Addison-Wesley.

Rényi, A., 1966, Statistics based on information theory. Presented at the European Meeting of Statisticians.

Samuelson, P., 1948, *Foundations of economic analysis*. Cambridge, Mass., Harvard University Press.

Savage, L.J., 1954. *The foundations of statistics*. New York, Wiley.

Savage, L.J., 1962, Bayesian statistics. In: *Recent Developments in Information and Decision Processes*, edited by R. F. Machol and P. Gray. New York-London, Macmillan.

Shannon, C.E., 1948, The mathematical theory of communication. *Bell System Technical Journal* (two papers, reproduced in the book of same title, by Shannon and Weaver, University of Illinois Press, 1949).

Shannon, C.E., 1960, Coding theorems for a discrete source with a fidelity criterion. In: *Information and Decision Processes*, edited by R. E. Machol. New York, McGraw-Hill, pp. 93-126.

Stigler, G., 1961, The economics of information. *Journal of Political Economy*, June.

Stigler, G., 1962, Information in the labor market. *Journal of Political Economy*, October (Supplement).

Theil, H., 1967, *Economics and information theory*. New York, Rand McNally.

Winter, S.G., 1966, Binary choice and the supply of memory. *Working Papers in Mathematical Economics and Econometrics* 97. Berkeley, Calif.

Wolfowitz, J., 1961, *Coding theorems of information theory*. Springer Verlag, Berlin.

COMMENTS BY DAVID W. PETERSON
Northwestern University

The following three general comments are of two types: the first two comments emphasize points which Professor Marschak has raised, while the third pertains to applications and developments to which his work appears to lead.

First, the present work, like many previous works bearing titles including the word "information", deals with certain aspects of information and its use without attempting to define it rigorously. Though this in no way detracts from the purpose of the paper (... "[to] study the rational choice-making of an individual from among available information systems..."), it seems worthwhile noting that the present effort is one more contribution to a general subject area which is as yet unfettered by a general theory. Thus Professor Marschak's tendency to use the term "symbol processing" to describe the object of his study is well-considered: his systems, like

Shannon's, involve symbols and their manipulation within sharply defined domains, and do not involve symbol meanings or syntax problems that arise in the general study of information.

Second, Professor Marschak correctly points out that the entropy function is just not capable of capturing all of the relevant aspects of information, or even of symbol processing. For some reason, there has been a tendency to regard the entropy function as being somehow synonymous with information, and also somehow (simultaneously) synonymous with the entropy to which the Second Law of Thermodynamics pertains. It appears more reasonable to consider the entropy function as a function defined on the set of discrete probability functions, which has properties relevant both to thermodynamics and to symbol processing. The thermodynamic entropy of a region in space is expressible (to within an additive constant) as a function of the heat and temperature distribution throughout the region. If a discrete probability function is chosen in a particular (deterministic) way, it happens that the entropy function applied to this probability function takes a value corresponding to the thermodynamic entropy of the region. In the area of symbol processing, the entropy function is useful as a measure of uncertainty associated with the anticipated occurrence of one of several possible events, very much as variance is used to describe the uncertainty associated with the anticipated valuation of a random variable. It happens that when used in the above context, the entropy function can be identified with the average volume required to store a uniquely decodeable representation of the event which most recently occurred. Viewed with this perspective, the entropy function appears to be a useful function in at least two areas, but there is no reason to suppose that it captures all relevant aspects of either area, or that it implies a particularly close relationship between the two areas.

Finally, we note that of the various theories and partial theories dealing with information, few if any have yet proved relevant to the man in the firm faced with problems of choosing a data processing facility or a management information system. Though some of the fault may be attributable to communication imperfections among theorists and practitioners, much of the disuse of the available work is due simply to their lack of relevance. What Professor Marschak has contributed in this present work, and the works leading to it, is a new, broad framework for analyzing symbol processing systems. The scope of this undertaking is sufficiently grand that it may represent, at last, the genesis of a useful theory of symbol processing.

Frontiers of Quantitative Economics, ed. M.D. Intriligator. © *North-Holland Publishing Company.*

CHAPTER 3

RECENT RESULTS IN THE THEORY OF VOTING*

CHARLES R. PLOTT

Purdue University

The theory of voting and public choice has been rapidly developing along several different lines. The purpose of this paper is to provide a review and synthesis of the recent results. "Recent" is taken to mean roughly since 1963. Excellent discussions of the developments prior to 1964 can be found in Arrow (1963), Rothenberg (1961), and Vickery (1960).

The materials are partitioned into three major sections. The first section pertains to the axiomatic formulation of the social choice problem. The second section deals exclusively with majority rule and the third section contains an examination of what could loosely be called the theory of political processes. The final section contains a few closing remarks.

0. Axiomatic formulation of the social choice problem

0.0. *Constitutions*

Roughly speaking a constitution is a social choice function together with the situations in which choice is to be exercised. From certain sets of alternatives, called agenda, it provides a choice—given the preferences of individuals. The choice can be considered as the "best" or "socially preferred" alternatives from those available but there is no need to restrict

* This research was supported, in part, by a Ford Foundation Faculty Research Grant and by a Krannert Research Grant. The author benefited from many stimulating conversations with M.D. Intriligator and R. Wilson while a visitor at Serra House, Stanford University. Responsibilities for the content remain with the author.

the interpretation so narrowly. The choice could also be considered as the outcomes of a game or the equilibriums of a decision process.

Before proceeding some notation is necessary. The empty set is $\emptyset$. If B and C are sets, then $B - C$ denotes set difference. A binary relation, R, over some set B is called "total" in case $(\forall xy)_{\substack{x\,y\in B \\ x\neq y}}[xRy \text{ or } yRx]$, "reflexive" in case $(\forall x)_{x\in B}[xRx]$ and "transitive" in case $(\forall xyz)_{x\,y\,z\in B}[xRy \ \& \ yRz \Rightarrow xRz]$. A total, reflexive, transitive binary relation is called a "weak order". S = the set of all social alternatives. $V = (v_1 \dots v_m)$ is a family of subsets of S. V will be termed the *admissible agenda*. $\mathfrak{R}$ = the set of weak orders over S. $\prod^{n} \mathfrak{R}$ = the n-fold cartesian product of $\mathfrak{R}$. This set is the set of *possible societies*. A *society d* is an element of this set, $d = (R_1 \dots R_n) \in \prod^{n} \mathfrak{R}$. R_i is the *preference relation* for the ith individual and R_{id} is the preference of i in society d. $\mathscr{D} \subset \prod^{n} \mathfrak{R}$ is the set of *admissible societies*. A *choice function* $C(v_i, d)$ is a non-empty subset of v_i defined for all elements of V and for all d in $\mathscr{D}$. A 4-tuple $\langle V, S, \mathscr{D}, C(v, d) \rangle$ is called a *constitution*.[1]

Several possible restrictions on constitutions are listed on Table 1. These restrictions, which are by no means exhaustive, have been partitioned into two main categories — properties of the domain and properties of choice. Restrictions on the domain of choice have received little attention other than to define the domain over which some *particular* choice function "works". Properties of the admissible agenda have been dictated by mathematical and logical conveniences as opposed to restrictions imposed by an interpretation. However, A1 can claim a particular distinction. If we are interested only in choosing from S, the set of all alternatives, then the only relevant choice is from S. The choice from subsets of S is irrelevant to this problem.

The restrictions on admissible societies listed on the table have been those found useful in finding the domain over which majority rule is not cyclic. The exception is of course B1, which requires all conceivable societies be admissible.

Properties of choice are classified as properties of $C(v, d)$ when v is fixed and d varies (aggregation properties) and those in which v varies while d is fixed (rationality properties).

---

[1] The term is Arrow's (1967). The formal statement is similar to what Richter (1966, 1967) refers to as a "choice" and Hansson (1968) calls a "choice structure".

Table 1

I. *Properties of domain*

(i) Properties of $V = \{v_1 \ldots v_m\}$
   A1. $V = \{S\}$
   A2. $\bigcup\limits_{v \in V} v = S$
   A3. $V = \{$all two element subsets of $S\}$
   A4. $V = \{$all two element subsets and S itself$\}$
   A5. $V = \{$all finite subsets of $S\}$

(ii) Properties of $\mathscr{D}$
   B1. $\mathscr{D} = \overset{n}{\prod} \mathfrak{N}$
   B2. value restriction: for "concerned"* individuals (i)
   $$\{(\forall i)[xP_i y \vee xP_i z]\} \vee \{(\forall i)[yP_i x \vee zP_i x]\} \vee \{(\forall i)[xP_i y \,\&\, xP_i z]\} \vee$$
   $$\{(\forall i)[yP_i x \,\&\, zP_i x]\}$$
   B.3 extremal restriction
   $$[(\exists i): xP_i y \,\&\, yP_i z] \Rightarrow (\forall_{j\; j\neq i})[zP_j x \Rightarrow zP_j y \,\&\, yP_j x]$$
   B4. limited agreement $(\forall xyz)\ (\exists \alpha\beta)\ \alpha\beta \subset \{xyz\}(\forall i)[\alpha R_i \beta]$
   B5. single peaked preferences

II. *Properties of choice*

(i) Aggregation properties, $C(v_0, d)$
   C1. weak pareto. $(\forall i)[xP_{id}y] \Rightarrow \{x \in v_0 \Rightarrow y \notin C(v_0, d)\}$
   C2. strong pareto. $\{(\forall i)[xR_{id}y] \,\&\, (\exists j)[xP_{jd}y]\} \Rightarrow x \in C(\{x, y\}, d)$
   C3. $\{(\forall i)[xP_{id}y]\} \Rightarrow \{y \in C(v_0, d) \Rightarrow [x \in v_0 \Rightarrow x \in C(v_0, d)]\}$
   C4. independence
   $$\{B \subset v_0 \,\&\, (\forall xy)_{xy\in B}\ (\forall i)[xR_{id}y \Leftrightarrow xR_{id'}y]\}$$
   $$\Rightarrow [B \cap C(v_0, d) = B \cap C(v_0, d') \text{ or one is empty}]$$
   C5. neutrality
   $(\forall xy)_{xy\in v_0}\ \forall i[xR_{id}y \Leftrightarrow f(x)\,R_{id'}, f(y)] \Rightarrow [x \in C(v_0, d) \Rightarrow f(x) \in C(v_0, d')]$,
   where $f(x)$ is a one-to-one function from v_0 onto v_0.
   C6. anonymity: let d' be a permutation of the elements in d.
   We have then $C(v_0, d) = C(v_0, d')$.
   C7. positive response.
   $(\forall i)\ (\forall xy)\{xP_{id}y \Rightarrow xP_{id'}y, xI_{id}y \Rightarrow xR_{id'}y,$ and for some k either
   $[xI_{kd}y$ and $xP_{kd'}\ y]$ or $[yP_{kd}x$ and $xR_{kd'}\ y]\}$
   $$\Rightarrow \{x \in C(\{x, y\}, d) \Rightarrow y \in C(\{x, y\}, d')\}$$
   C8. non-negative response. $\{$same antecedence as C7$\}$
   $\Rightarrow [y \notin C(\{x, y\}, d) \Rightarrow y \notin C(\{x, y\}, d)]$ and
   $$[x \in C(\{x, y\}, d) \Rightarrow x \in C(\{x, y\}, d')]$$
   C9. nondictatorship. $(\not\exists i)\ [(\forall xy)xP_{id}y \Rightarrow y \notin C(v_0, d)]$

(ii) Properties of rationality, $C(v, d_0)$
   D1. $v \subset v_0 \Rightarrow [C(v_0, d_0) \cap v \subset C(v, d_0)$ or $C(v_0, d_0) \cap v = \varnothing]$
   D2. $C(v, d_0)$ can be "rationalized" by a binary (total, reflexive) relation.
   D3. $C(v, d_0)$ can be "rationalized" by a quasi-transitive (total, reflexive) relation.
   D4. $C(v, d_0)$ can be "rationalized" by a weak order.

"Concerned" means "not indifferent".

The first three aggregation properties need little explanation. They are all variations of the Pareto principle. The fourth, C4, becomes Arrow's "independence of irrelevant alternatives" when B is restricted to $B = v_0$. This slight alteration of the Arrow axiom has an important consequence as will be indicated below. The next five are all variants of the axioms May (1952) found as necessary and sufficient conditions for simple majority rule. The last is Hansson's non-dictatorship axiom. There are dependences among these axioms, depending especially on the choice of V, but they will not be reviewed here.

The rationality properties of a constitution pertain to the behavior of the choice function over the agenda in a fixed society. *Rational choice* will simply mean the choice can be rationalized by a binary relation. That is, there exists a binary relation R (a *rationalization*) such that for every admissible agenda v, the choice, $C(v, d_0)$, is equal to the R-maximal elements of v.[2] The table lists several possible "degrees" of rationality — to use Richter's term. It is important to note that the relationship between these axioms varies with the choice of V. The first property D1 is the weakest [Chernoff (1954), Arrow (1959)]. It is implied by all of the others. All choice functions which have this property cannot, in general, be rationalized.[3] However, care should be exercised in interpreting these conditions since restrictions on V can force rationality.[4]

The second type of rationality D2 simply requires that choices be consistent with some binary (total, reflexive) relation. For finite S and sufficiently large V such as A5, this condition assures the "strong preference", P, of the rationalization will not be cyclic.[5] That is, with such admissible agenda $xPy \& yPz \& zPx$, cannot occur.

Sen (1969) introduced D3. This condition requires the induced strong preference of the rationalization to be transitive, $[xPy \& yPz] \Rightarrow xPz$. As a separate condition we could have required that the induced indifference relation be transitive.[6] Sen (1969) has shown that for finite S, quasi-transitivity together with transitive indifference implies that the rational-

---

[2] Any binary relation R such that $(\forall v)_{v \in V}[C(v, d_0) = \{x : x \in v \ \& \ (\forall y)_{y \in v} \ xRy\}]$ is called a "rationalization" of $C(v, d_0)$. See Hansson (1968), Richter (1966, 1967).

[3] Consider $C(xy) = \{xy\}$, $C(yz) = \{yz\}$, $C(xz) = \{xz\}$, $C(xyz) = x$.

[4] For example $C(v, d)$ satisfies D1-D4 in case A1 is assumed. If A3 is assumed, then $C(v, d)$ satisfies D2.

[5] Let R be a (total, reflexive) relationalization. Write xPy in case $\sim yRx$.

[6] If R is a rationalization write xIy in case $xRy \ \& \ yRx$. Transitive indifference requires $xIy \ \& \ yIz \Rightarrow xIz$.

ization R if complete and reflexive, is then transitive (that is, R is a weak order).

We are now at the "most rational" of rationality properties, D4. This axiom requires the existence of at least one weak order rationalization. Arrow required, in his statement of the problem, not only D4 but also the uniqueness of the rationalization. This requirement has been subject to recent debate.

0.1. *Constitutions with a problem*

The following theorems reveal some of the relationships among the axioms listed on table 1. Assume S is a finite[7] set with three or more elements. Arrow [General Possibility Theorem]:

$$\{\text{A5, B1, C1, C4, C9, D4}\} \text{ are inconsistent.} \tag{1}$$

Hansson (1969):

$$\{\text{A5, B1, C4, C5, C6, D4}\} \Rightarrow (\forall v)_{v \in V} (\forall d)_{d \in \mathcal{D}} C(v, d) = v. \tag{2}$$

These results have been criticized from several points of view. The most recent criticisms have been aimed at the requirements of "social rationality". Axiom D4 stipulates the existence of a weak order rationalization while from A5 it follows that any total, reflexive, rationalization is unique.

Two lines of argument appear depending upon the interpretation of the model. The first (Arrow 1950, p. 329; 1963, p. 2) is that Arrow has postulated existence of an entity termed "the social preference relation". By virtue of being a "preference relation" it should have the same properties as other "preference relations" in the system (those of individuals) — namely, being a binary relation with the properties of a weak order. The theorem simply establishes the impossibility of certain relationships between the "social preference" and the individuals' preferences.

Criticisms of the work which accept this interpretation fall in two classes. The first line of criticism has simply been to question the existence of an entity called "social preferences" (Buchanan 1954; Buchanan and Tullock 1962). The second, within limits, accepts the idea of "social preference" but would reject the properties required by Arrow. Schick (1969) apparently accepts

---

[7] This restriction can be dropped with suitable restrictions on V. The statements of the theorems in the cited papers do not depend upon the finiteness of S. Slightly different theorems are reported here for purposes of exposition and comparison.

the existence of "social preference" as a total binary relation but denies the transitivity of indifference as a property. For example, if the set of "social states" is interpreted as the set of "acts" available in a game against nature, there is no compelling reason (in the absence of knowledge of nature's choice) to assume that individuals, much less society, have weak orders over the "social states". Others (Pattanaik 1968a; Sen 1970) argue that the only requirement on the social preference relation should be the existence of R-maximal elements.[8] Only the maximal elements are of interest, it is argued, since these are all one needs for policy purposes.

In answer to criticisms of this nature Arrow appeals to a different interpretation (the second) of his model. His claim is that the non-existence of *decision processes* with certain attributes has been established.

> I would consider that it is indeed a social decision process with which I am concerned and not, strictly speaking, a welfare judgement by any individual. That said, however, I am bound to add that in my view a social decision process serves as a proper explication for the intuitive idea of social welfare. ... But where Bergson seeks to locate social values in welfare judgements by individuals, I prefer to locate them in the actions taken by society through its rules for making social decisions. (1963, p. 106).

In support of the strong rationality requirements he argues:

> Those familiar with the integrability controversy in the field of consumer's demand theory will observe that the basic problem is the same: the independence of the final choice from the path to it. Transitivity will insure this independence; from any environment, there will be a chosen alternative, and, in the absence of a deadlock, no place for the historically given alternative to be chosen by default. (1963, p. 120).

This argument appears to be in support of a requirement that the choice mechanism be one for which the equilibriums exist and have a property of stability similar, perhaps, to the relationship between the weak axiom of revealed preference, aggregate excess demand functions, and the stability and uniqueness of equilibrium.[9] The class of processes, which are being discussed are binary in the sense that binary choices exist and extend themselves to choice over larger sets, i.e.

$$C(v, d) = \{x : x \in v \,\&\, (\forall y)_{y \in v} \, x \in C(\{xy\}, d)\}$$

if this set is nonempty.

This property, taken with the transitivity of binary choice implies D4.[10]

---

[8] If R is a binary relation over S the R-maximal elements are $\{x : x \in S \,\&\, (\forall y)_{y \in S} \, xRy\}$.

[9] See Arrow and Hurwicz (1958), Theorem 2.

[10] See Fishburn (1970c). Transitivity of binary choice means
$\{x \in C(\{x, y\}, d) \,\&\, y \in C(\{y, z\}, d)\} \Rightarrow x \in C(\{x, z\}, d)$

Such a process will always attain an element of $C(S, d)$ as an *equilibrium* even though only binary choices are made — regardless of the sequence of such binary choices. The importance of this result would depend then, on the importance one attaches to the class of such binary group decision processes and this concept of equilibrium.

The work of Hansson is relevant particularly in view of the discussion of social rationality.

Hansson (1970):

$\{A1, B1, C1, C4, C9\}$ are inconsistent. (3)

$\{A1, B1, C4, C5, C6\} \Rightarrow (\forall d)_{de\,\mathcal{D}}\, C(S, d) = S.$ (4)

$\{A1, B1, C3, C4, C9\} \Rightarrow (\forall d)_{de\,\mathcal{D}}\, C(S, d) = S.$ (5)

The requirement that choice only be expressed for S means D4 is satisfied but there is no requirement about the uniqueness of the representation stemming from the domain of choice. However, as was mentioned above the independence axiom C4 is stronger than Arrow's. The following will indicate the rationality implications of this independence axiom.

Definition: $(\forall v)_{v \subset S}\, (\forall d)_{de\,\mathcal{D}}\, f(v, d) \equiv C(S, d_v),$

where d_v is a vector of preferences such that

(i) $xy \in v \Rightarrow (\forall i) x R_{id} y \Leftrightarrow x R_{id_v} y$

(ii) $xy \in S - v \Rightarrow (\forall i) x I_{id_v} y$

(iii) $x \in s,\ y \in s - v \Rightarrow (\forall i) x P_{id_v} y.$

Lemma: If $C(S, d)$ satisfies A1, C1, and C4, then $f(v, d)$ can be rationalized by a weak order and the rationalization is unique.

Proof: By C1 and the properties of d_v,

$(\forall v)_{v \subset S}(\forall d)_{de\,\mathcal{D}}[f(v, d) = v \cap C(S, d_v) \neq \emptyset].$

Suppose $v_1 \subset v_2 \subset S$. Note for any d, d_{v_1} and d_{v_2} "agree" over v_1 so by C4 $\{v_1 \cap C(S, dv_2) = v_1 \cap C(S, dv_1)$ or one is empty$\}$ substituting from line 1 $\{v_1 \cap f(v_2, d) = f(v_1, d)$ or the empty set$\}$. The latter statement is equivalent to the weak axiom of revealed preference. Since $f(\cdot, d)$ satisfies the weak axiom and S is finite we know from Arrow (1959, Theorem 3) there exists a unique, weak order rationalization of $f(\cdot, d)$.

Theorem (3) can be proved by establishing the statement; if $C(\cdot, \cdot)$ satisfies the conditions of (3) then the induced $f(\cdot, \cdot)$ satisfies the conditions of statement (1). Since Arrow has shown no constitution can satisfy the conditions of (1) the hypothesis of this statement cannot be satisfied.

For finite S Arrow's independence of irrelevant alternative axiom, i.e., C4 with B restricted to $B = v_0$, is equivalent to C4 in the presence of A5 and D4.[11] It has been the most controversial of all the axioms. Taken alone, however, the axiom is considerably more innocent than has been claimed. As a question of "ethics" the axiom simply says "best" depends upon preferences over candidates for "best" and not on unavailable alternatives. As a property of decision processes there are many processes which satisfy the axiom.[12] In fact the example Arrow gives as a process which does not satisfy the axiom actually satisfies it.[13] The example is worth considering in detail. Let the (finite) set of all alternatives be S. Each individual attaches a number to each element of v as follows. The least preferred elements of v get assigned 1, the next least 2, etc. Each alternative in v is given the sum of individual weights and $C(v, d)$ is the set of alternatives in v with the greatest sum. Note these numbers and thus $C(v, d)$, by construction, are independent of the preferences for alternatives in $S - v$.[14]

Part of the controversy concerning the independence of irrelevant alternatives axiom arose in discussions about the relationship between the Arrow construction and the idea of a "social welfare function". I interpret Samuelson (1967) as saying the Bergson-Samuelson social welfare function is any constitution which satisfies A5, $\mathscr{D} = d_0$, C_2, D_4. It is interesting to note the controversial axiom is satisfied vacuously.

---

[11] Note Arrow's axiom differs from Blau's binary choice axiom. See J. Blau, The existence of social welfare functions. *Econometrica*, April 1957.

[12] Consider processes which can be represented by a n-person, non-cooperative game. Let the outcomes be indexed by elements of $\prod_{i=1}^{n} S_i$, where S_i is the strategy set of i and assume $v \in V$ implies the projection of v on S_i $i = 1 \ldots n$, is a convex, compact set. So, for all $v \in V$ there is a game Γ_v. The constitution, where $C(v, d)$ is the Nash equilibriums of Γ_v, satisfies Arrow's independence of irrelevant alternatives. The competitive mechanism, to which Arrow refers (1963, p. 110) can be considered a special case of this example.

[13] The nature of the error is obliquely anticipated in Rothenberg (1961, pp. 131-32). While the process does not violate Arrow's independence of irrelevant alternatives, an example in R. Musgrave, *The theory of public finance* (p. 130) can be used to show, for some d, all of the rationality axioms are violated.

[14] A closely related process does violate the independence of irrelevant alternatives axiom. Suppose each individual numbers all elements of S according to their preference "level". $C(v, d)$ then is the numbers of v with the greatest sum. If preferences change for elements of $S-v$ the numbers attached to elements of v, and hence $C(v, d)$, will change.

0.2. *Aggregating over numbers*

There are many variables with which to tinker in order to get around the impossibility result. It is often argued that some notion of "intensity" of preference should be involved in group decision processes. The use of numbers would allow statements to be made about "intensity" of feeling between x and y in terms of some third commodity for example. The very construction of the constitution does not allow the use of numbers in the aggregation process (especially C4).

If numbers are admitted as data and we are given real valued functions to work with, several nice functions are available.[15] Functions like $\prod^n U^i(x)^K$ (see De Meyer and Plott 1970b; Nash 1950) or its additive version $\sum^n \alpha^i U^i(x)$ have almost any property[16] that has ever been demanded of an aggregation procedure, e.g., neutrality, anonymity, nondictatorship, Pareto optimality, rationality, independence (modified), defined for all preferences, etc. However, they are all subject to the same problem — interpretation of the numbers. Several interpretations have been suggested — probabilities (Intriligator 1968), Neumann-Morgenstern utilities (Hildreth 1953), discretion levels (Goodman and Markowitz 1952), cardinal utility (Nordin 1969), marginal rate of substitution (Inada 1964a). All are subject to the same ethical criticism — a man sufficiently "intense" on being greedy will get everything (Arrow 1963, p. 118).

1. Majority rule

Murakami's (1966) conceptualization of a *representative system* is essentially a set of "nested" simple majority voting operations. His definition is somewhat too complicated to cover completely here. It conveys, roughly, the idea of a hierarchy of councils. Since it is a binary process, the domain of choice is restricted to two element sets, the explanation will proceed in terms of an arbitrary two element set.

---

[15] Of course to stay within the framework above several axioms must be modified.

[16] Fishburn (1969) has provided necessary and sufficient conditions on an $n+1$-tuple $(R_1 \ldots R_n R_{n+1})$ of weak orders over a finite set S, for the existence of real valued functions $f_i(x)$ $i=1 \ldots n+1$ for which $f_i(x) \geq f_i(y) \Leftrightarrow xR_i y$ $i=1 \ldots n+1$ and $f_{n+1}(x) \equiv \sum_{i=1}^{n} f_i(x)$.

A majority voting operation is a function[17] $D = ((D_1 \ldots D_m))$ the arguments of which take values in the set $\{1, 0, -1\}$ and D takes values 1, 0, -1 as $\sum_{i=1}^{m} D_i > 0$, $= 0$, < 0, respectively. The arguments can represent another voting operation or the preferences of some individual. If D_j represents the preferences of individual k then D_j takes values 1, 0, -1 as $xP_k y$, $xI_k y$, $yP_k x$.

A representative system is a constitution satisfying A3, C4, C9 and $C(., .)$ is the choice function satisfying:

(i) For each pair xy, there exists a majority voting operation $((\ldots))$ such that

$$(\forall d)_{d \in \mathscr{D}} C(\{xy\}, d) = \{x\}, \{xy\}, \{z\} \text{ as } ((\ldots)) \text{ is } > 0, = 0, < 0.$$

(ii) The argument of any majority voting operation involved in $((\ldots))$ either represent the preferences of some individual in the society or another majority voting operation.

In a five person society consider as an example $((((D_1, D_1, D_2)), D_3, ((D_2, D_4, D_5))))$. The majority voting operation has three arguments. The first argument is a "committee" or "representative" controlled by individual 1. The second argument is simply individual 3's direct vote. The final argument is the "committee" or "representative" $((D_2, D_4, D_5))$. Note individual 2 has votes in both the first and third arguments. However his vote in the first "committee" can only be effective when $D_1 = 0$.

The following results, perhaps, provide more by way of explanation than the rather terse definition.

Theorem: Murakami (1966)

A constitution is a *representative* system only if it satisfied $\{A3, C4, C5, C8, C9\}$.

Theorem: Fishburn (1970b), Murakami (1968)

$\{A3, C4, C5, C7, C9\} \Rightarrow$ representative system.

In addition to these results Fishburn (1970b) has now supplied a set of necessary and sufficient conditions for a representative system.

It is of interest to compare these results with the classic result of May (1952) for simple majority rule. Notice, since C6 implies C9, simple majority decision is, as expected, a representative system.

---

[17] The notation $D = ((\ldots))$ rather than $D = F(\ldots)$ is used by Murakami for exposition convenience.

Theorem: A constitution is simple majority rule $\Leftrightarrow$ {A3, C4, C5, C6, C7}.

Considerable research has been expended on investigating the properties of simple majority rule. Perhaps because it is an esthetically pleasing function. One of the major subjects of inquiry has been the properties of $\mathscr{D}$ which would allow an expansion of V to A5 and also allow the addition of a rationality postulate.

This type of investigation introduces the possibility of confining the axioms to subsets of the domain of the constitution. We may want to specify different "ethics" for different societies.

In addition to a wealth of additional findings in Inada (1969) and Sen and Pattanaik (1969), the following fundamental results are stated.

Let $C^m(v, d)$ be a choice function which satisfies A3, C4, C5, C6 and C7 (it is the binary process of majority rule). Let $\Omega \subset \mathfrak{N}$ be a set of weak orders for which every triple $(x, y, z) \subset S$ satisfies B2, B3 or B4. Let $\mathfrak{S} = \{\Omega_1 \ldots \Omega_m\}$ be the family of all such sets.

In a sense conditions B2, B3 and B4 provide necessary and sufficient conditions over the domain of $C^m(v, d)$ for the choice to be rationalized. Recall, this is sufficient (together with A5) for cyclical majorities to be eliminated.

Theorem

$$(\forall B)_{B \subset \mathfrak{N}}[(\exists \Omega)_{\Omega \in \mathfrak{S}} : B \subset \Omega] \Rightarrow [(\forall d)_{d \in \overset{n}{\Pi} B} C^m(v, d) \text{ satisfies } A5 \text{ and } D2].$$

Furthermore

$$(\forall B)_{B \subset \mathfrak{N}}\{[(\not\exists \Omega)_{\Omega \in \mathfrak{S}} : B \subset \Omega] \Rightarrow [(\exists d_0)_{d_0 \in \overset{n}{\Pi} B} : C^m(v, d_0) \text{ does not satisfy}$$
$$A5 \text{ and } D2]\}.$$

In these societies there will always be a stable majority winner. For any other "configuration" of preferences there is always the "possibility" of instability.

The following results cover the case where majority rule is required to yield a weak order. Let $\Omega' \subset \mathfrak{N}$ be a set of weak orders which satisfy B3 and let $\mathfrak{S}' = \{\Omega'_1 \ldots \Omega'_m\}$ be the family of all such sets.

Theorem

$$(\forall B)_{B \subset \mathfrak{N}}[(\exists \Omega')_{\Omega' \in \mathfrak{S}'} : B \subset \Omega'] \Rightarrow [(\forall d)_{d \in \overset{n}{\Pi} B} C^m(v, d) \text{ satisfies } A5 \text{ and } D4].$$

Furthermore,

$$(\forall B)_{B \subset \mathfrak{R}}\{[(\nexists \Omega')_{\Omega' \in \mathfrak{S}'} : B \subset \Omega'] \Rightarrow [(\exists d_0)_{d_0 \in \overset{n}{\Pi} B} : C^m(v, d_0) \text{ does not satisfy}$$

$$A5 \text{ and } D4]\}.$$

The probability studies provide some insight into how restrictive these axioms might be. Examined is the case where the number of people is odd, preferences are strong orders (no indifferences), and people are multinomially distributed (with equal weights) over preferences. On table 2, n is the number of people, r is the number of alternatives, $Q(n, r)$ is the probability one issue wins by a majority over all others and $P(n, r)$ is the probability of no cycle at all. As can be seen the probabilities are very sensitive to the number of alternatives.[18]

Table 2*

r	3		4		5		15		∞	
n	Q	P	Q	P	Q	P	Q	P	Q	P
3	0.944	0.944	0.889	0.830	0.840		0.583		0	0
5	0.931	0.931	0.861	0.790					0	0
15	0.918	0.918							0	0
∞	0.915	0.915								

     * See DeMeyer and Plott (1970a), Garman and Kamien (1968), Niemi and Weisberg (1968).

If the commodity space is expanded to euclidian n-space Kramer (1969) has shown, in the case of differentiable, quasi-concave preferences the Inada-Sen-Pattanaik conditions are extremely restrictive.

---

[18] An interesting variation of this problem is found in Niemi (1969). He wants to know, in the case of three alternatives, the conditional probabilities that a cycle occur given a certain percentage of the population satisfied B5. The interpretation is thus a given percentage "agree on a norm" and thus a measure of the importance of "concensus" is obtained. This result is closely associated with that in Garman and Kamien (1968), where it is shown for some distributions over preferences the $\lim_{n \to \infty} Q'(n, 3) = 0$.

The foregoing discussion can be interpreted as an examination of the relationship between a system of ballots and social decision. "A system of ballots" is perhaps a less ambiguous interpretation than "a system of preferences" since the latter leaves open the problem of connecting preferences with choice over instruments of choice. The conditions of Inada, Sen and Pattanaik can then be viewed as the configurations of ballots for which a binary voting process will yield an "equilibrium" (an alternative which will beat any other by a majority).

In the case of a continuum of alternatives, where individual ballots (preferences) have quasi-concave, differentiable representations and no two individuals have the same point of satiation, Plott (1967a) has found a set of necessary and sufficient conditions for an alternative to be a "local equilibrium". The conditions are so strong they would appear to be satisfied in only exceptionally rare circumstances.[19] Expanding the problem to a case of a continuum of people Arrow (1969) has supplied a sufficient condition on preferences for the existence of a point which can receive a majority over all others.

2. Theory of political processes

The work on "equilibrium" and dominant points has proceeded without regard to the institutional setting of the decision process. By this I mean the method by which alternatives are considered for choice and the relationship between preferences and the actual ballots recorded.

One of the major contentions in the early work of Downs (1956) was that the politicians of two party systems, in their attempts to gain votes, would be forced to offer the platform desired by the median voter. The works of Davis and Hinich (1966, 1967, 1968, 1970) are in essence, attempts at modeling the possible "gravitation to the center"[20] in two party systems. No attempt will be made here to cover their many and varied results. Only a brief outline of the structure of their models will be presented.

[19] If a point is an equilibrium, then it is a maximum for at least one person. If this is true for only one person, then the point is an equilibrium if and only if the remaining people can be partitioned into pairs so that in each pair the normals (to the preference function) are parallel and in opposite directions.

[20] Simpson (1969) has recently isolated a set of points which has a special claim for dominance or "equilibriums". His min max set is the set of points $\hat{x}$ which minimize the maximum sized coalition that can be formed to move away from $\hat{x}$.

Individual preference relations R_i over E_n^+ (the positive orthant of euclidian n-space) are assumed to be represented by loss functions $L^i(x)$ of the form $L^i(x) = (x - \hat{x}^i)'\, A^i(x - \hat{x}^i)$. That is, for individual i,

$$xR_i y \Leftrightarrow [(x - \hat{x}^i)'\, A^i(x - \hat{x}^i)' < (y - \hat{x}^i)\, A^i(y - \hat{x}^i)] \equiv L^i(x) < L^i(y)$$

for some $\hat{x}^i$ and some matrix A^i (positive definite). A *society* is represented by a joint multivariate density $f(\hat{x}, A)$ with the probability of the event B, $P(B)$, interpreted as the proportion of people whose orderings can be represented by some $(\hat{x}, A) \in B$. It is assumed that $E(\hat{x} | A) = \mu$.[21] Two candidates, a and b, are assumed to offer *platforms* θ_a, $\theta_b \in E_n^+$. Candidate a wins,

written $\theta_a M \theta_b$, in case $P(\tilde{B}(\theta_a, \theta_b)) > \frac{1}{2}$, where

$$\tilde{B}(\theta_a, \theta_b) = \{(x, A) : (\theta_a - x)'\, A(\theta_a - x) < (\theta_b - x)'\, A(\theta_b - x)\}.$$

In order to establish the power of $E(x | A)$ in predicting the stands taken by politicians, they establish the following.

If the distribution of x given A is multivariate normal $N(\mu, \Sigma)$, then

$$(\forall \theta)_{\theta \in E_n^+}\, \mu M \theta.$$

Characterizing *societies* in which results of this nature hold is a major objective. However, many interesting features of the model have been and can be exploited — a political party can be characterized by a density and a multiparty political system by a convex combination of densities, platforms can be required to have "structural" similarities or differences, politicians can use statistical inference, etc.

In the Davis-Hinich model the politician has no motives other than his own desire to get elected. He has no preferences over social states. In addition people are assumed to have no reason to misrepresent their preferences — ballots represent preferences. With the assumed absence of strategic behavior models of decision processes are available for a wide class of preference orderings (Ledyard 1968; Plott 1967a; Thompson 1966). The ideas essentially involve finding the set of alternatives Pareto dominating a given point (the method of finding these points is part of the problem),

---

[21] The probability expression is the proportion of people whose preferences are within a given class of preferences. The assumption is that when we divide people into classes according to the shape of their indifference curves (defined by the matrix A) the average "most preferred point" is the same for every class. The assumption of a continuum of people in also made by Tullock (1967 a, b) and Arrow (1969).

choosing from among such points (how this is done depends on the models) and repeating the process. The motivation for such models is to be suggestive of possible institutional arrangements, which would direct the outcome of decision processes in a predictable way.

Along these lines the idea of vote markets has generated considerable interest even though little has been published. The motivation for these investigations is a feeling that a "logrolling process" will tend to exhaust "gains from exchange" much like a market exchange system.

Part of the problem of "vote markets" is the lack of a theory of why people vote[22] [Downs (1956) claims voting is irrational, given the cost of voting as opposed to the probability of affecting the election outcome]. This difficulty is compounded by the possibility of admitting strategic behavior into the analysis. Wilson (1969a) postulated a set of "reasonable" preference orders and "non-strategic" decision rules for individuals in their vote buying (or trading) activities. When he added the condition that the outcome of this process be pareto optimal he found the class of admissible individual preference orderings to be severely restricted.

When the class of decision rules is expanded to include strategic behavior the problem of logrolling and vote trading inherits many of the complexities and problems of the general theory of games. Nevertheless, some results have been forthcoming. As was mentioned above, the choice function of the constitution could well be some solution set to a game. Consequently, results here are of particular interest, especially since we are free to choose institutions in a way to influence solutions. Riker (1966) argues that the political game for the politicians (at least) is adequately represented by a n-person, zero-sum, cooperative, majority-rule game, with side payments. In addition, he argues the game has certain symmetric features which result in only minimum coalitions forming.

Wilson (1968, 1969b, 1970) has been expanding the model to cooperative, non-zero sum games without side payments. Before the decision makers is a set of bills. Each man has a vote on each bill. A social state then is the set of bills each of which passes by a majority. He notes that for some games of this form the Von Neumann-Morgenstern solutions (generalized to cooperative games without side-payments) contain only mixed strategies. Since a mixed strategy has no easy interpretation in a logrolling context, he concludes "no system of vote trading can achieve the solution".

---

[22] See Riker and Ordershook (1968).

3. Concluding remarks

Very little has been said about the nature of the "social alternatives". If alternatives have properties then, perhaps, these could be used in placing requirements on constitutions. An example given in the text pertained to the case where the alternatives were decision functions. Furthermore, a liberal might agree that each individual has a *right* to restrict social choices to certain classes of alternatives. Over *some* issues the individual should be a dictator. In this case the problem again takes the attributes of a game.[23]

Issues involved in the choice of a constitution are not completely resolved.[24] The role of the "status quo" has not been completely integrated into the analysis. Also involved is the interpretation of "non-unique" choices. Of course ideas of random choice and ideas of solutions to games may be potentially helpful here.

Finally there are whole classes of observations which may, and perhaps should, be integrated into the analysis. The information people have depends partially on the decision process. Not only tastes but ideas about states of nature influence balloting. People are willing to have others decide for them — widespread apathy may be a sign the system is functioning well. Certainly there may be the possibility of specialization, in group decision making, etc.

References

Arrow, K.J., 1950, A difficulty in the concept of social welfare. *Journal of Political Economy* 58.

Arrow, K.J., 1959, Rational choice functions and orderings. *Economica, N.S.* 26.

Arrow, K.J., 1963, *Social choice and individual values.* 2nd edition, New York, Wiley.

Arrow, K.J., 1967, Public and private values. In: *Human values and economic Policy,* edited by S. Hook. New York, University Press.

Arrow, K.J., 1968, Tullock and an existence theorem. *Public Choice* 6 (Spring).

Arrow, K.J. and L. Hurwicz, 1958, On the stability of competitive equilibrium. *Econometria* 26.

Black, D., 1969, On Arrow's impossibility theorem. *Law and Economics* 12.

Buchanan, J.M., 1954, Individual choice in voting and the market. *Journal of Political Economy* 62.

Buchanan, J.M., 1968, *The demand and supply of public goods.* Rand McNally & Co.

---

[23] Sen's discussion is a little different than what I have in mind. Simply view the problem as an *n*-person game where each individual's strategies are his "rights". In this particular instance the Nash construction does well but care must be exercised to avoid inconsistencies. See Sen (1970).

[24] See Buchanan and Tullock (1962), Buchanan (1968) and Rae (1969).

Buchanan, J.M. and Tullock, G., 1962, *The calculus of consent*. Ann Arbor, University of Michigan Press.

Chernoff, H., 1954, Rational selection of decision functions, *Econometrica* 22.

Coleman, J.S., 1966, The possibility of a social welfare function. *American Economic Review* 56.

Coleman, J.S., 1967, Social welfare function: reply. *American Economic Review* 57.

Davis, O.A. and M.J. Hinich, 1966, A mathematical model of policy formation in a democratic society. In: *Mathematical Applications in Political Science*, II, edited by J. Bernd, Dallas, Southern Methodist University Press.

Davis, O.A. and M.J. Hinich, 1967, Some results related to a mathematical model of policy formation in a democratic society. In: *Mathematical Applications in Political Science*, III, edited by J. Bernd. Charlottesville, University Press of Virginia.

Davis, O.A. and M.J. Hinich, 1968, On the power and importance of the mean preference in a mathematical model of democratic choice. *Public Choice* 5 (Fall).

Davis, O.A. and M.J. Hinich, 1970, Some extensions to a mathematical model of democratic choice. In: *Social choice*, edited by B. Lieberman. New York, Gorden & Breach Science Publishers (forthcoming).

DeMeyer, F. and C. Plott, 1970a, The probability of a cyclical majority. *Econometrica* (forthcoming).

DeMeyer, F. and C. Plott, 1970b, A social welfare function with "relative intensity" of preference. *Quarterly Journal of Economics* (forthcoming).

Downs, A., 1956, *An economic theory of democracy*. New York, Harper.

Encarnacion, Jose, 1969, On independence axioms concerning choice. *International Economic Review* 10.

Fishburn, P.C., 1969, Preferences, summation, and social welfare functions. *Management Science* 16.

Fishburn, P.C., 1970a, Intransitive individual indifference and transitive majorities. *Econometrica* (forthcoming).

Fishburn, P.C., 1970b, Theory of representative majority decision. *Econometrica* (forthcoming).

Fishburn, P.C., 1970c, Irrationality of transitivity in social choice. *Behavioral Science* (forthcoming).

Fishburn, P.C., 1970d, Comment on Hansson's "group preference". *Econometrica* (forthcoming).

Garman, M. and M. Kamien, 1968, The paradox of voting: Probability calculations. *Behavioral Science* 13.

Goodman, L.A. and H. Markowitz, 1952, Social welfare functions based on individual rankings. *American Journal of Sociology* 58.

Hansson, B., 1968, Choice structures and preference relations. *Synthese* 18.

Hansson, B., 1969, On group preferences. *Econometrica* 37.

Hansson, B., 1970, Voting and group decision functions. *Synthese* (forthcoming).

Harsanyi, J.C., 1955, Cardinal welfare, individualistic ethics, and interpersonal comparisons of utility. *Journal of Political Economy* 63.

Hildreth, C., 1953, Alternative conditions for social orderings. *Econometrica* 21.

Inada, K., 1964a, On the economic welfare function. *Econometrica* 32.

Inada, K., 1964b, A note on the simple majority decision rule. *Econometrica* 32.

Inada, K., 1969, On the simple majority decision rule. *Econometrica* 37.

Intriligator, M., 1968, A probabilistic model of social choice. (Mimeograph.)

Kramer, Gerald, 1969, On a class of equilibrium conditions for majority rule. Cowles Foundation Discussion Paper No. 284.

Ledyard, J.O., 1968, Resource allocation in unselfish environments. *American Economic Review*, May, 227.

May, K.O., 1952, A set of independent, necessary and sufficient conditions for simple majority decision. *Econometrica* 20.

Murakami, Y., 1966, Formal structure of majority decisions. *Econometrica* 34.

Murakami, Y., 1968, *Logic and social choice*. London and Dover, New York, Macmillan.

Nash, J.J., 1950, The bargaining problem. *Econometrica* 18.

Nicholson, M.B., 1965, Conditions for the voting paradox in committee decisions. *Metroeconomica* 42.

Niemi, R., 1969, Majority decision making with imperfect agreement on norms. *American Political Science Review*, June.

Niemi, R. and H. Weisberg, 1968, A mathematical solution for the probability of the paradox of voting. *Behavioral Sciences* 13.

Nordin, J.A., 1969, The normalized vote margins method of committee voting. *Rivista Internazionale di Scienze Economiche e Commerciali* 16.

Park, R.E., 1967, Comment (on Coleman). *American Economic Review* 57.

Pattanaik, P.K., 1968a), A note on democratic decisions and the existence of choice sets. *Review of Economic Studies* 35.

Pattanaik, P.K., 1968b, Risk, impersonality, and the social welfare function. *Journal of Political Economy* 76.

Plott, C., 1967a, A notion of equilibrium and its possibility under majority rules. *American Economic Review* 57.

Plott, C., 1967b, A method of finding acceptable proposals in group decision processes. *Papers on Non-Market Decision Making*.

Rae, D., 1969, Decision rules and individual values in collective choice. *American Political Science Review*, March.

Richter, M.R., 1966, Revealed preference theory. *Econometrica* 34.

Richter, M.R., 1967, "Rational Choice". Conference paper at meeting of Econometric Society, August.

Richter, M.R., Social choice, rationality and decentralization (unpublished manuscript).

Riker, W., 1966, A new proof of the size principal. In: *Mathematical applications in political science*, II, edited by J. Bernd. Arnold Foundation.

Riker, W. and P. Ordeshook, 1968, A theory of the calculus of voting. *American Political Science Review* 28.

Rothenberg, J., 1961, *The measurement of social welfare*. Englewood Cliffs, N.J., Prentice-Hall.

Samuelson, P., 1967, Arrow's mathematical politics. In: *Human values and economic policy*, edited by S. Hook. New York, University Press.

Schick, Frederik, 1969, Arrow's proof and the logic of preference. *Philosophy of Science*, June.

Sen, A.K., 1964, Preferences, votes and the transitivity of majority decisions. *Review of Economic Studies* 31.

Sen, A.K., 1966, A possibility theorem on majority decisions, *Econometrica* 34.

Sen, A.K., 1969, Quasi-transitivity, rational choice, and collective decisions. *Review of Economic Studies* 36.

Sen, A.K., 1970, The impossibility of a paretian liberal. *Journal of Political Economy* 78.

Sen, A.K. and P.K. Pattanaik, 1969, Necessary and sufficient conditions for rational choice under majority decision. *Journal of Economic Theory* 1.

Simpson, P., 1969, On defining areas of voter choice. *Quarterly Journal of Economics* 83.

Thompson, E., 1966, A Pareto optimal group decision process. *Papers on Non-Market Decisions.*

Tullock, G. 1967, *Towards a mathematics of politics.* Ann Arbor, University of Michigan Press.

Tullock, G., 1967b, The general irrelevance of the general possibility theorem. *Quarterly Journal of Economics* 81.

Wilson, R., 1970, A game-theoretic analysis of social choice. *Social choice,* edited by B. Lieberman, New York, Gordon and Breach (forthcoming).

Wilson, R., 1968, A class of solutions for voting games. Working paper 156, Stanford Business School, October.

Wilson, R., 1969a, An axiomatic model of logrolling. *American Economic Review* 59.

Wilson, R., 1969b, Stable coalition proposals in majority-rule voting. Working paper 167, Stanford Business School, November.

Vickery, W., 1960, Utility, stategy and social decision rules. *Quarterly Journal of Economics* 74.

COMMENTS BY PRASANTA K. PATTANAIK
Harvard University

Professor Plott has given us an integrated account of a large number of recent contributions in this field, within a very elegant framework. Most of these contributions are axiomatic in nature and exclude a number of issues which must be faced in a more realistic discussion of the theory of voting. There are, however, so many difficult problems even within the simplified structure that it may be useful to analyse them before we face the more complicated problems. I shall confine myself mainly to the axiomatic framework in my comments.

I am somewhat worried about the possible interpretations of S. Does S refer to the set of all conceivable social alternatives — or, does it refer only to the set of feasible alternatives — or, to some subset of the set of conceivable alternatives, not all the elements of which may be feasible.

Suppose S is interpreted as the set of all conceivable alternatives. At any given time the set of feasible alternatives will be a subset — and most likely, a proper subset — of S. The set of feasible alternatives can, however, change. In such a situation should we be satisfied if the constitution gives us a best alternative for each feasible set — or, should we go further and require these choices to be related in a certain way? Two important questions arise in this connection: whether we should require choice to be rationalized by a binary relation, and if so, whether we should require it to be rationalized by a weak ordering. The answer to these questions, it seems to me, will become somewhat easier if we logically factorize the properties involved. In particular, any deep justification for rationality in the classical sense of a weak ordering can come only by logically analysing it into more primitive components. As Professor Plott has rightly pointed out, such justification cannot be given either in terms of the existence of an equilibrium or in terms of stability. If the set of alternatives under consideration is infinite, then even a weak social ordering will not necessarily ensure the existence of an equilibrium. On the other hand if we make the usual assumption of a finite set of alternatives, then a binary and weak social preference relation ("at least as good as") which is reflexive and connected, and the strict social preference relation corresponding to which is "acyclic", will serve just as well for the existence of an equilibrium and for stability.

In discussing the problem of preference intensities, Professor Plott seems to be worried about the fact that if we incorporate preference intensities as an ingredient of social choice, then the preferences of "greedy" individuals will receive an undesirably high weight. I agree with him but only in so far as the preferences under consideration refer to "subjective preferences", to use the terminology of Harsanyi (1955). If, however, the preferences are interpreted as "ethical preferences", to use the terminology of Harsanyi (1955) again, then the objection based on the notion of greed seems to lose its force. The problem of course, remains as to what we mean by ethical preference and how to ascertain it in actual life. I shall not discuss this problem here. For, the point I want to make is that probably the crucial hurdle in this context is not the ethical problem of greed but the factual problem of measuring preference intensities and rendering them inter-personally comparable.

The distinction between subjective preferences and ethical preferences brings me to the question of what exacly we mean by the individual preferences that we are seeking to aggregate. It is clear that the individual preferences will differ depending on the context in response to which the individuals express their preferences. It is not quite clear that one type of individual preference is ethically as desirable as another, as the basis for social choice. If this is admitted, then the extent to which the mechanism for social choice leads individuals to express preferences of one type or another becomes a criterion of judging the mechanism itself. The problem of interpreting individual preferences also has relevance for the approach which emphasises similarities among individual preferences as a route of escape from Arrow's paradox. How similar the individual preferences are likely to be, depends on what type of individual preferences are in question. For example, if individual preferences are interpreted as referring to ethical preferences rather than to subjective preferences, a greater degree of similarity may be expected.

Finally, I would like to comment on the fourth theorem of section 4 of Professor Plott's paper which essentially deals with the sufficiency and necessity of value restriction, extremal restriction, and limited agreement, for the simple majority rule to generate a binary and weak social preference relation which defines at least one best alternative for every non-empty subset of S. Since for various reasons well known in the literature, the preferences of individuals may not satisfy transitivity, it will be of considerable interest to formulate similar necessary and sufficient conditions in a context where individual weak preference relations are not assumed to fulfill the property of transitivity. We can assume each R_i to be reflexive, connected, and quasi-transitive but not necessarily transitive. We may even go further, and assume only that each R_i is reflexive and connected, and each P_i is acyclic, though the problem becomes extremely difficult in this case.

Part 2

ECONOMETRIC TECHNIQUES

*Frontiers of Quantitative Economics, ed. **M**.D. Intriligator.* © *North-Holland Publishing Company.*

CHAPTER 4

FORECASTING AND POLICY EVALUATION USING LARGE SCALE ECONOMETRIC MODELS: THE STATE OF THE ART

LAWRENCE R. KLEIN
University of Pennsylvania

0. Recent developments

The impetus and environment associated with the first attempts (Tinbergen 1939) at large scale econometric model building were the business cycle problems of the Great Depression and the emergence of the Keynesian Revolution. These factors provided techniques in economic analysis, challenging unsolved problems in economic analysis, and natural areas of application. The next big developments were the provision of good data bases through the construction of national income accounting systems and the application of modern statistical inference to econometric theory (Haavelmo 1943, 1944; Koopmans 1950; Mann and Wald 1943). Although there was much interest in the subject during the late 40's and the entire decade of the 50's, active participation was sparse and few new techniques were forthcoming. Most of the developments represented largely the application of known techniques, both in economic analysis and statistical inference (Goldberger 1959; Klein and Goldberger 1955; Klein et al. 1961). Of course, the data base was continuously being improved and enlarged.

As the decade of the 60's draws to a close, however, we can look back on this period as marking a tremendous expansion in model building and applications. The developments of this decade will occupy the main attention of this paper.

A single development stands out as a breakthrough, namely, the development of the computer. It is true that computers were used for parts of the analysis of the Klein-Goldberger Model (Adelman and Adelman 1959; Goldberger 1959; Klein and Goldberger 1952) and the UK Model (Klein et al. 1961), but these were rudimentary applications. They were coupled with substantial amounts of hand labor, and the specification of models was distorted to accomodate them to simplistic methods of computation. We no longer shun nonlinearity, high dimensionality, covariance calculations, etc. This is all due to the development of computer technology.

During the 60's there was a substantial increase in the data base — in detail, quality, sophistication, area of coverage — but it was less of a breakthrough than a natural extension of what had been going on for 30 or more years. Similarly, economic analysis, both through knowledge of institutions and understanding of theory, saw no substantial new developments. In fact, there has been none since the Keynesian Revolution; there has simply been a gradual refinement and improvement.

In econometric theory, there was an improved understanding and ability to use the innovations of Haavelmo and Wald. The method of two-stage-least squares, which actually came in the 50's (Theil 1958), is simply a natural extension of known methods, such as instrumental variables; and the methods of three-stage-least-squares, various iteration techniques, simultaneous least squares, and other variants are not in the category of breakthroughs, but they all represent progress in the theory of our subject. There has been a steady improvement in sophistication, especially in dealing with nonlinearities, lag distributions, and time series analysis. To some extent these improvements have come about as a result of pure theorizing, but they emerged in good part as a result of the availability of the computer, since they often involve iteration or substantial amounts of computation, and the theorist need fear no longer that his ideas will be pushed aside as empty or impracticable because of difficulty in evaluation.

Computer methods put into widespread application during the last decade enabled us to deal with the following problems:

(1) Estimation of large systems. Most models currently in use consist of approximately 50 stochastic equations and as many as 100 is not unusual. The Brookings Model (Fromm and Taubman 1967) contains 200-300 equations in different versions. The estimation and application of such systems

would not have been impossible without the use of computers, but their proliferation would have been unlikely.[1]

(2) Treatment of nonlinearities. Maximum likelihood estimation for either linear or nonlinear systems posed nonlinear computation problems which have only recently been overcome (Bodkin and Klein 1967; Eisenpress and Greenstadt 1966). Methods for estimating lag distributions were formerly transformed into equivalent linear problems at the expense of misspecifying or complicating the stochastic structure. This is no longer necessary. Also correction for autocorrelated error structures is a nonlinear estimation problem that can, in many cases, be routinely handled now (Sargan 1961). Apart from nonlinearities at the stage of estimation, however, nonlinearities were serious for applications of estimated models. This problem was overcome in connection with research on the Brookings Model project (Fromm and Klein 1969).

(3) Sampling experiments. Monte Carlo type distributions of estimates to deal with theoretically intractable small sample problems appeared on a small scale before the last decade, but they are commonplace now and have greatly added to our understanding of small sample properties of alternative estimators or estimators in special situations. Stochastic simulation is a similar computer application that is now flowering. In addition to the pioneering studies with the Klein-Goldberger (Adelman and Adelman 1959) and Brookings Model (Nagar 1969), we now have stochastic simulations with replication and much more general variance-covariance-autocovariance properties of errors (Evans et al. 1969; Green 1969; Schink 1968). The magnitude of computation for sampling experiments or stochastic simulation is such that studies of this type could not have been undertaken without the technological breakthrough.

(4) Experimental calculation and hypothetical cases. The availability of the computer has brought a changed frame of mind to the practicing econometrician. If he has a plausible but dubious idea, he can now try it out. Formerly, we had to guess or estimate whether seemingly small changes would make a difference. Now calculations can be made so cheaply in a variety of ways that there is no need to make analytic short cuts to try to

---

[1] The first U.S. model by Tinbergen (Tinbergen 1939) was large, but it was some time before construction of an equally large system was tackled again. The forms of analysis used were severely limited, however, without the computer.

see through the implications of changes in big problems. At the stage of estimation this approach has both good and bad effects. It is certainly good to have an added degree of flexibility in order to consider a wide range of alternative specifications. We really do not know the true parametric structure of an economy; therefore exploration with alternatives can be helpful. The danger is that we may engage in "data-mining" and explore only up to the point of confirming pre-conceived biases. Also, in the language of Robert Summers, we may be developing a generation of students who find it easier to substitute THINK for *think*.

At the stage of model application, however, the ease of experimentation is almost entirely beneficial. The whole concept of multiplier analysis has been generalized to include complicated changes (in parameters or exogenous variables) over time. Many solutions, each representing different policy alternatives, can be studied in comparison with a baseline case. The uncertainty that must be attached to assumed values for many exogenous variables can be handled through the provision of computations for alternative cases. It was formerly painful to work through a single solution by hand calculation for moderately large models; now it is customary to work through 5-10 cases at a time to see the influence of alternative policies or alternative assumptions about uncontrolled exogenous variables.

1. The scale of models

The title of this paper focuses attention on "large scale" models. It also focuses attention on forecasting and policy evaluation. In the case of forecasting, there is a debatable issue on the question of choosing between large and small scale models, but in the case of policy evaluation, there is likely to be little place for small systems.

The "true" economy is a complicated Walrasian type model. To give a full mathematical representation would require millions or billions of equations as the critics of socialist planning once contended (Lange 1936). But if we drop the Walrasian objective and content ourselves with an aggregative system, where shall we draw limits on size? There is no unique aggregative representation of an economy. Many alternative versions provide different approximations to the "true" system. This is, indeed, one of the sources of error in the stochastic specification of models. Given the objectives for application of a model, a possible rule for *minimum* size in performing aggregation is to specify a model that will provide endogenous generation of all the variables in the objectives. If the objectives arc indefinite, and this is usually the case, a model should be specified at a size that is as large as can be handled without impairing precision through the use of faulty data or overly complicated processes and that can be managed in the sense of being up-dated and readily applied.

As a point of scientific principle, I take issue with the "law of parsimony" that seems attractive to many economists. Under this law, the empirical theoretical scheme that appears, in terms of manifest data, to account with a given degree of precision for selected endogenous variables with the least number of parameters is chosen as the best scheme. Minimization of a number of parameters is not an interesting objective for econometrics.

Following the "law of parsimony" or something like it, some economists have put forward small GNP models. These consist of fewer than 6 (or thereabouts) macroeconomic equations that purport to forecast GNP and other main economic magnitudes (Friend and Taubman 1964; Friend and Jones 1964). This view is taken to an extreme in the case of single equation models based on the quantity of money (Friedman and Meiselman 1963).

It is possible to demonstrate in terms of sample fit, and sample fit alone, that small models or single-equations formulas forecast GNP as well as large scale models do. In a complex modern industrial economy with many significant sectors, it is likely that different components of GNP will be of extreme importance during various periods of time. Small models that do not give separate treatment to many components are likely to miss important phases when some particular component that is buried in aggregation is responsible for unusual movement in the economy. There is bound to come a time when small models fail badly even though they provide a "good fit" for limited periods of time to historical data.

The likelihood of prediction error in the use of small forecasting systems is not their most serious deficiency. The trouble is that most users of economic forecasts want and need much more information than can be supplied by a small system. GNP forecasting is all right, by itself, but it is not enough. Users want information on profit, price level, interest rates, imports, exports, personal income, output in different industries, and many other variables. There is simply too little information in small systems, and user requirements push the econometrician towards the development of larger models. The trend is clear. Econometric models are bound to become larger and larger in the future.

The policy application of models, even more than the pure forecasting application, requires that the system be large — large enough to display a wide variety of policy parameters and variables. It is not only a question of displaying all the standard policy parameters and variables; it is also a question of being prepared for entrance into new specialized policy areas whose nature cannot be wholly foreseen in advance. Even the standard policies require separate tax equations, transfer payment equations, money supply equations, trade equations, and public expenditure equations. Models that bring all these aspects into display must have at least ten equations and probably need more. If more specialized policies for such things as accelerated depreciation, investment tax credit, farm price support, medicare, tariff rates, excise taxes, reserves for Eurodollar balances, ceilings on bank interest rates and other particular issues are to be dealt with through alternative simulations, we must use models that would be classified as large scale.

In making individual industry forecasts and simulations, it seems natural to combine a macroeconometric model with an input-output model. This is done in the Brookings Model (Fisher et al. 1965; Fromm and Klein 1969). With only a superficial industrial disaggregation into 8 I-0 sectors, the Brookings Model is large by any modern standards. If the industry detail were to be more complete, and this is the direction in which future research is going, the entire model will have to become very large. An industrial disaggregation into 35 sectors will require an enlargement to a model of one thousand equations. This is probably going to be the next quantitative step in the order of model building.

An original objective of econometric model building has been lost sight of recently. This objective is to test economic theory. Adequate tests of theory require refinement and detail. If testing is to be our objective, it can be expected that systems will become larger.

The arguments against bigness in model building are difficulty in comprehension, inaccuracy of detailed data, difficulty in model management, the spread of specification error, and the lack of degrees of freedom. While these are all real difficulties, they are being overcome. In defense of bigness, there may be some advantages of spreading risks. Highly aggregative relationships may appear to be smooth, tight-fitting, and well behaved, but when they go wrong; they often do so by wide margins. If one is dealing with many small components, errors may be offsetting in arriving at national totals and localized errors may not be serious for most of the system. Also, localized errors can often be readily detected and corrected.

The problem of degrees of freedom in large systems is a technical issue on which there is much confusion; therefore it is worthwhile considering the precise points at issue. In the fitting of single equations to sample data, the matter is clear. The number of observations minus the number of parameters to be estimated give the number of degrees of freedom. It is known that a linear function with n unknown coefficients parameters can be fit "perfectly" to n data points, leaving no degrees of freedom. This situation is unlikely to occur, however, since most econometric relationships have fewer than 10 unknown parameters (to be estimated) and more than 10 sample observations. In systems of equations, however, there may be many parameters. In systems of 100 equations, an altogether feasible size in current practice, there will be several hundred unknown parameters to be estimated. It is often the case that there are fewer than 100 sample observations. Does this situation imply a shortage of degrees of freedom? The answer is "not necessarily", and in all probability there will be ample degrees of freedom.

In the case of the single equation

$$y_i = \alpha_1 x_{1i} + \ldots + \alpha_n x_{ni} + e_i$$
$$i = 1, 2, \ldots, n,$$

we can write the system of n relationships for each sample point

$$y_1 = \alpha_1 x_{11} + \ldots + \alpha_n x_{n1}$$
$$y_2 = \alpha_1 x_{12} + \ldots + \alpha_n x_{n2}$$
$$\vdots$$
$$y_n = \alpha_1 x_{1n} + \ldots + \alpha_n x_{nn}.$$

This system will enable us to determine estimates of the unknown coefficients $\alpha_1, \ldots, \alpha_n$ with zero residual error. This procedure assumes that the data matrix for the explanatory variables is nonsingular.

$$\text{det. } x = \begin{vmatrix} x_{11} & \cdots & x_{n1} \\ x_{12} & \cdots & x_{n2} \\ \vdots & & \vdots \\ x_{1n} & \cdots & x_{nn} \end{vmatrix} \neq 0.$$

The estimates of $\alpha_1, \ldots, \alpha_n$ determined in this way provide a perfect fit and have no degrees of freedom. If the number of parameters exceed the number of sample points, it is possible to assign arbitrary values to some of the parameters and determine the remaining set so as to achieve a perfect fit. This procedure can be carried out in a variety of ways. In this case there is a shortage of degrees of freedom.

For the system of equations

$$Ay_t + Bx_t = e_t,$$

each *individual* equation may be written, in terms of the sample data, as

$$\alpha_{k1} y_{11} + \dots + \alpha_{kn} y_{n1} + \beta_{k1} x_{11} + \dots + \beta_{km} x_{m1} = 0$$
$$\vdots \qquad \vdots \qquad \qquad \vdots \qquad \qquad \vdots$$
$$\alpha_{k1} y_{1T} + \dots + \alpha_{kn} y_{nT} + \beta_{k1} x_{1T} + \dots + \beta_{km} x_{mT} = 0$$

$(k = 1, 2, \dots, n).$

In this representation there are n dependent variables and m independent variables. Apart from restrictions, and normalizations there are $n(n+m)$ unknown parameters with T observations on all variables, Even though

$$n(n+m) > T,$$

it does not follow that a perfect fit can be obtained because there are nT such equations written with zero residuals. There are T for each structural equation; therefore the *gross* number of degrees of freedom (before subtraction of the number of parameters) is nT. There are as many gross degrees of freedom as there are elements in the joint probability of the sample,

$$Pr(e_{11}, \dots, e_{1T}, e_{21}, \dots, e_{2T}, \dots, e_{n1}, \dots, e_{nT}).$$

To be very practical, $n+m$ will probably be less than 10 in each single equation after restrictions are taken into account. As long as $T > 10$, as will surely be the case, we shall have

$$10n < nT.$$

If we denote the number of unrestricted coefficients of the ith equation by $n_i + m_i$, we shall take the number of degrees of freedom for each single equation as

$$T - n_i - m_i.$$

There is not likely to be a shortage in this case.

Different methods of estimation, however, will require different numbers of degrees of freedom. A pure application of ordinary least squares (OLS) or instrumental variables (IV) methods of estimation to each equation of a complete system, would simply require that

$$T > n_i + m_i \quad i = 1, 2, \ldots, n.$$

This requirement will be readily met in practice with very large systems.

For the methods of two-stage-least-squares (TSLS) and limited-information maximum likelihood (LIML), however, there is an additional requirement that must be met, namely

$$T > m.$$

In the first stage of these two methods, the procedure is to regress the dependent on all the independent variables of the system in the unrestricted reduced form relationships

$$y_t = \Pi x_t + v_t.$$

In large systems, such as the Brookings Model (or even slightly smaller systems), it is not unlikely that we shall find

$$m > T.$$

A system with 200 equations might very well have $m = 200$, inclusive of lagged as well as independent variables, and $T < 100$, say merely 80 quarterly or 20 annual observations.

A way out of this difficulty is to form the first stage regressions on a small number of principal components of X_t (Kloeck and Mennes 1960) or on selected instruments chosen by rules of causation (Fisher 1965). Data reduction techniques for these regressions are needed if there is a shortage of degrees of freedom or if $X'X$ is ill-conditioned, say as a result of multi collinearity.

For the method of full-information-maximum likelihood, the restriction $T > m$ is needed, but an additional restriction is

$$T > n;$$

otherwise the likelihood function will have no maximum because

$$\text{est. } \Sigma = \left\| \frac{1}{T} \sum_{t=1}^{T} \hat{e}_{it} \hat{e}_{jt} \right\|$$

will be singular. This preceding inequality precludes the FIML estimation of a system as large as the Brookings Model from quarterly data unless the system is decomposable in special ways into subsystems. It can also be shown that we must have

$$T > m + n$$

for FIML estimation. The largest known system estimated by FIML methods contains 16 stochastic equations, with some decomposition (Klein 1969c).

2. Some applications

Originally, the building of dynamic macroeconometric models was associated with the testing of economic theory and the analysis of business cycles (Tinbergen 1939). The influence of the Keynesian theory of output and employment determination shifted emphasis towards application in the form of *prediction* in order to prescribe policy remedies for the economy. Prediction of GNP, unemployment, inflation rates, balance of trade, savings rates and similar variables has been a major issue in the USA since the end of World War II and the implementation of the Full Employment Act. In the decade of the 60's, it has become associated with the concept of "fine tuning" of the economy.

Prediction can be of a pure sort that attempts to foretell the results of tomorrow's economy. This is a widespread application in both government and business. For the dynamic model

$$\sum_{i=0}^{P} A_i y_{t-i} + B x_t = e_t,$$

in which A_i, B and the covariance matrix of e_t have been estimated from the sample $t = 1, 2, \ldots, T$; the prediction problem is one of determining Y_{T+1} from

$$y_{T+1} = -\hat{A}_0^{-1} \sum_{i=1}^{P} \hat{A}_i y_{T+1-i} - \hat{A}_0^{-1} \hat{B} x_{T+1}$$

on the basis of observed values for y_{T+1-i} and assumed values for x_{T+1}. The disturbance vector e_{T+1} is fixed at its mean value (0) for the prediction period in the absence of any specialized knowledge about error impacts.

After y_{T+1} is computed, it is used as lagged input for determining y_{T+2}, together with values for y_{T+2-i} and x_{T+2}. For as many future periods as necessary, the forecast solution is projected ahead in this way.

The making of point forecasts from large (nonlinear) systems in this way has been routinized. The computer has enabled us to overcome the difficulties of computing y_{T+k}, even if the system is nonlinear. In actual application of models to the forecasting problem, it has been found useful to try to estimate e_{T+k} on the basis of expert information and sample serial properties.

For single equation formulas in the static case the calculation of standard error of forecast is well known and easily applicable (Hotelling 1942-43). For dynamic systems used for *multiperiod* prediction ahead, there is an additional problem in accounting for the variability of y_{T+k-1}, y_{T+k-2}, etc., which may be "noisy" inputs for period $T+k$. Going beyond the well-known formulas for standard error of forecast in single equations, Goldberger, Nagar and Odeh have approximated the formulas for prediction from a complete system (Goldberger et al. 1962). Their methods are not easily applicable, especially for large nonlinear systems; therefore it appears that computer techniques of experimental sampling ought to be used for numerical approximation of the standard error of forecast (Schink 1968).

Perhaps more significant than applications of pure prediction have been simulation studies of alternative assumptions. These may be either alternative extrapolations beyond the sample span, in which case they are *conditional forecasts*, or they may be alternative interpretations of historical experience (within or before the sample). The latter are studies of what might have been. The best way of looking at the (alternative) simulation techniques is as a generalization of the multiplier concept. For the traditional multiplier, we look at the change in individual dependent variables associated with changes in a single independent variable. This involves evaluation of dy_{it}/dx_{jt} within an estimated model — linear or nonlinear. Such standard multipliers are computed as government expenditure multipliers, tax change multipliers, monetary policy multipliers, foreign trade multipliers, etc. Formula evaluation, as in the case of standard error of forecast, is difficult; therefore we turn to numerical simulation with the computer. For a fixed set of exogenous inputs $x^C_{t+1}, x^C_{t+2}, x^C_{t+3}, \ldots$, and given values for parameter estimates, we determine the *control* solution of a system over a finite period of time. For long run multiplier analysis, the long run solutions may cover 10 or 20 years. We then alter the inputs to $x^D_{t+1}, x^D_{t+2}, x^D_{t+3}, \ldots$ to obtain a *disturbed* solution. The disturbed solution may have changed parameter values as well as changed exogenous variables. The changes can be continuous, smooth, stepwise, alternating, or in any arbitrary time pattern. Also, the changes may be in several components of the vector x_t simultaneously and in several parameter values simultaneously. The comparison of two dynamic solution paths

$$y_{t+1}^C, \ y_{t+2}^C, \ y_{t+3}^C, \ \dots$$

$$y_{t+1}^D, \ y_{t+2}^D, \ y_{t+3}^D, \ \dots$$

provides us with a generalization of the multiplier concept. If the change in x_t is constant and confined to a single component, we have the usual multiplier formula from

$$\frac{y_{i,t+j}^D - y_{i,t+j}^C}{x_{k,t+j}^D - x_{k,t+j}^C} \ .$$

Short and long run multipliers for nonlinear dynamic systems have, in fact, been evaluated in this way (Evans and Klein 1968; Fromm 1969; Fromm and Taubman 1967). In the context of the U.S. economy, short run expenditure multipliers in the neighborhood of 1.6 and long run expenditure multipliers in the neighborhood of 2.0 appear to be common from several models. There is less agreement, however, on the comparative size of money market multipliers. Interesting comparisons have been made of multipliers for different countries using econometric model techniques (Evans 1966; Hickman 1969).

Multiplier calculations can be made in general terms so that rules of thumb are available to policy makers to apply to the judgment of the effects of their prospective decisions. But very specific policy actions can be separately programmed for intensive study. The types of studies that have been made in depth for specific policy changes are:

(1) The U.S. income tax cut of 1964 (Klein 1969a).

(2) The U.S. excise tax cut of 1965 (Fromm and Taubman 1967).

(3) Disarmament and Vietnamese peace settlements (Klein 1968b; Klein and Mori 1969).

(4) Revaluation of the West German mark (Krelle 1969).

This is by no means an exhaustive list of policy applications that can be studied by model simulation, but it is indicative of the type of issue that can be so treated. In case (1) the model is solved for the control solution with two sets of tax rates — these prevailing in 1963 before the cut and those prevailing in 1964 after the cut. This control solution should agree fairly closely with observed data from that time period. In the alternative solution, the parameters of the tax functions are kept constant, and the model is solved again for 1963-64. Comparison of the two solutions, variable by variable, shows the effect of the cut.

Excise taxes are highly specific, by commodity, and, in a macro model, must be approximated by broad commodity classes. In addition to the lack of correspondence between commodity classification for model structure and for tax law change there is much uncertainty about how much of the tax cut will be "absorbed" by producers and how much will be "passed on" to consumers. The effects of the excise tax cut are estimated by making alternative simulations, each assuming different portions of the tax cut to be passed on to consumers. The coming up of highly specific but significantly large excise tax cuts, after a model is already constructed and available for use shows how important it is to have a large detailed system. The greater the detail of the commodity classification in demand functions, the better the approximations for assessing the effects of the tax cut.

Disarmament and demobilization calculations require large packages of changes in exogenous variable inputs and parameter levels. The time table for demobilization of servicemen must be laid out for the exogenous variable on the size of the military labor force. Correspondingly, the public wage bill and military spending must be reduced each period by appropriate amounts. Orders for military goods, which affect inventories, must be altered for input values. Solutions can be made with offsetting rises in nondefense public expenditures, lowering of tax rates, and raising of transfer payments. These changes have been simultaneously placed into peace solutions over periods of 2 or more years for comparison with control solutions, where there is no cessation of hostilities.

General multiplier analysis or policy simulation, example by example, is similar. It involves the introduction of specific *a priori* changes among the inputs of a control solution, and an alternative is derived for comparative purposes. A fairly different approach to public policy analysis can also be followed in a search for optimal policies. Following the terminology of Tinbergen (1956), we classify variables into *targets* and *instruments*. *Targets* are dependent variables that we seek to have attain some given levels.

Targets of low unemployment rates, low inflation rates, high growth rates and large international payments surpluses, are typical. *Instruments* are independent variables over which public authorities or other decision makers can exercise control. All independent variables cannot be controlled, but those like tax rates, discount rates, budgeted levels of public spending, and open market operations can be controlled. The instruments, according to Tinbergen's analysis, are manipulated in order to reach targets.

In the formal application of macroeconometric models, the roles of dependent and independent variables are reversed for solution purposes. The targets (dependent variables) are fixed, and values for instruments (independent variables) are obtained from the solution. If there is equality between the numbers of targets and instruments, the problem is straight-forward. Values of the dependent variables are assigned input values at target levels, and the solution output values include the values of the instruments that must be fixed in order to arrive at the targets. If there is an excess of instruments or targets, reduction of their number by selection or by weighted or fractional combination is necessary. The interesting case is that in which there are surpluses of targets. These can be combined into a policy maker's preference function which can be maximized subject to the relationships of the system inplied by the model equations.

Within the framework of large econometric models there are few known applications of the general case in which optimal policies are sought, but for the simple case where there is equality between the number of instruments and targets, solutions have been obtained from slightly aggregated versions of the Wharton-EFU Model (Rahman 1968).

A fascinating type of analysis using large scale models is the attempt to reconstruct and re-orient history. The analyses of the income tax cut of 1964 and the excise tax cut of 1965 are reconstructions of history as well as studies in fiscal policy. The historical content is, however, subsidiary to the main purposes of the studies, and the historical epoch is quite brief and recent. Many other such policy simulations are accordingly reconstructions of history. A more pertinent example of historical analysis is the study of the 1929 depression through the device of an econometric model. This has been done by using revised and up-dated versions of the Klein-Goldberger Model (Klein 1966; Norman 1969). In the first instance the model is simulated through the 1929-33 downturn and the 1934-41 recovery. An analysis of the goodness of fit to these periods is first carried out; then alternative policies contrasting with those actually used are applied to money markets, transfer payments, and government expenditures to see if the depression could have been avoided or mitigated. These studies help us in understanding whether history is likely to repeat itself and show something about the effectiveness of different policies. In general, they show that the US economy has strong recovery power now and is likely to regain any level of activity very soon after displacement. They also indicate that simple monetary and fiscal policies could have mitigated the depression substantially.

Longer historical studies, reaching back into the 19th century, are best tackled through the construction of econometric growth models. Some modest attempts have been made at construction of long term growth models (Brown 1965; Klein and Kosobud 1961; Morishima and Saito 1964; Valavanis-Vail 1955), but this is, to a large extent, a field where much more needs to be done. Models of larger scale and more sophisticated econometrics need to be developed.

Closely allied, however, to model building for the study of long term historical growth is the building of models for developing economies. The data base is unfortunately recent and sparse. The researcher has to be content with limited samples of 15-20 annual time series observations. In some cases family budget surveys and other sources of cross-section data samples can be used to supplement the standard time series samples. Models have been built for a number of Latin American economies and also several countries in Africa, Asia, and Island chains (Behrman and Klein 1970; Marzouk 1969; UNCTAD 1968). These models can then be extrapolated forward in simulation calculations for periods of ten years or more in order to examine growth characteristics and growth policies.

The specifications of developing country models are different from those in most models of industrial economies. In the developing economy, more attention must be paid to the supply conditions of the economy. Needs are so great, that demand is assumed to take care of itself (in simple functional relationships). In addition, the following points should be kept in mind when modeling developing economies:

(1) Different supply sectors must be treated individually.

(2) Income distribution should be taken into account in spending equations.

(3) Demographic relations on population growth and internal migration (farm to city) should be included in the model.

(4) Export equations for major commodities should be linked to world market conditions.

The extensive world modeling by UNCTAD, covering models of more than 30 developing nations, was undertaken for *target* analysis. They were constructed for simulations to determine the size of the *trade* or *resource* "gaps" in a given year, such as 1980, that would be generated if the developing countries were to grow at targets rates per annum. A rate of 6% for real GNP would be considered favorable. The "gaps" are added over all developing countries to arrive at a total world figure. In addition to target simulation for the "gap" calculation, such models can be used for the evaluation of different growth policies.

The data are weak and too few. Large errors are associated with the sample observations of all variables, and the equations have non-negligible residual errors; nevertheless the estimated systems give plausible results and appear to be an excellent vehicle for research. They can obviously be improved upon through deeper efforts. Such systems can be verified and improved through continuous application to forecasting. The Division of Econometric Studies of Mexico in Wharton Econometric Forecasting Associates, Inc., regularly applies a large scale model to *ex ante* forecasting for Mexico in cooperation with major corporations in that country. The results are sufficiently encouraging that it does seem possible to model and predict developing economies.

A final area of application to be considered in this paper is cyclical analysis. This brings us back full circle to the original objectives of macro-econometrics, as stated at the beginning of this section. To make the ideas clear for this kind of analysis, let us write the general linear dynamic system as

$$\sum_{i=0}^{p} A_i y_{t-i} + Bx_t = A(L)y_t + Bx_t = e_t,$$

where $A(L)$ is a matrix polynomial in the lag displacement operator

$$L^i y_t = y_{t-i}.$$

The solution to this dynamic system can be written symbolically as

$$y_t = K\lambda^t - \frac{a(L)}{\Delta(L)} Bx_t + \frac{a(L)}{\Delta(L)} e_t,$$

where K is an $n \times np$ matrix depending on the initial conditions, λ is an np vector of roots of the characteristic equation of the homogenous systems, where $a(L)$ is the adjoint matrix of $A(L)$, and $\Delta(L)$ is the determinantal polynomial, det $A(L)$. Frisch (1933) appropriately distinguished between the "propagation problem" and the "impulse problem" in dynamic systems. The propagation component of the solution is $K\lambda^t$, while the impulse contribution is $-\dfrac{a(L)}{A(L)} Bx_t + \dfrac{a(L)}{A(L)} e_t$. In the early models of Tinbergen, attention was focussed on $K\lambda^t$. Using sample estimates of the parameters of the system, together with initial conditions, the expression $K\lambda^t$ can be evaluated. It has been computed on modern equipment for systems where $np = 43$ (Howrey 1969). It is, however, difficult to evaluate all the roots with good numerical precision. Frisch emphasized the point that cycles can be kept alive through exogenous and random impulses, which appear, in estimated form, as

$$-\frac{\hat{a}(L)}{\hat{A}(L)} \hat{B}x_t + \frac{\hat{a}(L)}{\hat{A}(L)} e_t,$$

but Slutsky (1937) provided much more insight when he proved his law of the sinusoidal limit for iterated moving averages of random numbers. The stochastic contribution to the solution

$$\frac{\hat{a}(L)}{\hat{A}(L)} e_t$$

is not exactly in the form of infinitely iterated moving averages, but in an unpublished paper, M. Otsuki of Pennsylvania and Osaka Universities has shown that there are sizable regions in the unit circle where roots $(\hat{\lambda}_1, \hat{\lambda}_2, .., \hat{\lambda}_{np})$ may be such that $(\hat{a}(L)/\hat{A}(L))e_t$ tends to a sinusoidal limit as $np \to \infty$. The distributed lag in e_t may be written as

$$\sum_{j=1}^{np} \sum_{i=0}^{t-np} \frac{\hat{\lambda}_j^i}{\prod\limits_{j\neq k=1}^{np} (\hat{\lambda}_j - \hat{\lambda}_k)} e_{t-i} = \frac{\hat{a}(L)}{\hat{A}(L)} e_t - \text{const.};$$

this is why the characteristic roots are of crucial importance in determining the nature of oscillations in the random component.

In modern cyclical studies, the emphasis has shifted from the propagation to the impulse component. Adelman and Adelman (1959) found that the Klein-Goldberger Model did not oscillate as a deterministic solution, either from the propagation component or from the exogenous impulse component. They found, however, that realistic oscillations did occur if the stochastic impulse component were added. This result was obtained by numerical simulation analysis in which random errors e_t were drawn to shock the individual structural equations

$$A(L)y_t + Bx_t = e_t.$$

The resulting stochastic solution showed realistic business cycle fluctuations about the deterministic solution. The latter was dominated by trend growth in the components of x_t. The propagation contribution to the solution was strongly damped. Subsequently, much larger systems have been shocked for the calculation of stochastic solutions. Nagar provided stochastic simulations of the 200 equation Brookings Model over the sample period. The Wharton-EFU Model, the new Brookings Model, and the Office of Business Economics Model have been solved stochastically for 100 future quarters, with replication to indicate sampling variability (Evans et al. 1969; Green 1969; Schink et al. 1969).

The Brookings, Wharton, and OBE stochastic simulations extend the procedures of Adelman and Adelman by drawing random errors so that all sample variances and covariances of equation residuals are preserved. We estimate the variance covariance matrices by

$$est \, \|Ee_{it} e_{jt}\| = \hat{\Sigma} = \left\| \frac{1}{T} \Sigma (res_{it})(res_{jt}) \right\|.$$

In the Adelman-Adelman simulation, the drawings for $\hat{\Sigma}$ made the matrix diagonal. Nagar developed a technique for drawing random numbers that have the covariance matrix $\hat{\Sigma}$, but his technique demands that

$$T > n,$$

where n is the number of stochastic equations in the system. In the Brookings model sample, $n > T$; therefore he had to compromise by retaining non-diagonality only within selected subblocks and assuming independence between blocks. This is clearly unsatisfactory, and the simulations of the Wharton and OBE Models draw the random numbers in another way. Let R be a matrix of equation residuals

$$R = \begin{pmatrix} r_{11} & \cdots & r_{1n} \\ r_{21} & \cdots & r_{2n} \\ \vdots & & \vdots \\ r_{T1} & & r_{Tn} \end{pmatrix}.$$

Let N be a $q \times T$ matrix of independent normal deviates with zero mean and unit variance. The number of future periods ahead that the simulation is to run will be q. The matrix

$$\frac{1}{\sqrt{T}} NR$$

has a variance-covariance matrix whose expected value is the same as the variance-covariance matrix of $\dfrac{1}{\sqrt{T}} R$. This is an extremely simple procedure, due to McCarthy (1969), that has no degrees-of-freedom restrictions. In addition, it has the remarkable property that sample serial covariances can also be imposed on the matrix of random errors. If the rows of N are

$$N = \begin{pmatrix} n_1 & n_2 & \dots & n_T \\ n_{T+1} & n_1 & \dots & n_{T-1} \\ \vdots & & & \vdots \\ n_{2T-1} & n_{2T-2} & \dots & n_1 \\ \vdots & & & \vdots \\ n_{T+q-1} & n_{T+q-2} & \dots & n_q \end{pmatrix},$$

the product

$$\frac{1}{\sqrt{T}} NR$$

will preserve all sample variances, covariances, and serial or auto-covariances. The best simulations of the Wharton, Brookings, and OBE Models, from the point of view of cyclical smoothness and regularity are obtained by using the error matrix with sample serial properties preserved. The other component of the solution, $[a(L)/\Delta(L)] Bx_t$, has yet to be fully investigated in the context of these simulations for its contribution to the cyclical process.

Extraction of roots for large systems, long simulations, drawing of random errors, and replication of experiment are made possible only by the use of the computer. Analysis has gone in this direction principally because of the availablity of facilities, and takes a different direction from earlier cyclical analysis mainly for this reason.

The analysis is explicit for linear systems. The solution can be written in closed form, and the separate components of the solution can be individually evaluated. In the case of stochastic nonlinear dynamic systems this is not generally possible. We proceed in a numerical way with nonlinear systems. The set of dynamic equations can be expressed as:

$$f_i(y_{1t}, \ldots, y_{mt}, \ldots, y_{1,t-p}, \ldots, y_{n,t-p}, x_{1t}, \ldots, x_{mt}) = e_{it}$$

$$(i = 1, 2, \ldots, n).$$

If the system can be expressed, as is usually the case, as

$$y_{it} = g_i(y_{it}, \ldots, y_{mt}, \ldots, y_{n,t-p}, x_{1t}, \ldots, x_{mt}) + e_{it}$$

we use a standard Gauss-Seidel iteration algorithm for solution,

$$y_{it}^{(r)} = \hat{g}_i(y_{1t}^{(r)}, \ldots, y_{it}^{(r-1)}, \ldots, y_{mt}^{(r-1)}, \ldots, y_{1t-p}, \ldots, y_{n,t-p}, x_{1t}, \ldots, x_{mt}).$$

We stop when

$$\left| \frac{y_{it}^{(r)} - y_{it}^{(r-1)}}{y_{it}^{(r-1)}} \right| < \varepsilon, \text{ for preassigned small } \varepsilon.$$

By forming successive solutions through time, substituting in each period the appropriate lag values computed from previous periods, we can develop an entire solution

$$y_{i1}, y_{i2}, y_{i3}, \ldots \qquad (i = 1, 2, \ldots, n).$$

This solution can be either deterministic or stochastic. In any event, we study the time pattern of the computed solution for its cyclical characteristics. In the case of linear systems, the stochastic solutions consist of two additive parts, the solution of the deterministic system

$$\hat{K}\hat{\lambda}^t - \frac{\hat{a}(L)}{\hat{A}(L)} \hat{B}x_t$$

and the stochastic contribution

$$\frac{\hat{a}(L)}{\hat{A}(L)} e_t.$$

The expected value of the solution is the deterministic part. In the case of nonlinear systems, the solution cannot generally be put into these two parts, but the departures from linearity are not usually so great, and, in fact, the mean solution, taken over replications, is close to the solution of the deterministic system.

A direct analytical method of studying periodicity in linear econometric models is provided by spectral analysis. The spectrum of the disturbance process, e_t, is transformed into the spectrum of the endogenous variables y_t by using the transfer function $\dfrac{\hat{a}(L)}{\hat{A}(L)}$. The spectrum of the disturbance process is estimated from the spectrum of equation residuals. This technique has been applied by Chow and Howrey to small and intermediate size systems (Chow and Levitan 1968; Howrey 1967). The same type of analysis for small systems where the spectral properties of the exogenuous variables is also taken into account is given by Dhrymes (1970).

There are some advantages in using a direct spectral analysis as outlined above because the results do not depend on the particular sample drawn as in the numerical simulation experiments described earlier. There is a sampling problem, however, because $\hat{a}(L)/\hat{A}(L)$ and the computed residuals, on which the spectral analysis rests, are sample estimates and are subject to error. Another problem that faces direct spectral analysis of models is that T is usually not very large (less than 80 in most cases of quarterly series and in some only as large as 50), while spectral analysis, to be meaningful, requires large samples. With annual data and standard cycles of 4-6 years, there will not be many periodicities to analyze unless T is more than 25. With quarterly data, the cycle length is 15-25 periods; therefore samples of length in excess of 100 are needed.

A combination of stochastic simulation and spectral analysis has many advantages. This is the method used for cyclical analysis of the Wharton-EFU, Brookings and OBE Models (Evans et al. 1969; Green 1969; Schink, et al. 1969). Stochastic solutions are obtained for the Models, as described above, over periods of 100 quarters. Longer simulations can also be made. These simulations are replicated — 50 times in the case of the Wharton and Brookings Models and 25 times in the case of the OBE Model. Spectral analyses are made of the solutions of the different variables in each simulation replication. The advantages of this approach are that the length of the series can be made long enough to make spectral analysis more reliable; the sampling variability of the spectrum can be studied from the several replications; the system need not be linear or linearly approximated;

any desired pattern — trend, cyclical, constant or random — can be given to the exogenous variables; it is simple to deal with serial covariance in the error process.

3. Degree of precision

It is difficult to summarize briefly the extent to which we have achieved a degree of scientific precision in econometric analysis through the use of large scale models because there are so many variables involved and so many different ways of measuring performance. In this discussion, attention will be centered on short and long run solutions, within and outside sample (fitting) periods, and solution *ex post* or *ex ante*.

Short run solutions are for periods of fewer than 5 years or 20 quarters. Long run solutions, except in the case of *hypothetical* business cycle and growth simulations, are usually not more than 20-25 years in length. That is the extent of the normal postwar sample period. Many long run solutions are for lengths of approximately 10 years.

Since most models are based on the national income and product accounts with a central objective being to forecast GNP, we may look at accuracy first in terms of that variable. Short run solutions *ex post*, for GNP reveal root-mean-square errors of $2-$8 billion. The lowest errors are for very short period solutions of 1 or 2 quarters, but the error grows as the solution lengthens. It tends to stabilize near $8 billion. In the neighborhood of cyclical turning points, the performance is less precise. For some cycles the root-mean-square error is greater than $10 billion. *Ex post* solution performance is better near troughs than near peaks.

There is wide divergence among components of GNP, but inventory and fixed investment solutions are comparatively poor (with errors almost as big as those in GNP) while consumption solutions show better performance. Wages and rentier income solutions track actual values better than do profits. Solutions for prices, interest rates, and wage rates are reasonably close during normal periods, but there is a tendency for models to underestimate extreme periods of inflation. Generally speaking, the solutions are smooth — especially the non stochastic variety — and extreme amplitudes are missed.

For solutions over the whole sample period or substantial portions of it, the root-mean-square error of GNP is $5-$10 billion. The size of the error depends on the period covered. Errors are especially large for the years immediately following World War II when shortages of durables and homes were severe, and for the Korean War years. During the Korean War there were extreme speculative waves, up and down, capacity pressure on the economy, unusual stock piling of strategic imports, and some direct controls.

Errors are also larger by $2-$3 billion if *ex post* extrapolations are made beyond the sample period. For most models, this introduces the period of strong inflation and War escalation. Extrapolations beyond the sample period can be made *ex post*, with correct inputs of lag values and exogenous variables. These are "psuedo forecasts" and have larger errors than those observed for sample period simulations.

These errors can be reduced by making autoregressive corrections on the basis of sample period serial correlations, by making minor adjustments to one or two equations that may have drifted from its period of fit, and by taking account of data revisions.

A more interesting measure of precision, however, is revealed by the error involved in genuine ex-ante forecasting. These errors are known for three U.S. Models — the annual Michigan Model, the Wharton-EFU Model and the OBE Model, which have been applied repeatedly to ex-ante forecasts. The Wharton and OBE Model forecasts of real GNP are usually under $3 billion for one quarter ahead. In current prices the average absolute error is less than $4.0 billion. Annual forecasts (made in December) of GNP in current prices are usually within $3 billion, and the performance of the Michigan Model is similar. Unusually large errors were made in 1968-69 for GNP in current prices, but real GNP forecasts were within the usual target area.

In many respects, *ex ante* prediction is more precise than ex post extrapolation, even though rough estimates of some lag values and incorrect exogenous assumptions are introduced in the former. A primary reason for the relatively good performance of the Wharton Model predictions *ex ante* is that they are made in collaboration with a number of cooperating experts from a wide range of private and public institutions. "Last minute", "inside" and "informed" *a priori* knowledge about possible values for $e_{it}(t = T+1, T+2, \ldots)$ are incorporated in the forecasts. On balance, the use of *a priori* information improves the predictions over mechanical application of *ex post* methods. Large scale models without informed judgment are not enough, and the informed judgment without formal models is inadequate. They complement each other well. The formal model provides a consistent framework within which to apply valuable judgmental information.

The success of trials in using models for public policy formation or business forecasting will not be shown entirely in their performance statistics such as root-mean-square error in comparison with other models, especially "naive" models. The latter are "no-change" estimates, "constant-change" estimates, or pure autoregressive estimates. The interesting issue is whether policy makers and business analysts find them helpful in their work. Their helpfulness will be judged by their performance *ex ante* in comparison with other models that are similarly available for *ex ante* applications. In this sense, it can be said that the Michigan, OBE, and Wharton Models have proved themselves in repeated application, continued over many years. Some individual periods have proved to be enigmatic, as in late 1968 and early 1969, but errors can readily be recognized and allowed for, so that a system that is temporarily off the track can readily be restored to the track; thus minimizing and confining failures.

4. Some new directions

The typical structure of models is presently undergoing change in well defined directions, with the outcome that the models of the future are sure to be much larger. Many models are expanding their treatment of the monetary sector and trying to forge better links between the monetary and real sectors. Monetary policy is being so actively pursued that models, to be useful in policy analysis, have to display the explicit parameters and variables of the money market. In this respect, as in others, there is a return to the spirit of Tinbergen's study for the League of Nations (Tinbergen 1939). Among American Models, the Federal Reserve-MIT-Pennsylvania Model has its primary emphasis on the money market (Ando and Modigliani 1969). In the case of the Wharton-EFU, the OBE, and the Michigan Models (Evans and Klein 1968; Green 1969) work is progressing towards building in more detailed processes of the financial sector. The Brookings Model from its very inception devoted much attention to the financial sector and received cooperation from the Federal Reserve in this work. In fact, the architect of the Brookings Model's financial sector (De Leeuw 1965) played a major role in developing the Federal Reserve-MIT-Pennsylvania Model.

Another direction in contemporary model building is to try to explain the balance of payments as well as the balance of trade. The Brookings Model is currently being extended in this direction. Such studies were undertaken at an early stage by Rhomberg for Canadian-U.S. capital flows (Rhomberg 1964), and work now being done for the Bank of Canada on their model is extending the trade and payments linkage between the two countries.

To build complete and detailed systems for financial and international payments sectors will practically double the size of most models. This will put most complete models in the range of more than 100 stochastic equations. Given that we can already handle much larger systems, from the points of view of data preparation, estimation, and simulation size is not going to be a major problem by itself.

The principal reason why the Brookings Model is so large is that it subdivides the producing sectors of the economy into eight groupings and combines a consolidated input-output matrix with the usual kind of final demand system. On the *supply* side of the model, however, there is separate explanation of employment, wage rate, price level, and capital formation by industrial sector. Future model analysis is undoubtedly going to go deeper into the supply side of the economy and combine, effectively, I-0 and traditional macroeconometric models. A reasonable aim would be to do this for two-digit manufacturing plus several nonmanufacturing industries. The number of sectors will be somewhere between 25 and 50. Some first attempts indicate substantial promise for this approach and show that it is technically feasible (Evans and Preston 1969; Saito 1969). The complete system in the form of an enlarged Brookings Model with something like 35 sectors will being us to the region of the 1000-equation model.

Another approach to sector analysis, either industrial or geographical sector, is to construct satellite models that are consistent with macro models of the economy as a whole. In these cases, there is no feedback from sector performance to national performance, while there is such feedback in the Brookings Model with its I-0 table to relate industrial sector performance to national performance. The construction of industry or regional models in depth, and grafting of them to master aggregative models are, however, being done and show good promise (Crow 1969; Glickman 1969; Klein 1969; L'Esperance et al. 1969).

During the last two decades, and especially during the past few years, models have appeared for almost all major economies. There are functioning models of excellent quality for Canada, the United Kingdom, The Netherlands, Belgium, Sweden, Israel, India, Japan, West Germany, Australia, Mexico, Brazil, and many other countries. Among these, the Dutch Model has a long and distinguished history. The U.K. and Japanese Models are used regularly in forecasting. The United Nations Conference on Trade and Development has constructed models of more than 30 developing nations (UNCTAD 1968). The application of models to problems of growth and development, both in industrial and emerging nations, is an area in which there is likely to be much further work. As the data base is improved and lengthened, it is becoming more possible to build reliable samples for parameter estimation. The problems of shortage of degrees of freedom are particularly severe in modeling the developing nations. Nevertheless, useful inferences can be made, and analysis of the development or growth process becomes clearer in the framework of the existing models.

Having the models of most of the large trading countries of the world, it appears possible to link them together into one system of world trade. Project LINK is trying to do just this (Social Science Research Council 1969). It is an econometric study group for building linkages, through compatible import and export equations, between models in the U.S.A., Canada, Japan, the United Kingdom, The Netherlands, Belgium, West Germany, Sweden and some other industrial market economies. The Rest-of-the-World and the developing countries will be separately grouped into rougher models to close the system. The objective of this econometric research will be to make simultaneous and consistent estimation of domestic and world trade flows for many countries. The nations included explicitly account for approximately two-thirds of world trade. This is on-going research, and concrete results are just now available.

These new directions — sector models, the combining of I-0 and macro-econometric analysis, development models, world systems — are largely substantive developments. Some new methodological developments also appear on the horizon. While the computer is here and being used in daily work, there are some new usages in prospect. Time sharing systems already exist on a small scale, whereby users in diverse parts of the country have instantaneous access, through ordinary telephone hook-up, with models, their data banks, their estimation programs, and their simulation programs. Participants can use existing models, can obtain latest up-dated inputs, can vary exogenous assumptions, can re-estimate equations, and can carry on general econometric model building research from remote areas. At present, business, government, and other institutional users are the main participants in such time sharing systems, but there is every reason to believe that academic centers of econometrics will soon be included for teaching and research uses.

It is not out of the question to think about the possibility that the internationally distributed members of project LINK in Philadelphia, Washington, San Francisco, Tokyo, London, Toronto, Ottawa, The Hague, Stockholm, Brussels, Bonn, and other centers will eventually have direct telephone access to the central file of data, models, simulations and programs for withdrawing information or executing calculations of world interest. This interchange is not yet at hand, but the hard and software components are all available, and it can be done.

The emphasis has properly been on digital calculation, but in this era in which we are reverting to older approaches, as in modern cycle analysis, there seems to be a need for a reconsideration of the role of the analog computer. In the early 1950's there was an interest in analog programming of dynamic economic models (Moorehouse et al. 1950, Strotz et al. 1953; Tustin 1953), but this work was not pursued. Recently, some work done at the Wharton School suggests that analog devices may have some important uses (Habibagahi and Klein 1969). A simple truncated version of an up-dated Klein-Goldberger Model has been programmed for simulation study, in deterministic and stochastic form, on a small analog computer. It is often claimed that everything that can be done by analog can be done better and more accurately by digital. The following points, however, seem to merit consideration:

(1) The analog is an excellent teaching device. A preprogrammed system can be altered readily by students with instantaneous results. The alterations may be changed input values of variables or changed parameter values. Changes can be made by simply turning knobs.

(2) Research experimentation for sensitivity of whole solution paths to parameter values can be readily conducted. It is possible to find out combinations of parameter values (knob setting) that give solution paths in good agreement with observed paths for specific variables.

(3) Phase diagrams and other frequency characteristics of systems can be readily obtained.

(4) Many types of nonlinear systems can be dealt with readily.

Analog equipment has become inproved in accuracy and larger in capacity. Large scale models can be programmed on the most sophisticated of such machines. A hybrid machine that links an analog and digital in use together can also be helpful. In addition to an analog display of a time path that is to be compared with a reference time path, we can evaluate differences between the two paths digitally. The fitting criterion can be studied directly as a number and used to guide the search being conducted on the analog for parameter values.

The solution to the general linear dynamic system was written as

$$y_t = K\lambda^t - \frac{a(L)}{\Delta(L)} Bx_t + \frac{a(L)}{\Delta(L)} e_t.$$

If elements of $A(L)$ and B are to be found that minimize

$$\sum_t \sum_i v_{it}^2 \, ; \, v_t = \frac{a(L)}{\Delta(L)} e_t \, ;$$

or some weighted version of this sum of squares, the problem is terribly difficult because of the nonlinearities involved. This would define optimal parameter estimates as those that minimize squared error about the simulation path. There are problems in the interpretation of such estimates because of the serial correlation in the series

$$\frac{a(L)}{\Delta(L)} e_t \, ;$$

nevertheless such estimates have much to recommend them. It seems that analog devices would be very helpful in searching for the appropriate elements of $A(L)$ and B. One can visually inspect the simulation paths for any set of parameter values, and these sets can be quickly altered.

This approach, whether pursued by analog or digital device, opens a fresh approach to the estimation problem, namely, one in which estimation can be tied directly to prediction, for dynamic prediction paths will be made from the solution

$$y_t = \hat{K}\hat{\lambda}^t + \frac{\hat{a}(L)}{\hat{\Delta}(L)} \hat{B}x_t$$

for $t = T+1, T+2, T+3, \ldots, T+k$ (Klein 1968a)

References

Adelman, I. and F.L. Adelman, 1959, The dynamic properties of the Klein-Goldberger model. *Econometrica* 27 (Oct.), 596-625.

Ando, A. and F. Modigliani, 1969, Econometric analysis of stabilization policies .*American Economic Review* 59 (May), 296-314.

Behrman, J. and L. R. Klein, 1970, Econometric growth models for the developing economy. In a collection of essays in honor of Sir Roy Harrod (in press).

Bodkin, R.G. and L.R. Klein, 1967, Nonlinear estimation of aggregate production functions. *Review of Economics and Statistics* 47 (February), 28-44.

Brown, T.M., 1965, *Canadian economic growth*. Ottawa, Royal Commission of Health Services.

Chow, G.C., 1968, The acceleration principle and the nature of business cycles. *Quárterly Journal of Economics* 82 (August), 403-18.

Chow, G.C. and R.E. Levitan, 1969, Nature of business cycles implicit in a linear economic model. *Quaterly Journal of Economics* 83 (August), 504-17.

Crow, R., 1969, An econometric model of the Northeast Corridor of the United States. Ph. D. Thesis, University of Pennsylvania.

De Leeuw, F., 1965, A Model of financial behavior. In: *The Brookings quarterly econometric model of the United States*. Chicago, Rand McNally.

Dhrymes, P., 1970, *Econometrics: statistical foundations and applications*. New York, Harper & Row.

Duggal, V., 1967, *Fiscal policy in economic stabilization: simulation with the Brookings quarterly econometric model*. Ph. D. thesis, Harvard.

Eisenpress, H. and J. Greenstadt, 1966, The estimation of non-linear econometric systems. *Econometrica* (October), 851-61.

Evans, M.K., 1966, Multiplier analysis of a post-war quarterly US model and a comparison with several other models. *Review of Economic Studies* 33, 337-60.

Evans, M.K. and L.R. Klein, 1968, *The Wharton econometric forecasting model*. Philadelphia, Economic Research Unit, University of Pennsylvania. 2nd enlarged ed.

Evans, M.K. and R.S. Preston, 1969, A new way of using aggregate economic models: Industry forecasts with econometric models. Discussion paper No. 138, Economics Department, University of Pennsylvania.

Evans, M.K., L.R. Klein, and M. Saito, 1969, Short and Long run simulations of the Wharton model. Paper presented to the Income and Wealth Conference, November.

Fisher, F.M., 1965, Dynamic structure and estimation in economy-wide econometric models. In: *The Brookings quarterly econometric model of the United States*. Chicago, Rand McNally.

Fisher, F.M., L.R. Klein, and Y. Shinkai, 1965, Price and output aggregation in the Brookings econometric model. In: *The Brookings quarterly econometric model of the United States*. Chicago, Rand McNally.

Friedman, M. and D. Meiselman, 1963, The relative stability of monetary velocity and the investment multiplier in the United States, 1897-1958. In: *Stabilization Policies* edited by E.C. Brown et al. Englewood Cliffs, N.J., Prentice-Hall Inc.

Friend, I. and R.C. Jones, 1964, Short run forecasting models incorporating, anticipatory data. In: *Models of income determination. Studies in income and wealth*,Princeton, N.J., Princeton University Press.

Friend, I. and P. Taubman, 1964, A short term forecasting model. *The Review of Economics and Statistics* 44 (August), 229-36.

Frisch, R., 1933, Propagation problems and impulse problems in dynamic economics. In: *Economic essays in honor of Gustav Cassel*. London, George Allen and Unwin.

Fromm, G., 1969, An evaluation of monetary instruments. In: *The Brookings model: some further results*, edited by J. S. Duesenberry et al. Chicago, Rand McNally.

Fromm, G. and L.R. Klein, 1969, Solutions of the complete system. In: *The Brookings model: some further results*, edited by J. S. Duesenberry et al. Chicago, Rand McNally.

Fromm, G. and P. Taubman, 1967, *Policy simulations with an econometric model*. Washington, Brookings.

Glickman, N., 1969, An econometric model of the Philadelphia region. Ph.D. Thesis, University of Pennsylvania.

Goldberger, A. S., 1969, *Impact multipliers and dynamic properties of the Klein-Goldberger model*. Amsterdam, North-Holland Publ. Co.

Goldberger, A. S., A. L. Nagar, and H. S. Odeh, 1962, The covariance matrices of reduced form coefficients and of forecasts for a structural econometric model. *Econometrica* 29 (October), 556-73.

Green, G., 1969, Short and long run simulations with the OBE model. Paper presented to the Income and Wealth Conference, November.

Haavelmo, T., 1943, The statistical implications of a system of simultaneous equations. *Econometrica* 11 (January), 1-12.

Haavelmo, T., 1944, *The probability approach in econometrics*. Supplement to *Econometrica* 12 (July).

Habibagahi, H. and L. R. Klein, 1969, Analog solution of econometric models. Discussion Paper No. 136, Philadelphia, Economics Department , University of Pennsylvania.

Hickman, B.G., 1969, Dynamic properties of macroeconometric models: An international comparison. In: *Is the business cycle obsolete?*, edited by M. Bronfenbrenner. New York, Wiley-Interscience.

Hotelling, H., 1942-43, Problems of prediction. *The American Journal of Sociology* 48, 61-76.

Howrey, E. P., 1969, Dynamic properties of a condensed version of the Wharton model. Paper presented at the Income and Wealth Conference, November.

Howrey, E. P., 1967, Stochastic properties of the Klein-Goldberger model. Research Memorandum No. 88, Princeton, N.J., Econometric Research Program.

Klein, L. R., 1966, On the possibility of another '29. Paper presented to the Conference on the Economic Outlook, Ann Arbor, Mich.

Klein, L.R., 1968, *An essay on the theory of economic prediction*. Helsinki, Yrjo Jahnssonin Säätiö.

Klein, L. R., 1968b, Economic consequences of Vietnam peace. *Wharton Quarterly* (Summer), 20-23.

Klein, L. R., 1969a, Econometric analysis of the tax cut of 1964. In: *The Brookings model: some further results*, edited by J. S. Duesenberry et al. Chicago, Rand McNally.

Klein, L. R. (ed)., 1969b, *Essays in industrial econometrics*. Philadelphia, Economic Research Unit, University of Pennsylvania. 2 vols.

Klein, L. R., 1969c, Estimation of interdependent systems in macroeconometrics. *Econometrica* 37 (April), 171-92.

Klein, L. R., R.J. Ball, A. Hazlewood, and P. Vandome, 1961, *An econometric model of the United Kingdom*. Oxford, Blackwell.

Klein, L. R. and A. S. Goldberger 1955, *An econometric model of the United States, 1929-1952*. Amsterdam, North-Holland Publ. Co.

Klein, L.R. and R.F. Kosobud, 1961, Some econometrics of growth: great ratios of economics. *Quarterly Journal of Economics* 75 (May), 173-98.

Klein, L. R. and K. Mori, 1969, The impact of disarmament on aggregate economic activity: an econometric analysis. Paper prepared for Arms Control and Disarmament Agency work group.

Kloeck, T. and L. B. M. Mennes, 1960, Simultaneous equations based on principal components of predetermined variables. *Econometrica* 28 (January), 45-61.

Koopmans, T. C. (ed)., 1950, *Statistical inference in dynamic economic models.* New York, John Wiley & Sons.

Krelle, W., 1969, The functioning of a prognostication model for the West German economy. Paper presented at the Project LINK Meetings.

Lange, O., 1936, On the economic theory of socialism. *The Review of Economic Studies* 4 (October), 53-71.

L'Esperance, W. L., G. Nestel and D. Fromm, 1969, Gross state product and an econometric model of a state. *Journal of the American Statistical Association* 64 (September). 787-807.

Mann, H. B. and A. Wald, 1943, On the statistical treatment of linear stochastic difference equations. *Econometrica* 11 (July-October), 173-220.

Marzouk, M., 1969, The predictability of predetermined variables in macro-econometric models. Ph. D. Thesis, University of Pennsylvania.

McCarthy, M. D., 1969, Some notes on the generation of pseudo structural errors for use in stochastic simulation studies. Paper presented to the Conference on Research in Income and Wealth, November.

Moorehouse, N. F., R. H. Strotz, and S. J. Horwitz, 1950, An electro analogue method for investigating problems in economic dynamics: inventory oscillations. *Econometrica* 18 (October), 313-28.

Morishima, M. and M. Saito, 1964, A dynamic analysis of the American economy, 1920-1952. *International Economic Review* 5 (May), 125-64.

Nagar, A. L., 1969, Stochastic simulation of the Brookings econometric model. In: *The Brookings model: some further results*, edited by J. S. Duesenberry et al. Chicago, Rand McNally.

Norman, M., 1969, The great depression and what might have been: an econometric model simulation study. Ph. D. Thesis, University of Pennsylvania.

Rahman, A., 1968, Determination of an ideal growth path of the U.S. economy with the help of an econometric model. Ph. D. Thesis, University of Pennsylvania.

Rhomberg, R. R., 1964, A model of the Canadian economy under fixed and fluctuating exchange rates. *Journal of Political Economy* (February).

Saito, M., 1969, An interindustry study of price formation. Discussion Paper No. 124. Philadelphia, Economics Department, University of Pennsylvania.

Sargan, J. D., 1961, The maximum likelihood estimation of economic relationships with autoregressive residuals. *Econometrica* 29 (July), 414-26.

Schink, G., 1968, Estimation of forecast error in a dynamic and/or non-linear econometric model. Paper presented to the Econometric Society, December.

Schink, G., G. Fromm, and L. R. Klein, 1969, Short and long term simulations with the Brookings model. Paper presented to the Conference on Research in Income and Wealth, November.

Slutsky, E., 1937, The summation of random causes as the source of cyclic processes. *Econometrica* 5 (April), 105-46.

Social Science Research Council, Committee en Economic Stability, 1969, Linkage of national econometric models; Project LINK. *Items.* report by B.G. Hickman, 23 (December), 54-56.

Strotz, R. H., and J. C. McAnulty, and J. B. Naines, Jr., 1953, Goodwin's non-linear theory of the business cycle: an electro-analog solution. *Econometrica* 21 (July), 390-411.

Suits, D.B., 1963, Econometric analysis of disarmament impacts. In: *Disarmament and the economy*. New York, Harper & Row.

Theil, H., 1958, *Economic forecasts and policy*. Amsterdam, North-Holland Publ. Co.

Tinbergen, J., 1939, *Statistical testing of business cycle theories*. vol. II: *Business cycles in the United States of America, 1919-1932*. Geneva, League of Nations.

Tinbergen, J., 1956, *Economic policy, principles and design*. Amsterdam, North-Holland Publ. Co.

Tustin, A., 1953, *The mechanism of economic systems*. Cambridge Mass., Harvard University Press.

UNCTAD Secretariat, 1968, *Trade prospects and capital needs of developing countries*. New York, United Nations.

Valavanis-Vail, S., 1955, An econometric model of growth, USA 1869-1953. *American Economic Review* 45 (May), 208-21.

COMMENTS BY DANIEL B. SUITS
University of California, Santa Cruz

Although the first econometric model was constructed by Jan Tinbergen and published in his famous *Statistical testing of business cycle theories* (Geneva, League of Nations, 1936), the modern era of econometric models received its greatest impetus from the work of Lawrence Klein, receiving its greatest push from the now classic Klein-Goldberger model that, I believe, included the first econometric forecast ever made. During the last 17 years, the large econometric model has risen from a mysterious academic curiosity understood by only a handful of mathematically minded economists to a position as standard tool of business and public policy analysis.

Klein has presented us here with a careful and thorough review of the present state and future prospects of large econometric models. Predictably his view is strongly affirmative. Equally predictably, I agree with most of what he said. Indeed, if I have any contribution to make in the short time allotted, it is merely to paraphrase some of the points he made and to provide a slightly different emphasis.

I should like first to comment on the increasingly serious problem posed by the ease with which large quantities of data can be processed by high-speed electronic computers. Human beings are prone to do whatever is easiest, and economic researchers are no notable exception to the rule. For this reason, those of us who did our graduate work before the computer came on the scene acquired a unique advantage, for anybody whose dissertation had to be done with the aid of nothing more advanced than a temperamental hand-cranked desk calculator found data manipulation a vastly greater chore than analysis of the problem itself. As a result, we tended to spend most of our time and effort on the relatively easy job of formulating the relationship, choosing the variables, and interpreting the results, and to postpone to the last possible point the unpleasant task of (literally) grinding out the final result. When regressions are time consuming and tedious to calculate, one considers carefully what the outcome is likely to mean before it is obtained, and to examine carefully whether, in fact, the computation is necessary at all. The result is an attitude toward statistical research that is not easily shaken, and one more easily acquired when it corresponds to the course of least effort into the bargain.

With the advent of the electronic computer and the canned program, the balance of effort has been completely shifted. It is now vastly easier to pump bales of data into a computer, flip the switch and stand by while the equipment spews out the answer a fraction of a second later. The easy course nowadays is to compute first and to postpone thinking about the matter until afterwards. Indeed, by the use of any one of a number of sequential regression programs, researchers can almost avoid thought altogether. The computer can be allowed to sort over the data and to decide for itself which things are important for the relationship in question and which are not. The greatest trouble with such programs is that, applied to economic data in which everything is highly correlated with everything else, it is a remarkable coincidence when the variables that actually belong in the relationship under study are also the ones that meet the significance criterion assigned to the computer. My own experience with such programs has led to the conviction that they are truly methods of *minimum* likelihood; the probability of a wrong answer being very high.

In addition, the disposition to compute first and think afterward often yields question-begging results that would have been revealed by a bare minimum of serious consideration, often without data, not to say elaborate computer programs. In the interest of long-standing friendships, I forebare from specific citations, but I have seen regression equations fitted to definitions. As another example, a recently published regression revealed that the cost per mile of highway construction depends partly on the number of lanes in the road. Needless to say, the result was complete with standard error, and the regression coefficient was highly significant.

All this is not to say that we must abandon computers, but it *is* to say that those of us who are engaged in teaching research methods have a serious obligation to place greater emphasis on the analysis of the structure of problems and on the insightful application of statistical tools before the computer is called in. We need to train students to see how far they can go in the solution of quantitative problems before they resort to purely statistical procedures and to concentrate on the proper interpretation of results once they are in.

Entirely aside from its other merits, the large econometric model provides an ideal training-ground for this purpose. One of the important advantages to disaggregation is that it brings the researcher closer to the structure under examination, and thus facilitates responsible formulation of relationships and insightful evaluation of results. Of course, the careful specification of structure and the careful construction of a number of relationships necessarily involves thinking. This is hard work, indeed, compared to working with a computer, but our job is to show students that it must be done.

The view of an econometric model as an effort to approximate the structure of an economic system has another important bearing on the size of the model. As soon as the object is to obtain the best representation of the system, the proper criterion of size becomes not the number of relationships and variables in the model, but the precision with which they correspond to the rich complexities of the real world. The target is not to limit the size of the model — this may be only another manifestation of the laziness syndrome — but rather to gain maximum insight into how the behavior of one group in society impinges upon and influences that of another, and to represent the system of mutually interdependent relationships in the greatest feasible detail. It is on precisely this point that I fail to understand some of the so-called "monetarists". I am perfectly prepared to be shown that money supply, appropriately defined and properly lagged is the most reliable predictor of the economic outlook. The question is, after all, an empirical one; there is no point in arguing about it, it can be settled only by comparing forecasts over a period of, say, 10 years. What I cannot understand are the groups that appear to treat money supply as some kind of spiritual force that hovers over the economy radiating its influence directly onto the GNP without the intervention of human agency or economic structure.

The important thing to those of us engaged with large econometric models is to approximate and capture the *structure* through which monetary

— or any other — conditions affect the investment behavior of business firms, the spending of consumers, the prices of products, and so on. To put it bluntly, a change in the money supply must affect *somebody*. It must make him act in a different way than before, and what we want to determine is *who* is affected, *how* he responds, and how his response affects others. These interesting and important questions cannot be studied without a model sufficiently detailed to distinguish one group from another and one response from another.

In any case, large and small models are not mutually exclusive like rival religious sects. The proper question is not *whether* to use a large or a small model, but *when* to use a large model and *when* to use a small one. For policy analysis, or even in terms of pure economic forecasting, there is more to the economic outlook than the GNP, and the greater the detail to be analyzed or forecast, the more elaborate the model must be. Clearly, an econometric model must be large enough to furnish the desired detail. One can hardly explore the outlook for the automobile market in a model that limits itself to a single consumption expenditure, lumping automobiles, ice cream and dental service along with everything else into an undifferentiated quantity.

At the same time, however, if only a general global view of the impact of a few highly important key factors is desired, analysis and forecasting by a very small model can be highly successful. I regularly resort to a small "back-of-the-envelope" model to get a quick evaluation of the economic outlook or to check the internal consistency of forecasts prepared by others. I have also found that a small but realistic model can be effectively employed as a "table of contents" to a larger model, and greatly facilitates the presentation of forecasts to students, businessmen, legislators or even fellow economists. An additional advantage to a small model is that it forces the forecaster to spend most of his care and effort in compiling the small amount of key information needed for inputs. Since, regardless of the size of the model, the forecast ultimately depends on the quality of a relatively small number of key variables that must be projected, if the basic structure of the economy is properly represented, a small model can accurately forecast the broad features of the economic outlook, but there is no way that complexity of structure can compensate for poor input information.

The final point I should like to raise involves the use of econometric models for policy formulation and analysis. As Klein has pointed out, models can be used in two different ways for this purpose. The direct application of the model involves the assignment of values to instrument variables in the model to represent the policy to be examined. The system is then solved to determine the implications of the policy for the endogenous variables. The second method is the inverse technique proposed by Jan Tinbergen. In this method, target values are assigned to endogenous variables — employment, growth rates, rate of inflation, balance of payments, etc. — and the system is solved to determine the values of policy instruments needed to produce the desired outcome. Since, however, certain combinations of values of endogenous variables are stru cturally inconsistent, a more sophisticated application of the inverse technique requires the establishment of a social welfare function whose arguments are the endogenous variables in the model. Values of variables representing policy instruments are then assigned so as to maximize the social welfare function.

Both these procedures are intimately affected by the size of the model. The "direct" application clearly requires a model large enough to encompass both the range of policy instruments to be evaluated and the range of endogenous consequences to be considered in the evaluation. A model whose structure fails to embody excise tax rates must remain silent on the effects of changes in such rates, and a model without a system of equations to determine the price level cannot indicate the impact of policy on the rate of inflation. Within these limitations, however, the model can function usefully and well, for neither excise taxes nor a price-determination sector are essential if all we want to know is the impact of changes in, say, government expenditures on, say, GNP and the level of employment. Moreover, as long as we realize that the model answers only the kind of question for which it has be designed, the results are unambiguous. The absence of an excise tax equation precludes the use of the model for the exploration of the impact of excise tax changes, but this obviously does not mean that excise taxes exert no effect on the economic system. Nor does the absence of a price-determination sector imply that government expenditure has no impact on price levels. A limited model can produce results that approximate the "truth", but they are necessarily far short of the "whole truth".

This limitation is obvious, and would hardly need to be pointed out except that the same qualifications tend to be overlooked when a model is applied in the inverse technique. Even the largest econometric models omit important aspects of economic life from the set of endogenous variables, and omit important policy instruments from the set of exogenous variables.

For example, all econometric models include GNP as an endogenous variable, but I know of none that represent the rate of resource exhaustion, or the impact of output on environmental pollution. Moreover, while most large econometric models include global instruments like tax rates, government expenditure, and monetary policy, they uniformly omit policies that might shift the position of the Phillips curve. It is a strange notion of social welfare, indeed, that permits destruction of the countryside in the interest of more jobs, or that is content to determine the "optimum" level of unemployment rather than to pursue steps to reduce the amount of inflation associated with low unemployment levels. The truth of the matter is that inverse applications of limited models can deliver only a maximum for a social "welfare" function in which important elements of welfare are given zero weight, attained by manipulation of a restricted set of policy variables from which many feasible and practical policy moves have been ruled out.

Given the natural disposition toward laziness which we agreed at the outset characterize even econometricians, there is a strong temptation to define this limited and myopic result as a serious policy prescription, and to present it as a substitute for the serious and agonizing effort needed to confront real policy issues on effective terms. This is a dangerous game in this increasingly technical age, and one that I, for one, will not play myself and — what is more to the point — one which I will earnestly discourage my students from playing.

COMMENTS BY STEPHEN M. GOLDFELD

Princeton University

Professor Klein has, as usual, provided us with an interesting and informative paper. The bulk of the paper is an occasionally nostalgic, but always optimistic, survey of developments in building and using large-scale econometric models. If the paper has a hero, it is certainly the "computer", although as Professor Klein recognizes, from the point of view of statistical methodology the computer is a mixed blessing. My aim in these brief remarks is selectively to play the devils advocate to Klein's optimism.

0. Degrees of freedom

Professor Klein neatly summarizes the computational problems presented by a limited number of observations and concludes (pun intended?) that "in all probability there will be ample degrees of freedom". It should be emphasized, however, that the "degrees-of-freedom" problem has more than computational aspects — it is intimately tied up with statistical significance tests of economic hypotheses. On this score there would appear to be a number of difficulties. We are all aware of the computerized-data-mining which econometricians are prone to do. In addition, empirical researchers often reestimate a previously successful specification with the addition of a few observations. Given the limited body of macroeconomic data, a truly "original" regression estimate is a rarity. Finally (and this is touched on a bit more below), there exist gaps in our knowledge of the small sample distributions of simultaneous equation estimators. These factors all suggest that from a statistical point of view we can hardly be sanguine about the adequacy of the small number of observations utilized by model builders. Some of these problems would be reduced if we adopted an explicitly sequential (Bayesian?) view of continually updated model estimates, but this is not an easy task for large models.

1. Estimation methods

Professor Klein reports, and not without justification, that computer-aided Monte Carlo studies have significantly added to our understanding of small sample properties of alternative estimators. Despite progress to date, however, we have a rather imperfect knowledge of which estimator is best in various small sample situations. Part of the reason for this is that virtually all of the empirical evidence comes from Monte Carlo methods applied to small models. Some recent theoretical work by Kadane[1] suggests that the ranking of alternative estimating methods can be quite sensitive to model size so that care is clearly needed in applying existing Monte Carlo results to realistic situations.[2]

As indicated above, we are also still on shaky grounds when it comes to the standard game of interpreting "t-statistics" in a simultaneous equation setting. The tendency is to pretend as if large-sample theory applied. While

---

[1] J.B. Kadane, Comparison of k-class estimators when the disturbances are small. Cowles Foundation Discussion Paper No. 269.

[2] Other theoretical work indicates that in some circumstances small sample distributions may not even have finite moments. This clearly also presents problems in interpreting Monte Carlo results.

the evidence is limited, Monte Carlo studies using comparably-sized small models suggest that what is a "large" sample varies from model to model, so that asymptotic results can only be applied cautiously.

A related issue concerns the success we have had in dealing with econometric problems other than simultaneous-equations bias. Klein again properly suggests that we have made significant progress in attacking problems presented by autocorrelation, distributed lags, covariances across equations, and nonlinearities. Nevertheless if, as is frequently the case, one is faced with several of these problems at once, tractability demands that significant compromises still have to be made. If I may venture a forecast, however, I think it reasonable to expect that developments in both numerical analysis and computer technology will make for significant advances in this area over the next few years.

2. Large vs. small models

While recognizing most of the main arguments against big models, Klein suggests that users of econometric models are demanding a degree of detail which is inevitably leading to larger and larger econometric models. For example, users want models which encompass both detailed industry variables as well as many policy parameters. Clearly large models are here to stay. They will undoubtedly grow even larger — there seems to be a Parkinson's law relating model size to existing computer capability. While Klein is undoubtedly correct in pointing out this tendency, I am somewhat uneasy about the wisdom of forging ahead with the thousand equation model which Klein suggests is the next step. Given our present state of knowledge, I would think rates of return would be higher in some other avenues of research, a few of which are mentioned below.

From a forecasting point of view, Klein indicates that the case for big models is less firm, but he clearly prefers big models for forecasting as well. In this context, he talks about the virtues of spreading "risks" over a larger number of equations. He clearly has in mind the extent to which undesirable aggregation may be producing untrustworthy equations. Pushing the portfolio analogy a bit further, however, we know that a sensible spreading of risks can only be achieved by disaggregation if all the covariances between different equations are properly considered. To date, at least, complete-system estimating techniques have not been applied to large models so that in forecasting with large-scale models researchers have not generally utilized such covariance information.

As a casual empirical observation, I would venture the proposition that despite the significant expansion of model sizes to date, the ability of existing models to forecast depends critically on a relatively small number of expenditure functions. Indeed models have expanded considerably less than proportionally with respect to expenditure functions. This is not to say that greater disaggregation of these functions would not improve matters but skepticism is certainly a respectable view on this score.

3. Nonlinearities

As suggested before, nonlinearities can present formidable estimation problems — especially if they occur in conjunction with other statistical difficulties. Aside from estimation problems, however, nonlinearities may also present difficulties in interpreting simulation results. As Howrey and Kelejian have illustrated, there are particular problems in interpreting nonstochastic or deterministic simulations of nonlinear models.[3] Their findings have implications for the growing use of simulation, *per se*, as well as for the increasing tendency to use simulation tracking ability as a criterion for the actual choice of parameter estimates.

Klein suggests that in his experience departures from linearity are not great, since the mean simulation solution taken over replications is similar to the nonstochastic simulation. This may not, however, say much about the degree of nonlinearity present in a properly specified econometric model. For one, researchers have generally avoided specifications which involve complex nonlinearities. Secondly, it is only recently (especially if we exclude the Korean war from our sample) that we have extreme observations on such things as price changes, interest rates, and unemployment rates. As a consequence, in the work to date many of the nonlinearities may be masked by the particular sample period used to estimate most econometric models.[4]

---

[3] E.P. Howrey and H.H. Kelejian, *Dynamic econometric models: simulations vs. analytical solution*, Duke University Press (forthcoming).

[4] For an example of the clear emergence of a nonlinear effect with the addition of most recent data, see R.C. Fair, The determination of aggregate price changes. *Journal of Political Economy* (forthcoming).

4. Some specification details

I think few model builders would disagree with the proposition that much work remains to be done to improve the specification of existing models. Below I have briefly listed some points which come immediately to mind but which hardly exhaust the needed menu of improvements.

(a) Disequilibrium phenomena such as credit rationing need to be dealt with in a more explicit and satisfactory way. It should be noted that the use of partial-adjustment mechanisms, while undoubtedly a move towards greater realism, still assumes that markets are cleared every period. Some recent work suggests that estimation problems presented by disequilibrium phenomena are interesting and complicated but still tractable.[5]

(b) In recent periods the expected rates of price increase, the expected course of monetary policy, and the "expected" termination of the tax surcharge (i.e., consumers regarding it as temporary) have all been cited as relevant factors explaining economic behavior. Nevertheless, model builders have done a rather imperfect job in dealing with expectational phenomena. Part of this reflects the state of knowledge of the theory of behavior under uncertainty, but more importantly it reflects the fact that expectations are generally unobserved. More work needs to be done in this area.

(c) Models which have been designed for short-term purposes have been increasingly used for long-run simulations. These simulations have driven home the extent to which models may violate desirable long-run steady state properties. Care is clearly needed on this score as well as in introducing long run supply considerations.

These comments have emphasized some of the difficulties in econometric model-building. Over the long run, of course, we all hope that Professor Klein's optimistic portrayal of the state of the art will be borne out.

COMMENTS BY ROBERT J. GORDON
University of Chicago

Klein's paper is an optimistic, almost sanguine report on the state of the art of building large-scale econometric models. His proposed agenda for

---

[5] See R. C. Fair and D. M. Jaffee, Methods of estimation for markets in disequilibrium. (Mimeographed).

the 1970's can be summarized: "more of the same, only bigger". But recently from two other sources have come strikingly less optimistic reports on the current state of the models. In its December 20 issue, *Business Week* ran a story titled "Bad Year for Econometrics" accompanied by two four-color cartoons, one titled "Poor forecasts have brought once high-flying econometricians closer back to earth" and another with the caption "The models had the right figures a few years back, but now their allure has dimmed". Another source of pessimism was the recent NBER-sponsored conference on econometric models and business cycles, at which various papers reported, among other things, that the models when simulated are generally unable to capture anything like the amplitude of postwar recessions like 1957-58 and in *ex post* experiments predict poorly only one or two quarters ahead.

Klein is not unaware of these problems, but he brushes them aside with disturbing complacency. About the recent forecasting difficulties, for instance, he states that "some individual periods have proved to be enigmatic, as in late 1968 and early 1969, but errors can readily be recognized and allowed for, so that a system that is temporarily off the track can readily be restored to the track; thus minimizing and confining failures". He apparently regards the recent record as calling only for *ad hoc* adjustments in the constants of weak equations, not for a fundamental reevaluation. Similarly, regarding the weakness in cyclical simulations, Klein admits that "in the neighborhood of cyclical turning points, the performance is less precise. For some cycles the root-mean-square error is greater than $10 billion". But again no mention is made of these errors when Klein presents his agenda for future research, which emphasizes further disaggregation and increased attention to explaining the balance of payments.

I concur with Klein's list of the four main purposes of large-scale models of countries like the U.S.A.: prediction, policy simulations (or "general multiplier analysis"), the search for optimal policies, and the reconstruction of history. But Klein appears to believe that we can use the models for policy and historical simulations even if they do not accurately reproduce the economy's behavior in postwar recessions, whereas I would not place much confidence in the general usefulness of the models until the problem areas are subjected to much more careful autopsies than have yet been performed. Before larger models are built, existing models should be subjected to "blockwise" simulations in which various *subsets* of equations are used to predict historical periods, both inside and outside of the sample period, with the variables which are endogenous to the model but explained in other subsets treated as exogenous. This procedure would allow us to determine whether weaknesses in the models are due to individual equations or the interaction of sets of equations, and we could then put first priority on intensive respecification and reestimation in the problem areas before further simulations are conducted. We might find, for instance, that prediction errors are caused by the cyclical insensitivity of inventory investment, and this would imply that until corrected the behavior of the inventory equations would tend to cause not only prediction errors, but also incorrect estimates of policy multipliers and business cycle simulations.

A very useful exercise, as yet scarcely attempted, would be the block-by-block comparison of alternative models. At the recent NBER conference simulation results using different models were compared, but no attempt was made to trace differing results to specific equations or groups of equations. As an example of what can be done, for instance, in a forthcoming review article of simulations with the Brookings model, I show that the high balanced budget multiplier in the Brookings model compared with other large models results almost completely from a particular misspecification in the Brookings demand for money equation.[1]

Modern computer technology would permit in many cases the substitution of an equation from one model into another, helping us to track down the equations which account for differences in the forecasts or policy multipliers yielded by alternative models.

This close and detailed comparison of alternative models should not be limited to the large-scale products like Brookings, Wharton-EFU, OBE, and MIT-FRB, but should include the revolutionary new one-equation model which was unveiled in St. Louis a year ago. Not only does a simple regression of changes in nominal GNP on current and lagged changes in the monetary base appear to outperform large models in predictions of the 1968-69 period, but the St. Louis approach also can track deep recessions like 1957-58 more accurately than the large models. While I do not accept the St. Louis conclusion that fiscal policy has no effect, partly because of the unresolved conflict between the low St. Louis fiscal policy coefficients and the almost unanimous empirical verdict that the demand for money is interest-elastic, I do feel that the St. Louis approach may have revealed an

---

[1] Robert J. Gordon, The Brookings model in action: a review article. *Journal of Political Economy*, May/June 1970.

important weakness in the monetary mechanism in the large-scale models. Klein's agenda for the future mentions the need for an expanded treatment of the monetary sector, but the direction he urges appears to be toward a very detailed description of the workings of the financial sector, whereas I think the greatest relative need is for a complete overhaul of the links between the financial and real sectors. Most models still introduce monetary impulses into the expenditure equations through nominal rather than real interest rate variables. This approach makes an increase in nominal interest rates during periods like 1968 act to reduce spending, whereas the increase in nominal rates may have reflected an increase in the expected rate of inflation accompanied by a constant or declining real rate of interest. Further, money or supply of credit variables need to be introduced directly in more models to represent the operations of wealth and credit rationing effects. More attention needs to be given to the effects of the supply of credit on consumption spending, particularly in light of the unstable behavior of the consumption function in 1968, one of the factors which invalidated the large-scale econometric forecasts for late 1968. Progress in this direction has extended furthest in the most recent versions of the MIT-FRB model, which is now attempting to take explicit account of changes in price expectations, and the kind of extensive disaggregation urged by Klein merely diverts attention from the most important weaknesses of the large models.

Even if a prediction and simulation competition between the St. Louis approach and the ultimate version of something like the MIT-FRB model were to declare the former as winner, a result I doubt will occur, large-scale econometric models will not be obsolete. The St. Louis approach only predicts changes in nominal GNP, and we will still need large models to predict changes in real GNP, prices, productivity, unemployment, and the income of various factors. Here I would again urge emphasis on careful blockwise simulation and prediction experiments with relatively small models, rather than an early push toward the 1000-equation model favored by Klein.

A careful distinction must be made between disaggregation by variable and disaggregation by industry. Klein presents a convincing case for models of, say, 50 equations, models which are large enough to "display a wide variety of policy parameters and variables". But these arguments do not support further disaggregation by industry, which tends to lead from 50 to 200 and ultimately to 1000 or so equations, Klein sees no reason why disaggregation should not be performed, and emphasizes advances in computer technology which make extensive disaggregation possible. But in place of abstract unsupported arguments in favor of either disaggregation for its own sake or the opposing "law of parsimony", I would urge that at each stage of disaggregation that the accompanying costs and benefits be calculated Do six Brookings-type equations explain the past behavior of *aggregate* investment better than one aggregate equation? If not, the benefits of industry disaggregation cited by Klein, which seem mainly to amount to the "satisfaction of user requirements", must be weighed against the cost of inaccuracy in describing the behavior of the aggregate economy. These cost-benefit calculations should be standard elements in preliminary analysis of any new econometric model which is larger than its predecessors.

There are several scattered pieces of evidence which indicate that the costs of extensive disaggregation may be high. First, scale itself appears to have been a major hurdle in the construction of the Brookings model. So much attention was devoted to compilation of a consistent model and the accompanying input-output tables that very little effort was devoted to careful analysis of the economic logic of the underlying equations. Contrary to Klein's claim, "localized errors" were in this case *not* "readily detected and corrected". Further, two pieces of evidence on the costs of disaggregation are presented in the recent volume, *The Brookings model: some further results*. Klein finds that the 1963-64 control solution of the relatively small Wharton-EFU model predicts actual values much more closely than that of the large Brookings model. Also, De Leeuw reports that in comparing financial market simulations of models using alternatively his large and small financial sectors, "The condensed model performs well in this test — better, in fact, than the larger model" (p. 296). These scattered findings do not appear to support Klein's unsupported claim that "In defense of bigness, there may be some advantages of spreading risks... If one is dealing with many small components, errors may be offsetting in arriving at national totals and localized errors may not be serious for most of the system".

I conclude, then, by proposing an agenda for the early 1970's which points in the opposite direction from Klein's. Large-scale econometric models have not been performing well lately, we should not be sanguine about their condition, and to remedy errors we need intensive repair work on relatively small systems which we can easily manipulate and understand rather than an indiscriminate push towards further disaggregation.

Frontiers of Quantitative Economics, ed. **M.D. Intriligator**. © *North-Holland Publishing Company*.

CHAPTER 5

THE BAYESIAN APPROACH AND ALTERNATIVES
IN ECONOMETRICS — I*

ARNOLD ZELLNER
University of Chicago

0. Introduction

The Bayesian approach and alternative approaches to the problems of inference and decision have been discussed at length in books and journals for quite a long time.[1] The subjects of these discussions are of fundamental importance for science in general since they involve consideration of conceptual frameworks and methods for analyzing data and making decisions. If, as Karl Pearson suggests, the unity of science is in the main unity in the methods employed in analyzing and learning from data, then the aforementioned discussions may have important implications for work in econometrics.[2]

---

* This work was financed in part by the National Science Foundation, Grant GS-2347, and by income from the H.G.B. Alexander Endowment Fund, Graduate School of Business, University of Chicago.

[1] See e.g., H. Jeffreys, *Theory of probability*. Oxford, Clarendon Press, 1939, 1948, 1961 and 1966, especially Chapters I, VII and VIII. — L.J. Savage et al., *The foundations of statistical inference*. London, Methuen, 1962. — D.V. Lindley, The use of prior probability distributions in statistical inferences and decisions. In: *Proceedings of the fourth Berkeley symposium on mathematical statistics and probability*, edited by J. Neyman, Vol. 1 (1961), 453-468. — J.W. Pratt, Bayesian interpretation of standard inference statements. *J. Royal Stat. Soc. B* 27 (1965), 169-203 (with discussion). — I.J. Good, A subjective evaluation of Bode's law and an "objective" test for approximate numerical rationality. *J. Am. Stat. Assoc.* 64 (1969), 23-49 (with discussion).

[2] K. Pearson, *The grammar of science*. Everyman edition, 1938, 16.

Ideally, it would be desirable to have a unified set of principles for making inferences and decisions which can be readily applied in a broad range of circumstances and fields to yield good results. One of the main points of this paper, and hardly a novel one, is that the Bayesian approach approximates this ideal much more closely than do non-Bayesian approaches currently in use in econometrics.[3] In fact, many non-Bayesian approaches in econometrics and elsewhere are rather good examples of what has been called a collection of "ad hockeries".[4] Some examples illustrating this point will be provided below.

The plan of the paper is as follows: In section 1 several key features of the Bayesian approach will be considered with main emphasis on illustrating its unity, generality and usefulness. Section 2 provides comparisons with other approaches utilized in econometrics. Last, section 3 contains some concluding remarks.

1. Aspects of the Bayesian approach[5]

The following are some key points which are relevant for comparing Bayesian and non-Bayesian approaches in econometrics.

(1) As Jeffreys and others have emphasized, the Bayesian approach to inference complements very nicely the activities of researchers.[6] A researcher is often concerned with the problem of how information in data modifies his beliefs about hypotheses and parameter values. In the Bayesian approach to inference, an investigator has formal and operational techniques for determining how sample information modifies his beliefs. That is, initial beliefs, represented by prior probabilities, are combined by means of Bayes' Theorem with information in data, incorporated in the likelihood function, to yield posterior probabilities relating to parameters or hypotheses.

---

[3] This point has been emphasized by Jeffreys, De Finetti, and others in connection with the Bayesian approach in general *vis-à-vis* other approaches.

[4] This phrase, used by B. de Finetti to describe non-Bayesian approaches at a meeting on Statistical Methods of Econometrics, sponsored by the Institute of Mathematics, Univ. of Rome, Frascati, June 1968, is probably due to I.J. Good.

[5] A number of these points were put forward earlier in A. Zellner, Bayesian inference and simultaneous equation econometric models. Paper presented to the First World Congress of the Econometric Society, Rome, September 1965.

[6] Cf. H. Jeffreys, *Theory of probability, cit. supra.*

In a fundamental sense, this Bayesian procedure for changing initial beliefs is a learning model of great value in accomplishing what Jeffreys and others consider to be a major objective of science, namely learning from experience.

(2) As regards statistical estimation, Bayes' Theorem (sometimes also called Bayes' Rule or the Principle of Inverse Probability) can and has been applied in analyses of all kinds of statistical models including regression models, time series models, Markov transition probability models, simultaneous equation models, errors in the variables models, etc. *In every instance*, the posterior probability density function (pdf) for parameters is proportional to the prior pdf times the likelihood function with the factor of proportionality being a normalizing factor. That one simple principle has such wide applicability is indeed appealing. Further, it should be noted that by appropriate choice of prior pdf an investigator can introduce as much or as little prior information in his analysis as he chooses. The likelihood function in Bayes' Theorem is known to incorporate all the sample information. Thus the posterior pdf for parameters of a model incorporates all the available information, prior and sample. In addition, the posterior pdf so obtained is an exact finite sample pdf which can be used to make exact finite sample posterior probability statements about parameters of a model. There is in general no need to rely on large sample approximations.[7]

Since the entire posterior pdf for a model's parameters, which incorporates both prior and sample information, is generally available, posterior beliefs about parameters are fully represented. If for some reason an investigator wishes to obtain a point estimate, the Bayesian prescription, choose the point estimate which minimizes expected loss, is a general, operational principle in accord with the expected utility hypothesis. For example, if the loss function is quadratic, the mean of a posterior pdf is optimal in general. Given an absolute error loss function, the optimal estimate is the median of a posterior pdf. The Bayesian point estimate is thus tailored to the particular loss function which is deemed appropriate and is an exact finite sample solution to the problem of point estimation. That Bayesian estimators are known to be admissible and consistent, and to minimize average risk are additional features which some point to in

---

[7] Of course, if the sample size is large, large sample approximations can be useful and are often convenient.

commending their use in practice.[8] Finally, in large samples under rather general conditions, posterior pdf's assume a normal form with mean equal to the maximum likelihood (ML) estimate. This dovetailing of Bayesian and ML results in large samples is indeed noteworthy. Jeffreys interprets this fact as providing a justification for the ML approach in large samples.[9]

(3) Bayesian methods for analyzing prediction problems are simple, operational, and generally applicable. Whatever the model, the predictive pdf for future observations is obtained.[10] This predictive pdf serves as a basis for making probability statements about future observations. Also, for a given loss function involving prediction errors, it is generally possible to obtain a point prediction which minimizes expected loss. As with point estimation, the solution to the point prediction problem is in accord with the expected utility hypothesis and is tailored to be appropriate for the loss function which is employed.

(4) In the area of control theory, Bayesian methods are particularly valuable in that their application yields a combined solution to the control and estimation problems.[11] For single period control problems, a Bayesian

---

[8] For consideration of these properties, see e.g., T.S. Ferguson, *Mathematical statistics: a decision theoretic approach*. New York, Academic Press, 1967. Note that these results are based on the assumed use of a *proper* prior pdf for parameters.

[9] See H. Jeffreys, *Theory of probability, cit. supra*, 193-194. Further work on the asymptotic properties of Bayesian procedures appears in D.V. Lindley, The use of prior probability distributions in statistical inferences and decisions, *cit. supra*, and L. Le Cam, On some asymptotic properties of maximum likelihood estimates and related Bayes estimates. *Univ. of California Publications in Statistics* 1 (1953), 277-330.

[10] If $\tilde{y}$ denotes a vector of future observations generated by a model with parameter vector θ, and the joint pdf for $\tilde{y}$ and θ, given the sample information, y, and prior information, I_0, is denoted $p(\tilde{y}, \theta | y, I_0)$, the predictive pdf is obtained by integrating this joint pdf with respect to the elements of θ. See e.g., H. Jeffreys, *Theory of probability, cit. supra.*—H. Raiffa and R. Schlaifer, *Applied statistical decision theory*, Cambridge, Mass., Harvard University Press, 1961.—D.V. Lindley, *Introduction to probability theory from a Bayesian viewpoint*, Part Two: *Inference*. Cambridge 1965, and A. Zellner, *Bayesian inference in econometrics* (forthcoming) for examples of predictive pdf's for a number of models.

[11] See M. Aoki, *Optimization of stochastic systems*. New York, Academic Press, 1967, for a valuable introduction to topics in the control area and an extensive list of references to earlier work. Some works by econometricians include W.D. Fisher, Estimation in the linear decision model, *Int. Econ. Review* 3 (1962), 1-29.—A. Zellner and V.K. Chetty, Prediction and decision problems in regression models from the Bayesian point of view. *J. Am. Stat. Assoc.* 60 (1965), 608-616.—A. Zellner and M.S. Geisel, Sensitivity of control to uncertaintly and form of the criterion function. In: *The future of statistics*, edited by D.G. Watts, New York, Academic Press, 1968, 269-289.—E.C. Prescott, Adaptive

solution incorporates both prior and sample information and involves due allowance for uncertainty about parameter values. For multi-period control problems, Bayesian principles can and have been employed to obtain optimal, computable solutions which not only take account of prior and past sample information and uncertainty about parameter values but also take account of new information as it becomes available and how settings of control variables affect the precision of information about parameter values. Thus solutions to adaptive control problems employing Bayesian methods are solutions to the joint problems of control, estimation and design of experiments.

(5) In the Bayesian approach, prior information about parameters or models can be flexibly and formally incorporated in analyses of estimation, prediction, control, and hypothesis testing problems. This flexibility of the Bayesian approach with respect to the incorporation of prior information in analyses contrasts markedly with currently available non-Bayesian techniques for using prior information in econometric analyses. (See the next section for examples.) Of course non-Bayesians use prior information extensively in their work. For example, exact prior restrictions on parameters are introduced to identify parameters of simultaneous equation models. In the errors in the variables model, prior information about parameter values, say the ratio of error terms' variances, is required to identify parameters. Often in analyses of Cobb-Douglas production function models, the prior assumption of constant returns to scale is introduced in an effort to deal with multicollinearity. What should be appreciated in these and other examples is that Bayesians can introduce such required information in a flexible manner which can more accurately reflect the prior information that we may have about parameter values.[12]

(6) The problem of nuisance parameters is solved quite straightforwardly and neatly in the Bayesian approach. Parameters not of interest to an investigator, that is nuisance parameters, can be integrated out of a posterior pdf to obtain the marginal pdf for the parameters of interest. This

---

decision rules for government and industry. Doctoral dissertation, Grad. Sch. of Ind. Administration, Carnegie-Mellon U., 1967.

[12] This point has been made by J. Drèze on many occasions. See e.g., his The Bayesian approach to simultaneous equations estimation. ONR Research Memo No. 67, The Technological Institute, Northwestern U., 1962.

marginal posterior pdf can then be employed to make inferences about the parameters of interest.[13]

(7) The Bayesian approach is convenient for the analysis of effects of departures from specifying assumptions. That is, use of conditional posterior pdf's enables an investigator to determine how sensitive his inferences about a particular subset of parameters are to what is assumed about other parameters. Such an approach has been used on a variety of problems.[14]

(8) In the Bayesian approach, inferences about parameters, etc., can be made on the basis of the prior and sample information which we have. There is no need to justify inference procedures in terms of their behavior in repeated, as yet unobserved, samples. This is not to say that properties of procedures in repeated samples are not of interest and, in fact, e.g., Bayesian estimators have several good sampling properties in that they are admissible and constructed so as to minimize average risk. However, in an inference situation, what is most relevant is the information at hand in the sample and in our prior beliefs.

(9) In the area of comparing and testing hypotheses and models, the Bayesian approach is distinguished from non-Bayesian approaches in that it associates probabilities with hypotheses and provides formal, operational techniques for modifying such probabilities in the light of new information. These posterior probabilities associated with hypotheses and models incorporate prior and sample information and are viewed by many Bayesians as representing degrees of belief. Then too, if one has explicit losses associated with actions, such as accepting or rejecting a particular hypothesis, and posterior probabilities associated with possible states of the world, he can act so as to minimize expected loss in testing hypotheses.[15]

---

[13] For an example, see A. Zellner and G. C. Tiao, Bayesian analysis of the regression model with autocorrelated errors. *J. Am. Stat. Assoc.* 59 (1964), 763-768.

[14] See e.g., G. E. P. Box and G. C. Tiao, A Bayesian approach to the importance of assumptions applied to the comparison of variances. *Biometrika* 51 (1964), 153-167. — A. Zellner and G. C. Tiao, Bayesian analysis of the regression model with autocorrelated errors, *cit. supra*. — V. K. Chetty, Bayesian Analysis of Haavelmo's models. *Econometrica* 36 (1968), 582-602.

[15] Some works dealing with comparing and testing hypotheses from the Bayesian point of view include H. Jeffreys, *Theory of probablity*, *cit. supra*. — D. V. Lindley, *Introduction to probability theory from a Bayesian viewpoint*. Part Two: *Inference*, *cit. supra*. — And A statistical paradox. *Biometrika* 44 (1957), 187-192 (see also M. S. Bartlett's

Having reviewed several important aspects of the Bayesian approach, a comparative review of the characteristics of some non-Bayesian approaches in econometrics will now be presented.

2. Non-Bayesian approaches in econometrics

Comparison of the Bayesian (B) approach with non-Bayesian (NB) approaches in econometrics is difficult since there are many formal and informal NB approaches utilized in econometrics. Some of these NB approaches are designed to handle specific types of problems and do not represent a unified set of principles which can be applied to a broad range of problems. Also, it is recognized that good researchers can sometimes obtain reasonable results even if they are not operating with an explicitly formulated set of principles. While this latter fact is recognized, what will emerge from the considerations presented below *is that there is no alternative set of principles currently being employed in econometrics which is as unified and as generally applicable as those embedded in the B approach.* To provide some structure to the discussion, a review of properties of NB approaches in econometrics to the issues and problems listed in section 1 will be presented.

(1) Above, it was pointed out that the Bayesian approach incorporates an explicit learning model which appears to complement the activities of researchers rather nicely. As of the present writing, it is a fact that NB approaches in econometrics do not incorporate learning models as fundamentally and as explicitly as is done in the B approach. For example, in NB approaches it is usually not considered meaningful to associate probabilities with hypotheses or models. Thus in NB approaches, it is impossible to quantify a statement of the type, "The permanent income hypothesis is probably true". Further, they can not formally allow for the modification of such probabilities in the light of new sample information.

---

comment on this paper in the same journal and volume, p. 533). — G.E.P. Box and W.J. Hill, Discrimination among mechanistic models. *Technometrics* 9 (1967), 57-91. — H. Thornber, Applications of decision theory to econometrics. Doctoral dissertation, U. of Chicago, 1966. — A. Zellner, *Bayesian inference in econometrics* (forthcoming). — M.S. Geisel, Comparing and choosing among parametric statistical models: A Bayesian analysis with macroeconomic applications. Doctoral dissertation, Univ. of Chicago (1970).

If the revision of such probabilities is regarded as a representation of the learning process in research, then, of course, NB approaches do not formally provide what is needed for this process. However, this is not to say that non-Bayesians do not engage in considerations concerning whether a particular hypothesis is probably true. They do so, but only in an informal and subjective manner.

That the B approach incorporates a formal and explicit learning model is not necessarily an advantage if, e.g., by doing so the B approach could not be applied fruitfully in practice. That this latter circumstance is not the case is easily established by noting that a wide range of problems has been analyzed from the B point of view without undue difficulty and, in fact, in many instances with less difficulty, both practically and theoretically, than is the case with NB approaches.

(2) In the area of econometric estimation, it was stated above that Bayes' Theorem is a simple and generally applicable principle which can and has been used to analyze estimation problems for a very wide range of models. In NB approaches in econometrics, the situation is quite different. There is a plethora of estimation principles, some more general than others. The following are a few principles which have been put forward: maximum likelihood, least squares, best linear unbiased estimation, generalized least squares, minimum absolute deviations, minimum chi-square, indirect least squares, instrumental variable methods, generalized classical linear estimation, two and three stage least squares, simultaneous equation least-squares, k-class estimation, double k-class estimation, minimal mean square error estimation, minimum variance unbiased estimation, best quadratic unbiased estimation, etc. While some of these methods produce satisfactory results in particular circumstances and for particular models, it is clearly the case that many are not generally applicable and are not related in any obvious way to a simple set of unified and generally applicable principles. This is one reason why many Bayesians regard current practice in econometrics and elsewhere to be rather *ad hoc*.

One of the more general principles listed above is the maximum likelihood (ML) method of estimation. It can and has been employed to produce estimates of parameters in many different kinds of econometric models. Usually in econometrics, estimators generated by ML are justified in terms of their sampling properties in large samples, e.g., consistency and large sample efficiency. As pointed out above, a ML estimate will be approximately equal to the mean of the Bayesian posterior pdf in large samples under general conditions. Thus, for many models, there is a compatibility between large sample Bayesian and ML results, although there is an important difference in interpretation of them. However, in "small" samples the situation is fundamentally different. ML estimators do not necessarily have good small sample sampling properties. For example, in the standard linear normal regression model, the ML estimator for the disturbance variance is usually discarded in favor of one with "better" properties. Recent work of Stein indicates that if there are three or more regression coefficients to be estimated, the ML estimator for the regression coefficients is inadmissible relative to a quadratic loss function.[16] Further, with regard to the log-normal distribution, it appears that there are estimators with better finite sample properties than possessed by the ML estimator. Last, in connection with parameters of simultaneous equation models, it is a fact that many econometricians use other than ML estimators for a variety of reasons.

Thus while the ML method of estimation is a general one and useful in quite a few circumstances, it is a fact that for quite a few important problems in econometrics it produces unsatisfactory small sample results according to sampling theory criteria and is often replaced by alternatives. This stands in contrast to Bayesian estimators which can be generated by simple principles and which have good sampling properties in that they are known to be admissible and minimize average risk (when it exists).

While not emphasized in much of the econometric literature, the likelihood approach of Barnard and others deserves some comment. In this approach great emphasis is placed on characterizing the shape and general features of the likelihood function without bringing in sampling properties of procedures.[17] That is, the likelihood function is considered in connection with data on hand and not with respect to other possible samples which could have arisen. The location of the mode of the likelihood function is just one feature, and perhaps not the most important feature, to be studied according to proponents of this approach. In this respect, most Bayesians would agree that a thorough study of the likelihood function is desirable.

---

[16] C. Stein, Multiple regression. In: *Contributions to probability and statistics: essays in honor of Harold Hotelling*, edited by I. Olkin. Stanford, Calif., Stanford Univ. Press, 1960, 424-443. See also S. L. Sclove, Improved Estimators for Coefficients in Linear Regression. *J. Am. Stat. Assoc.* 63 (1968), 596-606.

[17] See e. g., G. A. Barnard, G. M. Jenkins and C. B. Winsten, Likelihood inference and time series. *J. Roy. Statistical Society A* 125 (1962), 321-372 (with discussion).

However, without Bayes' Theorem, it appears necessary to entertain not only the concept of probability but also the concept of likelihood. By use of Bayes' Theorem the analysis can go forward in terms of the concept of probability alone which appears to be advantageous and which does not rule out the desirable practice of studying the form of the likelihood function.

While some Bayesians do not emphasize the sampling properties of B estimators, it should be recognized that B estimators have rather good sampling properties both in small and large samples. As pointed out above, the B estimator is the estimator which minimizes average risk. This is a well known exact finite sample property of B estimators which should be of great interest to NB's. Several Monte Carlo experiments have been performed to compare properties of B and NB estimators.[18] In all experiments to date, B estimators have performed as well or better than leading NB estimators. In one particularly outstanding study of an autoregressive model, risk functions and average risk associated with alternative B and NB estimators were estimated.[19] It was established that the properties of estimators for this "simple" model are quite different in small samples and that the B estimator's average risk is quite a bit smaller than of the ML estimator and several other popular NB estimators. Of course point estimation is just a part of the problem of inference. That the Bayesian approach provides the complete, finite sample posterior pdf for models' parameters and can be employed to make other kinds of inferences should not be overlooked.

(3) As pointed out above, the B approach provides a unified and operational approach to the problem of prediction. In NB approaches various principles are employed to generate "optimal" predictors which are not generally applicable. For example, in some situations NB econometricians use minimum variance linear unbiased predictors. It is well known that this principle can not be applied in the case of many important models used in econometrics. Further, the restrictions that a predictor be *linear* and *unbiased* can result in sub-optimal predictors in a number of

---

[18] See, e.g., A.Zellner, Bayesian inference and simultaneous equation econometric models, *cit. supra.* — V.K. Chetty, Bayesian analysis of some simultaneous equation models and specification errors. Doctoral dissertation, Univ. of Wisconsin, Madison, 1966. — H. Thornber, Finite Sample Monte Carlo studies: an autoregressive illustration. *J. Am. Stat. Assoc.* 62 (1967), 801-818. — J.B. Copas, Monte Carlo results for estimation in a stable Markov time series. *J. Roy. Stat. Soc. A* (1966), 110-116. — T.C. Lee, G.G. Judge and A. Zellner, Maximum likelihood and Bayesian estimation of transition probabilities. *J. Am. Stat. Assoc.* 63 (1968), 1162-1179.

[19] H. Thornber, *op. cit.*

cases.[20] Bayesians do not place such restrictions on their predictors and as a result can usually obtain point predictions which minimize expected loss. In addition, since the complete predictive pdf is in general available in the B approach, various probability statements about future observations can be made for a variety of models. These probability statements, made conditional upon the given sample and prior information, appear to be the kinds of statements which are of great value to economic forecasters. Needless to say, forecasters use a good deal of outside or prior information in their work. That the B approach provides a means of formally incorporating such information in forecasts and in probability statements regarding future outcomes is indeed fortunate and contrasts with what is currently available in NB approaches for accomplishing this objective.

(4) With respect to control problems in econometrics, it is probably accurate to state that approaches currently in use do not allow for uncertainty about values of parameters appearing in the equations of econometric models. This is the case in applications of "certainty equivalence" and "linear decision rule" principles which have appeared in the literature. Several studies have appeared which indicate that Bayesian solutions to control problems, which take account of uncertainty about parameter values, are different from certainty-equivalence solutions and provide lower expected loss particularly when sample information is not very extensive or precise.[21] In addition, B solutions to control problems reflect both sample and prior information (as much or as little of the latter as is judged reasonable to use). As regards multi-period control problems with unknown model parameters which must be estimated, it appears that there is no alternative to the B adaptive control solution in the econometric literature.

(5) On the question of introducing prior information in analyses, often this is done in an informal manner in NB approaches. For example, in regression problems some use the following procedure: If an independent variable's coefficient estimate turns out to have the "wrong" algebraic sign, the variable is dropped from the regression. This *ad hoc* procedure can yield good results in terms of, for example, a mean square error criterion. However, it is apparent that the resulting estimator is no longer a minimum

---

[20] See, e.g., A. Zellner, Decision rules for economic forecasting. *Econometrica* 31 (1963), 111-130.

[21] In particular see the work of Aoki, Fisher, Geisel, Prescott and Zellner cited in footnote 11 above.

variance linear unbiased estimator. Rather it is a biased, nonlinear estimator having a mixed distribution that is part discrete (some probability piled up at zero) and part in a truncated normal form.[22] Thus, obviously, there is no secure basis for the usual t tests and for constructing usual confidence intervals. This is then a good example of an *ad hoc* procedure which departs from what some regard as a fairly general principle (minimum variance linear unbiased estimation).

Another special method for incorporating subjective prior information in NB analyses which has appeared in econometrics texts and the literature is the "mixed linear estimation" procedure for the linear regression model,[23] $\tilde{y} = X\beta + \tilde{u}$. The subjective prior information about the non-stochastic, true parameter vector β, is represented by $\tilde{r} = R\beta + \tilde{v}$ where R is a matrix to be assigned by an investigator and a tilde denotes random variables. It is further assumed that $E\tilde{v} = 0$ and $E\tilde{v}\tilde{v}' = \Omega$, a matrix whose elements are assigned by an investigator. Then generalized least squares (GLS) is employed to combine the sample and prior information with the common variance of the elements of $\tilde{u}$ replaced by a sample estimate thereby getting an approximation to the GLS estimator. What appears not to have been recognized in this approach is that a rather stringent condition has been placed on the prior information. That is $E\tilde{r} = R\beta$, or if $R = I$, $E\tilde{r} = \beta$, the *true parameter* vector. That prior subjective information be unbiased is a severe restriction on the nature of such information, a restriction that is not imposed in the B approach. Further in analyzing the large sample properties of the linear mixed estimator, it has been customary to assume that $R'\Omega^{-1}R$ is of order T and that the prior subjective information grows with the sample size, T, and is not dominated by the sample information as the sample size grows large. That the precision of the prior subjective information depends on the sample size and that the sample information does not dominate in large samples are features of this approach which appear unsatisfactory from the B point of view.

---

[22] If $\hat{\beta}$ is the unrestricted least squares estimator, then a "sign-test" estimator, denoted $\beta*$, is given by

$$\beta* = \begin{cases} \hat{\beta} \text{ for } \hat{\beta} > 0 \\ 0 \text{ for } \hat{\beta} \leq 0. \end{cases}$$

[23] See e.g., A.S. Goldberger, *Econometric theory*. New York, Wiley, 1964, p. 261, and the references cited there.

Prior information in the form of exact constraints and/or inequality constraints can of course be introduced in B and NB approaches. In connection with inequality constraints, the criterion function (likelihood function, sum of squared errors, etc.) can be maximized (or minimized) subject to inequality constraints.[24] The resulting point estimators often have extremely complicated, unknown distributions. Testing and interval estimation procedures for the inequality constraint case remain to be worked out. Reliance is often placed on large sample approximations. However, if the sample is truly a large one, the prior information incorporated in the inequality constraints will often be unimportant. In the B approach inequality constraints can and have been introduced via an appropriate choice of prior pdf.[25] Posterior pdf's have been obtained in the usual manner and, as always, summarize the complete information (sample and prior) about parameters. If a point estimate is desired, it can be computed and has a finite sample justification, as explained above.

NB analyses of random parameter models superficially appear to resemble B analyses of fixed parameter models in that a pdf for parameters appears in a NB analysis. However, this pdf is not given the interpretation of representing subjective prior information and, further, B analyses of random parameter models involve placing a prior pdf on the parameters of the pdf for the random parameters.[26]

(6) The problem of nuisance parameters is a particularly thorny one in NB approaches in econometrics and elsewhere. For example, an optimal estimator, say a generalized least squares estimator, may depend on a disturbance autocorrelation parameter which is not of special interest to an investigator. Often a sample estimate of the nuisance parameter (or parameters) is inserted in the expression for an optimal estimator. This procedure produces an approximation to the optimal estimator which is

---

[24] Examples of such an approach appear in G. G. Judge and T. Takayama, Inequality restrictions in regression analysis. *J. Am. Stat. Assoc.* 61 (1966), 166-181. — T. C. Lee, G. G. Judge and A. Zellner, Maximum likelihood and Bayesian estimation of transition probabilities, *cit. supra.* — A. Zellner and M. S. Geisel, Analysis of distributed lag models with applications to consumption function estimation. Invited paper presented to the Econometric Society, Amsterdam, Sept. 1968, and to appear in *Econometrica*.

[25] See e. g., the last two references in footnote 24.

[26] These issues have been discussed by Lindley in connection with the paper D. V. Lindley and G. M. El-Sayyad, The Bayesian estimation of a linear functional relationship. *J. Roy. Stat. Soc. B* 20 (1968), 190-202. See also P. A. V. B. Swamy, Statistical inference in random coefficient models. Doctoral dissertation, Univ. of Wisconsin, Madison, 1968.

usually justified in terms of large sample theory. If the sample size is not large, there is a question about how good the approximation is. As mentioned above, Bayesians handle the nuisance parameter problem quite simply: such parameters are integrated out of a posterior pdf to yield the marginal posterior pdf for the parameter (or parameters) of interest.

(7) The effects of departures from specifying assumptions have been analyzed to some extent using B and NB approaches. If, e.g., disturbance terms in a regression model are thought to be autocorrelated, the model can be broadened to include a stochastic process, say a first order auto-regressive process, for the disturbance terms. Then under alternative assumptions about the value of the autoregressive parameter, both B and NB approaches can be utilized to assess how sensitive inferences about regression coefficients are to what is assumed about the autoregressive parameter. Similar calculations, involving introduction of a new parameter or two, can be performed in connection with possible departures from normality, linearity and homoscedasticity in regression models although in these cases it is difficult to obtain the exact finite sample distributions of NB unconditional estimators.[27] Since Bayesians and some likelihood advocates take the sample as given (not random), the relevance of these sampling distributions for the problems of inference and of investigating effects of departures in a particular analysis is unclear. Bayesians, in any event, can compute conditional posterior pdf's for parameters of interest given values of a parameter (or parameters) introduced to allow for a departure from specifying assumptions. This sort of analysis can generally be carried through without a need for approximations.

(8) The relevance for inference from given data of the criterion of performance in repeated samples, which is featured in many NB approaches in econometrics and elsewhere, has not received much attention in the econometric literature. Bayesians and some likelihood advocates emphasize that inferences from given data should be based on the information that is in the given data and, for Bayesians, on given prior information. The relevance of other possible samples for the problem of analyzing a given set of data is not clear. However, as pointed out above, Bayesian estimation procedures do have good properties in repeated samples. It appears that the question of how procedures perform in connection with random data

---

[27] See, e.g., G.E.P. Box and D.R. Cox, An Analysis of transformations. *J. Roy. Stat. Soc. B* 26 (1964), 211-243.

samples is an important issue before the data are drawn, for example in designing a survey. Once the data have been obtained, the problem of inference appears to be that of bringing the information in the given data to bear on beliefs about parameter values, etc.

(9) In the area of analyzing alternative hypotheses and models, it was pointed out above that Bayesians can compute probabilities associated with alternative hypotheses or models which reflect both prior and sample information and which can be regarded as measures of belief in alternative hypotheses or models. Posterior odds relating to two mutually exclusive hypotheses or models are given *in general* by the product of prior odds times a likelihood ratio factor. Further, if a decision has to be made, namely accept or reject, given a loss structure specifying the consequences of these acts, it is possible to act so as to minimize expected loss. NB approaches for analyzing alternative hypotheses and models do not involve introduction of probabilities associated with hypotheses or models. Rather what is involved in testing is the computation of a test statistic. If the test statistic assumes an "unusual" value under the null hypothesis, an investigator's view of the null hypothesis is somehow affected. The jump in logic from an unusual event under the null hypothesis to the conclusion that the null hypothesis is suspect is an issue that concerns many Bayesians. This is not to say that NB test procedures always or usually yield meaningless results. In fact under vague prior information, Lindley has provided a B rationale for usual tests (likelihood ratio, t tests, F tests, etc.).[28] On the other hand, as emphasized by Jeffreys and others, in testing situations our prior information is often not vague and it is important to take account of this fact in order to get meaningful results. Most, if not all, NB approaches to testing in econometrics do not appear at present to have the capability of formally introducing prior subjective information in testing hypotheses. Rather, such information tends to be used informally in viewing final results and, perhaps, in the choice of a significance level.

3. Conclusions

In a short paper, it is difficult to do justice to the delicate and deep issues involved in a comparison of alternative approaches in econometrics. What

---

[28] D. V. Lindley, *Introduction to probability theory from a Bayesian viewpoint*. Part Two: *Inference, cit. supra.*

has been presented is an overview of some distinctive characteristics of the B approach and a comparison of NB approaches in relation to these characteristics of the B approach. Further, it must be recognized that the B approach is in a stage of rapid development with work going ahead on many new problems and applications. While this is recognized, it does not seem overly risky to conclude that the B approach, which already has had some impact on econometric work, will have a much more powerful influence in the next few years. The most important consideration underlying this prediction is the fact that the B approach rests on a unified and relatively simple set of principles which are broadly applicable and produce good results. In addition, the considerations in sections 1 and 2 of this paper point up specific features of the B approach which commend it for use in econometrics and other areas of science.

Frontiers of Quantitative Economics, ed. M.D. Intriligator. © *North-Holland Publishing Company.*

THE BAYESIAN APPROACH AND ALTERNATIVES IN ECONOMETRICS — II

THOMAS J. ROTHENBERG

University of California, Berkeley

Should economists in the course of their empirical research use Bayesian methods of inference? This explicitly normative question is at the core of much current discussion in econometric methodology. Indeed, the question of the role of Bayesian techniques has been raised in nearly every application of statistics and has caused an enormous amount of controversy in each of them. I do not intend to survey this controversy over Bayesian methods — such a survey would be very lengthy and, in any case, would not be very fruitful. Nor will I try to present a convincing defense of my own answer to the question. Alas, I have none — neither a convincing defense, nor even an answer at all. It seems, however, that much of the controversy over Bayesian methods has been directed at false issues and has been based on misconceptions as to where the real difficulties lie. I would like, therefore, to indicate what are, for me, the crucial aspects of the debate between Bayesians and non-Bayesians.[1]

Before beginning, it is only fair that I state my current feelings about the role of Bayesian techniques in econometrics. Frankly, they are not altogether free from contradiction. I think that there is a set of important

---

[1] My thinking on these questions has been greatly influenced by the following: L.J. Savage, The Foundations of statistics reconsidered. In: *Studies in subjective probability*, edited by H. Kyburg and H. Smokler. New York, Wiley, 1964. — D.V. Lindley, Statistical inference. *Journal of the Royal Statistical Society B* 15 (1953). — R.A. Fisher, *Statistical methods and scientific inference.* New York, Hafner, 1956. — Karl Popper, *Conjectures and refutations. ...,* Basic Books, 1962.

problems where Bayesian techniques are clearly superior to any traditional alternatives. Some examples will be given later. I would suggest, however, that for many (perhaps most) statistical problems which arise in practice the difference between Bayesian methods and traditional methods is too small to worry about, and that when the two methods differ it is usually a result of making strongly different assumptions about the problem. Yet, I would also suggest that for certain key problems involving major changes in thinking, the difference between the Bayesian and traditional approaches is enormous and here the Bayesian approach is very unsatisfactory. These views will, I hope, become somewhat more clear as I proceed.

As a starting point in the discussion, I would like to quote some passages from a famous critic of an earlier version of Bayesian statistics (which then went under the name of "inverse probability"). In attacking the Bayesian approach in his 1935 book, *Design of experiments*, R. A. Fisher gave three basic arguments:

> 1. ... advocates of inverse probability seem forced to regard mathematical probability, not as an objective quantity measured by observable frequencies, but as measuring merely psychological tendencies, theorems respecting which are useless for scientific purposes.
> 2. ... it is the nature of an axiom that its truth should be apparent to any rational mind which fully apprehends its meaning. The axiom of Bayes has certainly been fully apprehended by a good many rational minds, including that of its author, without carrying this conviction of necessary truth.
> 3. ... inverse probability has been only very rarely used in the justification of conclusions from experimental facts, although the theory has been widely taught, and is widespread in the literature of probability. Whatever the reasons are which give experimenters confidence that they can draw valid conclusions from their results, they seem to act just as powerfully whether the experimenter has heard of the theory of inverse probability or not.[2]

Fisher, of course, was talking about a very primitive form of Bayesian analysis. It is of some interest to see how the modern mid-20th century version of Bayesianism stands up to his attacks. A first problem is that it is not altogether clear what one means by the modern Bayesian approach. The term "Bayesian" is used in a number of different ways by different people. All of these uses, however, have some common elements: Hypotheses about the state of nature are assigned probabilities. Sample evidence is viewed as a random variable whose probability distribution is conditional on the state of nature. By Bayes' formula one calculates a new probability

---

[2] Pages 6-7 in the 7th edition, printed in 1960 by Oliver and Boyd.

distribution for the hypotheses conditional on the sample data. This process of going from prior (before the data) probability distributions to posterior (after the data) probability distributions is the basis of inductive inference for a Bayesian.

This simple description leaves out two crucial steps in the inference procedure. First, how does one choose the prior distribution and, second, what does one do with the posterior distribution once one has it? Here is where there are differences of opinion among the Bayesians. One may distinguish two major schools of thought. The *decision theorists* (like Raiffa and Savage) argue that any specific inference problem involves a decision maker choosing among alternative actions where the degree of preference for the various possible actions can be expressed by a utility function which depends on the unknown state of nature. Given the posterior distribution the best act (and hence implicitly the best inference) is the one which maximizes expected utility. As for the prior distribution, the decision theorists argue as follows: people who make consistent choices in uncertain situations always behave as though they had a subjective probability distribution. Since decision makers do make decisions even in the absence of data, some *a priori* information is already available before experiments are made and this can be expressed as a prior probability distribution over the possible states of nature.

In contrast to the decision theorists, however, there are other Bayesians who do not assume a decision problem at all. These Bayesians, *canonical theorists* (like Jeffreys) argue that in those cases where there is little previous evidence available one should use as prior distribution a uniform distribution over alternative hypotheses. A somewhat more sophisticated version of this rule is provided by Jeffreys, who suggests an invariance procedure for obtaining prior distributions.[3] In either case, there is a canonical prior distribution determined by the likelihood function alone and not by any subjective beliefs. Since no decision problem is posed, the posterior distribution on the alternative hypotheses is the final product of this type of inference procedure.

Although there are great similarities between these two versions of Bayesianism (and it is possible to be a decision theorist for some problems and a canonical theorist for others), I shall treat these variants as quite

---

[3] Harold Jeffreys, *Theory of probability*, 3rd Edition. Oxford 1961, especially Chapter One.

separate. For they differ in one very important respect. Two decision theorists, looking at the same data and agreeing on the stochastic process which produced the data, could come to very different conclusions if they started with different prior beliefs or utility functions. Two followers of Jeffreys' invariance rule of induction, however, would always come to the same inference in this circumstance. Furthermore a canonical theorist can argue (along with non-Bayesians like Fisher) that inference and knowledge are quite different from behavior and decision, whereas a decision theorist treats the former as special cases of the latter.

The conclusion of this brief aside is that there are two sorts of Bayesians: (1) decision theorists who argue that inference should be thought of as action and that any prior probability which reflects one's beliefs can be used in deriving a posterior distribution, and (2) canonical theorists who argue that inference is meaningful even without action and that any specific problem gives rise to a specific set of prior probabilities to be used in Bayes' formula.

How, then, would these two types of Bayesians respond to Fisher's attacks? In regard to the first point — that Bayesians must give up a frequency interpretation of probability — both schools would agree. Indeed, both Savage and Jeffreys would argue that there are fundamental weaknesses in the frequency interpretation and that it has to be dropped in any case. Fisher's proposition that non-frequency interpretations are useless for scientific purposes is of course denied by Bayesians. Both decision theorists and canonical theorists would argue that statements like "it will probably rain tomorrow" are used constantly in scientific discourse and that such statements follow a precise logical structure. In some sense the Bayesians are clearly right: it *is* possible to develop a system of logic obeying the axioms of probability which is not based on relative frequencies. Both Savage and Jeffreys have produced such systems. Whether one should *use* such a system in scientific procedures, however, cannot be answered on purely logical grounds. After all, both Euclidean and non-Euclidean geometries are consistent logical systems. The usefulness of such a system must be judged at a different level.

Fisher's second argument — that the Bayesian axiom on the existence of prior probability distributions over states of nature is not readily apparent — is also answerable, at least by some Bayesians. The decision theorist can point to the fact that this axiom can be derived from a set of more basic postulates on the consistency of individual choices under uncertainty.[4] These latter postulates — although not accepted by everyone — are quite convincing to many rational minds (including this one). The canonical Bayesian theorists, however, have no clear answer to Fisher's objection. They simply argue that the axiom is indeed self evident; that there is a valid primitive idea expressing the degree of confidence that we may reasonably have in a proposition and further that there is a simple mathematical form for expressing the notion of complete ignorance. Here, unfortunately, I share Fisher's skepticism. Jeffreys' axioms do not possess the sure ring of truth, even though they may sometimes give rise to sensible statistical procedures. It is for this reason I believe that few people have been able to accept the Jeffreys analysis.

Finally, Fisher's third point — that in practice researchers do not defend their conclusions by Bayesian arguments — is in my opinion the crucial one. It is an argument that avoids tautologies and endless episto-mological debate. It is an argument consistent with a dictum of modern methodological research: to gain an understanding of the philosophy of science, one should study the history of science. Thus I would like to spend the rest of this paper exploring the question: is there compelling evidence in the history of science — in economics and elsewhere — that tends to support or contradict the Bayesian approach to learning from experience?

In this context it is possible to consider the original question in three parts. First, can most problems in scientific research be usefully classified as statistical decision problems? Second, if they can be so classified, is the Bayesian solution to the decision problem an accepted one? Third, if they cannot be so classified, do scientists use nondecision theoretic Bayesian arguments to justify their conclusions?

I would now like to take up these three questions, starting with the second one because it is in many ways the easiest. Suppose we argue that a given estimation problem does fall into the structure of statistical decision theory. That is, we have to guess the value of some parameter θ and that the cost of being wrong can be described by a loss function (say a quadratic function of the estimation error). We observe a sample which has a distri-bution completely known to us except for the parameter θ. Any estimator (i.e., any function of the sample values) has associated with it a mean

---

[4] See, e.g., J. Pratt, H. Raiffa, and R. Schlaifer, The foundations of decision under uncertainty: an elementary exposition. *J.A.S.A.*, 1964. — L.J. Savage, *The foundations of statistics*. New York, Wiley, 1954.

squared error which depends on θ. This expected loss, expressed as a function of θ, is called the risk function for the estimator. In general, the risk functions for various estimators will cross; that is, no risk function is, for all θ, uniformly below all the others. Thus we have a problem of choosing among the alternative risk functions.

The traditional solution is to restrict ourselves to unbiased estimators and hope that among estimators in the restricted class there is one which has uniformly smallest risk. Luckily, for many problems such a minimum variance unbiased estimate exists. But would anyone in a real decision context choose such a solution? It is hard to see why anyone should. Does a plant manager when making ordering decisions care that in some sense he will be right "on the average"? Won't he naturally use his rough information about the world, combine it with current data, and essentially act as a Bayesian? Surely people involved in real-world decision-making do possess enormous amounts of prior information. Furthermore, they very likely behave — or at least would like to behave — in a manner consistent with the "coherence" axioms of Savage. Thus I find very convincing the arguments of Savage, Raiffa, and others that Bayesian analysis is consistent with — indeed implied by — sensible decision making in practice. I will not try to defend this position here since it is persuasively done in the published literature. I shall simply state my view that, to the extent statistical problems truly are applied decision problems, I find the Bayesian approach more attractive than the traditional ones.

Some years ago I argued in an unpublished paper that the decision aspect of much economic research had been unfortunately ignored.[5] I took the view that a Bayesian approach to econometrics was needed so that this decision aspect could be incorporated into practical statistical procedures. Since that time enormous progress has been made in developing the tools for solving econometric decision problems. The excellent work of Dreze, Kaufman, Zellner and many others has brought us to the point where practical application of Bayesian methods in economics is now possible. Although many technical problems remain to be solved — convenient prior distributions when there are nuisance parameters have still to be developed, e.g. — the basic framework for Bayesian econometrics now exists. Textbooks in elementary economic statistics now treat Bayesian methods routinely.

---

[5] T.J. Rothenberg, A Bayesian analysis of simultaneous equation systems. Report 6315, Econometric Institute, Netherlands School of Economics, 1963.

The view that Bayesian decision theory is useful in economic research is widely accepted and no longer open to serious controversy.[6]

Why then is there controversy over Bayesian methods at all? Clearly because there is serious disagreement among statisticians over the usefulness of considering *all* inference problems as decision problems. Here we must be rather careful in defining our terms. Surely most textbook examples of point estimation and hypothesis testing problems do fit easily into the framework of decision theory. The modern textbook writers like Mood and Graybill and Lindgren specifically present these classical problems as special cases of the general decision problem. But does scientific research really proceed in the fashion described by these decision models? Is there not something rather artificial in this textbook treatment? I would suggest that recent work in the history and philosophy of science casts considerable doubt on the usefulness of the simple decision-theoretic model of scientific inference.

Let me suggest two different views on how scientists work.[7] Needless to say, these are highly stylized. One view, which I will call the incremental theory, sees intellectual development as a smooth piecemeal process by which facts and theories are added to the ever growing stockpile that constitutes scientific techniques and knowledge. The scientist learns from experience; and a natural way to describe the combining of past knowledge with current sample information is by Bayes' theorem. Thus each economist makes his small, but useful contribution by modifying his subjective probability distribution over the possible hypotheses concerning Nature. With more and more data posterior distributions become more and more concentrated and uniformity of opinion among economists is approached.

This charming and peaceful picture of progress through hard work and nice priors is of course a caricature. Yet it seems to fit the story told by Jeffreys, Savage, Zellner, and others. For example, Savage writes: "Inference means for us the change in opinion induced by evidence on the application of Bayes' theorem".[8] And De Finetti says: "Everything that does not reduce

---

[6] This is perhaps an exaggeration. See e.g., J. Wolfowitz, Bayesian inference and axioms of consistent decision. *Econometrica* 30 (1962).

[7] The following arguments are based on ones presented by Thomas Kuhn in *The structure of scientific revolution*. Chicago, University of Chicago Press, 1962—and by Paul Feyerabend in Problems of Empiricism. In: *Beyond the Edge of certainty*, edited by R. Colodny. Prentice-Hall, 1965. These authors do not draw the same conclusions from their arguments that I do; they are not, of course, responsible for what I say.

[8] The Foundations of statistics reconsidered, *op. cit.*, p. 178.

to a simple statement, to an isolated historical truth, ... constitutes a judgment of probability which is based, perhaps unconsciously and indistinctly, on the principles of the calculus of probability. This calculus thus constitutes the foundation of the greatest part of our thought, and we can well repeat with Poincaré, 'Without it, Science would be impossible'."[9]

If scientific progress is made by adapting prior beliefs as a result of new experimental evidence, one would expect development to occur smoothly. Intellectual life would be very peaceful; over time divergent opinions come closer together as scholars observe common new evidence. This view of scientific development seems to have some validity if one looks crudely over the general trend of history. Observational evidence has modified old beliefs to form new ones. Conflicting theories are merged into consistent ones as a result of cumulative evidence. Yet, as a description of the day to day work of scientists this incremental theory seems very misleading. It does not capture the arguments which researchers actually use in their discussions with colleagues.

A very different view on how science works is given by Karl Popper.[10] It is not continuity and accumulation which is emphasized, but quite the opposite. His dictum is: *We learn from our mistakes*. Progress is made by attack, by criticism, by attempted refutation of proposals. New truths are not produced by combining old ones with data. New truths are unjustified guesses, conjectures, which happen to survive severely critical tests. This point of view is well expressed by the quote:

> ... whenever we try to propose a solution to a problem, we ought to try as hard as we can to overthrow our solution, rather than defend it. Few of us, unfortunately, practice this precept; but other people, fortunately, will supply the criticism for us if we fail to supply it ourselves.[11]

Anyone who has had a lunchtime economics discussion with our good colleagues at the University of Chicago will see the truth — if not the fortune — of this last sentence!

Stronger versions of the Popper view are given by Kuhn and Feyerabend. Kuhn makes the (now famous) distinction between *normal science* — "a strenuous and devoted attempt to force nature into the conceptual boxes

---

[9] Bruno De Finetti, Foresight: its logical laws, its subjective sources. In: *Studies in subjective probability*, op cit., p. 156.

[10] The classic source is *The logic of scientific discovery*, Harper Torchbooks, 1965 (a translation of the 1934 German edition). A clearer presentation can be found in *Conjectures and refutations* cited earlier.

[11] K. Popper, *The logic of scientific discovery*, op. cit., p. 7.

supplied by professional education" — and *scientific revolutions* — "the extraordinary investigations that lead the profession at last to a new set of commitments, a new basis for the practice of science".[12] Normal science is a slow, incremental process of examining data and fitting them into the traditional paradigm. But scientific progress is not simply the cumulative result of normal scientific activity. The scientific revolutions, the great crises that occur when one paradigm collapses and another one takes its place — this does not fit easily into the incrementalist view of the world. As Feyerabend puts it:

> Now it is commonly assumed ... that crises are, or at least should be, *transitory stages* in the history of thought, that they are periods of disorder and embarrassment which are void of knowledge and provide no suitable basis for methodological discussions. ... The realization that alternatives precipitate progress suggests an evaluation of the relative merits of normal science and periods of crises that differs radically from [the above view.] Normal science, extended over a considerable time, now assumes the character of stagnation, of a lack of new ideas; it seems to become a starting point for dogmatism and metaphysics. Crises, on the other hand, are not accidental disturbances of a desirable peace; they are periods where science is at its best, exhibiting as they do the method of progressing through the consideration of alternatives.[13]

These scientific crises do not occur peacefully. The new paradigms are not related to the old ones by a generalized Bayes formula. As Kuhn quotes Max Planck, "a new scientific truth does not triumph by convincing its opponents and making them see the light, but rather because its opponents eventually die, and a new generation grows up that is familiar with it".[14] Although this is surely an exaggeration it does emphasize the crucial role played by criticism and intellectual antagonism in science. To summarize this crises theory in brief: Science at its best consists of two activities — imaginative, indefensible conjectures and ruthless attempts at refutation.

What does all this have to do with Bayesian econometrics? I think it has the following implications: If we accept the view that scientific progress results from criticism and attack, that scientific method consists of conjecture and refutation, then the naive view of a smooth transition via induction from prior probability to posterior probability must be rejected as historically invalid. Furthermore, the simple-minded decision models described in the textbooks must be rejected as a general framework for scientific work.

---

[12] T. Kuhn, *op. cit.*, pp. 5-6.

[13] P. Feyerabend, Problems of empiricism, *op. cit.*, pp. 167 and 172.

[14] T. Kuhn, *op. cit.*, p. 150. The citation is in the Max Planck, *Scientific autobiography and other papers.* New York 1949, pp. 33-34.

Although Bayesian methods are clearly useful for actual decision problems, they are not necessarily useful for fundamental economic research. Here Fisher's third argument has considerable force. It is, I think, factually correct to say that economists involved in basic empirical research do not justify their arguments on Bayesian grounds. The above arguments suggest there is no compelling reason why they should.

This position, however, does not constitute a general argument against the Bayesian approach. Even if science does consist of refutation rather than induction, rules for refutation must be established. Even if science is viewed as warfare among competing theories, some method for choosing among them is needed. It is simple enough to say that a theory should be rejected if it is inconsistent with the facts. But, as Kuhn emphasizes, all historically significant theories have agreed with the facts — more or less. The Bayesian framework does give us a basis for deciding which of two theories fits the facts best. Thus one may argue that Bayesian methods can play an important role even if one accepts Popper's view of science. This interpretation, however, has two weaknesses. First, it is very hard to place this role of Bayesian analysis into a decision context. I would have no idea how to specify a loss function or a prior probability distribution. One can resort, of course, to the Jeffreys type of analysis — but that has all the weaknesses discussed earlier. Second, most disagreements about fundamental ideas involve noncommensurabilities. "Neither side will grant all the non-empirical assumptions that the other needs in order to make its case", argues Kuhn.[15] Rarely can we specify completely and impartially the essential ideas underlying fundamental disagreements.

Although in principle Bayesian arguments might be useful in choosing among alternative theories, in practice they seem to play no important role. I would suggest the following analogy. In the theory of perfect competition under constant returns to scale, equilibrium is characterized by zero profits although profit seeking is the dynamic mechanism which produces this result. That is, the motivation of the individual participants is not reflected in the historical observations of equilibria. In a similar fashion, we may view the motivations of individual research workers. Each scientist behaves in the manner described by Popper, dogmatically asserting his positions and attacking the positions of others. The end result is a merging of views, a development which may, when viewed from afar, be described as learning

---

[15] *Ibid.*, p. 147.

from experience. Bayes' theorem may apply in the aggregate even though there are no Bayesian researchers!

As I said at the beginning, I do not have an answer to the question: "Should econometricians use Bayesian methods?". There are persuasive arguments on both sides of the question. I have presented here some views which I find relevant. If I have stimulated some interest in the issue, then I shall have succeeded in my task.[16]

*

COMMENTS ON THE TWO ABOVE PAPERS, BY GORDON M. KAUFMAN

Massachusetts Institute of Technology

Zellner and Rothenberg have presented two thoughtful provocative papers. Rothenberg has done an admirable job of putting into philosophical

---

[16] In the above analysis I have ignored a number of arguments that are often presented in discussions on Bayesianism. I should like to comment briefly on a few of them, although space does not permit a detailed study. One argument that frequently arises is that Bayesian inferences are based on the sample actually observed whereas traditional procedures depend also on samples that might have occured but did not. More technically, Bayesian procedures respect the "likelihood principle " and most traditional procedures do not. The likelihood principle is extremely attractive and at one time I was utterly convinced of its validity. Alas, conviction weakens with age. As is usual when principle clashes with prejudice, prejudice seems to win. In any case, I think that at the current state of affairs the war between Bayesians and non-Bayesians is better fought at a more practical level.

A second argument is that Bayesian methods yield exact finite-sample posterior distributions whereas traditional methods often result in sampling distributions too complex for analysis and hence asymptotic approximations are needed. Thus it is said that Bayesian methods are better because they are exact. I cannot accept this argument at all. In the first place, a Bayes procedure typically has a sampling distribution just as complex as the corresponding traditional procedure. If one judges procedures by their sampling distribution, then approximations are needed in both cases. If one judges procedures by posterior distributions, then there is nothing to compare since the traditional methods are ruled out by definition. In any case, experience has shown that in many problems with nuisance parameters the calculation of Bayesian posterior densities involves the same types of steps as calculating the exact sampling distributions of the traditional procedures.

Finally, some Bayesians have criticized traditional statistical procedures because their sampling distributions involve unknown population parameters. I had always thought that was an advantage. Indeed, unless the sampling distributions of statistics depend on the unknown parameters, classical inference is impossible. Of course the dependence of these sampling distributions on a large number of nuisance parameters may seriously complicate the analysis, but this does not stop us, at least in principle, from using the traditional inference procedures.

perspective a number of fundamental dilemmas that cannot be ignored — even by those of us who are firmly convinced that Bayesian methods have an important role to play in the future development of econometrics. Zellner has effectively summarized a battery of pro-Bayesian arguments that I find, in the main, compelling.

As Rothenberg points out, the Bayesian model of inference will not do as a vehicle for capturing the act of creativity underlying what he terms "scientific revolution": conceptualization of a testable model or hypothesis. But neither do any of the presently available alternate methodologies currently available. Until an implementable global model of inference that jives with all of the rigorous precepts governing a well constructed scientific philosophy is created — an unlikely event — we are forced to be pragmatic in the methodological tools we use.

None of this implies that a (non-Jeffreys) Bayesian approach is necessarily unattractive in implementing choice among alternative theories that are representable as *parametric* models. The posterior odds that Model A is true as against Model B has meaning and there is nothing incommensurable about such an expression of *relative* degree of belief after the objective evidence is in. Rather than reach a conclusion now about the viability of Bayesian methods in this context, I personally choose to defer judgment at this time and to wait and see how the Bayesian approach functions in some particular cases where such a choice is to be made. The work done by Geisel and Zellner on comparing and choosing among parametric statistical models is a promising start.

There are, however, two closely related *methodological* questions addressed by neither Zellner nor Rothenberg that loom large given the present state of development of the Bayesian approach. Before posing them let us assume that we are in the realm of *statistical decision*, so that we can all agree on the usefulness (in principle) of analysis à la Savage et al. The first is:

> *What methods should one use to elicit prior judgments about parameters of an econometric model?*

This question has a normative ring about it. In order to make it a valid one, then, we should prescribe the goals of such methods. One reasonable one suggested by Howard Raiffa is *empirical validity*. To see what it means consider a weather forecaster who, each day, states a probability of the event "snow on the morrow".

Suppose the forecaster restricts himself to asserting that the probability of snow is 0, 0.1, 0.2, ..., 1.0; i.e. to whole tenths and records for *each* of these eleven probabilities (a) the number of days that he asserted that probability and (b) the number of days among all such days that it *actually* snowed. When the total number of days he asserted that this probability is 0.3, say, becomes very large, we would hope that the proportion of these days that it *actually snowed* is very close to 0.3. If this is so for each of the eleven probabilities, then we assert that this forecaster *validates empirically.* This is very desirable.

In an econometric setting empirical validity has strong appeal. It can be interpreted as a measure of the degree to which an assessor is able to say what he really feels — provided that he has no clear motivation to state assessments different from those he believes. Experiments done by Raiffa at Harvard and replicated by others of us show that it is very difficult in general for an assessor to achieve empirical validity. His experiments show that most of us — even when of truly honest intent — are *strikingly* not empirically valid. A practitioner of Bayesian econometrics ought to take heed!

The second question is also about assessment of priors. It has to do with the tyranny of large numbers: to motivate it suppose we are interested in doing a Bayesian analysis of a simultaneous equation system with ten equations — not an unduly large number of equations. If one takes into account the normalization rule, but imposes no exact *a priori* constraints the number of functionally independent parameters in the 10×10 non-singular matrix premultiplying the exogenous variables is 90. One also has to worry about the remainder of the structure. I do not think anyone here seriously believes he can responsibly assess a joint density over 90 random variables. An appeal to natural conjugate analysis or its extensions helps somewhat, but not much. The question is then:

> *How can a Bayesian responsibly assess a prior for parameters of a large scale econometric model?*

One might argue that we are usually seriously interested in only a small subset of all such parameters. But this begs the question. Parenthetically, Jacques Drèze's work on a Bayesian analogue of limited information maximum likelihood estimation is indirectly addressed to this question in one special case.

I am not aware of any clear-cut general answer to the latter question.

These observations about practical problems that arise in assessing priors mirror, I believe, what may be a truly substantial barrier to widespread application of Bayesian methods in econometrics, except in the simplest of cases.

COMMENTS ON THE TWO ABOVE PAPERS, BY
JOHN W. PRATT

Harvard University

Ordinarily when I am invited to participate in a session of this kind I assume that I am supposed to represent the far left — or is it the far right — Bayesian view. When I was preparing my remarks, however, with only Zellner's paper in hand, I thought the other speakers would be all quite pro-Bayesian, so I planned to try to restore balance to the session by indicating some difficulties with Bayesian methods in practice. I was certainly wrong about the other speakers but I will make the remarks I had planned to make, anyway. Specifically, I will mention some problems which are important, but which are hard or impossible to handle by the Bayesian approach at present and whose future handling may involve us Bayesians in "ad hockeries" of our own.

(1) *Problems related to flat (diffuse) prior distributions.* Prior distributions are flexible, as Zellner said, but it is an inflexible requirement to have one. There is a great tendency to use "improper", flat prior distributions — even Zellner has this tendency. But the nice admissibility features Zellner mentions in several places hold in general only for proper prior distributions. In particular, Stein's inadmissibility results unfortunately apply to the usual (flat prior) Bayesian estimates. In fact, the usual Bayesian estimates coincide with classical estimates typically, and hence are neither better nor worse.

Choosing between models requires proper prior distributions, and the posterior probabilities of the models may be sensitive to their choice. What is crucial is something like the ratio of the heights of the prior densities of the parameters in the relevant regions under the two models. Here uncomfortable assessment problems cannot be avoided.

In this connection, in relation to Rothenberg's paper, it seems only fair to point out that the corresponding classical procedures, hypothesis tests and t-values, are not important in revolutionary science either. Regarding other difficulties with testing, I have already had my say to the Econometric Society in the previous paper mentioned by Zellner. That was two years ago, and I was not saying anything new even then.

One problem of choice of models receiving much attention nowadays is the problem of choice of subset regression. The advantage of parsimony, in terms of preferring a simpler explanation if it is almost as good, can be captured in a Bayesian analysis in various ways. But another aspect of this problem, expressed in classical terms, is that, when there are r parameters and n observations, the average over the n points of the variance of the usual (classical or Bayesian) estimate of the regression is $(r/n)\sigma^2$ and the corresponding average forecast variance is $(1+r/n)\sigma^2$. Adding more parameters to a model can therefore hurt. It cannot hurt a Bayesian in theory, if the assesses his "true" prior distributions. It can, however, if he uses flat prior distributions. Here I think we might look toward some kind of compromise, using prior distributions which are largely but not wholly conventional. This will inevitably be rather *ad hoc*.

(2) *Robustness problems*. It is generally agreed that randomization is nice if you can do it. In fact, the inability to randomize makes econometricians worry about their models much more than experimenters who randomize. (Notice, incidentally, that it is correspondingly hard to find a physically realizable frequency interpretation of classical statistical inference statements in typical practical econometric studies.) Classical methods appear to be able to make strong use of randomization if it has occurred, and generally, to permit inference statements which hold unchanged over a wide variety of models. To be sure, this is partly an illusion, because you would change the inference if you knew the model — not to mention that all classical inferences are an illusion anyway.

Bayesians have made some progress in using randomization (there has been special attention to this in the sample survey literature), but they have not explained its full appeal or exploited it fully.

One remark on robustness having nothing to do with randomization: the model you are using may cause you to estimate a population mean by a sample median or some other non-robust statistic — non-robust for estimating the mean. This may happen in both classical and Bayesian analysis, but the tendency is greater in Bayesian analysis since the Bayesian approach almost insists on taking the model literally and making full use of it. In my opinion, a Bayesian is really just as entitled as a classical statistician to use insufficient statistics, but he is less inclined to do so in many situations, because it makes his mathematics harder instead of easier.

I will now make three minor comments and then conclude.

(1) Estimates resulting from preliminary tests are not only biased and non-linear, they are even *discontinuous* functions of the observations.

(2) People often embarrass me by asking me for references to applications of Bayesian methods in practice, though I have never been so incautious as even to suggest I knew of many. I would be grateful for any references to reports on substantive problems where the primary analysis was Bayesian. (I am not talking about Bayesian re-analysis of data for methodological or illustrative purposes.)

(3) Raiffa's experiments on the difficulty of achieving empirical validity were perhaps not quite as striking as has been suggested by Kaufman, and a similar experiment this year is still less so. The tendency he observed is, however, certainly present.

Finally, lest all these comments on the limitations of the Bayesian approach lead you to think that I am not a Bayesian after all, let me alter de Finetti's famous remark and say that just because the Bayesian house is imperfect and not yet complete, I see no reason to move out of it and into a house with no foundation whatever.

COMMENTS BY
ARNOLD ZELLNER

I agree with Pratt that a prior pdf is required in a Bayesian approach and this is a reflection of the principle that you rarely, if ever, get something for nothing. On the other hand, non-Bayesians often use strong prior information, e.g. to identify parameters of errors-in-the-variables and "simultaneous equation" models. In such situations, use of prior pdf's may permit the required prior information to be represented more flexibly and suitably.

With respect to "flat" or "non-informative" prior pdf's, these are useful when we know little about parameter values or when we wish to have a posterior pdf reflect mainly just the information in the data. Of course if we have prior information about parameter values and wish to (or have to in order to identify parameters) incorporate it in an analysis, then of course we would not use a "flat" or "non-informative" prior pdf (see the paper by Geisel and myself for results of some analyses using several informative prior pdf's).

On the question of Stein's results on admissibility, Stein himself and Lindley (*J.R.S.S.*, *B*, 1962, 265-287) have indicated the prior pdf's which produce posterior pdf's having means close to or equal to Stein's estimates. The use of such *subjective* prior information to generate an estimator may disturb non-Bayesians. On the other hand, it must be recognized that Stein-like estimators can also be generated by a pre-testing procedure which, however, requires that informal prior information be employed in the selection of a significance level for the pre-test.

Frontiers of Quantitative Economics, ed. **M.D. Intriligator.** © *North-Holland Publishing Company.*

CHAPTER 6

POLICY SIMULATION EXPERIMENTS WITH MACRO-ECONOMETRIC MODELS: THE STATE OF THE ART*

THOMAS H. NAYLOR

Duke University and University of Wisconsin

0. Introduction

In recent years economists have made increasing use of policy simulation experiments with macro-econometric models to evaluate the effects of alternative economic policies on the behavior of the economy of an entire country. Although econometricians have devoted considerable time and effort to the solution of a multiplicity of problems related to the estimation of the parameters of econometric models, they have almost totally ignored some relatively serious methodological problems associated with policy simulation experiments with given econometric models. But some very real methodological problems do exist when one attempts to design and implement a simulation experiment with a large-scale, macro-econometric model. What are some of these problems? What are the possible consequences of ignoring these problems? What alternatives are available for circumventing these problems? In this paper we shall attempt to answer some of these questions.

---

* This research was supported by National Science Foundation Grant GS-1926.

1. Definition of the policy problem

Three alternative approaches have been proposed by economists for using macro-econometric models to evaluate the effects of alternative economic policies on the behavior of an economic system: (1) the Theil approach, (2) the Tinbergen approach, and (3) the policy simulation approach. Each of these approaches assumes that we begin with a given econometric model of the economy which is to be investigated. That is, it is assumed that the economy of the country in question can be described by a set of simultaneous equations of the following form,

$$AX_t + BY_t + \sum_{j=1}^{p} B_j Y_{t-j} + CZ_t + D = U_t, \tag{1}$$

where $X_t = $ an $m \times 1$ vector of exogenous variables; $Y_t = $ an $n \times 1$ vector of endogenous variables; $Y_{t-j} = $ an $n \times 1$ vector of lagged endogenous variables when $j = 1, \ldots, p$; $Z_t = $ a $q \times 1$ vector of policy instruments; $U_t = $ an $n \times 1$ vector of stochastic disturbance terms; $A, B, C, D = $ coefficient matrices whose parameters have been estimated by standard econometric techniques. (Of course, the model may also be nonlinear.)

1.0. *Theil approach (Fox et al. 1966)*

Theil assumes that we know the social welfare function W of the policy maker and that it may be expressed as a function of the target (endogenous) variables and the policy instruments,

$$W_t = W_t(Y_t, Z_t). \tag{2}$$

The problem of the policy maker is defined as one of finding the values of Y_t and Z_t which will maximize W_t subject to the constraints imposed by the econometric model (1) and given values of X_t, Y_{t-j}, and U_t.

This approach suffers from one major shortcoming. Namely, that in the real world we simply do not know the parameters or even the functional form of W_t for governmental policy makers. The Von Neumann-Morgenstern utility index and other techniques which have been proposed by economists for quantifying utility simply require too much information in order to obtain meaningful results — information that is not likely to be forthcoming from either present or future policy makers on the national, state, or local governmental levels. A policy maker whose principal concern is his own political survival is not going to reveal his utility function to you or me or any other economist.

Fromm (1969b), Fromm and Taubman (1968) and Shupp (1969) have proposed several examples of hypothetical utility functions for national policy makers. While these exercises may be of some interest to academic economists, they are not likely to do much for real world policy makers.

In summary, the Theil approach to the evaluation of economic policies with macro-econometric models is little more than an interesting exercise which offers only limited promise as a policy making tool. Economists would do well to spend less time trying to specify the social welfare functions of policy makers and spend more time seeking solutions to some of the problems of policy makers.

1.1. *Tinbergen approach (Fox et al. 1966)*

With the Tinbergen approach no knowledge of the policy maker's welfare function is assumed. This approach eliminates the maximization problem and instead assumes that the policy maker has specified a fixed target value for each of the endogenous variables. For given values of the exogenous, lagged endogenous, and stochastic variables, the equations of the econometric model (1) are then solved simultaneously for the set of values of the policy variables Z_t which is consistent with the targets.

If there are fewer policy variables than targets, then the number of unknowns (policy instruments) in the econometric model (1) is smaller than the number of equations and a solution is impossible except for special cases. On the other hand, if the number of policy instruments exceed the number of targets, the number of unknowns will exceed the number of equations, and an infinite number of solutions will be possible. Within the Tinbergen framework the first of these two problems can be resolved only by either increasing the number of policy instruments or reducing the number of target variables until there is an equal number of equations and unknowns in the system. In the case where there are more policy instruments than equations, the policy maker can assign arbitrary values to $q-n$ of the policy variables and the equation system can be solved for the remaining n policy variables.

Although the problem of balancing the number of equations and the number of policy variables may prove to be a serious limitation of the Tinbergen approach, there is, in my opinion, another problem which is even more serious. The assumption that in a country like the U.S.A. a policy maker is willing to commit himself to a specific set of target values for the endogenous variables is highly questionable.[1] Just as the policy maker is unlikely to provide the economist with enough information to glean his utility function, it is doubtful that the policy maker will reveal in a very precise manner the values of his targets. A methodology based on information (e.g., values of target variables) which is simply not available to the analyst cannot be expected to yield results which are particularly useful to the policy maker.

1.2. *Policy simulation approach*

There is yet a third approach to the problem of evaluating the effects of alternative economic policies on the behavior of the economy which does not assume prior knowledge of either the social welfare function or the targets of the policy maker. This approach is known in the literature as simulation. With simulation we can solve the set of simultaneous equations given by (1) for Y_t in terms of X_t, Y_{t-j}, Z_t and U_t and generate the time path of Y, for as long a period as we desire. The exogenous variables X_t are read into the computer as data, the values of Y_{t-j} generated in previous periods are fed back into the model in period t, the policy variables are specified by the analyst, and the stochastic disturbances may either be suppressed or generated by an appropriate computer subroutine (Naylor 1970). In the case of a linear econometric model the solution of the econometric model takes the following form,

$$Y_t = -B^{-1}AX_t - B^{-1}\sum_{j=1}^{p} B_j Y_{t-j} - B^{-1}CZ_t - B^{-1}D + B^{-1}U_t, \qquad (3)$$

where B^{-1} is the inverse of B. Since it is possible to invert very large matrices on today's digital computers in only a few seconds, it is relatively easy to generate the time paths of Y_t for linear models through the use of computer simulation techniques.

Therefore, for any given values of the policy instruments, we can generate the time paths of the endogenous variables. In other words, when we

---

[1] Admittedly, in a country like Holland or India, where economic planning is a generally accepted way of life, economic planners and policy makers may be willing to specify target values for the endogenous variables. But can you imagine a state legislator or even a U.S. Congressman in this country being willing to specify a set of policy targets?

approach the policy maker we ask him only two questions. First, "What output variables are of particular interest to you?". Second, "What sets of policy variables appear to be politically feasible?". With simulation we can then show the policy maker the consequences of the proposed policies. In addition, the economist may propose a few policies of his own for consideration by the policy maker. These policies may be put to a similar test. The policy maker then selects the policies which are most compatible with his preference function (which is unknown to the economist). The results of initial simulation runs may suggest other policy variable configurations to try.

There are two advantages of the policy simulation approach. First, it does not assume the availability of information about the policy maker's preferences that is impossible to obtain. Second, it provides the policy maker with the type of information which he is most likely to require in order to make decisions. In summary, while the Theil-Tinbergen approaches may be of considerable interest to economists from a purely theoretical standpoint, neither of these approaches provides operational solutions to policy problems. Therefore, policy simulation experiments may represent the only methodology currently available for obtaining practical solutions to real world policy problems.

We now turn our attention to several methodological problems associated with policy simulation experiments with macro-econometric models.

2. Solution of the model

If our econometric model is linear, then the solution is quite straightforward and is given by (3). Unfortunately, realistic econometric models are seldom linear. One example of nonlinearity which arises frequently in econometric models is the use of price times quantity terms in the identity defining Gross National Product in current prices. The Wharton Model (Evans 1969a; Evans and Klein 1968) contains several other examples of nonlinearities including: (1) relative prices in the consumption functions, (2) logarithmic treatment of the production function, (3) nonlinearity of the wage rate and capacity term in some of the price formation equations.

With the rediscovery by economists of the Gauss-Seidel method for solving systems of simultaneous nonlinear equations, nonlinearity no longer represents a serious computational problem. The paper by Evans (1969a) and the book by Klein and Evans (1969) provide complete descriptions of the Gauss-Seidel method. Although the convergence of this algorithm is influenced by (1) the type of normalization procedure used and (2) the ordering of the equations, practical experience with the algorithm indicates that convergence is usually not a problem.

In addition to the Gauss-Seidel method for solving nonlinear econometric models, Holt et al. (1967) have developed a special purpose simulation language called PROGRAM SIMULATE for generating the time paths of the endogenous variables of linear and non-linear econometric models.

For the sake of completeness, we should mention two other computational problems associated with the generation of the time paths of the endogenous variables of an econometric model with computer simulation techniques.

First, Goldberger (1962) has shown that when serial correlation is present in the error terms of an econometric model, the pattern of equation residuals over prior observations contains information which is useful in prediction. Through certain mechanical procedures which utilize information about the serial correlation in the observed residuals, it is possible to adjust the constant terms of regression equations and improve the predictive efficiency of the equations. Green (1969) has reported on the results of using four different mechanical adjustment procedures in simulation experiments with the OBE Model.

Second, with stochastic simulations with econometric models we frequently assume that the disturbance terms in (1) have a multivariate normal distribution with expected value of zero and a given variance-covariance matrix which has been estimated from the observed values of the residuals of the model. Provided the number of observations available to estimate the variance-covariance matrix is not less than the number of equations, then the technique for generating random variables with a multivariate normal distribution described in Naylor (1970) is appropriate. However, if the number of observations is less than the number of equations, then this technique breaks down and one of the procedures proposed by Nagar (1969) and McCarthy (in the appendix to Evans and Klein 1969) will be required.

3. Validation

The validity of an econometric model depends on the ability of the model to predict the behavior of the actual economic system on which the model is based. In order to test the degree to which data generated by simulation experiments with econometric models conform to observed data, two alternatives are available — historical verification and verification by forecasting. The essence of these procedures is prediction, for *historical verification* is concerned with retrospective predictions (*ex-post* simulations over the sample period) while *forecasting* is concerned with prospective predictions (*ex-ante* simulations beyond the sample period). In the paper by Naylor and Finger (1967) several criteria are suggested for deciding when the time paths generated by a simulation experiment agree sufficiently with the observed time paths so that agreement cannot be attributed merely to chance. Several specific measures and techniques are suggested for testing the "goodness-of-fit" of simulation results, i.e., the degree of conformity of simulated series to observed data.

Two recent studies by Cooper and Jorgenson (1969) and Stekler (1966, 1968) have attempted to evaluate the predictive behavior of several of the large-scale quarterly econometric models of the economy of the U.S.A. Cooper uses the mean-squared error as a goodness-of-fit criteria and Stekler uses the Theil inequality coefficient. Cooper concluded that,

> First, no single quarterly econometric model currently available is overwhelmingly superior to all other quarterly models in predicting the components of the national income and product accounts. Second, the econometric models are not, in general, superior to purely mechanical methods of forecasting. However, there are modules of the econometric models which are definitely superior to purely mechanical models. Third, the econometric models are, in general, structurally unstable (Cooper and Jorgenson 1969, p. 151).

Stekler (1968, p. 463) concluded that, "the results suggest that econometric models have not been entirely successful in forecasting economic activity". Cooper's study examined the predictive performance of seven different models, and Stekler considered six models. Both studies included earlier versions of the OBE (Liebenberg et al. 1966) and Wharton (Evans and Klein 1968) Models, but neither study treated the Brookings Model (Duesenberry et al. 1969) or the FRB-MIT-PENN Model (Ando et al. 1969).

4. Experimental design

In a computer simulation experiment, as any experiment, careful thought should be given to the problem of experimental design. Among the important considerations in the design of computer simulation experiments are: (1) factor selection, (2) randomization, (3) number of replications, (4) length of simulation runs, and (5) multiple responses.

4.0. *Factor selection*

In the language of experimental design, the policy variables in our model are usually called *factors* and the endogenous variables are known as *response* variables. A *full factorial* design involves selecting several values or levels for each of the factors (policy variables) in the experiment. By assigning to each factor one of its levels we generate a design point. If all the design points obtainable in this way are used, then we have a full factorial design. The total number of design points in the full factorial design is the product of the number of levels for each factor. It is clear that a full factorial design can require an unmanageably large number of design points if more than a very few factors are to be investigated. If we require a complete investigation of all the factors in the experiment, including main effects and interactions of all orders, then there is no solution to the problem of "too many factors". If, however, we are willing to settle for a less than complete investigation, perhaps including main effects and two-factor interactions, then there are designs which will accomplish our purpose which require fewer design points than the full factorial. Fractional factorial designs, including Latin square and Greco-Latin square designs, are examples of designs which require only a fraction of the design points required by the full factorial design. The papers by Hunter and Naylor in Naylor (1969) and Naylor et al. (1967) describe various experimental designs which may be useful with policy simulation experiments with macro-econometric models.

4.1. *Randomization*

There are at least three reasons why one might want to include stochastic disturbance terms in simulation experiments with nonlinear macro-econometric models.

First, as Howrey has pointed out in an unpublished paper entitled "Dynamic Properties of Stochastic Linear Econometric Models", if the long-term properties of an econometric model are to be investigated,

> ... it may not be reasonable to disregard the impact of the disturbance terms on the time paths of the endogenous variables. Neither the characteristic roots nor the dynamic multipliers provide information about the magnitude or correlation properties of deviations from the expected value of the time path.

Second, Howrey and Kelejian (1969) have demonstrated that, "the application of nonstochastic simulation procedures to econometric models that contain nonlinearities in the endogenous variables yields results that are not consistent with the properties of the reduced form of the model".

Third, by including stochastic error terms one can then replicate the simulation experiment and make statistical inferences and test hypotheses about the behavior of the system being simulated based on the output data generated by the simulation experiment.

4.2. *Number of replications*

If one is going to make inferences about the effects of alternative economic policies on the behavior of an economic system based on a computer simulation experiment, then the question of sample size or the number of replications of the experiment should be considered. It is well known that the optimal sample size (number of replications) depends on the answers one gives to the following questions: (1) How large a shift in population parameters do you wish to detect? (2) How much variability is present in the population? (3) What size risks are you willing to take?

Unfortunately, econometricians have tended to ignore the question of optimal sample size and to select some arbitrary number of replications for stochastic simulations with econometric models. Nagar (1969) for example, used twenty replications with his stochastic simulations with the Brookings Model. In more recent simulations with the Brookings (Fromm and Klein 1969), OBE (Green 1969), and Wharton (Evans and Klein 1969) Models, fifty replications were used. In none of these cases was any rationale whatsoever provided for the arbitrary sample size.

The paper by Gilman (1968) describes several rules for determining the number of replications of a simulation experiment when the observations are independent. (Observations obtained by replicating a simulation experiment will be independent provided one uses a random number generator which yields independent random numbers.)

4.3. *Length of simulation runs*

Another consideration in the design of simulation experiments is the length of a given simulation run. This problem is more complicated than the question of the number of replications because the observations generated by a given simulation rule will typically be autocorrelated and the application of "stopping rules" based on classical statistical techniques may underestimate the variance substantially and lead to incorrect inferences about the behavior of the system being simulated.

> In the large majority of current simulations, the required sample record length is guessed at by using some rule such as "Stop sampling when the parameter to be estimated does not change in the second decimal place when 1000 more samples are taken." The analyst must realize that makeshift rules such as this are very dangerous, since he may be dealing with a parameter whose sample values converge to a steady state solution very slowly. Indeed, his estimate may be several hundred percent in error. Therefore, it is necessary that adequate stopping rules be used in all simulations (Gilman 1968, p. 1).

To the best of my knowledge econometricians have not even acknowledged that the length of the simulation run might be a relevant consideration in the design of a policy simulation experiment. Gilman (1968) has described several "stopping rules" for determining the length of simulation runs with autocorrelated output data. Ling, in Naylor (1969), has also treated this problem.

4.4. *Multiple responses*

The multiple response problem arises when we wish to observe and evaluate many different response variables in a given simulation experiment. We previously alluded to this problem in our discussion of the Theil-Tinbergen approaches to the theory of quantitative economic policy. The multiple response problem is particularly acute with the Brookings, OBE, and Wharton Models, each of which has over fifty response variables. A question arises as to how one goes about validating multiple response simulation experiments and how one evaluates the results of the use of alternative policies in the case of policy simulation experiments. To solve the multiple response problem, the analyst must devise some technique for assigning weights to the different response variables before applying specific statistical tests. Fromm (1969b) and Fromm and Taubman (1968) have proposed the use of utility theory to evaluate the results of policy simulation experiments with the Brookings Model. The approach taken by most econometricians to the multiple response problem is to present the results of their experiments and let the policy maker assign his own weights to the different response variables. Given the practical and theoretical problems involved in assigning weights or utilities to different response variables, this approach is likely to prevail in the near future.

5. Data analysis

In a well-designed simulation experiment consideration must be given to methods of analyzing data generated by the experiment. Most of the classical experimental design techniques described in the literature are used in the expectation that the data will be analyzed by one or both of the following — regression analysis and analysis of variance. Regression analysis is a collection of techniques for data analysis which utilizes the numerical properties of the levels of quantitative factors. The analysis of variance is a collection of techniques for data analysis that are appropriate when qualitative factors are present, although quantitative factors are not excluded.

The papers by Burdick, Hunter, and Naylor in Naylor (1969) describe the use of response surface designs and regression analysis with computer simulation experiments with econometric models.

Several special cases of the analysis of variance have been applied to the analysis of data generated by simulation experiments with macro-econometric models. These techniques include the F-test, multiple comparisons, multiple ranking procedures, and spectral analysis. Although the F-test and multiple comparisons are well know to most economists, economists have made only limited use of multiple ranking procedures (Kleijnen and Naylor 1970).

Frequently, the objective of a computer simulation experiment with an econometric model is to find the "best", "second best", "third best", etc. policy. Although multiple comparison methods of estimating the sizes of differences between policies (as measured by population means) are often used as a way of attempting, indirectly, to achieve goals of this type, multiple ranking methods represent a more direct approach to the solution of the ranking problem. A good estimate of the rank of a set of economic policies is simply the ranking of the sample means associated with the given policies. Because of random error, however, sample rankings may yield incorrect results. With what probability can we say that a ranking of sample means represents the true ranking of population means? It is basically this question which multiple ranking procedures attempt to answer.

The F-test, multiple comparisons, and multiple ranking procedures have been used by Naylor et al. (1968) to evaluate the effects of alternative monetary and fiscal policies on the variance of national income with a simulation experiment with a macro-econometric model.

Another technique that has proved to be useful in analyzing data generated by computer simulation experiments with econometric models is spectral analysis. Spectral analysis was developed specifically to analyze time series data which are autocorrelated. For the purpose of describing the behavior of a stochastic variate (e.g., GNP) over time, the information content of spectral analysis is greater than that of sample means and variances. With spectral analysis it is relatively easy to construct confidence bands and to test hypotheses for the purpose of comparing the simulated results of the use of two or more alternative economic policies. Frequently, it is impossible to detect differences in time series generated by simulation experiments when one restricts himself to simple graphical analysis. Spectral analysis provides a means of objectively comparing time series generated with a computer model. Spectral analysis can also be used as a technique for validating an econometric model of an economic system. By comparing the estimated spectra of simulated data and corresponding real world data one can infer how well the model resembles the system it was designed to emulate.

Naylor et al. (1969) have used spectral analysis to analyze data generated by a simulation experiment with an econometric model. Spectral analysis was employed to compare the effects of alternative economic policies on national income generated by the simulation experiment.

6. Some unresolved problems

We shall conclude this paper by summarizing a number of methodological problems associated with policy simulation experiments with macro-economic models for which solutions do not presently exist.

6.0. *Simulation versus analytical solutions*

Explicit analytical solutions for the reduced form of simultaneous, nonlinear, stochastic difference equations are frequently difficult, if not impossible to obtain. For this reason economists have found it necessary to resort to numerical techniques or computer simulation experiments to validate these models and to investigate their dynamic properties. Howrey and Kelejian (1969) have recently raised some very interesting questions concerning the use of computer simulation techniques with econometric models. In general, they have suggested that the role of computer simulation as a tool of analysis of econometric models should be reconsidered. They have argued, "that once a *linear* econometric model has been estimated and tested in terms of the known distribution theory concerning parameter estimates, simulation experiments ... yield *no additional information* about the validity of the model". In addition, Howrey and Kelejian have pointed out that, "although some of the dynamic properties of linear models can be inferred from simulation results, an analytical technique (spectral analysis) based on the model itself is available for this purpose". Since any nonlinear econometric model can be approximated by a linear model through the use of an appropriate Taylor series expansion, the arguments of Howrey and Kelejian can also be extended to include nonlinear econometric models. The questions raised by Howrey and Kelejian are important ones and merit further theoretical and empirical consideration. In general, the whole question of when to use simulation rather than standard mathematical techniques is a question which needs further investigation, not only with econometric models but economic models of all types.

6.1. *Perverse simulation results*

Econometric models which have been estimated properly and are based on sound economic theory may yield simulation results which are nonsensical. That is, the simulations may "explode", and inherently positive variables may turn negative, leading to results which are in complete conflict with reality. We must learn more about the mathematical properties of our models with the hope of devising techniques which will enable us to spot these problems with our models analytically before running simulations with them. For example, Howrey and Kelejian (1969) have shown that the application of simulation techniques to non-stochastic econometric models that contain nonlinearities in the endogenous variables, "yields results that are not consistent with the properties of the reduced form of the model". What other information can be gleaned from the structure of econometric models prior to conducting simulation experiments?

There appears to be a definite need to combine the approaches of the econometrician and the systems analyst in formulating models of complex economic systems. To the systems analyst an economic model consists of a set of mathematical inequalities which reflect the various conditional statements, logical branchings, and complex feedback mechanisms that depict the economy as a dynamic, self-regulating system. Although economists have made considerable progress in building econometric models and developing techniques to estimate their parameters, little or no attention has been given to alternative model structures such as those used by systems analysts. The possibility of developing models of the economy as a whole which consist of structures other than simultaneous difference equations needs to be explored more fully. Special attention should be given to the types of logical models which have been developed by systems analysts. To use systems analysis to build macro-economic models which accurately reflect the underlying decision processes of the total economy, it may be necessary to draw heavily on other disciplines including sociology, psychology, and political science.

6.2. *Inadequate estimation techniques*

Although the static properties of simultaneous equation estimators such as OLS, 2SLS, LISE, FIML, and 3SLS are well known, we have no assurance whatsoever from econometric theory that a model whose parameters have been estimated by one of these methods will yield valid, dynamic, closed-loop simulations. That is, it is quite possible for a model which has been estimated by one of the aforementioned techniques to yield simulations which in no sense resemble the behavior of the system which they were designed to emulate. What is needed is a new estimation technique which uses as its criterion of goodness-of-fit, "How well does the model simulate?" rather than, "How well does the static model fit the historical data based on one-period predictions?". The question of whether poor simulation results with econometric models are due to improper methods of estimation or a misspecified model is a question which calls for further research.

6.3. *Unstable coefficients*

The simulation experiments of the Adelman's (1959, 1963) and others have demonstrated the effects of including additive stochastic error terms in econometric models. Howrey and Kelejian (1969) have also treated this question from a theoretical standpoint. What has not been considered is the question of what happens if we treat the coefficients of an econometric model as random variables in simulation experiments. Yet we know very well that these coefficients are indeed random variables and that they are not likely to remain constant over long periods of time. Preliminary experiments with this problem indicate that by shocking the coefficients of the Klein and Goldberger (1955) Model we encounter two different problems. First, we encounter serious difficulty in solving the model. Second, the results are quite different from the deterministic simulations as well as the simulations with additive shocks. Finally, the structure of the model may in reality evolve over time, and the assumption of constant coefficients, independent of time, may require review.

References

Adelman, Irma, 1963, Long cycles — a simulation experiment. In: *Symposium on simulation models*, edited by Austin C. Hoggatt and Frederick E. Balderston. Cincinnati, South-Western Publishing Co.

Adelman, Irma and Frank, 1959, The dynamic properties of the Klein-Goldberger model. *Econometrica*, Oct., 596-625.

Ando, Albert K., and Stephen Goldfeld, 1968, An econometric model for evaluating stabilization policies. In: *Studies in economics tabilization*. Washington, The Brookings Institution.

Ando, Albert K., Franco Modigliani and Robert Rasche, 1969, Economic theory in the FRB-MIT-PENN model. Conference on econometric models of cyclical behavior, Harvard University, November 14-15.

Cooper, Ronald L. and Dale W. Jorgenson, 1969, The predictive performance of quarterly econometric models of the United States. Conferences on econometric models of cyclical behavior, Harvard University, November 14-15.

DeLeeuw, Frank, 1964, Financial markets in business cycles: a simulation study. *American Economic Review* 54 (May), 309-323.

DeLeeuw, Frank and Edward Gramlich, 1968, The federal reserve-M.I.T. econometric model. *Federal Reserve Bulletin*, Jan., 1-40.

Duesenberry, James S., Gary Fromm, Lawrence R. Klein and Edwin Kuh, 1969, *The Brookings model: Some further results*. Chicago, Rand McNally.

Engle, R. F. and T. C. Liu, 1969, Effects of aggregation over time on dynamic characteristics of an econometric model. Conference on econometric models of cyclical behavior, Harvard University, November 14-15.

Evans, Michael, 1969a, Computer simulation of nonlinear econometric models. In: *The design of computer simulation experiments*, edited by Thomas H. Naylor. Durham, N.C., Duke University Press.

Evans, Michael K., 1969b, *Macroeconomic activity*. New York, Harper & Row.

Evans, Michael K. and Lawrence R. Klein, 1968, *The Wharton econometric forecasting model*. Philadelphia, Wharton School, University of Pennsylvania, 2nd edition.

Evans, M.K. and L.R. Klein, 1969, Short and long term simulations with the Wharton model. Conference on econometric models of cyclical behavior, Harvard University, November 14-15.

Evans, Michael K., Yoel Haitovsky, and George I. Treyz, 1969, An analysis of the forecasting properties of the U.S. econometric models. Conference on econometric models of cyclical behavior, Harvard University, November 14-15.

Fox, Karl, J.K. Sengupta, Erik Thorbecke, 1966, *The theory of Quantitative economic Policy*. Chicago, Rand McNally.

Fromm, Gary, 1969a, An evaluation of monetary policy instruments. In: *The Brookings Model: Some Further Results*, edited by J.S. Duesenberry et al. Chicago, Rand McNally.

Fromm, Gary, 1969b, Utility theory and the analysis of simulation output data. In: *The Design of Computer Simulation Experiments*, edited by Thomas H. Naylor. Durham, N.C., Duke University Press.

Fromm, Gary and Lawrence R. Klein, 1969, Short and long term simulations with the Brookings model. Conference on econometric models of cyclical behavior, Harvard University, November 14-15.

Fromm, Gary and Paul Taubman, 1968, *Policy simulations with an econometric model.* Washington, D.C., The Brookings Institution.

Geraci, Vincent J., 1969, On the simulation of dynamic econometric models. Econometric system simulation program, working paper No. 37, Durham, N.C., Duke University, August 15.

Gilman, Michael J., 1968, A brief survey of stopping rules in Monte Carlo simulations. *Digest of the Second Conference on Applications of Simulation*, December 2-4.

Goldberger, Arthur S., 1962, Best linear unbiased prediction in the generalized linear regression model. *Journal of the American Statistical Association* 57, June, 369-375.

Green, George, 1969, Short and long term simulations with the OBE econometric model. Conference on econometric models of cyclical behavior, Harvard University, November 14-15.

Griliches, Zvi, 1968, The Brookings model volume: A review article. *Review of Economics and Statistics* 50, May, 215-234.

Holt, Charles C. et al., 1967, PROGRAM SIMULATE II, Social Systems Research Institute, Madison, Wisc., April.

Howrey, E. Philip, 1969, Dynamic properties of a condensed version of the Wharton model. Conference on econometric models of cyclical behavior, Harvard University, November 14-15.

Howrey, Philip and H.H. Kelejian, 1969, Computer simulation versus analytical solutions. In: *The Design of Computer Simulation Experiments*, edited by Thomas H. Naylor. Durham, N.C., Duke University Press.

Kleijnen, Jack P. and Thomas H. Naylor, 1969, The use of multiple ranking procedures to analyze business and economic systems. *Proceedings of the American Statistical Association.*

Klein, Lawrence R., 1969a, An econometric analysis of the tax cut of 1964. In: *The Brookings model: some further results*, edited by J.S. Duesenberry et al. Chicago, Rand McNally.

Klein, Lawrence R., 1969b, Solutions of the complete system. In: *The Brookings model: some further results*, edited by J.S. Duesenberry et al. Chicago, Rand McNally.

Klein, Lawrence R. and Michael K. Evans, 1969, *Econometric gaming*. New York, Macmillan Company.

Klein, L.R. and A.S. Goldberger, 1955, *An econometric model of the United States, 1929-1952*. Amsterdam, North-Holland Publishing Co.

Liebenberg, M., A.A. Hirsch and P. Popkin, 1966, A quarterly econometric model of the United States. *Survey of Current Business* 46, May, 13-29.

Liu, Ta-Chung, 1969, A monthly recursive econometric model of the United states. *Review of Economics and Statistics* 51, February, 1-13.

Moore, Geoffrey H., Charlotte Boschan, and Victor Zarnowitz, 1969, Business cycle analysis of econometric model simulations. Conference on econometric models of cyclical behavior, Harvard University, November 14-15.

Nagar, A.L., 1969, Stochastic simulations of the Brookings econometric model. In: *The Brookings model: some further results*, edited by J.S. Duesenberry et al. Chicago, Rand McNally.

Naylor, Thomas H. (editor), 1969, *The design of computer simulation experiments*. Durham, N.C., Duke University Press.

Naylor, Thomas H., 1970, *Computer simulation experiments*. New York, John Wiley & Sons.

Naylor, Thomas H., Donald S. Burdick, and W. Earl Sasser, 1967, Computer simulation experiments with economic systems: the problem of experimental design. *Journal of the American Statistical Association* 62, Dec., 1315-1337.

Naylor, Thomas H. and J.M. Finger, 1967, Verification of computer simulation models. *Management Science* 14, Oct., 92-101.

Naylor, Thomas H., Kenneth Wertz and Thomas H. Wonnacott, 1968, Some methods for evaluating the effects of economic policies using simulation experiments. *Review of the International Statistical Institute* 184-200.

Naylor, Thomas H., Kenneth Wertz and Thomas Wonnacott, 1969, Spectral analysis of data generated by simulation experiments with econometric models. *Econometrica* 37, April, 333-352.

Shupp, Franklin R., 1969, Welfare functions and stabilization policies for a non-linear macroeconomic model. Quantitative Economics Workshop Paper No. 6903, University of Illinois, July.

Stekler, H.O., 1966, Forecasting with an econometric model: comment. *American Economic Review* 56, Dec., 1241-1248.

Stekler, H.O., 1968, Forecasting with econometric models: an evaluation. *Econometrica* 36, July-Oct., 437-463.

Suits, Daniel B., 1962, Forecasting and analysis with an econometric model. *American Economic Review* 52, March, 104-132.

Treyz, George I., 1969, *Computer problem booklet for economics*. New York, Macmillan Co.

SIMULATING A DEVELOPING AGRICULTURAL ECONOMY
METHODOLOGY AND PLANNING CAPABILITY

A. N. HALTER, M. L. HAYENGA, and T. J. MANETSCH*
Michigan State University

Simulation — a systems analysis approach — can provide a comprehensive view of a complex system (Forrester 1961; Halter and Miller 1966; Hayenga et al. 1968; Holland 1962, 1967; Holland and Gellespie 1963; Kresge 1967; Ligomenides et al. 1967; Simulatics Corp. 1966; Orcutt et al. 1961). In the case of development planning, we are interested in studying and approximating via a mathematical model those relationships within the economy which are important in the development process. By translating this model into a computer language, the likely end results of alternative development schemes can be evaluated through manipulation of the specified computer simulation model.

We are interested in exploring this approach to development planning because it might provide a more informed basis for planning development (Johnson 1966, 1967). The design of development, or planning, is especially important in less developed countries because they usually have comparatively few funds available relative to their apparent needs. Consequently, allocation mistakes appear to have a somewhat greater opportunity cost in terms of human well-being in the underdeveloped setting.

Planning in any country is a process fraught with uncertainty. Frequently,

---

* A. N. Halter is visiting professor of agricultural economics, M. L. Hayenga is assistant professor of agricultural economics, and T. J. Manetsch is associate professor of systems science, all at Michigan State University. The order of authorship does not necessarily imply degree of contribution. The three authors are members of a larger research team at Michigan State University. This paper was developed under a research contract from the U.S. Agency for International Development, contract number AID/ csd-1557.

there is uncertainty about likely immediate and longer range effects of development strategies. Further, the degree to which policies aimed at one set of economic phenomena may have unintended side effects on other aspects of the society is often uncertain. The paucity of information available for decision-making is often cited in developed countries, with even more frequent mention in less developed countries. Poor communication facilities, especially prevalent in LDC's often impede the accumulation of potentially available relevant information which might otherwise provide a reasonably well-informed basis for decision making. Given these difficulties and uncertainties, let us consider the utility of a systems analysis approach — simulation — in studying the dynamic interactions among variables affecting the rate of development and in subsequently planning development.

A systems analysis approach attempts to isolate and formulate into a mathematical model those sectors and components of the economy and those physical, biological, economic and social relationships within them which are most important in affecting the development effort. The systems analysis approach, in the development context, emphasizes those relationships which can be affected by or are vital to the evaluation of either public or private development policies. In the process of formulating the simulation model, relevant information is gathered and incorporated into the model. It is then available for analyzing alternative development strategies and assisting in the critical resource allocation decisions.

In this paper we first discuss simulation as a problem solving approach. We then illustrate the application of this approach to the development problems of the Nigerian agricultural economy. In so doing, we describe the route taken in formulating a simulation model of an economy primarily agricultural in nature. Finally, we comment on the potential planning capability of simulation models as applied to development planning.

0. Simulation methodology

Simulation is viewed here as an iterative problem solving process which involves problem formulation, mathematical modeling, refinement and testing of the resulting model, and creative design and execution of simulation experiments intended to provide answers to the questions posed. We conceptualize the process as shown in fig. 1. As the arrows indicate, the general movement of the process is from definition of the problem

A.N. Halter, M.L. Hayenga, T.J. Manetsch

toward model application, but the reverse arrows indicate that the process is iterative or "learning" in nature. A prior stage might have to be repeated on the basis of information acquired during a subsequent stage. In this manner changes in model structure, parameters etc., are introduced which lead to a better model. The "output" of a simulation is a set of system performance variables associated with each set of policies and/or strategies. This allows the decision maker to choose among a range of alternatives using his own criteria.

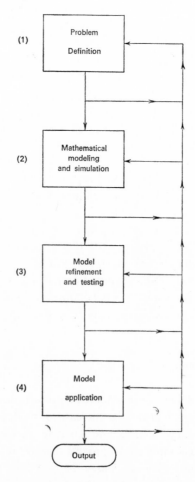

Fig. 1. Computer simulation as an iterative problem solving process.

1. Problem definition

Space and time are not available here to adequately describe "Problem Definition" and its fundamental importance to computer simulation of any system. The objective of this initial phase is to clearly specify the functions and mechanisms of the system, what measures of system performance are appropriate and what alternative means are available for achieving objectives — in a nutshell, to identify the major questions.

In our large-scale system study, effective problem definition required creative interaction among decision makers, planners, systems analysts and other specialists. The interdisciplinary research team at Michigan State University was fortunate in having available professionals with a backlog of experience in the Nigerian agricultural economy. The Consortium for the Study of Nigerian Rural Development (CSNRD), which was headquartered at Michigan State University, provided a substantial backlog of information about the country and served as a center for contacts with people in the U.S.A. and Nigeria who were knowledgeable about African agricultural and industrial development (Johnson et al. 1969). Further, the CSNRD collaborations with AID, FAO, and Nigerian planners and policy makers provided us with a fairly clear picture of the current governmental and planning institutions related to the agricultural economy and to the tools they use to influence the economy. This aided our selection of the planning clientele toward which this model should be oriented (Helleiner 1966; FAO 1966). As a consequence, the major policy questions and the corresponding relevant sectors, interrelationships, and variables in the Nigerian economy were isolated more easily than they might have been.

The following are examples of questions we proposed to answer. They illustrate the policy level at which we were aiming and, thereby, help to specify the level of aggregation toward which the simulation model is oriented.[1]

What would be the impact on farm income, national income, export earnings, level of demand for farm and non-farm products, and levels of employment of:

---

[1] The Nigerian model can be differentiated from the simulation models built by Holland for the Indian and Venezuelan economies and Kresge's model of the Pakistan economy (Holland 1962; Holland and Gellespie 1963; Kresge 1967) by its adaptability to questions which require either very macro or intermediate levels of aggregation in contrast to the macro considerations alone of the Holland and Kresge models.

(1) *increasing marketing board prices paid to export crop producers (i.e. reducing the spread between world and domestic prices)?*

(2) *increasing production research and extension efforts on export crops?*

(3) *increasing research on food crop varieties and production practices, and subsequently funding production campaigns to implement the most promising findings?*

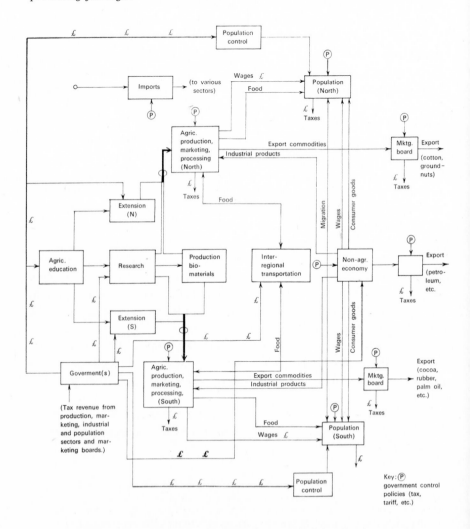

Fig. 2. Major sectors and flows of a simulation model of the Nigerian economy.

(4) *stimulating private investment or making public investments in agricultural input industries, storage and processing facilities, and required supporting infrastructure improvements?*

Specifying the relevant policy-making clientele and their most important questions determined which sectors and/or interrelationships needed particular attention within the model. The major sectors and flows as presently conceptualized within the simulation model of the Nigerian economy are shown in fig. 2. As can be seen from the diagram, our emphasis is on the agricultural sector which has been the major source of past economic growth. Since agriculture contains most of the productive resources in Nigeria (contributing 65% of the gross domestic product and 66% of Nigerian exports in 1962-63), its role in future growth will be very important. Some planners are interested in evaluating alternative policies affecting regional production specialization and trade. These typically involve likely farmer responses to various economic incentives or government assistance projects, etc. Consequently, our model has a commodity orientation, emphasizing export crops. To simply consider questions related to regional specialization and interregional trade, a two region (North and South) model is currently conceived. However, several ecological zones within each region are also differentiated to bring the model to a level at which many important policy decisions are being made.

Although this diagram shows the main components, sectors, and flows to be incorporated into the simulation model, it does not show the basic political decision mechanisms and their point of impact on the agricultural development and adjustment process in the Nigerian economy. In fig. 3, the relationship between specific policy variables and the components incorporating the main streams of economic activity are shown. These range from input allocation decisions to production results, following through the marketing process to consumption. The flows of material, money, price information and regulatory activities are shown. Thus, this general mechanism applies to virtually any commodity produced. Specifically it applies to staple food crops, livestock and the export crops (i.e. oil palm, ground nuts, cotton, cocoa and rubber) in the agricultural production and marketing sector of the model.

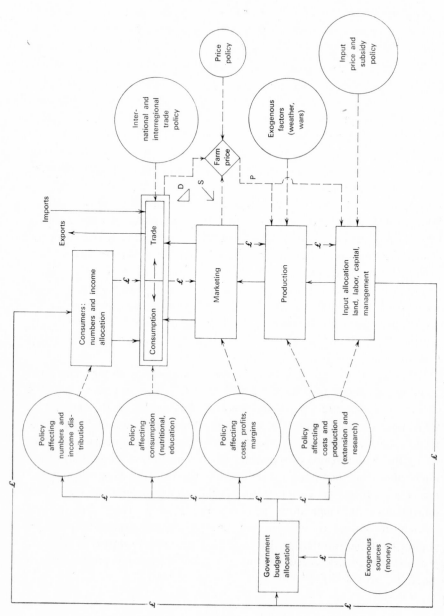

Fig. 3. Basic components of development model with main material, money, price, and regulation (information) flows.

2. Mathematical modeling and simulation

Conceptually, a simulation model of an economic system can be viewed in the following general mathematical form:

$$\psi(t+1) = F[\psi(t), \alpha(t), \beta(t), \gamma(t)]$$

$$\theta(t) \quad = H[\psi(t), \psi_w(t), \alpha(t), \beta(t), \gamma(t)]$$

$$\pi(t) \quad = G[\psi(t), \alpha(t), \beta(t), \gamma(t)],$$

where ψ = a vector (set) of variables which defines the state of the simulated system at any given time. Typical state variables might be production capacities, land allocated to various activities, prices, population by sub-groups, levels of technology, etc.

ψ_w = a vector of variables which describes the state of the system in the real world.

$\alpha(t)$ = a set of parameters that defines the structure of the system, e.g., technical coefficients, etc. (some of these may be subject to variation within the model).

$\beta(t)$ = a set of exogenous variables that influence system behavior, e.g., world prices, weather, etc.

$\gamma(t)$ = a set of policy variables which can be controlled to alter the system's performance in various directions, e.g., investment alternatives, tax policies, etc.

$\theta(t)$ = a set of intermediate output variables which measure how well the model of the system $\psi(t)$ corresponds to reality $\psi_w(t)$, e.g., residual sum of squares, R^2, etc.

$\pi(t)$ = a set of output variables which measure the system's simulated performance, e.g., profit, income, rates of growth, per capita income, foreign exchange earnings, etc.

The first equation is a difference equation formulation of the system model which describes the state of the system and subsequent performance at discrete points in time. This formulation is particularly amenable to digital computer solution. The second equation applies only in the model refinement and testing stage. The third equation is relevant in model application when the performance of the system is simulated over time under various policy alternatives.

This general formulation is exemplified in the hundreds of parameters and structural relationships which are actually incorporated in the model. Because space does not allow a detailed description of the entire computer program which makes explicit the components, variables and inter-relationships of the agricultural sector, fig. 4 depicts in more detail the major components of the Northern regional model previously mentioned. We will present in an Appendix some of the equations which explicate the details within one of the blocks of the diagram in fig. 4.[2]

3. The Northern Region model

The agricultural economy of Nigeria is broadly viewed as being comprised of two interacting regions, i.e., the southern tree and root crop region and the northern annual crop and livestock region.

The current model views Northern Nigeria (the old Northern Region) as being divided into four distinct sub-regions: (1) land area which is uniquely suitable for production of groundnuts or food crops, (2) land area suitable for the production of cotton or food crops, (3) an area on which groundnuts, cotton and food crops can compete with each other for the use of the land, and (4) land suitable only for food crops. The four production activities of these four regions are represented by the production and marketing blocks in fig. 4. The beef production block represents the other major agricultural producing activity of Northern Nigeria[3] which is assumed not to compete now or in the near future with crops for land resources.

In this part of the model, the major outputs are quantities of commodities from various production activities and other measures of system performance. These include level of gross domestic product, tax revenues, employment levels, foreign exchange earnings, per capita incomes and nutrition levels, and industrial good consumption levels. The planner can explore the impact of alternative development strategies upon these outputs. Major policy variables (from the user's standpoint) included are various modernization programs for the five production activities, marketing board producer price policies for groundnuts and cotton, and taxation policies.

---

[2] The computer program of the Nigerian model is written in FORDYN which is an adaptation of DYNAMO compatible with FORTRAN (Forrester 1961; Llewellyn 1966; Pugh 1963).

[3] The beef production activity was the first component developed by the Michigan State Research Team. It is reported elsewhere (Johnson et al. 1968; Manetsch et al. 1968a).

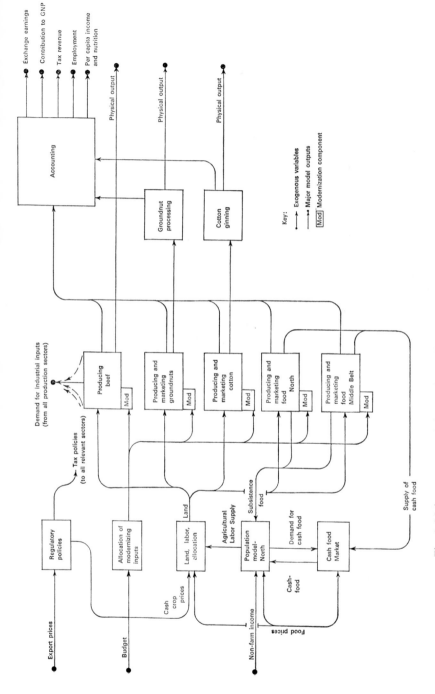

Fig. 4. Major sectors and interactions of the Northern Nigeria agricultural model.

A key component affecting the behavior of the model (and its ability to simulate real world behavior) is the land, labor allocation box in fig. 4. This component is explicated in its current form in the Appendix to illustrate the detailed structure of the model. To summarize those equations, the total arable land in the four sub-regions is determined by available labor, cash returns to labor, the proportion of the population active in the cash market, and a mechanization (or labor efficiency) coefficient (see Appendix). Given total arable land, land available for cash crops is computed as a residual after subsistence food needs have been provided.[4] The land allocation mechanism then allocates this residual to the viable alternatives in each of the four sub-regions on the basis of cash returns per unit of labor, the most restrictive resource. The model includes behavioral and production lags which provide for a smooth transition of allocatable land to the most profitable option available in each sub-region. The land allocation mechanism described determines the supply response and the Northern producers adjustment to changes in crop price and profit expectations. Since groundnut and cotton prices are established by Nigerian marketing boards, only cash food prices are determined endogenously in the model through the interaction of supply and demand. Demand for cash food in the model is determined as a function of non-farm income (assumed an exogenous variable at the present time), non-farm population, and food prices. Non-farm population and food prices are generated endogenously by the model.

The model incorporates a modernization component which can be used to evaluate the introduction of improved inputs or management practices to one or more of the crop components. The modernization component is a general purpose sub-routine which is called whenever a budget allocation has been made to stimulate the modernization of one or more crops. Modernization proceeds at a rate directly related to the level of profitability for the producer. This component also includes an innovation diffusion mechanism which allows for spontaneous (farmer to farmer) diffusion of modern techniques occurring over time, if necessary inputs, information requirements, etc. are available. The major outputs of the modernization component are changes in the average crop yields which currently are deterministic rather than probabilistic (i.e. weather influence is ignored) in the model.

---

[4] This describes the present behavioral situation in Northern Nigeria, but the model has the flexibility to allow cash food to replace subsistence food needs if socio-economic conditions change.

4. Model refinement and testing

Up to this point, we have used our theoretical and institutional understanding of the Nigerian economy to specify the major components or building blocks of the system and to initially specify the technological relationships, behavioral interrelationships, cultural and institutional constraints which might be manipulated by policy makers. In so doing we have (1) specified the structural interrelationships, (2) determined the important instrumental variables, (3) determined the directions of causation, (4) specified functional forms of the technological or behavioral relationships that seemed to fit the current and potential situations envisioned, and (5) tentatively specified the parameters and, thus, the shape of functional relations. Our sources of information and data have included CSNRD research, researchers and other professional personnel in the field, secondary data and previous research results. The above information was utilized in initially approximating the parameters and relationships in the components which we have completed. By computer simulation, we then checked the consistency of the various structural relationships and parameter values and made corrections in gross errors.

A procedure (illustrated below) known as "sensitivity analysis" tested the impact of changes in model parameters upon model behavior. These tests served at least two functions. They indicated what data were most important in affecting model behavior, thereby helping to establish priorities for additional data gathering activities. A second useful outcome of sensitivity analysis was identification of programs and policies which might significantly improve the performance of the system.

Those parameters which appear more sensitive will be investigated. The investigation may indicate that we need to instigate a special study or wait for new sources of information or for field surveys to become available. Alternatively, we may verify the reasonableness of the estimates by checking with experts or with data not previously utilized to establish the original parameters.

5. Preliminary tests of the Northern model

The major components of the system were modeled, simulated and tested individually as part of the overall model building process. During these tests, conceptual and programming errors were detected and corrected until the component appeared credible and ready for inclusion in larger models. The components were then integrated into the Northern regional model shown in fig. 4. Extensive model tests were continued within the context of the larger model to eliminate programming errors and inconsistencies between related model components. This refinement process led to a model which was deemed ready for preliminary comparison with time series data generated by the Northern Nigerian economy.

These initial comparisons served a number of purposes:

(1) They led to additional structural and parameter changes in the model which made it behave more realistically.

(2) They helped identify the model parameters which have the greatest impact on the performance of the economy as measured by such variables as income, foreign exchange earnings, value added, and so forth.

(3) They provided guidance in determining priorities for future data gathering activities.

Essentially the model (which at this time contains only "ball park" parameter estimates for the most part) was given farmer prices for groundnuts and cotton over the period 1953-65. Since these prices were determined largely by world prices and/or marketing board policies, they can be considered exogenously determined. The model then simulated this 13-year period, generating annual groundnut production, cotton production and an aggregate cash food price index for Northern Nigeria. The sum-of-squared errors between the simulated data and actual data was then calculated and aggregated. The following equations define this measure of model performance:

$$TSS = TSS_g + TSS_c + TSS_f,$$

where TSS = total sum of squared deviations of the model results from actual data.

TSS_g, TSS_c, TSS_f = total sum of squared deviations of groundnut, cotton and food series, respectively.

The individual squared deviations, TSS_g, TSS_c, and TSS_f are computed as follows:

$$TSS_i = \sum_{j=1}^{13} \left[\frac{X_{ij} - \hat{X}_{ij}}{\overline{X}_i} \right]^2,$$

where X_{ij} = real world observation in year j.

$$\overline{X}_i = \sum_{j=1}^{13} \frac{X_{ij}}{13} - \text{the mean of real world observations.}$$

$\hat{X}_{ij}$ = the simulated value of the ith time series in year j.

Division by the mean $\overline{X}_i$ in this equation normalizes the errors of each time series so they carry approximately equal weight in the overall measure of fit, *TSS*.

Given the performance measure *TSS*, the model was further refined and "uncertain" parameters were adjusted within the likely range of actual values until it roughly tracked real world data and produced a "respectable" value for *TSS*.[5] It was disturbing to note that the model could be made to look "respectable" in a number of different ways — some of them clearly unrealistic. Given more (than three) real world time series for comparison with the model, it would be more difficult to get a good model fit and this problem would be eased. The model was finally roughly tuned on the basis of the most reasonable and consistent set of underlying assumptions. Using the results of this procedure as a "base" run, a series of "sensitivity" runs of the model were made in which individual model parameters were varied by 20%. Some of the more important results of these sensitivity runs are shown in table 1.

The first run in table 1 provides a standard against which subsequent runs can be evaluated. In runs 2-13 the parameter listed in column 2 (and only that parameter) is changed by 20% and the impact upon measures of system behavior noted. In addition to a tabulation of values of *TSS*, TSS_f, TSS_c and TSS_g, which are measures of how well the model fits data from the Northern Nigeria economy, table 1 includes a number of economic measures which provide an indication of how important variations in any given parameter are in determining the performance of the economy. These are defined as follows:

CFICNA = Cash farm income from crops in Northern Nigeria accumulated over a 20-year simulation run — Billions of Nigerian pounds.

FOREXNA = Foreign exchange earnings from crops and beef in Northern Nigeria accumulated over a 20-year simulation run — Millions of pounds.

---

[5] As seen from the defining equation, perfect tracking would correspond to a *TSS* value of zero. If the model produced zero outputs, *TSS* would be approximately 39.

CFIPC = Cash farm income per capita in the rural economy of Northern Nigeria — £/person.

In all, 12 separate parameters are tested for sensitivity in table 1. These are defined as follows:

$APLO_1$ = Cultivated acres per equivalent man unit in region 1 (groundnut-food) with traditional mechanization and normal prices.

$APLO_2$ = Same as above for region 2 (cotton-food).

$EAP(1)$ = Percent of rural population that is economically active in region 1 (groundnut-food) at the beginning of the simulation run (1953).

$EAP(2)$ = Percent of rural population that is economically active in region 2 (cotton-food) at the beginning of the simulation run (1953).

$B(1,1)$ = Profitability elasticity (see equation (L4) in Appendix) for groundnuts when profitability index (PF_1) is greater than 1.

$B(1,4)$ = Profitability elasticity (equation (L4)) for food in region 4 when profitability index (PF_4) is greater than 1.

$B(2,1)$ = Profitability elasticity (equation (L4)) for groundnuts when profitability index (PF_1) is less than 1.

$C5$ = A parameter that controls the rate of food price adjustment in response to differences between supply and demand — Equation (L25).

P4(1), P4(2), P4(3), P4(4) = The productivities in yield per acre in the farm subregions of the northern model.

The runs tabulated are by no means exhaustive. Much more of this kind of testing needs to be done. The runs shown illustrate what can be learned from sensitivity analysis.

From runs 2-5 it is seen that variables such as acres cultivated per unit of labor and indices of economic activity are quite important in determining the performance of the model. This suggests that effort directed at obtaining better estimates of these parameters might substantially improve model accuracy. In fact, comparison of runs 2-5 with runs 6-8 suggests that labor utilization and economic activity parameters might be more important in determining system behavior than parameters which measure the impact of expected profitabilities upon subsequent enterprise selection decisions.

In run 9, the food price adjustment parameter $C5$ was examined for sensitivity and found to have a relatively weak influence upon model behavior. This suggests that data gathering efforts might be more profitably directed elsewhere.

Table 1

Selected results of Northern model sensitivity tests

Run no.	Run description	Base value of varied parameter	$CFICNA$ ($£ \times 10^9$)	$FOREXNA$ ($£ \times 10^6$)	$CFIPC$ ($£$)	TSS	TSS_f	TSS_g	TSS_c
1	Base Run		1.890	9.228	8.29	1.887	0.200	0.828	0.850
2	$APLO_1$ ↑ by 20%	6.0	2.026	172.7	8.57	4.896	0.200	3.837	0.859
3	$APLO_2$ ↑ by 20%	6.0	1.945	87.00	8.44	7.463	0.200	0.827	6.436
4	$EAP(1)$ ↑ by 20%	0.750	1.922	45.42	8.32	2.360	0.200	1.309	0.859
5	$EAP(2)$ ↑ by 20%	0.5	1.895	15.29	8.29	2.122	0.200	0.828	1.095
6	$B(1,1)$ ↑ by 20%	1.0	1.890	9.228	8.29	1.887	0.200	0.828	0.859
7	$B(1,4)$ ↑ by 20%	1.0	1.891	9.309	8.29	1.872	0.185	0.828	0.860
8	$B(2,1)$ ↑ by 20%	0.5	1.886	3.189	8.26	1.893	0.200	0.834	0.859
9	$C5$ ↑ by 20%	1.0	1.893	9.179	8.28	1.892	0.206	0.828	0.858
10	$P4(1)$ ↑ by 20%	700 lb./acre	1.989	130.3	8.51	3.699	0.200	2.639	0.859
11	$P4(2)$ ↑ by 20%	260 lb./acre	1.921	52.72	8.37	4.438	0.200	0.828	3.410
12	$P4(3)$ ↑ by 20%	700 lb./acre	2.007	156.7	8.54	5.452	0.200	2.428	2.825
13	$P4(4)$ ↑ by 20%	5320 lb./acre	1.890	8.386	8.25	1.949	0.248	0.828	0.874

Perhaps the most interesting simulation results contained in the table are those of runs 10-13. In these runs, it was assumed that yields per acre were increased by 20% for each of the four major cropping activities of Northern Nigeria. Run 10 (increased groundnut yield) showed significant increases in foreign exchange earnings and farm income. In run 11, the impact of a corresponding increase in cotton yield was less significant due to the smaller scale of cotton production.

In run 12, a 20% increase in the yield of food (mainly grains) grown *in competition with groundnuts and cotton* was postulated. The impact on foreign exchange earnings and farm income was greater than when either groundnut or cotton yields were increased by the same proportion. The increased food yields allowed farmers to release land and labor from food crops. Because of the very large acreage of food crops, the acreage and outputs of groundnuts and cotton increased more as substantial land and labor resources were freed from subsistence food crop production. These results focus attention on an important question: Should extension and research programs give more emphasis to food crops grown in competition with export crops such as groundnuts and cotton? In some situations, this might be preferable to aiming these resources directly at the export and import substitute commodities.

In run 13, the yield of food in the food-only zone was increased by 20%. Food prices were lowered and the impact on farm income and exchange earnings was neutral under the demand conditions currently specified in the region.

The tests described above represent a beginning. Much more testing is planned for the Northern model, including activation of the modernization components and exploration of alternative budget allocations.

6. Model validation

Once a model has undergone preliminary tests, attention turns to questions of validity.[6] Validation of a complex simulation model is by no means an easy task but certainly is of key importance if a model is to be used for

---

[6] The subject of model validation and the design of experiments to test for sensitivity and validity of model components has been examined more exhaustively by Naylor et al. (1967).

decision making. If the model describes an existing system, it is sometimes possible to rigorously compare the behavior of the model with the past behavior of the real world system and thereby gain insight into model validity. Prediction is, of course, an even better way to test a model — how well does the model predict how the real system is *going to* behave? Both these methods require considerable quantities of real world data which may be difficult or costly to acquire. The latter method involves a waiting period which may be intolerable in the situation at hand.

If the purpose of the model is to help plan a system that does not exist, the problem of validation can be even more formidable. In this case validation hinges on the laws, assumptions and logic embedded in the model and can be viewed as "validation by deduction". It is encouraging to note here that models *have* been useful in the design of new systems in many areas of activity. In any event, a simulation is *always* an approximation of reality. The question that must be answered is — is the model an acceptable approximation?

In many cases, it would seem, a pragmatic approach to the question of validation has been taken. People who are thoroughly acquainted with the way the real world behaves in the given problem situation can develop a "feel" for how well a model performs and to what extent they can allow it to enlarge their thinking and influence their decisions. In many situations, decision makers are forced to make important decisions on the basis of limited and perhaps questionable information. The question arises — can *better* decisions be made using a simulation? Are the decisions improved sufficiently to warrant the cost of simulation?

7. Model applications

At this point we assume that the simulation model has been refined, tested and judged to be credible in its representation of reality. What is its potential usefulness to decision makers?

A common use of a model is to provide the decision maker with a laboratory for exploring the alternative consequences of a wide range of alternative plans or management strategies. The decision maker has complete freedom to weight heavily only those benefits and costs which he considers important. In this mode of operation there must be close interaction between decision makers, systems analysts and computer specialists, as again the process is iterative in nature. One simulation experiment can lead to the creative design of a new and better one which will involve reprogramming or even, perhaps, basic modifications of the model. The development of a set of development strategies which are consistent, mutually reinforcing, and, thus, a more effective use of resources should be more readily achieved.

With current technology, simulation models can also be used in an optimization mode (Wilde and Beightler 1967). This approach pre-supposes some single criterion such as cost, profit, discounted present value, etc. to be maximized or minimized. In this mode the model is programmed to automatically search for the plans or policies which optimize the selected criterion. In many cases, one objective function may not be definable, or stable over time. Consequently, the multiple objective approach currently utilized in our model may be more useful, being sufficiently flexible that it is compatible with both different agencies and changes in goals as development progresses.

Due to the dynamic nature of system management, simulation models are often used on a more or less continuous basis through time. This implies periodic updating of input information and reevaluation of development strategies. Implicit in this is the monitoring of the real world behavior and using this information to keep the model realistic and credible to the decision maker clientele.

8. Planning capability

A computer simulation model of an economic system can have some conspicuous advantages for policy makers. It can serve as a means to experiment with and comprehensively analyze the complex relationships affecting the potential results of various policy alternatives. Undesirable economic situations or consequences can thus be foreseen and avoided. A simulation model can be a substantial assist in designing development plans if the major mechanisms constraining or accelerating development are adequately approximated within the model. However a substantial research investment may be necessary to adequately design and build a credible simulator. Substantial information reservoirs and research investigations are usually necessary in developing a reasonably complex and useful simulation model for regional or national development planning.

Current limiting resources in building realistic simulators for developing economies appear to be (1) the amount and breadth of applicable descriptive information available about the interrelationships within the economy, and (2) trained personnel.

Trained personnel, in combination with access to a large computer must be available to build and continually update the functional relationships within the model, to specify the possible impacts of new policies upon model structure and parameters, and to interpret the results of model experimentation for the decision maker.

For Nigeria, there was substantial descriptive information about the agricultural economy which was appropriate for fitting the functional interrelationships in the simulation model. However, much previous research and secondary data only related tangentially to our specific requirements. The behavioral dynamics of the system were probably the greatest single aspect of the model where initial approximations were most difficult. Here our resource personnel with Nigerian experience proved invaluable. Our current model and those which will follow in the coming year must be considered tentative and subject to revision in the light of new research findings and criticism from knowledgeable people. We recognize that the process of simulation model building and testing is iterative and that our work is only a stepping stone to an operational planning model. However, at each incremental step one must ask whether the benefits of increased model realism surpass the costs of data acquisition and greater modeling efforts.

A broader issue involves interpreting and implementing the results from simulation. Even with the best model that can be formulated from existing data, it must be pointed out that knowledge about an economic system is not at the same level as that known about most physical systems. The fact that results come from a computer certainly does not make them divine revelations or make them any more valid than the basic information inputs and perceived interrelationships determining the results. Also, we emphasize economic results of various development plans without specifying social and political implications. In actual implementation, each alternative and the associated economic results would have to be examined in more depth to provide an evaluation of their social and political consequences. We have not attempted to specify which politician or political group may be detrimentally affected if a technological change is promoted or what the political consequences may be with further governmental intervention in price determination. However, the likely economic opportunity costs associated with various alternatives may be useful information in the actual policy-maker's decision process.

9. Conclusion

The systems analysis approach to development planning provides a comprehensive view of a complex system. A simulation model can incorporate the most important mechanisms and the best available information within an economy to provide a readily available means of experimentation for various development policies. Information gaps can be spotlighted and research priorities can be more readily evaluated. In so doing, better-informed planning can be facilitated. Further, development bottlenecks can be diagnosed and policies tailored to alleviate problem situations. While no comprehensive simulation model of a national economy has yet been fully implemented and tested, it appears that the benefits involved include: (1) a clearer understanding of the important components and interactions within the economy and potential accelerators or constraints to development, (2) acquisition of relevant information in an "instant recall" model, and (3) a diagnostic tool which can point out likely undesirable economic results before policies are implemented. A simulation planning model tentatively seems to be a useful introduction of new technology into development planning where a substantial research and data base is available.

10. Appendix

10.0. *Land allocation*

The current model views Northern Nigeria as being made up of four distinct ecological sub-regions. In Venn diagrams it would appear as shown in fig. 5. The purpose of this component of the model is to simulate the behavior of Northern Nigerian farmers in allocating cultivated lands to: (1) subsistence food, (2) cash food, i.e., food that sells in the cash market (3) cash crops, i.e., groundnuts and cotton, within the sub-region which is appropriate. For example, in regions 1 and 2 the choice must be made between planting food for subsistence or for the cash market, or planting a cash crop.[7] The mathematical equations to follow describe the allocation mechanism between cash and non-cash crops and then cash crops for sub-regions 1 and 2, sub-region 3, and sub-region 4 in that order. Since the prices of groundnuts and cotton are set by marketing boards these are taken as policy variables; however, cash food prices are determined endogenously and the mechanism of cash food price determination is given in the last section.

1 Groundnut–food subregion
2 Cotton – food subregion
3 Groundnut – cotton – food subregion
4 Food only subregion

Fig. 5.

10.1. *Allocation between cash and non-cash crops within a sub-region*

The acres of land allocatible to cash crops is computed by equation (L1).

$$AL_i(t) = LABA_i(t) \times EAP_i(t) \times APL_i(t) \times PF_i(t)^B{}_i, \qquad (L1)$$

where AL_i = Land allocatible to cash crops in sub-region i ($i = 1, 2, 3, 4$).
$LABA_i$ = Effective labor available (man units) in sub-region i (computed in the population component).
EAP_i = Proportion of the population in sub-region i that is active in producing cash crops (see equation (L2)).
PF_i = A profitability index for sub-region i (see equation (L4)).
APL_i = Acres of cash crops cultivated per unit of labor at "normal" profitability ($PF_i = 1$) (see equation (L3)).
B_i = Parameters that determine the magnitude of responses to profitability.

The variable EAP (computed in equation (L2)) introduces the concept of an economically active population which includes those farmers who have responded to recently-learned opportunities to start growing and selling on the cash market.

$$EAP_i(t + DT) = EAP_i(t) + C7_i \times DT \times (1 - EAP_i(t)), \qquad (L2)$$

---

[7] The area of each region can contract but not expand in the time span of the model.

where EAP_i = Proportion of the population in region i that is economically active. $0 < EAP_i \leq 1$.

$C7_i$ = A model parameter that determines the rate at which farmers enter the economically active population.

DT = The basic time increment used in the simulation.

This equation is a crude model of a diffusion process which gradually increases the economically active proportion over time. EAP will gradually approach one in the limit as time increases. The parameter $C7_i$, which determines the speed of transition in each of the four regions, may be set at some constant value which approximates existing conditions or made dependent upon other variables such as extension expenditures, infrastructure developments, etc.

The variable APL_i in equation (L1) is an endogenous model variable computed by equation (L3):

$$APL_i(t) = \text{MAX } [APL_{0i} \times CM_i - SFL_i(t)/LABA_i, 0], \tag{L3}$$

where APL_i = Acres of cash crops per unit of labor in sub-region i.

APL_{0i} = *Total* acres cultivatible per unit of labor in sub-region i at a given level of mechanization.

CM_i = A mechanization coefficient that introduces the effect of labor saving investments.

SFL_i = Land required for food self-sufficiency in sub-region i (see equation (L5)).

$LABA_i$ = Total labor available in region i — man-units.

$\text{MAX } [a,b]$ = A function that takes the maximum of the terms in brackets.

The profitability indices in equation (L1) are determined as follows for sub-regions one and two (groundnuts — food and cotton — food):

$$PF_i(t) = \frac{(TLNF_i(t) \times CR_i(t) + TLCF_i(t) \times CRF_i(t))/AL_i(t)}{(TLNF_i(0) \times CR_i(0) + TLCF_i(0) \times CRF_i(0))/AL_i(0)}, \tag{L4}$$

where PF_i = Profitability indices for sub-regions one ($i = 1$) and two ($i = 2$).

AL_i = Total land allocated to cash earners in sub-region i.

$TLNF_i$ = Total land in non-food in sub-region i.

$TLCF_i$ = Total land in cash food in sub-region i.

CR_i = Net cash returns from non-food in sub-region i
($£$/man-year).

CRF_i = Net cash returns from cash food in sub-region i
($£$/man-year).

Similar equations compute profitability indices for sub-region 3 where cotton, groundnuts and food compete and sub-region 4 where food is the only cash earner.

The model next computes the subsistence food land required in each region.

$$SFL_i(t+DT) = SFL_i(t) + (DT/S3) (DEMR_i(t)/(CALA_i(t)) - SFL_i(t)).$$
$$(L5)$$

This equation determines, after an adjustment lag $S3$, the amount of land SFL_i required to satisfy the regional rural demand for calories, $DEMR_i$, given that $CALA_i$ calories per acre are produced in region i. Here again the index i ranges over the four regions included in the Northern model. $DEMR_i$, computed by the population component, is the total calorie requirement of farm families in region i, plus or minus an adjustment factor that can account either for a planned surplus or a planned deficit.[8]

Given the land required for food-self-sufficiency and the land allocated to cash crops in each region, total cultivated land is simply

$$TL_i(t) = AL_i(t) + SFL_i(t) \quad (AL_i(t) \geq 0),$$
$$(L6)$$

where AL_i = Allocatable land in region i.
TL_i = Total cultivated land in region i.
SFL_i = Total land required for substistence food in region i.

10.2. *Cash crops in sub-regions 1 and 2*

The model next allocates AL_1, AL_2, AL_3, and AL_4 to the competing cash crops in each region. It does this on the assumption that farmers will gradually move toward that crop which maximizes the net returns to labor. Land shifts to the more profitable crop at a rate that is proportional to:

---

[8] Currently the rural demand, $DEMR_i$, reflects the tendency of Northern Nigerian farmers to be food self-sufficient. Any changes in this behavior pattern would be reflected in changes in the variable $DEMR_i$.

(1) The percent difference in cash returns per unit of labor that exists between the two crops.

(2) The amount of land currently allocated to the less profitable crop.

(3) A model parameter, $C1$, which can be varied to match prevailing farmer behavior.

The equations that perform these functions for sub-regions 1 and 2 are:

$$R_i(t) = C1 \times (CR_i(t) - CRF(t)) \times XTL_i(t)/(CR_i(t)) + DAL_i(t)/DT, \quad \text{(L7)}$$

where R_i = The rate of change of non-food land (acres/year) for groundnuts ($i = 1$) and cotton ($i = 2$).

    CR_i = Net cash returns per unit of labor (lagged to include behavioral effects) (£/man-year).

    CRF = Net food cash returns per unit of labor also lagged (CR_1, CR_2, and CRF are computed by the production and marketing model component).

    XTL_i = Total allocatable land in cash food if $CR_i \geq CRF$; Total land in non-food in region i if $CR_i < CRF$.

    $C1$ = A model parameter that controls the speed of land adjustment.

The variable DAL_i in equation (L7) adds any net increase in allocatable land (AL_i) to the more profitable crop and subtracts any net decline from the less profitable crop via equation (L8).

$$\begin{aligned} DAL_i(t) &= \text{MAX}\,[(AL_i(t) - AL_i(t - DT)), 0] \\ &\quad \text{if } CR_i(t) \geq CRF(t) \\ &= \text{MIN}\,[(AL_i(t) - AL_i(t - DT)), 0] \\ &\quad \text{if } CR_i(t) < CRF(t). \end{aligned} \quad \text{(L8)}$$

Given the rate of change of non-food land from equation (L7) the model computes *total* non-food land (in regions one and two) as

$$TLNF_i(t) = \text{MAX}\,[(TLNF(t - DT) + DT \times R_i(t)), 0]. \quad \text{(L9)}$$

This equation essentially computes the time integral of $R_i(t)$, limited to preclude the possibility of negative land.

To complete the land allocation for regions one and two total cash food land is computed as a residual between total allocatable land, AL_i, and land allocated to non-food production, $TLNF_i$:

$$TLCF_i(t) = AL_i(t) - TLNF_i(t). \tag{L10}$$

10.3. *Cash crops in sub-region 3*

The mechanism for allocating land to the three cash earners in sub-region 3 is similiar to that described though considerably more complex. In words, this part of the model shifts land gradually to the crop with the greatest return per unit of labor. Any net increase in allocatible land in sub-region 3 (due to price incentives, population growth, etc.) is added to the land in the profitable crop. Any decreases in land over time are subtracted from the least profitable option if possible. If this is not possible the decrement is subtracted from the second least profitable crop and so forth. With three competitive crops there are six possible rankings with respect to profitability:

$$CR(1) \geq CR(2) \geq CRF$$
$$CR(1) \geq CRF \geq CR(2)$$
$$CR(2) \geq CR(1) \geq CRF$$
$$CR(2) \geq CRF \geq CR(1)$$
$$CRF \geq CR(1) \geq CR(2)$$
$$CRF \geq CR(2) \geq CR(1).$$

Here $CR(1)$, $CR(2)$ and CRF are respectively the current time averaged cash returns (£/man-year) for groundnuts, cotton and cash food respectively. The simulation model determines which of the six above cases applies and then allocates land, beginning with the least profitable crop. The following equations apply:

$$RJ3(t) = C4 \times TLJ3(t - DT) \times (CR3 - CR1)/CR3 + \text{MIN}[DAL_3(t), 0]/DT, \tag{L11}$$

where $RJ3$ = Rate of change of the least profitable crop in region 3 (the joint region in which groundnuts, cotton and food are grown).
$TLJ3$ = Total land currently in the least profitable crop in region 3 (acres).
$CR3$ = Cash returns for least profitable crop in sub-region 3 (£/man-year).

$CR1$ = Cash returns for the most profitable crop in sub-region 3 (£/man-year).

$C4$ = A model parameter that determines the speed of adjustment.

MIN = The minimum operation.

The variable, DAL_3, is the difference in allocatable land in region 3 in the past time interval and is given by

$$DAL_3(t) = AL_3(t) - AL_3(t - DT). \tag{L12}$$

Given $RJ3$, the model computes a new value for $TLJ3$ — the total land in the least profitable crop.

$$TLJ3(t) = \text{MAX} [TLJ3'(t), 0], \tag{L13}$$

where $TLJ3'(t) = TLJ3(t - DT) + DT \times RJ3(t)$.

Thus, equation (L13) computes $TLJ3$ as the time integral of $RJ3$, limited to preclude the possibility of negative land.

The model then allocates land to the second least profitable crop. This, again, assumes that land shifts to the most profitable in proportion to differential profitabilities that exist. In addition, any net *reduction* in total land area in the region (DAL_3) that could not be removed from the least profitable crop is taken out of this, the second least profitable crop. This behavior is described by the following equations:

$$RJ2(t) = C4 \times TLJ2(t - DT) \times$$
$$\times (CR2(t) - CR1(t))/CR2(t) + RESID(t)/DT, \tag{L14}$$

where $RJ2$ = Rate of change of the second most profitable crop (acres/year).

$TLJ2$ = Total land in the second most profitable crop (acres).

$CR2, CR1$ = Cash returns of second and most profitable crops respectively (£/man-year).

and

$$RESID(t) = \text{MAX} [\text{MIN} [TLJ3'(t), 0], \text{MIN} [DAL_3(t), 0]], \tag{L15}$$

where $TLJ3'$ and DAL_3 are defined in equations (L12) and (L13).

$$TLJ2(t) = \text{MAX} [TLJ2'(t), 0], \tag{L16}$$

where

$$TLJ2'(t) = TLJ2(t - DT) + DT \times RJ2(t). \tag{L17}$$

Again, a constraint is imposed so that land area is non-negative.

Land area in the most profitable crop $TLJ1$, is computed simply as the residual between total allocatable land AL_3 and $TLJ2$ and $TLJ3$:

$$TLJ1(t) = AL_3(t) - TLJ2(t) - TLJ3(t). \tag{L18}$$

Note that this equation allocates any net increase in allocatable land to the most profitable crop. Net decrease in AL_3, as described above, are removed from $TLJ3$ and $TLJ2$ if possible. If not, these latter areas are zero and the net decrease applies to $TLJ1$.

Given the total land areas according to a crop ranking on the basis of profitability, the model then translates these into areas of groundnuts, cotton and cash food by applying the known profitability ranking which currently pertain for the three crops. The following land areas are thereby defined:

$TLJG(t)$ = Total land in groundnuts in sub-region 3.

$TLJC(t)$ = Total land in cotton in sub-region 3.

$TLJF(t)$ = Total land in cash food in sub-region 3.

10.4. *Cash crops in sub-region 4*

Land allocation in sub-region 4 (the food-only zone) is trivial being simply the total allocatable land (if any) after the food needs of the regional population have been met.

$$TLMBCF(t) = MAX(AL_4(t), 0), \tag{L19}$$

where $TLMBCF$ is the total cash-food land in sub-region 4 allocated to cash food production.

10.5. *Totals of food and cash crops for Northern Nigeria*

With the above land allocations in the four sub-regions determined it is a simple matter to compute total areas for Northern Nigeria by crop. Total cash food land in the north, $TCFLN$ is given by:

$$TCFLN(t) = TCFL_1(t) + TLCF_2(t) + TLJF_3(t) + TLMBCF(t), \tag{L20}$$

where $TLCF_1, TLCF_2$ = Total land in cash food (sub-regions 1 and 2).

$TLJF_3$ = Total land in cash food (sub-region 3).

$TLMBCF$ = Total land in cash food (sub-region 4).

Total food land, $ZLC1$, is simply

$$ZLC1(t) = TCFLN(t) + SFL_1(t) + SFL_2(t) + SFL_3(t) + SFL_4(t), \quad \text{(L21)}$$

where SFL_i is the land required for food self-sufficiency in each sub-region (equation (L5)).

Total groundnut and cotton land, $TGLN$ and $TCLN$, are computed as

$$TGLN(t) = TLNF_1(t) + TLJG(t) \tag{L22}$$

$$TCLN(t) = TLNF_2(t) + TLJC(t), \tag{L23}$$

where $TLNF_1$, $TLNF_2$ = The total non-food land in sub-regions 1 and 2 respectively.

$TLJG$ = Total groundnut land in sub-region 3.
$TLJC$ = Total cotton land in sub-region 3.

10.6. *Price determination for cash food*

The land allocation component also contains the market mechanism for cash food. It is assumed that the weighted average price of cash food (subsistence foods including guinea corn, millet, yams and cassava) moves in response to differences between aggregate demand and supply. The aggregate supply of cash food, measured in calories per-year is computed by equation (L24).

$$SUPCFN(t) = CALAN(t) \times (TCFLN(t) - TLMBCF(t)) + \\ + CALAM(t) \times TLMBCF(t), \quad \text{(L24)}$$

where $SUPCFN$ = Supply of cash food in Northern Nigeria (calories/year).
        $CALAN$ = Calories per acre in the North excluding sub-region 4 (primarily from grain production).
        $CALAM$ = Calories per acre in sub-region 4 (primarily from root crops).
     $TLMBCF$ = Total land allocated to cash food in sub-region 4.
$TCFLM - TLMBCF$ = Total cash food land in the North excluding sub-region 4.

An unlagged food price is generated by equation (L25). This variable is lagged by equation (L26) to account for behavioral effects.

$$PFNU(t) = PFNU(t - DT) + DT \times C5 \times PFNU(t - DT) \times \\ \times (DEMCFN(t) - SUPCFN(t))/DEMCFN(t), \quad \text{(L25)}$$

where *PFNU* = Unlagged food price — £/# .

    DEMCFN = Demand for cash food in the North — Calories/year. (This variable is computed in the population component and is a function of non-agricultural population, income, and food price.)

    SUPCFN = Supply of cash food as determined by equation (L24).

    C5 = Price rate elasticity. (This parameter is the percent change in price *per unit time* per percent excess demand that exists in the market.)

$$PFN(t) = PFN(t-DT) + (DT/C6) \times (PFNU(t) - PFN(t-DT)), \qquad (L26)$$

where *PFN* = Price of food in Northern Nigeria (£/#).

    PFNU = Unlagged food price.

    C6 = A model parameter proportional to the behavioral lag between excess demand and price change.

This concludes a description of some of the most important features of the land allocation component of the model. For presentation here many details have been omitted.

References

Candler, Wilfred and Wayne Cartwright, 1969, Estimation of performance functions for budgeting and simulation studies. *American Journal of Agricultural Economics* 51 No. 1, 159-169.

Carroll, T.W., 1968, *Simulation of the diffusion of agricultural innovations in rural communities of transitional societies.* Ph.D. Thesis, MIT, Cambridge, Mass.

Forrester, J.W., 1961, *Industrial dynamics.* New York, John Wiley and Sons.

Hall, A.D., 1962, *A methodology for systems engineering.* Princeton, N.J., VanNostrand.

Halter, A.N. and G.W. Dean, 1965, *Simulation of a California range—feedlot operation.* Giannini Foundation Research Report 282, Univ. of Calif., May.

Halter, A.N. and S.F. Miller, 1966, *River basin planning—a simulation approach.* Oregon State University, Ag. Exp. Sta., Special Report 224, Nov.

Hayenga, M.L., T.J. Manetsch, and A.N. Halter, 1968, Computer simulation as a planning tool in developing economics. *American Journal of Agricultural Economics* 50, No. 5.

Helleiner, Gerald K., 1966, *Peasant agriculture, government and economic growth in Nigeria.* Homewood, Ill., Richard D. Irwin, Inc.

Holland, E.P., 1962, Simulation of an economy with development and trade problems. *American Economic Review* 52, No. 3.

Holland, Edward P., 1967, Principles of simulation. In: *The challenge of development: theory and practice,* edited by Richard J. Ward. Chicago, Aldine Publishing Company.

Holland, P. and Robert W. Gellespie, 1963, *Experiments on a simulated underdeveloped economy: development plans and balance-of-payments policies*. Cambridge, Mass., MIT Press.

Johnson, Glenn L., 1966, Quantitative problems in the simulation of the Nigerian agricultural economy. Michigan State University, East Lansing, Michigan, October. (Mimeographed.)

Johnson, Glenn L., 1967, Evaluation and development of analytical models for rural development. Michigan State University, East Lansing, Michigan. (Mimeographed.)

Johnson, G.L. et al., 1968, A simulation model of the Nigerian agricultural economy: Phase I. The Northern Nigerian beef industry, progress report submitted to the Agency for International Development, April.

Johnson, Glenn L. et al., 1969, Strategies and recommendations for Nigerian rural development. 1969/1985, CSNRD 33, Michigan State University, East Lansing, Mich.

Kresge, David T., 1967, A simulation model for economic planning: a Pakistan example, Economic development report No. 81, Development advisory service, Harvard University, Cambridge, Mass. (Mimeographed.)

Ligomenides, P.A., T.J. Manetsch, and F.A. Ramos, 1967, On the use of computer simulation models in planning development in Northeast Brazil. August. (Mimeographed.)

Llewellyn, R.L., 1966, FORDYN An Industrial Dynamics Simulator. Department of Industrial Engineering, University of North Carolina, Raleigh, N.C.

Manetsch, T.J., 1967, The United States plywood industry—a systems study. *IEEE Transactions on Systems Science and Cybernetics*, November.

Manetsch, T.J., M.L. Hayenga, and A.H. Halter, 1968a, A simulation model of the Nigerian beef industry. Michigan State University, East Lansing, Mich. (Mimeographed.)

Manetsch, T.J., F.A. Ramos, and S.C. Lenchner, 1968, Simulation of a program for modernizing cotton production in Northeast Brazil — working paper number three. Division of Engineering Research, Michigan State University, August.

McMillan, A. and R.F. Gonzales, 1968, *Systems-analysis — a computer approach to decision models*. Homewood, Ill., Richard D. Irwin, Inc.

Ministry of Economic Planning, 1964, *Development Plan, 1962-1968*. Kaduna, Northern Nigeria.

Naylor, Thomas H., 1969, Bibliography 19, Simulation and Gaming. *Computing Reviews*, January.

Naylor, Thomas H., Donald S. Burdick, and W. Earl Sasser, 1967, Computer simulation experiments with economic systems: the problem of experimental design. *Journal of American Statistical Association* 62, Dec., 1315-1337.

Naylor, Thomas H. and J.M. Finger, 1967, Verification of computer simulation models. *Management Science* 14, Oct.

Naylor, T.H. et al., 1966, *Computer simulation techniques*. New York, John Wiley and Sons.

Orcutt, G.H. et al., 1961, *Microanalysis of socio-economic Systems*. New York, Harper.

Pontificia Academia Scientiarum, 1965, *The econometric appoach to development planning*. Amsterdam, North-Holland Publishing Co.

Pugh, A.L., 1963, DYNAMO User's Manual. Cambridge, Mass., The MIT Press.

Simulatics Corporation, 1966, *Dynamic models for simulating the Venezuelan economy*. Centro de Estudios del Desarrollo (CENDES), Universidad Central de Venezuela, September.

U.N. Food and Agriculture Organisation, 1966, *Agricultural development in Nigeria, 1965-1980*. Rome, FAO.

Wilde, D.J. and C.S. Beightler, 1967, *Foundations of optimization*. Englewood Cliffs, N.J., Prentice-Hall.

COMMENTS ON THE TWO ABOVE PAPERS,
BY RICHARD H. DAY*

University of Wisconsin

An economic simulation model is a system of equations, a computer program or an analog device for representing the behavior of an economy or part of an economy. A simulation run is a particular finite sequence of values for a set of endogenous variables determined by the model for a given set of the initial conditions, parameters and exogenous variables.[1] Of the two papers considered here one presents a preliminary report on the development of a simulation model for Nigerian Agricultural Development, the second a discussion of general problems in the development and use of such models for policy purposes.

The field of simulation economics was established in the fifties, a period of work culminating in the books by Orcutt et al. (1961), Forrester (1961), and Cyert and March (1963). The decade of experience that has followed, with contributions far too numerous to catalog here, should provide perspective enough to review the current state of the art — or science. While the present papers have some shortcomings for this purpose, they do make it clear that simulation is alive and well. They also serve the occasion by illustrating some and outlining still more of the major problems in the field.

After a brief general critique of the papers, I review a series of specific questions raised by them. These involve the use of mnemonic notation, the simulation of rational behavior, several issues involving model evaluation,

---

* The author hopes these remarks have benefited from discussions with D.J. Aigner and A.S. Goldberger.

[1] According to Shubik (1960, p. 909) "simulation of a system or of an organism is the operation of a model or simulator which is a representation of the system or organism. The operation of the model can be studied and, from it properties concerning the behavior of the actual system or its subsystem can be inferred". Orcutt (1960, p. 893) defines simulation to be "...a general approach to the study and use of models". He goes on to observe that "an individual simulation run may be thought of as an experiment performed upon a model".

the measurement of policy preferences and a vision which I should like to name "a National Evolutionary Operations Procedure".

1. A general critique

The study of the Nigerian economy reported by Halter, Hayenga and Manetsch (H-H-M) is a direct descendent of Forrester's Industrial Dynamics and an explicit example of microanalytic simulation. It is also an outgrowth of a conference on simulation held at Michigan State University in 1966. It is gratifying to find that it is now "on the computer". Indeed, that an undertaking of this magnitude has reached the computing stage within a few years is in itself a significant fact that will no doubt encourage other efforts. Consequently, it is a disappointment that the authors devote so much space to a general description of simulation and systems analysis and so little to the details of their own study. The generalities are already available anyway in the excellent reviews by Orcutt (1960), Shubik (1960), Clarkson and Simon (1960), and Holland (1962). The functional notation and flowcharts are useful, but what a pity that the specific equations were relegated to an appendix. It is a little as if one had been sated with hors d'œuvres and then served the piece de resistance half-baked in place of liquor and coffee. What we should have liked instead was a report along the lines of Bonini (1963), Cohen (1960), or Clarkson (1962).

But while the tale told by H-H-M is incomplete, one feels there is more to it than in the telling. Microeconomic model building is an arduous task and the authors are to be congratulated for having got as far as they have. We will look forward to a more detailed account of the model, its evaluation and its application to policy.

Naylor's remarks by way of contrast are addressed to problems of simulating macroeconomic models, though most of them apply to micro-models as well. He covers problems of model evaluation and inference and raises some interesting issues connected with the utility functions of policy makers. However, it suffers from the same lack of specificity as its companion piece. A sampling of particular results accompanying the survey of concepts and bibliographical citations would have lent greater force to his obser-vations. Moreover, in view of the early work by Orcutt, Forrester, Cyert and March emphasizing microeconomic *systems* his accusation that "little or no attention has been given to ... model structures such as those used by systems analysts ... [based on] ... conditional statements, logical branchings, and complex feedback mechanisms..." is misleading. Indeed, the work cited involved the construction of computer models that represented the behavior of decision makers and their interaction in markets and complicated organizations using exactly these types of constructs. Its authors also shared his dismay at the limitations of macro models based on variables which are not in principle observable but which are the constructs of government statisticians.[2] Perhaps the simulation family has grown so big that one can no longer remember all of one's (even close) relatives!

But if Naylor has committed an oversight he has alerted us to a host of problems in simulation methodology and has informed us of some imaginative attempts to solve them. His contribution will be especially significant if it provokes econometricians to strike out from their comfortable linear establishment to seek radical new methods for estimation and inference in the simulation context.

2. Mnemonic notation

The mnemonic notation used by H-H-M is a convention often used by simulators following the authoritative precedent of Forrester himself. This is, of course, a matter of taste, but one wonders if the reason why simulation models are so often thought to be analytically intractable is because their basic structure is disguised in a language of use to computers but very poorly suited to the mathematician. It is this characteristic that probably explains why many econometricians and theoretical economists amongst us clearly seem to regard the field as a refuge for professional scoundrels. A combination of flowcharts and conventional mathematical notation could display a simulation model just as well and would be much more suggestive of the analytical possibilities.

3. The simulation of rational behavior

The H-H-M study incorporates a behavioral relation based on "the assumption that farmers will gradually move toward that crop which

---

[2] Orcutt, more than anyone has emphasized the potential increase in information from the "microanalytic" approach. See, e.g., Orcutt et al. (1968).

maximizes the net return to labor". The rationality hypothesis behind this has been pretty well confirmed by econometric studies of many different agricultural commodities in many different underdeveloped countries (e.g., Krishna 1963). This suggests the possibility of representing behavior with explicit optimizing or suboptimizing models based on budgeting, programming or optimal control arguments. Simulation models with these components have elsewhere been called "recursive programs", or "recursive programming models". General descriptions of applications to industry (Day et al. 1970) and to agriculture (Heidues 1970) are available. Such models have been shown to be amenable to an existence analysis (Day and Kennedy 1970), but because they are usually highly nonlinear their detailed study must draw on simulation methods of the kind under consideration here. They do have the theoretical advantage of incorporating economizing behavior explicitly.

4. Model evaluation: weighting errors

There is an economic reason for weighting errors in microanalytic models. Decision makers discriminate easily between important (read relatively profitable) variables and less easily between unimportant variables (variables with nearly zero profit or nearly the same profitability). In the former case decisions are definite and behavior predictable; in the latter decisions are ill-defined and behavior less determinate. Variables of large magnitude are likely to be or to have been important over relatively long periods, while those of small magnitudes are either newly profitable or have been unprofitable for a long period. Microanalytic models should predict important variables, or those of increasing importance, well, unimportant variables or those of declining importance not so well. A complete theory of evaluation for microeconomic models should therefore rest on a theory of decision-making that allows for the discriminating power of decision makers and on *non-stationary* processes. Some initial steps in this direction may be found in Klein (1968).

H-H-M, like various other authors, use a weighted squared error as an evaluation measure. Let x_{it}^*, x_{it}^0 be the model and observed values respectively of the tth observation of a variable x_i, $i = 1, \ldots, n$; $t = 1, \ldots, T$. Let $\varepsilon_{it} = (x_{it}^* - x_{it}^0)$, $\pi_{it} = \varepsilon_{it}/x_{it}^0$ and $\mu_i = (\Sigma_t x_{it}^0)/T$. The statistic used is then $TSS = \Sigma(\varepsilon_{it}/\mu_i)^2$ with the summation over i and t. It is intended to give each variable "approximately equal weight in the overall measure of fit". For a stationary process equal weights for each observation of a given variable as proposed here makes sense. However, in the present case, growth in some variables is anticipated while others should decline. Variables will change in relative importance as the composition of output changes. Hence, each observation should have a different weight. A measure corresponding to *TSS* but incorporating this idea is the squared relative error $SRE = \Sigma \pi_{it}^2$. Relative errors have the advantage of being "scale free" so that errors in variables measured in different units can be aggregated. This fact is not relevant in the present case because all the variables are measured in the same units. This measure implies that deviations are weighted inversely with their importance, i.e. since $SRE = \Sigma (\varepsilon_{it}/x_{it}^0)^2$ the less important the variable the more important its contribution to the evaluation statistic! "Less important" is meaningful here (again) because all variables have the same scale.

If on the other hand we weight *deviations* equally then we obtain the unweighted error $SE = \Sigma \varepsilon_{it}^2$. But since also $SE = \Sigma (x_{it}^0 \pi_{it})^2$ this implies a weighting of *relative* error in the direction of importance. But why not weight the deviations in the direction of importance too? We might consider $SWE = \Sigma (x_{it}^0 \varepsilon_{it})^2$. This implies $SWE = \Sigma [(x_{it}^0)^2 \pi_{it}]^2$, that is that the weight measuring the importance of relative error is the square of the observed variable level. I believe there is some intuitive appeal to the *SWE* statistic especially when the process modelled is nonstationary and variable levels are good proxies for "importance".

There is still another problem with the *TSS* statistic, which is also shared by *SRE*, *SE* and *SWE* in the present context. They are applied to field crop acreages which should satisfy "adding up" restrictions. If x_t^0 is the total acreage at time t then we should observe that $\Sigma_i x_{it}^0 = x_t^0$ and the model should satisfy the constraints $\Sigma_i x_{it}^* = x_t^*$, $t = 1, \ldots, T$. Errors are not independent and satisfy the equations $\varepsilon_t = \Sigma_i \varepsilon_{it}$. Moreover, small relative errors in important variables are likely to cause large relative errors in unimportant variables. All the more reason then to use the extreme weights recommended above. But a statistic *is* available that accounts for these constraints in Theil's Information Statistic (Theil 1967). It would seem particularly relevant here.

5. Model evaluation: the relevant comparisons

Some econometricians, e.g. Jorgenson and Nidiri (1967) have argued that a given econometric model should always be tested against an alternative model. While it has become fashionable to do so and Naylor cites a reference in case a strong qualification to the practice is needed. Policy models are designed to study the repercussion on various response variables of changes in particular exogenous or control variables. This policy purpose can be represented by a list of questions that a given model is constructed to answer. It places constraints on model comparison and evaluation. For example, a given model may not forecast as well as a "mechanical procedure" but one would scarcely reject it for that reason alone unless the only question to be put to it involved an unconditional forecast. Generally it can be said that one wants to know the degree of forecasting power possessed by a model in order to establish one's confidence or uncertainty about its application *to the purpose at hand*.

Microeconomic models particularly may not forecast the *levels* of the endogenous variables accurately, but grounds exist to justify their application to certain classes of policy questions. For example, a stabilization policy for a given commodity may have as its direct purpose to reduce the magnitude of an oscillation in price. A given dynamic model may not predict the price level accurately, but may simulate quite accurately its cyclical character. A control that stabilizes the simulated path might then appear to be an effective policy instrument to stabilize the real world counterpart. This reasoning suggests that models should be evaluated for their ability to simulate the dynamic structure of observed time series, i.e. their power spectra.

6. Model evaluation: comparative spectra

Naylor draws on his earlier work in suggesting that a comparison of the power spectra of two series or two sets of series can be used to evaluate a model and compare it with an alternative. Significance tests are available for this purpose. A model that produces spectra that do not depart substantially from those of a set of observed series might be thought "good" even if it forecast levels or turning points rather poorly. Likewise, alternative models could be tested for significant differences in their spectra. The relevance of this procedure is clear. The model that best represented the oscillatory characteristics of "reality" would presumably be the best candidate for simulating stabilization policies.

The use of the spectral inference theory rests on the necessity for the model to possess stochastic properties, i.e. to be simulated stochastically. It requires large samples, something that can be achieved only for models based on monthly or quarterly data. What is needed are small sample analogs, perhaps nonparametric in nature, that would allow similar inferences for models based on annual time periods.

7. Simulation experiments and policy inference

Economic policy makers possess a variety of controls and simulation models are often designed for repercussion studies including several of them. But when analytical solutions are unknown formidable problems of inference are present, even after one accepts the validity of the model for representing reality. Orcutt (1960, p. 893) observed that

> an individual simulation run may be thought of as an experiment performed upon a model. ... The problem of inferring general relationships from specific results obtained in individual experiments performed on a model is the same as that of inferring general relationships from specific experimental results in any of the inductive sciences.

Following this philosophy, Naylor reviews the application of experimental design to this problem of inference, noting that it requires stochastic simulation and replication. His comments and citations give one a start into the literature on the subject. I have nothing to add to them. Instead I should like to comment on two aspects of experimentation that he does not mention. The first involves the use of simulation to infer experimentally policy makers' (or citizens') preference structures. The second involves the construction of an EVOP for national planning. I take these up in turn.

8. The experimental inference of preferences for alternative policies

Naylor suggests that we do not know "... the parameters or even the functional form of the utility function for government policy makers..." and argues that "Economists would do well to spend less time trying to specify the social welfare functions of policy makers and spend more time seeking solutions to some of the problems of policy makers". On the contrary, he observes that when multiple responses are involved — as is usually the case — "... the analyst must devise some technique for assigning weights to the different response variables before applying specific statistical tests [for the purpose of discriminating amongst policies]". Value judgments will have their out and the preference of policy makers must clearly influence the optimal experimental design for simulation studies for policy.

In quite a different context, progress has been made on experimentally measuring preferences (Thurstone 1931; Davidson and Marshak 1959). Now why could not a policy simulation model be used as an experimental environment to measure the social preferences of policy makers or of voters? One might ask policy makers or voters to consider specific monetary and/or fiscal policy packages with specific budgets or costs to the government bureau or to the citizens. The model builder would then simulate the time paths implied by the policy. Indeed one might envisage a game to be played between a simulator like Naylor representing the economy and a policy maker or ordinary citizen who is to represent social values or his own private interest. By a series of experiments with the model the simulator could help the subject explore, indeed construct, his own social preference function.[3]

Something along this line was advocated by Ragnar Frisch some years ago at an international input-output conference.[4] Briefly Frisch suggested that models of the Norwegian economy be solved for different bills of goods and tax programs with a list being offered to voters. More recently, Encarnacion has explored the construction of social welfare functions by means of voting procedures.[5] It is curious that an approach so well suited to exploring technological and behavioral structures of the economy has not been turned to the study of the structure of preferences of decision makers.

---

[3] The investigation proposed would augment inferences about policy preferences obtained econometrically from the historical record, such as the study by Dewald and Johnson (1963).

[4] Oral remarks. Third International Input-Output Conference, United Nations. Also see Frisch (1961).

[5] Encarnacion (undated), ditto.

9. A national EVOP

One of the most interesting applications of experimental design to practical decision making is the so-called Evolutionary Operations Procedure, or EVOP initially developed by George Box (1957) for control of chemical production processes. Such processes are so complicated that plant production functions are unknown and economic optimization analytically intractable. Box's procedure involves the managers in a sequential game played with their own plant as the environment in which they experiment with controls to allow local estimation of the plant pay-off function and on the basis of which suboptimizing incremental changes in controls can be exercized.

Can we possibly look forward to a National Evolution Operations Procedure — a NAEVOP (pronounced Neevop) — in which (1) an initial set of simulation experiments are used to update and evaluate the current planning model; (2) a second round of experiments are conducted to form a broadly representative opinion survey about preferences of possible policy, economic-evolution combinations, (3) control modifications are attempted in a direction representing the current conception by policy makers of the public interest? One can imagine for NAEVOP a real-time fourway communication network between government planners, political representatives, other economic block representatives (labor unions, industrial executives), and private citizens.[6]

If life is a game then why not learn to play it well?

References

Bonini, C. P., 1962, *Simulation of information and decision systems in the firm.* Englewood Cliffs, Prentice-Hall, Inc.

Box, George, 1957, Evolutionary operation: a method for increasing industrial productivity. *Appl. Statist.* 6, 81-101.

Clarkson, G. P. E., 1962, *Portfolio selection: a simulation of trust investment.* Englewood Cliffs, Prentice-Hall, Inc.

Clarkson, G. P. E. and H. A. Simon, 1960, Simulation of individual and group behavior. *American Econ. Rev.* 50, December, 920-932.

Cohen, K. J., 1960, *Computer models of the shoe, leather, hide sequence.* Englewood Cliffs, Prentice-Hall, Inc.

Cyert, R. M. and J. G. March, 1963, *A behavioral theory of the firm.* Englewood Cliffs, Prentice-Hall.

---

[6] "But the preference function cannot be formulated in one stroke. It can only be done through a series of attempts based on a continuous cooperation between the responsible authorities and the analytical experts." Frisch (1961, p. 6).

Davidson, D. and J. Marshak, 1959, Experimental tests of stochastic decision theories. In: *Measurement, Definition and Theories*, edited by C.W. Churchman and P. Ratoosh. New York, John Wiley and Sons, Chapter 13, pp. 233-69.

Day, R.H. and P.E. Kennedy, 1970, Recursive decision systems: an existence analysis. *Econometrica* (forthcoming).

Day, R.H., M. Abe, W. Tabb, and C. Tsao, 1970, Recursive programming models of industrial development and technological change. In: *Input-Output Techniques*, edited by Carter and Brody. Amsterdam, North-Holland Publishing Co.

Dewald, W.G. and H.G. Johnson, 1963, An objective analysis of the objectives of American monetary policy, 1952-1961. In: *Banking and Monetary Studies*, edited by D. Carson. Homewood, Ill., Richard D. Irwin, Inc.

Encarnacion, J. (undated), On the specification of the social welfare function (ditto).

Forrester, J.W., 1961, *Industrial dynamics*. Cambridge, Mass., M.I.T. Press.

Frisch, R., 1961, A survey of types of economic forecasting and programming and a brief description of the Oslo channel model. Oslo, May. (Mimeographed.)

Heidues, T., 1970, Recursive programming in agricultural applications. In: *Input-Output Techniques*, edited by Carter and Brody. Amsterdam, North-Holland Publishing Co.

Holland, E.P., 1962, Simulation of an economy with development and trade problems. *Amer. Econ. Rev.* 52, June, 408-430.

Jorgenson, D.W. and M.I. Nidiri, 1967, The predictive performance of econometric models of quarterly investment behavior. Reprint 6813, Econometrics Institute, Netherlands School of Economics. (Mimeographed.)

Klein, L., 1968, *An essay on the theory of prediction*. Helsinki, The Academic Bookstore.

Krishna, R., 1963, Farm supply response in India-Pakistan: a case study of the Punjab region. *Economic Journal* 73, 477-87.

Naylor, T.H., K. Wertz, and T.H. Wonnacott, 1969, Spectral analysis of data generated by simulation experiments with econometric models. *Econometrica* 37, 333-352.

Orcutt, G.H., 1960, Simulation of economic systems. *Amer. Econ. Rev.* 50, December, 893-907.

Orcutt, G.H., M. Greenberger, J. Korbel, and A.M. Rivlin, 1961, *Microanalysis of socioeconomic systems: a simulation study*, New York, Harper.

Orcutt, G.H., H.W. Watts, and J.B. Edwards, 1968, Data aggregation and information loss. *American Econ. Review* 58, 773-787.

Shubik, M., 1960, Simulation of the industry and the firm. *Amer. Econ. Rev.* 50, December, 919-908.

Theil, H., 1967, *Economics and information theory*. Chicago, Rand McNally.

Thurstone, 1931, The indifference function. *Journal of Social Psychology* 2, 139-67. Reprinted as Chapter 12 in Thurstone, *The measurement of values*. Chicago, The University of Chicago Press, 1959.

COMMENTS ON THE TWO ABOVE PAPERS,
BY EDWARD P. HOLLAND
International Bank for Reconstruction and Development

On first impression these two papers seem to be concerned with different subjects. In part the difference is that one (Naylor's) is a general review of the state of the art of one aspect of simulation methodology, while the other (by Halter, Hayenga, and Manetsch) is a more specific exposition of some other aspects of simulation, illustrated by a particular case. Naylor's primary concern is the design of simulation experiments, with only secondary consideration of the nature of the model. Halter et al. give most of their attention to the formulation of a model, and their explanation of its use ignores a number of the problems Naylor regards as important.

But there are differences that interest me far more than the differences in coverage of the two papers. What interest me are the differences in treatment of some topics that *are* included in both papers and the differences in philosophy that I think are implicit in the discussions of procedures and in the definitions of problems.

I may be oversimplifying a little but I think it is fairly accurate to say that Professor Naylor represents the econometrician, viewing simulation as an extension of his formalized field — an extension that offers new opportunities but that should be exploited with care to maintain the values of a close connection with rigorous statistical theory. The Michigan State trio, on the other side, represent the system analysts, who believe they are making a model of "reality", uninhibited by the inflexibility of the econometrician's standard mathematical forms.

Obviously, there are some fundamental conflicts between these views of simulation. It is of more than casual interest to try to understand their differences and to speculate on the possibility of an eventual synthesis.

First, concerning the formulation of models, it would seem that Naylor regrets that he cannot keep his models linear, while the Michigan State group go in freely for exponential lags, branches, and multiplicative variables. It is not that Naylor does not recognize nonlinearity; in fact he says, "Unfortunately, realistic econometric models are seldom linear" and he speaks at several points about nonlinear models. But near the end, after quoting Howrey and Kelejian on the superfluity of simulation for linear models, he says, "Since any nonlinear econometric model can be approximated by a linear model ... the arguments of Howrey and Kelejian can also be extended to include nonlinear econometric models". If we try to imagine approximating all the different kinds of nonlinearity of the Nigeria model by "appropriate Taylor series expansions" in order to apply spectral analysis to the model, I think we must admit the prospect is not attractive. Moreover, such linearization is suitable only for small perturbations, whereas in studying development plans and policies, we are concerned with major changes in the variables.

As for the Michigan State group's approach to model formulation, I am sure it must make a good econometrician like Professor Naylor shudder to read, "Modernization proceeds at a rate directly related to the level of profitability for the producer. This component also includes an innovation diffusion mechanism which allows for spontaneous (farmer to farmer) diffusion of modern techniques occurring over time, if necessary inputs, information requirements, etc. are available". Imagine trying to verify that relation and estimate its parameters! But the defense of such *a priori* formulation is hard to overcome. If experienced observers believe that is the way things really work, that is the way they should be in the model, even if the parameters cannot be measured.

Experimental design is discussed by the Michigan State team only in terms of sensitivity tests and analysis. The system is treated as a non-stochastic or fully deterministic one for each run, with repetitions of runs made to investigate different *assigned* values of coefficients. These variations represent explorations of the effects of possible errors in estimating coefficients and explorations of the effects of changing policy elements. Presumably the results are analyzed by comparing the endogenous variables from pairs or very small groups of runs.

Naylor talks of experimental design in terms of multiple runs for each specification of inputs (policy etc.), as befits a stochastic model. Presumably, for any given policy combination one gets a probability distribution of results. How this would work in practice for a complex model with a large number of factors subject to randomization is hard to see. If the purpose of the experiments is to design policies or make plans by cut-and-try methods, and if random variations of some variable are not part of the essence of the problem, then it would seem just as valid and a lot less awkward to use a deterministic model with suitable sensitivity testing of selected policy comparisons. However, if random variations in a parameter or variable are likely to affect the choice of policies — e.g., if one plan of agricultural development is more sensitive than another to vagaries of the weather — it would seem necessary to include stochastic disturbances of that element and to make the large number of runs that are thereby required. Messrs. Halter, Hayenga, and Manetsch might well consider that possibility for future experiments.

I have discussed some differences between the viewpoints that are evident in the two papers. Now it may be a good thing to note their agreement on one very basic point — the value of simulation in the relation between analyst and policy maker. Both point out the advantage, inherent in simulation, of showing the policy maker the comparative results of alternative policies in terms of an array of familiar variables on which he can base a choice. The problem of communication between analysts and policy makers is one of great importance, and any one who thinks it is possible to formulate a policy maker's preference function or to establish a set of targets that will not be changed after the analysis has been made is out of touch with human psychology. The presentation of multi-variable outcomes of alternative policies and the question "what would happen if we changed such-and-such policy element?", followed by further tests, are by far the best forms thus far devised for these important communications.

Another topic on which the two papers seem to agree — up to a point — is the validation of models. Both speak of matching historical data and of verifying forecasts, judging the validity of the model by the fidelity with which it matches observed data. But this sort of validation is not sufficient; it misses a crucial point. The most important requirement of a simulation that is to be used for policy experiments is that it should respond correctly to changes in the policies at issue. For this purpose it is important that the mechanisms involved in the response should be right qualitatively as well as sufficiently accurate numerically. If similar policy changes have not occurred in the past, then matching past data is no indication that the response to policy change will be properly simulated. Recognizing the need for something more, Halter et al. write of "validation by deduction", but that is really no validation. That simply represents faith in the validity of the formulation. Naylor, in his list of unresolved problems, calls for a new criterion of goodness-of-fit: "How well does the model simulate?" rather than "How well does the static model fit historical data...?" But how can that be judged?

If we are optimistic we may hope that the systems analysts will learn to be more concerned about the problems of statistical estimation and validation and about the methodology of using their models, once they have been created. Some hope is already evoked for a possible synthesis by Professor Naylor's remarks about the need for combining the approaches of the econometrician and the systems analyst. But I believe that several of us economists in this session today are entitled to feel somewhat slighted by his statement that economists have given little or no attention to alternative model structures such as those used by systems analysts. I grant that we have not got far in developing new estimation methods, but we have been formulating the models. Of course there is room for still more economists giving attention to this subject, and we will welcome their help. There are plenty of problems. There is also a need for better communication about what we have been doing. Professor Naylor's final sentence suggests that just possibly we might have to consider using coefficients that vary with time. Well, some of us have been using them for a number of years.

COMMENTS ON THE TWO ABOVE PAPERS,
BY GLENN L. JOHNSON
Michigan State University

We have had two good, useful papers: Naylor's did a very nice job of comparing the Theil, Tinbergen and simulation approaches. In his written paper he calls for more attention "to the types of logical models which have been developed by systems analysts". Halter, Hayenga and Manetsch, provided us with an application of the system science approach, Manetsch being a member of the Department of Electrical Engineering and Systems Science in the College of Engineering.

Both papers contain much with which we can agree and which, if considered seriously, would improve the work of those using math. theory from various disciplines, and statistics in aiding decision makers such as farmers, business men, secretaries and ministries of various governmental units, Ministers of Economic Planning (abroad), and the Director of the Bureau of the Budget here at home.

In the Naylor paper, I was pleased with his clear comparison of the Theil, Tinbergen and "policy" simulation approaches. It was also good to read "economists would do well to spend less time trying to specify the social welfare functions of policy makers and spend more time seeking solutions to some of the problems of policy makers". I can only applaud Naylor's critical comments on the lack of attention to arbitrary sample sizes and lengths of simulation runs. He noted the importance of Howrey's and Kelejian's questions about the value of simulation experiments with econometric models in establishing the validity of econometric models. Also, I could only mutter a grateful Amen when I read in his discussion of systems analysis, "it may be necessary to draw heavily on other disciplines including sociology, psychology and political science". However, I would have been still happier if he had dropped the "may be", replaced the phrase with "is", and included the physical sciences.

Candidly, I am required to be careful and reserved in commenting favorably on the Halter et al. paper. It was written as part of a project which I direct and has already suffered from my criticisms and suggestions. Thus, there may be some sentences in it with which I agree more fully than the authors do. However, with this by way of warning, I will proceed with a few favorable comments. The first is that they have illustrated the substantial difference between the "systems" building-block approach and the simultaneous equations approach Naylor discussed. They have also stressed the importance for such work of the broad range of Nigerian experience available to them from the Nigerian Consortium. I would like to add that this experience also came from the MSU/U of Nigeria project and that it covers a wide range of disciplines including the crucial technical disciplines of animal husbandry, crop science and soil science. In his presentation, Hayenga skipped some of the details about the construction of the model and sensitivity tests. These are interesting, instructive and worth looking up in the longer paper. The stress on the iterative nature of the process of building a "systems" model was good — I might have given it even greater emphasis.

Despite the above favorable comments about the two papers, I must discuss some uneasy rumblings I have about computer simulations. Basically, these uneasy feelings involve simple ideas. We should not let simple ideas "turn us off", however, as so many of our useful techniques and theories are based on simple ideas. The "reduced form" idea, e.g., is a very simple one. So is the idea of errors of the first and second kinds which were recognized in Christian liturgies for centuries before incorporation into statistical theory, a theory which, to my knowledge, has not yet dealt with the somewhat more complex but still simple idea of six kinds of errors in choosing among three alternatives. In a broad sense, the basic idea in simulation is simple and has been employed for centuries. The idea is to determine the performance or characteristics of some system through a sequence of operations. Simulation was used to develop the wind tunnel, hydrological testing tanks, Boeing 747 pilot training simulator, a set of paper and pencil projections made for the Secretary of Agriculture to determine how changes in acreage allotments affect agriculture, a simultaneous equation system of the U.S. economy, and our system of equations for the Nigerian agricultural economy.

Like all of you I have been using various, more or less formal, and more or less computerized simulations for a long time. Some of these have assisted me in my own decisions, others have been done as teaching aids for my classroom, others have been parts of research projects designed to have general usefulness, while still others have been done to help specific decision makers handle specific problems. I believe we have much to learn from our successes and failures in carrying out such simulation and that much of what we learn will be simple, but have profound impacts on our quantitative, technical, methodological and philosophical approaches to problem-solving simulations.

Back in high school, my vocational agriculture teacher taught me how to budget farm businesses through time in order to study income flows, net worth accumulations, etc. I used what he taught me, and my paper and pencil computations indicated that I should leave the farm, a decision I have never regretted. When I think back I note five interesting things about the computations: (1) the information was interdisciplinary and technical as well as social, (2) they involved both simultaneous and non-simultaneous systems of relationships, (3) they utilized normative as well as non-normative concepts which were consistent with each other and with experience, clear and workable, (4) they were very creative, inventive and original in envisioning how the relevant physical, institutional and social worlds could be reorganized and controlled, and (5) important use was made of lagged endogenous variables.

We have had similiar experiences with architects in drawing house plans based on their inventories of our resources, income flows, needs, tastes and preferences. As an architect submits plans and then helps a family simulate living in the house, the family learns much, both normatively and non-normatively, technically and non-technically and certainly interdisciplinarily. One can appreciate the inventiveness, creativity and originality involved. The systems of simultaneous equations involve heat, air, electrical, economic and psychological phenomenon. But non-simultaneous equations and lagged endogenous variables are also applicable to the family living cycle.

If time permitted I could cite simulation experiences involving (1) paper, pencil and desk calculator projections in the U.S. Department of Agriculture for Congressional committees and the Secretary's office, (2) Navy supply corps instruction with simulated naval operations at the Harvard School of

Business Administration, (3) my own use of paper and pencil budget simulations in training farm managers, (4) simulations from systems of simultaneous equations of different parts of the U.S. agricultural economy, (5) the use of paper, pencil and desk calculator projections by the Nigerian Consortium and (6) our present computerized "systems science" simulation of the Nigerian agricultural economy. If I did go through all six of these in detail, I would encounter, each time, the same considerations I listed in budgeting my own decision to farm or not to farm as well as in the family house building determinations.

To reiterate, those five considerations were (1) interdisciplinary information, technical as well as non-technical, (2) non-simultaneous as well as simultaneous relationships, (3) the need to develop normative as well as non-normative concepts, (4) a major role for creativity, inventiveness, and originality, and (5) lagged endogenous variables. At more macro-levels I should also add that serious questions arise about decision-making rules — majority vote, maximization of the present values of expected future returns, minimaxing, etc.

Our two papers today have jointly, if not always singularly, handled the use of interdisciplinary and technical as well as social and economic (non-technical) information. Between them, they have handled non-simultaneous as well as simultaneous relationships. Both papers have recognized the need to exploit lagged endogenous variables.

My hesitations about the two papers involve normative information, creativity, and decision-making rules (as a special aspect of each of these).

In my opinion, Naylor has correctly rejected Theil's social welfare function approach as unrealistic and oversimplified. He has also rejected the Tinbergen approach of prior targets as failing to recognize that target selection is one of the tasks for which simulation is useful. The Halter et al. paper presents a rather complete diagram of the process, but does not explicitly discuss dealing with the normative in helping a decision-or policy-maker select targets, goals or objectives. When I am both simulator and decision-maker, the interaction between simulator and decision-maker is good. When I am simulator helping a decision-maker, the interaction is poorer and the iterations and interactions are harder to make. It is harder to picture the long-range "pros" and "cons" of the consequences of alternative decisions and policies, yet even more crucial that objective concepts be acquired of the "pros" and "cons".

The capacity of researchers to investigate the normative is often, in my opinion, restricted by the "thoughts of defunct" philosophers. One of the most restrictive philosophies is positivism, which seems to have peaked in agricultural economics and econometrics about 20-25 years after its decline in philosophic circles. As Naylor points out, Tinbergen's conditional normativism is also restrictive. In effect, both approaches put normative concepts beyond logical discussion and appeals to experience.

I wish one or both papers had investigated the role of interactions between simulators and decision-makers as an objective means of answering normative questions. Such a discussion would go deep into philosophy and is beyond the scope of a discussant's comments. However, it is needed badly by simulators under the influence of the lagged positivism so common among quantitative economists and econometricians.

I would like to comment briefly on creativity and originality. In solving problems, previously unconceived technological, institutional and behaviorial arrangements and patterns are often crucial. Free, uninhibited interaction between simulators and decision-makers is important for creativity. The interaction must also be on normative as well as non-normative questions if the originality is to be creative, not merely novel or possibly destructively novel as were some of Hitler's original ideas. In a sense, positivism is a deterrent to creativity. It precludes the possibility of objective normative knowledge. So is Tinbergen's conditional normativism.

Another constraint on creativity is disciplinary egocentrism. Simulators and decision-makers cannot be technologically creative while playing the sole role of economists. Nor can sociologically oriented, communication specialists be creative with respect to price control institutions while concentrating on sociology regardless of how much information is communicated by the price system.

I would fault Naylor's paper slightly because of his stress on experimental design. This can become a sort of disciplinary "hang up" for economists and statisticians. If this interest diverts attention away from creative interaction with decision- and policy-makers in conceiving new alternatives possible solutions to a problem, I am afraid opportunity costs could easily exceed returns to the experiment. The decision-maker needs to be part of the experimental design.

Part 3

QUANTITATIVE APPROACHES TO TRADITIONAL
TOPICS IN ECONOMICS

Frontiers of Quantitative Economics, ed. M.D. Intriligator. © *North-Holland Publishing Company*

CHAPTER 7

IS THERE AN OPTIMAL MONEY SUPPLY? — I

HARRY G. JOHNSON

London School of Economics and Political Science and University of Chicago

The title question of the papers in this section is provocative and interesting, inasmuch as it encapsulates a whole area of rapid recent development in monetary theory in an apparently simple question. Yet it is really a trick question, the answer to which must be yes if the terms are properly defined, and the difficulty of which inheres in such proper definition of the terms. Since the question has confused some theorists, I make no apology for spending much of this paper on clarification of the issues, even though this requires restatement of some elementary theoretical points.

To begin with — in case anyone is under any illusions on this point — the question has nothing to do with the optimal conduct of short-run stabilization policy. Instead it belongs to the pure theorists' world of continuous full employment of resources; as such, its policy relevance is to the framework of monetary organization and the long-run environmental objectives of monetary policy.

Within this frame of reference, the first point to be noticed is the elementary one that while the monetary authority fixes the nominal quantity of money, the public determines the quantity of real balances by driving the price level up or down until the real value of the given nominal money stock is what the public is content to hold. Since any nominal stock can provide any desired real stock through appropriate price level adjustment, it obviously makes no sense to ask whether there is an optimal money supply, if "money supply" is interpreted as it should be in terms of the nominal money supply that the authorities in fact control. The question has to be posed in terms of the real money supply. In fact there are two questions. First, is there an optimal real quantity of money generally different from what will be established by the actions of the public? Second, given that the monetary authorities cannot alter the real quantity of money directly by altering the nominal quantity of it, how can they alter it indirectly and what policy should they follow to establish the optimum quantity of real balances? To comprehend these two issues, the title question would better have been phrased "Is there an optimal money supply *policy?*"

This compound question can be approached from two different angles: by the construction and exploration of a model of a monetary economy, and by a welfare analysis of the existing monetary arrangements of actual economies. I begin with the former.

The simplest type of monetary model to construct is one that employs a non-interest-bearing fiat money — assumed costless to create — as a medium of exchange and store of value. The use of money, as contrasted with barter, must be motivated somehow — a point on which Tobin's important writings in this area can be faulted. Writers in the Chicago tradition of monetary theory — Friedman, Levhari-Patinkin and myself, among others — have recognized but by-passed this issue (the transition from a barter to a monetary economy) by treating money as both a consumers' good yielding a flow of services contributing to utility and a producers' good (an inventory) contributing to output.

Any problem of sub-optimality in the working of a competitive system can be put in terms of a divergence of private from social cost, or of the presence of externalities. In the fiat money model, sub-optimality of the stock of real balances arises from the fact that while by assumption money can be created at zero social cost, to the holder of it it has an alternative opportunity cost given by the yield on capital; hence less of it will be held than the socially optimal quantity, which would equate the marginal utility yield of money to consumers and the marginal productivity yield to producers to zero. Friedman has recently produced a suggestive supplementary explanation in terms of externalities: in order to accumulate extra cash balances the individual must forego real resources; but these resources accrue to his fellow-citizens through a (negligible) temporary fall in the price level, and do not constitute a social cost.

To attain optimality, it is necessary to provide a yield on real balances equal to the yield on real capital, in order to equate the marginal utility and productivity yields of money to zero and thus "satiate the demand for real balances". One way of doing this would be to pay interest on money equal to the real rate of return on real capital, financed by the usual hypothetical non-distorting lump-sum taxes. (As will be apparent immediately, this policy would have to be accompanied by a policy of monetary growth ensuring stability of prices over time.) An alternative possibility arises from the fact that, apart from their explicit zero nominal yield, in an economy in which inflation or deflation is going on *and is fully anticipated,* holders of cash balances knowingly bear a cost or enjoy a return from holding them equal to the expected (and actual) rate of inflation or deflation respectively. Hence, by providing a rate of monetary growth (or contraction) that will produce a rate of price deflation equal to the rate of return on real assets, the monetary authority can achieve the optimum stock of real balances. An alternative way of putting this point, for an economy containing bonds bearing a monetary rate of interest, is that formulated by Friedman, that monetary policy should aim at making the monetary rate of interest zero. In a growth model in which government simultaneously establishes a savings ratio consistent with the golden rule, as Patinkin and Levhari have shown, the appropriate monetary policy simplifies to keeping the money supply constant (since the rate of interest is equal to the rate of growth of output in golden rule conditions).

Both the payment of explicit interest on money, and the control of the behaviour of the nominal money stock over time, can and should be regarded as monetary policies. Hence there are two alternative policies available for achieving the optimum stock of real balances at every point in time — and of course these can be mixed in any desired proportion. In fact they are the extremes of the menu of possible mixtures: no deflation and an explicit rate of interest on money equal to the return on real capital, and no interest on money and deflation at a rate equal to the return on real capital. The possibility of achieving optimality of the money stock through interest payments as well as through deflation has generally been recognized as an afterthought in the literature, but put in the context of the difference between a competitive inside money system and an outside money system. As Pesek and Saving and I have shown, however, the difference essential for monetary theory is not between inside and outside money, but between non-interest-bearing and competitive interest-bearing money. There is, though, a serious practical problem about how to arrange interest payments on currency, a problem to which I shall return.

The alternative approach to the question of optimal money supply is through the welfare analysis of existing national monetary arrangements. These can be thought of, if we set aside the conventional conception of the government as something apart from its electorate that has been developed to justify the treatment of government liabilities to the public as "outside money" and hence to give empirical relevance to the Pigou effect, as an inside money system with certain distortions from the conditions of competitive optimality. Specifically, through its monopoly of legal tender, the government is able to force holders of currency to make it interest-free loans; similarly, through its monopoly of central banking, the government is able to force commercial bank holders of central bank deposits to make an interest-free loan directly to the central bank and indirectly to itself. Alternatively, the government is able through monopoly to impose a tax on the holding of these assets. To the extent that the prohibition of explicit interest on demand deposits is effective (which is doubtful), the government also levies a tax on deposit-holders for the benefit of the banks. It also taxes deposit-holders indirectly through other regulations and restrictions falling on banks and on bank entry. All these taxes imply sub-optimization of the stock of real balances held, by comparison with a situation in which commercial banks were free to compete for deposits (and obliged to do so by freedom of entry) and in which government paid commercial rates of interest on currency and on commercial bank deposits at the Federal Reserve. (The Federal Reserve could still control the nominal money supply in these circumstances.)

Elimination of restrictions and regulations and the payment of competitive interest rates on government and central bank obligations would achieve optimality of the real money stock, as in the fiat money model. The practical difficulty, which in this context is obviously practical and not introduced by extraneous assumption, is how to arrange payment of interest on government-issued currency. Presumably interest could be paid on the banks' vault cash, on the basis of average or daily figures; the problem is to devise a method of paying interest on the public's holdings of currency. Friedman has suggested giving banks permission to compete in the issuance of notes — as they used to do before the Bank Charter Act of 1844 in the United Kingdom and the National Banking Act of 1863 in the U.S.A. — and leaving them to figure out the technicalities of how to pay interest on such notes.

The alternative, as in the theoretical model, would be to manage the money supply so as to deflate prices at the rate required to make the money rate of interest zero, thus eliminating the monopoly profits now accruing to government, the central bank, and (possibly) the commercial banks. This is the policy recently recommended by Friedman, even though he has both to recognize the political and economic difficulties entailed in such a potentially major change from the present situation of price inflation ("potentially major" because he presents alternative calculations involving quite different rates of price deflation) and to admit to some embarrassment in reconciling this recommendation with his long-standing record of recommending pursuit of a monetary policy (adoption of a monetary rule) that would guarantee price stability. I would agree with Friedman that the step from monetary policy as presently conducted to a policy ensuring price stability is more potentially beneficial than the further step to a policy of price deflation at the appropriate rate; but I would argue further, against his general thesis, that if the steps that could feasibly be taken towards the establishment of competitive interest payments on money were in fact taken, there would probably be little further gain to be had from instituting the appropriate rate of price deflation.

It seems to me irrational to accept institutional arrangements that lead to economic inefficiency on the one hand, and on the other hand to try to persuade government to manipulate the growth of the money supply so as to offset the inefficiencies that result. Either government is unaware of the inefficiencies its practices cause, in which case it should be possible to persuade it to change those practices, specifically to terminate the prohibition of interest payments on demand deposits, to pay interest on reserve deposits of commercial banks at the Federal Reserve and on vault cash, and possibly to seek means of paying interest on the public's currency holdings. Or government is quite aware that it makes a profit out of these practices, and is determined to hold onto it, in which case, as controller of the behaviour of the money supply, it will certainly not act so as to deprive itself of those profits.

Assuming that government could be persuaded to eliminate the obviously and easily remediable institutional sources of inefficiency in the money supply — prohibition of interest on commercial bank demand deposits, non-payment of interest on commercial bank deposits at the Federal Reserve and on commercial bank cash — the remaining source of inefficiency in the provision of money (assuming for the moment the maintenance of price stability) would be the non-payment of interest on currency. Here there would be a double source of inefficiency: under present arrangements the holder of currency receives no interest but bears none of the costs of printing and minting required to create and to maintain the currency stock, whereas under efficient arrangements he would receive competitive interest on his bank deposit but pay charges for using bank money for payments. There would thus be incentives to economize on currency holding but to use currency rather than cheques for making payments.

Would the resulting welfare losses be sufficient to justify the adoption of a policy of deflating prices at the current rate of return on capital in order to avoid them? It seems very doubtful, though it may be worth someone's while to quantify. (With currency in circulation among the public running at about five per cent of G.N.P., and the elasticity of substitution between currency and interest-bearing bank deposits probably rather low, the welfare loss calculated on Friedman's lines would probably be a negligible fraction of national income.) The answer would be even more doubtful if, following Friedman's suggestion, commercial banks were allowed to experiment with the issue of interest-bearing notes.

As a digression on the question of interest-bearing currency, it should not be too difficult to devise it — any more than it has been difficult for the banks to develop new instruments such as certificates of deposit permitting them to pay higher interest on large savings deposits than on the ordinary savings deposits. In the early nineteenth century, after all, bills of exchange used to circulate in the North of England in place of money. Presumably banks would offer interest only on the higher denominations of notes, choose face values so that interest could be expressed as a gain in value of so many cents per week, and affix a maturity date so that if they overestimated the interest rate they could pay the holder could not extract indefinite ransom. (Actually, a return of so many cents per week would be a declining rate of weekly interest, so that this problem would take care of itself if the cents offered per week were constant.)

The payment of competitive interest on money, then, is one way of achieving the optimal money supply. Yet this proposition has recently encountered considerable opposition from monetary theorists. This opposition I believe to be mistaken.

One source of criticism is to be found in Pesek and Saving's book on *Money, wealth, and economic theory*, wherein it is argued that the essential characteristic of money is its non-interest-bearingness, and that if money were to bear interest it would cease to be used as money. One basis of this argument is a confusion between the two notions (1) that if banks were permitted to compete with each other in supplying socially costless money, they would expand the nominal money supply until its purchasing power fell to zero, and (2) that if they were allowed to compete with each other in supplying money within some overall constraint on the total quantity supplied, they would drive the rate of interest paid on deposits up to a level competitive with other yields, thereby reducing the value of the marginal liquidity services of money to zero. Another is the idea that if money had a yield people would not forego that yield for the sake of purchasing goods and services — an obvious fallacy since the function of all asset-holding is to carry purchasing power forward through time, and this implies no desire to hold forever an asset once acquired.

Another line of criticism focusses on the vagueness of the explanation of the function of money in a monetary economy, already mentioned in connection with writers in the Chicago tradition and perhaps even more characteristic of writers in the Keynesian tradition, and specifically on the possibility that the holding of a larger (optimum) quantity of real balances induced by the payment of interest on money may introduce an offsetting waste of resources through efforts to economize on the use of money in effecting transactions. This criticism was raised vehemently by Robert Clower, in connection with an effort by Paul Samuelson to state "What Classical and Neoclassical Monetary Theory Really Was". Samuelson's re-statement was admittedly faulty; but Clower has apparently recanted on his belief that there is something seriously wrong with the argument outlined above.

The issue can be put most clearly in terms of the Baumol-Tobin model of transactions demand for cash. That model assumes that transactions from money into goods occur in an even flow over time, and are costless. Holding all one's income in the form of money for the purposes of effecting this flow of transactions, however, means losing interest; money can be converted into interest-bearing assets and back again, but there is both a fixed and a proportional cost per such transaction; because of the fixed cost, there will be an optimum frequency of conversions of assets into cash and an optimum proportional cash balance holding varying inversely with income and the rate of interest on earning assets. Optimality would be achieved by paying interest on cash balances and so eliminating the real costs of conversions between cash and securities.

Now assume instead that there is no interest on cash, and that conversion of money into goods has both a fixed and a proportional cost. That is, there is an overhead time and real resource cost of going to the supermarket, and a time cost per item of shopping. These would indicate one trip per pay period; but there is also a storage cost proportional to their value on the holding of stocks of goods, which can be reduced by making more trips to market and holding a lower average stock of goods. Hence there is a total-cost-minimizing stock of goods in storage and of cash in hand.

It would appear that the payment of interest on money, by raising the alternative opportunity cost of holding stocks of goods, would reduce average stocks and so increase the real resources used in making trips to the supermarket, thereby wasting resources by comparison with the zero-interest-money situation. Hence the "optimum quantity of money" achieved by paying interest on money would appear to be socially suboptimal when the transactions costs of extra marketing induced by the payment of interest on money are taken into account.

But this conclusion would be correct only if the true social and private alternative opportunity cost of storing goods included only the real resources employed in storage, and not the interest on the resources invested in the stock itself. This is clearly not the case. Both society and the stockholding individual could convert the stocks into explicitly productive capital goods. Hence the storage cost of consumers' inventories already includes the interest rate, and is not increased by the payment of interest on money; and the payment of interest on money serves as before to eliminate the costs of converting cash into carning assets and vice versa (these costs may be thought of, following Samuelson, as the cost of shoe leather wasted on trips to the bank).

This point is illustrated by fig. 1, based on the Baumol-Tobin analysis of transactions demand for money. For the purposes of the diagram it is assumed that the individual receives an income per period of $2t$, which he receives either in interest-bearing assets or in money; that if he receives assets he earns an interest rate i per period on his average asset holding but he has an overhead charge per withdrawal of B and a proportional charge of $\frac{1}{2}K$ per unit of money withdrawn; that shopping involves an overhead cost b per shopping trip and a proportional cost of $\frac{1}{2}k$ per unit monetary value purchased; and that storage of goods (in amount g on the average) involves a proportional real cost of s per period and the interest charge i. If he receives no interest on money, it is assumed that he will choose to be paid in assets; it is also assumed for simplicity, at the cost of full generality, that he will combine trips to convert assets into money with trips to the

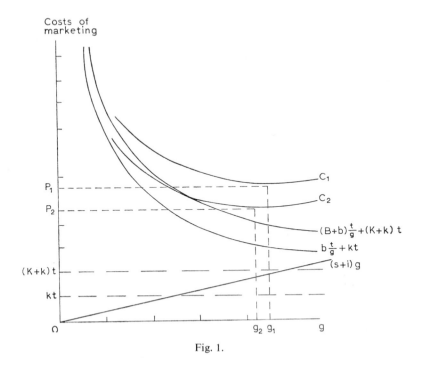

Fig. 1.

market to convert money into goods, to avoid interest loss on idle money. His cost curve as a function of his average stock of goods will be C_1, and his cost-minimizing average goods stock g_1. If, on the other hand, he received interest on money at the same rate as on earning assets, so that the could avoid conversions, his cost-minimizing stock of goods would be g_2, smaller than g_1. If, incorrectly, the rate of interest were not regarded as a proper social cost of stock-holding, and comparison were made between interest-paying and non-interest-paying money, there would be a third curve C_3 representing costs of holding stocks of goods excluding any interest rate cost of stock-holding, with a minimum point below and to the right of C_2, incorrectly suggesting a social waste from the payment of interest on money.

A final line of criticism contends that payment of competitive interest on money would lead to money replacing all other financial assets, and banks replacing all other financial intermediaries. This criticism seems to me quite unconvincing, unless the proposal is misinterpreted to mean that not only is interest to be paid on money, but that the rate is to be un-competitively high and that no charges are to be made for the use of money in making payments. The recommendation to pay interest on money equal to the rate of return on real capital is to be understood as a short-hand phrase that abstracts from various kinds of transactions and intermediation costs that would be taken account of in a fully competitive banking system.

References

Clower, R.W., 1969a, What traditional monetary theory really wasn't. *The Canadian Journal of Economics*, Vol. 2, no. 2, May, 299-302.

Clower, R.W., 1969b, On the technology of monetary exchange. (Mimeograph for the Southern Economic Association.)

Friedman, M., 1969, The optimum quantity of money. In: *The Optimum Quantity of Money and Other Essays*. Chicago, Aldine Publishing Co., Chapter 1, 1-50.

Johnson, H.G., 1967, Money in a neo-classical one-sector growth model. In: *Essays in Monetary Economics*. London, Allen & Unwin, 1967). Chapter IV, 143-178.

Johnson, H.G., 1968, Problems of efficiency in monetary management. *The Journal of Political Economy* 76, no. 5, September/October, 971-90.

Johnson, H.G., 1969a, Inside Money, Outside money, income, wealth and welfare in contemporary monetary theory. *Journal of Money, Credit, and Banking* 1, no. 1, February, 30-45.

Johnson, H.G., 1969b, Pesek and Saving's theory of money and wealth: a comment. *Journal of Money, Credit, and Banking* 1, no. 3, August, 535-7.

Levhari, D. and D. Patinkin, 1968, The role of money in a simple growth model. *The American Economic Review* 58, no. 4, September, 713-53.

Perlman, M., 1969, The roles of money in an economy and the optimum quantity of money. (Mimeograph.)

Pesek, B.P. and T.R. Saving, 1967, *Money, Wealth, and economic theory*. New York: Macmillan.

Samuelson, P.A., 1968, What classical and neoclassical monetary theory really was. *The Canadian Journal of Economics* Vol. 1, no. 1, February, 1-15.

Samuelson, P.A., 1969, Nonoptimality of money holdings under *Laissez faire. The Canadian Journal of Economics* Vol. 2, no. 2, May, 303-8.

Tobin, J., 1965, Money and economic growth. *Econometrica* 33, no. 4, October, 671-84.

Tobin, J., 1968, Notes on optimal monetary growth. *The Journal of Political Economy* 76, no. 4, Part III, July/August, 833-59.

*Frontiers of Quantitative Economics, ed. **M.D. Intriligator**. © North-Holland Publishing Company.*

IS THERE AN OPTIMAL MONEY SUPPLY? — II

ROBERT W. CLOWER

Northwestern University

The Pareto optimality of competitive equilibrium in a money economy is an interesting question not so much for its own sake as for the light that attempts to answer it have shed upon weaknesses in the foundations of contemporary monetary theory. More specifically, it seems to me that modern discussions of monetary optimality have so far yielded little more than a restatement of standard conclusions of welfare economics; for the conception of money implicit in most of these discussions does not permit us to distinguish analytically between "money" and any other commodity the demand for which depends partly on its usefulness as a store of value. Thus the question of an optimal supply of real money balances effectively has been disposed of as if it were equivalent to the question of an optimal supply of pearls or Old Masters.[1]

I am not suggesting that this procedure has generated false conclusions; on the contrary, my argument is simply that the premises explicitly adduced by previous writers are insufficient to support any definite conclusions about monetary optimality in a world where money commodities play a significant role as exchange intermediaries. In this paper, therefore, I propose to

---

[1] The literature on the subject is too extensive to be cited in detail here, but its essential flavor may be gleaned from the following sample: G.S. Tolley, Providing for growth of the money supply. *Journal of Political Economy* 65 (Dec. 1957), 477-84. — James Tobin, Notes on optimal monetary growth. *Journal of Political Economy* 76 (July/August 1968), 843-6. — A.L. Marty, The optimal rate of growth of money. *Journal of Political Economy* 76 (July/August 1968), 860-873. — P.A. Samuelson, What classical and neoclassical monetary theory really was. *Canadian Journal of Economics* 1 (Feb. 1968), 7-10. — Milton Friedman, The optimum quantity of money. In: *The optimum quantity of money and other essays*. Chicago, Aldine, 1969, pp. 14-21.

reconsider the entire question of an optimal supply of money, starting with what might be regarded as contemporary wisdom and ending with what I hope may be regarded as wisdom of a slightly higher order.

0. Monetary optimality: the contemporary paradigm

Perhaps the clearest statement of prevailing doctrine is provided by Samuelson's incidental remarks on the subject of monetary optimality in a recent paper on classical and neoclassical monetary theory.[2] Samuelson's discussion deals with an economy in which the representative transactor chooses optimal stationary values of consumption and money balances subject to a long-run budget equation in which the cost of holding money balances consists of virtual interest income foregone on alternative earning assets. In this model, equilibrium requires that the marginal utility of money be positive and proportional to the rate of interest. Having set out this result, Samuelson goes on to argue:

> Each man thinks of his cash balance as costing him foregone interest and as buying himself convenience. But for the community as a whole, the total (stock of money) is there and is quite costless to use. Forgetting gold mining and the historical expenditure of resources for the creating of (the money stock), the existing (stock) is, so to speak, a free good from society's viewpoint. Moreover, its *effective* amount can, from the community's viewpoint, be indefinitely augmented by the simple device of having a lower absolute level or *all* money prices.
>
> Evidently we have here an instance of a lack of optimality of *laissez-faire*: there is a kind of fictitious internal diseconomy from holding more cash balances, as things look to the individual. Yet if all were made to hold larger cash balances, which they turned over more slowly, the resulting lowering of absolute prices would end up making everybody better off. Better off in what sense? In the sense of having a higher (utility), which comes from having to make fewer trips to the bank, fewer trips to the brokers, smaller printing and other costs of transactions whose only purpose is to provide cash when you have been holding too little cash.
>
> From society's viewpoint, the optimum occurs when people are satiated with cash (so that the marginal utility of cash is zero). ... But this will not come about under *laissez-faire*, with stable prices.[3]

Samuelson's intuitive conception of a monetary economy presupposes that the main function of money is to serve as a medium of exchange; hence, his suggestion that larger holdings of cash balances will be associated with fewer trips to banks and brokers and so with smaller transaction costs per

---

[2] Cited in footnote 1, above.
[3] *Ibid.*, 9-10.

unit of time. But this presupposition is not embedded in Samuelson's formal model; strictly speaking, Samuelson's analysis does not permit us to assert even that money is used in exchange transactions, much less to say that the turnover rate of money will decrease if the effective quantity of money is increased. And if money is not used for transaction purposes, but is held simply as a store of value — the only possibility that is directly suggested by Samuelson's formal model — then any gain accruing to individuals through a rise in real money balances is just as much a social illusion as is the apparent cost to individuals of holding money balances.[4] Society cannot be shown to be "better off" in terms of any of the factors mentioned by Samuelson for the simple reason that these and other possible sources of real transaction costs nowhere enter his formal model.

I have singled out Samuelson's argument not because it is more open to objection than similar arguments advanced by other writers, but rather because no other writer has so carefully set out a formal model before proceeding to discuss the question of monetary optimality. Friedman's recent essay on "The Optimum Quantity of Money"[5], might have been chosen on similar grounds; but this would not have affected the outcome of our discussion in any significant respect, for Friedman's analysis, like Samuelson's, is vitiated by the absence of any explicit account of the relation between real money balances and real transaction costs.[6]

The same objection applies to all discussions of monetary optimality whose theoretical roots lie in the soil of conventional value theory; for conventional value theory is essentially a device for logical analysis of *virtual trades* in a world where individual economic activities are costlessly coordinated by a central market authority. It has nothing whatever to say about delivery and payment arrangements, about the timing or frequency of market transactions, about search, bargaining, information and other trading costs, or about countless other commonplace features of real-world trading processes.[7] In this respect, value theory is analogous to Newton's theory

---

[4] Compare K. Wicksell, *Lectures on political economy*. London, George Routledge and Sons, 1935, Vol. II, pp. 8-9.

[5] Cited in footnote 1, above.

[6] *Ibid.*, pp. 2-3. Like most other writers, Friedman refers verbally to transaction costs of various kinds (e. g., at p. 14 and at pp. 17-18); but his formal model is entirely innocent of such complications.

[7] This point has been made by many writers, but most especially by Sir John Hicks in his *Critical essays in monetary theory*. Oxford, The Clarendon Press, 1967, pp. 6-7. Interesting attempts to fill this gap in conventional theory have recently been made by

of a frictionless "ideal fluid" — an intellectually stimulating and conceptually fruitful model the implications of which are seriously at variance with the most elementary facts of experience. Hydrodynamic theory began to bear significant practical fruit only after Newton's model was generalized around the turn of this century to deal explicitly with non-ideal, viscous fluids — such fluids being the only kind that exist in actual fact.[8] A similar generalization of value theory is evidently required if we are ever to establish an acceptable theoretical foundation for explicit analysis of monetary exchange processes. The problem of monetary optimality is just one of many issues the solution to which must remain in doubt in the meantime.

1. The technology of monetary exchange

It is one thing to recognize a problem, another to solve it. Ideally, transaction and other costs of market exchange should be introduced into microeconomic analysis via the formulation of an explicit dynamic model in which holdings of commodity and money inventories at any given point in time are a function of planned intertemporal patterns or market purchases and sales. The conceptual and mathematical difficulties of this procedure are too great, however, for it to be regarded as a practical possibility at this time. A far from ideal, but currently feasible alternative, is to introduce trading costs into statical representations of stationary solutions to implicit dynamical models. The objection to this approach is that it takes for granted that which cannot be proved, namely, the existence and qualitative characteristics of stationary solutions to dynamical models the precise characteristics of which are never specified. Since the practical force of this objection can be gauged only in the light of experience, however, we need not regard it as fatal.

Proceeding as suggested, let me begin by considering the qualitative properties of the stationary solution to a dynamical problem the details of which are reasonably clear, at least to me: namely, the problem of managing

---

Armen Alchian, T.R. Saving, Karl Brunner and Allan Meltzer, Joseph Ostroy, Jack Hirshleifer, Jurg Niehans, Preston Miller, E. Feige, and M. Parkin, to mention just those authors whose work I have been privileged to see. As of this time, however, no writer has provided an entirely satisfactory conceptual framework for analyzing the phenomena in question.

[8] Cf. G. Birkhoff, *Hydrodynamics*. Princeton, N.J., Princeton University Press, 1960, pp. 3-5; L. Prandtl and O.G. Tietjens, *Hydro- and aeromechanics*. New York, McGraw-Hill, 1934, Vol. I.

my own finances. As most of my friends know, my expenditures tend always to exhaust my income, and my income, particularly in recent years, has been regrettably constant. So my holdings of assets — mostly negative — are, on average, constant over time although my holdings of money and consumer good inventories fluctuate considerably from day to day and week to week. All things considered, therefore, my "state" as an economic man is effectively stationary.

Now, the most notable fact about my asset position concerns my holdings not of currency, demand deposits, bonds or jewels, but rather my holdings of consumer good inventories. My average inventory of money is normally miniscule compared with the dollar value of my holdings of canned goods, milk, soap, cigarettes, bread, coffee, gasoline, shirts, typing paper, razor blades, etc. In holding physical commodity inventories, I obviously incur some storage and deterioration charges as well as costs in terms of foregone interest income. To justify what at first sight might be regarded as irrational behavior on my part, I have only to remark that *not* to hold sizeable inventories of most of the goods I regularly consume would cost me dearly in terms of time and effort spent in frequent trips to market. Rational behavior on my part requires that my average holdings of consumption good inventories be maintained at a level such that the value to me of their imputed marginal yield of leisure and energy is at least as great as the direct marginal cost of holding them.

Unfortunately, my recurrent shopping activities involve certain indirect as well as direct inventory costs; for in order to purchase goods regularly, I have to carry a certain inventory of cash as a passport for entry into this organized market provided by local markets. Since any money I have on hand adds something to the interest cost of my current overdraft, I attempt to keep my average holdings of cash as small as possible. But this does not mean that I shop and pay bills only on pay day — the one procedure that would effectively reduce my average cash balance to zero — for this would force me to carry huge inventories of consumer goods through most of the month, and the costs of doing this would outweigh any real or monetary savings associated with lower cash balances and less frequent trips to market. What I in fact do is to choose the frequency and timing of my shopping trips in the light both of direct costs of holding commodity inventories and related indirect costs of holding money balances.

This personalized description of the factors governing my choice of commodity and money inventories may be clarified by a diagram. Let the trading cost curve $T(q^0)$ in fig. 1 indicate the dollar cost per unit of time of leisure and energy devoted to trade, corresponding to alternative possible dollar values of average holdings of consumption good inventories, Q, and some given flow of consumption expenditure, q^0. The trading cost curve is drawn on the assumption that trading costs depend partly on the frequency of market purchases per unit trade period (for which the ratio q^0/Q is a convenient proxy), partly on the quantity of goods purchased per shopping trip (for which Q is a proxy). Up to a point, therefore, there are economies of scale in holdings of commodity inventories; but the trading cost curve ultimately reaches a minimum and thereafter rises without limit.

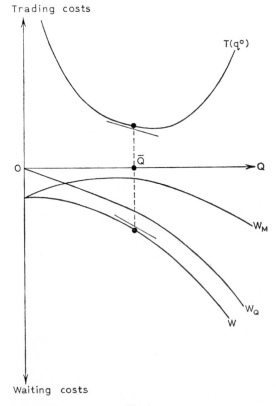

Fig. 1.

Direct waiting costs associated with alternative holdings of commodity inventories are shown in fig. 1 by the curve W_Q, indirect waiting costs by the curve W_M, and total waiting costs (the vertical sum of W_Q and W_M) by the curve W. The amount of indirect waiting costs (interest income foregone) corresponding to any given value of Q depends on the timing and frequency of purchases in relation to the timing and frequency of income receipts, and upon money prices. In general, these costs will decline, up to a point, as purchases and sales become more closely synchronized, but will thereafter rise indefinitely, as suggested by the form of the curve W_M. Direct waiting costs (interest income foregone, plus storage and other charges) are, of course, a strictly increasing function of the dollar value of average inventory holdings as indicated by the curve W_Q. Except in special cases, indirect waiting costs will be relatively small compared with direct waiting costs since money costs little or nothing to store whereas storage and other costs of holding commodity inventories may loom very large in relation to costs in terms of foregone interest income. In general, therefore, the curve W will differ only moderately from the curve W_Q.

The choice of an optimal average stock of commodity inventories (equivalently, the choice of an optimal average transaction period) requires that the individual minimize total marketing costs, $T + W_Q + W_M$. The solution to the problem is defined in the usual way by the condition that the marginal yield on average holdings of commodity inventories (represented by the absolute slope of the trading cost curve T) be equal to marginal direct waiting costs plus marginal indirect waiting costs (represented by the absolute slope of the waiting cost curve W). As the curves in fig. 1 are drawn, the optimal average inventory is $\bar{Q}$, and the corresponding optimal average transaction period is $2\,\bar{Q}/q^0$.[9]

The preceding diagram grossly oversimplifies even the statics of monetary exchange. What I have described as a single decision process involving aggregate values of inventory holdings would appear in a disaggregated model as a description of just one among many interrelated decision processes, one for each commodity purchased or sold. Trade being a two-way street, we could infer from a more general model alternative values of an

---

[9] The model outlined here bears an obvious resemblance to the classic inventory models of Baumol and Tobin. The essential difference lies in the addition to the present model of relevant indirect waiting costs — an item that is entirely overlooked in earlier discussions of the problem. The crucial point is simple that every exchange involves at least two commodities; hence, holdings of inventories of one exchangeable commodity (money or goods) entails holdings of inventories of at least one other commodity. On this, see R. W. Clower, *Readings in Monetary Theory*. London, Penguin Books, 1969, pp. 7-14.

individual's holdings of money balances from knowledge about the frequency and money value of his purchases and sales of commodities. Average holdings of cash as a "temporary abode of purchasing power"[10] would then be determined along with average holdings of commodity inventories by the requirement that cash holdings be minimal relative to any given set of values of production and consumption flows.

The elaboration of a full scale model along the lines suggested poses no problems of principle, but neither is it likely to yield any essentially new information. One can only go so far with statical techniques of analysis — especially when the dynamics remain shrouded in intuition. In any event, we have gone far enough to assert what is important for present purposes, namely, that equilibrium holdings of real money balances are inextricably linked with equilibrium holdings of commodity inventories, and *vice versa*. We may also assert that the link between real money balances and commodity inventories is much too complex to permit us to infer anything either about turnover rates of inventories from information about real cash balances, or about average holdings of real cash balances from information about commodity inventories. More pointedly, it is incorrect to suggest — as numerous writers have done — that real transactions balances can be produced at no cost to society; for, in general, every change in real balances will be associated with changes in socially costly holdings of commodities inventories. Moreover, it is incorrect to suggest that a change in interest rates that makes money balances less costly for individuals to hold will tend to increase equilibrium holdings of real money balances; for it is entirely possible that interest-induced changes in equilibrium holdings and turnover rates of commodity inventories will produce exactly the opposite effect.[11]

2. Monetary optimality: an alternative view

The central point that emerges from the preceding discussion is that real marketing costs depend in an essential way on turnover rates of commodity inventories and cannot be inferred directly from information about individual or aggregate holdings of real money balances. On this view, the question

---

[10] The phrase is Friedman's, and aptly characterizes the essential function of money as an exchange intermediary.

[11] For examples of the assertions in question, see any of the papers cited in footnote 1, above.

of an optimal supply of money should be rephrased to read: "Is there an optimal supply of money and other trade inventories?" The answer to this question is provided, at least in principle, by the diagrammatic argument of the preceding section. What is required for Pareto optimality is that the marginal cost of holding commodity and money inventories, as viewed by individuals, should accurately reflect corresponding marginal social costs. Now, this condition will be satisfied only if marginal *indirect* waiting costs associated with holdings of transactions balances correspond to social opportunity costs; for unless this requirement is met, the real rate of return on some commodities held as trade capital will exceed the real rate of return on the same commodities used as capital goods in production. Thus a transfer of commodity inventories from the trading sector to the production sector of the economy, even though it entails an increase in trading costs via increased turnover rates of trade inventories, will yield a marginal increase in aggregate output of goods and services.

This conclusion obviously accords with that reached by Friedman, Samuelson, Tobin, Johnson, Marty, Phelps, Levhari and Patinkin, and other writers who have approached the problem of monetary optimality by a more conventional route.[12] In the present case, however, the conclusion can be justified by reference to identifiable sources of social cost and benefit. In effect, our analysis supplies a needed theoretical rationale for the intuitive ideas that underlie earlier discussions of the monetary optimality problem.

It is an altogether more difficult matter to determine the practical circumstances in which marginal indirect waiting costs will accurately reflect social opportunity costs. Presumably this condition will be satisfied under *laissez faire* in an economy where transactions balances consist entirely of "inside money", e.g., of privately issued bonds or of privately produced nuggets of gold. And presumably the condition will not be

---

[12] See the papers cited in footnote 1, above; also H.C. Johnson, Money in a neo-classical one-sector growth model. In: *Essays in Monetary Economics*. London, Allen and Unwin, 1967, p. 170. — E.S. Phelps, Anticipated inflation and economic welfare. *Journal of Political Economy* 73, (Feb. 1965), 8-12. — D. Levhari and D. Patinkin, The role of money in a simple growth model. *American Economic Review* 53 (Sept. 1968), 713-53. — For contrary, but apparently erroneous views, see R.W. Clower, What traditional monetary theory really wasn't. *Canadian Journal of Economics* 2 (May 1969), 299-302, — and B.P. Pesek, Comment on the optimal growth rate of money. *Journal of Political Economy* 76 (July/August 1968), 885-892. Mention should also be made of the stimulating but rather equivocal discussion of the problem by S.C. Tsiang, A critical note on the optimum supply of money. *Journal of money, credit and banking* 1 (May 1969), 266-80.

satisfied in an economy where the supply of means of payment is determined by government fiat and consists of commodities that do not bear interest. But the world as we know it contains many kinds of money commodities, some provided by government, some by banks and other business concerns. In recent years, e.g., any household transactor that wished to economize on cash could do so fairly effectively by arranging appropriate non-interest bearing lines of credit with department stores, banks, and credit card companies. Such action should, in principle, yield a more optimal allocation of resources within the household sector, but its effect on other sectors of the economy, particularly when we consider administrative and other costs connected with credit means of payment, might well be adverse. Apparently this example involves a problem of second best, but is this not typical of the world in which we live?

Even if it were possible accurately to identify situations in which holdings of commodity and money inventories were Pareto nonoptimal, there would still be serious question whether anything should be done to move the economy in the direction of optimality. For example, suppose it were feasible to pay direct interest subsidies to holders of money balances or, alternatively, suppose it were feasible to induce a steady rate of price deflation by imposing appropriate lump sum taxes on money holdings of individuals. Then, in principle, waiting costs on currency and demand deposits could be reduced to zero, and technical efficiency considerations would seem to favor action to accomplish this result. In practice, however, no program of government intervention is costless. Moreover, since direct waiting costs on holdings of commodity inventories are likely to be vastly greater than indirect waiting costs associated with holdings of transactions balances, it is not at all clear that the complete elimination of indirect waiting costs would have any appreciable effect upon inventory turnover rates nor, therefore, on social welfare. In general, mere ability to identify Pareto nonoptimal situations provides no basis whatever for policy prescriptions.

3. Conclusion

Let me end on the note with which I began. The question of monetary optimality, like most questions in welfare economics, is important not so much for its own sake as for the stimulus it has given to monetary theorists to re-examine the foundations and strengthen the superstructure of their subject. As of the present time, the optimality question has provoked more assertion than analysis, more confusion than enlightenment, and more controversy than agreement; but that is just what has long been needed to rescue monetary theory from the arid wastes of post-Keynesian general equilibrium analysis.[13] Perhaps we shall never have a definitive answer to the optimality problem, but we shall certainly have many attempts at it. And in the process we shall get what is most urgently needed: an improved theoretical understanding of the actual working of the economy in which we live.

COMMENTS ON THE TWO ABOVE PAPERS,
BY ALLAN H. MELTZER*
Carnegie-Mellon University

There are two distinct ways of interpreting the question that serves as a title for this session. On one interpretation, the question asks whether recent advances in the theories of growth and money include the development of a set of necessary and sufficient conditions for an optimum. Although I shall comment briefly on the implications of theoretical work at this level of abstraction, the second interpretation of the question interests me more. On that interpretation, the title asks whether the conclusions of the analysis are applicable, perhaps with minor change, to a money using economy. I shall discuss only one aspect of this question, whether the analysis recognizes the essential difference between a monetary and a non-monetary economy. This is a very basic question, as Clower has reminded us on this and on other occasions.

First a few words about the implications and conclusions. For as long as most of us can remember, monetary theorists have been exhorted to dispense with "ad hockery" and apply the standard principles and practices used in

[13] Cf. Axel Leijonhufvud, *Keynesian economics and the economics of Keynes*. New York, Oxford University Press, 1968, Chapters 1 and 2.

* The comments in this paper are the result of lengthy discussions of the issue and many years of joint work with Karl Brunner. I want to acknowledge, also, financial assistance from the National Science Foundation and the Ford Foundation's Distinguished Research Professorship at Carnegie-Mellon University.

other branches of economic theory. Research on the optimal stock of money is responsive to that demand. Money is generally outside fiat paper money and is produced at zero marginal social cost. The private marginal opportunity cost of holding money is made positive and equal to the rate of interest on non-money assets. As in other applications of standard welfare theory, any difference between private and social marginal cost gives rise to an external economy or diseconomy that can be removed, in principle, by imposing an appropriate tax or granting a subsidy. To attain an optimal allocation of resources, the government must pay interest to money holders and it is generally recommended that this be done by forcing a rate of deflation that drives the nominal rate of interest to zero. By assumption the marginal social cost of deflating the economy is zero, so the marginal net social benefit per period is the amount of resources that are released from their previous use — economizing on cash balances. The alternative policy and the one recommended by Harry Johnson, is to pay interest on reserves, on currency and on deposits if the latter exist.

A second main conclusion of the analysis is that the tax or subsidy through inflation or deflation has an allocative effect. This conclusion is implicit in the argument for the existence of an optimum, but the explicit proof of the allocative effect — or as it is known, the non-neutrality of monetary policy in a growing economy — necessarily precedes the discussion of means of achieving an optimal allocation. The proof of non-neutrality has not been reached by applying the relevant portions of the theory of public finance and taxation, but the main point can be grasped readily within that framework.[1] In the theory of public finance, any tax borne entirely by owners or holders of a specific type of asset has an allocative effect unless the tax falls on pure Ricardian rents or the profits of a pure, profit maximizing monopolist. The tax on cash balances does not meet these requirements for neutrality, hence the choice of a rate of monetary growth and rate of inflation is not neutral.

The practical force of these conclusions, however, is weakened by the failure to consider differences between anticipated and actual rates of price change and the private and social costs of acquiring information, adjusting portfolios, and adjusting rates of consumption and allocations between labor and leisure. These costs of adjustment must be counted as the price

---

[1] For references see my survey Money, intermediation and growth. *Journal of Economic Literature*, March 1969.

society pays to reach an optimum. If costs of acquiring information are high and adjustment is slow, the cumulated present value of the resource cost of moving from a market equilibrium to an optimum may exceed the present value of the resources released by the recommended policy of satiating cash balances.

My reason for bringing up this point is not simply to note that like all pathbreaking analysis, research on optimal monetary policy raises more new and interesting questions than it answers. The problem is more basic. By neglecting transaction costs, including under that heading costs of acquiring information about market prices and the qualities of goods, the analysis of optimal monetary policy misses the essential difference between money and other assets and between a monetary and a barter economy.[2] The missing elements are explanations of the role of money, of the services provided by the asset called money and the difference between money and bonds. Both the Clower and Johnson papers make clear that the discussion of optimal money has focussed almost entirely on social and private costs and very little on the sources of productivity or utility, whereas it is from the differences in the services rendered by money and bonds that we can expect an explanation of the coexistence of these two assets in portfolios containing real assets and equities.

Let me summarize the principal arguments. For Samuelson,[3] the use of money saves shoe leather by reducing the number of trips to the bank. Money is an inventory used to bridge the gap between receipts and payments. Presumably, money, bonds and real assets coexist in his analysis, and money is held as an alternative to "bonds" for the usual (Baumol-Tobin) reasons. Both Clower and Johnson rely on the Baumol-Tobin argument but restrict their analyses to a world in which there are two types of assets one of which is a real consumer good. The other is either money or bonds. Instead of saving shoe leather by reducing the number of trips to the bank, individuals now reduce transactions costs, still measured in inches of shoe leather, by reducing the number of trips to the supermarket. Costs of acquiring information and arranging payments schedules are neglected in the new, as in the

---

[2] See Karl Brunner and Allan H. Meltzer, The uses of money: money in a theory of exchange, presented at the Southern Economic Association meeting, St. Louis, November 1969 (multilithed) — and Thomas R. Saving, Transaction costs and monetary theory. *ibid.* — See also Jurg Niehans, Money in a static theory of optimal payment arrangements. *Journal of Money, Credit and Banking*, November 1969.

[3] Paul A. Samuelson, Nonoptimality of money holdings under *laissez-faire. Canadian Journal of Economics*, May 1969.

older, application of the inventory model. There is no explanation of why the economy continues to use money once it has remained for some time on an optimal growth path.

What is the difference between interest bearing money and interest bearing bonds in this analysis? There is no uncertainty; payments schedules are fixed; information is a free good; and all price changes are fully and instantaneously anticipated. Each of these potential explanations of the productivity of money and the use of money as a medium of exchange is ruled out. Yet money is used and held. If the only service rendered by money is the synchronization of receipts and payments, why are payments not made in interest bearing bonds, produced at zero marginal social cost? Why do money and bonds coexist when the economy reaches and remains at a static equilibrium or moves along an optimal growth path? The latter is an important question that Pesek and Saving tried to raise with their argument about the productivity of money.[4] The fact that their answer is dismissed as unacceptable does not give us a reason to dismiss the question.

Friedman's attempted answer is most explicit and therefore most revealing.[5] He invokes a non-observable, non-pecuniary yield to summarize the services rendered by money and assumes that at any positive rate of interest, a dollar of real money balances provides more of these non-pecuniary services than a dollar of real bonds or other real assets. If optimal monetary policy drives the market rate of interest to zero, the *marginal* non-pecuniary services of money and bonds are zero. Money and bonds continue to be held, however, because the cumulated sum of the pecuniary and non-pecuniary returns on the infra-marginal units make the real stocks of both assets sources of utility. If we accept these arguments, money and bonds remain in portfolios. Johnson and Marty make essentially the same argument about the services of money but are less explicit about the services of bonds.[6]

Note that the entire argument depends, as Friedman recognizes, on the assumption that a dollar of real money balances is a better sources of non-

---

[4] Borris Pesek and Thomas R. Saving, *Money, wealth and economic theory.* New York, The Macmillan Co., 1967.

[5] Milton Friedman, The optimum quantity of money. In: *The optimum quantity of money and other essays.* Chicago, Aldine Publishing Co., 1969, Chapter 1.

[6] Harry G. Johnson, Money in a neo-classical one-sector growth model. In: *Essays in monetary economics.* London, Allen and Unwin, 1967, Chapter 4. — Alvin Marty, The optimal rate of growth of money. *Journal of Political Economy,* suppl. August, 1968.

pecuniary services than a dollar of other real assets.[7] To justify the assumption, Friedman appeals to our intuitive belief that "money is a more efficient carrier of non-pecuniary services" such as pride of possession, and feelings of security that he and others summarize in the overworked, undefined term "liquidity".

This seems a weak foundation on which to rest both the entire distinction between a monetary and a non-monetary economy and the conclusion about optimal monetary policy. Accepting the appeal to intuition is particularly difficult in this case because in the economy under discussion all market exchange ratios are known, all price changes are correctly foreseen and the only service of money is to serve as an inventory. In the economy, why cannot the inventory gap be closed by holding verbal promises to pay, produced whenever they are required without any trips to the bank. Interest bearing government perpetuities, produced at zero marginal social cost, can be used to make payments. Once again, why do money and bonds coexist?

Money emerged in most societies at a very early stage of man's social development, and using money as a medium of exchange appears to have been an important means of reducing the cost of making payments. The development of money and a lower cost payment mechanism, in turn, made trading and exchange less costly. Trade expanded and with the expansion came further development of the payments mechanism, including the use of bonds, credit and other means of deferring payments. The fairs of the Middle Ages provide impressive evidence of ways in which the use of money as a medium of exchange and as a unit of account contributed to the development of market economies. The acceptance of gold as an international medium of exchange and the basis of the 19th century payments system is additional evidence of the connection between the use of a common money and the expansion of trade. More recent evidence comes from the discussions of the importance of a stable, generally accepted, international money for the expansion of trade and the development of institutions like the Eurodollar market to produce money services. Traditional explanations of the services of money — particularly the use of money as a medium of exchange and unit of account — provide the base on which to build an explanation of the productivity of money and the difference between money and bonds. In all but the most primitive economies, a small group of assets

---

[7] Friedman, *op. cit.*, pp. 25-26.

with very similar properties functions as mediums of exchange. One task of monetary theory is to explain why this is so.

The conclusions about optimal monetary policy may provide important implications for the conduct of actual policy, as Johnson suggests. Or, the proof of optimality may be no more than a demonstration that the economy discussed in our theory is not a monetary economy. I do not think we can find the means of choosing between these two answers until we leave the two asset world and provide more information about the properties of assets.

I have come to a stopping place, but I do not want to end on a negative note. We can judge how far events and analysis have brought us by recalling that only a generation ago, interest payments on demand deposits were outlawed and taxes on money balances were urged as desirable. Theoretical work on money and growth is a major forward step in the development of monetary theory as a part of economic theory. From these developments, we can expect to obtain a firmer foundation for social policy. Meanwhile, I believe we can accept some of the main policy conclusions — the advantages of permitting competitive banking, removing the prohibition against interest payments on demand deposits, and steady, or a least steadier, growth of money — on the basis or analysis that is much less restrictive and better validated than the theory used to establish the set of propositions we now call optimal monetary policy.

COMMENTS ON THE TWO ABOVE PAPERS,
BY WARREN L. SMITH
University of Michigan

The subject under discussion is, to say the least, a peculiar one — or perhaps it is more accurate to say that it is a familiar subject that has been given a peculiar twist. At the beginning of his paper, Professor Johnson says, "The question has nothing to do with the optimal conduct of short-run stabilization policy. Instead it belongs to the pure theorists' world of continuous full employment of resources; as such, its policy relevance is to the framework of monetary organization and the long-run environmental objectives of monetary policy." However, this view of the problem can be traced to the context in which Milton Friedman took it up in his important paper on the subject.[1] Viewed in a different light, the issue is of more immediate significance and does, as I shall show, have relevance for the conduct of short-run stabilization policy.

The problem is that unless money yields a positive rate of return to its holders, the quantity of real cash balances held will be less than the welfare-maximizing amount, and an inordinate amount of real resources will be employed in economizing the use of bank deposits and currency which cost virtually nothing to create. Friedman's solution, which seems to be correct in the context of long-run full employment when the rate of inflation or deflation is fully anticipated and there is therefore no trade-off between inflation and unemployment, is to deflate the price level at a rate sufficient to make the monetary interest rate on bonds equal to zero. However, it has not been demonstrated conclusively that such a deflationary policy could be achieved without significant real costs in terms of lost output and employment even in the long run. And it is perfectly clear that there would be heavy costs involved in getting from the present inflationary environment to such a deflationary one. Moreover, as Friedman's own calculations show, there is a wide range of uncertainty about the rate of deflation that would be needed to eliminate the welfare loss. This uncertainty, together with the high probability that the required rate of deflation might vary substantially through time, argues in favor of reliance on the market to solve the problem rather than altering the government's policies to achieve an appropriate rate of deflation. The means of achieving at least a crude solution through the market lie readily at hand:

(1) Eliminate the present prohibition of the payment of interest on demand deposits. The prevailing degree of competition for funds would probably assure the payment of a suitable market-determined return on demand deposits. What would probably emerge would be a system under which interest was paid on the average balance in an account, combined with charges to compensate the bank for services rendered to the account holder.

(2) Some procedure should be adopted to provide the banks with a suitable return on their cash reserves, thereby enabling them to pay higher interest to their depositors. One step that could be taken would be to reduce

---

[1] Milton Friedman, The optimum quantity of money. In: *The optimum quantity of money and other essays*. Chicago, Aldine Publishing Co., 1969, pp. 1-50.

reserve requirements sharply. If reserve requirements had been 5% for demand deposits and 1% for time deposits in 1968, required reserves would have averaged about $8 billion during that year. Interest on this amount of reserves at 5% would have amounted to about $400 million. The total expenses of the Federal Reserve banks, a large proportion of which were incurred in the process of rendering services to member banks, amounted to $242 million in 1968. Thus, a mere lowering of reserve requirements to the indicated levels would reduce the net burden on the member banks of carrying cash reserves to an inconsequential level even without the payment of interest on reserve balances.

(3) The third aspect of the problem would be to arrange for appropriate interest payments on the public's holding of currency. It is primarily the difficulty of solving this problem that leads Friedman to propose his policy of price deflation. However, as Friedman points out and Johnson also mentions, an alternative approach would be to go back to arrangements similar to those that prevailed under the National Banking System prior to the establishment of the Federal Reserve, under which currency is issued by the commercial banks rather than by the central bank.[2] Under such a system, competition among banks would establish an incentive for banks to devise means to pay a suitable rate of interest on currency. If the welfare losses from failure to pay interest on currency are in fact substantial, this would presumably imply a market environment in which the incentives to the banks to devise a way of paying interest on currency would be strong. And recent experience with respect to bank competition for funds suggests that if the incentives were strong, the banks would be ingenious enough to find a solution to the problem.

The welfare gains that would be achieved through the adoption of the proposals I have just mentioned are, so far as I can see, independent of the kind of monetary policy followed. Johnson says that a policy of paying interest on money "would have to be accompanied by a policy of monetary growth ensuring price stability over time". However, in a regime containing

---

[2] A further advantage of such an arrangement is that it would facilitate the establishment of fractional reserve requirements for currency equal to those applicable to demand deposits. Such an equalization of reserve requirements for currency and demand deposits would somewhat simplify the conduct of monetary policy by eliminating the effects on the total supply of credit and on interest rates that now arise as a result of shifts in the composition of the money stock between demand deposits and currency.

money, bonds, and real capital, payment of interest on money at a rate equal to the interest on bonds would appear to be optimal even with a positive rate of inflation in the sense of leading to expansion of real money holdings to the point at which the marginal non-pecuniary benefits of holding money were reduced to zero.

The adoption of procedures which would result in the payment of interest on money at rates which adjusted in response to changing market conditions would add to the short-run effectiveness of monetary policy. When, e.g., a restrictive monetary policy caused market interest rates to rise, the interest rate on money would also rise, reducing the incentive to economize money and thereby dampening the tendency of velocity to rise. This improvement in the effectiveness of monetary policy would accrue to the system whether a discretionary policy was followed or a monetary rule adopted. Thus, I do not agree with Johnson's statement that the subject under discussion "has nothing to do with the optimal conduct of short-run stabilization policy".

As far as the welfare economics aspect of the problem discussed by Professor Clower is concerned, it seems to me that under a regime such as the present one in which demand deposits and currency do not bear interest, transactors should be viewed as holding transactions balances consisting partly of demand deposits and currency and partly of interest-bearing financial assets, the mix of the two being determined by a balancing of interest returns against transactions costs. If money paid interest at a rate which moved with other market rates, the shifts in transactions balances between money and securities should wholly or largely cease. The resources that are used to economize cash balances under the present system would be set free for some other use, a clear social gain. The net return on transactions balances would be somewhat higher than it is now (because costs that now have to be incurred to earn these returns would be eliminated). Consequently, transactors would hold somewhat larger transactions balances. This would presumably imply the holding of somewhat smaller inventories of commodities and the making of somewhat less frequent trips to the bank and more frequent trips to the market. As Johnson points out, the capital released from commodity inventories would be available for use elsewhere in the economy. As far as I can see, the calculus governing decisions about holdings of transactions balances, holdings of commodity inventories, frequency of trips to the bank, and frequency of trips to the market would be exactly the same as it is now. The gain would come from the release of resources that are now employed in the process of economizing the use of demand deposits and currency.[3]

With respect to the point raised at the end of Johnson's paper regarding the possibility of banks replacing other financial intermediaries, I think it would probably be an improvement if this did occur. The existence of specialized financial institutions subject to legal constraints has served to compartmentalize the capital market, leading to significant differences in the rate of return on real capital in different uses. Developments which widened the scope of operation of commercial banks, or made other financial institutions behave more like banks, would probably add to the efficiency of the financial system and improve capital allocation.

---

[3] The institution of the new regime would presumably cause some rise in market interest rates, because the practice the holding some fraction of transactions balances in securities would come to an end, theory reducing the demand for securities. As I view monetary policy, therefore, the Federal Reserve would have to expand bank reserves and the supply of money somewhat to offset this effect if the same monetary policy was to be maintained. Or, to put it another way, the demand for money at a given level of real income and prices would be increased, and the Federal Reserve would have to accommodate this demand if a deflationary effect was to be avoided. But, in principle, this adjustment would involve no difficulties.

Frontiers of Quantitative Economics, ed. M.D. Intriligator. © *North-Holland Publishing Company.*

CHAPTER 8

EFFICIENT CAPITAL MARKETS: A REVIEW OF
THEORY AND EMPIRICAL WORK*

EUGENE F. FAMA
University of Chicago

0. Introduction

The primary role of the capital market is allocation of ownership of the economy's capital stock. In general terms, the ideal is a market in which prices provide accurate signals for resource allocation: that is, a market in which firms can make production-investment decisions, and investors can choose among the securities that represent ownership of firms' activities under the assumption that security prices at any time "fully reflect" all available information. A market in which prices always "fully reflect" available information is called "efficient".

This paper reviews the theoretical and empirical literature on the efficient markets model. After a discussion of the theory, empirical work concerned with the adjustment of security prices to three relevant information subsets is considered. First, *weak form* tests, in which the information set is just historical prices, are discussed. Then *semi-strong form* tests, in which the concern is whether prices efficiently adjust to other information that is obviously publicly available (e.g., announcements of annual earnings, stock splits, etc.) are considered. Finally, *strong form* tests concerned with whether

───────────

* Research on this project was supported by a grant from the National Science Foundation. I am indebted to Arthur Laffer, Robert Aliber, Ray Ball, Michael Jensen, James Lorie, Merton Miller, Charles Nelson, Richard Roll, William Taylor, and Ross Watts for their helpful comments.

given investors or groups have monopolistic access to any information relevant for price formation are reviewed.[1] We shall conclude that, with but a few exceptions, the efficient markets model stands up well.

Though we proceed from theory to empirical work, to keep the proper historical perspective we should note that to a large extent the empirical work in this area preceded the development of the theory. The theory is presented first here in order to more easily judge which of the empirical results are most relevant from the viewpoint of the theory. The empirical work itself, however, will then be reviewed in more or less historical sequence.

Finally, the perceptive reader will surely recognize instances in this paper where relevant studies are not specifically discussed. In such cases my apologies should be taken for granted. The area is so bountiful that some such injustices are unavoidable. But the primary goal here will have been accomplished if a coherent picture of the main lines of the work on efficient markets is presented, along with an accurate picture of the current state of the arts.

1. The theory of efficient markets

1.0. *Expected return or "fair game" models*

The definitional statement that in an efficient market prices "fully reflect" available information is so general that it has no empirically testable implications. To make the model testable, the process of price formation must be specified in more detail. In essence we must define somewhat more exactly what is meant by the term "fully reflect".

One possibility would be to posit that equilibrium prices (or expected returns) on securities are generated as in the "two parameter" Sharpe (1964) — Lintner (1965a, b) world. In general, however, the theoretical models and especially the empirical tests of capital market efficiency have not been this specific. Most of the available work is based only on the assumption that the conditions of market equilibrium can (somehow) be stated in terms of expected returns. In general terms, like the two parameter model such theories would posit that, conditional on some relevant information set,

---

[1] The distinction between weak and strong form tests was first suggested by Harry Roberts.

the equilibrium expected return on a security is a function of its "risk". And different theories would differ primarily in how "risk" is defined.

All members of the class of such *"expected return theories"* can, however, be described notationally as follows:

$$E(\tilde{p}_{j,t+1}|\Phi_t) = [1+E(\tilde{r}_{j,t+1}|\Phi_t)]p_{jt}, \tag{1}$$

where E is the expected value operator; p_{jt} is the price of security j at time t; $p_{j,t+1}$ is its price at $t+1$ (with reinvestment of any intermediate cash income from the security); $r_{j,t+1}$ is the one-period percentage return $(p_{j,t+1}-p_{jt})/p_{jt}$; Φ_t is a general symbol for whatever set of information is assumed to be "fully reflected" in the price at t; and the tildes indicate that $p_{j,t+1}$ and $r_{j,t+1}$ are random variables at t.

The value of the equilibrium expected return $E(\tilde{r}_{j,t+1}|\Phi_t)$ projected on the basis of the information Φ_t would be determined from the particular expected return theory at hand. The conditional expectation notation of (1) is meant to imply, however, that whatever expected return model is assumed to apply, the information in Φ_t is fully utilized in determining equilibrium expected returns. And this is the sense in which Φ_t is "fully reflected" in the formation of the price p_{jt}.

But we should note immediately that, simple as it is, the assumption that the conditions of market equilibrium can be stated in terms of expected returns elevates the purely mathematical concept of expected value to a status not necessarily implied by the general notion of market efficiency. The expected value is just one of many possible summary measures of a distribution of returns, and market efficiency *per se* (i.e., the general notion that prices "fully reflect" available information) does not imbue it with any special importance. Thus, the results of tests based on this assumption depend to some extent on its validity as well as on the efficiency of the market. But some such assumption is the unavoidable price one must pay to give the theory of efficient markets empirical content.

The assumptions that the conditions of market equilibrium can be stated in terms of expected returns and that equilibrium expected returns are formed on the basis of (and thus "fully reflect") the information set Φ_t have a major empirical implication — they rule out the possibility of trading systems based only on information in Φ_t that have expected profits or returns in excess of equilibrium expected profits on returns. Thus let

$$x_{j,t+1} = p_{j,t+1} - E(\tilde{p}_{j,t+1}|\Phi_t). \tag{2}$$

Then:

$$E(\tilde{x}_{j,t+1} | \Phi_t) = 0, \tag{3}$$

which, *by definition*, says that the sequence $\{x_{jt}\}$ is a *"fair game"* with respect to the information sequence $\{\Phi_t\}$. Or, equivalently, let:

$$z_{j,t+1} = r_{j,t+1} - E(\tilde{r}_{j,t+1} | \Phi_t). \tag{4}$$

Then:

$$E(\tilde{z}_{j,t+1} | \Phi_t) = 0, \tag{5}$$

so that the sequence $\{z_{jt}\}$ is also a "fair game" with respect to the information sequence $\{\Phi_t\}$.

In economic terms, $x_{j,t+1}$ is the excess market value of security j at time $t+1$: it is the difference between the observed price and the expected value of the price that was projected at t on the basis of the information Φ_t. And similarly, $z_{j,t+1}$ is the return at $t+1$ in excess of the equilibrium expected return projected at t. Let:

$$\alpha(\Phi_t) = [\alpha_1(\Phi_t), \alpha_2(\Phi_t), ..., \alpha_n(\Phi_t)]$$

be any trading system based on Φ_t which tells the investor the amounts $\alpha_j(\Phi_t)$ of funds available at t that are to be invested in each of the n available securities. The total excess market value at $t+1$ that will be generated by such a system is:

$$V_{t+1} = \sum_{j=1}^{n} \alpha_j(\Phi_t) [r_{j,t+1} - E(\tilde{r}_{j,t+1} | \Phi_t)],$$

which, from the "fair game" property of (5) has expectation:

$$E(\tilde{V}_{t+1} | \Phi_t) = \sum_{j=1}^{n} \alpha_j(\Phi_t) E(\tilde{z}_{j,t+1} | \Phi_t) = 0.$$

The expected return or "fair game" efficient markets model has other important testable implications, but these are better saved for the later discussion of the empirical work.[2] Now we turn to two special cases of the

---

[2] Though we shall sometimes refer to the model summarized by (1) as the "fair game" model, keep in mind that the "fair game" properties of the model are *implications* of the assumptions that (i) the conditions of market equilibrium can be stated in terms of expected returns, and (ii) the information Φ_t is fully utilized by the market in forming equilibrium expected returns and thus current prices. — The role of "fair game" models in the theory of efficient markets was first recognized and studied rigorously by Samuelson (1965) and Mandelbrot (1966). Their work will be discussed in more detail later.

model, the submartingale and the random walk, that (as we shall see later) play an important role in the empirical literature.

1.1. *The submartingale model*

Suppose we assume in (1) that for all t and Φ_t:

$$E(\tilde{p}_{j,t+1} \mid \Phi_t) \geq p_{jt}, \text{ or equivalently, } E(\tilde{r}_{j,t+1} \mid \Phi_t) \geq 0. \tag{6}$$

This is a statement that the price sequence $\{p_{jt}\}$ for security j follows a *submartingale* with respect to the information sequence $\{\Phi_t\}$, which is to say nothing more than that the expected value of next period's price, as projected on the basis of the information Φ_t, is equal to or greater than the current price. If (6) holds as an equality (so that expected returns and price changes are zero), then the price sequence follows a *martingale*.

A submartingale in prices has one important empirical implication. Consider the set of "one security and cash" mechanical trading rules by which we mean systems that concentrate on individual securities and that define the conditions under which the investor would hold a given security, sell it short, or simply hold cash at any time t. Then the assumption of (6) that expected returns conditional on Φ_t are non-negative directly implies that such trading rules based only on the information in Φ_t cannot have greater expected profits than a policy of always buying-and-holding the security during the future period in question. Tests of such rules will be an important part of the empirical evidence on the efficient markets model.[3]

1.2. *The random walk model*

In the early treatments of the efficient markets model, the statement that the current price of a security "fully reflects" available information was assumed

---

[3] Note that the expected profitability of "one security and cash" trading systems vis-à-vis buy-and-hold is not ruled out by the general expected return or "fair game" efficient markets model. The latter rules out systems with expected profits in excess of equilibrium expected returns, but since in principle it allows equilibrium expected returns to be negative, holding cash (which always has zero actual and thus expected return) may have higher expected return than holding some security. — And negative equilibrium expected returns for some securities are quite possible. For example, in the Sharpe (1964) — Lintner (1965a, b) model the equilibrium expected return on a security depends on the extent to which the dispersion in the security's return distribution is related to dispersion in the returns on all other securities. A security whose returns on average move opposite to the general market is particularly valuable in reducing dispersion of portfolio returns, and so its equilibrium expected return may well be negative.

to imply that successive price changes (or more usually, successive one-period returns) are independent. In addition, it was usually assumed that successive changes (or returns) are identically distributed. Together the two hypotheses constitute the *random walk model*. Formally, the model says:

$$f(r_{j,t+1} \mid \Phi_t) = f(r_{j,t+1}), \tag{7}$$

which is the usual statement that the conditional and marginal probability distributions of an independent random variable are identical. In addition, the density function f must be the same for all t.[4]

Expression (7) of course says much more than the general expected return model summarized by (1). For example, if we restrict (1) by assuming that the expected return on security j is constant over time, then we have:

$$E(\tilde{r}_{j,t+1} \mid \Phi_t) = E(\tilde{r}_{j,t+1}). \tag{8}$$

This says that the mean of the distribution of $r_{j,t+1}$ is independent of Φ_t, the information available at t, whereas the random walk model of (7) in addition says that the entire distribution is independent of Φ_t.[5]

We argue later that it is best to regard the random walk model as an extension of the general expected return or "fair game" efficient markets model in the sense of making a more detailed statement about the economic environment. The "fair game" model just says that the conditions of market equilibrium can be stated in terms of expected returns, and thus it says little about the details of the stochastic process generating returns. A random walk arises within the context of such a model when the environment is (fortuitously) such that the evolution of investor tastes and the process generating new information combine to produce equilibria in which return distributions repeat themselves through time.

---

[4] The terminology is loose. Prices will only follow a random walk if price changes are independent, identically distributed; and even then we should say "random walk with drift" since expected price changes can be non-zero. If one-period returns are independent, identically distributed, prices will not follow a random walk since the distribution of price changes will depend on the price level. But though rigorous terminology is usually desirable, our loose use of terms should not cause confusion; and our usage follows that of the efficient markets literature. — Note also that in the random walk literature, the information set Φ_t in (7) us usually assumed to include only the past return history, $r_{j, t}, r_{j, t+1}, \cdots$

[5] The random walk model does not say, however, that past information is of no value in *assessing* distributions of future returns. Indeed since return distributions are assumed to be stationary through time, past returns are the best source of such information. The random walk model does say, however, that the *sequence* (or the order) of the past returns is of no consequence in assessing distributions of future returns.

Thus it is not surprising that empirical tests of the "random walk" model that are in fact tests of "fair game" properties are more strongly in support of the model than tests of the additional (and, from the viewpoint of expected return market efficiency, superfluous) pure independence assumption. (But it is perhaps equally surprising that, as we shall soon see, the evidence against the independence of returns over time is as weak as it is.)

1.3. *Market conditions consistent with efficiency*

Before turning to the empirical work, however, a few words about the market conditions that might help or hinder efficient adjustment of prices to information are in order. First, it is easy to determine *sufficient* conditions for capital market efficiency. For example, consider a market in which (i) there are no transactions costs in trading securities, (ii) all available information is costlessly available to all market participants, and (iii) all agree on the implications of current information for the current price and distributions of future prices of each security. In such a market, the current price of a security obviously "fully reflects" all available information.

But a frictionless market in which all information is freely available and investors agree on its implications is, of course, not descriptive of markets met in practice. Fortunately, these conditions, while sufficient for market efficiency, are not necessary. For example, as long as transactors take account of all available information, even large transactions costs that inhibit the flow of transactions do not in themselves imply that when transactions do take place, prices will not "fully reflect" available information. Similarly (and speaking, as above, somewhat loosely), the market may be efficient if "sufficient numbers" of investors have ready access to available information. And disagreement among investors about the implications of given information does not in itself imply market inefficiency unless there are investors who can consistently make better evaluations of available information than are implicit in market prices.

But though (i) transactions costs, (ii) information that is not freely available to all investors, and (iii) disagreement among investors about the implications of given information are not necessarily sources of market inefficiency, they are *potential* sources. And all three exist to some extent in real world markets. Measuring their effects on the process of price formation is, of course, the major goal of empirical work in this area.

2. The evidence

All the empirical research on the theory of efficient markets has been concerned with whether prices "fully reflect" particular subsets of available information. Historically, the empirical work evolved more or less as follows. The initial studies were concerned with what we call *weak form* tests in which the information subset of interest is just past price (or return) histories. Most of the results here come from the random walk literature. When extensive tests seemed to support the efficiency hypothesis at this level, attention was turned to *semi-strong form* tests in which the concern is the speed of price adjustment to other obviously publicly available information (e.g., announcements of stock splits, annual reports, new security issues, etc.). Finally, *strong form* tests in which the concern is whether any investor or groups (e.g., managements of mutual funds) have monopolistic access to any information relevant for the formation of prices have recently appeared. We review the empirical research in more or less this historical sequence.

First, however, we should note that what we have called *the* efficient markets model in the discussions of earlier sections is the hypothesis that security prices at any point in time "fully reflect" *all* available information. Though we shall argue that the model stands up rather well to the data, it is obviously an extreme null hypothesis. And, like any other extreme null hypothesis, we do not expect it to be literally true. The categorization of the tests into weak, semi-strong, and strong form will serve the useful purpose of allowing us to pinpoint the level of information at which the hypothesis breaks down. And we shall contend that there is no important evidence against the hypothesis in the weak and semi-strong form tests (i.e., prices seem to efficiently adjust to obviously publicly available information), and only limited evidence against the hypothesis in the strong form tests (i.e., monopolistic access to information about prices does not seem to be a prevalent phenomenon in the investment community).

2.0. *Weak form tests of the efficient markets model*

2.0.0. *Random walks and fair games: a little historical background*

As noted earlier, all of the empirical work on efficient markets can be considered within the context of the general expected return or "fair game" model, and much of the evidence bears directly on the special submartingale expected return model of (6). Indeed, in the early literature, discussions of the efficient markets model were phrased in terms of the even more special random walk model, though we shall argue that most of the early authors were in fact concerned with more general versions of the "fair game" model.

Some of the confusion in the early random walk writings is understandable. Research on secuirty prices did not begin with the development of a theory of price formation which was then subjected to empirical tests. Rather, the impetus for the development of a theory came from the accumulation of evidence in the middle 1950's and early 1960's that the behavior of common stock and other speculative prices could be well approximated by a random walk. Faced with the evidence, economists felt compelled to offer some rationalization. What resulted was a theory of efficient markets stated in terms of random walks, but usually implying some more general "fair game" model.

It was not until the work of Samuelson (1965) and Mandelbrot (1966) that the role of "fair game" expected return models in the theory of efficient markets and the relationships between these models and the theory of random walks were rigorously studied.[6] These papers came somewhat after the major empirical work on random walks. In the earlier work, "theoretical" discussions, though usually intuitively appealing, were always lacking in rigor and often either vague or *ad hoc*. In short, until the Mandelbrot-Samuelson models appeared, there existed a large body of empirical results in search of a rigorous theory.

Thus, though his contributions were ignored for 60 years, the first statement and test of the random walk model was that of Bachelier (1900). But his "fundamental principle" for the behavior of prices was that speculation should be a "fair game"; in particular, the expected profits to the speculator should be zero. With the benefit of the modern theory of

---

[6] Basing their analyses on futures contracts in commodity markets, Mandelbrot and Samuelson show that if the price of such a contract at time t is the expected value at t (given information Φ_t) of the spot price at the termination of the contract, then the fututes price will follow a martingale with respect to the information sequence $\{\Phi_t\}$; that is, the expected price change from period to period will be zero, and the price changes will be a "fair game". If the equilibrium expected return is not assumed to be zero, our more general "fair game" model, summarized by (1), is obtained. — But though the Mandelbrot-Samuelson approach certainly illuminates the process of price formation in commodity markets, we have seen that "fair game" expected return models can be derived in much simpler fashion. In particular, (1) is just a formalization of the assumptions that the conditions of market equilibrium can be stated in terms of expected returns and that the information Φ_t is used in forming market prices at t.

stochastic processes, we know now that the process implied by this fundamental principle is a martingale.

After Bachelier, research on the behavior of security prices lagged until
the coming of the computer. In 1953 Kendall examined the behavior of
weekly changes in nineteen indices of British industrial share prices and in
spot prices for cotton (New York) and wheat (Chicago). After extensive
analysis of serial correlations, he suggests, in quite graphic terms:

> The series looks like a wandering one, almost as if once a week the Demon of Chance
> drew a random number from a symmetrical population of fixed dispersion and added
> it to the current price to determine the next week's price. (Kendall 1953, p. 13).

Kendall's conclusion had in fact been suggested earlier by Working (1934),
though his suggestion lacked the force provided by Kendall's empirical
results. And the implications of the conclusion for stock market research
and financial analysis were later underlined by Roberts (1959).

But the suggestion by Kendall, Working, and Roberts that series of
speculative prices may be well described by random walks was based on
observation. None of these authors attempted to provide much economic
rationale for the hypothesis, and, indeed, Kendall felt that economists
would generally reject it. Osborne (1959) suggested market conditions,
similar to those assumed by Bachelier, that would lead to a random walk.
But in his model, independence of successive price changes derives from the
assumption that the decisions of investors in an individual security are
independent from transaction to transaction — which is little in the way
of an economic model.

Whenever economists (prior to Mandelbrot and Samuelson) tried to
provide economic justification for the random walk, their arguments usually
implied a "fair game". For example, Alexander (Cootner 1964, p. 200) states:

> If one were to start out with the assumption that a stock or commodity speculation
> is a "fair game" with equal expectation of gain or loss or, more accurately, with
> an expectation of zero gain, one would be well on the way to picturing the behavior
> of speculative prices as a random walk.

There is an awareness here that the "fair game" assumption is not sufficient
to lead to a random walk, but Alexander never expands on the comment.
Similarly, Cootner (1964, p. 232) states:

> If any substantial group of buyers thought prices were too low, their buying would
> force up the prices. The reverse would be true for sellers. Except for appreciation
> due to earnings retention, the conditional expectation of tomorrow's price, given today's
> price, is today's price.

In such a world, the only price changes that would occur are those that result from new information. Since there is no reason to expect that information to be non-random in appearance, the period-to-period price changes of a stock should be random movements, statistically independent of one another.

Though somewhat imprecise, the last sentence of the first paragraph seems to point to a "fair game" model rather than a random walk.[7] In this light, the second paragraph can be viewed as an attempt to describe environmental conditions that would reduce a "fair game" to a random walk. But the specification imposed on the information generating process is insufficient for this purpose; one would, e.g., also have to say something about investor tastes. Finally, lest I be accused of criticizing others too severely for ambiguity, lack of rigor and incorrect conclusions:

> By contrast, the stock market trader has a much more practical criterion for judging what constitutes important dependence in successive price changes. For his purposes the random walk model is valid as long as knowledge of the past behavior of the series of price changes cannot be used to increase expected gains. More specifically, the independence assumption is an adequate description of reality as long as the actual degree of dependence in the series of price changes is not sufficient to allow the past history of the series to be used to predict the future in a way which makes expected profits greater than they would be under a naive buy-and-hold model. (Fama 1965, p. 35).

We know now, of course, that this last condition hardly requires a random walk. It will in fact be met by the submartingale model of (6).

But one should not be too hard on the theoretical efforts of the early empirical random walk literature. The arguments were usually appealing; where they fell short was in awareness of developments in the theory of stochastic processes. Moreover, we shall now see that most of the empirical evidence in the random walk literature can easily be interpreted as tests of more general expected return or "fair game" models.[8]

2.0.1. *Tests of market efficiency in the random walk literature*

As discussed earlier, "fair game" models imply the "impossibility" of various sorts of trading systems. Some of the random walk literature has

---

[7] The appropriate conditioning statement would be "Given the sequence of historical prices".

[8] Our brief historical review is meant only to provide perspective, and it is, of course, somewhat incomplete. For example, we have ignored the important contributions to the early random walk literature in studies of warrants and other options by Sprenkle, Kruizenga, Boness, and others. Much of this early work on options is summarized in Cootner (1964).

been concerned with testing the profitability of such systems. More of the literature has, however, been concerned with tests of serial covariances of returns. We shall now show that, like a random walk, the serial covariances of a "fair game" are zero, so that these tests are also relevant for the expected return models.

If $\{x_t\}$ is a "fair game", its unconditional expectation is zero and its serial covariance can be written in general form as:

$$E(\tilde{x}_{t+\tau}\,\tilde{x}_t) \;=\; \int_{x_t} x_t E(\tilde{x}_{t+\tau}\,|\,x_t)\,f(x_t)\,dx_t,$$

where f indicates a density function. But if $\{x_t\}$ is a "fair game"[9]:

$$E(\tilde{x}_{t+\tau}\,|\,x_t) = 0.$$

From this it follows that for all lags, the serial covariances between lagged values of a "fair game" variable are zero. Thus, observations of a "fair game" variable are linearly independent.[10]

---

[9] More generally, if the sequence $\{x_t\}$ is a fair game with respect to the information sequence $\{\Phi_t\}$ (i.e., $E(\tilde{x}_{t+1}\,|\,\Phi_t) = 0$ for all Φ_t), then $\{x_t\}$ is a fair game with respect to any Φ'_t that is a subset of Φ_t (i.e., $E(\tilde{x}_{t+1}\,|\,\Phi'_t) = 0$ for all Φ'_t). To show this, let $\Phi_t = (\Phi'_t, \Phi''_t)$. Then, using Stieltjes integrals and the symbol F to denote cumulative distribution functions, the conditional expectation

$$E(\tilde{x}_{t+1}\,|\,\Phi'_t) = \int_{\Phi''_t} \int_{x_{t+1}} x_{t+1}\,dF(x_{t+1}, \Phi''_t\,|\,\Phi'_t)$$
$$= \int_{\Phi''_t} \left[\int_{x_{t+1}} x_{t+1}\,dF(x_{t+1}\,|\,\Phi'_t, \Phi''_t) \right] dF(\Phi''_t\,|\,\Phi'_t).$$

But the integral in brackets is just $E(\tilde{x}_{t+1}\,|\,\Phi_t)$ which by the "fair game" assumption is zero, so that:

$$E(x_{t+1}\,|\,\Phi'_t) = 0 \text{ for all } \Phi'_t \subset \Phi_t.$$

[10] But though zero serial covariances are consistent with a "fair game", they do not imply such a process. A "fair game" also rules out many types of nonlinear dependence. Thus using arguments similar to those above, it can be shown that if x is a "fair game", $E(\tilde{x}_t\tilde{x}_{t+1} \ldots \tilde{x}_{t+\tau}) = 0$ for all τ, which is not implied by $E(\tilde{x}_t\tilde{x}_{t+\tau}) = 0$ for all τ. For example, consider a three-period case where x must be either ± 1. Suppose the process is $x_{t+2} = \text{sign}\,(x_t x_{t+1})$, i.e.,

x_{2t}	x_{t+}	$\rightarrow x_{t+1}$
+	+	→ +
+	−	→ −
−	+	→ −
−	−	→ +

But the "fair game" model does not necessarily imply that the serial covariances of *one-period returns* are zero. In the weak form tests of this model the "fair game" variable is (cf. footnote 9):

$$z_{j,t} = r_{j,t} - E(\tilde{r}_{j,t} \, r_{j,t-1}, r_{j,t-2}, \ldots).$$ (9)

But the covariance between, e.g., r_{jt} and $r_{j,t+1}$ is:

$$E([\tilde{r}_{j,t+1} - E(\tilde{r}_{j,t+1})] \, [\tilde{r}_{jt} - E(\tilde{r}_{jt})])$$

$$= \int_{r_{jt}} [r_{jt} - E(\tilde{r}_{jt})] \, [E(\tilde{r}_{j,t+1} \mid r_{jt}) - E(\tilde{r}_{j,t+1})] \, f(r_{jt}) \, dr_{jt},$$

and (9) does not imply that $E(\tilde{r}_{j,t+1} \mid r_{jt}) = E(\tilde{r}_{j,t+1})$: In the "fair game" efficient markets model, the deviation of the return for $t+1$ from its conditional expectation is a "fair game" variable, but the conditional expectation itself can depend on the return observed for t.[11]

In the random walk literature, this problem is not recognized, since it is assumed that the expected return (and indeed the entire distribution of returns) is stationary through time. In practice, this implies estimating serial covariances by taking cross products of deviations of observed returns from the overall sample mean return. It is somewhat fortuitous, then, that this procedure, which represents a rather gross approximation from the viewpoint of the general expected return efficient markets model, does not seem to greatly affect the results of the covariance tests, at least for common stocks.[12]

For example, table 1 (taken from Fama 1965) shows the serial correlations between successive changes in the natural log of price for each of the thirty

---

If probabilities are uniformly distributed across events,

$$E(\tilde{x}_{t+2} \mid x_{t+1}) = E(\tilde{x}_{t+2} \mid x_t) = E(\tilde{x}_{t+1} \mid x_t) = E(\tilde{x}_{t+2}) = E(\tilde{x}_{t+1}) = E(\tilde{x}_t) = 0,$$

so that all pairwise serial convariances are zero. But the process is not a "fair game", since $E(\tilde{x}_{t+2} \mid x_{t+1}, x_t) \neq 0$, and knowledge of (x_{t+1}, x_t) can be used as the basis of a simple "system" with positive expected profit.

[11] For example, suppose the level of one-period returns follows a martingale so that:

$$E(r_{j,t+1} \mid r_{jt}, r_{j,t+1} \ldots) = r_{jt}.$$

Then covariances between successive returns will be nonzero (though in this special case first differences of returns will be uncorrelated).

[12] The reason is probably that for stocks, changes in equilibrium expected returns for the common differencing intervals of a day, a week, or a month, are trivial relative to other sources of variation in returns. Later, when we consider Roll's (1968) work, we shall see that this is not true for one week returns on U.S. Government Treasury Bills.

stocks of the Dow Jones Industrial Average, for time periods that vary slightly from stock to stock, but usually run from about the end of 1957 to September 26, 1962. The serial correlations of successive changes in $\log_e$ price are shown for differencing intervals or 1, 4, 9, and 16 days.[13]

Table 1 (from Fama 1965)

First-order serial correlation coefficients for 1, 4, 9, and 16 day changes in $\log_e$ price

Stock	Differencing Interval (Days)			
	One	Four	Nine	Sixteen
Allied Chemical	0.017	0.029	−0.091	−0.118
Alcoa	0.118*	0.095	−0.112	−0.044
American Can	−0.087*	−0.124*	−0.060	0.031
A.T. & T.	−0.039	−0.010	−0.009	−0.003
American Tobacco	0.111*	−0.175*	0.033	0.007
Anaconda	0.067*	−0.068	−0.125	0.202
Bethlehem Steel	0.013	−0.122	−0.148	0.112
Chrysler	0.012	0.060	−0.026	0.040
DuPont	0.013	0.069	−0.043	−0.055
Eastman Kodak	0.025	−0.006	−0.053	−0.023
General Electric	0.011	0.020	−0.004	0.000
General Foods	0.061*	−0.005	−0.140	−0.098
General Motors	−0.004	−0.128*	0.009	−0.028
Goodyear	−0.123*	0.001	−0.037	0.033
International Harvester	−0.017	−0.068	−0.244*	0.116
International Nickel	0.096*	0.038	0.124	0.041
International Paper	0.046	0.060	−0.004	−0.010
Johns Manville	0.006	−0.068	−0.002	0.002
Owens Illinois	−0.021	−0.006	0.003	−0.022
Procter & Gamble	0.099*	−0.006	0.098	0.076
Sears	0.097*	−0.070	−0.113	0.041
Standard Oil (Calif.)	0.025	−0.143*	−0.046	0.040
Standard Oil (N.J.)	0.008	−0.109	−0.082	−0.121
Swift & Co.	−0.004	−0.072	0.118	−0.197
Texaco	0.094*	−0.053	−0.047	−0.178
Union Carbide	0.107*	0.049	−0.101	0.124
United Aircraft	0.014	−0.190*	−0.192*	−0.040
U.S. Steel	0.040	−0.006	−0.056	0.236*
Westinghouse	−0.027	−0.097	−0.137	0.067
Woolworth	0.028	−0.033	−0.112	0.040

* Coefficient is twice its computed standard error.

---

[13] The use of changes in $\log_e$ price as the measure of return is common in the random walk literature. It can be justified in several ways. But for current purposes, it is sufficient to note that for price changes less than 15%, the change in $\log_e$ price is approximately the percentage price change or one-period return. And for differencing intervals shorter

The results in table 1 are typical of those reported by others for tests based on serial covariances. (Cf. Kendall (1953); Moore (1962); Alexander (1961), and the results of Granger and Morgenstern (1963) and Godfrey et al. (1964) obtained by means of spectral analysis). Specifically, there is no evidence of substantial linear dependence between lagged price changes or returns. In absolute terms the measured serial correlations are always close to zero.

Looking hard, though, one can probably find evidence of statistically "significant" linear dependence in table 1 (and again this is true of results reported by others). For the daily returns eleven of the serial correlations are more than twice their computed standard errors, and twenty-two out of thirty are positive. On the other hand, twenty-one and twenty-four of the coefficients for the 4 and 9 day differences are negative. But with samples of the size underlying table 1 ($N = 1200$-1700 observations per stock on a daily basis) statistically "significant" deviations from zero covariance are not necessarily a basis for rejecting the efficient markets model. For the results in table 1, the standard errors of the serial correlations were approximated as $(1/(N-1))^{1/2}$, which for the daily data implies that a correlation as small as 0.06 is more than twice its standard error. But a coefficient this size implies that a linear relationship with the lagged price change can be used to explain about 0.36% of the variation in the current price change, which is probably insignificant from an economic viewpoint. In particular, it is unlikely that the small absolute levels of serial correlation that are always observed can be used as the basis of substantially profitable trading systems.[14]

It is, of course, difficult to judge what degree of serial correlation would

---

than one month, returns in excess of 15% are unusual. Thus Fama (1965) reports that for the data of table 1, tests carried out on percentage or one-period returns yielded results essentially identical to the tests based on changes in $\log_e$ price.

[14] Given the evidence of Kendall (1953), Mandelbrot (1963), Fama (1965) and others that large price changes occur much more frequently than would be expected if the generating process were Gaussian, the expression $(1/(N-1))^{1/2}$ understates the sampling dispersion of the serial correlation coefficient, and thus leads to an overstatement of significance levels. In addition, the fact that sample serial correlations are predominantly of one sign or the other is not in itself evidence of linear dependence. If, as the work of King (1966) and Blume (1968) indicates, there is a market factor whose behavior affects the returns on all securities, the sample behavior of this market factor may lead to a predominance of signs of one type in the serial correlations for individual securities, even though the population serial correlations for both the market factor and the returns on individual securities are zero. For a more extensive analysis of these issues see Fama (1965).

imply the existence of trading rules with substantial expected profits. (And indeed we shall soon have to be a little more precise about what is implied by "substantial" profits.) Moreover, zero serial covariances are consistent with a "fair game" model, but as noted earlier (footnote 10), there are types of nonlinear dependence that imply the existence of profitable trading systems, and yet do not imply nonzero serial covariances. Thus, for many reasons it is desirable to directly test the profitability of various trading rules.

The first major evidence on trading rules was Alexander's (1961, 1964). He tests a variety of systems, but the most thoroughly examined can be described as follows: If the price of a security moves up at least $y\%$, buy and hold the security until its price moves down at least $y\%$ from a subsequent high, at which time simultaneously sell and go short. The short position is maintained until the price rises at least $y\%$ above a subsequent low, at which time one covers the short position and buys. Moves less than $y\%$ in either direction are ignored. Such a system is called a $y\%$ filter. It is obviously a "one security and cash" trading rule, so that the results it produces are relevant for the submartingale expected return model of (6).

After extensive tests using daily data on price indices from 1897 to 1959 and filters from 1 to 50%, and after correcting some incorrect presumptions in the initial results of Alexander (1961) (see footnote 25), in his final paper on the subject, Alexander concludes:

> In fact, at this point I should advise any reader who is interested only in practical results, and who is not a floor trader and so must pay commissions, to turn to other sources on how to beat buy and hold. The rest of this article is devoted principally to a theoretical consideration of whether the observed results are consistent with a random walk hypothesis. (Cootner 1964, p. 351).

Later in the paper Alexander concludes that there is some evidence in his results against the independence assumption of the random walk model. But market efficiency does not require a random walk, and from the viewpoint of the submartingale model of (6), the conclusion that the filters cannot beat buy-and-hold is support for the efficient markets hypothesis. Further support is provided by Fama and Blume (1966) who compare the profitability of various filters to buy-and-hold for the individual stocks of the Dow-Jones Industrial Average. (The data are those underlying table 1.)

But again, looking hard one can find evidence in the filter tests of both Alexander and Fama-Blume that is inconsistent with the submartingale efficient markets model, if that model is interpreted in a strict sense. In particular, the results for very small filters (1% in Alexander's tests and 0.5, 1.0, and 1.5% in the tests of Fama-Blume) indicate that it is possible to devise trading schemes based on very short-term (preferably intra-day but at most daily) price swings that will on average outperform buy-and-hold. The average profits on individual transactions from such schemes are miniscule, but they generate transactions so frequently that over longer periods and ignoring commissions they outperform buy-and-hold by a substantial margin. These results are evidence of persistence or positive dependence in very short-term price movements. And, interestingly, this is consistent with the evidence for slight positive linear dependence in successive daily price changes produced by the serial correlations.[15]

But when one takes account of even the minimum trading costs that would be generated by small filters, their advantage over buy-and-hold disappears. For example, even a floor trader (i.e., a person who owns a seat) on the New York Stock Exchange must pay clearinghouse fees on his trades that amount to about 0.1% per turnaround transaction (i.e., sales plus purchase). Fama-Blume show that because small filters produce such frequent trades, these minimum trading costs are sufficient to wipe out their advantage over buy-and-hold.

Thus the filter tests, like the serial correlations, produce empirically noticeable departures from the strict implications of the efficient markets model. But, in spite of any statistical significance they might have, from an

---

[15] Though strictly speaking, such tests of pure independence are not directly relevant for expected return models, it is interesting that the conclusion that very short-term swings in prices persist slightly longer than would be expected under the martingale hypothesis is also supported by the results of non-parametric runs tests applied to the daily data of table 1. (See Fama 1965, Tables 12-15.) For the daily prices changes, the actual number of runs of price changes of the same sign is less than the expected number for 26 out of 30 stocks. Moreover, of the eight stocks for which the actual number of runs is more than two standard errors less than the expected number, five of the same stocks have positive daily, first order serial correlations in table 1 that are more than twice their standard errors. But in both cases the statistical "significance" of the results is largely a reflection of the large sample sizes. Just as the serial correlations are small in absolute terms (the average is 0.026), the differences between the expected and actual number of runs on average are only 3% of the total expected number. — On the other hand, it is also interesting that the runs tests do not support the suggestion of slight negative dependence in 4 and 9 day changes that appeared in the serial correlations. In the runs tests such negative dependence would appear as a tendency for the actual number of runs to exceed the expected number. In fact, for the 4 and 9 day price changes, for 17 and 18 of the 30 stocks in table 1 the actual number of runs is less than the expected number. Indeed, runs tests in general show no consistent evidence of dependence for any differencing interval longer than a day, which seems especially pertinent in light of the comments in footnote 14.

economic viewpoint the departures are so small that it seems hardly justified to use them to declare the market inefficient.

2.0.2. *Other tests of independence in the random walk literature*

It is probably best to regard the random walk model as a special case of the more general expected return model in the sense of making a more detailed specification of the economic environment. That is, the basic model of market equilibrium is the "fair game" expected return model, with a random walk arising when additional environmental conditions are such that distributions of one-period returns repeat themselves through time. From this viewpoint violations of the pure independence assumption of the random walk model are to be expected. But when judged relative to the benchmark provided by the random walk model, these violations can provide insights into the nature of the market environment.

For example, one departure from the pure independence assumption of the random walk model has been noted by Osborne (1962), Fama (1965, Table 17 and Figure 8), and others. In particular, large daily price changes tend to be followed by large daily changes. The signs of the successor changes are apparently random, however, which indicates that the phenomenon represents a denial of the random walk model but not of the market efficiency hypothesis. Nevertheless, it is interesting to speculate why the phenomenon might arise. It may be that when important new information comes into the market, it cannot always be immediately evaluated precisely. Thus, sometimes the initial price will overadjust to the information, and other times it will underadjust. But since the evidence indicates that the price changes on days following the initial large change are random in sign, the initial large change at least represents an unbiased adjustment to the ultimate price effects of the information, and this is sufficient for the expected return efficient markets model.

Niederhoffer and Osborne (1966) document two departures from complete randomness in common stock price changes from transaction to transaction. First, their data indicate that reversals (pairs of consecutive price changes of opposite sign) are from two to three times as likely as continuations (pairs of consecutive price changes of the same sign). Second, a continuation is slightly more frequent after a preceding continuation than after a reversal. That is, let $(+|++)$ indicate the occurrence of a positive price change, given two preceding positive changes. Then the events

$(+|++)$ and $(-|--)$ are slightly more frequent than $(+|+-)$ or $(-|-+)$.[16]

Niederhoffer and Osborne offer explanations for these phenomena based on the market structure of the New York Stock Exchange (N.Y.S.E.). In particular, there are three major types of orders that an investor might place in a given stock: (a) buy limit (buy at a specified price or lower), (b) sell limit (sell at a specified price or higher), and (c) buy or sell at market (at the lowest selling or highest buying price of another investor). A book of unexecuted limit orders in a given stock is kept by the specialist in that stock on the floor of the exchange. Unexecuted sell limit orders are, of course, at higher prices than unexecuted buy limit orders. On both exchanges, the smallest non zero price change allowed is $\frac{1}{8}$ point.

Suppose now that there is more than one unexecuted sell limit order at the lowest price of any such order. A transaction at this price (initiated by an order to buy at market[17]) can only be followed either by a transaction at the same price (if the next market order is to buy) or by a transaction at a lower price (if the next market order is to sell). Consecutive price increases can usually only occur when consecutive market orders to buy exhaust the sell limit orders at a given price.[18] In short, the excessive tendency toward reversal for consecutive non zero price changes could result from bunching of unexecuted buy and sell limit orders.

The tendency for the events $(+|++)$ and $(-|--)$ to occur slightly more frequently than $(+|+-)$ and $(-|-+)$ requires a more involved explanation which we shall not attempt to reproduce in full here. In brief, Niederhoffer and Osborne contend that the higher frequency of $(+|++)$ relative to $(+|+-)$ arises from a tendency for limit orders "to be concentrated at integers (26, 43), halves ($26\frac{1}{2}$, $43\frac{1}{2}$), even eighths and odd eighths in descending order of preference".[19] The frequency of the event $(+|++)$,

---

[16] On a transaction to transaction basis, positive and negative price changes are about equally likely. Thus, under the assumption that price changes are random, any pair of non zero changes should be as likely as any other, and likewise for triplets of consecutive non zero changes.

[17] A buy limit order for a price equal to or greater than the lowest available sell limit price is effectively an order to buy at market, and is treated as such by the broker.

[18] The exception is when there is a gap of more than $\frac{1}{8}$ between the highest unexecuted buy limit and the lowest unexecuted sell limit order, so that market orders (and new limit orders) can be crossed at intermediate prices.

[19] Their empirical documentation for this claim is a few samples of specialists' books for selected days, plus the observation (Osborne 1962) that actual trading prices, at least for volatile high priced stocks, seem to be concentrated at integers, halves, quarters and odd eighths in descending order.

which usually requires that sell limit orders be exhausted at at least two consecutively higher prices (the last of which is relatively more frequently at an odd eighth), more heavily reflects the absence of sell limit orders at odd eighths than the event $(+|+-)$, which usually implies that sell limit orders at only one price have been exhausted and so more or less reflects the average bunching of limit orders at all eighths.

But though Niederhoffer and Osborne present convincing evidence of statistically significant departures from independence in price changes from transaction to transaction, and though their analysis of their findings presents interesting insights into the process of market making on the major exchanges, the types of dependence uncovered do not imply market inefficiency. The best documented source of dependence, the tendency toward excessive reversals in pairs of non zero price changes, seems to be a direct result of the ability of investors to place limit orders as well as orders at market, and this negative dependence in itself does not imply the existence of profitable trading rules. Similarly, the apparent tendency for observed transactions (and, by implication, limit orders) to be concentrated at integers, halves, even eighths and odd eighths in descending order is an interesting fact about investor behavior, but in itself is not a basis on which to conclude that the market is inefficient.[20]

The Niederhoffer-Osborne analysis of market making does, however, point to the existence of market inefficiency, with respect to *strong form* tests of the efficient markets model. In particular, the list of unexecuted buy and sell limit orders in the specialist's book is important information about the likely future behavior of prices, and this information is only available to the specialist. When the specialist is asked for a quote, he gives the prices and can give the quantities of the highest buy limit and lowest sell limit orders on his book, but he is prevented by law from divulging the

---

[20] Niederhoffer and Osborne offer little to refute this conclusion. For example (1966, p. 914): "Although the specific properties reported in this study gave a significance from a statistical point of view, the reader may well ask whether or not they are helpful in a practical sense. Certain trading rules emerge as a result of our analysis. One is that limit and stop orders should be placed at odd eighths, preferably at 7/8 for sell orders and at 1/8 for buy orders. Another is to buy when a stock advances through a barrier and to sell when it sinks through a barrier." The first "trading rule" tells the investor to resist his innate inclination to place orders at integers, but rather to place sell orders $\frac{1}{8}$ below an integer and buy order $\frac{1}{8}$ above. Successful execution of the orders is then more likely, since the congestion of orders that occur at integers is avoided. But the cost of this success is apparent. The second "trading rule" seems no more promising, if indeed it can even be translated into a concrete prescription for action.

book's full contents. The interested reader can easily imagine situations where the structure of limit orders in the book could be used as the basis of a profitable trading rule.[21] But the record seems to speak for itself:

> It should not be assumed that these transactions undertaken by the specialist, and in which he is involved as buyer or seller in 24 per cent of all market volume, are necessarily a burden to him. Typically, the specialist sells above his last purchase on 83 per cent of all his sales, and buys below his last sale on 81 per cent of all his purchases. (Niederhoffer and Osborne 1966, p. 908.)

Thus it seems that the specialist has monopoly power over an important block of information, and, not unexpectedly, uses his monopoly to turn a profit. And this, of course, is evidence of market inefficiency in the strong form sense. The important economic question, of course, is whether the market making function of the specialist could be fulfilled more economically by some non-monopolistic mechanism.[22]

2.0.3. *Distributional evidence*

At this date the weight of the empirical evidence is such that economists would generally agree that whatever dependence exists in series of historical returns cannot be used to make profitable predictions of the future. Indeed, for returns that cover periods of a day or longer, there is little in the evidence that would cause rejection of the stronger random walk model, at least as a good first approximation.

Rather, the last burning issue of the random walk literature has centered on the nature of the distribution of price changes (which, we should note immediately, is an important issue for the efficient markets hypothesis since the nature of the distribution affects both the types of statistical tools relevant for testing the hypothesis and the interpretation of any results obtained). A model implying normally distributed price changes was first

---

[21] See, Niederhoffer and Osborne (1966, p. 908). But it is unlikely that anyone but the specialist could earn substantial profits from knowledge of the structure of unexecuted limit orders on the book. The specialist makes trading profits by engaging in many transactions, each of which has a small average profit; but for any other trader, including those with seats on the exchange, these profits would be eaten up by commissions to the specialist.

[22] With modern computers, it is hard to believe that a more competetive and economical system would not be feasible. It does not seem technologically impossible to replace the entire floor of the N.Y.S.E. with a computer, fed by many remote consoles, that kept all the books now kept by the specialists, that could easily make the entire book on any stock available to anybody (so that interested individuals could then compete to "make a market" in a stock) and that carried out transactions automatically.

proposed by Bachelier (1900), who assumed that price changes from transaction to transaction are independent, identically distributed random variables with finite variances. If transactions are fairly uniformly spread across time, and if the number of transactions per day, week, or month is very large, then the Central Limit Theorem leads us to expect that these price changes will have normal or Gaussian distributions.

Osborne (1959), Moore (1962), and Kendall (1953) all thought their empirical evidence supported the normality hypothesis, but all observed high tails (i.e., higher proportions of large observations) in their data distributions vis-à-vis what would be expected if the distributions were normal. Drawing on these findings and some empirical work of his own, Mandelbrot (1963) then suggested that these departures from normality could be explained by a more general form of the Bachelier model. In particular, if one does not assume that distributions of price changes from transaction to transaction necessarily have finite variances, then the limiting distributions for price changes over longer differencing intervals could be any member of the stable class, which includes the normal as a special case. Non-normal stable distributions have higher tails than the normal, and so can account for this empirically observed feature of distributions of price changes. After extensive testing (involving the data from the stocks in table 1), Fama (1965) concludes that non-normal stable distributions are a better description of distributions of daily returns on common stocks than the normal. This conclusion is also supported by the empirical work of Blume (1968) on common stocks, and it has been extended to U.S. Government Treasury Bills by Roll (1968).

Economists have, however, been reluctant to accept these results, primarily because of the wealth of statistical techniques available for dealing with normal variables and the relative paucity of such techniques for non-normal stable variables.[23] But perhaps the biggest contribution of

---

[23] Some have suggested that the long-tailed empirical distributions might result from processes that are mixtures of normal distributions with different variances. Press (1968), e.g., suggests a Poisson mixture of normals in which the resulting distributions of price changes have long tails but finite variances. On the other hand, Mandelbrot and Taylor (1967) show that other mixtures of normals can still lead to non-normal stable distributions of price changes for finite differencing intervals. — If, as Press' model would imply, distributions of price changes are long-tailed but have finite variances, then distributions of price changes over longer and longer differencing intervals should be progressively closer to the normal. No such convergence to normality was observed in Fama (1953) (though admittedly the techniques used were somewhat rough). Rather,

Mandelbrot's work has been to stimulate research on stable distributions and estimation procedures to be applied to stable variables. (See, e.g., Wise (1963), Fama and Roll (1968), and Blattberg and Sargent (1970), among others.) The advance of statistical sophistication (and the importance of examining distributional assumptions in testing the efficient markets model) is well illustrated in Roll (1968), as compared, e.g., with the early empirical work of Mandelbrot (1963) and Fama (1965).

2.0.4. *"Fair game" models in the treasury till market*

Roll's work is novel in other respects as well. Coming after the efficient markets models of Mandelbrot (1966) and Samuelson (1965), it is the first weak form empirical work that is consciously in the "fair game" rather than the random walk tradition.

More important, as we saw earlier, the "fair game" properties of the general expected return models apply to:

$$z_{jt} = r_{jt} - E(\tilde{r}_{jt} | \Phi_{t-1}). \tag{10}$$

For data on common stocks, tests of "fair game" (and random walk) properties seem to go well when the conditional expected return is estimated as the average return for the sample of data at hand. Apparently the variation in common stock returns about their expected values is so large relative to any changes in the expected values that the latter can safely be ignored. But, as Roll demonstrates, this result does not hold for Treasury Bills. Thus, to test the "fair game" model on Treasury Bills requires explicit economic theory for the evolution of expected returns through time.

Roll uses three existing theories of the term structure (the pure expectations hypothesis of Lutz (1940) and two market segmentation hypotheses, one of which is the familiar "liquidity preference" hypothesis of Hicks (1946) and Kessel 1965) for this purpose.[24] In his models r_{jt} is the rate observed from the term structure at period t for one week loans to commence at

---

except for origin and scale, the distributions for longer differencing intervals seem to have the "high-tailed" characteristics as distributions for shorter differencing intervals, which is as would be expected if the distributions are non-normal stable.

[24] As noted early in our discussions, all available tests of market efficiency are implicitly also tests of expected return models of market equilibrium. But Roll formulates explicitly the economic models underlying his estimates of expected returns, and emphasizes that he is simultaneously testing economic models of the term structure as well as market efficiency.

$t+j-1$, and can be thought of as a "futures" rate. Thus $r_{j+1,t-1}$ is likewise the rate on one week loans to commence at $t+j-1$, but observed in this case at $t-1$. Similarly, L_{jt} is the so-called "liquidity premium" in r_{jt}; that is:

$$r_{jt} = E(\tilde{r}_{0,t+j-1} \mid \Phi_t) + L_{jt}.$$

In words, the one-week "futures" rate for period $t+j-1$ observed from the term structure at t is the expectation at t of the "spot" rate for $t+j-1$ plus a "liquidity premium" (which could, however, be positive or negative).

In all three theories of the term structure considered by Roll, the conditional expectation required in (10) is of the form:

$$E(\tilde{r}_{j,t} \mid \Phi_{t-1}) = r_{j+1,t-1} + E(L_{jt} \mid \Phi_{t-1}) - L_{j+1,t-1}.$$

The three theories differ only in the values assigned to the "liquidity premiums". For example, in the "liquidity preference" hypothesis, investors must always be paid a positive premium for bearing interest rate uncertainty, so that the L_{jt} are always positive. By contrast, in the "pure expectations" hypothesis, all liquidity premiums are assumed to be zero, so that:

$$E(\tilde{r}_{jt} \mid \Phi_{t-1}) = r_{j+1,t-1}.$$

After extensive testing, Roll concludes (i) that the two market segmentation hypotheses fit the data better than the pure expectations hypothesis, with perhaps a slight advantage for the "liquidity preference" hypothesis, and (ii) that as far as his tests are concerned, the market for Treasury Bills is efficient. Indeed, it is interesting that when the best fitting term structure model is used to estimate the conditional expected "futures" rate in (10), the resulting variable z_{jt} seems to be serially independent! It is also interesting that if he simply assumed that his data distributions were normal, Roll's results would not be so strongly in support of the efficient markets model. In this case taking account of the observed high tails of the data distributions substantially affected the interpretation of the results.[25]

---

[25] The importance of distributional assumptions is also illustrated in Alexander's work on trading rules. In his initial tests of filter systems, Alexander (1961) assumed that purchases could always be executed exactly (rather than at least) $y\%$ above lows and sales exactly $y\%$ below highs. Mandelbrot (1963) pointed out, however, that though this assumption would do little harm with normally distributed price changes (since price series are then essentially continuous), with non-normal stable distributions it would introduce substantial positive bias into the filter profits (since with such distributions price series will show many discontinuities). In his later tests, Alexander (1964) does indeed find that taking account of the discontinuities (i.e., the presence of large price changes) in his data substantially lowers the profitability of the filters.

2.0.5. *Tests of a multiple security expected return model*

Though the weak form tests support the "fair game" efficient markets model, all of the evidence examined so far consists of what we might call "single security tests". That is, the price or return histories of individual securities are examined for evidence of dependence that might be used as the basis of a trading system for *that* security. We have not discussed tests of whether securities are "appropriately priced" vis-à-vis one another.

But to judge whether differences between average returns are "appropriate" an economic theory of equilibrium expected returns is required. At the moment, the only fully developed theory is that of Sharpe (1964) and Lintner (1965a, b) referred to earlier. In this model (which is a direct outgrowth of the mean-standard deviation portfolio models of investor equilibrium of Markowitz (1959) and Tobin (1958)), the expected return on security *j* from time *t* to *t*+1 is:

$$E(\tilde{r}_{j,t+1} \mid \Phi_t) = r_{f,t+1} + \left[\frac{E(\tilde{r}_{m,t+1} \mid \Phi_t) - r_{f,t+1}}{\sigma(\tilde{r}_{m,t+1} \mid \Phi_t)} \right] \frac{\mathrm{cov}(\tilde{r}_{j,t+1}, \tilde{r}_{m,t+1} \mid \Phi_t)}{\sigma(\tilde{r}_{m,t+1} \mid \Phi_t)}, \tag{11}$$

where $r_{f,t+1}$ is the return from *t* to *t*+1 on an asset that is riskless in money terms; $r_{m,t+1}$ is the return on the "market portfolio" *m* (a portfolio of all investment assets with each weighted in proportion to the total market value of all its outstanding units); $\sigma^2(\tilde{r}_{m,t+1} \mid \Phi_t)$ is the variance of the return on *m*; $\mathrm{cov}(\tilde{r}_{j,t+1}, \tilde{r}_{m,t+1} \mid \Phi_t)$ is the covariance between the returns on *j* and *m*; and the appearance of Φ_t indicates that the various expected returns, variance and covariance, could in principle depend on Φ_t. Though Sharpe and Lintner derive (11) as a one-period model, the result is given a multi-period interpretation in Fama (1970). The model has also been extended to the case where the one-period returns could have stable distributions with infinite variances by Fama (1971).

In words, (11) says that the expected one-period return on a security is the one-period riskless rate of interest $r_{f,t+1}$ plus a "risk premium" that is proportional to $\mathrm{cov}(\tilde{r}_{j,t+1}, \tilde{r}_{m,t+1} \mid \Phi_t)/\sigma(\tilde{r}_{m,t+1} \mid \Phi_t)$. In the Sharpe-Lintner model each investor holds some combination of the riskless asset and the market portfolio, so that, given a mean-standard deviation framework, the risk of an individual asset can be measured by its contribution to the standard deviation of the return on the market portfolio. This contribution is in fact cov $(\tilde{r}_{j,t+1}, \tilde{r}_{m,t+1} | \Phi_t)/\sigma(\tilde{r}_{m,t+1} | \Phi_t)$.[26] The factor:

$$[E(\tilde{r}_{m,t+1} | \Phi_t) - r_{f,t+1}]/\sigma(\tilde{r}_{m,t+1} | \Phi_t),$$

which is the same for all securities, is then regarded as the market price of risk.

Published empirical tests of the Sharpe-Lintner model are not yet available, though much work is in progress. There is some published work, however, which, though not directed at the Sharpe-Lintner model, is at least consistent with some of its implications. The stated goal of this work has been to determine the extent to which the returns on a given security are related to the returns on other securities. It started (again) with Kendall's (1953) finding that though common stock price changes do not seem to be serially correlated, there is a high degree of cross-correlation between the *simultaneous* returns of different securities. This line of attack was continued by King (1966), who (using factor analysis of a sample of monthly returns on sixty N.Y.S.E. stocks for the period 1926-60) found that on average about 50% of the variance of an individual stock's returns could be accounted for by a "market factor" which affects the returns on all stocks, with "industry factors" accounting for at most an additional 10% of the variance.

For our purposes, however, the work of Fama et al. (1969) (henceforth FFJR) and the more extensive work of Blume (1968) on monthly return data is more relevant. They test the following "market model", originally suggested by Markowitz (1959):

$$\tilde{r}_{j,t+1} = \alpha_j + \beta_j \tilde{r}_{M,t+1} + \tilde{u}_{j,t+1}, \tag{12}$$

where $r_{j,t+1}$ is the rate of return on security j for month t, $r_{M,t+1}$ is the corresponding return on a market index M, α_j and β_j are parameters that can vary from security to security, and $u_{j,t+1}$ is a random disturbance. The tests of FFJR and subsequently those of Blume indicate that (12) is well specified as a linear regression model in that (i) the estimated parameters $\hat{\alpha}_j$ and $\hat{\beta}_j$ remain fairly constant over long periods of time (e.g., the entire post-World War II period in the case of Blume), (ii) $r_{M,t+1}$ and the

---

[26] That is,

$$\sum_j \text{cov}\,(\tilde{r}_{j,t+1}, \tilde{r}_{m,t+1} | \Phi_t)/\sigma(\tilde{r}_{m,t+1} | \Phi_t) = \sigma(\tilde{r}_{m,t+1} | \Phi_t)$$

estimated $\hat{u}_{j,t+1}$, are close to serially independent, and (iii) the $\hat{u}_{j,t+1}$ seem to be independent of $r_{M,t+1}$.

Thus the observed properties of the "market model" are consistent with the expected return efficient markets model, and, in addition, the "market model" tells us something about the process generating expected returns from security to security. In particular,

$$E(\tilde{r}_{j,t+1}) = \alpha_j + \beta_j E(\tilde{r}_{M,t+1}). \tag{13}$$

The question now is to what extent (13) is consistent with the Sharpe-Lintner expected return model summarized by (11). Rearranging (11) we obtain:

$$E(\tilde{r}_{j,t+1} \,|\, \Phi_t) = \alpha_j(\Phi_t) + \beta_j(\Phi_t) E(\tilde{r}_{m,t+1} \,|\, \Phi_t), \tag{14}$$

where, noting that the riskless rate $r_{f,t+1}$ is itself part of the information set Φ_t, we have:

$$\alpha_j(\Phi_t) = r_{f,t+1}[1 - \beta_j(\Phi_t)], \tag{15}$$

and:

$$\beta_j(\Phi_t) = \frac{\text{cov}\,(\tilde{r}_{j,t+1}, \tilde{r}_{m,t+1} \,|\, \Phi_t)}{\sigma^2(\tilde{r}_{m,t+1} \,|\, \Phi_t)}. \tag{16}$$

With some simplifying assumptions, (14) can be reduced to (13). In particular, if the covariance and variance that determine $\beta_j(\Phi_t)$ in (16) are the same for all t and Φ_t, then $\beta_j(\Phi_t)$ in (16) corresponds to β_j in (12) and (13), and the least squares *estimate* of β_j in (12) is in fact just the ratio of the sample values of the covariance and variance in (16). If we also assume that $r_{f,t+1}$ is the same for all t, and that the behavior of the returns on the market portfolio m are closely approximated by the returns on some representative index M, we will have come a long way toward equating (13) and (11). Indeed, the only missing link is whether in the estimated parameters of (12):

$$\hat{\alpha} \cong r_f(1 - \hat{\beta}_j). \tag{17}$$

Neither FFJR nor Blume attack this question directly, though some of Blume's evidence is at least promising. In particular, the magnitudes of the estimated $\hat{\alpha}_j$ are roughly consistent with (17) in the sense that the estimates are always close to zero (as they should be with monthly return data).[27]

In a sense, though, in establishing the apparent empirical validity of the "market model" of (12), both too much and too little have been shown *vis-à-vis* the Sharpe-Lintner expected return model of (11). We know that during the post-World War II period one-month interest rates on riskless assets (e.g., government bills with one month to maturity) have not been constant. Thus, if expected security returns were generated by a version of the "market model" that is fully consistent with the Sharpe-Lintner model, we would, according to (15), expect to observe some non-stationarity in the estimates of α_j. On a monthly basis, however, variation through time in one-period riskless interest rates is probably trivial relative to variation in other factors affecting monthly common stock returns, so that more powerful statistical methods would be necessary to study the effects of changes in the riskless rate.

In any case, since the work of FFJR and Blume on the "market model" was not concerned with relating this model to the Sharpe-Lintner model, we can only say that the results for the former are somewhat consistent with the implications of the latter. But the results for the "market model" are, after all, just a statistical description of the return generating process, and they are probably somewhat consistent with other models of equilibrium expected returns. Thus the only way to generate strong empirical conclusions about the Sharpe-Lintner model is to test it directly. On the other hand, any alternative model of equilibrium expected returns must be somewhat consistent with the "market model", given the evidence in its support.

2.1. *Tests of martingale models of the semi-strong form*

In general, semi-strong form tests of efficient markets models are concerned with whether current prices "fully reflect" all obviously publicly available

---

[27] With least squares applied to monthly return data, the estmate of α_j in (12) is

$$\hat{\alpha}_j = \bar{r}_{j,t} - \hat{\beta}_j \bar{r}_{m,t},$$

where the bars indicate sample mean returns. But, in fact, Blume applies the market model to the wealth relatives $R_{jt} = 1 + r_{jt}$ and $R_{mt} = 1 + r_{mt}$. This yields precisely the same estimate of β_j as least squares applied to (12), but the intercept is now

$$\hat{\alpha}_j = \bar{R}_j \bar{R}_{Mt} = 1 + \bar{r}_{jt} - \hat{\beta}_j (1 + \bar{r}_{Mt}) = 1 - \hat{\beta}_j + \hat{\alpha}_j.$$

Thus, what Blume in fact finds is that for almost all securities, $\hat{\alpha}_j + \hat{\beta}_j \cong 1$, which implies that $\hat{\alpha}_j$ is close to 0.

information. Each individual test, however, is concerned with the adjustment of security prices to one kind of information generating event (e.g., stock splits, announcements of financial reports by firms, new security issues, etc.). Thus each test only brings supporting evidence for the model, with the idea that by accumulating such evidence the validity of the model will be "established".

In fact, however, though the available evidence is in support of the efficient markets model, it is limited to a few major types of information generating events. The initial major work is apparently the study of stock splits by FFJR, and all the subsequent studies summarized here are adaptations and extensions of the techniques developed in FFJR. Thus, this paper will first be reviewed in some detail, and then the other studies will be considered.

2.1.0. *Splits and the adjustment of stock prices to new information*

Since the only apparent result of a stock split is to multiply the number of shares per shareholder without increasing claims to real assets, splits in themselves are not necessarily sources of new information. The presumption of FFJR is that splits may often be associated with the appearance of more fundamentally important information. The idea is to examine security returns around split dates to see first if there is any "unusual" behavior, and, if so, to what extent it can be accounted for by relationships between splits and other more fundamental variables.

The approach of FFJR to the problem relies heavily on the "market model" of (12). In this model if a stock split is associated with abnormal behavior, this would be reflected in the estimated regression residuals for the months surrounding the split. For a given split, define month 0 as the month in which the effective date of a split occurs, month 1 as the month immediately following the split month, month -1 as the month preceding, etc. Now define the average residual over all split securities for month m (where for each security m is measured relative to the split month) as:

$$u_m = \sum_{j=1}^{N} \frac{\hat{u}_{jm}}{N},$$

where $\hat{u}_{jm}$ is the sample regression residual for security j in month m, and N is the number of splits. Next, define the cumulative average residual

U_m as:

$$U_m = \sum_{k=-29}^{m} u_k .$$

The average residual u_m can be interpreted as the average deviation (in month m relative to split months) of the returns of split stocks from their normal relationships with the market. Similarly, U_m can be interpreted as the cumulative deviation (from month -29 to month m). Finally, define u_m^+, u_m^-, U_m^+, and U_m^- as the average and cumulative average residuals for splits followed by "increased" $(+)$ and "decreased" $(-)$ dividends. An "increase" is a case where the percentage change in dividends on the split share in the year after the split is greater than the percentage change for the N.Y.S.E. as a whole, while a "decrease" is a case of relative dividend decline.

The essence of the results of FFJR are then summarized in fig. 1, which shows the cumulative average residuals U_m, U_m^+, and U_m^- for $-29 \le m \le 30$. The sample includes all 940 stock splits on the N.Y.S.E. from 1927-59, where the exchange was at least five new shares for four old, and where the security was listed for at least 12 months before and after the split.

For all three dividend categories the cumulative average residuals rise in the 29 months prior to the split, and in fact the average residuals (not shown here) are uniformly positive. This cannot be attributed to the splitting process, since in only about 10% of the cases is the time between the announcement and effective dates of a split greater than 4 months. Rather, it seems that firms tend to split their shares during "abnormally" good times — that is, during periods when the prices of their shares have increased more than would be implied by their normal relationships with general market prices, which itself probably reflects a sharp improvement, relative to the market, in the earnings prospects of these firms sometime during the years immediately preceding a split.[28]

---

[28] It is important to note, however, that as FFJR indicate, the persistent upward drift of the cumulative average residuals in the months preceding the split is not a phenomenon that could be used to increase expected trading profits. The reason is that the behavior of the average residuals is not representative of the behavior of the residuals for individual securities. In months prior to the split, successive sample residuals for individual securities seem to be independent. But in most cases, there are a few months in which the residuals are abnormally large and positive. The months of large residuals differ from security to security, however, and these differences in timing explain why the signs of the residuals are uniformly positive for many months preceding the split.

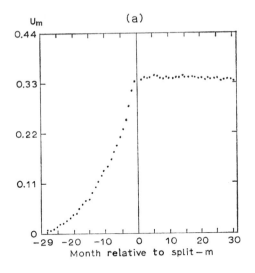

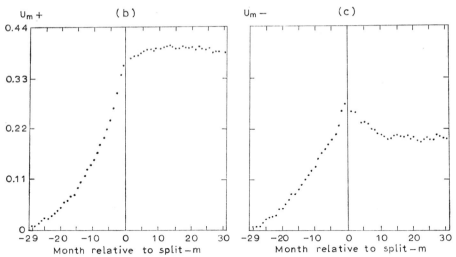

Fig. 1. Cumulative average residuals: (a) all splits. — (b) for dividend "increases". — (c) for dividend "decreases".

After the split month there is almost no further movement in U_m, the cumulative average residual for all splits. This is striking, since 71.5% (672 out of 940) of all splits experienced greater percentage dividend increases in the year after the split than the average for all securities on the

N.Y.S.E. In light of this, FFJR suggest that when a split is announced the market interprets this (and correctly so) as a signal that the company's directors are probably confident that future earnings will be sufficient to maintain dividend payments at a higher level. Thus the large price increases in the months immediately preceding a split may be due to an alteration in expectations concerning the future earning potential of the firm, rather than to any intrinsic effects of the split itself.

If this hypothesis is correct, return behavior subsequent to splits should be substantially different for the cases where the dividend increase materializes than for the cases where it does not. FFJR argue that in fact the differences are in the directions that would be predicted. The fact that the cumulative average residuals for the "increased" dividends (fig. 1b) drift upward but only slightly in the year *after* the split is consistent with the hypothesis that when the split is *declared*, there is a price adjustment in anticipation of future dividend increases. But the behavior of the residuals for stock splits associated with "decreased" dividends offers even stronger evidence for the split hypothesis. The cumulative average residuals for these stocks (fig. 1c) rise in the few months before the split, but then fall dramatically in the few months after the split when the anticipated dividend increase is not forthcoming. When a year has passed after the split, the cumulative average residual has fallen to about where it was 5 months prior to the split, which is about the earliest time reliable information about a split is likely to reach the market. Thus by the time it becomes clear that the anticipated dividend increase is not forthcoming, the apparent effects of the split seem to have been wiped away, and the stock's returns have reverted to their normal relationship with market returns.

Finally, and most important, although the behavior of post-split returns will be very different depending on whether or not dividend "increases" occur, and in spite of the fact that a large majority of split securities do experience dividend "increases", when all splits are examined together (fig. 1a), subsequent to the split there is no net movement up or down in the cumulative average residuals. Thus, apparently the market makes unbiased forecasts of the implications of a split for future dividends, and these forecasts are fully reflected in the price of the security by the end of the split month. After considerably more data analysis than can be summarized here, FFJR conclude that their results lend considerable support to the conclusion that the stock market is efficient, at least with respect to its ability to adjust to the information implicit in a split.

2.1.1. *Other studies of public announcements*

Variants of the method of residual analysis developed in FFJR have been used by others to study the effects of different kinds of public announcements, and all of these also support the efficient markets hypothesis.

Thus using data on 261 major firms for the period 1946-66, Ball and Brown (1968) apply the method to study the effects of annual earnings announcements. They use the residuals from a time series regression of the annual earnings of a firm on the average earnings of all their firms to classify the firm's earnings for a given year as having "increased" or "decreased" relative to the market. Residuals from regressions of monthly common stock returns on an index of returns (i.e., the market model of (12)) are then used to compute cumulative average return residuals separately for the earnings that "increased", and those that "decreased". The cumulative average return residuals rise throughout the year in advance of the announcement for the earnings "increased" category, and fall for the earnings "decreased" category.[29] Ball and Brown (1968, p. 175) conclude that in fact no more than about 10-15% of the information in the annual earnings announcement has not been anticipated by the month of the announcement.

On the macro level, Waud (1970) has used the method of residual analysis to examine the effects of announcements of discount rate changes by Federal Reserve Banks. In this case the residuals are essentially just the deviations of the daily returns on the Standard and Poor's 500 Index from the average daily return. He finds evidence of a statistically significant "announcement effect" on stock returns for the first trading day following an announcement, but the magnitude of the adjustment is small, never exceeding 0.5%. More interesting from the viewpoint of the efficient hypothesis is his conclusion that, if anything, the market anticipates the announcements (or information is somehow leaked in advance). This conclusion is based on the non-random patterns of the signs of average return residuals on the days immediately preceding the announcement.

Further evidence in support of the efficient markets hypothesis is provided in the work of Scholes (1969) on large secondary offerings of common stock (i.e., large underwritten sales of existing common stocks by individuals and institutions) and on new issues of stock. He finds that, on average,

---

[29] But the comment of footnote 28 is again relevant here.

large secondary issues are associated with a decline of between 1 and 2%
in the cumulative average residual returns for the corresponding common
stocks. Since the magnitude of the price adjustment is unrelated to the size of
the issue, Scholes concludes that the adjustment is not due to "selling
pressure" (as is commonly believed), but rather results from negative
information implicit in the fact that somebody is trying to sell a large block
of a firm's stock. Moreover, he presents evidence that the value of the
information in a secondary depends to some extent on the vendor. As might
be expected, by far the largest negative cumulative average residuals occur
where the vendor is the corporation itself or one of its officers, with
investment companies a distant second. But the identity of the vendor is not
generally known at the time of the secondary, and corporate insiders need
only report their transactions in their own company's stock to the S.E.C.
within 6 days after a sale. By this time the market on average has fully
adjusted to the information in the secondary, as indicated by the fact that
the average residuals behave randomly thereafter.

Note, however, that though this is evidence that prices adjust efficiently
to public information, it is also evidence that corporate insiders at least
sometimes have important information about their firm that is not yet
publicly known. Thus Scholes' evidence for secondary distributions provides
support for the efficient markets model in the semi-strong form sense, but
also some strong-form evidence *against* the model.

Though his results here are only preliminary, Scholes also reports on an
application of the method of residual analysis to a sample of 696 new issues
of common stock during the period 1926-66. As in the FFJR study of splits,
the cumulative average residuals rise in the months preceding the new
security offering (suggesting that new issues tend to come after favorable
recent events)[30] but behave randomly in the months following the offering
(indicating that whatever information is contained in the new issue is on
average fully reflected in the price of the month of the offering).

In short, the available semi-strong form evidence on the effects of various
sorts of public announcements on common stock returns is all consistent
with the efficient markets model. The strong point of the evidence, however,
is its consistency rather than its quantity; in fact, few different types of
public information have been examined, though those treated are among
the obviously most important. Moreover, as we shall now see, the amount

---

[30] Footnote 28 is again relevant here.

of semi-strong form evidence is voluminous compared to the strong form tests that are available.

2.2. *Strong form tests of the efficient markets models*

The strong form tests of the efficient markets model are concerned with whether all available information is fully reflected in prices in the sense that no individual has higher expected trading profits than others because he has monopolistic access to some information. We would not, of course, expect this model to be an exact description of reality, and indeed, the preceding discussions have already indicated the existence of contradictory evidence. In particular, Niederhoffer and Osborne (1966) have pointed out that specialists on the N.Y.S.E. apparently use their monopolistic access to information concerning unfilled limit orders to generate monopoly profits, and Scholes' (1969) evidence indicates that officers of corporations sometimes have monopolistic access to information about their firms.

Since we already have enough evidence to determine that the model is not strictly valid, we can now turn to other interesting questions. Specifically, how far down through the investment community do deviations from the model permeate? Does it pay for the average investor (or the average economist) to expend resources searching out little known information? Are such activities even generally profitable for various groups of market "professionals"? More generally, who are the people in the investment community that have access to "special information"?

Though this is a fascinating problem, only one group has been studied in any depth — the managements of open end mutual funds. Several studies are available (e.g., Sharpe (1965, 1966) and Treynor (1965)), but the most thorough are Jensen's (1968, 1969), and our comments will be limited to his work. We shall first present the theoretical model underlying his tests, and then go on to his empirical results.

2.2.0. *Theoretical framework*

In studying the performance of mutual funds the major goals are to determine (a) whether in general fund managers seem to have access to special information which allows them to generate "abnormal" expected returns, and (b) whether some funds are better at uncovering such special information than others. Since the criterion will simply be the ability of funds to produce higher returns than some norm with no attempt to determine what is responsible for the high returns, the "special information" that leads to high performance could be either keener insight into the implications of publicly available information than is implicit in market prices or monopolistic access to specific information. Thus the tests of the performance of the mutual fund industry are not strictly strong form tests of the efficient markets model.

The major theoretical (and practical) problem in using the mutual fund industry to test the efficient markets model is developing a "norm" against which performance can be judged. The norm must represent the results of an investment policy based on the assumption that prices fully reflect all available information. And if one believes that investors are generally risk averse and so on average must be compensated for any risks undertaken, then one has the problem of finding appropriate definitions of risk and evaluating each fund relative to a norm with its chosen level of risk.

Jensen uses the Sharpe (1964) - Lintner (1965a, b) model of equilibrium expected returns discussed above to derive a norm consistent with these goals. From (14)-(16), in this model the expected return on an asset or portfolio j from t to $t+1$ is:

$$E(\tilde{r}_{j,t+1} \mid \Phi_t) = r_{f,t+1}[1 - \beta_j(\Phi_t)] + E(\tilde{r}_{m,t+1} \mid \Phi_t)\,\beta_j(\Phi_t), \tag{18}$$

where the various symbols are defined as in section 2.0.5. But (18) is an *ex ante* relationship, and to evaluate performance an *ex post* norm is needed. One way the latter can be obtained is to substitute the realized return on the market portfolio for the expected return in (18) with the result[31]:

$$E(\tilde{r}_{j,t+1} \mid \Phi_t, r_{m,t+1}) = r_{f,t+1}[1 - \beta_j(\Phi_t)] + r_{m,t+1}\beta_j(\Phi_t). \tag{19}$$

Geometrically, (19) says that within the context of the Sharpe-Lintner model, the expected return on j (given information Φ_t and the return $r_{m,t+1}$ on the market portfolio) is a linear function of its risk:

$$\beta_j(\Phi_t) = \text{cov}\,(\tilde{r}_{j,t+1}, \tilde{r}_{m,t+1} \mid \Phi_t)/\sigma^2(\tilde{r}_{m,t+1} \mid \Phi_t),$$

as indicated in fig. 2. Assuming that the value of $\beta_j(\Phi_t)$ is somehow known, or can be reliably estimated, if j is a mutual fund, its *ex post* performance

---

[31] The assumption here is that the return $\tilde{r}_{j,t+1}$ is generated according to:

$$\tilde{r}_{j,t+1} = r_{f,t+1}[1 - \beta_j(\Phi_t)] + r_{m,t+1}\beta_j(\Phi_t) + \tilde{u}_{j,t+1},$$

where

$$E(\tilde{u}_{j,t+1} \mid r_{m,t+1}) = 0 \text{ for all } r_{m,t+1}.$$

from t to $t+1$ might now be evaluated by plotting its combination of realized return $r_{j,t+1}$ and risk in fig. 2. If (as for the point a) the combination falls above the expected return line (or, as it is more commonly called, the "market line"), it has done better than would be expected given its level of risk, while if (as for the point b) it falls below the line it has done worse.

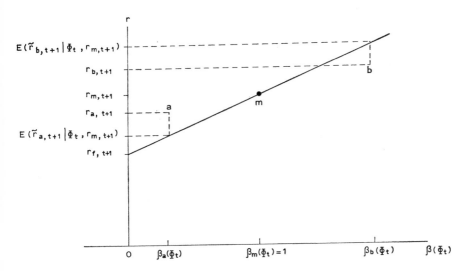

Fig. 2. Performance evaluation graph.

Alternatively, the market line shows the combinations of return and risk provided by portfolios that are simple mixtures of the riskless asset and the market portfolio m. The returns and risks for such portfolios (call them c) are:

$$r_{c,t+1} = \alpha r_{f,t+1} + (1-\alpha) r_{m,t+1}$$

$$\beta_c(\Phi_t) = \frac{\text{cov}(\tilde{r}_{c,t+1}, \tilde{r}_{m,t+1} | \Phi_t)}{\sigma^2(\tilde{r}_{m,t+1} | \Phi_t)} = \frac{\text{cov}((1-\alpha)\tilde{r}_{m,t+1}, \tilde{r}_{m,t+1} | \Phi_t)}{\sigma^2(\tilde{r}_{m,t+1} | \Phi_t)} = 1-\alpha,$$

where α is the proportion of portfolio funds invested in the riskless asset. Thus, when $1 \geq \alpha \geq 0$ we obtain the combinations of return and risk along the market line from $r_{f,t+1}$ to m in fig. 2, while when $\alpha < 0$ (and under the assumption that investors can borrow at the same rate that they lend) we obtain the combinations of return and risk along the extension of the line through *m*. In this interpretation, the market line represents the results of a naive investment strategy, which the investor who thinks prices reflect all available information might follow. The performance of a mutual fund is then measured relative to this naive strategy.

2.2.1. *Empirical results*

Jensen uses this risk-return framework to evaluate the performance of 115 mutual funds over the 10-year period 1955-64. He argues at length for measuring return as the nominal 10-year rate with continuous compounding (i.e., the natural log of the ratio of terminal wealth after 10 years to initial wealth) and for using historical data on nominal 1-year rates with continuous compounding to estimate risk. The Standard and Poor Index of 500 major common stocks is used as the proxy for the market portfolio.

The general question to be answered is whether mutual fund managements have any special insights or information which allows them to earn returns above the norm. But Jensen attacks the question on several levels. First, can the funds in general do well enough to compensate investors for loading charges, management fees, and other costs that might be avoided by simply choosing the combination of the riskless asset *f* and the market portfolio *m* with risk level comparable to that of the fund's actual portfolio? The answer seems to be an emphatic no. As far as net returns to investors are concerned, in 89 out of 115 cases, the fund's risk-return combination for the 10-year period is below the market line for the period, and the average over all funds of the deviations of 10 year returns from the market time is -14.6%. That is, on average the consumer's wealth after 10 years of holding mutual funds is about 15% less than if he held the corresponding portfolios along the market line.

But the loading charge that an investor pays in buying into a fund is usually a pure salesman's commission that the fund itself never gets to invest. Thus one might ask whether, ignoring loading charges (i.e., assuming no such charges were paid by the investor), in general fund managements can earn returns sufficiently above the norm to cover all other expenses that are presumably more directly related to the management of the fund portfolios. Again, the answer seems to be no. Even when loading charges are ignored in computing returns, the risk-return combinations for 72 out of 115 funds are below the market line, and the average deviation of 10 year returns from the market line is -8.9%.

Finally, as a somewhat stronger test of the efficient markets model, one would like to know if, ignoring all expenses, fund managements in general showed any ability to pick securities that outperformed the norm. Unfortunately, this question cannot be answered with precision for individual funds since, curiously, data on brokerage commissions are not published regularly. But Jensen suggests the available evidence indicates that the answer to the question is again probably negative. Specifically, adding back all other published expenses of funds to their returns, the risk-return combinations for 58 out of 115 funds were below the market line, and the average deviation of 10 year returns from the line was -2.5%. But part of this result is due to the absence of a correction for brokerage commissions. Estimating these commissions from average portfolio turnover rates for all funds for the period 1953-58 and adding them back to returns for all funds increases the average deviation from the market line from -2.5% to 0.09%, which still is not indicative of the existence of special information among mutual fund managers.

But though mutual fund managers in general do not seem to have access to information not already fully reflected in prices, perhaps there are individual funds that consistently do better than the norm, and so provide at least some strong form evidence against the efficient markets model. If there are such funds, however, they escape Jensen's search. For example, for individual funds, returns above the norm in one subperiod do not seem to be associated with performance above the norm in other subperiods. And regardless of how returns are measured (i.e., net or gross of loading charges and other expenses), the number of funds with large positive deviations of returns from the market line of fig. 2 is less than the number that would be expected by chance with 115 funds under the assumption that fund managements have no special talents in predicting returns.[32]

Jensen argues that though his results apply to only one segment of the

---

[32] On the other hand, there is some suggestion in Scholes' (1969) work on secondary issues that mutual funds may occasionally have access to "special information". After corporate insiders, the next largest negative price changes occur when the secondary seller is an investment company (including mutual funds), though on average the price changes are much smaller (i.e., closer to 0) than when the seller is a corporate insider. — Moreover, Jensen's evidence itself, though not indicative of the existence of special information among mutual fund managers, is not sufficiently precise to conclude that such information never exists. This stronger conclusion would require exact data on unavoidable expenses (including brokerage commissions) of portfolio management incurred by funds.

investment community, they are nevertheless striking evidence in favor of the efficient markets model:

> Although these results certainly do not imply that the strong form of the martingale hypothesis holds for all investors and for all time, they provide strong evidence in support of that hypothesis. One must realize that these analysts are extremely well endowed. Moreover, they operate in the securities markets every day and have wide-ranging contacts and associations in both the business and financial communities. Thus, the fact that they are apparently unable to forecast returns accurately enough to recover their research and transactions costs is a striking piece of evidence in favor of the strong form of the martingale hypothesis at least as far as the extensive subset of information available to these analysts is concerned (Jensen 1969, p. 170).

3. Summary and conclusions

The preceding analysis can be summarized as follows: in general terms, the theory of efficient markets in concerned with whether prices at any point in time "fully reflect" available information. The theory has empirical content, however, only within the context of a more specific model of market equilibrium, that is, a model that specifies the nature of market equilibrium when prices "fully reflect" available information. We have seen that all of the available empirical literature is implicitly or explicitly based on the assumption that the conditions of market equilibrium can be stated in terms of expected returns. This assumption is the basis of the expected return or "fair game" efficient markets models.

The empirical work itself can be divided into three categories depending on the nature of the information subset of interest. *Strong-form* tests are concerned with whether individual investors or groups have monopolistic access to any information relevant for price formation. One would not expect such an extreme model to be an exact description of the world, and it is probably best viewed as a benchmark against which the importance of deviations from market efficiency can be judged. In the less restrictive *semi-strong-form* tests the information subset of interest includes all obviously publicly available information, while in the *weak form* tests the information subset is just historical price or return sequences.

Weak form tests of the efficient markets model are the most voluminous, and it seems fair to say that the results are strongly in support. Though statistically significant evidence for dependence in successive price changes or returns has been found, some of this is consistent with the "fair game" model and the rest does not appear to be sufficient to declare the market inefficient. Indeed, at least for price changes or returns covering a day or longer, there is not much evidence against the more ambitious offspring of the "fair game" model, the random walk.

Thus, there is consistent evidence of positive dependence in day-to-day price changes and returns on common stocks, and the dependence is of a form that can be used as the basis of marginally profitable trading rules. In Fama's (1965) data the dependence shows up as serial correlations that are consistently positive but also consistently close to zero, and as a slight tendency for observed numbers of runs of positive and negative price changes to be less than the numbers that would be expected from a purely random process. More important, the dependence also shows up in the filter tests of Alexander (1961, 1964) and those of Fama and Blume (1966) as a tendency for very small filters to produce profits in excess of buy-and-hold. But any systems (like the filters) that attempt to turn such short-term dependence into trading profits of necessity generate so many transactions that their expected profits would be absorbed by even the minimum commissions (security handling fees) that floor traders on major exchanges must pay. Thus, using a less than completely strict interpretation of market efficiency, this positive dependence does not seem of sufficient importance to warrant rejection of the efficient markets model.

Evidence in contradiction of the "fair game" efficient markets model for price changes or returns covering periods longer than a single day is more difficult to find. Cootner (1962), and Moore (1962) report preponderantly negative (but again small) serial correlations in weekly common stock returns, and this result appears also in the 4-day returns analyzed by Fama (1965). But it does not appear in runs tests of Fama (1965), where, if anything, there is some slight indication of positive dependence, but actually not much evidence of any dependence at all. In any case, there is no indication that whatever dependence exists in weekly returns can be used as the basis of profitable trading rules.

Other existing evidence of dependence in returns provides interesting insights into the process of price formation in the stock market, but it is not relevant for testing the efficient markets model. For example, Fama (1965) shows that large daily price changes tend to be followed by large changes, but of unpredictable sign. This suggests that important information cannot be completely evaluated immediately, but that the initial (first day's) adjustment of prices to the information is unbiased, which is sufficient for the martingale model. More interesting and important, however, is the Niederhoffer-Osborne (1966) finding of a tendency toward excessive reversals in common stock price changes from transaction to transaction. They explain this as a logical result of the mechanism whereby orders to buy and sell at market are matched against existing limit orders on the books of the specialist. Given the way this tendency toward excessive reversals arises, however, there seems to be no way it can be used as the basis of a profitable trading rule. As they rightly claim, their results are a strong refutation of the theory of random walks, at least as applied to price changes from transaction to transaction, but they do not constitute refutation of the economically more relevant "fair game" efficient markets model.

Semi-strong form tests, in which prices are assumed to fully reflect all obviously publicly available information, have also supported the efficient markets hypothesis. Thus Fama *et al.* (1969) find that the information in stock splits concerning the firm's future dividend payments is on average fully reflected in the price of a split share at the time of the split. Ball and Brown (1968) and Scholes (1969) come to similar conclusions with respect to the information contained in (i) annual earning announcements by firms and (ii) new issues and large block secondary issues of common stock. Though only a few different types of information generating events are represented here, they are among the more important, and the results are probably indicative of what can be expected in future studies.

As noted earlier, the strong-form efficient markets model, in which prices are assumed to fully reflect all available information, is probably best viewed as a benchmark against which deviations from market efficiency (interpreted in its strictest sense) can be judged. Two such deviations have in fact been observed. First, Niederhoffer and Osborne (1966) point out that specialists on major security exchanges have monopolistic access to information on unexecuted limit orders, information they use to generate trading profits. This raises the question of whether the "market making" function of the specialist (if indeed this is a meaningful economic function) could not as effectively be carried out by some other mechanism that did not imply monopolistic access to information. Second, Scholes (1969) finds that, not unexpectedly, corporate insiders often have monopolistic access to information about their firms.

At the moment, however, corporate insiders and specialists are the only two groups whose monopolistic access to information has been documented. There is no evidence that deviations from the strong form of the efficient markets model permeate down any further through the investment community. For the purposes of most investors the efficient markets model seems a good approximation to reality.

In short, the evidence in support of the efficient markets model is extensive, and (somewhat uniquely in economics) contradictory evidence is sparse. Nevertheless, we certainly do not want to leave the impression that all issues are closed. The old saw, "much remains to be done", is certainly relevant here. Indeed, as is often the case in successful scientific research, now that we know where we have been in the past, we are able to pose and, hopefully, to answer an even more interesting set of questions for the future. In this case the most pressing field of future endeavor is the development and testing of models of market equilibrium under uncertainty. When the processes generating equilibrium expected returns are better understood, we will have a better framework for more sophisticated tests of market efficiency.

References

Alexander, Sidney S., 1961, Price movements in speculative markets: trends or random walks. *Industrial Management Review* 2, May, 7-26. Reprinted in Cootner (1964), 199-218.

Alexander, Sidney S., 1964, Price movements in speculative markets: trends or random walks, No. 2. In: Cootner (1964), 338-72.

Bachelier, Louis, 1900, *Théorie de la spéculation.* Paris, Gauthier-Villars. Reprinted in English in Cootner (1964), 17-78.

Ball, Ray and Philip Brown, 1968, An empirical evaluation of accounting income numbers. *Journal of Accounting Research* 6, Autumn, 159-78.

Beaver, William, 1968, The information content of annual earnings announcements. In.: *Empirical research in accounting: selected studies*, supplement to Vol. 7 of the *Journal of Accounting Research*, 67-92.

Blattberg, Robert and Thomas Sargent, 1970, Regression with non-Gaussian disturbances: some sampling results. *Econometrica* (forthcoming).

Blume, Marshall, 1968, The assessment of portfolio performance. Unpublished Ph. D. thesis, University of Chicago. A paper summarizing much of this work has appeared in *Journal of Business*, April 1970.

Cootner, Paul, 1962, Stock prices: random vs. systematic changes. *Industrial Management Review* 3, Spring, 24-45. Reprinted in Cootner (1964), 231-52.

Cootner, Paul (ed.), 1964, *The random character of stock market prices.* Cambridge, Mass., The M.I.T. Press.

Fama, Eugene F., 1965, The behavior of stock market prices. *Journal of Business* 38, January, 34-105, 1971.

Fama, Eugene F., 1970, Multiperiod consumption-investment decisions. *American Economic Review*, March, 163-74.

Fama, Eugene F., 1971, Risk, return and equilibrium. *Journal of Political Economy*, January-February.

Fama, Eugene F. and Marshall Blume, 1966, Filter rules and stock market trading profits: *Journal of Business* 39 (Special Supplement, January), 226-41.

Fama, Eugene F., Lawrence Fisher, Michael Jensen, and Richard Roll, 1969, The Adjustment of Stock Prices to New Information. *International Economic Review* 10, February, 1-21.

Fama, Eugene F. and Richard Roll, 1968, Some properties of symmetric stable distributions. *Journal of the American Statistical Association* 63, September, 817-36.

Godfrey, Michael D., C.W.J. Granger, and O. Morgenstern, 1964, The Random Walk Hypothesis of Stock Market Behavior. *Kyklos* 17, 1-30.

Granger, C.W.J. and O. Morgenstern, 1963, Spectral analysis of New York stock market prices. *Kyklos* 16, 1-27. Reprinted in Cootner (1964), 162-187.

Hicks, John R., 1946, *Value and capital*. Oxford, The Clarendon Press.

Jensen, Michael, 1968, The performance of mutual funds in the period 1945-64. *Journal of Finance* 23, May, 389-416.

Jensen, Michael, 1969, Risk, the pricing of capital assets, and the evaluation of investment portfolios. *Journal of Business* 42, April, 167-247.

Kendall, Maurice G., 1953, The analysis of economic time-series. Part I : prices. *Journal of the Royal Statistical Society* 96, Part I, 11-25,

Kessel, Reuben A., 1965, The cyclical behavior of the term structure of interest rates. National Bureau of Economic Research Occasional Paper No. 91. New York, Columbia University Press.

King, Benjamin F., 1966, Market and industry factors in stock price behavior. *Journal of Business* 39 (Special Supplement, January), 139-90.

Lintner, John, 1965a, Security prices, risk, and maximal gains from diversification. *Journal of Finance* 20, December, 587-615.

Lintner, John, 1965b, The valuation of risk assets and the selection of risky investments in stock portfolios and capital budgets. *Review of Economics and Statistics* 47, Februay 13-37.

Lutz, Friedrich A., 1940-41, The structure of interest rates. *Quarterly Journal of Economics* 40.

Mandelbrot, Benoit, 1963, The variation of certain speculative prices. *Journal of Business* 36, October, 394-419.

Mandelbrot, Benoit, 1966, Forecasts of future prices, unbiased markets, and martingale models. *Journal of Business* 39 (Special Supplement, January), 242-55.

Mandelbrot, Benoit and Howard M. Taylor, 1967, On the distribution of stock price differences. *Operations Research* 15, November-December, 1057-62.

Markowitz, Harry, 1959, *Portfolio selection: efficient diversification of investment*. New York, John Wiley & Sons.

Moore, Arnold, 1962, A statistical analysis of common stock prices. Unpublished Ph. D. thesis, Graduate School of Business, University of Chicago.

Niederhoffer, Victor and M.F.M. Osboirne, 1966, Market making and reversal on the stock exchange, *Journal of the American Statistical Association* 61, December, 897-916.

Osborne, M.F.M., 1959, Brownian motion in the stock market. *Operations Research* 7, March-April, 145-73. Reprinted in Cootner (1964), 100-28.

Osborne, M.F.M., 1962, Periodic structure in the brownian motion of stock prices. *Operations Research* 10, May-June, 345-79. Reprinted in Cootner (1964), 262-96.

Press, S. James, 1968, A compound events model for security prices, *Journal of Business* 40, July, 317-35.

Roberts, Harry V., 1959, Stock market 'patterns' and financial analysis: methodological suggestions. *Journal of Finance* 14, March, 1-10.

Roll, Richard, 1968, The efficient market model applied to U.S. treasury till rates. Unpublished Ph. D. thesis, Graduate School of Business, University of Chicago.

Samuelson, Paul A., 1965, Proof that properly anticipated prices fluctuate randomly. *Industrial Management Review* 6, Spring, 41-9.

Scholes, Myron, 1969, A test of the competitive market hypothesis: the market for new issues and secondary offerings. Unpublished Ph. D. thesis, Graduate School of Business, University of Chicago.

Sharpe, William F., 1964, Capital asset prices: a theory of market equilibrium under conditions of risk. *Journal of Finance* 19, September, 425-42.

Sharpe, William F., 1965, Risk aversion in the stock market, *Journal of Finance* 20, September, 416-22.

Sharpe, William F., 1966, Mutual fund performance. *Journal of Business* 39 (Special Supplement, January), 119-38.

Tobin, James, 1958, Liquidity preference as behavior towards risk. *Review of Economic Studies* 25, February, 65-85.

Treynor, Jack L., 1965, How to rate management of investment funds. *Harvard Business Review* 43, January-February, 63-75.

Waud, Roger N., 1970, Public interpretation of discount rate changes: evidence on the "Announcement effect". *Econometrica* 38, March, 231-50.

Wise, John, 1963, Linear estimators for linear regression systems having infinite variances. Unpublished paper presented at the Berkeley-Stanford Mathematical Economics Seminar, October.

Working, Holbrook, 1934, A random difference series for use in the analysis of time series. *Journal of the American Statistical Association* 29, March, 11-24.

COMMENTS BY WILLIAM F. SHARPE

University of California, Irvine

Professor Fama deserves considerable praise for this excellent summary. He and his students have provided much of the key work in the area; it is thus fitting that he should be the first to bring the material together and to show so clearly the relationships of the various parts to the overall subject.

I find it worthwhile to step back from this subject every now and then, to see just what is being considered. Simply put, the thesis is this: in a well-functioning market, the prices of capital assets (securities) will reflect predictions based on all relevant and available information. This seems almost trivially self-evident to most professional economists — so much so, that testing seems rather silly. On the other hand, the idea seems truly revolutionary to the traditional security analyst. Only the most exhaustive testing could possibly convince some die-hard practitioners of the merits of the approach. Interestingly, professional economists appear to think more highly of professional investors than do other professional investors.

The replacement of the random-walk model with the more appealing martingale model seems very desirable. And I find the proposed classification scheme appealing, although the definition of a semi-strong martingale is clearly open to dispute (When is information publicly available? Which investors are in the public? How soon must the information be available? — at what price?).

The idea of a weak martingale is more clear-cut. As I understand it, the concept assumes the full use of past data concerning the factor being predicted. Since return is the object of primary interest, a careful formulation of the weak martingale should be based on past *returns* (i.e. prices *and* dividends), not just on prices. In fact, this is often done via "prices adjusted for dividends". But I would hope that in the future there will be more talk of *returns* and less of *prices per se*.

As Professor Fama indicates, the random-walk thesis requires much more than one would expect from market equilibrium conditions alone. Moreover, it is often misstated and/or misinterpreted (as is the more general martingale process). Let me illustrate. Assume that past data are properly reflected in current prices. Then, in a sense, the price of a security tells everything. But in another sense, it tells nothing. In a world in which there is risk-aversion, one should somehow find out which securities are more risky (and thus promise a relatively high expected return), and which are less risky (and thus promise a relatively low expected return). If security characteristics are reasonably stable over time, past data can be used to differentiate securities from one another in this respect. One could estimate risk directly, but it might be simpler to estimate expected return, since equilibrium conditions suggest that it is a good surrogate for risk. An obvious, and apparently sensible, procedure is to simply use the average return during some past period. This suggests that the *order* of the past data (returns) may not be important, although the data themselves will be. Thus it hardly follows (as some assert) that one should not look at past data at all. Only in a world in which investors are indifferent to risk would this be the case (since every security would then have the same expected return). This is not a very interesting world; but some statements in the literature make little sense in any other environment.

The idea of using past data to represent *ex ante* predictions raises some interesting questions. Two interpretations may be offered. One holds that predictions remain relatively constant over time, and that the data represent unbiased samples of those predictions. The other interpretation holds that investors do, in fact, make predictions by simply extrapolating past data. If so, past data provide estimates of the predictions currently being made by investors.

Both interpretations raise a crucial question. What, if any, reason does a corporation have to keep its securities from changing significantly over time? The empirical evidence suggests considerable stability — most notably in security risk (the β_j term in Professor Fama's paper). Why might this be so? I suspect that it arises because corporate officers know that significant changes in security characteristics impose costs on investors. There is the cost of not realizing that a change has occurred, as well as the cost associated with the set of transactions required to re-establish one's preferred position regarding risk vis-à-vis expected return. The true extent of this stability and the reasons for it clearly deserve additional investigation, as do the implications for the field of corporate finance.

The role of the specialist and his possible replacement by a computer-cum-algorithm raise some interesting (and essentially unanswered) questions. The current procedure leads to certain types of investor behavior. Most notably, a large majority of orders are placed "at market". If a computer were in charge, there might be a larger proportion of limit orders. Moreover, if the "book" were public knowledge, the number of limit orders might be further affected, since the submission of such an order would have two effects, one of which (conveying information directly to many other investors) is now absent. It is thus very difficult to predict the full implications of any particular proposed scheme (computer algorithm), let alone suggest the best procedure.

This is not the place to enter into the controversy concerning distributions of return. One potentially bothersome implication requires comment, however. In his dissertation, Blume suggests that the residuals around a security's characteristic line (i.e. the μ_j term in the "market model" described by Professor Fama) may follow a stable Paretian distribution with a characteristic exponent less than 2. This suggests that least-squares procedures may give poor estimates of security or portfolio volatility. As an alternative, one might fit a line that minimizes the sum of the absolute deviations. This is relatively simple, but the resulting estimates lack some of the key characteristics attributed to the model (in particular, the slope parameter of a portfolio may not equal the appropriately weighted average of the slope parameters of its component securities). Clearly, we could use a healthy dose of empirical research in this area.

Professor Fama differentiates "single security tests" from tests involving intersecurity comparisons. As an economist, I find the latter far more interesting. If there is risk-aversion, expected return should be correlated with risk. The key question concerns the appropriate measure of risk. As indicated, there is only one well-developed theory to cope with this problem. I am beginning to think of it as the "hyphenated theory", since it is usually titled by connecting several names with hyphens. Professor Fama has used Sharpe and Lintner, but others have added (quite rightfully) the names of Treynor and Mossin, as well as those of Markowitz and Tobin. In any event, the theory proposes a simple yet convincing measure of risk. I call it *volatility*, following Treynor; others call it simply *beta*. Whatever it is called, it measures the responsiveness of a security or portfolio's return to changes in the return on the market as a whole.

The crucial question is not what to name risk, but how to measure it. Since the riskless interest rate does, in fact, change from time to time, it may be preferable to regress excess return on the excess return on the market, thus:

$$(R_{it} - p_t) = b_i(R_{Mt} - p_t) + e_t,$$

where R_{it} = the return on security or portfolio i at time t; R_{Mt} = the return on the market at time t; p_t = the riskless or pure interest rate at time t; b_i = the volatility of security or portfolio i; and e_t = a residual or error term with (in theory) a mean value of zero.

But this is only one of a number of possible decisions one can make. Here are some others:

(1) *How should observations be weighted?*

Are more recent ones more important than less recent ones? How much more important? How long a period should be considered?

(2) *How often should observations be taken?*

Is the best differencing interval monthly, quarterly, annually?

(3) *Should one use return or the logarithm of the value relative?*

Is the appropriate differencing interval infinitely small? If so, a continuously compounded rate of return may be most appropriate. The logarithm of the value relative (to base *e*) provides such a value.

(4) *Should one use before-tax or after-tax values, and if the latter, at what tax rate?*

Virtually none of the theoretical or empirical work performed to date adequately accounts for income and capital-gains taxes; but differential treatment of these two components of return suggests that different results might be obtained if taxes were taken into account. Can a "representative" tax rate suffice for this purpose? How different will the results be?

(5) *What index should one use for the "market"?*

The Dow-Jones Industrial Average, Standard and Poor's 500 stocks, the average return on the securities on the New York stock exchange, or perhaps the return on any portfolio of 30 or more securities chosen at random?

(6) *What measure should one use for the "riskless" rate?*

Treasury Bill rates, the "prime" rate? Should bid prices be used, or ask prices, or an average of the two?

(7) *How should characteristic lines be estimated?*

Least-squares or mean-absolute deviation? Returns or excess returns? Should the line be forced through the point at which both returns equal the pure interest rate, or should it be allowed to go above or below that point?

(8) *How should one compute, interpret, and use "confidence" limits on estimated volatility?*

All these questions are undergoing empirical test, not only in academe, but also in the investment industry. We seem to have left the era of testing for serial correlation of security prices and to have entered the era in which we confront head-on the question of risk at both a theoretical and an empirical level. We have come a long way in the last few years. But, fortunately for our employment prospects, we still have a long way to go.

COMMENTS BY ROBERT A. SCHWARTZ
New York University

Professor Fama has successfully synthesized a large body of material in his review of theoretical and empirical work on financial capital markets.

Studies of (a) the random walk and martingale processes, (b) the effects of announcements of stock splits, of earnings, etc., and (c) the relative profitability of mutual funds, all have implications about the efficiency with which the capital market functions, and it is under the "roof" of efficiency implications that Fama has achieved a most valuable integration of studies which might otherwise appear to be quite disparate.

I wish to focus my comments on the efficiency implications derived from the analyses Professor Fama has discussed. While Fama appears to conclude that the capital market is basically efficient, I feel that, in relation to this most important and complex institution, questions of a critical disposition can and should be raised. I believe that Fama's very successful review would have been further enhanced by the inclusion of such questions; their articulation could, furthermore, usefully suggest future research.

Fama's definition of efficiency is simple and, for his purpose, serviceable. Fundamentally, he posits that the capital market is efficient (a) if all security prices fully reflect all known market information, and (b) if no traders in the market have monopoly control of information. He then presents a tri-chotomization of information: (1) a *strong form*, which encompasses all information, including that possessed by insiders; (2) a *semi-strong form*, which includes all public information; and (3) a *weak form*, which includes only that information which can be gleaned from an examination of an historical series of security prices. He uses this trichotomy to structure his discussion according to three classes of market studies.

Clearly, if markets are efficient in the strong form, then they must, as well, be efficient in both the semi-strong and weak forms. While noting the paucity of strong form oriented analyses, Fama presents evidence (the Neiderhoffer-Osborne, and Scholes studies) which he feels is sufficient to reject the hypothesis of strong form efficiency. On the other hand, he cites Jensen's mutual fund studies which quite strongly suggest that deviations from complete efficiency do not extend very far through the investment community.

In any event, Fama suggests that efficiency in the strong form is not clearly met, and we are thus led to consider analyses of the semi-strong form. Here, Fama cites his own study (with Fisher, Jensen and Roll) of the reaction of security prices to stock splits, Ball and Brown's study of price reaction to earnings announcements, Ward's examination of the effect of discount rate changes by the Federal Reserve banks, and Scholes' analysis of the effect on prices of large secondary offerings of common stock. In all cases, the observed affect on stock prices appears to preceed the event in issue; e.g., prices are observed to incorporate, fully and early, new information of the type considered in these studies. For instance, in their study of the effect of the announcement of stock splits, Fama et al. present evidence which suggests that investors cannot systematically realize profits from split securities, not only after the effective date of the split, but after the date of the announcement of the split. Security prices thus appear, not only to adjust to new information, but to anticipate new information.

While Fama rightly points out that analyses of the semi-strong form have been "limited to only a few major types of information generating events", he does suggest that the evidence supports the semi-strong efficiency model. This conclusion appears, to me, to be only partially valid. Anticipatory price adjustments do indicate that, on average, new information is quickly gleened and responded to by the investment community. This aspect of efficiency, however, is not an explicit part of Fama's definition; furthermore, it does not suggest the manner in which new information is *dispersed* among traders. Yet, the dispersal of information (or, the across-trader variance in receipt time) is more clearly related to Fama's efficiency definition which focuses upon the absence of monopoly control of information. Relatively early receipt of information gives a trader a transitory monopoly position; persistently early receipt of a stream of information, to a trader, suggests superior access to sources of information which give the trader a market advantage that Fama would, presumably, consider inefficient in the semi-strong form.

Again, let us consider Fama's analysis of the effect of stock splits. He employs the "market model" originally suggested by Markowitz to calculate residual return behavior. In this review, he shows that for a sample of 940 stocks, the average residual return becomes positive 29 months before the split date, and remains positive (and, in fact, increases) up to the split date, at which time it returns to zero. While the market adjustment is thus completed before the occurrence of the event which stimulates it, this evidence also indicates that the process of adjustment takes place over a 29 month period.

Fama et al. refer, as well, to the behavior of the residuals computed for specific stocks, and note that, preceeding the split state, successive residuals are not serially dependent, and tend to be "abnormally large and positive" for only a few months. Apparently, the few months of large, positive residuals varies from stock to stock, and thus the average, across stocks, is observed to be positive over the longer time span. This suggests that the adjustment process spans a few months rather than a 29 month period.

The length of the adjustment process is relevant for considerations of market efficiency, and a few months might appear long enough to suggest inefficiency. Because the Fama et al. study utilized monthly price data, it does not provide a sufficiently precise measure of the length of the adjustment period which might be of about a month's duration. Thus, it does not yield evidence for or against efficiency in this particular sense. Further examination, utilizing, perhaps, weekly data, might clarify the issue. One would also like to have knowledge of the systematic dispersion of information during the adjustment period before formulating a final judgment of market efficiency.

This leads us, therefore, to a consideration of efficiency in the weak form. The volume of research in this area far outnumbers the more recent semi-strong and strong form studies. In essence, these studies consider whether information gathered from analyses of historical price movements can enable traders to realize above normal returns. If the market does operate efficiently (in the sense of setting prices that fully reflect all information) one would expect that these studies would not yield information that could be used for the formulation of investment strategies. Fama reasons in the opposite direction: if historical price studies do not yield useful information, the market must, in the weak form at least, be efficient. While this logic is correct, the empirical approach is most challenging.

Autoregressive tests, filter analyses, and runs tests do yield, quite consistently, evidence of "positive dependence in day-to-day price changes and returns on common stocks". Fama concludes, however, that "this positive dependence does not seem of sufficient importance to warrant rejection of the martingale efficient markets model", Yet, this methodology can yield a "proof" only if the tests are all inclusive. Unfortunately, an alternative way of examining past data might always be conceived by future analysts. Thus, the debate between chartists on the one side, and random walkers and fundamentalists on the other, will never be fully settled until we are willing to accept the statement, to paraphrase John Stuart Mill, "happily there is nothing in the laws of the historical behavior of stock prices which remains for the present or any future writer to clear up; the theory of the subject is complete".

For instance, some further characteristic of the distribution of stock prices, such as the variance, might yield serial dependence. The volatility of prices, however, is not a simple, unambiguous statistic as is the level or the first differences of price. A variety of approaches to defining and measuring volatility exist; some, such as high — low spreads or ratios are quite simple, while others employ rather sophisticated econometric techniques. The complexity surrounding this characteristic of the distribution of stock prices causes me to have little *a priori* conviction that market prices fully reflect the type of information which a volatility analysis might yield.

If there are persistent inter-stock volatility differences, and if, for a stock, volatility does behave in a stable fashion over time, a trader might be able to utilize information distilled from an analysis of historical price series. He might be able to formulate profitable strategies, not on the basis of expectations of a specific directional price change, but rather on the expectation that one stock's price is simply more apt to change than another's. The ability to predict future price volatility from past volatility could lead to the development of strategies for the trading of options, particularly spreads and straddles.

The implication this would have for market efficiency, in terms of Fama's formulation, is not clear. Is the market more efficient when no traders have knowledge of a particular type of serial dependence in price changes, then when *some* of the traders obtain this information? One might hold that markets are efficient in some narrow sense of the term if there is an equal or non-monopolized distribution of existing knowledge; yet, they might be efficient in a broader sense if more complete knowledge, regardless of its distribution, is developed. These are definitional issues which should be clarified.

Fama has attempted to evaluate the efficiency of the market by considering the extent to which prices reflect knowledge. One might also attempt to consider, more directly, the actual dynamic processes by which new market information is distributed throughout the investment community.

By so clearly synthesizing the objectives and results of a major number of stock market studies, Professor Fama has accomplished much in this review. He has also provided a valuable service by so strongly focusing attention on the fundamental issue of market efficiency. If, this focus, along with clarifying existing issues, causes new questions to be raised, I believe his work should be doubly valued.

Frontiers of Quantitative Economics, ed. M.D. Intriligator. © *North-Holland Publishing Company.*

CHAPTER 9

QUANTITATIVE STUDIES OF INDUSTRIAL ORGANIZATION

LEONARD WEISS*

University of Wisconsin

0. Introduction

In a famous article of 30 years ago E. S. Mason laid out the plan for systematic study of what was to become industrial organization (Mason 1939). He and his colleagues were to examine in depth a large enough number of industries with various structures to permit generalizations about relationships between the several leading elements of structure and performance. Over the next two decades the right and proper thing for a sincere young disciple was to thoroughly study some industry from the background of economic analysis. By the start of this decade, however, it seemed clear that the case study approach had yielded a great richness of special considerations, but had provided little basis for the hoped-for generalizations.

The alternative, to treat much of the rich detail as random noise, and to evaluate hypotheses by statistical tests of an inter-firm or inter-industry nature, also had a start in the late 1930's, but was long questioned. In a review of the TNEC Papers George Stigler (1942) concluded that, "It is

---

* The author is professor of economics at the University of Wisconsin. At present he is on temporary leave at the Department of Justice where he serves as special economic advisor to the Assistant Attorney General for Antitrust. The views in this paper are his own and do not necessarily reflect those of the Anti-Trust Division. He is indebted to Charles Holt and Edward Heiden for comments on this paper and to George Burch and Lawrence Hexter for help in the computations. Some of the computations were financial under NSF grant GS 2454.

doubtful whether the monopoly question will ever receive much illumination from large scale statistical investigations". Most of the profession seemed to agree. Industrial organization was one of the last fields of economics to be touched by the econometric revolution, and even now we use relatively unsophisticated tools.[1] Yet the fairly simple econometric techniques applied in the field over the last 10 or 15 years have yielded a set of generalizations that, to my mind, surpass in concreteness and certainty those attained by the preceding case studies. The statistical work in the field covers a range of topics much too broad for this paper. I will limit myself to the major structure-performance hypotheses.

1. Concentration and profits

1.0. *Bain and Stigler*

The classic hypothesis of monopoly theory dealt with profits. The structure-profits relation was the first area of industrial organization to be systematically studied and has been by far the most thoroughly plowed field since. Although oligopoly theories could be constructed that would point in almost any direction, most practitioners assumed[2] that successful (tacit or explicit) collusion would approach joint maximization and that the ability to collude increases with concentration. Industries so unconcentrated that collusion was impossible were expected to yield only opportunity costs to all factors plus random deviations reflecting unanticipated changes in demand and/or cost. Profit rates were expected to increase with concentration as collusion became more successful until they reached a maximum attainable with given demand, cost, and entry conditions, again with short run profit differences due to unanticipated changes in demand and/or cost.

---

[1] To some extent our relatively simple methods may reflect the rudimentary preparation in econometrics received by many of us, but that was never true of all and is certainly not so of the younger men in the field today. I believe that a more basic explanation is that important contributions could be made with fairly simple techniques because of the character of our hypotheses and data. Most of our work led naturally to cross section rather than time series regressions, so we have been spared many of the pains of serial correlation and distributed lags. We have seldom been faced with the situation that seems common in time series work where a series of alternative and sometimes contradictory hypotheses all yield high R^2's.

[2] The assumptions of the concentration-profits model are often not spelled out. I am following Bain who was much more explicit than most of us (Bain 1951).

A more complete model involves the determinants of that maximum profit level: the elasticity of demand, the pattern of long run marginal costs, and the conditions of entry. For lack of systematic data, we have almost all assumed that elasticity is unrelated to other structural variables. A fair amount of evidence points to constant long run marginal costs over wide ranges of output in manufacturing (Johnston 1960, ch. 5) and this convenient condition has been generally assumed in cross section studies. Of course, Bain did explicitly include entry barriers in his model.

There have been at least thirty-two tests of some form of the classic profit-determination hypothesis over the last 18 years, and the number seems to be accelerating if anything (Bain 1951, 1956; Schwartzman 1959; Levinson 1960; Fuchs 1961; Sato 1961; Minhas 1963; Stigler 1963, 1964; Weiss 1963; Sherman 1964, 1968; Mann 1966; Collins and Preston 1966, 1968, 1969; Food Marketing Commission 1966; Asch 1967; Kilpatrick 1967, 1968; Miller 1967; Hall and Weiss 1967; Comanor and Wilson 1968; George 1968; Kamerschen 1969; Kelly 1969; and, as yet unpublished theses or papers by Solomon, 1967; Arnould, 1968; Gambeles, 1969; Telser, 1969; Long, 1970; and Imel, 1970).

Bain was the first to formulate and test an operational concentration-profits hypothesis (Bain 1951). He carefully sorted relevant data that had been generated by the late New Deal (the 1935 concentation ratios tabulated by the National Resources Committee, 1939, and the 1936-40 profit data compiled by the SEC). He limited himself to 42 industries that corresponded to well-defined national markets for which at least three corporate series were available. Within this sample he found a barely significant positive linear relation between eight firm concentration and a weighted industry average of 5-year average rates of return on equity, but there appeared to be a highly significant positive difference between industries with eight firm concentration ratios above and below 70. He reported that the effect of concentration could not be explained by firm size, percentage overhead, capital-output ratios, product durability, or type of buyer. These explanatory variables where apparently examined one at a time. Of course he subsequently (Bain 1956, ch. 7) went on to cross tabulate 1936-40 and 1948-51 profit rates against concentration and his estimates of barriers to entry and found a positive effect for both variables (see below).

Stigler, on the other hand, could find little or no statistical support for the traditional hypothesis (Stigler 1963, ch. 4). He worked with income tax data for IRS minor industries using average four firm concentration ratios weighted by value added within these industries and assigning those with average concentration in excess of 60 to a group that he considered "concentrated", these below 50 (or below 20 in industries that sell primarily on local or regional markets) to the "unconcentrated" category, and consigned the remainder to an "ambiguous" purgatory. The concentrated industries showed higher average rates of return (on total investment) in 1938-41 and after 1948, but only in the periods 1951-53 and 1954-56 were these differences statistically significant. Moreover, when he corrected for excessive entrepreneurial withdrawals, he found no significant relation at all.

He felt he had found support for two related hypotheses, however — that profit rates would be more dispersed among concentrated industries where high profits would attract less entry, and that inter-industry profit differences would persist longer in concentrated industries for the same reason. The former held up passably once allowance was made for entrepreneurial withdrawals. The latter was tested by correlating current and lagged profit rates using various lags for all possible pairs of years within each concentration class. The correlation coefficients fell off much more rapidly in the unconcentrated class as the lag was increased. This result is most striking in 1938-47, but it is suspect because of the transition from depression and war in that period. The difference between the concentrated and unconcentrated classes in 1948-57 seems to be almost entirely explainable by differences in the number of degrees of freedom. In both classes the correlation falls to non-significance after 8 years.[3]

In general Stigler found ambiguity where others found a clear cut positive effect. Kilpatrick tried to rework Stigler's study (Kilpatrick 1968). He argued that Stigler's correction for entrepreneurial withdrawals had probably eliminated much of the effect of concentration on profits because of the correlations among concentration, firm size, and such withdrawals. He tried two alternatives, in one introducing the percentage of net worth assignable to small firms as an additional variable, and in the other, eliminating small firms from the study completely. The latter seems particularly well designed, both because it eliminates the effect of entrepreneurial withdrawals and because it drops the firms most likely to be suboptimal (or misclassified). The concentration-profits hypothesis does not refer to fringe firms. The results of Kilpatrick's reconstruction of Stigler was itself equivocal because he did not use precisely the same years as Stigler and

---

[3] *Ibid.*, pp. 69-71.

because he did not find a very high correlation in 1950. However, his IRS data showed a clear cut positive relationship in 1956 and 1963.

Bain thought that Stigler's weak results were due to his having used weighted averages of uncorrected concentration ratios (Bain 1968, p. 451).[4] Averaging can distort if the underlying relation is not linear, and the census concentration ratios are certainly not pure, but others have derived quite significant relationships of the expected sort using similar data (Sherman 1964, 1968; Kilpatrick 1968).

My guess is that the difference between Stigler and the rest of us is more a matter of timing than of technique. In a recent thesis, Gambeles (1969) correlated profit rates and concentration for FTC-SEC 2 digit industries on an annual basis and found significant positive correlations in 1949 and 1952-65, but virtually zero and even negative relationships in the years of open inflation or price controls: 1947-48, 1950-51 and now in 1965-67. The concentration-profits hypothesis apparently does not hold up well in such periods, and every period examined by Stigler except the last (1955-57) contained a preponderance of such years.[5]

1.1. *Price-cost margins*

The collection by the census of gross book values of fixed capital in 1958 and from 1963 on has permitted studies at a 4-digit level, thus avoiding the weighted averages on which many studies have rested. The most comprehensive work along these lines has been that of Collins and Preston (1966, 1968, 1969). Their dependent variable was an approximation to

$$\left(\frac{\text{Price-Marginal Cost}}{\text{Price}} \right)$$

which they were at some pains to show "is most closely related to the

---

[4] Bain also objects to the arbitrary cutoffs at concentration ratios of 50 and 60 though these translate fairly closely to the eight firm concentration ratio of 70 which he had invented. And he complains about Stigler's use of rates of return on assets rather than on equity, a point on which we agree (Hall and Weiss 1967, p. 321). Industries differ in their stability and growth rates and, therefore, in their ability to borrow. Rates of return on assets are apt to reflect the latter in part. It is rates of return on equity which should be eqalized in competitive industries in the long run.

[5] This may account for his different results from Bain's for the pre-war years. Bain used 1936-40 so that 45 of the 60 months covered were late depression. Stigler used 1938-41 so that 28 of his 48 months were during the first part of World War II.

theoretical prediction ...."[6] I am skeptical about this claim. The normal return to be equalized in unconcentrated industries would surely be a yield on capital, not sales, and the ability to successfully collude would increase yields above those available to all on competitive markets. Nevertheless, they do find that weighted average concentration ratios and weighted average capital-output ratios taken together "explain" a larger percentage of the variance in the profit-sales ratio than in the rates of return on equity or assets among SEC-FTC 2 digit industries.

The variable used in their regressions was not the profit-sales ratio, but "price-cost margins" — i.e. the difference between value of shipments and direct cost (labor and materials costs) as a percentage of shipments. The numerator in this variable is interpreted as "profits before taxes plus quasi-rents (depreciation)", but it contains a good deal more than that, most notably purchased services and central office expenses. Advertising is the most obvious of the purchased services. Central office expenses often include such items as research and development, sales, and general administrative expenses. In the 1969 article (though not the book) it also included non-wage labor costs. Advertising[7] seems to be associated with large firms (Comanor and Wilson 1969), central office expenses probably are (Gort 1962, pp. 87-91), and one would expect the same of fringe benefits. Margins should increase with concentration because of the relation of concentration and firm size, if for no other reason.

---

[6] Collins and Preston 1968, pp. 13-4. This ratio would be a correct statement of optimal margin if entry were blockaded so that margin depended on demand elasticity, but blockaded entry seems to be rare outside of regulated industries. I believe that conditions of entry rather than elasticity is the main determinant of optimal margin in most markets. The entry-inducing price yields a normal return on total investment (including entry costs) to the most likely entrant. The optimal price is a function of the entry-inducing price. It should yield a correspondingly higher return on equity to insiders the higher the barriers to entry and the greater the insiders' ability to collude.

[7] Because of the inclusion of advertising in margins, one would expect higher gross margins for differentiated goods, and, if advertising increases with concentration (Mann et al. 1967), one would expect higher regression coefficients as well. Preston's and Collin's concentration-margin relationships for consumers good industries were (Preston and Collins 1969):

High and moderately differentiated $M = 18.7 + 0.189CR$.
Low differentiation $\qquad\qquad\qquad M = 17.4 + 0.150CR$.

The difference in estimated margins (M) comes to 1.26% when CR is zero, 3.21% when it is 50, and 5.16% when it is 100. These differences are in the same ballpark with the advertising-sales ratios for differentiated consumer goods.

There is a good possibility that some net effect of concentration on profits is also detected, however. Telser (1969) attempted to allow for central office expenses by assigning those reported in *Enterprise Statistics* to 4-digit industries associated with an enterprise product class. He still found a significant positive effect of concentration on the remaining overhead even after controlling for payroll, inventory, and fixed capital. Payroll should pick up most of the fringe benefit costs, so the relation between concentration and overhead must reflect profits, taxes, depreciation, and purchased services such as advertising.

Collins and Preston regressed margins on concentration, capital-output ratios, and plant dispersion for 2-digit industries separately and for all industries taken together. The 2-digit regressions were mixed, yielding significant relationships about half the time. I have argued elsewhere (Weiss 1962) that 2-digit industries are particularly poor (and hardly random) samples of industries for tests of hypotheses in which changes in demand or cost are important, because they are fairly homogeneous with respect to concentration, perhaps reflecting related technologies, but are extremely heterogeneous with respect to change in output, perhaps reflecting intrasector competition. Within the 2-digit sectors we are apt to observe only a limited variance in concentration but a large variance in another important element in profits — changing demand or cost. The inevitable result is poorer fits, a point briefly acknowledged (Collins and Preston 1968, p. 96). A much closer fit was observed when the same industries were combined. (The *t* ratio for concentration rose to 6.8 against an average of 1.8 in the sector regressions.) Spurious correlation could be a problem in these studies, since value of shipments is the denominator in the margin, the capital output ratios, and the concentration ratio. However, Telser avoided this problem and still found a significant effect (Telser 1969).

In their recent article (Collins and Preston 1969) they experimented with similar regressions for samples of industries where concentration was rising, stable or declining and where the margins of the largest four firms were high or low relative to the industry as a whole. Some plausible reasons are suggested for why margins should be high in consumer goods industries where concentration has risen or is stable, but further tests should be found for these seemingly after-the-fact hypotheses.

1.2. *Firm studies*

Most past profit studies have used industries as observations, but current studies seem to use individual firms as observations instead. The industry make up of firms is estimated using directory data or interviews and weighted averages of appropriate industry variables are then assigned to the firms. In addition to the study that Marshall Hall and I published in 1967, I know of four theses (Solomon 1967; Arnould 1967; Kelly 1969; Imel 1970) that have taken a similar approach in at least some segments of manufacturing. The results have generally been conventional. Heteroskedasticity is a problem in these studies, since smaller firm size classes have a greater variance in profit experience than do large firms (Alexander 1949; Stekler 1964, Stigler 1963, p. 48), due, presumably, to less diversification. When Hall and I corrected for heteroskedasticity we detected a net positive effect of size on profit along with the expected effects of concentration, output growth, and leverage. Its effect was more strongly positive than that found in previous single-variable studies based on IRS asset size classes (Crum 1939; Alexander 1949; Stekler 1963; Stigler 1963). Some subsequent studies have shown equivocal results within individual 2-digit or IRS minor industries (Marcus 1969; Kelly 1969), but these are not wholly inconsistent with our hypothesis.[8] We expected size to affect profits in broad, inter-industry studies, since large firms have access to a wider range of industries than small and may be expected to invest in those industries with high prospective profits. On the other hand, our results may derive primarily from the peculiarities of the years studied, 1956-62, a relatively depressed period when the advantages of size and diversification might be most substantial.

1.3. *The low R^2's*

The typical result of concentration-profits studies, especially those based on firms, has been a significant but fairly weak positive relationship. The weakness of the relationship has several sources. First, the data is poor.

---

[8] Samuels and Smyth (1968) found a negative relation between size and profits, but I believe this is due to a bias in their sample. It was drawn from Moody's which will contain almost all large firms but only publicly listed small firms. The more profitable small firms seem more likely to be listed, and as a result of the heteroskedasticity of profit rates with respect to size the most profitable small firms earn more than the average large firm.

We measure the ability to collude very imperfectly with four firm concentration in 4-digit products, accounting profits are far from economic profits and contain a large random element due to the variety of accounting conventions in use, and the link between firm accounting and product data is inaccurate because of diversification. Our data are surely worse than the macro-aggregates used in estimating consumption or investment functions or the price, output, inventory, and input data available to agricultural or public utility economists. The resulting large random error element in our data biases the relationship toward zero.

Second, accounting procedures probably bias reported profit rates toward equality because large and profitable firms have the most to gain in tax avoidance and public relations by the understatement of profits, some corporate assets are revalued when they change hands or are written down if profit prospects are low, and original cost asset valuation plus inflation leads to the relative overstatement of rates of return in slowly growing firms (which are usually relatively unprofitable).[9]

Third, much of the inter-industry and more of the inter-firm variance in profit rates reflects unexpected shifts in demand or cost or managerial errors in location, technique, product design or leverage. Some of these may be roughly allowed for by additional variables in multiple regressions, but never very precisely. Concentration is generally only a secondary reason for inter-industry or inter-firm profit differences, so R^2's are bound to be fairly low.[10]

Fourth, high prices may induce high costs, perhaps because they protect suboptimal, excess, or obsolete capacity, perhaps because of internal or union-induced incentives to pay high wages, or perhaps because of managerial preferences for certain expenses. The profit and margin studies probably miss some of the allocative effect of concentration as a result. In general, we can probably conclude that any relationships between profit

---

[9] The accountants' practice of "expensing" intangibles may overstate or understate profit rates, but it is more likely to overstate, the more slowly intangible expenditures grow (Weiss 1969).

[10] The higher R^2's found in regressions using weighted averages for 2-digit industries probably reflect (a) the more accurate assignment of firms to 2- than to 4-digit industries, (b) the averaging out of random influences, and (c) the elimination of much of the effect of changing demand and cost. Two-digit industries are fairly homogeneous with respect to concentration but the variance of output change is almost as great within such industries as in manufacturing generally. Two-digit averages therefore retain much more of the underlying variance in concentration than in output change (Weiss 1963).

and concentration, barriers, and/or output change that we observe are real and are probably badly underestimated.

1.4. *Developing more precise parameters for policy*

Almost all of the 32 concentration-profits studies except Stigler's have yielded significant positive relationships for years of prosperity or recession, though they have depended on a wide variety of data and methods.[11] I think that practically all observers are now convinced that there is something to the traditional hypothesis. This is a considerable accomplishment. Two decades ago Congress passed the anti-merger act with little more than some merger statistics and economic theory to guide it. Nevertheless, I doubt that we need many more general concentration-profits studies.

What we *do* need still is a precise statement of what elements of concentration are important and over what range. This may seem humdrum, but it is highly practical. Life would be much easier at the Anti-Trust Division if we knew whether (a) there really is a critical level of concentration, (b) if it exists, whether concentration makes a difference above and/or below that level, and (c) how much difference is made by larger market shares for the third or sixth or ninth firms in the market. These questions arise continuously and I hope that sometime in the next few years we will at last have some fairly definite answers.

Profit rates, at least in stable prosperity or mild recession, have come to serve as a sort of thermometer to evaluate market power (Bain 1956; Weiss 1963; Comanor and Wilson 1967; Miller 1968; Preston and Collins 1969). This seems quite legitimate. Like the expansion of mercury in the thermometer, we have good theoretical reason to expect profits to increase with market power and have observed it many times. We should now use the established relationship to answer the practical questions.

Bain invented the critical concentration ratio. He found, on an after-the-fact basis, distinctly higher profit rates in industries where eight firm concentration exceeded 70 (1951). Several others adopted this cutoff or its four firm equivalent of 50 (Kaysen and Turner 1959, ch. 2; Schwartzman 1959; Levenson 1960; Stigler 1963; Mann 1966; Comanor 1967;

---

[11] The relationship became non-significant in (Comanor and Wilson 1967) when entry barriers were introduced, see p. 199.

Kamerschen 1969), but only a few have tested it. Kilpatrick (1967) and Collins and Preston (1969) both attempted simple regressions with dummy variables for concentration greater than 50 and arrived at R^2's lower than those found for concentration as a continuous variable. Kilpatrick tried several alternative cutoffs as well. His R^2 reached a maximum when the critical value was 50 for profit rate level and when it was 75 for profit rate changes between 1949 and 1954 (p. 259) though the differences from other cutoffs were not significant. These tests do not seem conclusive for two reasons. Kilpatrick was comparing average profit rates and average concentration ratios for IRS minor industries. Even if a dichotomous relationship existed for realistic markets, it could tend to disappear when they were averaged. Collins and Preston use 4-digit industries and are less vulnerable on this point, but their profit variable is crude. Second, both studies ignore the possibility that slopes may differ substantially below and/or above the critical level. This could make a dichotomous subdivision consistent with a closer fit for a continuous than for a simple shift variable.[12]

The question of what level of concentration is important was also approached by Kilpatrick (1967) and by Miller (1967). Kilpatrick tried four firm, eight firm, and twenty firm concentration ratios as alternative variables and found he could "explain" a slightly larger percentage of the variance in 1950-57 average profit rates and of the change in profit rates between 1949 and 1954 with four firm than with eight firm concentration, and more with the eight firm than with the twenty firm concentration. Again the differences between the correlation coefficients were not significant. This seems to imply that the shares of the fifth through eighth firms and those of the ninth through twentieth firms add nothing to the determination of profit rates.

Miller (1967) resurrected[13] the "marginal concentration ratio" and found that with the four firm concentration given, the share of the fifth through eighth firms had a significant *negative* effect. He suggested a plausible interpretation — that an industry with four leaders and many small followers could collude more readily than one with eight leaders and many small followers. Preston and Collins (1969) have since pointed out that the marginal concentration ratio is a biased measure, since its value is

---

[12] Telser did distinguish industries where $CR \leq 25$, $25 < CR \leq 50$, and $CR > 50$ and found progressively steeper slopes (1969).

[13] As far as I can tell, Gort invented it (1963).

constrained by $MCR \leq CR$ for $CR \leq 50$ and by $MCR \leq (100 - CR)$ for $CR \geq 50$. They attempted two makeshift alternative variables and found that the effect of marginal concentration was equivocal. One of their tabulations seems to show that marginal concentration has a positive effect, if anything, in the ranges where it is most constrained ($CR < 30$ and $CR > 70$) though it may have a negative effect where $30 \leq CR \leq 70$.

This range contains most of the important cases since few of us worry much about markets where $CR < 30$, and there just are not many markets where $CR > 70$.

I tried a rerun using Collins' and Preston's 1958 data (1968) and marginal concentration ratios from their sources. MCR had a non-significant negative effect on margins:

$$M = 15.17 + 0.125\,CR - 0.058\,MCR - 0.015\,D + 0.013\,\frac{K}{VS} \quad \begin{matrix} R^2 = 0.12 \\ \mathrm{d}f = 286 - 5 = 281, \end{matrix}$$
$$\quad\ (1.55)\ (0.021)\quad (0.079)\qquad (0.014)\quad (0.022)$$

where D is their dispersion index and K/VS is their capital-output ratio. The negative effect of MCR is enhanced when the range of CR is limited to $30 \leq CR \leq 70$:

$$M = 9.04 + 0.289\,CR - 0.266\,MCR - 0.032\,D + 0.060\,\frac{K}{VS} \quad \begin{matrix} R^2 = 0.16 \\ \mathrm{d}f = 117 - 5 = 112. \end{matrix}$$
$$\quad\ (4.15)\ (0.068)\quad (0.127)\qquad (0.024)\quad (0.033)$$

To eliminate the constraint completely, I substituted a variable V equal to MCR/CR when $CR \leq 50$ and to $MCR/(1 - CR)$ when $CR > 50$. V can range from zero to 100 just as CR can. It yields:

$$M = 13.85 + 0.121\,CR + 2.02\,V - 0.017\,D + 0.010\,\frac{K}{VS} \quad \begin{matrix} R^2 = 0.12 \\ \mathrm{d}f = 286 - 5 = 281. \end{matrix}$$
$$\quad\ (1.74)\ (0.021)\quad (2.28)\quad (0.014)\quad (0.022)$$

The main result from all this would seem to be that MCR has little effect one way or another.

There would be a clear cut policy implication of a negative coefficient for MCR — that the anti-trust authorities should *encourage* mergers among smaller firms. I do not feel that we know enough to give such advice until a more thorough exploration of this ground is done. Specifically, I would like to know if it makes any difference whether we are dealing with differentiated goods sold to consumers or standardized industrial materials. At the moment the most I can tell the Anti-Trust Division is that it does not look as if a merger among the smaller firms in a market would make a lot of difference so long as the four firm concentration ratio does not change. Even that is an enormous increase on what we could say on the subject 3 years ago.

Work on the parameters of the concentration-profits relationship has been woefully free of theory, with the one elegant and largely ignored exception of Stigler (1964). His proposition was that the success of oligopolistic collusion depends on the individual seller's ability to detect chiseling and that ultimately this depends on his ability to distinguish non-random sales losses. The implication, spelled out with mathematical precision, is that the ability to collude depends heavily on the number and relative size of sellers, falling off rapidly as firm sizes approach equality and as numbers rise. The concentration index directly derivable from his theoretical construct was the Herfindahl index rather than the conventional concentration ratio[14], and he showed that for a group of 17 industries where concentration exceeded 63, profit rates were more closely related to this index than to four firm concentration.

If Stigler's hypothesis were supported, the implications for policy would be striking. It means that we should be very concerned about the shares of the top one or two firms and that the shares of any firm beyond about the fourth cannot make much difference.[15] Moreover, since the Herfindahl index increases with the square of the concentration ratio, if the degree of inequality is given[16], it also implies that we should put most of

---

[14] The Herfindahl index seems also to be implied in the Cournot hypothesis (Long 1969 and Stigler 1968, ch. 4)

[15] If $K = X_n/X_{n-1}$, where X is market share and n is the rank of the firm in question, then the Herfindahl index is: $H = X_1^2 (1 + K^2 + K^4 ...) = X_1^2 \dfrac{1}{1-K^2}$, and the value of H determined by the top t firms is:

$$V = X_1^2 \frac{1 - K^{2 \cdot t}}{1 - K^2}.$$

The ratio of $V/H = (1 - K^{2 \cdot t})$. The share of the top two firms in the index ($t = 2$) is then 0.67 for $K = 0.7$, 0.94 for $K = 0.5$ and 0.99 for $K = 0.3$. The share of the top four firms is 0.94, 0.996 and 0.999994 for the same K's.

[16] Using the same notation as the previous footnote,

$$CR = X_1(1 + K + K^2 + K^3) = \frac{1 - K^4}{1 - K} X_1 \text{ or } X_1 = \frac{1 - K}{1 - K^4} CR$$

$$H = X_1^2 \frac{1}{1 - K^2} = (\frac{1 - K}{1 - K^4} CR)^2 \frac{1}{1 - K^2} = \frac{1 - K}{(1 - K)(1 - K^4)^2} CR^2.$$

Since the ratio on the left is assumed a constant, H increases with CR^2 which, of course, ranges trom 25 to 100 when CR goes from 50 to 100.

our emphasis on mergers where the four firm concentration ratio exceeds 50. The familiar ring of these two cutoff points suggest that Stigler might be right.

Some more general and sophisticated tests of the Herfindahl index are obviously in order. Although both Nelson's tabulation of 1954 Herfindahl indexes (1963) and Stigler's theory (1964) have been available for a half decade, no systematic tests of its effect have been attempted to my knowledges I tried an unsophisticated test using Collins' and Preston's 1958 margins and Nelson's 1956 Herfindahl indexes for 34 industries where all data were available. The Herfindahl index yielded a lower R^2 (0.070) than CR did (0.082) and CR^2 did better than either (0.097). This does not support Stigler very well, but the evidence is at least as tenuous as his was.

Stigler also felt that the number and size of *buyers* was of crucial importance for the ability of insiders to collude (1964, pp. 47-8), large numbers of small buyers per seller making secret price concessions infeasible. Preston and Collins, in effect, tested this by running separate regressions for producer and consumer goods industries. They found a much sharper effect of concentration in the latter case ($\partial M/\partial CR = 0.033$ for producer goods and 0.199 for consumer goods where M is price cost margin). An alternative hypothesis, that it was product differentiation rather than numbers of buyers that control, did not show up well.

2. Conditions of entry

2.0. *Concentration, barriers to entry and profits*

It is customary to acknowledge that concentration is only one dimension of market structure, but the attempts to allow for barriers to entry have been few and usually rudimentary. Bain, himself, made qualitative judgments about the conditions of entry and concentration, and showed an apparently systematic effect of barriers (1956, pp. 199-201) on profits for 1936-40 and 1947-51. The second period is striking in view of the usually poor effect of concentration in "explaining" profits during open inflations. Michael Mann reproduced the experiment using profit rates for 1950-60 and mildly revised and expanded estimates of entry conditions, obtaining similar results (Mann 1966). Neither study attempted any statistical tests of the results.

In the basic model rising concentration increases the ability of industry members to cooperate and to approach the maximum profit rates permitted by entry conditions. Thus profits should rise more rapidly with concentration, the higher the barriers to entry, so that an appropriate model might be:

$$\frac{\Pi}{E} = a + b_1 B_{\text{I}} CR + b_2 B_{\text{II}} CR + b_3 B_{\text{III}} CR \,, \tag{1}$$

where B_{I}, B_{II}, and B_{III} are dummies with a value of 1 when barriers to entry are "low to moderate", "substantial" or "high" respectively. The intercept term presumably represents "normal profits". When Bain's and Mann's data were inserted into such a model, they yielded the expected results:

Bain
1936-40 $\dfrac{\Pi}{E} = 3.82 + 0.069\,CR \cdot B_{\text{I}} + 0.078\,CR \cdot B_{\text{II}} + 0.194\,CR \cdot B_{\text{III}}$ $\quad R^2 = 0.78$
$\phantom{\dfrac{\Pi}{E} =}$ (0.044) $\qquad$ (0.034) $\qquad$ (0.031) $\qquad\qquad\;\; \mathrm{d}f = 20 - 4 = 16.$

Bain
1947-51 $\dfrac{\Pi}{E} = 9.26 + 0.060\,CR \cdot B_{\text{I}} + 0.062\,CR \cdot B_{\text{II}} + 0.119\,CR \cdot B_{\text{III}}$ $\quad R^2 = 0.47$
$\phantom{\dfrac{\Pi}{E} =}$ (0.050) $\qquad$ (0.039) $\qquad$ (0.036) $\qquad\qquad\;\; \mathrm{d}f = 20 - 4 = 16.$

Mann
1950-60 $\dfrac{\Pi}{E} = 7.83 + 0.047\,CR \cdot B_{\text{I}} + 0.050\,CR \cdot B_{\text{II}} + 0.103\,CR \cdot B_{\text{III}}$ $\quad R^2 = 0.51$
$\phantom{\dfrac{\Pi}{E} =}$ (0.033) $\qquad$ (0.027) $\qquad$ (0.024) $\qquad\qquad\;\; \mathrm{d}f = 30 - 4 = 26.$

The results are roughly those that Bain had perceived but had not tested statistically. The effect of concentration seems to be about the same in industries with moderate and with substantial barriers to entry but a good deal greater where barriers are high.

2.1. *Continuous entry variables*

A few attempts have been made to introduce the various barriers as continuous, independent variables. If these can be measured, it may be possible to quantify the barriers to entry, permitting us to judge their relative importance and to add them up. A simple model might be:

$$\frac{\Pi}{E} = a + b_1 B_1 CR \, \dots \, b_i B_i CR \, \dots, \tag{2}$$

where B_i is a continuously measurable barrier such as optimal scale as a percent of market size (MES/VS) or the capital requirement for optimal plants ($MES \cdot K/VS$). The coefficients in such a model would be hard to estimate because of multicollinearity, and they would reflect only crudely Bain's hypothesis that expected profits rise with barriers at an increasing rate. Moreover, it is overall barriers that counts, not any one barrier individually.

A logarithmic regression would preserve the multiplicative relation between concentration and barriers:

$$\frac{\Pi}{E} = kCR^a B_1^{b_1} \dots B_i^{b_i} \dots , \tag{3}$$

but it would not permit profits to rise at an increasing rate with barriers, and it would make the effect of each barrier depend on the levels of other barriers. A better model would be:

$$\frac{\Pi}{E} = KCR^a [b_1 B_1 + \dots + b_i B_i \dots]^c. \tag{4}$$

The value of c should exceed 1.0 if industries with low barriers charge entry-inducing prices while those with higher barriers charge entry-impeding prices as Bain surmises. This would be hard to estimate. One possibility would be to first estimate equation (2) and then use the resulting b_i's to define the bracketed aggregate entry barrier variable used in estimating equation (4).

To my knowledge, no one has ever pursued this approach, but Comanor and Wilson (1967) estimated equations of types (2) and (3) for a group of 41 IRS minor industries that produce primarily consumer goods. The major entry barriers seemed to be those associated with advertising and capital requirements, the latter depending mainly on the auto industry. The scale barrier played a minor role, and concentration had a non-significant and sometimes negative effect. This was due in part to the close correlation between concentration and barriers as measured. Perhaps these are indistinguishable in consumer goods industries, or perhaps a more accurate estimate of the scale and capital barriers might be less closely related to concentration and would yield a different result.[17] I would be

---

[17] Their scale barrier is the average size of the plants accounting for half of shipments divided by total industry shipments. This has the same denominator as concentration and numerator which is correlated with the shipments of the four largest firms. They acknowledge this point (footnote 28, p. 345).

reluctant to reject the independent importance of concentration short of a more extensive investigation covering producer as well as consumer goods. A recent FTC study based on individual firm data in the food industries (Kelly 1969) yielded substantial positive effects for both concentration and advertising intensity.

A possible reason for the strong effect of advertising is the accounting treatment of advertising as current expense. To the extent that ads have lasting value, such accounting practice results in an understatement of both profits and equity. If advertising grows at a constant percentage rate, r, it can be shown that the rate of return on equity will be overstated if $\Pi/E > r/(1+r)$ and vice versa (Telser 1969; Weiss 1969). I reworked Comanor and Wilson's results and found a significant positive effect of advertising intensity on profits even after correcting the profits and equity for previous ads and their depreciation (Weiss 1969). One reason was that r was high during the period covered so that profit rates were not greatly affected by the adjustment. This suggests that the barrier is real.

2.2. *Vertical and conglomerate size*

All studies reviewed to this point have tested some aspect of the classic concentration-barriers-profits hypothesis where empirical studies can now offer at least some guidance for policy, but current merger policy extends to some vertical, market and product extension, and pure conglomerate mergers as well. No one has presented tests of the vertical foreclosure, potential entry, and reciprocity theories that underly many of these merger cases. Perhaps the size-profits studies can be thought of as partial tests of some aggregate economic power theory, though I interpreted a positive relationship as an index of the capital cost barrier (Hall and Weiss 1967). At any rate, the effect of size on profits is still far from established (Alexander 1949; Stigler 1963; Kelly 1969).

The one explicit attempt to test an aggregate concentration argument of which I know is in the new FTC conglomerate merger study (FTC 1969, Appendix, Table 4-4). They regressed the absolute change in 4-digit four firm concentration from 1947 through 1966 on the share of 4-digit industry value added accounted for by firms among the top 200 corporations in 1963. Their data consisted of all 55 industries for which such comparisons are possible, and they controlled for initial concentration, growth, and a high or moderate product differentiation dummy. The large firm variable had a significant positive effect. Since this variable had to be based on membership in the top 200 near the end of the period, increasing industry concentration might have played a role in putting a firm in that category. This possible bias seems remote, however. It is unlikely to account for all of the quite large observed effect

$$\frac{\partial \Delta CR}{\partial Pct\ 200} = 0.191,\ t\text{-ratio} = 2.44.$$

The aggregate economic power hypothesis seems to have been supported[18], but we need a great deal more work on the subject.

3. Competition and labor markets

3.0. *The monopoly wage hypothesis*

An association between concentration and wage rates has been expected by many though such a relation does not derive easily from conventional theory of the firm. A few early tests using only simple correlations (Weiss 1963) wage changes (Garbarino 1950; Levinson 1960) and international comparisons (Schwartzman 1959) yielded unconvincing evidence. My own paper, or at least the data I developed for it, seems to have played a role here (Weiss 1966). I studied annual earnings and estimated average hourly earnings in four broad sex-occupation groupings and ten narrow groupings from the 1/1000 sample of the 1960 Census. When these were regressed on weighted averages of corrected concentration ratios and collective bargaining coverage, earnings seemed to be strongly affected by both variables in most occupations. The addition of other industry variables such as establishment size, employment growth, and various labor force characteristics did not alter this seriously, but when personal characteristics such as race, education, age, region, urban-rural residence, and family status were introduced, the effect of concentration disappeared. I doubt

---

[18] The FTC used the absolute change in concentration which would tend to be large in concentrated industries and might reasonably be deflated by initial concentration. I attempted a regression for a roughly random sample of 25 industries using $\dfrac{CR_{66} - CR_{54}}{CR_{54}}$ and the dependent variable and got results similar to theirs. For what it is worth, the same sample showed no relationship between top 200 participation and price-cost margins.

that this was due merely to inaccurate measurement of concentration. The effect of unionism, which was less well measured, held up for most production workers and showed values near those commonly found in the unionism-wage rate studies — 6-8% for operatives and 8-15% for craftsmen (Lewis 1963, ch. V; but see Stafford 1968). I conclude that while concentrated industries pay higher wage rates, they also hire "superior" personnel whose incomes contain few monopoly rents. There were faults in this study which the subsequent work of Victor Fuchs avoided (Fuchs 1968, Ch. 6). If I were repeating it, I would now put primary emphasis on average hourly earnings. I would use a logarithmic form and would experiment with transformations of the concentration variable, but I doubt that these changes would change the basic results.

3.1. *Labor turnover*

The main line of research in this area today seems to be converging on a study of quit rates. The three studies of which I am aware are those of Stoikov and Raimon (1968), Burton and Parker (1969), and Telser (1969). The first does not introduce market structure variables except for plant size (which has a non-significant, negative effect). They reject concentration as having no theoretical basis, but they show the expected negative effect of wage rates on quits in a relatively prosperous period. The second considers concentration relevant because of a greater possibility of slack, no-raiding agreements, and high quality of labor in concentrated industries. As it turned out, concentration had a significant, negative effect which held up in a variety of models with up to 13 additional variables including unionism and a variety of labor force and dynamic variables (layoffs, accessions, and wage changes). When wage levels were introduced, the effect of unionism largely disappeared but that of concentration was little affected. They concluded that unionism did not impede mobility, but that monopoly did. I would reverse this. Unionism raises wages above the opportunity cost of labor and in the process impedes mobility, but the high wages of concentrated industries are in line with the "quality" of labor hired. Important features of that high "quality" are age, race, sex, family status, and education, all of which are associated with stable employment. Masters, Burton and Parker, and I had all pointed to this aspect of a high "quality" — high wage policy (Masters 1969, pp. 342-3; Burton and Parker 1969, p. 206; and Weiss 1966b, p. 97).

Telser (1969) makes several points which may suggest some connection among concentration, wages and quit rates. He finds that various measures of payroll have significant positive effects on the difference between sales and direct costs after controlling for capital and concentration, which, he believes, reflects specific human capital — i.e., training that is specific to the firm involved. Where training costs are high, the firm should be willing to pay high wages to prevent labor turnover. Telser argues that concentration encourages investment in such forms because it reduces intra-industry mobility and permits the firm to capture much of the gain from even industry-specific human capital. This argument accounts for the otherwise mysterious concentration-quit rate relationship and suggests that the effect may be socially useful.

Yet another aspect of concentration and labor "quality" has come to light. Some have argued that monopolistic industries might take profits in such forms as "socially acceptable" staff (Alchian and Kessel 1960), which could mean racial discrimination. Shepherd found some basis for the assertion — in a simple regression the percentage of executive personel that was Negro was systematically lower in concentrated than unconcentrated 2-digit industries if we ignore the telephone company (Shepherd 1969). Strauss (1970) found such a relationship for various well-paid occupations — managers, clerical workers, and craftsmen — in multiple regression analyses, though it was largely eliminated once he controlled for education-skill class. My guess is that race is at least partly a proxy for quality of education and that large firms in concentrated industries are buying a stable labor force once more, but there may be an element of managerial preference for whites present as well. One wonders to what extent Telser's specific human capital takes such forms.

3.2. *Executive compensation*

An element of labor cost which most economists would probably expect to contain some profits is executive compensation. In small firms the manager and owner are often identical, and in large firms, the separation of ownership and control may provide leeway for officers to absorb some profits. No study attacks this directly, but Williamson produced some relevant results (1963a). His hypothesis was that managers would favor expenses that enter their utility functions. The most obvious is executive compensation. He expected and found a significant positive relation between the top executives' salaries and both concentration and Bain's entry barriers after allowing for general and selling expense as an index of administrative responsibility. The relation with market structure variables was somewhat closer than with profit rates in 1953 and 1961 and roughly similar in 1957. In his view, concentration and barriers show the profit rates available to the firm, some of which are appropriated by its executives. Reported profits would be less likely to determine executive prerequisites than the profit opportunities themselves. This concept is potentially important but it should be tested more thoroughly. The model was well specified (e.g. concentration and barriers were introduced multiplicatively) but he had only 26-30 observations and rather crude data. Executive compensation was limited to salary and bonus, and stockholder control was represented by the inside character of the board of directors. Extensive information on other forms of executive income and on stock diffusion is now available for more than 100 firms (Lewellen 1968; Larner 1966, 1968) and should be used.

The salary and bonus of the chief executive is itself a small portion of corporate profits, but the total cost involved may be large since salaries throughout the corporate hierarchy rise with those at the top of the pyramid.

The main effect of the labor and executive compensation studies is to reinforce the concentration — profits relationship. Some work in this area is useful as an offset to Harberger (1954), but I do not see much concrete policy application for it.

4. Other expenses

4.0. *Advertising*

One of the most controversial expenses is advertising. It has been treated both as an element of product differentiation and hence, of structure, and as a type of performance. A tendency for concentration to result in heavy advertising is an old hypothesis. Dorfman and Steiner's model (1954) where the ratio of marginal net revenue to marginal selling cost is equated with elasticity, suggests that firms in atomistic markets will find advertising less profitable. To this might be added Williamson's analysis of conditions in which it is profitable to advertise to increase entry barriers (Williamson 1963b). Telser (1962) makes the further point that if ads serve partly to enhance the demand for a generic product, then the profitability of advertising will rise with market share.

Another group of hypotheses suggest that heavy advertising causes high concentration. Firms that win strong consumer loyalties are apt to win large market shares in the bargain, and it is commonly supposed that the economies of scale in advertising are often large relative to economies in production.[19]

Both sets of hypotheses suggest a net positive relation between concentration and advertising intensity, but it has been hard to find. Telser (1964) worked with 44 IRS minor industries which sell primarily consumer goods, relating their advertising-sales ratios to weighted averages of four firm concentration in 3 census years and found a non-significant positive effect in each case.[20] He went on to show some evidence that brand market shares were less stable for heavily advertised products, but one wonders how valuable unstable market shares are as a element of performance. He pointed out that average concentration ratios may not reflect extreme values but claims that this does not bias his results since the dependent variable is averaged in a similar way. This is correct only if the underlying relationship is linear. Moreover, misdefinition of component markets makes no difference in computing average advertising but creates errors in average concentration. Precisely the same points can be made about an average concentration-profits relationship, however, and it usually does hold up. If there were a relationship present that Telser was unable to detect, it was probably due to an omitted variable, "differentiability" (Caves 1962, pp. 48-54), or, more precisely, the capability for differentiating the product via advertising. Casual observation suggests that this variable, while elusive and difficult to quantify, is large for a small number of products.

Mann et al. (1967) approached the same problem using firm data. They limited themselves to 14 4-digit industries for which data for two or more fairly specialized firms was available. They found a strong positive relationship between average firm advertising rate and concentration in

---

[19] Comanor and Wilson (1969) tested this using 41 IRS minor industries that sell primarily consumer goods. They estimated minimum efficient firm size (*MEF*) by regressing profit rates on size in 29 industries where profits rise with size. Average advertising rates were relatively low in the other 12. They then attempted to "explain" the ratio of *MEF* to industry size in a cross-industry regression using estimated minimum efficient plant size (*MES*) and advertising intensity. A logarithmic interaction term provided the best (though quite weak) fit, suggesting that advertising increases *MEF* more when *MES* is low than when it is high.

[20] Doyle (1968) arrived at similar results with more detailed British data.

each year covered. These results are also open to question, however, since their sample excluded drugs and toiletries, just the industries which combine high advertising rates with moderate 4-digit concentration ratios.

The expected relationship between concentration and promotion has not been confirmed. Perhaps it cannot be, but some improvements on the model could alter the picture. It is essentially a simultaneous equation problem, one hypothesis pointing to concentration as a determinant of advertising intensity along with product differentiability and the other, to advertising as a determinant of concentration along with the ratio of optimal scale relative to market size. An appropriate model might then be:

$$\begin{cases} \dfrac{A}{S} = k(CR)^b \left(\dfrac{C}{S}\right)^c & (5) \\[4mm] CR = g\left(\dfrac{A}{S}\right)^h \left(\dfrac{MES}{S}\right)^i, & (6) \end{cases}$$

where A is advertising expenditures, S is sales, C is final consumption expenditures, and MES is the value of shipments of a plant of minimum efficient scale. A multiplicative form is used on the assumptions that the effect of concentration on advertising would be quite different for producer goods and that the effect of advertising on optimal scale is larger the smaller is the optimal plant size (Comanor and Wilson 1969). This simultaneous equation model is itself a simplification. In particular, concentration may well depend on a distributed lag series of advertising, as market share does in most intra-industry studies (Nerlove and Waugh 1961, Telser 1962, Palda 1964; Lambin 1969; Peles 1969). Introducing a distributed lag would result in a complex, dynamic model that would be difficult to estimate.

4.1. *Other costs*

Market structure has been expected to affect costs in a variety of other ways as well. High prices associated with high concentration or product differentiation may attract or support excess capacity if barriers to entry are low and may prevent the elimination of excess or suboptimal capacity regardless of entry conditions. To my knowledge, no one has done any convincing empirical work on either hypothesis, presumably for lack of reliable data.

Then there is X-efficiency — the ability of firms to attain minimum costs for their given scales and techniques. Leibenstein's (1966) hypothesis does not directly deal with market structure, but he and Comanor have proposed that the ability or willingness of firms to attain minimum unit costs depends heavily on structure (Comanor and Leibenstein 1969). While this is plausible, no evidence has been presented to support it. I presume the correct test would depends on intra-industry differences in productivity or unit cost for many different industries which could then be compared in a simple model of the sort:

Variance of Productivity $= a + bCR$.

The Bureau of the Census has the wherewithal to run such a regression; I do not know who else can. The effect of competition on cost is potentially important if it ever can be measured because it involves direct welfare losses due to excessive costs in addition to allocative losses.

5. Stability

The belief that industrial concentration contributes to economic instability is as old as the concentration ratio (National Resources Committee 1939). It has been resurrected in various forms as our experience with the cycle has changed. I will leave the role of price rigidity in the great depression to history (summarized in Ruggles 1955). The "administered inflation" hypothesis of the 1950's still seems to affect policy proposals, and it may well reappear once more in the 1970's. Less publicized but potentially as important is the unpredictable character of investment in oligopolistic industries.

5.0. *Administered inflation*

Gardner Means, using his 30-year-old classification of industries into those with administered prices, "mixed", and market-determined prices testified in the late 1950's that industries with administered prices had played a minor role in the postwar inflation, but had been the primary element in what came to be known as the administered inflation of the 1950's (Means 1957, 1959).

George Stigler challenged the administered inflation hypothesis as illogical, because profit maximizing monopolists do not raise prices indefinitely. He cited evidence that BLS wholesale price indexes tend to understate price flexibility in concentrated industries and that those indexes rose no more in concentrated than other industries (Stigler 1962). DePodwin and Seldon correlated BLS wholesale price relatives for 1959 based on 1953 with various concentration measures for 5-digit and again, 4-digit manufactured products where BLS and SIC definitions could be matched. When they worked with the entire range of manufactured products they found a mild positive effect of concentration on price change, but it was always weak and usually non-significant. Regressions within the larger 2-digit industries yielded seven negative and four positive relations — all but one non-significant again. They concluded that the administered inflation hypothesis could be rejected.

As in the Collins and Preston study discussed above, DePodwin's and Selden's 2-digit results should carry little weight because such samples minimize the variability in concentration while keeping a high variability in output change. The major problem with their study was their failure to allow for changes in cost and demand. I reworked their data for all their 4-digit industries that had comparable SIC definitions in 1953 and 1959, regressing price changes on changes in deflated shipments, unit materials cost, and unit labor cost as well as concentration (Weiss 1966b). Concentration then turned out to have a significant positive effect similar to that proposed by Means. In similar regressions for 1959-63, changes in output and unit material and labor costs had about the same coefficients as in the previous period, but concentration now had a non-significant negative effect. Taking the whole 1953-63 period together, concentration had about the same effect as in the 1950's, suggesting that there had been a once-for-all increase in BLS wholesale prices in concentrated industries relative to the less concentrated in the 1950's. This result would be consistent with profit maximization if the concentrated industries were not taking full advantage of their position at the end of the Korean War. Then the administered inflation would amount to a tendency for oligopoly prices to respond to inflationary pressures with a lag.[21] One problem with my administered price study, however, was that the dependent variable was used to deflate output, unit material cost, and unit labor cost. The coefficients of these variables may be biased upward and R^2 may be exaggerated if there were errors in these

---

[21] W. J. Yordan had already shown that for 14 industries, the main effect of market structures on price was to produce relatively great lags between cost and price change (Yordan 1961).

price relatives. This bias should not affect the main result, however, since the price change and concentration variables were derived independently.

5.1. *Wage rate changes*

The difficult wage change element of administered inflation is still unsettled. There is a long tradition in labor economics that wage rates rise faster in concentrated industries (summarized in Allen 1968, pp. 353-7). This barely makes sense as a continuous phenomenon, though it could apply in the 1950's if wage levels were initially less than optimal from the point of view of the affected unions.

Several studies have shown significant positive relationships between concentration and wage changes in the 1930's (Garbarino 1950), and the 1950's (Levinson 1960; Bowen 1960; Yordan 1961a; Weiss 1963, 1966b), though negative relationships appear to be common in 1923-29 (Lewis 1963, pp. 158-9) and 1940-47 (Weiss 1963; Lewis 1963, pp. 159-60). Lewis felt that the positive effect of concentration in the 1930's was due to its correlation with the growth in unionism. Bowen and Levinson also introduced employment growth, profit rates, and unionization in explaining wage changes at 2-digit levels for various short periods from 1947 through 1959. The net effect of concentration was ordinarily positive though there was some instability in the relationship due probably to colinearity among the profit, concentration, and unionism variables.

As with the administered prices, the tendency for wage rates to rise faster in concentrated sectors in the 1950's may have been a temporary phenomenon. Allen (1968) related wage changes to concentration on a 3- or 4-digit level on a year-to-year basis from 1949 on and found a non-significant effect in the Korean War Period (1949-51) and the early 1960's (1961-64). My guess is that in the recent inflation the relation will turn out to be negative again. Administered wages like administered prices seem to respond to changing market conditions with a lag. We can probably expect another period of moderate "administered inflation" in the early 1970's along with demands for more guideposts or even direct controls. The basic problem is simply that prices and wages are sticky in the monopolistic sectors.

I have excluded the enormous literature on the Phillips curve from this discussion. Their results, which seem commonly to show an overall inflationary bias are consistent with only periodic and temporary administered inflations in concentrated sectors. Prices as a whole may rise persistently, but prices in monopolistic sectors only rise with the rest, on the average.

5.2. *Investment*

Scherer introduced another role for market structure in stability last year when he examined the effect of concentration on industrial investment. He found a few scraps of hypotheses on the subject in previous literature, some of which pointed to more stable and some to less stable investment in concentrated markets. Scherer's basic test consisted of a regression covering 80 4-digit industries for which investment series were available.[22] His dependent variable was the standard error of estimate around logarithmic trends of industry capital expenditures; and his explanatory variables were four firm concentration, variability of man-hours around its logarithmic trend, capital-value added ratio, industry size, and dummies for durables, consumer goods, and intermediate materials. The cross-industry regressions yielded a fairly large positive effect for concentration, but it was of only borderline significance. Although concentration is not closely correlated with anyone of the other explanatory variables, the significance of its relationship to investment variability falls off rapidly as they are added. In interpreting this, he emphasized the common effects of industry size and concentration, feeling that they tend both to measure diversity of decision making. Finally he examined the residuals from investment functions for 13 2-digit industries estimated by Jorgenson and Stephenson (1967). The standard errors of estimate from these investment functions, expressed as ratios to mean investments, were regressed on weighted average concentration. The errors were positively correlated with concentration,[23] perhaps supporting the contention that investment in concentrated industries is particularly unstable. Or perhaps, as he says, that the Jorgensen-Stephanson model is misspecified in concentrated industries.

---

[22] His data was from the *Annual Surveys of Manufactures*. In industries where probability sampling is important, investment series from this source may be irregular merely because of periodic sample changes. Probability sampling is important in some unconcentrated but almost never in concentrated industries.

[23] The relation to a simple weighted average of concentration ratios was stronger than for a set of weighted averages I had constructed in which I had attempted to correct for non-competing subproducts, inter-industry competition, and the regional character of

Scherer's paper should eliminate any notions of concentration contributing to stability due to coordination of investment. On the other hand, the instability of investment within concentrated industries is probably not very serious since many such industries, taken together, contain many decision centers, even if any one does not.

Altogether, concentration seems to contribute to short term price and wage stability, though I doubt that this is a virtue, and may make investment somewhat less predictable.

6. Progressiveness

Technological progressiveness seems to be the most important area for industrial organization research for the future. Its main elements are research and development, innovation, and diffusion. The seminal work was that of Schumpeter (1942), who emphasized firm size and market power in explaining each of these, but more recent work has gone far beyond him.

6.0. *Research and size*

There seems to be agreement that the benefits of basic research are unpredictable and inappropriable for most private enterprise. Only a broadly based monopolist would find such investment profitable. It happens that our most broadly based monopolist, the telephone company, *is* the leading business contributor to basic research.

Most empirical work has dealt with applied research and development where we have more degrees of freedom. Firm size is the favorite variable, presumably because it can be used within industries, thus finessing the problem of interindustry differences in technological opportunity. Most

---

the market (Weiss 1963). This could mean that my corrections merely introduced random noise. On the other hand, if the greater stability of investment in unconcentrated industries is due to diversity of decision-making rather than reduced monopoly power, then the uncorrected concentration ratios would be the superior measure. Diversity due to regional fragmentation of the market or non-competing sub-products should be just as successful in reducing the standard error of investment as is diversity due to competition within markets. This suggests that Scherer might be able to distinguish between the effects of concentration and diversity in his four digit data by using corrected and uncorrected concentration ratios.

studies show strong positive effects of size on R and D employment or expenditures within broadly defined industries but weak, and often negative effects of size on R and D intensity (Worley 1961; Horowitz 1962; Hamberg 1962, reproduced in 1966, pp. 46-63; Mansfield 1962, reproduced in 1968, p. 39; Scherer 1965; Comanor 1967; Grabowski 1968). The positive effect of size is exaggerated in some broad-based studies because of the high proportion of large-firm research that is financed by government. On the other hand, the samples used in most of these studies contain biases against the size-R and D hypothesis, excluding small firms or, worse, including only those small firms with research staffs. There are other problems[24] in individual studies, but the consistent result is impressive.

These studies cover R and D inputs, which seem less significant from a public viewpoint than the output of new knowledge. Numbers of patents have sometimes been used as proxies for the latter, and small manufacturing firms (less than 5000 employees) play a larger role here, accounting for only 14% of R and D expenditures but around 40% of both manufacturing patents and sales (Scherer 1965, pp. 1104-5). The difference may reflect some bias in the propensity to patent (Schmookler 1966, pp. 32-5) but another element is the dependence of small firms on part time research done by managerial or sales staff (Schmookler 1959).

The most thorough patent numbers study was Scherer's (1965). He was able to "explain" a remarkably large percentage of inter-firm variance in patent numbers among 352 large industrials by regressing patents on firm size within 2- or 3-digit industries. Interindustry differences in the regression slopes were interpreted as differences in technological opportunity. Using these slopes, he then combined his observations into four fairly homogeneous groupings and tested a cubic sales-patents model and a quadratic R and D intensity-patent intensity model within each grouping. Diminishing returns to sales size and to the R and D personnel-sales ratio were evident

---

[24] One problem deserves mention because it arises fairly commonly in industrial organisation research and has received little attention. Both Mansfield (1962) and Grawbowski (1968) used pooled cross sections. I have used similar data (Hall and Weiss 1967), but it is quite tricky. It is apt to involve serial correlation because consecutive observations of the same firm are often more closely correlated with each other than with those of other firms. As a result, conventional t-ratios may exaggerate the significance of coefficients for slowly changing variables such as size or concentration. Mansfield's 150 observations obtained for 10 firms in 15 years were surely less distinct than 150 different firms, but we are likely to apply the same significance test to both sets of data.

over most of the observed range in most groupings. Diversification seemed to reduce patent output in technically progressive groupings, to increase it in the others and to have little overall effect. Altogether, Scherer seems to show that size adds even less to patent output than to R and D input, and that conglomerate bigness has a de minimus effect.

A major problem with patent numbers studies is the varying quality of patents involved.[25] Mansfield tried to avoid this by tracking down the most important inventions in chemicals, petroleum, and steel (Mansfield 1964, reproduced in 1968, pp. 40-2). He regressed the sum of these (weighted by the number of times they were mentioned by experts) on the firm's R and D expense, its R and D expense squared, and an R and D-size interaction. He imposed a zero intercept without giving any reason and he suppressed several non-significant coefficients — a dangerous practice when colinearity is as likely as it is here. But this is carping. The amazing thing is that he detected any relationship at all with only 10 observations in chemicals, 8 in petroleum, and 11 in steel.

Comanor's pharmaceutical industry study was based on more convincing data (Comanor 1965). He worked with 57 firms and could distinguish all new chemical entities, weighting them by their first two years' sales, a seemingly more objective basis for evaluating inventions. His model was unfortunately very complex:

$$\frac{N}{S} = f\left(\frac{R}{S}, \frac{R^2}{S}, S, R \cdot S, D\right),$$ (7)

where N is the weighted sum of new chemical entities, S is sales, R is numbers of professional research personnel, and D is diversification within ethical drugs. After estimating the coefficients, he multiplied through by S in order

---

[25] The propensity to patent appears to vary systematically over time (a downward trend), between individuals and corporations (higher for individuals) and among industries (Schmookler 1966, pp. 23-56). At least within the drug industry (Comanor and Scherer 1969) inter-firm variations in patent numbers seem to be significantly correlated with the weighted sum of new products, but they are better correlated with total R and D staff, and the latter "explains" as much of the variance in new product as patents do. These results suggest that high R and D intensity is positively related to the propensity to patent. Moreover, patents correlate more closely with total R and D personnel than with professionals and more closely with all new products (including those already marketed in other dosages or combinations or under other brands) than with new chemical entities. All this suggets that patents reflect new R and D input better than significant R and D output.

to estimate the marginal product of R, so that:

$$N = f(S, R, R^2, S^2, R \cdot S^2, D \cdot S).$$ (8)

The results were similar to Mansfield's chemical industry results: both show increasing returns to research intensity[26] and a decline in the marginal product of R and D at any level of R and D as size grows. Rough calculations using Comanor's regressions suggest that dN/dS is also positive, but this is uncertain because no values are reported for D or for dR/dS, both of which are needed to find dN/dS.

6.1. *Market structures and R and D*

Schumpeter emphasizes market power as well as size as determinants of progressiveness. Both Hamberg (1966, pp. 63-5) and Horowitz (1962) found significant positive effects of concentration on R and D expenditure at two digit levels using NSF and early post war surveys. Scherer (1965, pp. 1116-1121) identified the four leading firms in 48 narrower industries within his moderately or highly progressive groupings and regressed their 1954 patents appropriate to the industry involved on sales size, concentration, and chemical and electrical industry dummies. Concentration had a mild positive effect. In another test two years later (Scherer 1967) he used the numbers of scientific and engineering personnel by industry from the 1960 population census corrected for government-financed research and the percentage of such personnel in formal R and D activities. The ratio of this scientific and engineering personnel variable to total industry employment rose with both size and concentration. Most of the correlation between R and D intensity and concentration occurred within the sector that he had identified as "traditional", where there was little opportunity for progressiveness. Comanor (1967) found a similar result when he distinguished differentiated durables, where design competition is important, from material inputs and consumer non-durables. Concentration had a positive effect in the latter but no effect in the technologically more progressive differentiated durable goods industries.

---

[26] The line of causation may be reversed here. Grabowski quite plausibly makes R and D intensity a function of patent productivity of the firm's scientific personnel (Grabowski 1968).

Perhaps because I am a relative outsider in this area, I finish reading each of the size or concentration — R and D input or output studies with some skepticism, but, taken together, they are more convincing. Most studies show that within their range of observation, size adds little to research intensity and may actually detract from it in some industries. A common caveat is that a threshold size is probably required for many important types of R and D. Most studies are based mainly on firms from the top 500 industrials and are not well designed to detect that threshold (Markham 1965). The failure to detect the R and D size threshold is probably not very important for policy, however, since merger policy is normally oriented toward the leading firms in an industry. A strict policy at that level apparently cannot do much damage to privately financed R and D effort.

On the other hand, I draw the tentative verdict that concentration is positively related to R and D intensity. Perhaps, as some have suggested (Horowitz 1962; Phillips 1966; Comanor 1967; Scherer 1967) we have the line of causation at least partially reversed, with technological progressiveness contributing to concentration. If so, a simultaneous equation model along the line of the following seems in order:

$$\begin{cases} R/S = f(CR, \text{Technological Opportunity}) \\ CR = f(R/S, MES/VS). \end{cases}$$

A logically superior alternative might be a dynamic system where concentration is dependent on distributed lags of R/S and is a partial determinant of current R/S, but such a model would be difficult to estimate.

Even if concentration has a significantly positive effect on R and D, it does not follow that oligopoly would increase productivity growth in presently unconcentrated industries. It seems common for process R and D to be centralized in equipment industries, so that many processing and consumer goods industries could be unconcentrated with little or no loss in inventive output.

Finally, there is the effect of diversification. I cannot find any good way to reconcile Grabowski's positive effect with Comanor's negative effect and Scherer's roughly neutral effect.[27] At present, I judge that the issue is

---

[27] In both Comanor and Grabowski (1965; and 1968) diversification is a determinant of R/S while in Scherer (1965) it is related to R. Comanor's data seem cleaner than Grabowski's. He has far more observations and his diversification variable is based on 40 classes of drugs instead of the nine 5-digit products used by Grabowski. Scherer's data were for one year rather than several, his diversification measure referred to four

unsettled and a good candidate for more work, especially in view of its potential relevance to the conglomerate merger debate.

6.2. *Innovation*

Schumpeter put great emphasis on the innovation decision but data problems have virtually limited us to historical case studies and Mansfield's extensive and ingenious research. In his fundamental study Mansfield (1963; reproduced in 1968, Ch. 5) developed a list of major innovations in steel, petroleum and coal in 1919-38 and 1939-58 and found the first commercial user of each. The four largest firms had a larger share of total innovations than of capacity in petroleum and coal but less than their share in steel. He also estimated the mean investment and asset size required to introduce each industry's innovations in each period, and developed a model where the four industry leaders' share of innovations depended on their size relative to other firms above the threshold and on the investment requirements relative to threshold size. The model was estimated using steel and petroleum process and product innovations in the two periods. It seemed to predict passably when later applied to the railroads. The analysis is impressive, but the empirical estimates based on five *possibly* independent degrees of freedom are inherently unconvincing.

He went on to regress numbers of innovations on the log of asset size in a cubic model for each type of innovation in each industry and period. The coefficients suggested diminishing returns to size after some point for most products except coal. He had plenty of degrees of freedom this time, but the dependent variable was zero and size was apparently small in about 95% of the cases. His evidence of diminishing returns depended on the upper tail of the distribution where he again had only a few observations.

Mansfield's remarkable study was partially reconstructed by Williamson (1965), who used it to test the hypothesis that leading firms were more likely to innovate than small firms as concentration increased. He found that the ratio of the top four firms' share of innovations to their share of capacity declined as concentration increased with an almost perfect correlation ($R^2 = 0.985$). Adding Mansfield's later data on railroads would re-enforce this result if a national concentration ratio were used, but using

---

digit or broader classes and extended beyond the drug field. I can reconcile Scherer with either Grabowski or Comanor but not with both.

regional concentration would reduce the correlation to non-significance. At any rate, the Schumpeterian hypothesis is not supported.

Between them, Mansfield and Williamson have wrung more results from the same 4 or 5 degrees of freedom than you commonly see in print. While in much of industrial organization research the theory has been weaker than the data, this case is at the opposite extreme. I should think that it would be possible to develop more lists of major innovations for maybe 20 industries and to identify the innovators so that at least some of the ingeneous hypotheses in these papers could be properly tested. This enterprise would seem the natural subject for Ph.D. theses.

We have little more than hypotheses now, but it should be feasible to find enough data to test them. Until we do the correct statement is that we *probably* need not worry about the effect on innovation of merger policy within the range in which it operates.

6.3. *Diffusion*

The speed with which an industry adopts new techniques once they have been introduced is the final element of progressiveness. It is the crucial element in a competitive industry serviced by technologically progressive suppliers.

The classic study of diffusion was Griliches' work on hybrid corn (1957) in which he fit logistic curves to hybrid corn planting within states. The three parameters of the logistic, its origin, slope, and ceiling, then became dependent variables for further analysis. In a series of cross-state regressions he let the origin depend on variables likely to affect the initial entry of seed producers into a state and the initial adoption of the product by farmers. Similarly, the slope and the ceiling of the logistic curve depended on indexes of the profitability of the change in the various states. He concluded that corn growers had responded in a way that might be expected of rational profit-maximizers.

Mansfield adapted this model to the industrial sector. He decomposed diffusion into imitation, the initial adoption by a firm of a new technique, and intra-firm diffusion.

His imitation study (Mansfield 1961; reproduced in 1968, Ch. 7) traced the percentage of major firms adopting each of 12 innovations from four industries. He fit a logistic function to each imitation series, and made their slopes dependent on the size of the initial investment relative to assets per firm, the profitability of the new investment relative to industry expected profitability, and industry dummies. He then examined those industry dummies and felt that he saw the speed of imitation increasing with competitiveness. As usual, the model was brilliant and the fit was remarkable, but the second regression was based on 5 degrees of freedom, and the implicit regression of speed of imitation on competitiveness[28] may have had 2! We obviously need more observations, which should mean more Ph.D. theses.

Using similar data, he later showed (Mansfield 1963b, reproduced in 1968, Ch. 9) that individual large firms are, on the average, quicker to imitate than smaller firms, though he did not feel he had enough observations to answer the more basic question of whether the larger firms were quicker to imitate than groups of smaller firms with about the same number of investment decisions to make.

I wonder if the problem was all that difficult. He had almost 300 observations for 14 innovations. I should think that he could have grouped smaller firms to create combinations equal in size to the largest firm in each industry. Assuming each firm to be half the size of the next, he would have had 4 or 5 observations per innovation. He could have then regressed imitation delay on the average size of firm in a grouping, perhaps pooling innovations with dummies for each industry or even each innovation. He would have been able to say with unaccustomed certainty whether the speed of imitation was enhanced or delayed by having an industry of large firms.[29]

Finally, Mansfield studied intra-firm diffusion using the case of the diesel locomotive (1963c, reproduced in 1968, Ch. 9). He again fit logistic curves within each firm and was able to "explain" 69% of the interfirm variance in the slope parameters using four plausible variables. The diesel locomotive, on the average, was diffused more slowly within larger firms. This size effect was non-significant where diffusion was measured in

---

[28] His two independent variables cast some light themselves. For any given innovation, imitation response would be slower, the greater the average expected rate of return in an industry. It will also be slower, the smaller the average assets of major firms. Competition affects both of these variables, so there may be some case for regressing the slope coefficients on concentration directly.

[29] In the one case for which data is given — dieselization (1968, p. 182) — a simple regression of group imitation lag on average firm size within the yields a significant tendency for large firms to delay longer ($R^2 = 0.62$ with $7 - 2 = 5$ degrees of freedom).

numbers of locomotives, but significant, though small, when measured in ton-miles hauled.

The upshot of the diffusion studies is that smaller firms and competitive industries do at least as well as large and oligopolistic firms in adopting new techniques once they have been introduced, but as usual, the evidence is based on a handful of instances. I would think that future work on this subject will often be easier if imitation and intra-firm diffusion are melded as they were in Griliches' study. Mansfield's distinction is conceptually useful, but the data probably will not allow it very often.

Altogether, the analysis of technological progressiveness has been more imaginative than that in much of the rest of industrial organization, but the data (except for patents) has been hard to come by, so the tests are often not convincing. Since I suspect the performance payoff from market structure could be great in this area, a high priority should be given to digging out enough data to make the conclusions credible.

7. Omissions

I have intentionally limited this paper to the market structure-performance relationship as probably the most critical for public policy. One element of performance — the social and political impact of the large or monopolistic firm — is omitted merely because statistically oriented economists have left it untouched, though it abounds in untested hypotheses. I have also left out the burgeoning studies of managerial motivation (Williamson 1963a; Larner 1968; Kamerschen 1968; Monsen et al. 1968). In addition I have largely ignored our spotty attempts to explain industry structure: (a) the still fairly blank field on economies of scale and of long production runs, (b) an occasional study of mergers that gets beyond the descriptive level, and (c) our enormous, intellectually elegant literature on the log normal distribution of firm sizes, the next important policy implication of which will be its first. I have also left out the industry studies completely — the annual, ever more precise, cost or production function for electric power (Johnston 1960, Ch. 4-1; Kimiya 1962; Nerlove 1963; Barzel 1964; Dhrymes and Kurz 1964; Ling 1964; Galatin 1968); Fisher's careful estimates of the elasticity of supply of oil and gas exploratory drilling (1964); MacAvoy's ingeneous methods for detecting monopoly or competition in gas fields and ancient railroad documents (1964, 1965); Caves' study of air transport

(1962); or Meyer et al.'s potentially revolutionary examination of rail and truck costs (1959). Such studies are of great importance — in regulated industries in particular — and their payoff may well exceed anything we can accomplish in the unregulated sector, merely because performance in the regulated sectors seems so unsatisfactory. Perhaps the right next step is back to the industry study, but this time with regression in hand.

References

Alchian, A. and R.A. Kessel, 1960, Competition, monopoly, and the pursuit of money. In: Universities — National Bureau, *Aspects of Labor Economics*. Princeton, N.J., Princeton University Press, 70-81.

Alexander, S.S., 1949, The effect of size of manufacturing corporations on the distribution of the rate of return. *Review of Economics and Statistics* 31, No. 3 (August), 229-235.

Allen, B.T., 1968, Market concentration and wage increases: U.S. manufacturing, 1947-1964. *Industrial and Labor Relations Review* 21, No. 3 (April), 353-366.

Arnould, R.J., 1968, The effect of market and firm structure on the performance of food processing firms. Ph. D. Thesis, Iowa State Univ., Ames.

Asch, P., 1967, Industry structure and performance: some empirical evidence. *Review of Social Economy* 25, No. 2 (Sep.), 167-182.

Bain, J.S., 1951, Relation of profit rate to industry concentration: American manufacturing 1936-1940. *Quarterly Journal of Economics* 65, No. 3 (August), 293-324.

Bain, J.S., 1956, *Barriers to new competition*. Cambridge, Mass., Harvard University Press.

Bain, J.S., 1968, *Industrial Organization*, Second Edition, New York: John Wiley and Sons.

Barzel, Y., 1964, The production function and technical change in the steam power industry. *Journal of Political Economy* 72, No. 2 (April), 133-150.

Bowen, W.G., 1960, *Wage behavior in the post war period*. Princeton, N.J., Princeton University Press.

Burton, J.F. jr. and J.E. Parker, 1969, Inter-industry variations in voluntary labor mobility. *Industrial and Labor Relations Review* 22, No. 2 (January), 199-216.

Cabinet Committee on Price Stability, 1969, *Studies by the staff*. Washington, Government Printing Office.

Caves, R., 1962, *Air transport and its regulators*. Cambridge, Mass., Harvard University Press.

Collins, N.R. and L.E. Preston, 1966, Concentration and price cost margins in food manufacturing industries. *Journal of Industrial Economics* 14, No. 3 (July), 226-42.

Collins, N.H. and L.E. Preston, 1968, *Concentration and price cost margins in manufacturing industries*. Berkeley, Calif., University of California Press.

Collins, N.H. and L.E. Preston, 1969, Price — cost margins and industry structure. *Review of Economics and Statistics* 51, No. 3 (August), 271-286.

Comanor, W.S., 1965, Research and technical change in the pharmaceutical industry. *The Review of Economics and Statistics* 47, No. 2 (May), 182-90.

Comanor, W.S., 1967, Market structure, product differentiation, and industrial research. *Quarterly Journal of Economics* 81, No. 4, (November), 639-657.

Comanor, W.S. and H. Leibenstein, 1969, Allocative efficiency, x-efficiency and the measurement of welfare loss. *Economica*, New Series 36, No. 143 (August), 304-309.

Comanor, W.S. and F.M. Scherer, 1969, Patent statistics as a measure of technical change. *Journal of Political Economy* 77, No. 3 (May/Je), 392-98.

Comanor, W.S. and T.A. Wilson, 1967, Advertising, market structure, and performance *Review of Economics and Statistics* 49, No. 4 (November), 423-440.

Comanor, W.S. and T.A. Wilson, 1969, Advertising and the economics of scale. *American Economic Review* 59, No. 2 (May), 87-98.

Crum, W.L., 1939, *Corporate size and earning power*. Cambridge, Mass., Harvard University Press.

DePodwin, H.J. and R.T. Selden, 1963, Business pricing policies and inflation. *Journal of Political Economy* 71, No. 2 (April), 110-127.

Dhrymes, P. and M. Kurz, 1964, Technology and scale in electricity generation. *Econometrica* 32, No. 3 (July), 287-314.

Dorfman, R. and P.O. Steiner, 1954, Optimal advertising and optimal quality. *American Economic Review* 54, No. 5 (December), 826-836.

Doyle, A., 1968, Advertising expenditures and consumer demand. *Oxford Economic Papers*, New Series 20, No. 3 (November), 395-416.

Fisher, F.M., 1964, *Supply and costs in the U.S. petroleum industry*. Resources for the Future. Baltimore, Johns Hopkins Press.

Food Marketing Commission Technical Study No. 8, 1966 *The structure of food marketing*. Washington, Government Printing Office.

Fuchs, V.R., 1961, Integration, concentration and profits in manufacturing industries. *Quarterly Journal of Economics* 75, No. 2 (May), 278-290.

Fuchs, V.R., 1968, *The service economy*. New York, Columbia University Press.

Galatin, M., 1968, *Economies of scale and technological change in thermal power generation*. Amsterdam, North-Holland Publishing Company.

Gambeles, G., 1969, Structural determinants of profit performance in United States manufacturing industries, 1947-1967. Ph. D. thesis, University of Maryland.

Garbarino, J.W., 1950, A theory of interindustry wage variation. *Quarterly Journal of Economics* 64, No. 2 (May), 299-305.

George, K.D., 1968, Concentration, barriers to entry, and Rates of return. *Review of Economics and Statistics* 50, No. 2 (May), 273-275.

Gort, M., 1962, *Diversification and integration in American industry*. Princeton, N.J., Princeton University Press.

Gort, M., 1963, Analysis of stability and change in market shares. *Journal of Political Economy* 71, No. 1 (February), 51-63.

Grabowski, H.G., 1968, The determinants of industrial research and development: a study of the chemical, drug and petroleum industries. *Journal of Political Economy* 76, No. 2 (March/April), 292-306.

Griliches, Z., 1957, Hybrid corn: an exploration in the economics of technological change. *Econometrica* 25, No. 4 (October), 501-522.

Hall, M. and L. Weiss, 1967, Firm size and profitability. *Review of Economics and Statistics* 49, No. 3 (August), 319-331.

Hamberg, D., 1966, *R and D, essays on the economics of research and development*. New York, Random House.

Harberger, A.C., 1954, Monopoly and resource allocation. *American Economic Review* 44, No. 2 (May), 77-97.

Horowitz, I., 1962, Firm size and research activity. *Southern Economic Journal* 28, No. 3 (January), 298-301.

Imel, B., 1970, Structure-profits relationships in the food processing sector. Ph. D.Thesis, Univ. of Wisconsin.

Johnston, J., 1960, *Statistical cost analysis*. New York, McGraw Hill.

Jorgenson, D.W. and J.A. Stephenson, 1967, The time structure of investment behavior in U.S. manufacturing, 1947-1960. *Review of Economics and Statistics* 49, No. 2 (February).

Kamerschen, D.R., 1969, The determination of profit rates in 'oligopolistic'industries *Journal of Business* 42, No. 3 (July), 293-301.

Kaysen, L. and D. Turner, 1959, *Anti-trust economics*. Cambridge, Mass., Harvard University Press.

Kelly, W. (FTC), 1969, *Economic report on the influence of market structure on profit performance of food manufacturing firms*. A Federal Trade Commission economic report. Washington, Government Printing Office.

Kilpatrick, R.W., 1967, The choice among alternative measures of industrial concentration. *Review of Economics and Statistics* 44, No. 2 (May), 258-60.

Kilpatrick, R.W., 1968, Stigler on the relationship between industry profit rates and market concentration. *Journal of Political Economy*, 76, No. 3 (May/June), 479-488.

Komiya, R., 1962, Technical progress and the production function in the United States steam power industry. *Review of Economics and Statistics* 44, No. 2 (May), 156-66.

Lambin, J.J., 1969, Measuring the profitability of advertising: an empirical study. *Journal of Industrial Economics* 17, No. 2 (April), 86-103.

Larner, R.J., 1966, Ownership and control in the 200 largest non-financial corporations, 1929 and 1963. *American Economic Review* 56, No. 4 (September), 777-87.

Larner, R.J., 1968, Separation of ownership and control and its implications for the behavior of the firm. Unpublished Ph. D. Thesis, University of Wisconsin,

Leibenstein, H., 1966, Allocative efficiency vs. x-efficiency. *American Economic Review* 56, No. 3 (June), 392-415.

Lerner, A., 1933, The concept of monopoly and the measurement of monopoly power. *Review of Economic Studies* 1, No. 3, 157-175.

Levinson, H. M., 1960, Post war movements in prices and wages in manufacturing industries. Joint Economic Committee, *Study of Income, Employment, and Prices*. Study Paper No. 21, Washington, Governement Printing Office.

Lewis, H.G., 1963, *Unionism and relative wages in the United States*. Chicago, University of Chicago Press.

Lewellen, W.G., 1968, *Executive compensation in large industrial corporations*. National Bureau of Economic Research, New York, Columbia University Press.

Ling, S., 1964, *Economies of scale in the steam electric power generating industry*. Amsterdam, North-Holland Publishing Company.

Long, W., 1970, An econometric study of performance in American manufacturing. Ph. D. thesis, University of California.

MacAvoy, P.W., 1962, *Price formation in natural gas fields*. New Haven, Conn., Yale University Press.

MacAvoy, P.W., 1965, *The economic effects of regulation: the trunk line railroad cartels and the Interstate Commerce Commission before 1900*. Cambridge, Mass., The MIT Press.

Mann, H.M., 1966, Seller concentration, barriers to entry, and rates of return in thirty industries, 1950-1960. *Review of Economics and Statistics* 48, No. 3 (August), 296-307.

Mann, H.M., J.A. Hennings, and J.W. Meehan, Jr., 1967, Advertising and concentration: an empirical investigation. *Journal of Industrial Economics* 16, No. 1 (November), 34-45.

Mansfield, E., 1961, Technical change and the rate of imitation. *Econometrica* 29, No. 4 (October), 741-766.

Mansfield, E., 1963 a, Intrafirm rates of diffusion of an innovation. *Review of Economics and Statistics* 45, No. 4 (November), 348-359.

Mansfield, E., 1963b, Size of firm, market structure, and innovation. *Journal of Political Economy* 71, No. 6 (December), 556-576.

Mansfield, E., 1963c, The speed of response of firms to new techniques. *Quarterly Journal of Economics* 77, No. 2 (May), 290-311.

Mansfield, E., 1964, Industrial research and development expenditures: determinants, prospects, and relation to size of firm and inventive output. *Journal of Political Economy* 72, No. 4 (August), 319-340.

Marcus, M., 1969, Profitability and size of firm. *Review of Economics and Statistics* 51, No. 1 (February), 104-107.

Markham, J. W., 1965, Market structure, business conduct and innovation. *American Economic Review* 55, No. 2 (May), 323-332.

Mason, E. S., 1939, Price and production policies of large scale enterprise. *American Economic Review* 29, No. 1 (March), 61-74.

Masters, S. H., 1969, An inter industry analysis of wage and plant size. *Review of Economics and Statistics* 51, No. 3 (August), 341-345.

Means, G., 1957, Before the senate judiciary, sub-committee on anti-trust and monopoly. *Hearings on Administered Prices*, Washington, Government Printing Office. Part I, 124-5. Part IX (do., 1959), 4746-58. Part X (do., 1959), 4897-4910.

Meyer, J. R., M. J. Peck, J. Stenason and C. Zwick, 1959, *The economics of competition in the transportation industries*. Cambridge, Mass., Harvard University Press.

Miller, R. A., 1967, Marginal concentration and industrial profit rates. *Southern Economic Journal* 24, No. 4 (October), 259-268.

Minhas, B. S., 1963, *An international comparison of factor cost and factor use*. Amsterdam, North-Holland Publishing Company, 82-84.

Monsen, R., J. S. Chiu, and D. E. Cooley, 1968, The effect of separation of ownership and control on the performance of the large firm. *Quarterly Journal of Economics* 82, No. 3 (August), 435-451.

National Resources Committee, 1939, *The structure of the American economy*. Part I: *Basic characteristics*. Washington, Goverment Printing Office.

Nelson, R. L., 1963, *Concentration in the manufacturing industries of the United States*. New Haven, Conn., Yale University Press.

Nerlove, M., 1963, Returns to scale in electricity supply. *Measurement in economics — Studies in mathematical economics and econometrics in memory of Yehuda Grunfeld*. Stanford, Calif., Stanford University Press, 167-198.

Nerlove, M. and F. V. Waugh, 1961, Advertising without supply control. *Journal of Farm Economics* 43 (November).

Palda, K. S., 1964, *The measurement of cumulative advertising effects*. Ford Doctoral Dissertation Series. Englewood Cliffs, N. J., Prentice Hall.

Peles, Y., 1969, Rates of amortization of advertising expenditures. Unpublished Ph. D. thesis, Graduate School of Business, University of Chicago.

Phillips, A., 1966, Patents, potential competition, and technical progress. *American Economic Review* 56, No. 2 (May), 301-31.

Reder, M., 1962, Wage differentials, theory and measurement. In: Universities — National, Bureau. *Aspects of Labor Economics*. Princeton, N. J., Princeton University Press, 285-286.

Ross, A. M. and W. Goldner, 1950, Forces affecting the interindustry wage structure. *Quarterly Journal of Economics* 64, No. 2 (May), 280-281.

Ruggles, R., 1955, The nature of price flexibility and the determinants of relative price changes in the economy. In: Universities — National Bureau, *Business Concentration and Price Policy*. Princeton, N.J., Princeton University Press, 441-495.

Sato, Kazuo, 1961, Price-cost structure and behavior of profit margins. *Yale Economic Essays* 1, No. 2 (Fall), 361-418.

Samuels, J. M. and D. J. Smyth, 1968, Profits, variability of profits, and firm size. *Economica* New Series 35, No. 138 (May), 127-149.

Scherer, F. M., 1965, Firm size, market structure, opportunity and the output of patented inventions. *American Economic Review* 55, No. 5, Part I (December), 1097-1125.

Scherer, F. M., 1967, Market structure and the employment of scientists and engineers. *American Economic Review* 57, No. 3 (June), 524-531.

Scherer, F. M., 1969, Market structure and the stability of investment. *American Economic Review* 59, No. 2 (May), 72-79.

Schmookler, J., 1959, Bigness, fewness, and research. *Journal of Political Economy* 67, No. 6 (December), 628-632.

Schmookler, J., 1966, *Invention and economic growth*. Cambridge, Mass., Harvard University Press.

Schumpeter, J., 1942, *Capitalism, socialism and democracy*. New York, Harper.

Schwartzman, D., 1959, The effect of monopoly on price. *Journal of Political Economy* 67, No. 4 (August), 352-62.

Segal, M., 1964, The relation between union wage impact and market structure. *Quarterly Journal of Economics*, 78 (February), 96-114.

Shepherd, W. G., 1969, Market power and racial discrimination in white collar employment. *Anti-Trust Bulletin* 14, (Spring), 141-161.

Sherman, H. J., 1964, *Macro-dynamic economics*. New York, Appleton-Century-Crofts, Ch. 8.

Sherman, H. J., 1968, *Profits in the United States*. Ithaca, Cernell Univ. Press, Ch. 3.

Solomon, B., 1967, Determinants of interfirm differences in profitability among the largest 500 U.S. industrial firms. Ph.D. thesis, University of California.

Stafford, F., 1968, Concentration and labor earnings: comment. *American Economic Review* 58 (March), 174-181 and my reply, 181-185.

Stekler, H. O., 1963, *Profitability and size of firm*. Berkeley, Calif., Institute of Business and Economic Research, University of California.

Stekler, H. O., 1964, The variability of profitability with size of firm 1947-1958. *Journal of the American Statistical Association* 59, No. 308 (December), 1183-1193.

Stigler, G., 1942, The extent and bases of monopoly. *American Economic Review* 32, No. 2, Part 2 (June), 1-22.

Stigler, G., 1950, Monopoly and oligopoly by merger. *American Economic Review* 40, No. 2 (May), 23-34.

Stigler, G., 1956, The statistics of monopoly and merger. *Journal of Political Economy* 64 (February), 33-40.

Stigler, G., 1962, Administered prices and oligopolistic inflation. *Journal of Business* 35, No. 1 (January), 235-251.

Stigler, G., 1963, *Capital and rates of return in manufacturing industries*. Princeton, N.J., Princeton University Press for NBER.

Stigler, G., 1964, A theory of oligopoly. *Journal of Political Economy* 72, No. 1 (February), 44-61.

Stigler, G., 1968, *The organization of industry*. Homewood, Ill., Irwin.

Stoikov, V. and R. L. Raimon, 1968, Determinants of differences in the quit rate among industries. *American Economic Review* 58, No. 5, Part I (December), 1283-1298.

Strauss, R.P., 1970, Discrimination against Negroes in the labor Market. Ph. D. thesis, Univ. of Wisconsin.

Telser, L., 1962, Advertising and cigarettes. *Journal of Political Economy* 70, No. 5 (October) 471-499.

Telser, L., 1964, Advertising and competition. *Journal of Political Economy* 72, No. 6 (December), 537-562.

Telser, L., 1969, Some determinants of the returns to manufacturing industries. Report No. 6935. Center for Mathematical Studies in Business and Economics, University of Chicago. (Unpublished.)

Throop, A.W., 1968, The union-non union wage differential and cost-push inflation. *American Economic Review* 58, No. 1 (March), 83-4.

Watson, D. and M. Holman, 1967, Concentration of patents from government financed research in industry. *Review of Economics and Statistics*, August, 375-381.

Weiss, L.W., 1963, Average concentration ratios and industry performance. *Journal of Industrial Economics*, No. 3 (July), 247-252.

Weiss, L.W., 1966a, Concentration and labor earnings. *American Economic Review* 56, No. 1, (March), 95-117.

Weiss, L.W., 1966b, Business pricing policies and inflation reconsidered. *Journal of Political Economy* 74, No. 2 (April), 177-187.

Weiss, L.W., 1969, Advertising, profits and corporate taxes. *Review of Economics and Statistics* 51, No. 4 (November), 421-430.

Williamson, O.E., 1963a, Managerial discretion and business behavior. *American Economic Review* 52, No. 5 (December), 1032-1057.

Williamson, O.E., 1963b, Selling expense as a barrier to entry. *Quarterly Journal of Economics* 77, No. 1 (February), 112-128.

Williamson, O.E., 1965, Innovation and market structure. *Journal of Political Economy* 73, No. 1 (February), 67-73.

Worley, J.S., 1961, Industrial research and the new competition. *Journal of Political Economy* 59, No. 2 (April), 183-6.

Yordan, W.J., 1961a, Another look at monopoly and wages. *Canadian Journal of Economics and Political Science* 27, No. 3 (August), 372-9.

Yordan, W.J., 1961b, Industrial concentration and price flexibility in inflation: Price response rates in fourteen industries, 1947-1958. *Review of Economics and Statistics* 43, No. 3 (August), 287-294.

COMMENTS BY WILLIAM S. COMANOR[*]
Stanford University

Professor Weiss' paper is a useful review of much of the econometric work which has been done in the field of industrial organization. It is an accurate and well balanced survey, and as such there is little to criticize which refers specifically to the paper. This comment, therefore, is reserved for the body of material which is covered.

---

* I am grateful to Bridger M. Mitchell and Robert Wilson for helpful discussion which preceded the preparation of these comments.

Industrial organization is an area of applied research, which traditionally has been closely tied to questions of public policy. Despite the original prescriptions of Edward Mason, practitioners in this area have moved away from an early reliance on case studies and towards the use of econometric methods of analysis. To a large extent, therefore, a review of econometric studies of industrial organization is a review of much of the content of the field.

As Weiss accurately indicates, a large share of this recent work has investigated the relationship between various dimensions of market structure and different indices of market performance. This focus has flowed directly from the original emphasis placed on questions of public policy. Although our primary concern may be with economic performance, there are generally few levers which can be used directly to influence performance. Government policies, in contrast, are generally applied to specific structural or behavioral characteristics of markets which only indirectly affect performance. We are therefore obliged to be concerned with the nature of this relationship.

The primary concern with investigating how structure affects performance implies a great deal about both the strengths and weaknesses of much of the work which has been carried out — especially in terms of the empirical methodology which has been pursued. What has followed from this concern are studies which have a large inductive flavor. Workers in this area have little confidence in their ability to derive much about the nature of the underlying relationships from general principles and so they examine the statistical regularities with the hope of being able to infer some more general results. Their objective is to discover how the conduct of individual firms, independently and in concert with others, and as influenced by different elements of market structure, affects various dimensions of economic performance.

It is interesting that nearly every study which Weiss reports, and which is carried out at the industry level, looks at the impact of concentration ratios. Despite their pervasive use, these ratios are admittedly an *ad hoc* measure of only one dimension of industry structure and have little or no theoretical justification. At the same time, their use cannot be easily dismissed, for we *are* interested in determining the effect that concentration is likely to have on performance. This interest follows not so much from the influence of economic theory as from the concern paid to questions of public policy.

To be sure, many of the studies reported by Weiss go beyond this point. They move beyond an analysis of the data and an attempt to explain the regularities which are found, so that they are not fully inductive in spirit. Many contain considerable discussion and justification of the underlying hypotheses, where the hypotheses are derived not only from economic theory but also from some knowledge of the relevant institutions as well as from *a priori* reasoning which has not been embodied in the mainstream of economic thought. In addition, of course, some hypotheses are derived directly from policy considerations and are of concern precisely because the relevant independent variables appear amenable to policy control. The emphasis here is placed generally on the testing of relevant hypotheses which are expressed in terms of the effect of one variable on another.

This methodological spirit can be contrasted with that embodied in econometric research which has been carried out in other areas. In the case, e.g., of research on demand curves and production functions, the emphasis is much more on specifying explicitly an underlying model and estimating the parameters of that model. In much of this work, the structure of the model is derived directly from economic theory. When hypotheses are put forward, these are generally stated in terms of the size or sign of specific parameters, and they often assume a more secondary character. This distinction can be over-emphasized, and there certainly exists a continuum in that most studies include both types of statistical problems. Nevertheless there does appear to be a greater concern with structural estimation, in contrast to the emphasis on hypothesis testing dominant in industrial organization. Such research has a largely deductive spirit — even where the analysis is carried out predominantly in the form of single equation models.

Accepting that these differences exist, we need to ask why such different methodological approaches have evolved. Why is it that different areas of econometric research have developed with different empirical methodologies? While many reasons could be offered, clearly a dominant element results from a second distinction which can be drawn among the various areas of research. In the case of demand equations and production functions there is wide acceptance both of the general form of the basic models and of their underlying assumptions. In industrial organization, on the other hand, there exist no generally agreed upon basic models of economic behavior, and the underlying assumptions are often contested. As a result the different areas are concerned with answering significantly different types of empirical questions.

Most significant in the case of industrial organization is that there is no generally agreed upon theory of oligopoly from which models of market behavior can be deduced. It is not a matter that there are no theories of oligopoly behavior, but rather that the theories which exist require more specific — and less general — assumptions regarding economic conduct than those for pure competition and monopoly. What is required are assumptions dealing with how firms react to the recognition of mutual interdependence, specifically the strategies they follow in circumstances where not all of the important decision variables lie within their control. Since there are no agreed upon rules of behavior in these circumstances, we obtain a different theory for each different postulated rule of behavior.

In this context, it is not surprising that practitioners of industrial organization are forced to take a more inductive approach. They have used the theories which exist, together with some assumed rules of behavior, to develop specific hypotheses regarding market outcomes, which are then subject to empirical testing. Precisely because these assumed rules of behavior are not completely general, their behavioral implications are rarely developed into fully specified models. On the contrary, investigators appear content to study one aspect of the total picture at a time, to investigate the impact of one variable on another, with the hope that at some later point, the pieces will be fitted together into a consistent whole.

A second set of factors which has led to this methodological approach is the existence of conflicting theories in a number of areas. The classic case here concerns the Schumpterian hypothesis regarding the impact of market structure on innovation and technical change. As is well known, in contrast to the Schumpterian position, others have argued that more competitive market structures lead to faster rates of technical change. As expected, these differences stem from alternate assumptions which underlie the two models, and one approach would be to test the validity of the various assumptions. Whatever its justification, this approach is generally not feasible since the different assumptions result from different behavioral rules which are difficult to isolate and observe. What can be observed, however, are the results of this behavior, and therefore it has been far more fruitful to test the alternate implications of the conflicting theories.

By way of contrast, other areas of econometric research have more solid theoretical foundations. With reference to demand analysis, it seems clear that, whatever its problems, it provides some reasonably well established propositions. Investigators do not feel compelled to test whether incomes and prices determine the quantities demanded, but rather are concerned with estimating the size of the underlying parameters. Similarly, in the case of production functions, investigators are not generally concerned with the question of whether inputs affect outputs. Their concern is rather with estimating the parameters of the underlying relationship.

In industrial organization, investigators simply do not have the same degree of confidence in their theoretical constructs as exists in other areas. In many respects the theoretical problems are less tractable, and, as a result, the theoretical apparatus is in a more rudimentary state. We are therefore forced to be more inductive in our approach.

Given that differences exist, what inferences should be drawn from their presence? At this point, it is useful to ask whether any general conclusions can be reached regarding the state of econometric research in this area.

Among some economists, there is a tendency to regard more deductive methods of analysis as somewhat superior to their more inductive counterparts. The latter is regarded as "numbers" without "theory", and the empirical findings are therefore more questionable. Whatever the validity of this view of a purely inductive approach, there is a middle ground between the two extremes which is reached by many of the studies reviewed by Weiss. This middle position is occupied by those who use econometric methods to test propositions which are derived at least partially from an underlying theoretical structure. A theoretical framework is used to derive the propositions which are tested, although this framework is clearly placed in a more secondary role than would be the case in a more deductive approach. Nevertheless, this middle ground may indeed be the most fruitful one for work on the problems posed in industrial organization.

At the same time, it must be admitted that this approach has provided a shield behind which a considerable amount of sloppy work has been carried on. Even though our basic concern is not with estimating the structural parameters of a multi-equation model because of the inherent difficulties involved, we still need to worry about the econometric techniques which are used and whether they are not too simple to provide accurate estimates of the test statistics. For example, we need to be concerned about including endogenous variables on the right-hand sides of our equations in circumstances where there is likely also to be substantial reverse causality, and then proceeding to estimate the coefficients by standard single equation methods. Here the problem is not so much that of going back to an underlying structure as with dealing with the bias created by ignoring these relationships. Where multi-equation bias exists, moreover, we need to examine whether it is likely to invalidate our results. While we may still decide to proceed with single equation methods, a more explicit discussion of these questions is probably in order.

An example of this problem can be found in the largest single area of study as reported by Weiss. This concerns the numerous studies which have tested the effect of concentration on profit rates. It might be asked: should not profits also affect concentration? Since high profits attract new firms into an industry, and since this entry would then reduce concentration levels, it might be argued that high profits should lead to lower concentration ratios. It is interesting that this question has been singularly ignored in the studies reported by Weiss. Furthermore there are other areas where similar questions arise, and indeed some of the problems created by the presence also of reverse causality were noted by Weiss in his review. For this reason, perhaps some greater emphasis on specifying the underlying relationships would be helpful even when the primary concern remains with hypothesis testing rather than with structural estimation. By so doing we could have a greater degree of confidence in the empirical results obtained.

COMMENTS BY OLIVER E. WILLIAMSON
University of Pennsylvania

Leonard Weiss is to be commended for his impressive review of an extensive literature. I am prepared indeed to predict that it will become a standard reference — one that we will both require of our students and recommend to our colleagues. My comments will be restricted mainly to the policy related statements of the paper and to the matter of directions for future research.

0. Cross-section studies and antitrust

As Weiss indicates, a shift away from industry studies in favor of cross-section studies has occurred in the past 30 years. The need for this has been manifold — although, as Weiss also indicates, the two techniques are really complementary and one would hope that neither would become so fashionable as to supplant the other. Among the advantages of cross-section studies is that they help to restore (or maintain) perspectives. (Many of the critics of antitrust would, if they could, rest their case on references to conspicious exceptions. The frequency with which Bell and General Electric Labs are cited as "typical" in the dialogue dealing with progressiveness in relation to firm size is an illustration. To cite counterexamples is mere disputative. A dispassionate view of the evidence such as cross-sectional analysis potentially affords is in these circumstances clearly indicated.)

Such studies are also useful for purposes of overall policy design. (The Merger Guidelines of the Department of Justice is an example.) Three reservations should nevertheless be expressed in this respect. First, a sensitivity to variance as well as average tendencies is important. Enforcement officials, whose natural posture is one of advocacy, may need to be cautioned in this regard lest empirical results be "used" with excessive zeal. Second, and related, average tendency analysis should not be permitted to suppress a sensitivity to the existence of genuine exceptions. Uniform policies are easy to enforce but may also, occasionally, be counterproductive. Notable exceptions and the reasons therefore ought presumably to be recognized where this is feasible and the main policy is not seriously compromised in the process. Third, the quest for a "critical" concentration ratio that intrigues Weiss and many others seems ill-advised. Making life at the Antitrust Division easy is a commendable objective, but it can also be misleading. Surely the evidence that market performance rests on a variety of structural influences, of which concentration is only one, is at this point decisive.

1. Policy-relevant studies

Antitrust proceeds for the most part on the basis of individual cases. Although cross-section studies may be of great help in this connection, industry studies may frequently be more productive of useful policy results — especially for the "big" cases. Attention should presumably be directed at those industries which pose or prospectively pose monopoly problems — electronic data processing, CATV, commercial airline manufacturing, etc. being examples.

Also, whereas most cross-section studies are concerned with associations between structure and performance, it is also of interest to consider specific practices and examine the relations between structure and conduct. The first question to be addressed here is what practices are to be considered offensive and for what reasons. The problem, thus, is to distinguish truly offensive from allegedly offensive behavior. Insistence that objectionable practices pass a viability test — which is to say that nonrationality arguments (under any reasonable specification of the firm's utility function) ought to be regarded as inherently suspect — may permit many fabricated claims to be dismissed from the outset. For those practices that pass a viability test, the question becomes one of *discriminating* between circumstances in which the practice is really objectionable from those in which it is innocent or altogether beneficial. (For example, in what circumstances does the operation of a franchise system raise nontrivial entry barriers? When does advertising have offensive economic consequences?) This question may be partly answered by *a priori* reasoning, but empirical studies will also be needed. The more productive of these, both from a statistical and policy point of view, are apt to be ones which focus on the objectionable subset rather than condemn the practice quite generally on the basis of average tendencies.

2. Some conceptual considerations

"Everyone knows" that firms specialize according to characteristic strengths. Still, there is a common tendency among economists in general and industrial organization specialists in particular to disregard this truism and evaluate each firm with respect to all performance dimensions. Consider the "optimum" firm size dispute. Large firms which have access to economies of scale in production and marketing are sometimes discredited on account of their inferior progressiveness characteristics. The question is then put: What are the *net* economic consequences of large size considering both scale economies and progressiveness performance? But the question, often, is misdirected. If the large enterprise has an advantage in managing proven resources while the small firm enjoys an advantage with respect to inventive activity, *and if* a transfer process exists which permits innovations to be exchanged or acquired, the net consequences of large size cannot be established in this way. The relevant issue is whether the *system* of large and small firms operates effectively, which shifts attention to consideration of factors that impair its effectiveness. (For example, to what extent does high concentration and very large size inhibit entry and in this way impair the transfer process from operating as described?) This is a different issue altogether from the netting out procedure described above.

A second conceptual issue that Weiss' discussion raises is the measurement problem. The progressive refinement of measuring advertising effects that he describes is one example. A second, and one where I differ with Weiss, is in measuring the rate of return. Weiss favors the use of rate of return on equity because "industries differ in their stability and growth rates and, therefore, in their ability to borrow. Rates of return on assets are apt to reflect the latter in part. It is rates of return on equity which should be equalized in competitive industries in the long run." From the standpoint of allocative efficiency, however, it is rates of return on capital, not on any particular kind of capital, that is of interest. Also, as Baumol and Malkiel have pointed out, the well-managed firm will ordinarily be levered to capacity.[1] If then the debt-equity ratio is a proxy for management excellence, measuring the rate of return on equity will magnify these management differences and could lead to erroneous conclusions if management excellence and concentration were to be positively correlated, which seems not implausible.

Finally, with respect to data collection, I would support F. M. Scherer's plea for greater access to industry data collected by the government. But special studies by academics may frequently be even more productive. The success of Edwin Mansfield in his small sample studies of innovation bears testimony to the merits of collecting special purpose data using refined techniques. His experience and that of others who have collected original data reveals, I think, that, contrary to allegation, businesses often will cooperate with academics if an earnest effort is made to secure their support.

---

[1] William Baumol and Burton Malkiel, The firm's optimal debt-equity combination and the cost of capitals. *Quarterly Journal of Economics* 81, November 1967, 547-78,

Frontiers of Quantitative Economics, ed. M.D. Intriligator. © *North-Holland Publishing Company.*

CHAPTER 10

ECONOMETRIC STUDIES OF HISTORY

GAVIN WRIGHT

Yale University

0. The "new economic history"

No one who has had any contact with American economic history during the past decade can be unaware of the great changes in approach which the field has experienced nor of the methodological controversies which this shift has left in its wake. "New economic historians" have both called for, and brought forth, a body of literature which makes intensive use of quantification, economic theory, and statistical tools.[1] Critics of these approaches have maintained that the study of deductive models and counterfactual situations is a kind of "quasi-history" which cannot replace the real thing (Redlich 1965, 1968); or that economic theory in its present state is not adequate to the tasks of history (Desai 1968; Hacker 1966). Skeptics from within have argued that economic historians should not view themselves as "users of economic theory", but should rather, through "the determination of what of significance actually happened in economic history", serve as active critics of "economic laws" (Basmann 1965). The rejoinder to these views has been that most statements of interest about what "actually happened" involve *implicit* theory and measurement and assertions about

---

[1] Methodological articles include Conrad and Meyer (1957), Conrad (1968), Davis et al. (1960), Fogel (1966), and North (1966, ch. 1).

counterfactual states (Fogel 1967). "Moderates" in the debate maintain that "cliometric" methods are appropriate for some historical questions but not for others (Cochran 1969).

To the practicing economic historian, at least to those who have received their training in economics departments, much of this debate has an abstract, ethereal tone. An economist who consults this literature in search of guidance on fruitful methods of approaching economic history is likely to be disappointed. For most of us it goes without saying that economic subjects are quantitative; and since we accept the "social science" label without grumbling, we have no qualms in principle about the use of deductive theory and the study of counterfactual states. What is of concern, however, to anyone planning research in historical economics is the practical question of the type of quantitative methods to use, especially the level of sophistication in econometric technique which is called for. Is there a major intellectual "return" to the application of formal estimation procedures to elaborate mathematical models? Or does the shortage of historical data indicate that relatively "low-power" methods of statistical testing make more sense? Are the established methods of econometrics inappropriate in some ways for historical studies, either because of the lack of data or because of the sorts of questions historians ask? This paper attempts to shed some light on these questions by examining critically several recent studies which do attempt to apply relatively sophisticated techniques to historical problems.

The spirit of the inquiry is strictly pragmatic: the question we are concerned with is the extent to which "econometric studies of history" have succeeded in providing convincing answers to questions of interest to economic historians. But how do we determine whether conclusions are convincing? Can we really proceed without clearer standards of evaluation? We do, of course, have some "objective" standards for judging econometric studies — e.g., the tests for statistical significance of coefficients, goodness of fit, and serial correlation of residuals and, more loosely, the adequacy of the specification and the "realism" of any assumptions involved. But the evaluation has several unavoidably subjective dimensions and I think it is best to recognize these frankly. The facts of life of practical econometric work are that we are always forced to proceed on the basis of assumptions — especially assumed specifications of structural relationships, which may not be fully realized. Even the "tests" typically depend for their validity on assumptions of normality which we frequently have almost no hope of verifying. The difficulty of being sure of the "true" degree of uncertainty which attaches to a conclusion derived from an econometric fit is compounded by the fact that, in history, we have no clear standard as to what constitutes an acceptable degree of accuracy. For policy-oriented studies we have at least the hypothetical check of prediction; or, in the case of structural estimation, the (again possibly hypothetical) possibility that some measure of policy will be based on the estimates. These points of focus and the implicit loss functions attached to wrong predictions or misguided policies provide at least some economic basis for judging how close is "close enough". But in econometric history there are no such "outside" constraints. Some may look to history for policy guidance of a general sort, of course, but it seems most unlikely that any cliometrician will ever have to answer to a policy-maker because of a grossly misestimated coefficient.

In these circumstances, it is clear that opinions will differ on whether or not a given conclusion is "convincing". Still more subjective is the question whether a finding is "of interest to economic historians". If you are not especially interested in the causes of cotton-price fluctuations in the 1830's, then you will not be very impressed by a model which successfully explains them.[2] It may seem unfair to ask that a cliometrician should meet anyone else's standards of "interest". But the question cannot be avoided, because of the frequent assertion that only a limited range of historical questions lends itself to econometric analysis.

My only justification for proceeding in the light of these observations, is that I think most of us share enough subjective standards at least to communicate on these matters. We are often able to agree that certain models are "very" misspecified in certain situations, and we usually recognize greater and lesser degrees of care in testing the sensitivity of conclusions with respect to the less plausible assumptions. It is not so clear, however, that our "interests" are the same; nor is it clear that we are agreed on just what it is that we expect to gain from the study of history. In all of these matters, I hope that I am explicit enough in the statement of my own standards to make the exercise useful even for those who disagree. "Consumer Reports" can be valuable even if you don't accept their ratings, as long as they explain their reasons for rating products as they do.

---

[2] A common ploy in this regard is to state that the method of analysis if of great interest even if the findings are not. This claim may salvage an article, but it really does not gain much ground overall: at some point the methods cease to be interesting if they never give interesting results.

In much of the foregoing it may be observed that the evaluation is as much of "econometrics" as of "econometric history", and it may be argued that this is inappropriate. It is reported that a midwestern farmer once explained that it made no sense for him to study the latest agricultural methods because "I already know better than I'm doing". It may be said that we are in a similar position, the level of econometric sophistication among economic historians being so clearly below that of econometricians. Perhaps we should concentrate on "closing the gap" before venturing to criticize econometrics itself.

But just as the farmer's comment is hard for an economist to fathom, so the argument is misguided, and comments which reflect on the adequacy of econometric methods in general are fair game. The reason for studying history is to improve our understanding of the past, and if econometric methods will not do that for us, it is more important to know *that*, than to know whether the technique is the "best" available. There is always the possibility, of course, that a "better" method will "succeed" where another "failed", but some of us suspect that the enthusiasm of book-jacket writers for "modern econometric techniques" carries as many dangers as the implicit theorizing of the older school.

The paper makes no claim to completeness in its coverage of econometric historical studies. Indeed there is no clear line between "applied econometrics" and "econometric history", and certain exclusions of border-line cases are bound to be arbitrary. Thus, two recent historical studies of railroad investment behavior are concerned in part with evaluating a study published by Klein in 1951, which applied to time-series data going up to 1941; it is doubtful that Klein believed he was writing "economic history" at the time. But how "old" do data have to be before they become "history"?[3] Furthermore, this review is concerned almost exclusively with American economic history, and hence I omit such promising new work as Kelley's (1965, 1968) articles on Australian migration, and research by McCloskey (1969) and others on British economic history.

Perhaps more serious are the omissions of many studies which are as yet unpublished but which will appear in the next few years.[4] Many of these

---

[3] This is not to deny that there may be differences in orientation between economic historians and "applied economists", and that these differences may affect the appropriateness of certain techniques.

[4] Notable pieces include McCloskey (1969) and Zevin (1969). See also the many unpublished papers and dissertations listed in Fogel (1966) and Fogel and Engerman (1969)

I have not read, and it would hardly be fair to criticize those which I have read prior to their publication. The reader is warned, therefore, that the overall complexion of the field may change considerably in a short time. Nevertheless, we now have a sufficient number of studies published to make an intensive review worthwhile, even if the review itself may become obsolete sooner than I care to reflect. For the benefit of non-cliometricians, however, I begin with a survey of the variety of methods which have so far been employed.

1. Varieties of econometric history

In writing a review of this kind, one is immediately confronted with the realization that much of what is referred to as "econometric history" is hardly recognizable to econometricians as such. In reviewing Robert Fogel's study of the impact of the railroads on American economic growth (one of the most daring works of the new genre). Marc Nerlove wrote: "An econometrician reading the book may be shocked, as I was, at how limited indeed are the uses of econometric technique and how simple minded are those tools actually used" (Nerlove 1966, p. 107). The distinctive contribution of the New Economic History has not been so much the use of "econometrics" but the use of *economics* — the application of standard economic reasoning in the posing and answering of historical questions. Many historical issues have been substantially clarified simply by analytical thinking and measurement, without any complex or elaborate quantitative methods. Most of these studies bear a closer methodological resemblance to present-day cost-benefit studies than to the methods covered in a typical course or textbook in econometrics. The approach usually is to estimate values for various parameters directly from historical documents, secondary sources, or data fragments, and to use a theoretical (or accounting) framework to summarize this information in a sensible way. Most frequently, structural coefficients which cannot be ascertained directly are not "estimated"; rather, *a priori* beliefs about them are used to assess the direction of "bias" in the result.

Many of the best-known works of the new economic history are "cost-benefit" studies in purpose as well. This characterization applies, I believe, to Conrad and Meyer's estimation of the profitability of slavery and to subsequent revisions.[5] It certainly applies to Thomas' (1965) estimation of the cost of British imperial policy to the American colonies[6]; to Lebergott's (1966) estimate of the potential profitability of the antebellum railroads as seen by an investor; and to Temin's (1964) calculation of the profit rates on different types of blast furnaces in the antebellum period (pp. 51-81). One might characterize as strictly "benefit" studies those which attempt to calculate the direct "social saving" from an innovation, such as those by Fogel (1964) and Fishlow (1965) on the railroad, and that of Ransom (1964) on the canals. An example of a study within an accounting framework is North's (1968) recent examination of the sources of productivity change in ocean shipping. While most calculations of "profitability" are forced to construct estimates for a "typical" or "representative" firm, Swieringa (1968) has arrived at separate rates of return for each member of a large sample of land speculators in central Iowa.

As is often true in cost-benefit work, many of these writers use a variety of ingenious theoretical devices to estimate implicit costs and benefits. Thus, Fogel (1964) examines insurance rates to estimate the cost of the relative "riskiness" of canals, and he accounts for the relative speed of the canals by estimating the cost of holding inventories (ch. II). However, in none of the articles mentioned is there an "estimation" of a behavioral or technical relationship, in the sense of a statistical inference from a number of observations. At most, the sensitivity of conclusions is tested by varying the assumed parameter values, or the conclusion is given added confidence by consistently biasing the choices against it

I want to emphasize that I do not mean to dismiss these studies as inherently "inferior" either in methodological ingenuity or in "results". While many particular efforts have been shown to be quite wide of the mark, this does not necessarily reflect on the methods; and in cases where only scattered scraps of data are available it is often hard to know what more can be done. If "econometrics" in the broadest sense is the technique of drawing inference from non-experimental data, then such studies certainly qualify. It is quite plain, however, that such methods fall short of providing knowledge of underlying economic structure and of the interplay of market

---

[5] See Conrad and Meyer (1958). Revised calculations may be found in Evans (1962), Foust and Swan (1970), Saraydar (1964), and Sutch (1965). Conrad and Meyer mistakenly believed that their test was relevant for the issue of the viability of slavery. For a correction see Yasuba (1961).

[6] Thomas' methods and findings are criticized in McClelland (1969) and Ransom (1968).

forces which we would like to have. Indeed, one really needs econometric estimates of the relevant economic functions in order to carry out a cost-benefit calculation accurately. The emphasis in this review, therefore, will be on those writers who have managed to assemble enough data to use "econometrics" in the narrower sense.

There is an intermediate class of studies, however, which deserves attention: those which use regression or curve-fitting methods in order to estimate figures for which no direct sources are available. The method is in some sense peculiar to economic history — or at least to fields in which data-sparseness is often the most pressing problem — and much cliometric work has taken this form. Many examples may be cited: Fogel (1964), in his chapter on the position of rails in the market for American iron (ch. V), fits a second-degree time trend to six observations on the share of Pennsylvania in total national output of pig iron in order to complete an annual series for the national total. In the same chapter, Fogel uses fragmentary evidence on the average and range of rail life as a rationale for the use of a log-normal curve to estimate annual requirements for rail replacements. (He experiments with alternative parameters and a normal distribution is order to ensure that the results are fairly insensitive to such changes.) Fishlow (1965) uses a cubic time trend in a somewhat different way: to convert knowledge of cumulative railroad investment expenditures into an annual series (p. 384). His description of the actual estimation of the equation, however, is somewhat obscure. Other investigators have fitted regressions to relationships between variables (rather than to time) for the same purpose. Temin, e.g., regresses the quantity of rolled steel products on the outputs of ingots and castings in order to complete a series of the former.[7] Davis and Legler (1966) have estimated an annual series of local tax receipts from a regression on a set of regional dummy variables, a variable representing urbanization, and state tax receipts. In this case, the full cross-section data are available for only 6 years, and the equation is fitted without distinguishing the observations by year. (They observe in a footnote: "Inclusion of time improves the R^2 significantly ... but produces insurmountable problems of interpretation.") Since state receipts are available on an annual basis, Davis and Legler are able to derive an annual series for local receipts.

---

[7] Appendix C. From the description of the regression in the text, it appears that there is a typographical error in the reported version of the equation.

Two final examples may be cited: Poulson (1969) uses a regression of the value of manufacturing output on other manufacturing series for the period 1849-1899 in order to estimate the value of manufacturing output for the earlier period 1809-39; and Cranmer (1960) estimates a cost curve for canal construction in order to compute total canal investment between 1815 and 1860.[8]

The most important observation to be made about these procedures, it seems to me, is that they have very little economic content, and in some cases none at all. Fogel likens his role to that of a paleontologist who wants to reconstruct an entire animal, having only a single tooth and perhaps other scattered fragments of other points in the anatomy. The comparison may not be entirely apt, however, since presumably the paleontologist would employ some kind of theory or accumulated knowledge about the structural relationships of animals in general. He would not simply fit a curve joining his set of points. No theory is involved in such statements as: "Taken as a group, the six ratios suggest that the changing position of Pennsylvania in the national market would be well described by a second degree equation" (Fogel 1964, pp. 162-163). Similarly, there is no real "model" of the distribution of rail wear, only a curve specified which "connects points" in a more general sense. Regressions between economic variables may embody some substantive relationship: the regressions of Cranmer and Temin cited above clearly involve functional connections, and the statement quoted from Davis and Legler indicates that they do intend their prediction equation to have some economic meaning. But in most cases there is no attempt to argue that an economic mechanism is being described; one merely hopes for a regularity of relationship.

I do not mean to suggest that these authors masquerade their estimates as solid and reliable — indeed, more often they are at pains to emphasize the tentative character of the figures — nor by any means that the estimates are without value. Certainly the flexibility of form allowed by regressions and other curves is a great improvement over the assumption of proportionality so common in earlier years, as Fogel (1967) and Poulson (1969) have emphasized. But it is important that the procedures be recognized as forms of interpolation, and not much more.

A second observation is that, in general, such efforts are "worth it"

---

[8] Cranmer's equation is plagued by heteroscedasticity. A possible correction is described in Von Tunzelman (1968).

only if the resulting numbers have some meaning which will be generally recognized. Once you have estimated a series by assuming that the variable bore a regular empirical relationship to others that you can measure, it is a risky business indeed to use those figures in subsequent research. Some uses may be appropriate, but certainly it is illegitimate to use them in "econometric" estimation of functional relationships, within the same system. Thus Fogel is able to use his derived estimates to refute the "gross theory" that railroad demand must have been a great stimulus to iron because of its sheer volume relative to total iron production, but he is not able to evaluate the many theoretically interesting ways which he outlines in which a *small* addition to demand could have had major consequences for the industry. The problem of evaluating the significance of such results is well illustrated by Fishlow's (1965) alternative calculations of the share of railroad demand in iron production (p. 142). Fishlow objects to Fogel's application of "long-term homeostatic principles to short-run events" and prefers his own figures, which are "rooted directly in the financial expenditures for iron reported by individual roads" (p. 147). Yet, issues of methodology aside, much of the dispute seems to be that Fogel and Fishlow began their efforts with different prior conceptions of what constitutes a "large" or "small" share. In the end, Fishlow asserts that *both* sets of figures show a "large and increasing role for railroad demands" (p. 149). But in the absence of knowledge of the functional relationships relevant for understanding the interaction of the two industries, do we have any objective basis for such a statement? It not, then are we even in a position to evaluate assertions about the "relative insensitivity" of the results with respect to various assumptions?[9]

These comments are intended more as observations than as criticisms of principle because I believe it is quite wrong to argue that we never have any shared standards of "how large is large". Having gleaned our so-called "*a priori*" notions from observing the same universe, we do have some area of agreement on what are "fast" and "slow" rates of growth, and there are many instances where most of us can agree that an important distinction can be made between positive or rising and negative or falling numbers. And

---

[9] A similar argument appears in Desai (1968). Perhaps it should be stated explicitly that the difficulties noted here cannot be resolved by tests of the "statistical significance" of differences. Such tests tell us at best only whether apparent differences are "true" ones. A number, coefficient, or a difference can be statistically significant and economically insignificant.

if these roughly shared feelings of "what was hitherto believed" are not immediately at the top of our heads, it may be possible to evoke them by drawing comparisons with other historical periods or with the present day. Indeed, many of the historical revisions which have most forcefully reshaped our thinking about the past have simply been the estimation of numbers which all of us agree are important, such as the rate of growth of output during the Civil War, or prior to 1840. It seems to be a respectable opinion among some cliometricians that discovering "what actually happened" is as important as attempting to specify and estimate models.[10] And if it is true that this distinction is not really possible in principle or in practice, nevertheless the very fact that the statement is so frequently made suggests that it is expected that we will have some shared reaction to whatever numbers are produced. It is an open question at this point which kind of research will yield higher returns in terms of these expectations.

Several other intermediate varieties of "econometric history" should be mentioned. The first is curve-fitting, not for purposes of interpolation, but for characterizing an observed frequency distribution in summary form, and perhaps also as a means of devising statistical tests of changes in the distribution. The methods are well known to students of industrial concentration and income inequality, but they have not been in general use among economic historians. Soltow (1969) has fit inverse-Pareto curves to data taken from returns of the federal income tax of 1866-71, the abortive tax of 1894, and the post-1913 income tax, in an effort to assess long-run changes in income inequality in the U.S.A.[11] He found substantial inequality after the Civil War, and a slow trend to equalization since then. However, his figures are limited to upper-income groups, and the evidence from 1894 is extremely fragmentary. No test of the statistical significance is supplied, though Soltow makes no claim that the observed fall in inequality is important. In my own work (Wright 1969, 1970), I have attempted to fit

---

[10] Cf., e.g., Davis and Legler (1966), p. 256: "... we need to know a good deal more about what actually happened during the nineteenth century before we can say much more about the economic history of the period", or Basmann's contention (1965, p. 178) that "the determination of what of significance actually happened in economic history" is just as fundamental as "the derivation of prediction statements (mathematical economics) and the manipulation of statistical computations (econometric statistics)." In this connection there is a certain irony in the reference to "the ubiquity of the weighting problem" (Fogel 1967) as a factor *favoring* the econometric approach to history; I would have said that the ubiquity and the general lack of concern over the problem are indicative of the kind of "suspension of disbelief" under which econometricians operate.

[11] Soltow (1968) applies similar procedures to British data going back as far as 1436.

log-normal and incomplete-beta distributions to data on farm size and agricultural wealth in the antebellum South, primarily for the purpose of developing statistical tests of differences in concentration between regions and over time. The results were of interest, but they were hardly satisfying methodologically, since in many cases the form of the distribution — that is, the degree to which it was well-approximated by one of the two distributions — changed markedly between 1850 and 1860.

Such formal methods of measuring inequality are clearly an improvement over the size-class distributions which led Owsley (1949) and his students astray.[12] But, as before, the economic content is small. While it is possible to construct probabilistic models which generate log-normal or other convenient distributions, little connection has so far been found between these models and real world processes. Identifying such mechanisms would obviously require much more "econometric" methods than curve-fitting.

A second intermediate "stage" in historical econometric method is what might be called the "casual" use of regression analysis, simply to verify certain correlations which may be present in a body of data, but without a serious effort to specify a "model" or to identify functional relationships. An illustration of what I have in mind is Fishlow's regression of school enrollment rates, average daily attendance, and expenditure per pupil by state on per capita income and on the share of income emanating from agriculture, applied to cross-section data for 1900 (Fishlow 1966). The regressions are not at all the main focus of the article, which is to estimate levels of investment in education, and he makes no effort to describe the coefficients as parameters in a demand function (which would not be accurate). Nevertheless, the regressions do convey information: he finds that enrollment rates are unrelated to per capita income and highly correlated with the share of agriculture, but that the reverse pattern is true for average daily attendance and expenditures per pupil. Fishlow's explanation for these apparently inconsistent results — that the opportunity cost burden of schooling was low in rural areas because of the seasonality of agriculture (hence the high enrollment), but the schools were of poor quality precisely because of the unwillingness to extend the school year — is eminently sensible; but my point here is simply that this

---

[12] Briefly and somewhat unfairly summarized, the Owsley procedure was to draw conclusions about the "importance" of the small yeoman farmers for the South, by looking at the high percentage of farms which appeared in the lower size classes.

conclusion is certainly not inferred in any way from the regressions. A similar study, which devotes more attention to the regression equations, is that of Davis and Legler (1966). They regress levels of state expenditure against time, urbanization, regional location, and income. One could hardly say — and Davis and Legler certainly do not claim — that a "model" of state spending is described.

I do not mean the term "casual" to be one of abuse. Both of the studies mentioned are competent, common-sense jobs, and the use of regressions is informative. Certainly the use of regressions, simply as a check on the consistency of correlations, is a great improvement over the vague description of "general tendencies" (with exceptions explained by special factors) common to previous generations of economic historians.[13] But without greater attention to the model-building side of econometrics, regressions do not go very far in telling us "how the system worked".

One class of studies — the last of my "intermediate" stages — illustrates that it is sometimes possible to construct the model so cleverly or to choose assumptions so powerful in their implications, that you can reach highly "econometric" conclusions without resort to regressions at all. The "sometimes" in the preceding sentence should be underlined, since experience has shown that assumptions which have such power are apt to be challenged. Nevertheless, it is often surprising how far a few simple arguments can take you.

Consider first Temin's (1964) resolution of the identification problem confronting him in his study of the antebellum iron industry (pp. 29-34). There are two phenomena to be explained: a steady fall in the price of wrought iron relative to that of cast iron, and a rise in the relative quantity of cast iron consumed. With only the price and quantity information, it is not possible to judge whether either of these developments resulted from shifts in supply or shifts in demand, or both. The established econometric answer to the problem is to bring more information to bear on the problem, but evidently in this case there are no good statistical series of variables which might have shifted either of the curves. The problem is resolved by the following "qualitative" assertions:

> The supply curves of both wrought iron and cast iron were quite elastic, if a few years — say two — are allowed for new firms to enter the industry. The industry was

---

[13] Cf., e. g., the description of Lewis Cecil Aray's explanation of the degree of concentration of slaveholdng in different counties of the South in Wright (1969).

composed of a great number of small firms, each exploiting the raw material locally available with the aid of skills that were widely known. As it was quite easy for iron production of both types to be started or discontinued, and the unit of production was small relative to the total volume of production, the industry approximated the conditions of constant costs and had very elastic supply curves. The demand for wrought and cast iron was undoubtedly more sensitive to prices. The level of prices certainly influenced the nature and extent in which these materials were used; their demand curves, in other words, were relatively inelastic. (Temin 1964, p. 32).

This paragraph is all that is required to answer both questions originally posed: if the supply curves are infinitely elastic, then the fall in relative price must be due to a shift in the relative position of the supply curves alone; the explanation of the shift in relative quantities falls on the demand side. Temin goes on to describe a basis for these respective shifts, a description which would seem much less plausible in the absence of the preceding demonstration.

The only important methodological comment to be made is simply that it is fine to make such bold assumptions if there is really a basis for them, and if they will be generally accepted. Indeed, if we were willing in general to accept such arguments on an *a priori* basis, we could get along very well without econometric estimation at all. In this case, however, one wonders how firm the basis for the assumption is after all. It is quite unsettling to have the relative inelasticity of the demand curve justified on the basis that demand was "undoubtedly *more* sensitive to prices". Unless I have seriously misread the argument, it is backward, and this raises the question whether there really is any prior knowledge about the demand curve at all. In any case, the critical assumption on the demand side is the *similarity* of the elasticity in the two markets, which is much harder to have prior feelings about. Further problems are raised by the likelihood that the cross-elasticity of demand between the two types of iron was high. The argument on the supply side is certainly plausible, but even here no very strong reason is given for the belief that the long-run supply curve is approximated over short periods of time. Fogel and Engerman (1969) have laid much stress on the distinction between long-run and short-run equilibrium in their model of the antebellum iron industry.

An even more striking simplification is achieved by David (1966), in his explanation of the forces behind the adoption of the reaper in the 1850's. From the secondary literature, David gleans two possible hypotheses (1) that the labor supply was inelastic relative to the supply of reapers, and hence the expansion of demand for wheat forced up wages, making the substitution profitable, and (2) the expansion of the scale of farms in response to the rise in demand made adoption of the reaper profitable, once some "threshold" level was reached. David then combines the two arguments by noting that the threshold scale is inversely related to the wage level. The calculation of the threshold is carried out in an extremely simple manner, by assuming that the cost curves are linear over the relevant range. Then the threshold scale — the point at which the farmer is just indifferent between methods — is given by the equation

$$c = S_T L_S w$$

where c is the fixed annual money cost of a reaper; S_T is the threshold scale; L_S is the number of man-days of labor dispensed with by mechanizing, per acre harvested; and w is the money cost of a man-day of harvest labor. By assuming that c is given by a straight line depreciation of the purchase price of the reaper, David is able to calculate S_T in terms of five parameters, for which estimates are available. Observations on average farm size then suggest that this average did indeed surpass S_T for the first time during the 1850's, with two-thirds of the change resulting from the decline in S_T.

Thus David's "estimation procedure" is no more complex than the "cost-benefit" studies discussed above. The important point, however, is that this simplification was achieved by means of some carefully chosen steps. One might, of course, insist that the parameter values be rigorously estimated by regression methods, but actually only the technical coefficient L_S is not observed directly, and no one, to my knowledge, has argued that David's figure is far off. Where, then, is the price paid for these powerful conclusions? Once again, if the "prior" knowledge brought to bear is accurate and acceptable, then a little information can go a long way. But there are some questions which might be raised. The first is that it is somewhat disturbing theoretically to see that the model does not really explain the choice of scale on the part of the farmer; this choice is taken as a "given" (from the census average) and the deduction is that *if* farmers decided to expand their farms (as in fact they did) *then* it also made sense to buy reapers. But if there were savings to be realized by this combination of choices, why didn't the expansion come earlier? David, of course, is aware of this implication of the model, and he argues that the wheat price had to rise sufficiently to cover the *initial* costs of the expansion (the costs of "acquiring, clearing, and fencing new land, or even preparing land already held"). In theory, even if existing farms are stuck with old methods, new entrants should force the adoption of the most efficient technology, but in this case any farmer (new or old) had to undergo transition costs to establish a farm above threshold size. I have no particular reason to quarrel with this answer, but one might argue that this rather terse argument is the main point of interest of the paper — the point at which David is not "applying theory" but explaining why the predictions of theory are not realized. That is why diffusion is of interest in the first place. This much is largely a question of emphasis. But Davis (1968) and Bogue have been unwilling to accept even the applicability of a threshold model, arguing that the services of a reaper were not indivisible, and that there were in fact many cases of cooperative purchase.[14]

This is not the place to resolve this issue, but my point is simply that we seldom get any free lunch in econometric history. I have no objection to the approaches of Temin, David, and others who have tried similar methods. When adequate data simply are not available, we have to let assumptions (or theory) substitute for data. It is often said that the "art" of econometrics is in choosing simple but powerful assumptions; and a good artist can do very well with no internally estimated parameters at all. But just as there are few objective standards in art, so one has to be prepared for a lack of general convincement in response to such efforts. Assumptions so powerful are likely to be challenged by someone. The question to which I turn in the next section is whether, when enough data for more formal estimation procedures are available, the results can be made more generally convincing.

2. Selected studies in econometric history

It would not be wise to draw too sharp a distinction in principle between the studies discussed below and those covered in the preceding section. Many econometricians are skeptical of our ability to estimate true structures at any time,[15] let alone with nineteenth-century data. Even with a carefully specified model, one often has to insert observed variables which one knows to be inappropriate, and even "econometrically estimated" models can

---

[14] In Davis (1968) Bogue is quoted as follows (p. 87): "I gave this problem to a graduate student one morning at eight o'clock and he was back in my office by ten with a long list of cooperative purchases." Note is made of the fact that the graduate student had special expertise in this area.

[15] See, e.g., Kuh (1965) and Nerlove (1965b).

involve some drastic simplifying assumptions. Nevertheless, I believe most readers will agree that a distinction is called for in that the studies covered in this section are characterized *both* by extended consideration of a model and by its estimation by formal methods. In the absence of more compelling distinctions than this one, the studies are discussed roughly in order of their appearance.

2.0. *The success of railroad price-fixing*

MacAvoy (1965) has used econometric methods to assist in the identification of periods of success and failure of railroad rate-fixing agreements before 1900, especially before and after the establishment of the Interstate Commerce Commission. The word "assist" is used intentionally since the analysis and argument of the book is not limited to the regression results, but includes also a wealth of information from railroad journals, cartel records, ICC reports, etc. Indeed, I should note at the outset that MacAvoy states in his preface: "This study is not history, nor is it econometrics" (p. v). But, MacAvoy's methods *look* much more econometric than those of many studies which confidently accept the name, and hence it would hardly do to omit the book because of this disclaimer. Indeed, considerable space is devoted to explaining the regressions to be run, and to a lesser degree the "expected" coefficient values.

The first regression equation is designed to test loyalty to cartel agreements by comparison of the official (cartel) rates with those reported by the Chicago Board of Trade — that is, by the consumers of railroad services. Hence, the following regression is run:

$$R_T = \alpha + \beta R_o \tag{1}$$

where R_T = rates reported by Board of Trade; R_o = official (cartel) rates. The equation is fit to weekly data for successive summer and winter seasons in an effort to identify periods of breakdown in the cartel. Since complete loyalty requires that rates change only through changes in R_o, it is stated (p. 28) that if there is no cheating we should have $\alpha = 0$ and $\beta = 1.00$, and, indeed, $R^2 = 1.00$. If there is cheating, on the other hand, β will be less than unity (since R_T will tend to run below R_o) and R^2 will be low, "since some proportion of the variation in R_T followed from cheating rather than from changes in R_o".

An additional pair of regressions is employed to assess the effects of the collusive rates on grain markets. In these regressions railroad rates are entered as independent variables in an attempt to explain differences in grain prices between Chicago and New York. The first regression assumes instantaneous adjustment:

$$P_g^* = \alpha + \beta R, \tag{2}$$

where P_g^* = the weekly New York-Chicago grain price difference. (This equation is modified to include the lake-rail rate (R_L) during summer seasons, in addition to R.) A second version assumes that there is a lagged adjustment to an equilibrium price difference:

$$P_{g,t} = P_{g,t-1} + e(P_g^* - P_{g,t-1}), \tag{3}$$

where $P_{g,t}$ = observed price difference at time t, and P_g^* = equilibrium price difference. Equation (3) is computed in the form

$$P_{g,t} - P_{g,t-1} = \Delta P_g = -eP_{g,t-1} + e(\alpha + \beta R), \tag{4}$$

which is to say that P_g^* is given by a (hypothetical) instantaneous adjustment to a level given by an implicitly estimated α and β[16].

Equation (1) is the most clearly motivated of the tests, but it nonetheless has two severe shortcomings: (1) the success of the cartel depends upon the *level* of R_o as well as "loyalty": if the cartel is so weak that it can only enforce a rate close to marginal cost, then "loyalty" has little relevance; (2) changes initiated by R_T — i.e., cheating — may also be reflected in subsequent changes in R_o, as the cartel attempts to "punish" the cheater (or simply adjusts itself to a new, more realistic level). Taken together, these arguments imply that $\beta = 1.00$ and high R^2 values are neither necessary nor sufficient conditions for cartel success. Both problems are recognized by MacAvoy, but he offers no specific remedy.

Conceptual shortcomings notwithstanding, the initial results for the period 1871-74 seem quite promising. The R^2 values are all high and the t-test

---

[16] The estimating procedure is not very clearly described. MacAvoy regresses ΔP_g on $P_{g,t-1}$ and R. The coefficient of $P_{g,t+1}$ is taken as $-e$, and it is then possible to calculate α and β by dividing the other coefficients by e. The "results" of the equations are reported in the somewhat confusing form

$$P_{t,t} = (1-e) P_{g,t-1} + e(\alpha + \beta R),$$

with the standard error listed below e. The assumption is that the disturbances are added to P^*, the equilibrium value, and not to the observed P. One obtains no real inkling, from this information, of the statistical significance of α and β.

of the difference of β from 1.00 shows it to be insignificant.[17] It is even noted that the high degree of serial correlation in the residuals may exaggerate the t-ratio, a bias which in this case would, if corrected, strengthen his conclusion[18] that there was little cheating during the period. One might be troubled slightly by what appear to be large values for the constant term — three negative and one positive — but, perhaps this is a small point.[19] Furthermore, there is quite a striking contrast between these results and those of the winter season of 1874-75 (at which time the $B\&0$ completed a direct line to Chicago) when both β and R^2 values fall to 0.00.

So far so good. However, these standards of econometric performance are slowly eroded over time, until they virtually disappear altogether. As the years roll by, each one represented by its set of regressions, it becomes apparent that no consistent interpretation is given to the results of equation (1), and they are of almost no use in "dating" periods of break-down. The proposed test that $\alpha = 0$ is never mentioned again, and only occasionally are tests of $\beta = 1.00$ reported. Instead, MacAvoy identifies periods of breakdown primarily from "outside" evidence and then refers to the regressions for illustrative comment when they appear to fit with the narrative. In light of the two objections raised above, this is as it should be, in the sense that it would be far worse to rely mechanically on the results of poorly specified regressions. But one wonders whether the regressions add anything at all to the analysis, given that, in 23 of the 50 seasons covered, the results of equation (1) are completely trivial — the R^2 values are either 0.00 or 1.00, either because $R_T = R_o$ in every week, or because R_T varied while R_o did not. One hardly needs a regression model to understand that.

But it is actually unfair to draw these conclusions with respect to equation (1) only, since consideration of equations (2)-(4) occupies considerably more space. The relationship of these equations to the question of cartel success — i.e., the expected results in the presence of loyalty and cheating — is never stated clearly beforehand, but in practice the main use seems to be to compare R^2 values for the regressions using first R_o and

---

[17] One might raise the question of the meaning of a statistical test of the difference between β and unity. Either $R_T = R_0$ or not, and if not, loyalty was imperfect. To salvage the test, one must argue that R_T was subject to random influences, which were as likely to raise R_T above R_0 as the reverse.

[18] Unfortunately, no tests of serial correlation are reported, so the reader cannot make a judgment as to the severity of this problem.

[19] "Appear to be" because the standard error of the constant term is not reported.

then R_T: if cheating is present, one would expect P_g to be more responsive to R_T. This comparison does help to supplement the rather empty results of (1), and offers some hope of a clear standard, but the use made of (2)-(4) is no more consistent than that of (1). The information contained in the historical narrative seems so much more reliable than the model that MacAvoy persistently refuses to accept the implications of the regressions. For example, the cartel would appear to be much more successful from the summer of 1875 through the summer of 1876 than it had been during the winter of 1874-75, yet the discussion does not recognize any improvement at all. Of the six relevant pairs of R^2 values, only one shows any significant "advantage" of R_T over R_o, and this difference (in the lagged version for winter, 1875-76) is hardly greater than the difference in the opposite direction in the same equation for the preceding season. Again, the great disruptions of the summer of 1881 (as described in the text) show no impact whatsoever in the regression results — and this fact is not taken as any reason to challenge the narrative.

One reason for the looseness of the interpretation is that two alternate models of price adjustment are carried throughout the book. Now I can think of two possible reasons for estimating more than one form of a model: one might wish to ascertain which model is "better", and to make a choice between them on the basis of their performance; or, one might wish to focus on the conclusions, and to verify that a conclusion holds for both forms. But MacAvoy does neither. He is willing to cite R^2 values for the lagged-adjustment equations when they support him and to shift to the instantaneous model when it is more congenial. Thus if the two models are at all points equally usable, one might be able to draw the opposite conclusions by making the opposite respective choices of equation. In fact, we have not two but an infinity of models because, in the lagged adjustment equation a new "average lag" is calculated for each and every season. These highly variable lengths of time are reported throughout the book without any recognition of the implausibility of the notion that the true structure of market adjustment could have changed so erratically from year to year.

It should be noted that MacAvoy does attempt a kind of justification of his procedure in his preface, by stating that the study is "not econometrics" in that it relies on "simple regression analyses as means for summarizing, rather than on econometric techniques as means for testing specific hypotheses". But it is an illusion that such a distinction is genuine. In fact the book *does* contain "specific hypotheses", and the regression results are frequently cited in support of them. The erratic shifting of criteria from case to case (and the introduction of new criteria applied only to isolated cases) is simply not a valid logical procedure, and it cannot be justified by calling it "summarizing".

This is not to say that the book has no value, nor that the regression models should not have been tried. The book's narrative account is very well done; and, since the history of cartel success and failure appears to be so well known without any true help from econometrics, the study might well have been cast as an attempt to test whether the regressions would yield true predictions — perhaps as a test of the use of the model in other situations. Unfortunately, the results of such a test would have been negative.

2.1. *The growth of cities*

The failure to place interpretive focus on econometric results can hardly be charged to Williamson and Swanson (1966) in their examination of the bases of urbanization in the American Northeast, 1820-70. The meticulous attention which they devote to the construction of their model and the interpretation of the results makes their study extremely valuable for anyone planning to attempt econometric history. Nevertheless, the extent to which the paper succeeds in increasing our understanding of the process of urbanization merits further consideration.

The major question in the paper is the "scale hypothesis" that the growth of cities is related to economies of scale in terms of urban size. After much ground-clearing and preliminary discussion, Williamson and Swanson present their model for testing the hypothesis as follows: They argue that according to the scale hypothesis the "long-run average cost" of city output will be described by a U-shaped curve, reaching a minimum point at the optimum size C_t^* for a given technology. Entrepreneurs will be attracted by low levels of average-cost, and hence the growth rate of each city will be proportional to the reciprocal of the city's average cost:

$$g(C_i) = k(AC_i)_t^{-1} \tag{5}$$

for each city i at time t, with k a "small positive constant with slight variance". Because of the U-shaped cost curve, the "growth rate curve" will then have an inverted U-shape, represented by a quadratic function of city size C_i:

$$g(C_i) = a_1 + b_1 C_{i,t} + d_1 (C_{i,t})^2 + u_i. \tag{6}$$

This much of the model is a test of the scale hypothesis. However, because other factors will be involved in determining a city's growth, several other variables are added before the regression is run: (1) the proportion of the labor force in manufacturing (M/L), because aggregate data indicate a relative shift out of the urban service sector into the manufacturing sector between 1820 and 1860 so that cities committed to industry should have enjoyed faster growth during the period; (2) the proportion of the labor force in agriculture (A/L), since a larger agricultural share would imply a "more provincial outlook" and hence "more sluggish growth"; (3) the growth rate of the agricultural population of the state ($g(R_j)$), since city growth will depend also on the demand placed upon it by the surrounding area; and (4) the age of a city or its "date of entrance", because those cities established in 1810-20 developed economic structure well-suited for commercial, trade-oriented growth, and not for manufacturing.

The regression is run on cross-section data for three separate-decades: 1820-30, 1840-50, and 1860-70. The independent variables are valued at the start of the decade. Their main finding is the surprising one that no significant scale effect appears. The age of the city does show a negative relationship to growth. The effects of the "hinterland" are positive for 1820-30 and (surprisingly) for 1860-70. The orientation toward manufacturing (M/L) has a significant effect only for 1840-50.

Before commenting on the conclusions, I would like to raise several points about the model itself. With respect to the influence of scale, I am not satisfied that a clearly formulated hypothesis is being tested, despite all the attention paid to model contruction. In their introduction, they speculate on a variety of ways in which urban size might affect industrial choices, but in the end the model comes down to one proposition: low levels of average cost attract industry into cities. Now in their text they state (p. 29): "As we move toward optimum city size, city urban [sic] growth rates begin to decline." This statement suggests that we are dealing with some kind of equilibrium model in which city size will tend to converge at some point. The *actual* formulation of the model, however, suggests that the sentence is merely a slip of the pen, because in fact the model holds that the growth rate is *maximized* at the "optimum" scale, with no tendency to convergence but rather the extremely pessimistic implication that there will be a chronic tendency to "over-expansion" of cities. Such a pattern of behavior is certainly a possibility, but it is not clear to me that this is what a reasonable advocate of the scale hypothesis would have in mind. He might hold, e.g., that cities above a certain scale would take steps to limit their own size or that entrepreneurs were able to judge something about the direction of a city's growth as well as its average cost level.

A related point is whether absolute or percentage growth rates are appropriate, a question which receives virtually no discussion. *Percentage growth rates* are used throughout, a fact which makes the pessimistic predictions of the model much worse: not only do cities continue to grow beyond the optimum size, but it appears that even more firms are attracted to cities that are "too large" than to cities with the same average costs which are "too small". The only statement related to this question which I am able to find[20] is their justification in an appendix for a geometric definition of city size classes (p. 80): "Such scaling is in the tradition of Hart and Preis and is based on the notion that each city would have an equal chance at relative growth." But is it really so obvious that equal relative growth is the norm? This implicit assumption that "size breeds growth", to my mind, takes much of the interest and a good deal of the content out of a study of the "growth of cities". The oft-heard statement that an abnormally high growth rate can be "explained" by "it started from a low base" suggests that intuition is not a safe guide in this matter. But without a more detailed specification of entrepreneurial and individual choice, it is difficult to go much beyond this complaint.[21]

In passing, certain objections might be raised with respect to the additional variables. The rationale for inclusion of M/L is not entirely convincing: the presumption seems to be that the character of economic growth is given exogenously, and the cities react to it — that is, those cities best suited to the "going trends" in the economy will grow fastest. But no real theory or structural argument is presented in support of this view,

---

[20] In a sense, Williamson and Swanson do answer the question implicitly in their introductory sections, when they reject the presumption that the mere increase in size of cities over time implies economies of scale: "Even if every city grew at a constant and equal rate, regardless of their initial sizes, the average city size would increase unless the rate of new city entrance was especially rapid." But the sentence has no substantive content — it merely restates the implicit notion that a phenomenon of equal percentage growth rates of cities does not require explanation, a notion which, as we have seen, is not really axiomatic.

[21] It is possible that the negative correlation between "age" and growth reflects in part the "punishing" of large cities by making them grow faster (absolutely) just to keep pace. In this regard, Williamson and Swanson do state: "A more general life cycle approach might appear to be more relevant but no attempt was made to do so [sic]."

other than the observation that output shifted in the direction of manufacturing at this time. Is this really enough? If output shifts in the direction
of hats rather than coats, then those cities specializing in hats will be likely
to show faster growth, but this correlation may have nothing to do with
any structural advantages. Of course the Williamson and Swanson argument
is more plausible than that, but we should be wary of attributing independent
"influence" to M/L simply on the basis of a correlation. Furthermore, one
can construct a plausible argument for a certain simultaneity — that the
pattern of output occurred in part because of the economies which were
possible because of cities.

With respect to A/L, the reference to "provincial outlook" seems
completely out of keeping with the approach of the rest of the paper;
surely the reason for including the variable would be that farm workers
living in cities are not really "urban workers". Finally, I have some difficulty
understanding their approach to the "hinterland" variable. They fully
recognize the distortion involved in using a state total — especially serious
for large states like New York and Pennsylvania — and they simply accept
the shortcoming as a rough approximation. But I find hard to accept the
transition involved in the following two sentences (p. 41): "The larger the
city the larger the market for which it produces and thus the smaller the
impact which local conditions should play in determining the growth
performance of the city. ... Given the declining importance of 'small' cities
in the Northeast, one would predict that rural population ('local' hinterland)
growth rates would play a diminishing role in explaining overall city growth
performance." It seems to me that the clear implication of the first sentence
is that the relationship is nonlinear — for *any* city, regardless of the average
of all cities. To employ instead a linear relation expected to be of declining
importance over time is to accept a substitute inferior to that suggested by
their own argument.

The comments of the preceding paragraph are of relatively minor
importance, relating as much to the argument as to the specification itself.
There are, however, two aspects of the estimation procedure which may
have serious consequences. The first relates to the disturbance term in the
regression. At one point in the paper (pp. 44-47) Williamson and Swanson
raise high hopes that they will develop some way of incorporating information about the "immense range of variables" which have not been
included explicitly, which they refer to as z-variables: "Estimation of the
model requires careful attention to the manner in which the z-variables

affect city growth." The hopes are raised here, because not only is it true that assumptions about such disturbance terms can drastically affect the estimation, but it is also true that we hardly ever have any intelligent *a priori* information about them. These raised hopes are soon dashed, however, with the commonplace conclusion: "Specifically, we assume that the influence of $z_1, z_2 \ldots z_n$ on city growth rates can be represented by a random variable." Now it is not much of a criticism to say that Williamson and Swanson make the most convenient assumption about disturbances, just as almost everyone else does. The disappointment is heightened, however, by the fact that there is a fairly obvious observation which can be made about the disturbances in their model, which could seriously affect the results. The problem is that a "disturbance" which affects the growth rate of a city in decade one does not have its effect in decade one and then disappear. Instead, it leaves the city at a larger size than it "should" have in terms of its characteristics and hence, one would expect slower growth in the succeeding decade. It is easy to see that this effect, if it occurred, would weaken the observed relationship between scale and growth. Just as the "permanent income effect" reduces the observed slope of the consumption function, so this "return to normal" effect would reduce the magnitude of the scale relationship and make it more difficult to isolate statistically.[22] Williamson and Swanson do, of course, separate their decades of observation by 10-year intervals, but this does not disturb my argument, which applies to the cross-section regressions in any decade.

It is possible to argue that this is not a real problem, because the disturbance is added to the growth *rate*, and the growth-scale association should hold, if it is a true technical association, regardless of the reason for the city's size at the start of the decade. This brings me to my second point. The cross-section regressions must assume that the optimum scale is the same for each city, and indeed, that the growth-size function is the same for each city. It is not hard to think of purely geographical reasons which inherently limit the growth of certain cities, or which at least affect the optimum size — the ruggedness of the terrain, or the existence of physical

---

[22] The *t*-values will be reduced because the effect is to introduce a second "true" correlation of opposite direction to the first "true" correlation, blurring the statistical difference from zero. This effect is unambiguous only if most cities are below the "optimum" size at which the growth curve turns down. This level we, of course, do not know, but the levels implied by the (not statistically significant) Williamson and Swanson coefficients are all well above the average size.

barriers to expansion in certain directions, e.g. More important is the question whether it is really reasonable to view the independent variables and the disturbance terms as factors which raise or lower the growth *rate*, leaving the growth-size function unchanged. In the case of M/L and age, it seems to me that the logic of the argument is that these variables will shift the *average cost* curve, not the growth rate directly. Furthermore, I would argue that this is also true for many of the "disturbance" terms, such as geographical obstacles to growth. But if this is the case, then it will not be valid to assume a single optimum; and, indeed, single-equation cross-section models will not be able to identify the function at all.[23]

Williamson and Swanson cannot with justice be accused of claiming too much for their model. They state in their conclusion (p. 66): "We would be less than candid with our patient readers if we left this study without sounding a note of disappointment. No one realizes more clearly than we just how vulnerable we are to attack from both the methodological right and left. ... The cleometrician [sic] ... is likely to respond with his traditional trilogy of criticism: inadequate specification, over-aggregation, and model simplistics." Nonetheless this modesty sits strangely beside their assertion (p. 67): "We have shown conclusively that size distribution by itself calls for rejection of the urban economies hypothesis." This confidence seems especially misplaced in light of the fact — which they note — that the coefficients of the scale variables are always of the right sign, with not unreasonable values for the optimum size. While I am thus not convinced of their conclusions, I do think the Williamson and Swanson study is a hopeful one. They have covered many of the considerations which will have to be included in more elaborate models; and many of my criticisms, if valid, appear to be correctable. There is some promise, therefore, that continued econometric work on these important questions will yield more convincing results.

2.2. *The determinants of investment*

Several studies have employed regression models to explain the investment behavior of firms in a historical context. For the most part the procedures follow methodological paths which have been well trod by contemporary

---

[23] This identification problem is analogous to the difficulty of estimating Cobb-Douglas production functions with cross section data. See Nerlove (1965a).

investment studies; hence the discussion here will be brief. Some interesting questions of historical approach are raised, however, in a study by Kmenta and Williamson (1966) of the determinants of railroad investment, 1872-1941. Kmenta and Williamson argue that these determinants will change according to the "phase of the industry's life cycle". They divide the period into three such phases: adolescence, 1872-95; maturity, 1896-1914; senility, 1922-41. These dates are chosen from a perusal of the overall railroad investment trends relative to the entire economy, from the changing regional nature of investment, and from changes in methods of finance. Using a recently estimated railroad investment series due to Ulmer (1960), Kmenta and Williamson justify three separate regression equations in the following way:

$$I_t = \alpha_0 + \alpha_1(\delta_1 X_{t-2} - K_{t-2}) + \alpha_2(\pi^*/K)_{t-2} + \alpha_3(\pi^*_{t-1} - \pi^*_{t-2}), \qquad (7)$$

where I = net investment; X = output; K = capital stock at start of period; π^* = net operating income after depreciation. The rationale for the first term on the right-hand side is that an accelerator mechanism is likely to be working during a period of high investment and expansion; but the profit variables will also be important because of their role in attracting new firms into the industry. The two-year lag "is likely to be most appropriate" because of the length of time required for receiving information and carrying out plans. After 1896, new entry becomes extremely rare, and hence "the profit variables are less likely to be relevant". Therefore the second equation is written as follows:

$$I_t = \beta_0 + \beta_1(\delta_2 X_{t-2} - K_{t-2}). \qquad (8)$$

For the stage of senility, the capital-stock adjustment becomes irrelevant because the capital stock is already at the saturation level. Only the level of the capital stock is relevant, because a higher stock means a lower average age of capital, and hence less need for replacement. The third regression is:

$$I_t = v_0 + v_1 K_{t-1} + v_2 \pi^{**}_{t-1}, \qquad (9)$$

where π^{**} = *net* income, including non-operating income. The change in the definition of income occurs because its role now is that of a *financial* variable for existing firms, not an incentive for new firms. The lag is shortened to one year, because of "increased efficiency of communications, management and capital market transactions, and the secular decline in the importance of railroad investment of longer gestation".

While it may be unfair to do so, one is strongly tempted to raise one's eyebrows at this point. Regression studies of investment are known chiefly for the hairline distinctions which must be made in judging competing hypotheses and for the strong tendency for a wide variety of variables to successfully "explain" investment. Hence it is difficult to understand the apparent confidence of Kmenta and Williamson in their procedure, which involves *a priori* information of an extremely rough character. The changes in the length of the lag in particular seems to involve only the haziest sort of guess-work.

But it is hard to argue with success, and each of the equations does predict moderately well for its own period. An alternative equation that Klein had used for 1922-41, which included the average yield on railroad bonds and a price index for railroad capital goods, did very poorly in each period, with wrong signs appearing for both the bond yield and the price index. Furthermore Kmenta and Williamson note that they did try each of the three equations for all three periods, and in each case the model had "poor explanatory power" outside of its proper period.

These findings, if valid, have quite hopeful implications for historical econometrics. Several writers have argued for the importance of using information from the more traditional sources of economic history in model-building (Nerlove 1956; Wright 1969), and Kmenta and Williamson appear to have demonstrated the point with great power. Still, one cannot help doubting whether their "prior" information was really strong enough to justify their boldness — which is to say, one wonders if they were not just lucky. A point which hints in this direction is their note that they did try changing the lag in (9) from 1 to 2 years, with the result that the R^2 value was reduced and serial correlation was present in the residuals (though the coefficients did not change much). If they had tried a 2-year lag first, would it have been so clear that their expectations had been realized?

A much stronger challenge to Kmenta and Williamson comes from a study by Neal (1969) of the middle period, 1897-1914. Neal quarrels with the Kmenta and Williamson basis for the separation of "stages", arguing that in fact a major financial reorganization was taking place during 1894-1907 — the period of "Morganization" of railroads, reduction of high interest debt and increasing equity. Hence, Neal maintains not only that Kmenta and Williamson do not divide their time periods appropriately, but also that financial inducements to increase investment were critical during precisely the period when they disappear completely from the Kmenta and Williamson equations. How is it then that these authors obtained the results they did? Because, Neal argues, they used faulty data. Now this may seem like something of a low blow to an applied econometrician; Kmenta and Williamson recognized certain shortcomings in Ulmer's data, but believed it would be excessively timid to abstain from their use. This is not the place to enter into a description of the data themselves, but suffice it to say that Neal makes several quite reasonable adjustments and submits his new series to three tests, all of which lend some credence to its validity. Re-estimating the regressions with the revised figures, Neal obtains results which bear no resemblance to those of Kmenta and Williamson. He finds that none of the three Kmenta and Williamson equations predicts at all well for 1897-1914, and that (8) — designed especially for the period — does worst of all. Neal substitutes an extremely simple equation:

$$I^t = \alpha_0 + \alpha_1 X_{t-1} + \alpha_2 \pi_{t-1}^{***} - \alpha_3 i_{t-1}^e, \tag{10}$$

where $X =$ output; $\pi^{***} =$ retained earnings, $i^e =$ equity yield. All of the signs obtained are correct, α_1 and α_3 are significantly different from zero, and $R^2 = 0.87$. When the regression is run for 1897-1907 only, as Neal's argument would indicate, the importance of the equity yield becomes still more pronounced. Finally, Neal goes on to estimate three more general models from recent investment studies — Klein's model, the neoclassical model of Jorgensen, and Eisner's distributed lag accelerator — and finds that all do reasonably well for 1897-1914, at least as well as (8). These results, while hardly pinpointing a "correct" answer, tend to confirm the worst fears about Kmenta and Williamson's original formulation.

There is considerable irony in Neal's concluding comment on "the value of paying attention to the major features of an industry's economic history when attempting to explain its investment behavior. Such attention to economic history might also mitigate [sic] against facile acceptance of faulty data and the misleading results they produce" (p. 135). But this was precisely the burden of Kmenta and Williamson's argument — that they were bringing historical considerations to bear on econometric analysis, adjusting their regression equations to account for "the major features of an industry's economic history". The moral of Neal's work, if any, is that you have to be very careful in such a business, especially of applying *a priori* arguments based on very loose and general arguments of plausibility. The two studies taken together do not give much grounds for belief that we will be able to be more certain about investment functions in history than we have been in the present.

Somewhat more clear-cut answers are provided, however, in an analysis of the dividend and investment behavior of 19th-century textile firms by McGouldrick (1968). This study is deserving of special attention because it appears to be the most "vertically integrated" study of econometric history to date. McGouldrick has performed every "stage of production" himself, from the basic source work with a sample of Waltham-Lowell type textile firms (1836-86) to sorting out the various conceptual problems involved in measuring the capital stock, output, capacity, etc., and finally, to regression analysis of dividend and investment behavior. The econometric portion of the study yields "Charles River" results throughout: he concludes in favor of a "basic Lintner hypothesis" of partial adaption to a desired dividend payout ratio, and in favor of a primarily "profits" explanation of capital spending. The methodological features of the regression analysis do not differ in any major way from recent investment studies, and since the issues involved have been discussed extensively (if not conclusively) in the current literature, I will not attempt an evaluation of the approach. The remarkable point is that McGouldrick is able to perform the tests over such a long period, going back so far into the 19th century. There is no mystery, however, about the reason for his ability to do this, which is simply his willingness to do his own ground work.

2.3. *The supply of and demand for education*

Some recent work by Lewis Solmon (1970) presents an interesting example of an attempt to apply an equilibrium framework to the explanation of observed levels of education in 1880. Solmon is critical of "models" of state differences in education which simply list factors thought to influence education in some way and then use these variables in regressions to "explain" levels of education by state. He points out first that the state is not a good unit of observation, because of clear differences between urban and rural areas. A second and more theoretically interesting point is that levels of education are influenced by both supply and demand factors, and hence an appropriate "model" must explain the interworking of these two sides. Solmon employs the analysis of Becker, in which the level of education is determined by the intersection of a demand-like curve of negative slope between the quantity of education and the marginal benefit (or rate of return R), and a supply-like curve of positive slope relating quantity and the marginal financing cost (or the interest rate I). Assuming constant elasticities, the curves may be represented by:

$$Q_D = D \cdot R^{-r} \qquad (11)$$

$$Q_S = S \cdot I^i, \qquad (12)$$

where D and S are the shift variables for each function, and r and i are the elasticities. In equilibrium, $Q_D = Q_S$ and $R = I$, so that the reduced form solution for Q is

$$\log Q = \frac{i}{r+i} \log D + \frac{r}{r+i} \log S. \qquad (13)$$

The main problem is to specify the shift variables D and S. Solmon distinguishes three types of shift variables: those which affect only the demand curve (A), those which affect only the supply curve (B), and those which affect both (C). He thus writes:

$$D = dA_1^{\alpha_1} A_2^{\alpha_2} C_1^{\alpha_3} \qquad (14)$$

$$S = sB_1^{\beta_1} B_2^{\beta_2} C_1^{\beta_3}. \qquad (15)$$

Hence the general form for the multiple regressions is given by the reduced form:

$$\log Q = \log K + a\alpha_1 \log A_1 + a\alpha_2 \log A_2 + b\beta_1 \log B_1$$
$$+ b\beta_2 \log B_2 + (a\alpha_3 + b\beta_3) \log C_1, \qquad (16)$$

where K is a constant, and $a = i/(r+i)$, $b = r/(r+i)$.

This formulation carries the important implication that the coefficient of income in a regression of education on several variables should not be interpreted as an "income elasticity of demand for education". In fact, income will shift both the supply and demand curves; high income may cause the gross "returns" (psychic or pecuniary) from education to rise, but it also raises the opportunity costs; furthermore, high income areas should have more private financing available, and hence a lower supply curve. This much can be seen from theoretical analysis alone.

Unfortunately, the "price" variables in this system are not observed. Thus only the reduced form for quantity can be run, and Solmon is not able to get back to the structural coefficients. The income variables have positive coefficients, but as we have seen this reflects a combination of influences. In fact, as Solmon points out, there is an additional element of simultaneity, because education is also a productive input in the determination of income. This element is more important in practice than in principle: education as

a factor of production is a stock variable, the cumulated human capital
from past investment. However, all of the variables available to represent
education flows — percentage enrollment, man-days attended per capita,
total costs of education per capita, etc. — are highly correlated with stock
variables (e.g., literacy), as Solmon shows. Solmon does manage to illustrate
the role of opportunity costs in one way: by showing a negative correlation
between education and days available for farm work, when the regression
was run for rural data. But in no other way — as Solmon recognizes — are
the various effects of income successfully distinguished.

Solmon uses "direct costs per student" as a proxy for the quality of
schooling, a variable which should shift the demand curve upward. In fact,
some positive correlation does appear for this variable, though only for the
urban regressions is it clear that this is not mainly a spurious correlation
with "costs per school age population", one of the variables used to
represent "education". Several other variables were also included in the
regression, but in no case is it possible to give a convincing "prior"
explanation of the nature of their impact. In the case of such variables as the
percentage of immigrants in the population, urbanization, and illiteracy, it
is possible to construct arguments for both positive and negative influence
and the empirical results are also by and large inconclusive. Population
density is positively correlated with education, and a variety of possible
reasons for this fact are explored. There is a negative relationship
between education and the percentage of farm land in corn and wheat;
but the "prior" reasons for including this variable are not very clear, and
Solmon is not sure whether the explanation has to do with lower returns or
higher costs.

In the end, the question must be asked whether we have come out with
a better understanding of education in 1880 than we would have with the
time-honored combination of ordinary-least-squares and common sense. In
one sense, the answer must be yes, since the analysis does reveal the complexity involved in interpreting the regression coefficients and cautions
against jumping to quick and possibly erroneous conclusions. But in terms
of the quest with which this survey is concerned — the accumulation of
historical knowledge from putting theory into quantitative terms — the
implications of the paper are pessimistic. It seems that in spite of the careful
attention devoted to the preparation of the model, we end up making the
same kind of speculations about the meaning of the coefficients that occurs
in what I have called the "casual" use of least-squares fits. It would be

premature to assert that there is no prospect of going further in the study of education, but at this time it appears that the problem is fundamentally in the nature of the available data in relation to theory. Too many of the relevant variables are unobserved for one to be hopeful about efforts to identify functional relationships. This is not to say that Solmon has claimed great achievements for his models. He is quite modest about his results, and one hopes he will continue to develop his work along these lines.

2.4. *Cotton-price fluctuations*

To this point all of the studies considered have been single-equation regression models, or models which are collapsed into a single-equation regression for purposes of estimation. In several cases it has been shown that the coefficients in such systems cannot be interpreted unambigously, because the analysis really involved more than one fundamental relationship. Recently, some efforts have been made to estimate historical models of more complexity. One of these is an effort by Temin (1967) to explain the causes of cotton-price fluctuations during the 1830's. Temin's particular point of focus is the thesis — most recently advanced by North — that the explanation lies in the "shape of the supply curve of cotton ... and the way in which the supply curve shifted". North (1961) had argued that this supply curve "was highly elastic over a range which included all the available land which had been cleared and readied for crop production and was suitable for cotton. ... When the growth of demand for cotton finally brought all this potential capacity into production, a further increase in demand resulted in substantial price increases as the supply curve became increasingly inelastic" (pp. 71-73). These high prices brought about a lagged but substantial "expansion of capacity" — reflected in increased sales of federal lands — and a period of depression as the elastic region again came into effect. Temin rightly objects that this analysis involves implicit theorizing about the behavior of demand and that both sides of the market must be identified.

The first step in Temin's alternative approach is to establish that there was a "world price" of cotton; that is, that the British price (P_B) and the American price (P_A) were closely linked, so that one may treat the two countries as two sides of one market. This proposition is tested by a regression of P_A on P_B, as well as on the British tariff on cotton (F) and on time (t), as a test of whether falling freight rates, the lowered tariff, or the reduced gold content of the dollar (as of 1834) resulted in a change in the differential. The regression result, with standard errors in parentheses below the coefficients, is:

$$P_A = 1.60 + 1.52 P_B - 2.85 F - 0.04 t \qquad R^2 = 0.77 \qquad (17)$$
$$(0.17) \quad (2.32) \quad (0.05) \qquad D - W = 2.1$$

Because the correlation is high and because the coefficients of F and t are not significant, the point is taken as established and only the two prices are continued into the subsequent analysis.

At this point some relatively minor objections may be raised to the procedure. First, the variable t is not really appropriate for the kind of discontinuous change represented by a devaluation. Second, Temin seems to extend the role of "significance tests" beyond what is warranted. Is our *a priori* knowledge really so weak that we have to "test the hypothesis" that a tariff will influence price differentials between two countries? Whether or not the tariff — or either of the other influences for that matter — had a "statistically significant effect" on price differentials really has nothing to do with whether the two countries were part of a unified market in the economic sense. A better procedure would be to add the tariff to P_A and run the regression on the adjusted price. The impact of the tariff was probably not too important, but a similar argument can be made with respect to freight rates, which did not change uniformly over time, and for which North has compiled annual figures. Such adjustments could conceivably affect Temin's conclusions, because the regression of log P_A on log P_B, the logarithmic version of (14) with F and t omitted, appears as one of three equations in his general model.

The main part of the model, however, consists of the equations depicting supply and demand. Temin argues that the output of cotton was not influenced by current year prices; cotton was planted in the previous year, and there is no evidence that crop abandonment was ever widespread (variable costs being low), nor that farmers held inventories of cotton over from one crop year to the next. Hence only a lagged price is included in the supply function. Temin argues that secular shifts in the supply curve should be represented by the growth of the labor force, since land was not a constraining factor of production.[24] Since we have figures on population only

---

[24] See Temin (1967), p. 648: "If we assume that there was an upper bound to the amount of land a given number of workers could farm efficiently, then the speed at which new land could be settled would depend on the rate of growth of the potential labor force, i.e., the population."

at 10-year intervals, there is no "loss of accuracy" in substituting a time trend. Hence the supply function is:

$$\log Q = b_0 + b_1 \log P_{A-1} + b_2 t + v. \tag{18}$$

With quantity thus predetermined in any year, the demand curve now becomes a price-determination equation. The hypothesis is that price will be determined by three variables: the size of the cotton crop, the secular increase in income and population (represented by a time trend), and the cyclical changes in income (represented by the price of bread in London, B). The last variable is admittedly quite a crude proxy, but it has a rationale in the importance of the harvest for British prosperity. The demand curve is thus:

$$\log P_B = a_0 + a_1 \log Q + a_2 t + a_3 \log B + \log R + u, \tag{19}$$

where R is an index of British prices.

The three-equation system is estimated by ordinary-least-squares, on the grounds that it is not simultaneous. The endogenous mechanism works as follows: lagged price determines current output through (18); output determines P_B through (19); and P_B is transmitted to the U.S.A. through the modified version of (17):

$$\log P_A = c_0 + c_1 \log P_B. \tag{20}$$

Now it may be valid to estimate these equations as a recursive system by ordinary-least-squares, but it is important to note that an additional assumption about the disturbance term is required. One must assume that the variance-covariance matrix of the disturbances is diagonal, which is to say that there is no correlation between disturbances in any pair of equations. It may be plausible to assume no correlation between the disturbances for (19) and (18), but it is not quite so clear that the same is true for (19) and (20). It is difficult to say anything precise about this, because it is not clear what kind of "structural" mechanism is described by (20). But Temin does make use of the residuals from (20) as an estimate of the impact of "American demand" on P_A, and if this interpretation is correct then it hardly seems safe to assume that there will be no correlation with disturbances in British demand.

Using the regression estimates for the period 1820-59, Temin is able to decompose the fluctuations in the cotton price into percentages "caused" by each of several factors. The most striking finding is that shifts in the supply curve — indicated by the residuals in (18) — acted to *depress* the price level throughout the period of high prices, 1834-37; the high prices resulted from unusual demand factors. The North model is plainly rejected, as may be seen from the estimated supply function:

$$\log Q = 5.37 - 0.05 \log P_{A-1} + 0.06t \qquad R^2 = 0.96. \tag{21}$$
$$ (0.09) \phantom{\log P_{A-1} +} (0.002)$$

The wrong sign[25] and lack of significance of the price elasticity leads to the conclusion that "there is no evidence that the size of the cotton crop in the U.S.A. was at all responsive to price". Temin states in his conclusion: "The hypothesis of price rises based on periodic exhaustion of capacity accordingly should be abandoned."

The closely reasoned and judicious model construction offered by Temin is, I believe, a major step forward in historical econometrics. But I am not persuaded that his model is an adequate test of North's hypothesis, and I would like to describe an alternative model which produces a more balanced view of events.[26] North's main piece of evidence for his interpretation was the observed correlation between cotton prices and federal land sales in the cotton regions. While Temin's specification of this supply curve does allow for a "short-run" elasticity, it does not allow for a "long-run" elasticity of the sort North seems to have in mind. The labor force was probably not very responsive to the price of cotton, and, in any case, a time trend will certainly not show any response.

Even if the labor force data were available, it is questionable whether "the speed at which new land could be settled would depend on the rate of growth of the potential labor force". What North describes is an *economic* decision to undertake the cultivation of new cotton lands, a decision which was not based on the physical supply of labor available, but on prices and expected prices, especially the price of cotton.

---

[25] Temin states that the coefficients "all have appropriate signs", but unless there is a mistake in the reporting, the sign of the price elasticity is wrong.

[26] A detailed presentation of the full model may be found in Wright (1969). An early version of the model was developed independent of Temin's work. This was subsequently expanded and modified, in part as a response to criticism and suggestions from Professor Temin, to whom I am grateful.

With these considerations in mind I have estimated several versions of the following pair of equations:

$$\log Q = a_1 + a_2 \log P_{A-1} + a_3 \log L_{-3} \tag{22}$$

$$\log S = b_1 + b_2 P_A + b_3 t, \tag{23}$$

where S is the annual volume of federal land sales in the cotton regions, L_{-3} is lagged cumulative land sales in these regions, and the other variables follow Temin's notation. The variable L should not be viewed as the factor of production "land" but rather as a reflection of the extent to which expansion had taken place.

Equation (23) was estimated as part of a larger simultaneous system not shown here; equation (22) was estimated by ordinary-least-squares, since (as in Temin's model) it is entirely predetermined in the absence of serially correlated disturbances. In (22), lags of 2, 3, and 4 years were run; and (23) was estimated in geometrically distributed lag form as well. Estimates of b_2, the cotton-price elasticity of demand for land, range from 0.60 to 2.10 for equation (23), and from 1.50 to 2.91 in the "long-run", under the distributed lag assumption. Furthermore, when L is substituted for t in the supply function, a modest but identifiable 1-year supply elasticity appears, with estimates ranging from 0.09 to 0.27. Taken together, these results cannot be viewed as a confirmation of the notion of a "periodic exhaustion of capacity", but they are certainly much more favorable to North's hypothesis than is Temin.

In addition to the argument presented above concerning the use of a time trend, Temin has presented two arguments against the use of federal land sales as I have. The first is that acreage sold by the federal government is not identical with the increase in cotton land. The second is that land may have been purchased for speculative purposes. Using census years as benchmarks, I have tried to allow for the first argument by estimating two polar-case land sales series: the first assumes that the "rate of settlement" of land other than federally-sold land showed no responsiveness to cotton prices — i.e., it increased uniformly over time. The second assumes that the two categories of cotton land showed precisely the same degree of responsiveness. The range of estimates quoted above includes the results of both series.

With respect to the second argument, we do have some evidence that land which was purchased in large blocks by speculators was not held for long periods of time, but was quickly sold to farmers.[27] Temin has argued that unreasonably large amounts of land were sold during the peak year of 1835-36 — that is, more land than could be brought into cultivation in 1 year — but with a 2-4 year lag in the model (and with the recognition that at all times during the antebellum period only a fraction of the land on farms was improved), this argument loses much of its force. Finally, we note that when both L and t are included in the supply equation, they divide the correlation more or less equally, with a slight improvement in the R^2 value over either (21) or (22).

Having said all this, one must admit that the arguments are not conclusive and that Temin and others may be unconvinced. This state of things might be taken as an indication of the hopeless character of historical econometrics — since at this stage we have just about exhausted the statistical sources and indicators — but such a view is too pessimistic. One should not overlook the broad areas of agreement between the two versions: both find very low levels of supply elasticity in cotton, and my analysis is quite consistent with Temin's explanation for the price rise from 1834 to 1837. One cannot infer from high land sales elasticities in (23) that the "long-run" elasticity of cotton supply was large, because new land sales were only a fraction of the total acreage in cotton in any year; in most years this fraction was extremely small. Indeed, the only major difference in prediction between the two models is for the years 1838-40: Temin explains the low price of 1838 and 1840 and the sharp but temporary recovery of 1839 in large part by "sharp but fluctuating harvests" which are not explained in his model. But the large crops and low prices of 1838 and 1840 are explained very nicely by (22) as a result of the preceding land sales boom. In my model the large negative residual for 1839 requires special explanation, but contemporary evidence of a "drought almost unprecedented in its disaster" during that year makes this a not difficult task. Thus, the way that we seem to accumulate "knowledge" through historical econometrics is not necessarily through the achievement of a "correct" — or universally accepted — specification by one investigator, but through the emergence of an area of agreement on findings of those approaching the problem in very different ways. Looked at in this way, these studies have hopeful implications for returns to future work.

---

[27] See Swieringa (1968) and Young (1961), pp. 101-102, 113.

2.5. *The expansion of the antebellum iron industry*[28]

The last study considered in this review is an attempt by Fogel and Engerman (1969) to explain the expansion of the American iron industry from 1842 to 1858. One reason for special interest in the article is that their model is presented as a general model of industrial expansion, of wide applicability during the 19th century. Fogel and Engerman juxtapose their approach with what "every schoolboy has been taught about the mechanical inventions of the industrial revolution", and the slighting of other expansive factors in historical research. With this introduction, it comes as something of a jolt to read: "The model is applicable to competitive industries characterized by constant returns to scale." In light of all that has been written about the great changes in industrial concentration during the 19th century — based in part upon economies of scale resulting from technological change — it is difficult to share this optimism with respect to the simplest market structure and production function that theory has given us. It is quite clear, e.g., that such a model is applicable for only a fleeting period to the American iron industry. This is not the place for a lengthy discussion of the subject, so I will simply express my opinion that I am not hopeful in general that competition and Cobb-Douglas will take us very far in unraveling the mysteries of the industrial revolution.

But these comments are alien to the spirit of this review, which is to approach the subject pragmatically, asking what specifically has been accomplished in economic history to date. The assumption of competition does seem valid for the period covered; and, in the absence of prior information about the form of the production function, Cobb-Douglas may be a reasonable starting point. Furthermore, the Fogel and Engerman approach does have at least two novel features which are important in practical work: the abandonment of the assumption of long-run equilibrium, for which they substitute a series of short-run equilibria; and a "data-saving" innovation in their method of estimation. Hence I will concentrate on their application.

Fogel and Engerman wish to estimate the following structural equations:

Demand $\qquad Q = (bI^{\psi} P_i^{\varepsilon_i}) P^{-\varepsilon}$ (24)

Supply $\qquad Q = (mA^{1/\alpha_3} w^{-\alpha_1/\alpha_3} r^{-\alpha_2/\alpha_3} K) P^{\gamma}$ (25)

---

[28] I am grateful to William Nordhaus, Craig Swan, and Robert Fogel for advice in the writing of this section.

where Q = output of pig iron; I = gross domestic investment; P_i = price of imported iron; P = domestic price of pig iron; A = index of productive efficiency; W = wage rate; r = unit cost of raw materials; K = input of capital; and the remaining symbols are the parameters of the two functions. The economic content of the system is conventional enough, but one might raise a question about the inclusion of P_i, the price of imported iron, as an exogenous variable. There is no question that the demand curve for domestic iron will depend on P_i; the problem is the statistical possibility that P_i will be correlated with the disturbance term in (24). This will clearly be the case if the U.S.A. was large enough to influence P_i; for then P and P_i would be determined simultaneously, and the estimate of ε_i will be biased. Fogel and Engerman justify the equation with the statement that it seems to "fit the data quite well", but this is not very reassuring with respect to bias from simultaneity.[29] Even if the U.S.A. were small enough relative to the world market that the supply of imports may be regarded as completely elastic, there will be a bias if P and P_i are influenced by common disturbance factors not included in the model. The only remedy for either of these problems, unfortunately, is expansion of the model.

Fogel and Engerman are not able to estimate the variable A and K, so they substitute the general shift variable S into (25). With disturbance terms included, the structure is then:

$$Q = (bI^{\psi} P_i^{\varepsilon_i}) P^{-\varepsilon} e^{u} \tag{26}$$

$$Q = SP^{\gamma} e^{v}, \tag{27}$$

where u and v are uncorrelated random variables. For purposes of estimation the equations are solved for the reduced form, i.e., solution for endogenous variables in terms of exogenous variables. In logarithmic form this is:

$$\log Q = \frac{\gamma}{\gamma + \varepsilon} \log b + \frac{\gamma \psi}{\gamma + \varepsilon} \log I + \frac{\gamma \varepsilon_i}{\gamma + \varepsilon} \log P_i + \frac{\varepsilon}{\gamma + \varepsilon} \log S + \frac{\gamma u + \varepsilon v}{\gamma + \varepsilon} \tag{28}$$

$$\log P = \frac{1}{\gamma + \varepsilon} \log b + \frac{\psi}{\gamma + \varepsilon} \log I + \frac{\varepsilon_i}{\gamma + \varepsilon} \log P_i - \frac{1}{\gamma + \varepsilon} \log S + \frac{u + v}{\gamma + \varepsilon}. \tag{29}$$

---

[29] They state in the text: "When applied to the iron industry, the assumption that the demand function is linear in logs yields a regression in which the correlation coefficient is equal to 0.98." This statement is apparently referring to an ordinary-least-squares estimate of (24) which is not shown; but the goodness-of-fit criterion has no particular relevance to simultaneous-equation bias.

Because the variable S is not observed, Fogel and Engerman rewrite equation (24) as:

$$Se^v = \frac{Q}{P^\gamma} \tag{30}$$

and proceed to apply two ingenious estimates for γ, the elasticity of supply: the first is estimated from the 1860 census data on factor shares, on the assumption of constant returns to scale and Cobb-Douglas; the second is based on the Hicks-Slutsky condition that the sum of the elasticities of substitutes must be equal and opposite to the price elasticity.[30] With the values substituted for S in (28) and (29), the regressions can be run, with the following results obtained (with *t-ratios* in parentheses below each coefficient):

$$\log Q = 1.292 + 0.441 \log I + 1.212 \log P_i + 0.273 \log S \qquad R^2 = 0.79 \ (31)$$
$$(2.94) \qquad (4.82) \qquad (2.61) \qquad D - W = 1.09$$

$$\log P = 0.309 + 0.106 \log I + 0.290 \log P_i - 0.174 \log S \qquad R^2 = 0.96 \ (32)$$
$$(2.94) \qquad (4.82) \qquad (6.95) \qquad D - W = 1.09.$$

Coefficients under the alternative assumption for γ are similar. From these equations the structural parameters are obtained. With this information, Fogel and Engerman are able to reach a number of conclusions, the most striking of which is that all of the growth of output from 1842 to 1858 is a result of the expansion of supply. By running the regressions separately for charcoal and for anthracite furnaces, however, Fogel and Engerman find that demand *was* important. The anthracite sector was especially sensitive to the price of imported iron, and hence the fall in the tariff was responsible for the apparent slow growth of "demand" for anthracite iron. In the charcoal sector, supply-side expansion accounted for the rise in output, while demand was falling. Hence the hypothesis of Taussig — that the tariff had little effect on anthracite, and merely allowed the construction of inefficient charcoal furnaces during 1843-46 — must be rejected.

These conclusions are of interest in themselves, but the method bears closer scrutiny since the procedure and its justification may not be completely

---

[30] The fact that Fogel and Engerman make recognition in this way of the substitutability of domestic and imported iron does not affect my earlier argument concerning a possible statistical bias associated with the variable P_i.

clear. The essential problem is that there are no observations of the shift variable S. Equation (30) does not supply such observations; instead it gives us values for Se^v, the "shift" term *including the random error component*. Thus it is not quite correct to write the fourth regression coefficient in (28) and (29) as a coefficient of "log S", since the variable is really "log $S+v$". If, in (28) and (29), one writes "log $Q-\gamma$ log P" in place of "log S", and then solves through for Q, it becomes evident that these two equations are not really the reduced-form for a simultaneous-system; they are instead identical demand equations, with terms shifted around. The solution in both cases is:

$$\log Q = \log b + \psi \log I + \varepsilon_i \log P_i - \varepsilon \log P + u. \tag{33}$$

Fogel and Engerman do state in a footnote that they did expect the t-ratios for log I and log P_i to be identical in the two equations, but it may not be clear to the reader that (31) and (32) are merely different forms of the same regression. It is not true in general, of course, that alternative algebraic statements of the same equation will yield equivalent regression estimates; but it is true here because one is minimizing the same error term in each case.

But all of the preceding comment relates only to the exposition; what Fogel and Engerman have done is to use "outside" information to collapse a simultaneous system to a single equation, which is then estimated by ordinary-least-squares. The real question is whether this procedure will bias the estimates. The key point here is that Fogel and Engerman have not run a regression of the form (33), which would clearly lead to biased estimates; instead they have run the following regression:

$$\log Q = \frac{\gamma}{\gamma+\varepsilon} \log b + \frac{\gamma\psi}{\gamma+\varepsilon} \log I + \frac{\gamma\varepsilon_i}{\gamma+\varepsilon} \log P_i$$

$$+ \frac{\varepsilon}{\gamma+\varepsilon} [\log Q - \gamma \log P] + \frac{\gamma u}{\gamma+\varepsilon}. \tag{34}$$

At first glance the simultaneous-equations bias appears still to be present, because there are still endogenous variables on both sides of the equation.[31] However, Fogel and Engerman have not inserted *one* endogenous variable on the right-hand-side, but rather an expression involving two endogenous

---

[31] This was my first reaction. I owe the revised version in the text to correspondence with Professor Fogel.

variables; and it may be shown, by dividing the reduced-form solution for Q by that for P^γ, that even though both P and Q will be correlated with u and v, the expression Q/P^γ (or $\log Q - \gamma \log P$) will be correlated only with v. Thus it does appear that Fogel and Engerman have successfully managed to estimate a demand equation by ordinary-least-squares and at the same time avoid simultaneous-equations bias.

This procedure does depend on the accuracy of the estimate for γ. If γ is wrong, there will be errors-in-the variables, though this will probably be a minor source of bias compared to the direct effects of the mistaken value of γ. However, the insensitivity of the conclusions with respect to the two estimated values of γ does give reassurance on this score — though of course one might not be so fortunate in a different application. It should perhaps be noted that the coefficient of "$\log S + v$" will probably not be the same as what one would obtain if one knew the true values for S; but it is not clear to me that this will bias the estimates of the parameters. A similar comment may be made about the rates of growth for S quoted by Fogel and Engerman in Tables 4, 5, and 6. They are actually rates of growth for Se^v; but here again I do not see a reason for bias, so long as there is no serial correlation in v.

On the whole, then, Fogel and Engerman have an imaginative and hopeful contribution. The appropriateness of the method in other contexts will have to be studied further, but they have certainly shown the relevance of econometric models to a question in traditional economic history, and they have presented substantial evidence for their historical interpretation.

3. Concluding comments

The question with which this review began was whether one can draw any conclusions about the returns to econometric history on the basis of a survey of recent studies. Have econometric methods made major substantive contributions to historical understanding, and do they offer promise for the future? Unfortunately, I think the answer must be both yes and no. Looking at the firm conclusions which can be drawn from the studies discussed, it is very hard to argue that much progress has been made; certainly, those findings which can be stated with confidence — if indeed there are any — do not compare in interest or importance with those which have been achieved in recent years by much simpler statistical methods. If these results were explainable simply in terms of carelessness or lack of sophistication, the message would be clear; but such factors are only a small part of the story, and it is not at all clear to me what general methodological message is appropriate. I do feel safe in predicting that econometrics is not going to revolutionize our understanding of the past very soon. Certainly no one should believe something simply because "modern econometric techniques" have been used on it.

On the other hand I do not think that these conclusions are any grounds for giving up the enterprise. This survey has encountered some hopeful starts as well as some dead ends, and there are a great many unexplored areas which offer new possibilities. Furthermore, as was shown earlier in the paper, a great many historical questions will never be answered *until* we have satisfactory econometric models. Related to this point is the observation that formal econometrics can be of value simply in explaining what kinds of procedure and estimates are *not* unbiased or accurate.

In no particular order, and with no particular attempt at rigorous demonstration, I offer the following thoughts on the problems and prospects of econometric history:

(1) The difficulties of econometric history result in many ways from shortcomings of theory and of econometric methods. Textbooks of econometrics almost always begin with the assumption of a known structure, whereas what we really want to do is usually to *test* structure. This we can get around by trial-and-error methods, but outside of pure competition we do not get much real help from theory. Nor are the dynamic characteristics of even this theory well developed outside of the simplest cases. Satisfactory theories of technical change and diffusion are yet to come.

(2) But the problems of historical econometrics are still more severe. As stated, we usually want to know the structure — to find out "how the system worked" rather than to make predictions — and hence we cannot satisfactorily rely on the inclusion of any and all variables which improve R^2 values. Still more pressing is the fact that we so often have only scraps of data, and formal econometrics gives little help on what to do with these. Hence we can expect to continue to see a variety of ingenious new methods and *ad hoc* devices, simply in order to allow the work to go ahead. This trend should certainly be encouraged, but if we do so we had better prepare ourselves for a continued flow of studies with unacceptable and sometimes bizarre conclusions.

(3) "Progress" in econometric history will depend not only on new

econometric devices and on theoretical advances, but also on a willingness to undertake extensive historical research of a more conventional sort — not just in the collection of data, but also for help in formulating and specifying models. There is really almost no such thing as *a priori* knowledge in economic history, and most of what is called "*a priori* knowledge" is derived from works of the "old economic history", which will continue to be useful. But since specifications are highly uncertain in almost every case, substantive progress — "convincing answers to questions of interest to economic historians" — will probably come only with a great expansion in the number of studies, as an area of agreement slowly converges from a great variety of models.

(4) One implication of the preceding point is that there will continue to be plenty of room for many types and varieties of work in economic history. We have already seen some of the benefits of the division of labor between data collection and model-building. While there is some room for methods of "prediction" as tools in estimating unavailable data, the results are not too helpful as inputs in structural estimation, and the older methods will remain valuable.

A more important reason for my statement, however, is that econometric studies have not yet come close to giving answers to the kind of questions which bring many people into the field of economic history. Econometric methods are well designed for analyzing relatively narrow-gauge relationships, such as the determinants of investment by firms, elasticities of supply and demand in competitive markets, and, with more difficulty, cost curves and production functions. With the more abundant data of the post-Civil War era, we may even be able to develop a macro-econometric history. All of these are "historical" points of interest which match closely the concerns of non-historical economists. But what is the point of studying economic history anyway? I am not interested in defining a "role of the economic historian" if that implies that we should all share the same interests. But many economic historians would say that their purpose is to achieve a *broadening* of the economist's perspective, an appreciation of the minute fraction of man's economic past which the modern economy society represents — above all, some understanding of the great social transformation involved in the process of economic development, and of the cumulative bases for the striking economic contrasts in the world today. Some, indeed, are less interested in explaining the *economic* experience of the past as in understanding the ways in which economic factors influence social and political developments. I think we have to admit that econometrics has not gone very far in advancing understanding of these historical processes. This admission is not really surprising when one considers that econometrics — and to some extent economic theory itself — has developed in response to policy-making needs within a relatively narrow set of surrounding institutions and attitudes.

It is less obvious than it may appear that this will always be so. Good econometricians have a way of breaking down grand historical processes into more workable parts, and we have already had econometric investigations into such areas as urbanization and education, which might earlier have seemed impossible. As the new economic history continues to insist that wide-ranging, imaginative hypotheses about history be rigorously stated and theoretically consistent, it may be that more and more subject matter will come within operational reach.[32] But for the foreseeable future, within these bounds of clarity and consistency, there will be plenty of room for old-fashioned speculations about history, even if we econometricians will not really believe any of it.

References

Basmann, R. L., 1965, The role of the economic historian in predictive testing of proffered "economic laws". *Explorations in Entrepreneurial History*, Second Series, II (Spring/ Summer).

Cochran, T. C., 1969, Economic history, old and new. *American Historial Review* 74 (June).

Conrad, A., 1968, Econometrics and southern history. *Explorations in Entrepreneurial History*, Second Series, VI (Fall).

Conrad, A. and John Meyer, 1957, Economic theory, statistical inference and economic history. *Journal of Economic History* 17 (December). Reprinted in Conrad and Meyer, *The Economics of Slavery and Other Studies in Econometric History*. Chicago, Aldine Publishing Company, 1964.

Conrad, A. and John Meyer, 1958, The economics of slavery in the ante bellum South. *Journal of Political Economy* 66 (April). Reprinted in Conrad and Meyer, *The Economics of Slavery*.

Cranmer, H. Jerome, 1960, Canal investment, 1815-1860. In: National Bureau of Economic Research, *Trends in the American Economy in the Nineteenth Century* (Studies in Income and Wealth Volume 24). Princeton, N.J., Princeton University Press.

---

[32] See Thernstrom (1968) for a survey of a variety of techniques used by quantitative political and social historians. Many of these studies have invaded territory previously thought to be restricted to "literary" historians.

David, Paul, 1966, The mechanization of reaping in the ante-bellum Midwest. In: *Industrialization in two systems*, edited by Henry Rosovsky. New York, Wiley & Sons, Inc.

Davis, L., 1966, Professor Fogel and the new economic history. *Economic History Review* 19 (December).

Davis, L., 1968, "And it will never be literature": the new economic history: a critique. *Explorations in Entrepreneurial History*. Second Series, VI (Fall).

Davis, L., J. R. T. Hughes, and S. Reiter, 1960, Aspects of quantitative research in economic history. *Journal of Economic History* 20 (December).

Davis, L. and J. Legler, 1966, The government in the American economy, 1815-1902. *Journal of Economic History* 26 (December).

Desai, M., 1968, Some issues in econometric history. *Economic History Review* 21 (April).

Evans, Robert Jr., 1962, The economics of American negro slavery, 1830-1860. In: National Bureau of Economic Research, *Aspects of Labor Economics*. Princeton, N. J., Princeton University Press.

Fishlow, Albert, 1965, *American railroads and the transformation of the ante-bellum economy*. Cambridge, Mass., Harvard University Press.

Fishlow, Albert, 1966, Levels of nineteenth-century American investment in education. *Journal of Economic History* 26 (December).

Fogel, R. W., 1964, *Railroads and American economic growth*. Baltimore, Johns Hopkins Press.

Fogel, R. W., 1966, The new economic history: its findings and methods. *Economy History Review* 19 (December).

Fogel, R. W., 1967, The specification problem in economic history. *Journal of Economic History* 27 (September).

Fogel, R. W. and S. L. Engerman, 1969, A model for the explanation of industrial expansion during the nineteenth century with an application to the American iron industry. *Journal of Political Economy* 77 LXXVII (May/June).

Foust, James and Dale Swan, 1970, The productivity of ante-bellum slave labor: a micro approach. *Agricultural History* 44 (January).

Hacker, L. M., 1966, The new revolution in economic history: A review article based on railroads and American economic growth: essays in econometric history, by Robert William Fogel. *Explorations in Entrepreneurial History*, Second Series, III (Spring).

Kelley, A. C., 1965, International migration and economic growth. Australia: 1865-1935. *Journal of Economic History* 25 (September).

Kelley, A. C., 1968, Demographic change and economic growth: Australia, 1861-1911. *Explorations in Entrepreneurial History* 5 (Spring/Summer).

Kmenta, J. and J. G. Williamson, 1966, Determinants of investment behavior: United States railroads, 1872-1941. *Review of Economics and Statistics* 48 (May).

Kuh, E., 1965, Econometric models: is a new age dawning? *American Economic Review* 55 (May).

Lebergott, Stanley, 1966, United States transport advance and externalities. *Journal of Economic History* 26 (Decemb er).

MacAvoy, Paul, 1965, *The economic effects of regulation: trunk-line railroad cartels and the interstate commerce commission before 1900*. Cambridge, Mass., the M. I. T. Press.

McClelland, Peter, 1968, Railroads, American growth, and the new economic history: a critique. *Journal of Economic History* 28 (March).

McClelland, Peter, 1969, The cost to America of British imperial policy. *American Economic Review* 59 (May).

McCloskey, Donald, 1969, Did Victorian Britain fail? Paper presented to the January 1969 Purdue Conference on the Application of Economic Theory and Quantitative Techniques to Problems of Economic History; "Britain's Loss from Foreign Industrialization: A Provisional Estimate". (Unpublished paper.)

McGouldrick, Paul, 1968, *New England textiles in the nineteenth century: profits and investment.* Cambridge, Mass., Harvard University Press.

Neal, Larry, 1969, Investment behavior by American railroads: 1897-1914. *Review of Economics and Statistics* 51 (May).

Nerlove, Marc, 1965a, *The estimation and identification of Cobb-Douglas production functions.* Chicago, Rand-McNally and Company.

Nerlove, Marc, 1965b, Two models of the British economy: a fragment of a critical survey. *International Economic Review* 5 (May).

Nerlove, Marc, 1966, Railroads and American economic growth. *Journal of Economic History* 26 (March).

North, Douglass, 1961, *The economic growth of the United States, 1790-1860.* Englewood Cliffs, N. J., Prentice-Hall.

North, Douglass, 1966, *Growth and welfare in the American past.* Englewood Cliffs, N. J., Prentice-Hall.

North, Douglass, 1968, Sources of productivity change in ocean shipping, 1600-1850. *Journal of Political Economy* 76 (September/October).

Owsley, Frank, 1949, *Plain folk of the Old South.* Baton Rouge, La., Louisiana State University Press.

Poulson, Barry, 1969, Estimates of the value of manufacturing output during the early nineteenth century. *Journal of Economic History* 29 (September).

Ransom, Roger, 1964, Canals and development: a discussion of the issues. *American Economic Review* 54 (May).

Ransom, Roger, 1968, British policy and colonial growth: some implications of the burden from the navigation acts. *Journal of Economic History* 28 (September).

Redlich, Fritz, 1965, "New" and traditional approaches to economic history and their interdependence. *Journal of Economic History* 25 (December).

Redlich, Fritz, 1968, Potentialities and pitfalls in economic history. *Explorations in Entrepreneurial History*, Second Series, VI (Fall).

Saraydar, E., 1964, A note on the profitability of ante bellum slavery. *Southern Economic Journal* 30 (April).

Solmon, L.C., Opportunity costs and models of schooling in the nineteenth century. *Southern Economic Journal* 37 (July).

Soltow, Lee, 1968, Long-run changes in British income inequality. *Economic History Review* 21 (April).

Soltow, Lee, 1969, Evidence on income inequality in the United States, 1866-1965. *Journal of Economic History* 29 (June).

Sutch, Richard, 1965, The profitability of ante bellum slavery — revisited. *Southern Economic Journal* 31 (April).

Swieringa, Robert, 1968, *Pioneers and profits: land speculation on the Iowa farm.* Ames, Iowa State University Press.

Temin, Peter, 1964, *Iron and steel in nineteenth century America.* Cambridge, Mass. The M.I.T. Press.

Temin, Peter, 1967, The cause of cotton price fluctuations in the 1830's. *Review of Economics and Statistics* 49 (November).

Thernstrom, Stephan, 1968, Quantitative methods in history: some notes. In: *Sociology and History: Methods*, edited by S. M. Lipset and R. Hofstadter. New York, Basic Books, Inc.

Thomas, R. P., 1965, A quantitative approach to the study of the effects of British imperial policy upon colonial welfare: some preliminary findings. *Journal of Economic History* 25 (December).

Von Tunzelman, G. N., 1968, The new economic history: an econometric appraisal. *Explorations in Entrepreneurial History*, Second Series, V (Winter).

Williamson, J. G. and J. A. Swanson, 1966, The growth of cities in the American Northeast, 1820-1870. *Explorations in Entrepreneurial History.* Second Series, IV (Supplement).

Wright, Gavin, 1969, The economics of cotton in the antebellum South. Unpublished Ph. D. dissertation, Yale University.

Wright, Gavin, 1970, "Economic democracy" and the distribution of agricultural wealth in the Cotton South, 1850-1860. *Agricultural History* (January).

Ulmer, M. J., 1960, *Capital in transportation, communications, and public utilities*. Princeton N. J., Princeton University Press.

Yasuba, Yasukitchi, 1961, The profitability and viability of plantation slavery in the United States. *Economic Studies Quarterly* 12. To be reprinted in *The Reinterpretation of American economic history*, edited by R. W. Fogel and S. L. Engerman. New York, Harper & Row (forthcoming).

Young, Mary E., 1961, *Redskins, ruffleshirts and rednecks. Indian allotments in Alabama and Mississippi, 1830-1860*. Norman, Okla., University of Oklahoma Press.

Zevin, Robert B., 1969, The growth of cotton textile production after 1815. In: Fogel and Engerman, *The Reinterpretation of American economic history*.

COMMENTS BY PAUL A. DAVID

Stanford University

Gavin Wright's admirable survey of econometric work in economic history presents an almost insuperable challenge to a commentator of my disposition. I must confess that by nature I am slow to praise and inclined to compliment my colleagues' work in only the most backward manner — by spending time trying to take it to bits. For me to be presented a virtually seamless garment, which simply will not unravel and can therefore only be held up for admiration is thus most frustrating.

My embarrassment extends beyond that of having vainly tried to find something significant that is "wrong" with Wright's paper. My real plight lies in the fact that I also concur in the general spirit of the critical appraisal Wright offers of the work that has been done to date. Equally, I share his views of the problems and prospects for future undertakings in the application of econometric methods to historical questions. Thus far, it seems to me, the achievements have been limited and very uneven. Moreover, because the most serious deficiencies (to which this survey rightly draws attention) have sprung from inadequacies in the *economic* analysis of the phenomena under examination, there is scant reason to think that an improvement of average performance will automatically attend the application of more sophisticated methods of quantitative analysis, or the more widespread use of the regression techniques now coming into fashion among economic historians.

Indeed, the appeal of greater econometric "rigor" may perversely elicit from readers of the new economic history such a willing suspension of disbelief that the most improbable simplifications of the past will be entertained on the strength of their empirical or analytical convenience alone. To cite two instances of this incipient trend, I need hardly range beyond the collection of papers that have deservedly won favorable comment in Wright's review. My first illustration is drawn from the work of Engerman and Fogel (1969), who ingeniously propose to identify the supply parameter of an otherwise under-identified model of the ante bellum market for pig iron by imposing the (Hicks-Slutsky) condition that a derived demand function — for investment inputs in their particular case — must be zero-order homogeneous in prices. Specifically, they appeal to this condition to support the restriction that the price elasticities of demand for domestic pig iron and imported pig iron must have been of equal magnitude and opposite sign. But for us to accept this we must grant Engerman and Fogel the preposterous assumption that the elasticity of substitution between pig iron inputs and all other goods and services flowing into the production of the aggregate bundle of domestic investment goods in the U.S.A. during the years 1840-60 was identically zero! If they protest that the assumption is not preposterous because we are familiar with Leontief-type, fixed-coefficient models of production, my reply must surely be that as history is an empirical subject its practitioners ought to be willing to assume the burden of empirical proof. Why not explicitly introduce the prices of say, lumber products and labor into the (derived) demand equation for domestic pig iron, and test whether the coefficients of those price variables are significantly different from zero in the quasi-reduced form regression equation of the sort estimated by Engerman and Fogel?[1]

---

[1] I cannot accept Engerman and Fogel's (1969) deflation of pig iron prices by the wholesale price index as meeting the objection to the exclusion of the prices of other inputs into gross domestic investment from the quasi-reduced form regression model. That deflation would be justified only if two conditions were met:

In view of the attention Wright has directed to the methodological contribution made by the Engerman and Fogel study, I may perhaps be indulged a footnote-like digression on a technical point. It is easy enough to see that the Hicks-Slutsky restriction on the elasticities provides an estimation method, *à la* Fogel and Engerman, that generalizes to m substitutes for the commodity under study. If the demand and supply equations are (extending the notation employed in Wright's equations (26) and (27)) respectively,

$$Q = bI^{\psi}P^{-\varepsilon}\left\{\prod_{j=i}^{m}P_{j}^{\varepsilon_{j}}\right\}e^{u}, \tag{1}$$

and

$$Q = SP^{\gamma}e^{v}, \tag{2}$$

solving first for the reduced-form expression for log (Q), and substituting in that for the composite variable (log $S + v$) derived from the supply relation, (2) yields:

$$\log Q = \{\gamma/(\gamma+\varepsilon)\}\log b + \{\gamma\psi/(\gamma+\varepsilon)\}\log I + \{\gamma/(\gamma+\varepsilon)\}\sum_{j=i}^{m}\varepsilon_{j}\log P_{j}$$

$$+\{\varepsilon/(\gamma+\varepsilon)\}[\log Q - \gamma\log P] + \{u/(\gamma+\varepsilon)\}. \tag{3}$$

The analogous expression may be obtained for log P — paralleling Wright's equation (29) as equation (3) here parallels his equation (28). Note then that the Hicks-Slutsky restriction takes the general form:

$$\left\{\sum_{j=i}^{m}\varepsilon_{i}\right\} - \varepsilon = 0. \tag{4}$$

This permits the supply elasticity to be identified by dividing the *sum* of the m coefficients of the substitute-price variable — log (P_{j}) — by the

---

(a) if $(\varepsilon_{i}-\varepsilon)=\varepsilon_{w}$, which relationship would hold among the price elasticities of the Hicksian demand function, only if the wholesale price index (P_{w}) was a geometrically weighted index in which the weights were proportional to the price elasticities of the (derived) demand for those goods in the investment goods sector — which is certainly not the case;

(b) if $\varepsilon_{w}=0$, when Engerman and Fogel impose the restriction $\varepsilon_{i}=\varepsilon$. Since the wholesale price series in not the weighted index described above, the test of the significance of the coefficient it takes when allowed to appear in the regression explicitly is not relevant as a defense against may objection to the omission of say, wage rates and lumber prices from the regression equations. (The notation used here is the same as that employed in the text below.)

coefficient of the constructed variable ($\log Q - \gamma \log P$). The parameter thus obtained is $+\gamma$.

From this last it is evident that Wright has been a little too generous (on page 453) in crediting Engerman and Fogel with having "successfully managed to estimate a demand equation by ordinary least-squares and at the same time avoid simultaneous-equations bias". The point ought to have been made that their method called for *constrained* least-squares estimation, namely constraining the parameter γ implied by the restriction on the regression coefficients to be identical to the $-\gamma$ value employed in generating the variable ($\log Q - \gamma \log P$). Observe that this constraint must be enforced even if one relies on an independent estimate of the supply elasticity parameter (γ), at least so long as it is maintained that the demand equation for the commodity in question (pig iron here) is derivable from some set of continuously differentiable isoquants — or, in the case of a final consumer good, indifference contours. Alternatively, it should be possible (and seems preferable) to secure a maximum likelihood estimate of the parameter γ, along with the other constrained parameters, by using non-linear regression methods to estimate the quasi-reduced-form equations for $\log Q$ and for $\log P$ *simultaneously*.[2] As Wright's paper so aptly puts it, "there is no free lunch in econometric history". To the extent that Engerman and Fogel estimated their model by ordinary, unconstrained least-squares, they have erred precisely in becoming bemused by the "free lunch" fallacy.

But, to return now to further illustrate the basis of my concern over the willing suspension of disbelief engendered by econometric history exercises, consider Peter Temin's (1967) study of the cotton market in the ante bellum era. Temin asks us to regard an exponential time trend as a reasonable proxy for the agricultural labor force available to the South during 1820-60, and, arguing that the effective long-term capacity constraint on the growth of the cotton supply was not land but the growth of the available labor force, he estimates a "supply function" by regressing the logarithm of the U.S. cotton crop on the logarithm of the previous year's (American) price for cotton and an index of calendar time. In justification for introducing the exponential trend, Temin notes (1967, p. 468) that the U.S. southern

---

[2] I am grateful to Warren C. Sanderson, of the National Bureau of Economic Research, for an algebraic demonstration that when the "quantity" relation — given by equation (3) above — is estimated singly, the maximum likelihood value for the price elasticity of supply is $\hat{\gamma} = 0$, as that will provide an exact fit to the data leaving all residuals equal to zero.

population was growing *steadily*, at a rate between 2 and 3% per annum, from decade to decade during this period; as far as numbers are concerned, my own estimates of the *agricultural labor force* in the southern states for census dates in the period 1800-60 indicates even greater stability of the growth rate during the decades 1820-60 — in the range from 2.0-2.4% per annum.[3] So far so good. Why, then, does the supply function estimated by Temin shift outward at the rate of 6.0% with each passing year?[4] If we are really to believe that the time trend is — as Temin tells us — nothing more than a proxy for the steady growth of the labor supply constraint on cotton production, it is thus necessary to imagine that the long-run elasticity of U.S. cotton output with respect to the input of labor was approximately 2.7! And if it will be suggested that the time variable picks up the influence of the secular advance in labor productivity as well as the growth of the labor force, surely it is bizarre to depict the growth of supply as being "constrained" by the labor force growth when cotton output per worker was rising so much faster than the labor force itself. Indeed, the rapidity of the implied pace of productivity advance — still following Temin's interpretation — might suggest another route through which the opening up of more fertile western lands played a role governing the expansion of long-run supply. But the pace implied, being upwards of 3.5% per annum, is simply too rapid a rate of advance in cotton labor productivity to be reconciled with our general quantitative impressions of the growth of southern agriculture, or the national economy for that matter, during the period in question.[5] All this simply suggests that the rationale Temin puts forward for the presence of the exponential time trend is highly suspect.

My point in these two examples is not merely that the justifications of Engerman and Fogel's and Temin's interpretations of their respective econometric results hinge upon bold simplifications of historical experience which seem difficult to credit. Rather, the feature I find noteworthy — and

---

[3] The labor force estimates referred to are those underlying Appendix Table II of David (1967), p. 197. The full set of figures, and the method of their derivation, are available from the author (upon request) in the form of Stanford Research Center in Economic Growth, Research Memorandum 53-A (December 1966, mimeo., 33 pp.).

[4] Not only does the price elasticity coefficient estimated by Temin's equation, which Wright, reproduces as equation (21), have the wrong sign, the coefficient of "t" is 0.06 — with a standard error of 0.002 — a magnitude which one would have thought would have attracted notice before now.

[5] Cf., e.g., David (1967), esp., pp. 174-86.

unhappily symptomatic of more widespread tendencies in the recent writing of quantitative economic history — is that in neither case has an effort been made to reconcile the obvious empirical implications of the "simplifying" premises with anything else that happens to be known about the economy under examination. Could the long-run elasticity of cotton output with respect to labor inputs have been anything like as high as 3? Was not iron substituted for wood in investment goods as the relative price of the former declined during the pre-Civil War period? It used to be the vogue for champions of "the new economic history" to belabor their more "traditional" brethren for passing off, under cover of literary license, all sorts of unfounded quantitative statements about the past. An uncharitable observer might conclude that it will be the peculiar achievement of the new economic historians to have demonstrated that this can also be managed without benefit of a readable prose style.

Now I suppose that my lament is bitter because I am disappointed to see so much of the work in the new, econometric history — including some of the most important contributions — succumbing to a malady already virtually endemic in applied economic exercises, particularly applied econometrics, but against which I used to believe economic historians would be able to muster effective resistance. The illness in question is a form of intellectual tunnel vision. It manifests itself most frequently in a penchant for focusing exclusive attention upon the confrontation between a terribly restricted set of observations and an equally narrowly specified hypothesis concerning some facet of economic behavior; typically, the victim fixes upon some partial aspect of a body of quantitative findings which he construes as most directly germane to a "test" of his hypothesis, *and* will utterly neglect the implications of any corollary empirical results, ostensibly because securing them was not the immediate object of the exercise. In combating this malady, the economic historian, I should have thought, would be aided by those special interests that distinguish him from the general run of economists, applied and otherwise — interests that properly should serve as an antidote to this pathological fixation with verifying a particular theoretical formulation rather than asking what the attempt to verify it discloses about past and present economic experience.

Yes, there are, after all, some significant differences separating Economic History from the larger discipline of Economics. These reside not in matters of general methodology but in the nature of the problems that have long been the fundamental concern, and until rather recently the special province of economic historians. What, then are these fundamental concerns? As Ashton (1946) maintained, economic history is preoccupied with — should one say motivated by? — the search for an understanding of processes of economic change that are played out over comparatively long spans of time. In my view, the length of time required for completion of these processes is not itself crucial. Rather, it is the nature of the changes with which we are concerned that matters — and their nature appears to militate against their being achieved overnight. The sort of changes I have in mind here might be summarily described as *alternations in the structure of economic relationships*.

It should immediately be appreciated that by this I do not simply refer to changes in industrial structure, in the narrow sense of shifts in the composition of output, or in the relative sizes and relations among productive units (firms) selling in more-or-less well defined markets. Instead, I find it helpful, as does Wright, to use "structure" in something very close to the Cowles Commission sense: "Structure" subsumes an account of the relationships among the relevant variables of an economic system in existence at a specific moment in time. Structural change thus comprises many things: (1) It refers to alterations in the parameter values of behavioral equations specified for components of an economic system, such as changes in the long-run propensity to save out of personal disposable income. (2) It must also include the appearance of new behavioral equations within the system: commutation of agricultural labor services into money wage payments, or the large-scale manumission of slaves, will require a rewriting of micro- and macro-supply and demand equations for labor. Equally, the emergence of banks of issues, generating new debt instruments in the form of notes, should occasion a revision of the asset supply and demand equations. (3) Structural change, further, encompasses the supplanting of one variable by another among the arguments of a particular behavioral equation, for economic development involves the disappearance of some relationships as well as the addition of new ones. Thus, at various times during the 19th century, I daresay, industrial employment rate fluctuations supplanted harvest yield- and grain price-movements as proximate determinants of the variations of marriage rates in Western European countries. (4) Finally, structural change subsumes alterations in the weights attached to different behavioral equations within the system, so that drifting values of parameters in the more highly aggregated functional relations such as aggregate investment demand equations may simply reflect, say, the secular decline of the relative importance of inventory change and the rise of fixed investment.

The very terms in which I have described what I mean by structural change suggest that these problems are not alien to the applied economist-econometrician. He is almost certain to encounter them as he searches for stable relationships in data drawn from the experience of societies that have been undergoing such transformations. Yet, I think it is fair to say that for the ordinary applied econometrician such problems are primarily a source of annoyance. He tends to be looking for a simple, comprehensive, descriptive structure, and so tries to take account of them as best he can by allowing for parameter shifts in the regression equations he estimates. An equation that fits the data well for half the period and not for the rest is, for him, a failure. But for the economic historian it is, or should be regarded as, nothing less than a triumph — in the sense that by indicating that a structural change occurred it signals that he must set to work to learn what happened in history.

I think it is instructive to envision the economic historian's world as a succession of working models, each appropriate to a particular social, temporal and technological setting. His ultimate task is to explain the sequence of different models. Why do they change the way they do? What determines the rate at which one supplants another? You may say that really the historian is searching for some stable set of general relations governing the succession of particular representations of states of economic life. In practice, however, such a system is too complex, and involves too many non-economic variables, to be worth trying to formalize in a closed form. And so, rather than obscure the developments in which he is interested, the economic historian may be quite content to try to accumulate a sequence of partial models, each of which has been found to be consistent with as much of the evidence as is available for some historical settings, and rather less appropriate as a rationalization for our empirical knowledge about others.

This last marks a critical difference I hope I still perceive in the attitudes of historians who use econometric methods and those revealed by your run-of-the-mill applied economist. The applied economist may draw upon historical data to test a hypothesis, but he is not terribly bothered about the dates attached to the observations — simply because he is not worried about how his partial model will square with other things known or conjectured concerning that period, and about the position it will occupy in a sequence of such models. Furthermore, what he really wants — or so it often seems — is to find any set of data for which the model "works", and he does not as a rule label tested models according to when they *do not* work. Indeed, the conventional (95%) confidence levels that have been established for significance tests in most econometric investigations seem to reflect the majority-sentiment that real tragedy consists in the rejection of a true hypothesis, whereas the historians (who are, and will most likely remain a minority among the users of *t*-statistics) might be better served by tests that possess greater power against errors of Type II. Certainly, the demonstration that a particular model fails to rationalize the available observations for certain societies, or periods in the history of one society, will be viewed by econometric historians as of no less interest than the finding that there is *some* body of data to which the model is appropriate.

Much of the econometric historian's time necessarily will be spent in doing the same sort of thing that applied economists do — looking for a structure descriptive of a given set of data. It does not follow that their ultimate purposes are identical, or that it is desirable for econometric historians to assimilate majority-attitudes concerning such undertakings. If they spend their time piecing together an appropriate structure, historians ought not be encouraged to suppress their ultimate interest in discovering the limits of its applicability.

Reflecting upon the ecumenical spirit of the occasion, I suppose it is only fitting that Gavin Wright's survey for the Econometric Society eschewed exposition of those subtle differences in orientation which might be expected to distinguish economic historians from the majority of the users of econometric methods. But perhaps it will be agreed after all that it is better for these not to be wholly suppressed, lest economic historians themselves forget the peculiar purposes for which they sought to employ these new and more precise tools of empirical analysis.

References

Ashton, T.S., 1946, The relationship of economic history to economic theory. *Economica* (May).

David, P.A., 1967, The growth of real product in the United States before 1840: new evidence, controlled conjectures. *Journal of Economic History* 26 (June).

Engerman, S.L. and R.W. Fogel, 1969, A model for the explanation of industrial expansion during the nineteenth century: with an application to the American iron industry. *Journal of Political Economy* 77 (May/June).

Temin, P., 1967, The causes of cotton price fluctuations in the 1830's *Review of Economics and Statistics* 49 (November).

SUBJECT INDEX

Please note my continuation order for following series:

☐ **Studies in Mathematical and Managerial Economics, from vol. .... onwards.**

☐ **Contributions to Economic Analysis, from vol. .... onwards.**

Please send prospectuses in the following fields:

Name   Full Address *(block letters please)*:

☐	**Economic Planning, Statistics**
☐	**Economic Theory, Mathematical Economics**
☐	**Econometrics**
☐	**International Economics, Economics of Developing Countries**
☐	**Welfare Economics**
☐	**Monetary Economics, Banking, Business Finance**
☐	**Industrial and Labour Economics**
☐	**Transport Economics**
☐	**Distribution and Consumer Research**
☐	**Business and Industrial Administration**
☐	**Personnel Management Commercial Studies**

Please mention your institute or organisation and position held.

P 20 M I270 E

(B 1035)   Printed in Belgium by Ceuterick s.a.
Brusselse straat 153   3000-Louvain
Adm.-dir. L. Pitsi   Bertemse baan 25   3008-Veltem-Beisem